Praise for *3D User Inter*
Second Edition

"An essential guide for anyone developing interfaces for Virtual and Augmented Reality gaming experiences."

—Richard Marks, Director of Magic Lab, Sony PlayStation

"An incredible resource for 3D interaction researchers and practitioners, made all the more timely and valuable with today's renewed interest in Virtual and Augmented reality platforms. Everyone in VR and AR can benefit from the decades of research thoughtfully organized and presented in this updated edition."

—Andy Wilson, Microsoft Research

"This is an essential book for researchers and developers creating 3D user interfaces. If you're developing Virtual Reality or Augmented Reality experiences, or even mobile and desktop 3D applications, you need to buy this book."

—Mark Billinghurst, University of South Australia

3D User Interfaces
Second Edition

3D User Interfaces

Theory and Practice
Second Edition

Joseph J. LaViola Jr.
Ernst Kruijff
Ryan P. McMahan
Doug A. Bowman
Ivan Poupyrev

Addison-Wesley

Boston • Columbus • Indianapolis • New York • San Francisco
Amsterdam • Cape Town • Dubai • London • Madrid • Milan
Munich • Paris • Montreal • Toronto • Delhi • Mexico City
São Paulo • Sidney • Hong Kong • Seoul • Singapore • Taipei • Tokyo

For information about buying this title in bulk quantities, or for special sales opportunities (which may include electronic versions; custom cover designs; and content particular to your business, training goals, marketing focus, or branding interests), please contact our corporate sales department at corpsales@pearsoned.com or (800) 382-3419.

For government sales inquiries, please contact governmentsales@pearsoned.com.

For questions about sales outside the U.S., please contact intlcs@pearsoned.com.

Visit us on the Web: informit.com/aw

Library of Congress Control Number: 2016961395

ISBN-13: 978-0-13-403432-4

ISBN-10: 0-13-403432-5

1 17

Editor-in-Chief
Mark Taub

Senior Acquisitions Editor
Laura Lewin

Development Editor
Susan Zahn

Managing Editor
Sandra Schroeder

Project Editor
Lori Lyons

Production Manager
Dhayanidhi

Copy Editor
Warren Hapke

Indexer
Erika Millen

Proofreader
Sam Sunder Singh

Technical Reviewer
Andy Wilson

Publishing Coordinator
Olivia Basegio

Cover Designer
Chuti Prasersith

Compositor
codeMantra

To my family, with love—they are my life.

—Joe

To my wife and kids, for their love and support.

—Ernst

To my parents, who always encouraged me.

—Ryan

To Dawn and all the kids under the Bowman bigtop,
with all my love.

—Doug

To my parents, for bringing me up, and to
my wife forputting up with me.

—Ivan

Contents at a Glance

Contents

Contents

FOREWORD TO THE SECOND EDITION

It seems like yesterday that the first edition of this book was published. However, yesterday was over a dozen years ago—just in time for me to adopt it for the 3D user interface course I have been teaching ever since. The first edition was the ambitious and successful first text devoted to this subject. A timely and welcome gift to our field, it was the product of a team of authors actively engaged in leading-edge research, who codified and successively refined their work through the development of a series of tutorials out of which their book grew.

As Jim Foley wrote in his foreword to the first edition, "Three-dimensional user interfaces are finally receiving their due!" But, exhilarating though the times were then, the intervening years have brought us even more exciting advances. As I write this, virtual reality is becoming consumer reality, with tethered head-worn displays connected to desktop computers and mobile head-worn displays powered by phones—all superior in many ways to the orders-of-magnitude more expensive systems that were found in research labs back when the first edition appeared. Meanwhile, hand-held augmented reality games have become international sensations, downloaded hundreds of millions of times, and early commercial head-worn augmented reality displays are already in the hands and on the heads of eager developers.

Simply put, the processing and display technology needed for interactive 3D is now commonplace. The graphics power of current smartphones is comparable to that of full-size game consoles that debuted after the first edition was published. Hardware and software for accurately tracking the 3D position and orientation of a smartphone or a user's head and for capturing full hand and body pose are now integrated into an increasing number of those phones. Even smartwatches can run 3D applications.

But amidst this thrilling democratization of 3D, there is a problem. Powerful processors, high-quality displays, responsive interaction devices, and efficient software by themselves are not enough to make 3D useful. These technologies need to be combined together in the right way to create effective 3D user interfaces. However, the vast majority of user interface designers and developers are only knowledgeable about and comfortable with 2D user interfaces. What can be done about this?

That's where this book comes in. Joe LaViola, Ernst Kruijff, Doug Bowman, and Ivan Poupyrev—the authors of the first edition—have joined with Ryan McMahan. Together, they have given us this extensively updated second edition, which provides the thorough background needed to understand current 3D user interfaces and the software and hardware from which they are built. Like its predecessor, the second edition teaches the reader how to design, implement, and evaluate 3D user interfaces, summarizing and categorizing decades of ongoing research and practice. Two extended application case studies are threaded throughout the book, offering substantial examples of how to make appropriate choices from among the possibilities described, whether high-level design, displays, input devices, interaction techniques, or evaluation approaches.

Many of the technologies underlying 3D user interfaces are different from those used in 2D user interfaces, have not undergone the same level of standardization, and are more actively evolving. Yet there is one constant: people. Recognizing this, the authors dedicate several substantial chapters to the perceptual, cognitive, and physical bases, as well as to the principles of human–computer interaction for how we interact in and with the 3D world. By grounding the book in a principled understanding of users, they help guide us toward the design of effective 3D user interfaces that honor our abilities and respect our limitations.

I'm looking forward to using the second edition in my course at Columbia. And whether you're a seasoned researcher or practitioner, or a fresh convert to the power of 3D interaction, you're also in for a treat!

Steve Feiner
Department of Computer Science
Columbia University
January 2017

FOREWORD TO THE FIRST EDITION

Three-dimensional user interfaces are finally receiving their due! Research in 3D interaction and 3D display began in the 1960s, pioneered by researchers like Ivan Sutherland, Bob Sproull, Fred Brooks, Andrew Ortony, and Richard Feldman. Although many commercially successful 3D applications exist—computer-aided design and simulation, radiation therapy, drug discovery, surgical simulation, scientific and information visualization, entertainment—no author or group of authors has written a comprehensive and authoritative text on the subject, despite a continuing and rich set of research findings, prototype systems, and products.

Why is that? Why is it that this book by Doug Bowman, Ernst Kruijff, Joe LaViola, and Ivan Poupyrev is the first thorough treatment of 3D UIs?

Perhaps it was our digression during the last 20 years to the WIMP GUI. After all, the Windows, Icons, Menus, and Pointers GUI is used very widely by millions of users. Mac OS and Microsoft Windows users know it well, as do many UNIX users. Indeed, every user of the Web works with a GUI, and this year there are many hundreds of millions of them. Two-dimensional GUIs will be with us for a long time. After all, a lot of the workaday world with which we deal is flat—not just our Web pages but our documents, presentations, and spreadsheets too. Yes, some of these can be extended to 3D, but most of the time, 2D is just fine, thank you very much. Furthermore, pointing and selecting and typing are relatively fast and relatively error-free—they work, and they work well.

Perhaps it is that not as many people use 3D GUIs as use the 2D WIMP GUI, and so they are not thought to be as important. But the above list of 3D applications involves multibillion-dollar manufacturing industries, such as aerospace and automotive, and equally large and even more important activities in the life-saving and life-giving pharmaceutical and health care industries.

Perhaps it was that we needed the particular set of backgrounds that Doug, Joe, Ivan, and Ernst bring to the table. Doug comes out of the GVU Center at Georgia Tech, where he worked on 3D UIs with Larry Hodges and others and learned the value of careful user studies and experimentation, and he is now a member of an influential HCI group at Virginia Tech; Joe works at Brown with Andy van Dam, a long-time proponent of rich 3D interaction; Ivan comes from the HIT Lab at the University of Washington, where he worked with Tom Furness and Suzanne Weghorst, and now works with Jun Rekimoto at Sony CSL; and Ernst works with Martin Goebel in the VE Group at Fraunhofer IMK in Germany.

Whatever the case, I am excited and pleased that this team has given us the benefit of their research and experience. As I reviewed the draft manuscript for this book, I jotted down some of the thoughts that came to my mind: comprehensive, encyclopedic, authoritative, taxonomic; grounded in the psychological, HCI, human factors, and computer graphics literature; grounded in the personal research experiences of the authors, their teachers, and their students.

I myself have long preached the importance of integrating the study of the computer with the study of the human. Indeed, this is the key premise on which I built the GVU Center at Georgia Tech. This book certainly follows that admonition. There are numerous discussions of human issues as they relate to 3D navigation and interaction, drawing on references in psychology and human factors.

This is indeed a book for both practitioners and researchers. The extensive literature reviews, examples, and guidelines help us understand what to do now. Combined with the research agenda in Chapter 13, The Future of 3D User Interfaces (now Chapter 12), the material also helps us have a sense of what it is that we do not yet know.

I particularly commend to readers the Chapter 11 discussion of evaluating 3D UIs. We in the computer graphics community have tended to design devices and techniques and then "throw them over the wall" to the user community. This is not the route to success. Careful study of user needs coupled with evaluation as part of the ongoing design cycle is much more likely to lead to effective techniques. The authors, all of whom have grappled with the difficult task of designing 3D interfaces, know from first-hand experience how crucial this is. Their section 11.4, on the distinctive characteristics of the 3D interface evaluation process, is a wonderful codification of that first-hand knowledge.

Thanks to Doug and Ernst and Joe and Ivan!

Jim Foley
GVU Center
College of Computing
Georgia Tech
March 2004

PREFACE TO THE SECOND EDITION

It has been more than 10 years since the first edition of *3D User Interfaces: Theory and Practice*, and the field has certainly changed over that time. The original edition was highly regarded, but perhaps ahead of its time since 3D user interfaces were confined to university research labs and some industrial research labs. However, over the last 10 years with technological breakthroughs in both hardware and software, we see that the commercial sector has brought virtual and augmented reality displays, mobile devices, gaming consoles, and even robotic platforms to market that require 3D user interface technology to provide useful, powerful, and engaging user experiences in a variety of different application domains. Meanwhile, this commodity hardware and software has revitalized university research labs doing work with 3D user interfaces and is now making it more affordable to set up virtual and augmented reality labs in the classroom, making the technology much more accessible to students at the graduate, undergraduate, and high school levels. These developments make the content of this book more relevant than ever and more useful to a wider audience of researchers, developers, hobbyists, and students. Thus, we believe releasing a second edition now is timelier than ever.

Given the changes described above, we needed to significantly revamp the book to not only reflect current needs of our readers (both old and new), but to update the material given the plethora of research into 3D user interface hardware and software that has been performed over the last decade. In addition, we decided to make the book application agnostic, since 3D user interfaces can be applied almost anywhere, given appropriate sensors to determine someone or something's position, orientation, and/or motion in space. We have made several changes in this edition that we feel make the book more inclusive and timely, while still maintaining its strength in discussing 3D user interface design from hardware to software to evaluation of 3D user interface techniques and applications.

This edition is organized into six distinct parts. Three chapters from the first edition—on wayfinding, symbolic input, and augmented reality—no longer stand on their own but have been fused into other parts of the book. We added two completely new chapters on human factors and general human-computer interaction to provide the reader with a more solid foundational background that can be used as base material for the 3D user interface chapters. We have also significantly revised each chapter with new material based on the latest research developments and findings. In addition, we felt it was important to have better cohesion between chapters from an application development perspective, so we decided to introduce two running case studies that describe a mobile augmented reality application and a first-person virtual reality gaming application. The content of these case studies will appear at the end of each chapter in Parts III, IV, and V of the book so the reader can see how the material can be utilized in these specific applications and how 3D user interface design is employed in each part of the 3D application.

In this edition, Part I has two chapters. The first is an introduction to the concepts of 3D user interfaces, while Chapter 2 provides a historical background into the field and lays out a roadmap for 3D user interfaces and how they relate to other fields. This is also where we introduce the two case studies that will be discussed throughout the book. Part II provides background material on the human factors aspects of interfaces in general and 3D user interfaces in particular, with emphasis on the human sensory system and human cognition (Chapter 3) and a general introduction to the field of human-computer interaction (Chapter 4) that can be used as a basis for understanding the various 3D user interface concepts and ideas we present in later parts of the book. Part III delves into 3D user interface hardware, including output devices for the visual, auditory, and haptic/tactile systems (Chapter 5), and input devices used in 3D user interfaces, with specific emphasis on obtaining 3D position and orientation and motion information about the user in physical space (Chapter 6). We consider Part IV the core of the book because its focus is on the fundamental 3D interaction tasks used in the majority of 3D user interfaces. In this part, Chapter 7 describes techniques for 3D object selection and manipulation while Chapter 8 delves into navigation and wayfinding techniques for moving through both virtual and physical spaces. Finally, Chapter 9 focuses on different system control techniques that can be used to change application state, issue commands and provide overall input to a 3D application. Part V describes strategies for 3D user interface design and evaluation, with Chapter 10 examining different design strategies for choosing and developing 3D user interfaces, and Chapter 11 covering the all-important aspects of 3D user interface evaluation, a critical component of the development of a 3D user interface technique or application. Finally, Part VI contains Chapter 12, which looks into the future of 3D user interfaces by providing a discussion of the open research problems that we need to solve to move the field forward.

As with the first edition, we offer numerous **guidelines**—practical and proven advice for the designer and developer. Guidelines are indicated in the text like this:

> **Tip**
>
> Follow the guidelines in this book to help you design usable 3D UIs.

The second edition of *3D User Interfaces: Theory and Practice* can be used in several different ways, depending on the reader's goals and intentions. For the student with no experience in human-computer interaction, the entire book can be used in an introductory 3D user interface design course at the graduate or undergraduate level. Those students who have had some background in human-computer interaction could essentially skip Part II of the book without loss of generality to support a more detailed course on 3D user interfaces.

Developers and 3D application designers can use the book for inspiration and guidance in the design, implementation, and evaluation of applications with 3D UIs. In the design process, developers can choose appropriate hardware from Part III, choose specific interaction techniques from Part IV, and learn how to evaluate their techniques and applications from Part V. Developers can also get inspiration from Chapter 10 on how best to go about designing their 3D application. It is our hope that developers, especially in the virtual and augmented reality communities, will use this material so they don't have to "reinvent the wheel" when developing their applications.

Finally, researchers can use the book as a comprehensive collection of related and prior work to help them understand what has been done in the field, ensure their research ideas are novel, get inspiration to tackle new problems in 3D user interfaces, and act as a one-stop shop for all things 3D UI. Chapter 12 would be especially useful for researchers who are looking for significantly challenging problems to explore.

Register your copy of *3D User Interfaces: Theory and Practice* at informit.com for convenient access to downloads, updates, and corrections as they become available. To start the registration process, go to informit.com/register and log in or create an account. Enter the product ISBN 9780134034324 and click Submit. Once the process is complete, you will find any available content under "Registered Products."

PREFACE TO THE FIRST EDITION

An architect sits in her home office, putting the final touches on the design of the new entrance to the city park. A three-dimensional virtual model of the park appears in front of her on the desk's surface. She nudges a pathway slightly to the right to avoid a low-lying area, and then makes the model life-size so she can walk along the path to view the effect. "Those dark colors on the sign at the entrance are too foreboding," she thinks, so she quickly changes the color palette to brighter primary colors. She looks up and notices that the clients are arriving for the final design review meeting. They are located in other offices around the city, but they can all view the 3D model and make suggested changes, as well as communicate with one another. "What's the construction plan?" asks one of the clients. The architect starts an animation showing the progress of the project from start to finish. "That first step may not work," says the client. "The excavation is much too close to the existing playground. Let me show you." He looks out his window, which has a view of the park, and overlays the virtual construction plan on it. "You're right," says the architect, "let's plan to move the playground slightly—that will be much cheaper than changing the construction site." After viewing the effects of the change, all agree that this plan will work, and the meeting adjourns.

This scenario and others like it illustrate the enormous potential of 3D environments and applications. The technology to realize such a vision is available now, although it will certainly be improved. But the scenario also leaves out a great deal of information—information that is crucial to making this dream a reality. How did the architect load the park model, and how does she manipulate her view of it? What technique is used to change the pathway? How can multiple clients all manipulate the model at the same time? How do the participants appear to each other in the virtual space? How is the speed and playback of the animation controlled? How did the client instruct the system to merge the real and virtual scenes?

These questions all relate to the design of the user interface (UI) and interaction techniques for this 3D application, an area that is usually given only a cursory treatment in futuristic films and books. The scenarios usually either assume that all interaction between the user and the system will be "natural"—based on techniques like intuitive gestures and speech—or "automatic"—the system will be so intelligent that it will deduce the user's intentions. But is this type of interaction realistic, or even desirable?

This book addresses the critical area of **3D UI design**—a field that seeks to answer detailed questions, like those above, that make the difference between a 3D system that is usable and efficient and one that causes user frustration, errors, and even physical discomfort. We present practical information for developers, the latest research results, easy-to-follow guidelines for the UI designer, and relevant application examples. Although there are quite a few books devoted to UIs in general and to 2D UI design in particular, 3D UIs have received significantly less attention. The results of work in the field are scattered throughout numerous conference proceedings, journal articles, single book chapters, and Web sites. This field deserves a reference and educational text that integrates the best practices and state-of-the-art research, and that's why this book was created.

How This Book Came to Be

The story of this book begins in April 1998, when Ivan Poupyrev and Doug Bowman were doctoral students at Hiroshima University and Georgia Tech, respectively, working on 3D interaction techniques for object manipulation in virtual environments (VEs). We started a lively email discussion about the design and usability of these techniques and about 3D UIs in general. Ivan, who was at the time a visiting research student at the University of Washington, suggested that the discussion would be even more profitable if other researchers in this new area could join in as well, and so the 3D UI mailing list was born. Since that time, over 100 researchers from around the globe have joined the list and participated in the discussion (to see an archive of all the list traffic or to join the list, check out http://www.3dui.org). Joe LaViola and Ernst Kruijff were two of the first people to join the list.

In August of that same year, Doug forwarded to the list a call for tutorials for the upcoming IEEE Virtual Reality Conference. After some discussion, Joe, Ivan, and Ernst agreed to join Doug to organize a tutorial on "The Art and Science of 3D Interaction." The tutorial was a big hit at the conference in Houston, and the four of us continued to present courses on the topic at ACM Virtual Reality Software and Technology 1999, IEEE VR 2000, and ACM SIGGRAPH 2000 and 2001.

After developing a huge amount of content for the notes supplements of these courses, we decided it would be silly not to compile and expand all of this information in book form. Furthermore, there was no way to include all the information available on 3D UIs in a one-day course. And that's why you're holding this book in your hands today—a book containing information on 3D UIs that can't be found in any other single source.

ACKNOWLEDGMENTS

This book would not have been possible without the hard work, support, and intelligence of a large group of people.

First, we offer our gratitude to the reviewers who gave their time and energy in improving the quality of the book. Their comments and suggestions have made the book more complete, more readable, and more useful. Thanks to Ben Shneiderman, Harry Hersh, D. Jay Newman, Jeff Pierce, Dieter Schmalstieg, and Bob Zeleznik for providing this invaluable service. Special thanks go to Jim Foley for his encouragement and support.

Next, we would like to thank our original editor at Addison-Wesley, Peter Gordon, for his invaluable advice and encouragement. The rest of the staff who worked on the first edition, including Bernie Gaffney, Amy Fleischer, Julie Nahil, Heather Mullane, and Curt Johnson have also been extremely helpful. Thanks also to Simone Payment and Carol Lallier for their competent and professional work during the production phase.

We thank Laura Lewin for her work on the second edition, in addition to Olivia Basegio and Susan Zahn. Getting this significantly updated new edition to print was almost as large of a task as a brand new book!

All of us would like to personally thank our colleagues in the 3D UI community for their fruitful discussions and collaborations. They include Mark Mine, Robert Lindeman, Matthew Conway, Ken Hinckley, Shumin Zhai, Kiyoshi Kiyokawa, Chris Shaw, Mark Billinghurst, Rudy Darken, Pablo Figueroa, Bernd Fröhlich, Steve Feiner, Wolfgang Stürzlinger, Martin Hachet, Yoshifumi Kitamura, Eric Ragan, Tobias Höllerer, Ravin Balakrishnan, and many others.

Portions of this material are based upon work supported by the National Science Foundation. Any opinions, findings and conclusions, or recommendations expressed in this material are those of the author(s) and do not necessarily reflect the views of the National Science Foundation (NSF). Portions of this material are based on work supported by the Office of Naval Research. Any opinions, findings, conclusions, or recommendations expressed in this material are those of the author(s) and do not necessarily reflect the views of the Office of Naval Research (ONR).

Joe LaViola: During the writing of the first edition of this book, I was just a PhD student, and over the last decade or so, having become a professor, my work in 3D user interfaces has been more about my students' efforts here at the University of Central Florida than anything I could have done myself. Thus, I want to thank the students who have worked in the Interactive Systems and User Experience Lab including but not limited to Paul Varcholik, Emiko Charbonneau, Jared Bott, Salman Cheema, Jeff Cashion, Brian Williamson, Tad Litwiller, Andrew Miller, Arun Kulshreshth, Sara Buchanan, Travis Cossairt, Eugene Taranta, Corey Pittman, Kevin Pfeil, Andres Vargas, Seng Lee Koh, Conner Brooks, Michael Hoffman, Jim Crowley, and Juliet Norton. I also want to thank Chad Wingrave who was a postdoc with me for several years and was instrumental in moving 3D user interface research forward in my lab.

I want thank my PhD thesis advisor, colleague, and friend, Andries van Dam, for mentoring me over the years and always giving me goals to shoot for. Thanks also go to my family for their love and support, including my wife, Michelle, and my two beautiful daughters, Juliana, and Josephine, my Mom and Dad, my brother, Jamie, and the rest of my extended family. Without them, I could not have taken on such a large project.

I need to also thank my current and former friends and colleagues at Brown University, including John Hughes, David Laidlaw, Robert Zeleznik, Daniel Keefe, Daniel Acevedo Feliz, Andrew Forsberg, Loring Holden, Tim Miller, Steve Dollins, Lee Markosian, David Karelitz, Tim Rowley, Christine Waggoner, and all the members of the Brown University Computer Graphics Group. They were instrumental in helping with the first edition of this book.

Finally, I want to thank my coauthors, Doug, Ernst, Ivan, and Ryan, for their friendship and collaboration on the second edition of *3D User Interfaces: Theory and Practice*. It took us over a decade to decide to do this revision, and it felt almost as long to finish, but the results, in my opinion, are quite thorough and valuable to the community. Their contributions to this effort make the book what it is.

Ernst Kruijff: First of all, my thanks go to Joe, Ryan, Doug, and Ivan for their great cooperation, help, and extensive discussions. Thanks also go to my wife and kids, my parents, my brother, and my sister-in-law for their support, each in their own way. Furthermore, my thanks go to my colleagues at igroup / Bauhaus University Weimar, the Virtual Environments group at Fraunhofer IMK, the Augmented Reality group at TU Graz, CURE, and the Institute of Visual Computing at BRSU. Special thanks (in chronological order) for extensive collaboration, support and inspiration to Holger Regenbrecht, Jakob Beetz, Hartmut Seichter, Martin Göbel, Bernd Fröhlich, Gerold Wesche, Gernot Heisenberg , Aeldrik Pander, Steffi Beckhaus, Dieter Schmalstieg, Eduardo Veas, Alexander Bornik, Erick Mendez, Manuela Waldner, Daniel Wagner, André Hinkenjann, Jens Maiero, Christina Trepkowski, Alexander Marquardt, Saugata Biswas, as well as external collaborators Bernhard Riecke, Wolfgang Stuerzlinger, Rob Lindeman, Ed Swan, Steve Feiner, Jason Orlosky, and Kiyoshi Kiyokawa.

Ryan McMahan: First, I would like to thank Doug, Joe, Ernst, and Ivan for including me on this little adventure. It was a great honor to work with these aficionados. I especially need to thank

Amanda, my fiancée, for enduring the weekends of writing and my battles with deadlines. Her unwavering love kept me motivated. Thanks go to my mother, JoAnn McMahan, my family, and my friends for their continued support and encouragement. I would also like to recognize my colleagues and students at UT Dallas, especially the members of the Future Immersive Virtual Environments (FIVE) Lab. Finally, I am extremely grateful to my father, the late Ralph McMahan.

Doug Bowman: Much gratitude is due to Joe, Ivan, Ernst, and Ryan for seeing this project through and for all their years of friendship and collaboration. I especially appreciate Ryan stepping in and making such a big contribution to this second edition when my bandwidth was so limited. I greatly appreciate my closest collaborators: Tobias Höllerer and Chris North; thanks to both of you for pushing me beyond where I thought I could go, challenging my thinking, providing opportunities, picking up my slack, and (most importantly) being my friends. Thanks also go to my colleagues and students at Virginia Tech, including Jake Socha, David Hicks, Todd Ogle, David Cline, Ben Knapp, Ron Kriz, Mehdi Setareh, Walid Thabet, Thomas Ollendick, David Cox, Debby Hix, John Kelso, Joe Gabbard, Chad Wingrave, Jian Chen, Nicholas Polys, Wendy Schafer, Marcio Pinho, Eric Ragan, Felipe Bacim, Regis Kopper, Tao Ni, Yi Wang, Bireswar Laha, Andrew Ray, Bert Scerbo, Cheryl Stinson, Mahdi Nabiyouni, Panagiotis Apostolellis, Wallace Lages, and Run Yu. Thanks to the whole Center for HCI community for their support, in particular to Andrea Kavanaugh. Past colleagues at Georgia Tech also deserve thanks. They include Larry Hodges, Drew Kessler, David Koller, Donald Johnson, Donald Allison, Brian Wills, Jean Wineman, Jay Bolter, Elizabeth Davis, Albert Badre, and Ben Watson. There are many other colleagues and friends who have shaped my career and helped me to where I am now—thanks for your many contributions.

Finally, I would like to thank my wife, Dawn, for her unfailing love and support. My kiddos—Drew, Caroline, Lucy, Laken, and David—have made my life full during this project. Thanks also to my extended family and friends, especially those at Grace Covenant Presbyterian Church. My work and life are all due to the grace of God. *Soli Deo gloria.*

Ivan Poupyrev: This book is result of many years of collaboration and friendship with my coauthors, and needless to say this book would be never possible without them. This collaboration started and grew while I was doing my PhD research that was conducted jointly between Hiroshima University in Japan and Human Interface Technology Laboratory (HIT Lab) at the University of Washington in Seattle. Thus, I am deeply indebted to everyone who supported me during my Hiroshima and Seattle years, including but not limited to Professor Tadao Ichikawa, who supervised my PhD thesis at Hiroshima University, Masahito Hirakawa, Bryn Holmes, Suzanne Weghorst, and Professor Tom Furness III who accepted me to the HIT Lab family, as well as Mark Billinghurst, Mark Phillips, Jennifer Feyma, and Chris Airola for being collaborators and friends who gave me life outside the lab. I am grateful to the Japanese government for providing me with the Monbusho Scholarship for conducting graduate studies in Japan.

Parts of the augmented reality material were developed as a part of my postdoctoral research conducted at ATR Media Integration and Communication Research Labs in Kyoto. I am grateful to the ATR community and leadership of Ryohei Nakatsu, Jun Ohya, Nobuji Tetsutani, as well as collaborators and friends including Jun Kurumisawa, Tatsumi Sakaguchi, Keiko Nakao, Lew Baldwin, Desney Tan, Sidney Fels, Michael Lyons, Tal Shalif, and many others.

The first edition of the book itself was written while I was a Researcher at the Sony Computer Science Laboratories in Tokyo, and I would like to extend my gratitude to Jun Rekimoto, Mario Tokoro, Hiroaki Kitano, and Yuimko Kawashima for their guidance and patience.

For the second edition of this book, my deepest gratitude goes to my coauthors, who carried the absolute majority of efforts in preparing this substantial revision of the book. The project started when I moved to Google ATAP with a mission to build and grow a new research initiative that subsequently spanned into product efforts which consumed all my time, severely limiting my ability to contribute to the second edition efforts. I am humbled and indebted to my coauthors for their understanding and support during my rollercoaster years at Google ATAP.

ABOUT THE AUTHORS

JOSEPH J. LAVIOLA, JR., Associate Professor of Computer Science, directs the Interactive Systems and User Experience Research Cluster of Excellence at the University of Central Florida.

ERNST KRUIJFF, Interim Professor for Computer Graphics and Interactive Systems at the Institute of Visual Computing, Bonn-Rhein-Sieg University of Applied Sciences, leads the 3DMi group's design of multisensory 3D user interfaces.

RYAN P. McMAHAN, Assistant Professor of Computer Science and of Arts, Technology, and Emerging Communication at UT Dallas, directs its Future Immersive Virtual Environments (FIVE) Lab.

DOUG A. BOWMAN, Professor of Computer Science at Virginia Tech, directs its 3D Interaction Research Group and Center for Human-Computer Interaction. He is an ACM Distinguished Scientist.

IVAN POUPYREV is Technical Program Lead working on advanced interaction research at Google's Advanced Technology and Products (ATAP) division.

PART I

FOUNDATIONS OF 3D USER INTERFACES

Part I introduces you to the topic of 3D user interfaces (3D UIs). Chapter 1, "Introduction to 3D User Interfaces," explains what 3D UIs are and why they are important. It also introduces some key terminology used throughout the book and presents some applications that use 3D UIs. Chapter 2, "3D User Interfaces: History and Roadmap," provides a brief history of 3D UIs and a roadmap of related areas, positioning the topics covered in this book within a larger context.

CHAPTER 1

INTRODUCTION TO 3D USER INTERFACES

On desktop computers, good user interface (UI) design is now almost universally recognized as a crucial part of the system development process. Almost every computing-related product touts itself as "easy to use," "intuitive," or "designed with your needs in mind." For the most part, however, desktop user interfaces have used the same basic principles and designs for the past decade or more. With the advent of virtual reality (VR), augmented reality, ubiquitous and mobile computing, and other "off-the-desktop" technologies, three-dimensional (3D)

UI design is now becoming a critical area for developers, students, and researchers to understand. In this chapter, we answer the question, "What are 3D user interfaces?" and provide an introduction to the terminology used throughout the book. We describe the goals of 3D UI design and list some application areas for 3D user interfaces. Keeping these applications in mind as you progress through the book will help provide a concrete reference point for some of the more abstract concepts we discuss.

1.1 What Are 3D User Interfaces?

Modern computer users have become intimately familiar with a specific set of UI components, including *input devices* such as the mouse and touchscreen, *output devices* such as the monitor, tablet, or cell phone display, *interaction techniques* such as drag-and-drop and pinch to zoom, *interface widgets* such as pull-down menus, and *UI metaphors* such as the Windows, Icons, Menus, Pointer (WIMP) desktop metaphor (van Dam 1997).

These interface components, however, are often inappropriate for the nontraditional computing environments and applications under development today. For example, a virtual reality (VR) user wearing a fully immersive head-worn display (HWD) won't be able to see the physical world, making the use of a keyboard impractical. An HWD in an augmented reality (AR) application may have limited resolution, forcing the redesign of text-intensive interface components such as dialog boxes. A VR application may allow a user to place an object anywhere in 3D space, with any orientation—a task for which a 2D mouse is inadequate.

Thus, these nontraditional systems need a new set of interface components: new devices, new techniques, new metaphors. Some of these new components may be simple refinements of existing components; others must be designed from scratch. Because many of these nontraditional environments work in real and/or virtual 3D space; we term these interfaces **3D user interfaces** (a more precise definition is given in section 1.3).

In this book, we describe and analyze the components (devices, techniques, metaphors) that can be used to design 3D user interfaces. We also provide guidance in choosing the components for particular systems based on empirical evidence from published research, anecdotal evidence from colleagues, and personal experience.

1.2 Why 3D User Interfaces?

Why is the information in this book important? We had five main motivations for producing this book:

- **3D interaction is relevant to real-world tasks.**

  Interacting in three dimensions makes intuitive sense for a wide range of applications (see section 1.4) because of the characteristics of the tasks in these domains and their match with the characteristics of 3D environments. For example, virtual environments (VEs) can provide users with a sense of *presence* (the feeling of "being there"—replacing the physical environment with the virtual one), which makes sense for applications such as gaming, training, and simulation. If a user can interact using natural skills, then the application can take advantage of the fact that the user already has a great deal of knowledge about the world. Also, 3D UIs may be more direct or immediate; that is, there is a short "cognitive distance" between a user's action and the system's feedback that shows the result of that action. This can allow users to build up complex mental models of how a simulation works, for example.

- **The technology behind 3D UIs is becoming mature.**

  UIs for computer applications are becoming more diverse. Mice, keyboards, windows, menus, and icons—the standard parts of traditional WIMP interfaces—are still prevalent, but nontraditional devices and interface components are proliferating rapidly, and not just on mobile devices. These components include spatial input devices such as trackers, 3D pointing devices, and whole-hand devices that allow gesture-based input. Multisensory 3D output technologies, such as stereoscopic projection displays, high-resolution HWDs, spatial audio systems, and haptic devices, are also becoming more common, and some of them are now even considered consumer electronics products.

- **3D interaction is difficult.**

  With this technology, a variety of problems have also been revealed. People often find it inherently difficult to understand 3D spaces and to perform actions in free space (Herndon et al. 1994). Although we live and act in a 3D world, the physical world contains many more cues for understanding and constraints and affordances for action that cannot currently be represented accurately in a computer simulation. Therefore, great care must go into the design of UIs and interaction techniques for 3D applications. It is clear that simply adapting traditional WIMP interaction styles to 3D does not provide a complete solution to this problem. Rather, novel 3D UIs based on real-world interaction or other metaphors must be developed.

- **Current 3D UIs either are straightforward or lack usability.**

  There are already some applications of 3D UIs used by real people in the real world (e.g., entertainment, gaming, training, psychiatric treatment, and design review). Most of these applications, however, contain 3D interaction that is not very complex. For example, the interaction in current VR entertainment applications such as VR films is largely limited to rotating the viewpoint (i.e., turning the head). More complex 3D interfaces (for applications such as modeling and design, education, scientific visualization, and psychomotor training) are difficult to design and evaluate, often leading to a lack of usability or a low-quality user experience. While improved technology can help, better technology will not solve the problem—for example, over 40 years of AR technology research have not ensured that today's AR systems are usable. Thus, a more thorough treatment of this subject is needed.

- **3D UI design is an area ripe for further work.**

  Finally, development of 3D UIs is one of the most exciting areas of research in human–computer interaction (HCI) today, providing a new frontier for innovation in the field. A wealth of basic and applied research and development opportunities are available for those with a solid background in 3D interaction.

It is crucial, then, for anyone involved in the design, implementation, or evaluation of nontraditional interactive systems to understand the issues discussed in this book.

1.3 Terminology

The technology sector loves acronyms and jargon, and precise terminology can make life easier as long as everyone agrees about the meaning of a particular term. This book is meant to be accessible to a broad audience, but we still find it useful to employ precise language. Here we present a glossary of some terms that we use throughout the book.

We begin with a set of general terms from the field of HCI that are used in later definitions:

- **human–computer interaction (HCI)**

  A field of study that examines all aspects of the interplay between people and interactive technologies. One way to think about HCI is as the process of *communication* between human users and computers (or interactive technologies in general). Users communicate actions, intents, goals, queries, and other such needs to computers. Computers, in turn, communicate to the user information about the world, about their internal state, about the responses to user queries, and so on. This communication may involve explicit dialog, or turn-taking, in which a user issues a command or query, the system responds, and so on, but in most modern computer systems, the communication is more implicit, free form, or even imperceptible (Hix and Hartson 1993).

- **user interface (UI)**

  The medium through which the communication between users and computers takes place. The UI translates a user's actions and state (inputs) into a representation the computer can understand and act upon, and it translates the computer's actions and state (outputs) into a representation the human user can understand and act upon (Hix and Hartson 1993).

- **input device**

  A physical (hardware) device allowing communication from the user to the computer.

- **degrees of freedom (DOF)**

  The number of independent dimensions of the motion of a body. DOF can be used to describe the input possibilities provided by input devices, the motion of a complex articulated object such as a human arm and hand, or the possible movements of a virtual object.

- **output device**

  A physical device allowing communication from the computer to the user. Output devices are also called *displays* and can refer to the display of any sort of sensory information (i.e., not just visual images, but also sounds, touch, taste, smell, and even the sense of balance).

- **interaction technique**

  A method allowing a user to accomplish a task via the UI. An interaction technique includes both hardware (input/output devices) and software components. The interaction technique's software component is responsible for mapping the information from the input device (or devices) into some action within the system and for mapping the output of the system to a form that can be displayed by the output device (or devices).

- **usability**

  The characteristics of an artifact (usually a device, interaction technique, or complete UI) that affect the user's use of the artifact. There are many aspects of usability, including ease of use, user task performance, user comfort, and system performance (Hix and Hartson 1993).

- **user experience (UX)**

  A broader concept encompassing a user's entire relationship with an artifact, including not only usability but also usefulness and emotional factors such as fun, joy, pride of ownership, and perceived elegance of design (Hartson and Pyla 2012).

- **UX evaluation**

  The process of assessing or measuring some aspects of the user experience of a particular artifact.

Using this HCI terminology, we define 3D interaction and 3D user interface:

- **3D interaction**

  Human–computer interaction in which the user's tasks are performed directly in a real or virtual 3D spatial context. Interactive systems that display 3D graphics do not necessarily involve 3D interaction; for example, if a user tours a model of a building on her desktop computer by choosing viewpoints from a traditional menu, no 3D interaction has taken place. On the other hand, 3D interaction does not necessarily mean that 3D input devices are used; for example, in the same application, if the user clicks on a target object to navigate to that object, then the 2D mouse input has been directly translated into a 3D virtual location; we consider this to be a form of 3D interaction. In this book, however, we focus primarily on 3D interaction that involves real 3D spatial input such as hand gestures or physical walking. Desktop 3D interaction requires different interaction techniques and design principles. We cover some desktop and multi-touch 3D interaction techniques in Chapters 7–9 but emphasize interaction with 3D spatial input throughout the book.

- **3D user interface (3D UI)**

  A UI that involves 3D interaction.

Finally, we define some technological areas in which 3D UIs are used:

- **virtual environment (VE)**

  A synthetic, spatial (usually 3D) world seen from a first-person point of view. The view in a virtual environment is under the real-time control of the user.

- **virtual reality (VR)**

  An approach that uses displays, tracking, and other technologies to immerse the user in a VE. Note that in practice VE and VR are often used almost interchangeably.

- **augmented reality (AR)**

  An approach that uses displays, tracking, and other technologies to enhance (augment) the user's view of a real-world environment with synthetic objects or information.

- **mixed reality (MR)**

  A set of approaches, including both VR and AR, in which real and virtual information is mixed in different combinations. A system's position on the mixed reality continuum indicates the mixture of virtuality and reality in the system (with the extremes being purely virtual and purely real). Mixed reality systems may move along this continuum as the user interacts with them (Milgram and Kishino 1994).

- **ubiquitous computing (UbiComp)**

  The notion that computing devices and infrastructure (and access to them) may be mobile or scattered throughout the real environment so that users have "anytime, anyplace" access to computational power (Weiser 1991).

- **telerobotics**

  The ability to control a robot that is geographically separated from the user, thus requiring remote operation. Robots often have many degrees of freedom and operate in the physical world, making 3D UIs applicable to their operation.

1.4 Application Areas

3D interaction and the principles we discuss in this book can be employed in a wide variety of application domains. Keep these application examples in mind as you read through the various sections of the book. We discuss this list of application areas in greater detail in Chapter 2. 3D UI application areas include:

- **Design and prototyping**
- **Heritage and tourism**
- **Gaming and entertainment**

- **Simulation and training**
- **Education**
- **Art**
- **Visual data analysis**
- **Architecture and construction**
- **Medicine and psychiatry**
- **Collaboration**
- **Robotics**

1.5 Conclusion

In this chapter, we introduced 3D UIs—their importance, terminology, and applications. In Chapter 2, "3D User Interfaces: History and Roadmap," we step back to look at the bigger picture—the history of and context for 3D UIs.

CHAPTER 2

3D USER INTERFACES: HISTORY AND ROADMAP

The field of 3D user interfaces, like human–computer interaction (HCI) in general, draws from many disciplines and lacks well-defined boundaries. In this chapter, we briefly describe some of the history of 3D UIs to set the stage for the rest of the book. We also present a 3D UI roadmap that positions the topics covered in this book relative to associated areas.

2.1 History of 3D UIs

The graphical user interfaces (GUIs) used in today's personal computers have an interesting history. Prior to 1980, almost all interaction with computers was based on the command line—the user was required to type complicated commands using a keyboard. The display was used almost exclusively for text, and when graphics were used, they were typically noninteractive. But around 1980, several technologies, such as the mouse, inexpensive raster graphics displays, and reasonably priced personal computer parts, were all mature enough to enable the first GUIs (such as the Xerox Star). With the advent of GUIs, UI design and HCI in general became a much more important research area because the research affected everyone using computers. HCI is an interdisciplinary field that draws from existing knowledge in perception, cognition, linguistics, human factors, ethnography, sociology, graphic design, industrial design, and other areas.

In a similar way, the development of 3D UIs as an area of research and practice has to a large degree been driven by technologies, including 3D graphics technology, augmented reality and virtual reality technology, and (especially) 3D position- and orientation-tracking technologies. As each of these technologies matured, they enabled new types of applications, leading in turn to previously unexplored user tasks, new challenges in UI design, and unforeseen usability issues. Thus, 3D UI research became necessary. In the rest of this section, we chronicle the development of some of these areas and show how advances in technology produced a need for 3D UI research.

In the late 1960s, Ivan Sutherland developed a vision for a whole new type of computing platform (Sutherland 1965) in which computers were not primarily for number crunching, but instead for interactive experiences in a simulated reality and for visual analysis of data. A few years later, he took the first steps towards achieving this vision with the first tracked head-mounted display (Sutherland 1968), which was capable of both VR and AR and included a precise, but cumbersome, mechanical head tracker. This use of head-tracking data to interactively determine the viewing angle, in such a way that users would just move their heads to look at different parts of the world naturally, was possibly the first 3D interaction technique (and is still a fundamental technique today).

Sutherland was ahead of his time, but finally in the late 1980s and early 1990s, it became more practical to build VR systems. The technologies that enabled this vision included 3D stereoscopic computer graphics, miniature CRT displays, position-tracking systems, and interaction devices such as the VPL DataGlove. Although many of the uses of VR technology didn't involve much 3D interaction beyond head tracking, early experiments looked at how to enable users to interact with the world through tracked hands and tools. Interestingly, when VR first entered the public consciousness through Jim Foley's article in *Scientific American* (Foley 1987), the cover image showed not a display system or a complex graphical environment but rather the DataGlove—a whole-hand input device-enabling users to interact with and manipulate the virtual world.

At first, 3D interaction technologies were strictly the domain of computer scientists and engineers (mostly in the computer graphics community) and were used for relatively simple applications. Visualization of 3D scientific datasets, real-time walkthroughs of architectural structures, and VR games were interesting and useful applications, and they provided plenty of research challenges (such as faster, more realistic graphics; more accurate head-tracking; lower latency; and better VR software toolkits). These applications, however, were relatively impoverished when it came to user interaction. The typical application only allowed the user to interactively navigate the environment, with a few providing more complex interaction, such as displaying the name of an object when it was touched.

As 3D tracking and display technology continued to improve (e.g., decreased latency and improved accuracy in position and orientation tracking), researchers wanted to develop more complex applications with a much richer set of interactions. For example, besides allowing an architect to experience his building design in a virtual world by looking around with head tracking and doing simple navigation, we could allow him to record and play audio annotations about the design, to change the type of stone used on the façade, to move a window, or to hide the interior walls so that the pipes and ducts could be seen. The problem, however, was that there was no knowledge about how to design such complex 3D interaction so that it was usable and effective. Technology had improved to a point where such applications were possible, but 3D UI research was needed to make them plausible.

Fortunately, because of the earlier focus on interfaces for personal computers, the field of HCI had a reasonable level of maturity when 3D applications experienced their "interface crisis." HCI experts had developed general principles for good interface design (Nielsen and Molich 1992), design and development processes aimed at ensuring usability (Hix and Hartson 1993), and models that explained how humans process information when interacting with systems (Card et al. 1986).

The application of existing HCI knowledge to 3D interfaces helped to improve their usability. But there were some questions about 3D UIs on which traditional HCI was silent. Consider a simple example: the user wants to explore a 3D medical dataset on a desktop display using a tracked 3D device. Traditional HCI might tell us that direct manipulation of the dataset—rotating the visualization by rotating the device, let's say—will be intuitive and efficient. But although the general principle is simple, the devil is in the details. How should the direct manipulation mapping be implemented? Can we scale the rotation so that the user doesn't get fatigued? What do we do when the wires attached to the device get in the way? What happens when the user needs to set the device down to type on the keyboard? How does the user point to a particular 3D location in the dataset to annotate it? The questions go on and on.

Beyond these low-level design questions, designers of 3D UIs were (and still are) faced with technological limitations, such as input latency, limited 3D workspace, tracking dropouts, and cumbersome devices that must be worn, held, or attached. Thus, a great design on paper couldn't always be implemented the way it was envisioned. In addition, researchers found that the design space for 3D interaction was huge, with a virtually unlimited number of possibilities due to the expressiveness of 3D input and the ability to design all sorts of "magical" interactions. How can a designer possibly choose the best 3D UI design (or even a reasonable one) from this large space?

Questions such as these indicated that a new subfield of HCI was needed to address the issues specific to the design of interfaces using 3D input in VR, AR, wearable computing, and other platforms. The common theme of all of these interactive technologies is interaction in a 3D context. Thus, the new subarea of HCI is termed **3D interaction, 3D user interface design,** or **3D HCI**.

Today, the field of 3D UI is becoming more mature. Researchers and practitioners around the globe, and from many different backgrounds, are designing, evaluating, and studying 3D interaction. Research is published in a wide variety of academic conferences and journals (the IEEE Symposium on 3D User Interfaces and the ACM Symposium on Spatial User Interaction are two venues we recommend in particular). Moreover, because robust 3D input technologies like the Nintendo Wii Remote, the Microsoft Kinect, the Leap Motion Controller, and Oculus Touch have become available to consumers, there are hundreds of demonstrations, apps, and homebrew projects involving 3D interaction. It's extremely difficult to find and understand all that's been done in this fascinating field. And that's why we wrote this book—to distill the ideas and findings of 3D UI researchers into a single source.

In the next section, we look at the types of research problems addressed and approaches used in 3D UI work and position them with respect to related work in other fields.

2.2 Roadmap to 3D UIs

To help you understand the material in this book in its proper context, it's important to discuss what topics are squarely within the 3D UI area, what makes up the background for 3D UI work, and what impact 3D UIs have on other areas. In this section, therefore, we present brief snapshots of a wide variety of topics with some connection to 3D UIs. Figure 2.1 illustrates our basic organizational structure. In the following lists of topics, we provide at least one important reference for most topics or, if applicable, a pointer to a particular chapter or section of the book where that topic is covered.

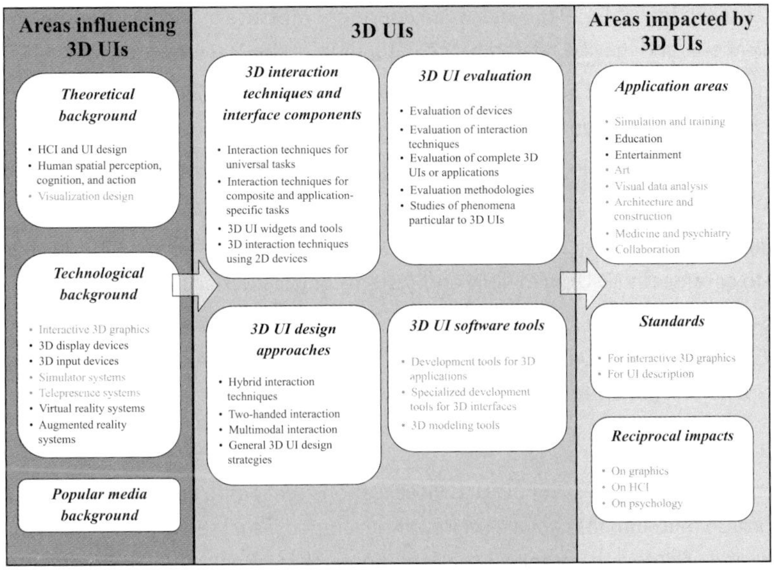

Figure 2.1 Roadmap to 3D UIs. Topics shown in darker text are covered in this book.

2.2.1 Areas Informing the Design of 3D UIs

We can draw upon many areas of research when considering the design of 3D UIs. The following sections discuss the theoretical, technological, and popular media background for the topics covered in this book.

Theoretical Background

The relevant theoretical background comes from work in the following areas: basic principles of HCI and UI design; human spatial perception, cognition, and action; and visualization design.

Human Spatial Perception, Cognition, and Action

The defining feature of 3D UIs is that users are viewing and acting in a real and/or virtual 3D space. Thus, psychology and human factors knowledge about spatial perception; spatial cognition; and human navigation, movement, and manipulation in 3D space contain critical background information for 3D UI design. We cover much of this background in more detail in Chapter 3, "Human Factors Fundamentals." Examples of such knowledge and theories include

- Visual perception and 3D depth cues (Bruce and Green 1990; Kosslyn 1993; see Chapter 3, "Human Factors Fundamentals," section 3.3 and Chapter 5, "3D User Interface Output Hardware," section 5.2), which are important when designing 3D worlds, objects, and visual feedback in 3D space
- Spatial sound perception (Durlach 1991; see Chapter 5, section 5.3), which is used to design audio feedback and data sonification

- Presence (Slater et al. 1994), which is an important measure of success in some applications, and may be related to the naturalism of the 3D UI
- Human spatial abilities and individual differences in abilities (Shepard and Metzler 1971), which inform the design of spatial interaction techniques
- Formation of spatial knowledge about 3D environments (Thorndyke and Hayes-Roth 1982; see Chapter 8, "Travel," section 8.9), which is critical in the design of wayfinding aids
- Cognitive planning of actions (Card et al. 1983; see Chapter 3, section 3.4), which is important to consider in 3D UIs generally and system control interfaces particularly
- Properties of manual reaching and grabbing (MacKenzie and Iberall 1994; Marras 1997; see Chapter 7, "Selection and Manipulation"), which inform the design of 3D selection and manipulation techniques

Visualization Design

An important application area for 3D UI is visualization—changing abstract data into a perceptual form so that humans can use their well-developed visual sense to find patterns, detect anomalies, and understand complex situations. Research in visualization therefore informs and complements 3D UI design. Example topics include

- Principles of visual data representation (Tufte 1990)
- Information or data visualization techniques (Ware 2000)
- Scientific visualization techniques (McCormick et al. 1987)
- Interaction techniques for visualization (Shneiderman 1996)

Basic Principles of HCI and UI/UX Design

A great deal of knowledge, theory, and practical advice has been generated by researchers in HCI. Although some is particularly focused on traditional desktop UIs, much can be generalized to apply to 3D UIs as well. We cover this background in more detail in Chapter 4, "General Principles of Human–Computer Interaction." Examples include

- Generic heuristics or guidelines for UI/UX design, such as visibility, affordances, and constraints (Nielsen and Molich 1992; Norman 1990), all of which are also critical for 3D UIs
- Models and theories of HCI, such as activity theory, GOMS (Goals, Operators, Methods, and Selection Rules), and scenario-based design (Bødker 1991; Card et al. 1980; Rosson and Carroll 2001), which can be used to understand, design, and evaluate 3D interaction
- UI design and evaluation techniques such as hierarchical task analysis, ethnographic analysis, heuristic evaluation, cognitive walkthrough, and usability studies (as found in HCI textbooks such as Shneiderman 1998; see Chapter 11, "Evaluation of 3D User Interfaces"), which can be applied directly to or adapted for 3D UIs
- Methods for managing the entire UX design lifecycle, such as the Wheel methodology (Hartson and Pyla 2012).

Technological Background

There are many areas of technology that are relevant to 3D UI design. They include interactive 3D graphics, 3D display devices, and 3D input devices, plus systems for simulation, telepresence, virtual reality and augmented reality.

Interactive 3D Graphics

Producing realistic but synthetic 3D images on a computer screen has been a focus of computer science research for more than 50 years. One particular line of research has focused on interactive 3D graphics—images that are rendered in real time so that users can interact with them directly (i.e., user input determines what is drawn, as in video games). This technology provides the environment in which 3D UI designers do their work. We do not cover 3D graphics background in this book, but there are many excellent textbooks on the subject (Hughes et al. 2013). Some representative advances in interactive 3D graphics are

- Fast line and polygon rendering algorithms (Bresenham 1965)
- Texture-mapping procedures (Watt and Watt 1992)
- Real-time lighting methods (Bishop and Weimer 1986)
- Dedicated graphics processors for fast hardware-based rendering (Olano and Lastra 1998)
- Algorithms for drawing stereoscopic images (Davis and Hodges 1995)
- Shader algorithms for fast, customizable rendering on graphics processing units (GPUs) (Nguyen 2007)
- High-level graphics software toolkits and integrated development environments (Unity3D and the Unreal Engine)

3D Display Devices

All visual displays used with computers today are capable of displaying 3D graphics (i.e., 2D images that are drawn with proper 3D perspective). Often, however, 3D UIs make use of more advanced displays that provide stereo viewing (slightly different images for the left and right eyes, producing an enhanced depth effect) or spatial immersion (being surrounded by a virtual environment). In addition, many 3D UIs make use of nonvisual displays—displays that present information to other senses. Here is a short list of such advanced 3D displays:

- Stereoscopic displays for desktop computers (Schmandt 1983)
- Walkaround 3D displays (Bimber et al. 2001)
- Head worn displays (HWDs; Melzer and Moffitt 2011), including see-through HWDs for augmented reality (Azuma 1997)
- Projection-based spatially immersive displays (Cruz-Neira et al. 1993)
- 3D spatial sound systems (Kapralos et al. 2003)
- Force-feedback, tactile, and other haptic displays (Burdea 1996)

We cover 3D displays in detail in Chapter 5.

3D Input Devices

Computer systems have traditionally used text-based input (keyboards), and one- degree of freedom (DOF) (dials, sliders) or 2-DOF (mouse, joystick, trackball) input devices. Three-dimensional input devices provide more DOF for the user to control simultaneously. These 3D spatial devices are the foundational technology for 3D UIs of the type we discuss in this book; they are the means by which the user interacts directly in a physical 3D spatial context. Examples of 3D input device types include

- Position- and orientation-tracking sensors (Meyer and Applewhite 1992; Turk and Fragoso 2015; Welch and Foxlin 2002)
- Posture- and gesture-sensing devices, often for human hands (Sturman and Zeltzer 1994)
- Multiple-DOF joysticks (Zhai et al. 1999) and 3D mice (Simon and Fröhlich 2003)

We discuss 3D input devices at length in Chapter 6, "3D User Interface Input Hardware."

To this point in the technological background, we have been discussing component technologies used to build 3D UIs. Now we turn our attention to whole technological systems built of these components. These systems provide platforms for 3D UI design.

Simulator Systems

Before the term VR was ever used, simulator systems pioneered the use of large, immersive, interactive displays of 3D computer graphics. Simulators have been used for many applications, including flight simulation, tank and military vehicle simulation, space vehicle simulation, and simulators for entertainment (Pausch et al. 1993).

Telepresence Systems

Telepresence systems enable a user in one real-world location to feel as if he were in a different real-world location. They combine sensors (cameras, microphones, etc.) on the remote side with displays (visual, auditory, haptic) and interactive controls (e.g., for rotating the camera) on the local side. Telepresence technology is similar to VR (see the following section) in many ways (Stassen and Smets 1995), except that real-world data, rather than synthetic data, is being displayed.

Virtual Reality Systems

Immersive VR systems combine interactive 3D graphics, 3D visual display devices, and 3D input devices (especially position trackers) to create the illusion that the user is inside a virtual world. Some important VR systems have included

- Sutherland's original head-mounted display system (Sutherland 1968)
- VPL's HMD and DataGlove (Zimmerman et al. 1987)
- The Cave Automatic Virtual Environment (CAVE), originally developed at the University of Illinois-Chicago's Electronic Visualization Laboratory (Cruz-Neira et al. 1993)

Augmented Reality Systems

AR uses most of the same technologies as VR but displays a combination of real and virtual imagery to give the impression that the user's real-world view is augmented, enhanced, or modified. 3D UI design for AR is especially challenging because the user must interact with both real-world and virtual objects, perhaps using different techniques. Examples of AR systems include

- HWD-based AR, such as Columbia University's MARS system (Höllerer et al. 1999)
- Spatial AR, where the virtual objects are projected onto the real world (Bimber and Raskar 2005)
- Handheld mobile AR, popular on smartphones and tablets (Schmalstieg and Wagner 2007)

Popular Media Background

A very different source of inspiration and vision for 3D UI work has been popular books (especially science fiction), films, and other media. Much of this vision has involved fully "natural" interaction with intelligent interfaces in perfectly realistic environments. Some specific examples are

- Books such as *Snow Crash* (Stephenson 1992), which describes the "Metaverse," a futuristic, immersive version of the Internet; *Neuromancer* (Gibson 1984), which coined the term **cyberspace;** and *Disclosure* (Crichton 1994), which features a VR system with natural physical movement and natural-language interaction.
- Television shows such as *Star Trek*: The *Next Generation*, which features the "Holodeck," a fully immersive synthetic environment that looks, feels, acts, and reacts just like the physical world.
- Films such as *Minority Report* and *Iron Man 2*, which envision advanced 3D interaction with data based on in-air gestures and body movements.

2.2.2 3D UI Subareas

In this section, we describe the various subparts of the field of 3D UIs. These subareas, described only briefly here, make up the bulk of the content of this book. We provide references in this section only when a topic is not covered later in the book.

3D Interaction Techniques and Interface Components

Just as 2D UIs are built from components such as windows, scrollbars, and menus and interaction techniques such as point-and-click, pinch-to-zoom, and drag-and-drop, 3D UIs are composed of a large number of techniques and components.

Interaction Techniques for Universal Tasks

Selection, manipulation, navigation, and system control are common, low-level user tasks in 3D interfaces. For each of these tasks, there is a large number of possible interaction techniques (combinations of input device and UI software). Interaction techniques may be based on real-world actions, or they may involve "magical" interactions that enhance capability. Chapters 7–9 discuss the design space of these techniques in detail, forming the core of this book.

Interaction Techniques for Composite and Application-Specific Tasks

More complex tasks in 3D UIs are often composed of the universal tasks described above. For example, the task of changing an object's color might involve choosing a color picker item from a menu (system control), pointing out an object (selection), and positioning a marker in a 3D color space (manipulation). The low-level interaction techniques for these subtasks can be composed to form a high-level interaction technique for the composite task. Other tasks are specific to a particular application. For example, the task of cloning objects in space could be seen as a composite task involving selection, system control, and manipulation, but there are benefits to considering this task independently and designing specific interaction techniques for it (Chen and Bowman 2009).

3D UI Widgets and Tools

Not all 3D interaction operates directly on the objects in the world. For many complex tasks, we need specialized objects that are not part of the environment but that help the user to interact with the environment. For example, a virtual knife might help a designer to slice through an automobile model to see a particular cross-section, or a small icon representing a piece of paper could be attached to a building to indicate the presence of textual information about it. Such tools are discussed in Chapter 9, "System Control," section 9.4.

3D Interaction Techniques Using 2D Devices

As we discussed in Chapter 1, "Introduction to 3D User Interfaces," 3D interaction takes place in a physical 3D spatial context (i.e., uses 3D spatial input devices), a virtual 3D spatial context (i.e., a 3D virtual world), or both. In this book, we focus on the design of 3D UIs using 3D spatial input devices. 3D interaction techniques that operate in a 2D input context (i.e., using devices such as a mouse or touchscreen) are another subarea of 3D UIs. For example, in 3D modeling programs running on desktop computers, we need a way to map 2D mouse input to the six degrees of freedom (DOF) of a 3D object. We do not cover this form of 3D interaction in this book. For the reader interested in this area, we recommend checking out research in desktop 3D interaction (Conner et al. 1992; Zeleznik and Forsberg 1999) and touch-based 3D interaction (Wigdor and Wixon 2011).

3D UI Design Approaches

Low-level interaction techniques and interface components are the building blocks of complete 3D UIs, but it is not trivial to put these elements together in a usable and understandable way. Thus, we need higher-level approaches or strategies for developing 3D interfaces.

Hybrid Interaction Techniques

One way to improve on the usability of individual interaction techniques is to combine the best parts of existing techniques. For example, the HOMER manipulation technique (see Chapter 7, section 7.4.5) is a hybrid of two other types of techniques: ray-casting and arm-extension. Another hybrid interaction approach is to combine 2D and 3D UIs together, taking the strengths of each one to create a more robust interface. This type of interaction is often done in system control (see Chapter 9).

Two-Handed Interaction

3D UIs can take advantage of a much richer set of inputs than can 2D interfaces. One powerful approach is to develop interactions that enable the user to use both hands in a complementary way. Taking this approach even farther, 3D UIs can be designed around whole-body interaction. See Chapter 10, "Strategies in Developing and Designing 3D User Interfaces," section 10.2 for a discussion of this and similar strategies.

Multimodal Interaction

Another design strategy that makes sense for 3D UIs is to use more than one input modality at the same time—so-called **multimodal interaction**. For example, combining hand-based gestures with speech input provides a powerful and concise way to specify complex actions. Multimodal interfaces are covered in Chapter 9, "System Control," section 9.9.

General 3D UI Design Strategies

Overall strategies for designing 3D UIs, discussed in Chapter 10 and in the case studies throughout the book, include

- Using real-world metaphors that help guide the user to the correct actions
- Using physical props or physics-based constraints to lessen precision requirements
- Applying principles of aesthetics and visual design
- Basing UI design on formal taxonomies of devices or interaction techniques
- Basing UI design on guidelines developed by researchers
- Using "magic" to allow the user to go beyond the perceptual, cognitive, or physical limitations of the real world
- Intentionally violating assumptions about the real world in the virtual world

3D UI Software Tools

Tools are needed to turn conceptual UI designs into concrete prototypes and implementations. This area changes rapidly, so we do not discuss specific tools, languages, development environments, or standards in this book. We note at least three important categories of tools.

Development Tools for 3D Applications

A wide variety of software libraries, toolkits, application programming interfaces (APIs), and integrated development environments (IDEs) exist that enable programmers to develop 3D graphical applications. Typically, these applications are written in a standard programming language such as C++ and make use of special APIs for 3D graphics (e.g., OpenGL), 3D device drivers, and so on.

Specialized Development Tools for 3D Interfaces

Fewer tools are designed specifically to aid the implementation of 3D UIs. Some 3D toolkits include default interaction techniques or interface widgets. Also, some work has been done on 3D UI description languages. Standards such as Virtual Reality Modeling Language (VRML) and Extensible 3D (X3D) include some interaction functionality, although the implementation of this functionality is left up to the browser or viewer developers.

3D Modeling Tools

All 3D UIs include 3D geometric objects and/or scenes. We are not aware of any 3D modeling tools aimed specifically at 3D UI visual design, but modeling tools used in other domains, such as animation, architecture, and engineering, can also be used to develop the objects and elements in a 3D UI.

3D UI Evaluation

As in all user experience work, usability evaluation is a critical part of 3D UI design. Evaluation helps designers pursue good ideas and reject poor ones, compare two or more alternatives for a particular UI component, validate the usability of a complete application, and more. We cover 3D UI evaluation in detail in Chapter 11.

Evaluation of Devices

In 3D UIs, evaluation must start at the lowest level because the UI components are almost always novel and unfamiliar. Thus, comparisons of the usability of various input and output devices are necessary. For example, one might compare the performance of different device types for a simple 3D rotation task (Hinckley, Tullio et al. 1997).

Evaluation of Interaction Techniques

As new 3D interaction techniques are developed for universal or application-specific tasks, simple usability studies can help to guide the design of these techniques. When there are many possible techniques for a particular task, a comparative evaluation can reveal the tradeoffs in usability and performance among the techniques (Bowman and Hodges 1997).

Evaluation of Complete 3D UIs or Applications

At a higher level, UX evaluation can be used within the design process (formative evaluation) or at its end (summative evaluation) to examine the quality of the user experience provided by a fully integrated UI or complete 3D application.

Evaluation Methodologies

Some researchers have investigated generic methodologies for evaluating the usability of 3D interfaces. For example, in test-bed evaluation (Chapter 11, section 11.6), researchers compare interaction techniques by having subjects use them in a wide variety of different tasks and situations so that a complete picture of the technique's quality can be obtained.

Studies of Phenomena Particular to 3D UIs

Most usability evaluations measure things like time to complete a task, perceived ease of use, satisfaction, or error rates. There are some metrics, however, that are unique to 3D UIs. One of these is **presence**—the feeling of "being there" that you get when immersed in a virtual 3D world (Slater et al. 1994). Because presence is not a concept that applies to most UIs, researchers have only recently begun to define it precisely and devise methods for measuring it. Another unique phenomenon is **cybersickness**—feelings of physical discomfort brought on by the use of immersive systems (Kennedy et al. 2000). Again, precise definitions and metrics for cybersickness are just beginning to emerge. Finally, since many 3D UIs attempt to replicate real-world interaction or are inspired by actions common in the physical world, studies of **interaction fidelity**—the level of realism of the UI—have become important (McMahan et al. 2012).

2.2.3 Areas Impacted by 3D UIs

This section addresses the impact of 3D UIs on other domains. This impact is felt mainly in the applications that are enabled by 3D UIs.

Application Areas

3D interaction can be used in a wide variety of application domains. We describe many of the most important ones briefly below.

Design and Prototyping

A 3D UI can be used to allow designers of real-world artifacts to work directly in a realistic 3D context (Weidlich et al. 2007). For example, an architect can navigate through a proposed new building and make changes to its design directly rather than working in the traditional 2D medium of drawings and plans (Bowman, Wineman, et al. 1998). The scenario in the preface illustrates the types of design problems and tasks a 3D UI might help to address.

Heritage and Tourism

Visiting historical sites can often be disappointing. Buildings have crumbled, cities have grown up around the site, and information is difficult to obtain. AR technology can address some of these issues by allowing a visitor to see directly what the site might have looked like in earlier times. The combination of real-world images and synthetic images seen from a first-person point of view can be quite compelling (Wither et al. 2010). 3D UIs can be used, for example, to set the time period the user wants to view or to navigate through text, audio, or image information related to the site (Gleue and Dahne 2001).

Gaming and Entertainment

An added component in video games is the ability to interact spatially in 3D (Norton et al. 2010). This type of interaction provides not only natural interaction metaphors, such as hitting a virtual tennis ball or steering a virtual car with a real steering wheel, but also more magical interfaces such as using 3D gestures to cast spells or to fly through a VE. Other examples include drawing in 3D to create 3D sculptures and using virtual walking techniques to move through first-person VR games. We discuss the design of a gaming 3D UI in one of the running case studies.

Simulation and Training

Three-dimensional environments based on virtual or augmented reality can be used for simulations of military operations, robotic agent actions, or the spread of a disease within the body, just to name a few. Training in a 3D environment for tasks such as surgery, spacewalks, or piloting an aircraft can also be very effective. In most cases, simulation and training applications need interactive capabilities and thus need 3D UI design.

Education

Students can learn topics from Newton's laws to historical inquiry in 3D virtual worlds and augmented real-world environments. If the worlds are highly interactive, students can experiment with a range of situations to help them construct their own mental models of how something works or to explore and analyze artifacts and information.

Art

Three-dimensional worlds provide artists a new canvas for new types of expression. Although some of today's 3D art is passive, most of it is interactive, responding to viewers' positions, gestures, touch, speech, and so on.

Visual Data Analysis

Scientists, engineers, business analysts, and others all work with large, complex 3D (or higher-dimensional) datasets. This data can be visualized using 3D graphics, providing understanding and insight that could not be obtained from looking at numeric results. With 3D UI components, the user can interactively navigate through the data, query various points in the visualization, or even steer the simulation computation (Bryson 1996). The mobile AR case study we present in later chapters of the book fits into this category.

Architecture and Construction

Architectural design and construction projects are organized around large 3D physical environments. With 3D interfaces, architects can visualize and modify their designs directly, contractors can address the coordination of construction equipment on a worksite, or interior designers can try hundreds of combinations of wall colors, furniture, and lighting and see the results immediately.

Medicine and Psychiatry

Three-dimensional applications are being used in the medical domain for telemedicine (remote diagnosis and treatment), 3D visualization of medical images such as MRIs, and psychotherapy, just to name a few examples. Virtual medicine and psychiatry can be less expensive, less embarrassing, and less dangerous. VR can also be used for pain control as part of physical therapy (Hoffman et al. 2008). A 3D UI can be used to allow the patient to interact with the environment. For example, someone with a fear of snakes might be able to pick up and handle a virtual snake with a combination of 3D input devices and a realistic toy snake.

Robotics

As robotic technologies become more prolific in society, designers need to provide methods for guiding and controlling them easily and intuitively (Pfeil et al, 2013). These robots might be humanoid, unmanned aerial vehicles (UAVs), or mobile manipulators. 3D UIs can be used to control these robots in a number of different ways. For example, 3D hand gestures can be used to control a UAV, or a user's arm and hand can act as a 3D proxy for a robot's gripper in mobile manipulation tasks. 3D UIs can be used for direct teleoperation, or to guide a robot to move in a general direction, or to point at physical objects that the robot should interact with.

Collaboration

More and more of our work is done in groups or teams, and often these groups are geographically scattered rather than located in a single office. This situation has led to the rise of a whole new software industry focused on collaborative applications, including videoconferencing, online presentations and classes, collaborative document editing, and design reviews (Cao et al. 2006). There are many ways 3D UIs can be used for collaborative work in a number of the application domains above (Prince et al. 2002). For example, a virtual meeting can be held in a 3D environment, providing more of the spatial and visual richness of a face-to-face meeting, or collaborators can enter a 3D environment to work together on the design of a new car.

Standards

There are no standard 3D UIs today in the sense of de facto standards (as the desktop metaphor is a de facto standard in 2D GUIs) or in the sense of documented standards (such as ISO standards). However, 3D UI work has had impact (that will continue to grow) on certain areas of standardization.

For Interactive 3D Graphics

The World Wide Web Consortium (W3C) defines international standards for many aspects of the Internet, including interactive 3D graphics. This work has led to the VRML specification and its successor, X3D. These standards provide a well-defined method for describing interactive 3D environments and indicate the features and functionality that 3D Web browsers need to implement. Although they focus on geometry, appearance, and organization, these standards do include some interactive components, and more are being added all the time.

For UI Description

The HCI community has worked to develop methods for the abstract, platform-independent description of UIs, and several have been produced for 2D GUIs (Hartson and Gray 1992). Although these could not yet be called standards, that is their intent. The 3D UI community has also seen the need for such description languages (Figueroa et al. 2001), and we expect that this will be a focus area in the future.

Reciprocal Impacts

Finally, we note that 3D UI research has influenced some of the areas from which it sprang. These reciprocal impacts indicate that 3D UI work has had an effect beyond itself, revealing gaps in our knowledge of other areas.

On Graphics

To be usable, 3D UIs often require complex visuals. For example, the principle of feedback indicates that the visual display should show users information about their actions both during and after the users' input. This means that during 3D object manipulation, we should provide users with sufficient depth and position cues to understand where the object is in relation to the target location. These cues might include subtle lighting effects, realistic shadows, or various levels of transparency, all of which require complex real-time graphics algorithms. In this and many other ways, the requirements of 3D UIs can drive graphics research.

On HCI

The study of 3D UIs has revealed many areas not addressed by traditional HCI. For example, what metrics should be used to study the user experience of a system? In typical UIs, metrics such as speed, accuracy, satisfaction, and perceived ease of use may be sufficient; in 3D UIs, we also need to assess things like physical comfort and presence. The development of heuristics or guidelines for good UI design is another area that has been studied thoroughly in traditional HCI but that requires further thought and expansion for 3D UIs.

On Psychology

As we noted above, the design of 3D UIs is heavily dependent on knowledge from perceptual and cognitive psychology. In an interesting way, even these areas have benefited from 3D UI research. One issue in perceptual psychology, for example, is the design of valid and generalizable experiments studying visual perception, because it's very hard to tightly control what a person sees in a real-world setting and because some visual stimuli are hard to produce in the real world. In a synthetic 3D VE, however, we can remove all the real-world visual stimuli and replace them with anything we like, producing an extremely powerful environment for studying topics like human navigation (Riecke et al. 2002). Interactive virtual worlds also provide an ideal platform for studying human behavior in a variety of situations (Blascovich et al. 2002)

2.3 Scope of this Book

This book is about the design of 3D user interfaces, and therefore we focus on the content that is specific to 3D UIs. This roughly corresponds to the topics in section 2.2.2 (3D UI Subareas, excluding the software tools topics). We also discuss some of the background and application topics from sections 2.2.1 and 2.2.3 when appropriate. For example, Chapters 3 and 4 cover some basic background on human factors and HCI, respectively, and the case studies that run throughout the book discuss the design of virtual reality and mobile augmented reality applications.

Of course, this book can't cover everything in the roadmap. Some specific items that are not covered include

- An in-depth discussion of presence and cybersickness
- Technical information on the design or workings of various devices
- Graphics algorithms and techniques for rendering 3D environments
- Information on the usage of particular 3D toolkits, APIs, or modeling programs

For information on these topics, refer to the references above and to the recommended reading lists in each chapter.

For a visual representation of the book's coverage, see Figure 2.1. The items shown in bold text in the figure are discussed in some detail, while the gray items are not covered or are mentioned only briefly.

We already noted that there are several different platforms for 3D UIs, including VR, AR, and traditional desktop computers. In this book, we strive to be as general as possible in our descriptions of interaction techniques and UI components, and the principles and guidelines we provide are usually applicable to any 3D UI. However, we recognize that there are some interaction techniques that are specifically designed for one platform or another. We call out such special cases as they arise.

2.4 Introduction to Case Studies

Throughout the book, we will be presenting running case studies that are used to reinforce concepts presented in each chapter, starting with Chapter 5. These case studies are meant to provide examples for how a 3D UI application is designed, built, and evaluated. In this section, we introduce the two case studies that we will use; the first one is a VR game and the second is a mobile AR application.

2.4.1 VR Gaming Case Study

When we think of highly interactive VR experiences, gaming comes to mind immediately. The current renaissance of interest and investment in VR is largely driven by gaming and other entertainment applications, so it's natural for us to consider the design of a 3D UI for a VR game as one of the case studies for this book. As we dive deeply into this topic, we'll see that there are a multitude of interesting and potentially thorny 3D interaction issues to explore.

Unlike our mobile AR case study (see section 2.4.2), the VR gaming case study is purely hypothetical and speculative. We have not prototyped or studied such a game; the design we present is only a first "paper prototype." Still, the design we discuss here is not ad hoc, but is based on reasoning from research and experience—what we know about effective 3D interaction techniques. We also recognize that 3D interaction design is not the only, or even the primary, criterion determining the success of a VR game. Clearly, creative decisions about concept, storyline, characters, and visual/sound design also play a huge role. At the same time, interaction design and game mechanics can be important differentiators, especially when designing games for new technologies (cf. the interaction techniques used in the Nintendo Wii as compared to previous console game UIs).

For the case study, we've chosen to design the interaction for a VR version of the classic action-adventure game genre. Notable examples of this genre include the Portal series, the Legend of Zelda series, and the Tomb Raider series. This type of game is slower paced than pure action games like first-person shooters, emphasizing puzzle solving and action planning, but also includes elements of physical skill and timing. This seems to be an ideal fit for VR, where it's fun to have the player physically involved in the game and interacting with the game in real time but where rapid movements and quickly changing environments are problematic, because they might lead to physical sickness or injury.

We need a goal for the player and a minimal story outline to serve as context for our game design decisions. Because we want to include some physical navigation, we need a virtual environment that's extensive but also compartmentalized (moving physically through a very large outdoor environment is problematic), so let's say that the game takes place in a large building broken up into many rooms—perhaps a spooky old hotel. The player starts out on the ground floor, which is surrounded by monsters or other baddies, and it becomes clear that the only way of escape is to make it to the roof, where the good guys can come to rescue you in a helicopter. But getting to the roof requires the player to collect items and solve puzzles that will open locked doors, provide a way to cross giant chasms in the floor, and get the elevator working. All the while, the player must be wary of monsters sneaking up on them. Think Luigi's Mansion, but in realistic first-person VR.

In the upcoming chapters, we'll explore the 3D UI issues related to this VR game, from the choice of input devices to the design of menus and much more.

2.4.2 Mobile AR Case Study

Powerful mobile devices and sensor networks enable the development of increasingly complex mobile graphical information system (GIS) applications. In this case study, we present the HYDROSYS system (Nurminen et al. 2011), a mobile AR system tailored to environmental analysis (Veas et al. 2013). The system, which was developed by Kruijff and his colleagues, supported groups of users in analyzing environmental processes on-site, that is, in the actual location these processes occur (see Figure 2.2).

Analysis at the actual location the event occurred can offer the user substantial insights that would be difficult to gain while working in an office. For example, consider the case where someone wants to analyze the situation after a flood or avalanche has damaged a built environment. It is often hard to do an accurate analysis of such complex processes without visiting the site itself. Remote analysis often lacks information about the latest state of the environment: even though the environment itself may be changing continuously, the models that represent these environments are often updated only irregularly.

In HYDROSYS, users performed simple observations of data like temperature distributions or snow characteristics, as well as detailed and complex analyses of large-scale processes such as those occurring after a natural disaster. End-users included not only environmental scientists but also government employees, insurance personnel, and the general public. Each group posed quite different requirements on the usage of the system due to different levels of experience with environmental data, as well as widely varying spatial abilities that affect the interpretation of the spatial data.

Figure 2.2 User holding the handheld AR device and the sensor station in an alpine usage environment of HYDROSYS (image courtesy of Erick Mendez).

To provide the user with an accurate representation of an environmental process requires capturing and processing of data from different kinds of sensors. Preferably, this is achieved through a high-density network of sensors. In HYDROSYS, we placed up to 15 sensor stations at relatively small exploration sites (maximum several square kilometers), providing high-resolution data. In comparison, during normal weather monitoring for your daily weather update, a single weather station often monitors several tens of square kilometers. Each of these sensor stations was equipped with around 10 sensors, ranging from basic weather sensors to specialized hydrological equipment. Sensor stations sent their readings over a wireless network to a central server at a regular interval, up to once a minute. From the central server, data could be accessed directly or transferred to a simulation server that would process the data. While in the field, users could access both the latest sensor readings as well as the processed data, which could range from a simple temperature distribution map up to complex forecast visualizations.

These data could not only be observed from a first-person perspective but also through the eyes of other users or camera systems. The most innovative feature of HYDROSYS was a multi-camera system that could be used to assess the site from different perspectives so as to improve spatial awareness. Each user was equipped with a wearable AR setup containing a camera, while other cameras were mounted on sensor stations or tripods. We also deployed a seven-meter blimp that was used to capture thermal data and reconstruct the environment to create up-to-date 3D models. Users could switch through the various camera video streams to obtain a better impression of the site—aiding the process of building up spatial awareness—while discussing observations with other users using a teleconference system.

The HYDROSYS system posed numerous challenges, ranging from the development of ergonomic but robust handheld AR platforms that could withstand harsh environments to the design of effective navigation methods for multi-camera viewpoint transitions. As such, it provides an exciting example of the various issues you may encounter when designing systems with similar requirements. In the following chapters, we look at many of these issues.

2.5 Conclusion

In this chapter, you've taken a tour through some of the history of 3D interaction and seen glimpses of the many facets of this rich and interesting area. In Parts II and III, we provide more detail on the theoretical, practical, and technological background for 3D UI design.

PART II

HUMAN FACTORS AND HUMAN-COMPUTER INTERACTION BASICS

Understanding 3D UIs, and the remainder of this book, requires a solid understanding of fundamental principles from human factors and HCI. For the reader unfamiliar with these principles, we offer an overview in the following two chapters.

CHAPTER 3

HUMAN FACTORS FUNDAMENTALS

This chapter explores human factors issues that typically affect the design of a 3D UI. We focus on how users process information. Additionally, perception, cognition and physical ergonomics issues are explored, which will be reflected in the subsequent chapters on interaction technology and techniques.

3.1 Introduction

When a novel 3D interaction device or technique is being designed, it is important to consider the human factors that affect its usability and performance. While not always discussed or analyzed in much detail, human factors are an important cornerstone of a user-centered design process. The term "human factors" refers to the capabilities, characteristics, and limitations of the human user, and includes considerations related to the body (acting), the senses (perceiving), and the brain (thinking). An understanding of human factors is used for the design of systems in pursuit of safe, efficient, and comfortable use.

So, what is good human-factors-driven design? This question is not easy to answer: it highly depends on the use case and users involved. Some issues that interaction designers might address include the visibility issues affecting the perceptual optimization of augmented reality interfaces, the study of knowledge transfer in training applications, or the analysis and design of ergonomic grips for interaction devices. In general, human-factors-driven design means analyzing the true capabilities of the human body (and mind) and making use of the enormous potential of human beings to improve design. Design processes driven by human potential can lead to highly innovative and engaging interfaces, in particular those that are applied in the games and arts sectors (Beckhaus and Kruijff 2004; Kruijff 2013). The consideration of human factors issues can be seen as a critical part of user-centered interface design and can be integrated directly into the usability engineering processes we introduce in Chapter 4, "General Principles of Human–Computer Interaction."

The analysis of human factors issues requires a good understanding of general evaluation methodologies. Hence, we also recommend that you look closely at Chapters 4 and 11, "Evaluation of 3D User Interfaces." It's often a good idea to isolate human factors issues to reduce the overall complexity of a study, as many human factors are interconnected. As we will see later in the analytical methods sections, practical concerns may actually limit the choice of method, as not all methods can readily be deployed in every situation. For example, it may be difficult to deploy certain psycho-physiological methods in outdoor validations, as even in controlled environments they are usually difficult to use. For a thorough discussion of performing human factors and ergonomics studies, we recommend that you read Jacko et al. (2012).

In this chapter, we give an overview of the human factors that affect the design of many interfaces. After introducing higher-level issues related to the processing of information (section 3.2), we focus on three interconnected human factors categories: perceptual (section 3.3), cognitive (section 3.4), and physical ergonomics issues (section 3.5). For example, you will be confronted with these issues when you want to analyze a specific display device (perception), evaluate how much cognitive load a user experiences when performing certain tasks (cognition), or study the effect of posture fatigue in full-body interfaces (physical ergonomics). As we go through these categories, we explain the psycho-physiological foundations and identify major human factors related problems and methods to analyze these issues. While discussing the human factors issues, we also deal with processes at a neurological level, which is important for understanding brain-computer interfaces, systems that trigger the nervous system to produce auditory or vestibular events, or the usage of bio-signals to address arousal or cognitive load issues.

This chapter provides a foundation for most of the upcoming chapters. Throughout the remainder of the book, we refer to the specific human factors sections. So even if you don't read this chapter as a whole, you may want to read specific sections to help you understand later material.

3.2 Information Processing

In this section we provide an overview of the basic concepts surrounding human Information processing.

3.2.1 Foundations

To understand the mechanisms underlying human-factors-driven design, it is important to have a basic knowledge of how users process information into useful (inter)actions. This process is generally referred to as information processing, and it is closely tied to the discussion of interaction loops we will discuss in Chapter 4. During interaction with a system, users continuously perceive information from various sources, encode and transfer the information in different forms, and take actions based on the processed information. In return, they receive feedback on their actions, which is fed back into the information-processing loop. Within these processes, information must be transformed—this takes time and may produce errors, two main sources that define the performance of a user interface.

While multiple models of information-processing exist, we adapted the high-level staged model that was introduced by Wickens and Carswell (1997) by mapping it to the three main factors discussed in this chapter: perception, cognition, and physical ergonomics. If you are interested in different views on information processing, Wickens and Carswell also briefly explain other models. Our adapted model, shown in Figure 3.1, shows the various stages of information processing and how they are related to the three main human factors categories we will address in this chapter.

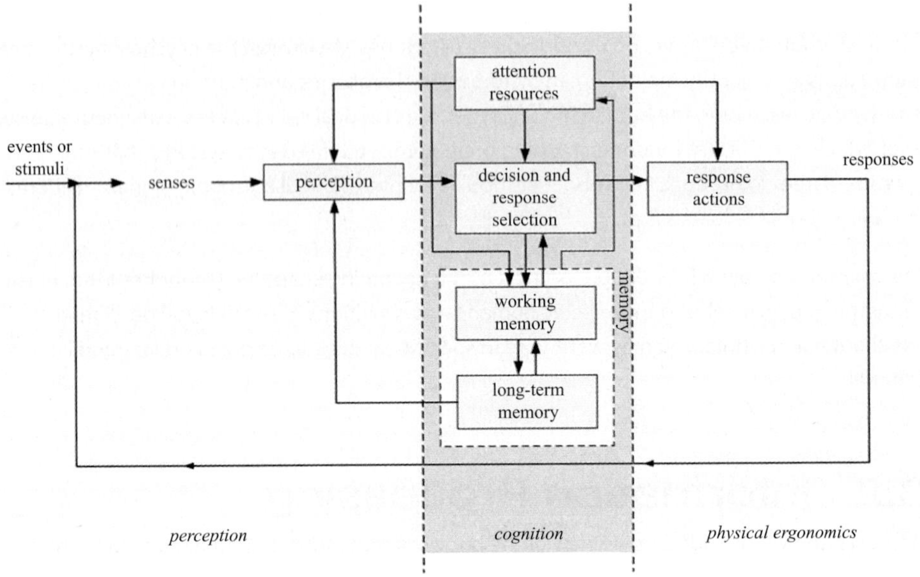

Figure 3.1 Information processing and related human factors issues. Adapted from (Wickens and Carswell 1997).

In this model, stimuli or events are sensed and perceived, that is, provided with a meaningful interpretation based on memories of past experiences. In response to what is perceived, actions may get selected and executed or information may get stored in working memory, also known as short-term memory. Working memory has limited capacity and is highly influenced by attention resources (i.e., to keep something in working memory, one must be attending to it). In contrast, the capacity of our long-term memory is vast, storing information about our world, concepts, and procedures while not being directly affected by attention. As a result of performed actions, users may receive feedback, which is fed back into the information-processing loop.

3.2.2 Attention

Within the information-processing system, attention affects several subprocesses. Understanding attention helps interface designers. For example, attention affects how users search in analytical applications, influences which information we gather from dynamic spatio-temporal environments, and can be used to draw our focus to specific (urgent) information in a large information space.

While attention is still not fully understood, evidence indicates that it has three components: orienting to sensory events, detecting signals for focused processing, and maintaining a vigilant or alert state (Posner and Boies 1971). Attention is a major component in processing visual stimuli and search behavior (Treisman and Gelade 1980). It involves the selection of some information for further processing and inhibiting other information from receiving further processing (Smith and Kosslyn 2013).

Attention can take different forms in information-processing tasks (Wickens and Carswell 1997):

- *Selective attention* is the choosing of which events or stimuli to process.
- *Focused attention* is the effort to maintain processing of these elements while avoiding distraction from other stimuli or events.
- *Divided attention* is the ability to process more than one event or stimulus at a given point in time.

As such, attention can be seen conceptually as a selection process. However, analyzing and describing attention at a neurological level is a difficult task. Current research focuses on analyzing so-called event-related potentials (ERPs) using neuro-imaging methods. While we briefly look at ERPs in the validation sections, for now it suffices to understand that attention involves three mental operations: disengaging attention from the current location, moving attention to a new location, and reengaging attention in a new location to support processing in that location (Posner and Cohen 1984). It has been shown that attention in one sensory channel can trigger attention within another channel (Driver and Spence 1998). For example, consider a busy train station—a friend may be waving and, once you focus your attention on her, you may notice she is also calling your name. Interestingly, many links seem to exist between the different sensory modalities. We attend to these issues in various sections of this chapter, in particular section 3.3.5, which deals with multisensory processing.

However useful attention is in our daily life, its processes are unfortunately prone to errors, which can be increased by certain bottlenecks. Examples of such bottlenecks are limitations in our sensory systems (e.g., the low acuity of our peripheral vision) or the split of attention in divided attention tasks. Such errors, or failures, tend to happen either at a spatial or temporal level and may be strengthened by the mode of attention. For example, while walking through a busy street, you are presented with a vast amount of information at different spatial locations, which is impossible to notice all at once. This information overload may produce errors to surprising magnitudes, including the inability to notice visual changes (change blindness, Simons and Rensink 2005). For example, consider continuity errors in movies that often go unnoticed, even though changes may be large. Change blindness occurs not only in vision but also in audition, known as change deafness (Vitevitch 2003). Similarly, errors occur on a temporal basis, especially when rapid sequences of stimuli occur.

3.2.3 Decision-Making, Behavior, and Skills

As we can see in Figure 3.1, decision-making processes are in the center of information processing and depend on capturing, organizing, and combining information from various sources. Decision-making is the process of choosing between two or more alternatives, resulting in real or imaginary consequences (Lehto et al. 2012). The process itself is based on the identification of the current situation, potential actions, and the consequences thereof. The speed of decision-making processes varies widely, and is affected by conflicts, complexity, or uncertainty of either the information being processed or the detection of the possible outcome. Decision-making often depends on problem solving and reasoning methods; the boundary between these processes often cannot be drawn clearly.

A typical method to visually define the structure of decisions is a so-called decision tree. However, similar to attention, the modeling of decision-making processes is a complex undertaking. A good overview of different theories can be found in Lehto et al. (2012). They identify three possible models. The normative model applies methods from statistics and economics and is built around the notion of rationality. Behavioral models, in contrast, take into account human limitations and model decision-making around heuristics. Finally, naturalistic decision models try to define how people make decisions about (complex) tasks in realistic situations.

There are two issues deeply embedded in decision-making that are worth a brief look: **behavior** and **skills**. In the context of decision-making, behavior refers to the usage of specific strategies to make decisions that may be formed through experience and can be affected by culture, belief, habits, social norms, or attitudes. Our behavior can be adjusted by our emotional state. Some effects that have been shown are temporal discounting (i.e., the devaluing of outcomes that are further in the future) and dynamic inconsistencies (i.e., making different choices in similar conditions, defying direct logic) (Smith and Kosslyn 2013). User behavior can also be affected by *conditioning*, which has become infamous through the experiments of Russian psychologist Ivan Pavlov, in which responses are triggered by specific stimuli (Pavlov 1927). Conditioning should not be mistaken with *habituation*, a process occurring in long-term memory in which an organism decreases its response or even stops responding to a stimulus after repeated presentation (Kandell et al. 2000). Habituation has successfully been used in VR applications to treat disorders such as phobias (Garcia-Palacios et al. 2001). In the context of decision-making, looking deeper at user behavior may potentially reveal such issues as variances in taking decisions or the general risk attitude. In HCI, researchers have tried to model user behavior using complex models of user intent, in particular search behavior, while interacting with systems. Within 3DUIs, behavior often informs the design of natural user interfaces, such as those that use gestures (Wigdor and Wixon 2011).

User behavior is often affected by skills. Skills allow users to make more accurate and quicker responses and can be acquired over time by repeatedly performing similar actions (Fitts and Posner 1967). As such, they tie into decision-making, memory, and motor processes. Fitts and Posner (1967) identified three different stages in acquiring skills. The cognitive stage represents declarative knowledge and often relates to a conscious set of instructions. Gradually, users may move into the associative stage, in which behavior is getting tuned and error rates go down. Finally, over time users enter the autonomous stage, in which actions can be accurately and rapidly executed. Skills are thought to be stored as nondeclarative knowledge in our long-term memory (Kandell et al. 2000; see section 3.4.1).

Skills can be a major focus of a 3DUI. Functional sets or particular actions can be difficult to learn and thus require skill to be mastered. Furthermore, skill transfer is an important factor in many VR training applications, with the expectation that skills learned in a VE can also be applied in the real world (Philbin et al. 1998; Hughes et al. 2005). Good examples can be found in medicine (Torkington et al. 2001; Jack et al. 2001), engineering (Loftin and Kenney 1995), and firefighting (Tate et al. 1997).

3.2.4 Selection and Control of Action

Selection and control of action are closely tied to decision-making, as they involve the selection and performance of a response based on certain stimuli. It is not always easy to separate the two processes, since they seem to tie into each other seamlessly. In general, decision-making is a higher-level cognitive process that may involve "deeper thinking," while action selection is a lower-level, more automatic process that only involves simple cognition.

The speed and accuracy of responses are dependent on various factors. First of all, they depend on the *stimulus-response compatibility,* which refers to specific combinations of stimuli and responses that may be more natural and as a result may lead to faster or more accurate performance (Fitts and Seeger 1953). Furthermore, responses to stimuli are faster when the stimuli and response are the same as in the preceding trial (Bertelson 1961). In contrast, response times increase when users need to switch between tasks. Finally, stimulus-response times can be affected by uncertainty and precueing (Sanders 1998).

Selection and control of action are inherently bound to user performance. Speed is affected by accuracy: when speedy responses are required, speed can be traded for accuracy, a mechanism also known as the speed-accuracy trade-off (Pachella 1974). The selection and control of action are affected by Fitts's law, affecting control performance (Proctor and Vu 2012).

Motor control is a crucial aspect of many 3DUIs and is generally believed to take two different forms: open-loop and closed-loop control. Open-loop control is based on an internal model, referred to as a motor program or plan, which defines a set of movement commands. In contrast, closed-loop control is dependent on sensory feedback, making adjustments of control along the way. Fitts's law has been a key in describing the performance of many motor actions and has been used in numerous evaluations. It describes the time to make aimed movements to a target location (Fitts 1954). The original Fitts's law formula is defined as follows:

$$MT = a + b \log_2 (2D/W)$$

where MT is movement time, a and b are constants (model parameters), D is the distance to the target, and W is the target size. Fitts's law identifies two important performance factors for aimed movement: performance time increases both by increasing the distance towards a target and decreasing the target width. The formula thus also defines a speed-accuracy relationship: the more precise our movements need to be, the longer the movements will take. Movements can be divided into two phases: a fast motion towards the target (also known as the ballistic phase) and a corrective movement, used to home in on the target once it's nearby. The latter relates directly to the *index of difficulty* (ID), the quantity of information transmitted (in units of bits) by performing the task, which can be defined by

$$ID = \log_2 (2D/W)$$

where the ID is the same as the entirety of the Fitts's law equation after the constant *b*. The index is a metric to quantify the difficulty of selecting a target. Subsequently, both metrics can be combined to form the *index of performance* (IP), defined as

$$IP = (ID/MT)$$

The IP is expressed in bits per second and has been used to define the performance of many input devices. In one study, the hand itself was found to have an IP of 10.6 bits/s, a mouse 10.4 bits/s, a joystick 5.0 bits/s, and a touchpad 1.6 bits/s (MacKenzie 1992).

It should be noted that multiple factors affect performance, including the method of visual feedback, the selection method, the coordination between different motor actions, the latency of the input device, and the actual sequence in which tasks are performed. Specific spatial and motor symmetries have also been shown to affect performance—one known example is the coordination between hand and feet (Proctor and Vu 2012).

Finally, the *steering law* is highly relevant to various tasks performed in a 3D UI. The steering law is a predictive model that describes the time to steer (move or navigate) through a tunnel. The tunnel can be understood as a path or trajectory with a certain width. The model is associated with the task of moving through the tunnel as quickly as possible without crossing the boundaries. For example, in a VR game, a user might be required to navigate through a corridor without touching the walls. For complex, curvilinear paths, the steering law can be defined as

$$T = a + b\int_C \frac{ds}{W(s)}$$

where T is the average time to move through the path, C is the path parameterized by s, $W(s)$ is the width of the path at s, and a and b are experimentally fitted constants. For simple paths (i.e., straight tunnels with a constant width W), the steering law can be represented as

$$T = a + b\frac{A}{W}$$

where A is simply the length of the path. Interestingly, in the formula we can see a speed-accuracy trade-off similar to Fitts's Law.

3.3 Perception

Now that we have reviewed overall information-processing principles, let us take a closer look at the three different stages in the information-processing cycle, namely perception (section 3.3), cognition (section 3.4), and physical ergonomics (section 3.5).

A good understanding of perceptual mechanisms is important to choose or design effective interfaces and will help make sense of the 3D UI guidelines we present in later chapters. In the following sections, we will describe the foundations of each perceptual channel as well as the main cues that are involved. For a thorough introduction to some of the terminology, we refer the reader to Goldstein (2014), Smith and Kosslyn (2013), and Siegel and Shapru (2010).

3.3.1 Vision

In this section, we introduce the basics of visual perception and the various cues that are processed when interacting with a real or virtual environment.

Foundations

The processing of visual information depends on a complex pattern of intertwined pathways. At the lowest level, features of a visual scene such as light intensity and edges form an image on the retina, which is captured by a layer of cells called photoreceptors and by nerve cells at the back of the eye. The distribution of the different kinds of photoreceptors (rods and cones) results in different abilities of the visual system in the center and the periphery. While in central vision we are able to see colors, shapes, and text, towards the periphery these abilities deteriorate quickly. However, peripheral vision is still reasonably good in processing motion; this is important for our fast reaction to moving objects. As we will see later, these abilities are important in display systems that offer a wider field of view.

The photoreceptors and nerve cells convert light into electrical signals and transmit them to the brain's primary visual cortex via the optic nerves. Within the primary visual cortex, there are two pathways: the dorsal pathway, which is import for processing information about object locations and how they may be acted upon, and the ventral pathway, which deals with the recognition and identification of objects. These pathways are bidirectional and have an important role in how information is processed: bottom-up processes are driven by information in the world being observed, while top-down processes interpret sensory information on the basis of knowledge, expectations, beliefs, and goals; they are thus connected to cognitive processes (Goldstein 2014; Smith and Kosslyn 2013).

Visual Cues

Within a spatial application, users often need to interpret a visual scene correctly for effective use, and this is achieved through visual cues in the displayed content. For example, users need to have a good understanding of the spatial structure of a 3D scene, which is supported by depth cues. Depth information will help the user to interact with the application, especially when performing 3D selection, manipulation, and navigation tasks. Depth cues may conflict, leading to false assumptions. Therefore, understanding what depth cues the human visual system uses to extract 3D information and how visual displays provide such cues is another important tool for analyzing these devices.

More detail on visual depth cues can be found in Goldstein (2014); May and Badcock (2002); Wickens, Todd, and Seidler (1989); Sedgwick (1988); and Sekuler and Blake (1994).

Monocular, Static Cues

Monocular, static depth cues refer to depth information that can be inferred from a static image (normally viewed by a single eye). Because they can be seen in a still picture, static cues are also called pictorial cues. These cues include relative size, height relative to the horizon, occlusion, linear and aerial perspective, shadows and lighting, and texture gradients.

With no information about the absolute size of an object, its **relative size** can be used as a depth cue. For example, if a scene contains a group of increasingly smaller circles placed against a blank background, the smaller circles appear to be farther away (see Figure 3.2). An object's **height relative to the horizon** can also influence a viewer's depth perception. Objects viewed below the horizon in the lower part of the visual field appear closer to the viewer than objects higher in the visual field. This effect is reversed for objects above the horizon.

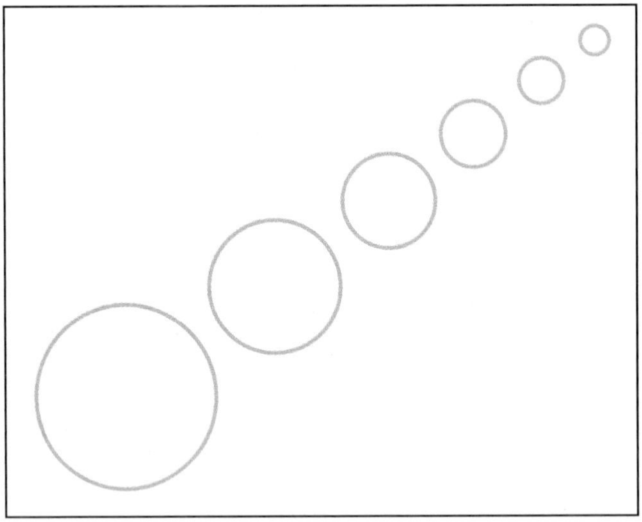

Figure 3.2 Relative size as a visual depth cue.

Occlusion (also called contour interruption or interposition) is the phenomenon in which an object closer to the user partially obstructs the view of an object farther away. When one opaque object occludes another, the user knows that the first object is closer (see Figure 3.3).

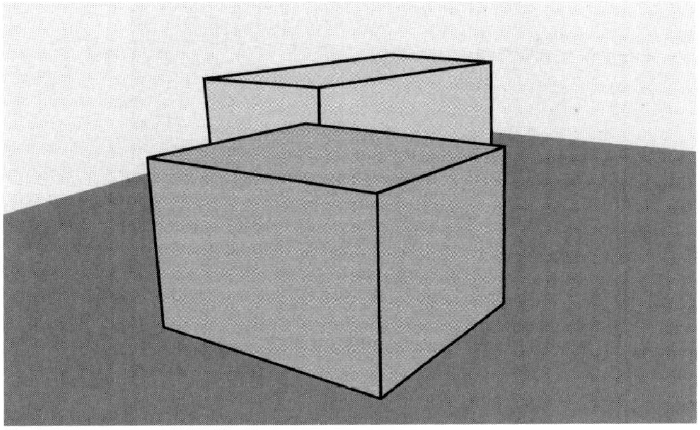

Figure 3.3 Occlusion and linear perspective.

Linear perspective is the phenomenon that makes parallel lines appear to converge as they move away from the viewer. The closer the lines get to one another, the farther they appear to be from the viewer. In addition to showing occlusion, Figure 3.3 shows an example of linear perspective.

Aerial perspective (also called atmospheric attenuation) is a cue that gauges relative distance by measuring the scattering and absorption of light through the atmosphere. For example, a nearer object will have more color saturation and brightness, while a more distant object will be duller and dimmer.

Shadows and lighting also play a role in helping the viewer to determine depth. Shadows convey depth as they fall on other objects or are cast from an object to adjacent surfaces. The viewer estimates the location of the light sources in the scene to determine how far an object is from an adjacent surface (see Figure 3.4). Lighting conveys depth because objects that have more illumination are generally closer to the viewer.

Figure 3.4 How shadows give the illusion of depth: the rectangle on the right appears to be much higher off the page than the rectangle on the left.

Many surfaces and objects have patterns associated with them. When these patterns are projected onto a 2D surface, the density of the surface or object texture increases with the distance between the surface and the viewer. This phenomenon is called an object's **texture gradient** and provides relative depth cues (see Figure 3.5).

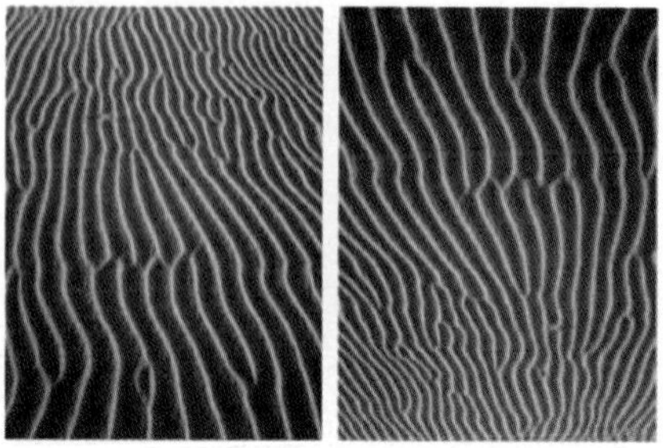

Figure 3.5 Effects of texture gradient: the image on the right is simply the left image inverted. In both cases, depth is conveyed.

Oculomotor cues

Oculomotor cues (illustrated in Figure 3.6) are depth cues derived from muscular tension in the viewer's visual system, called accommodation and vergence. **Accommodation** is the physical stretching and relaxing of the eye lens caused by the eye muscles when focusing on an image. The state of these eye muscles in stretching and relaxing provides the viewer a cue as to the distance of the focused object. When an object is far away, these muscles relax, resulting in the lens being more spherical. When an object is close to the viewer, the eye muscles pull on the lens, flattening it out. **Vergence** is the rotation of the viewer's eyes so images can be fused together at varying distances. The muscular feedback from this rotation is also a cue as to the depth of the object. A viewer's two eyes converge when viewing near objects and diverge when viewing far objects.

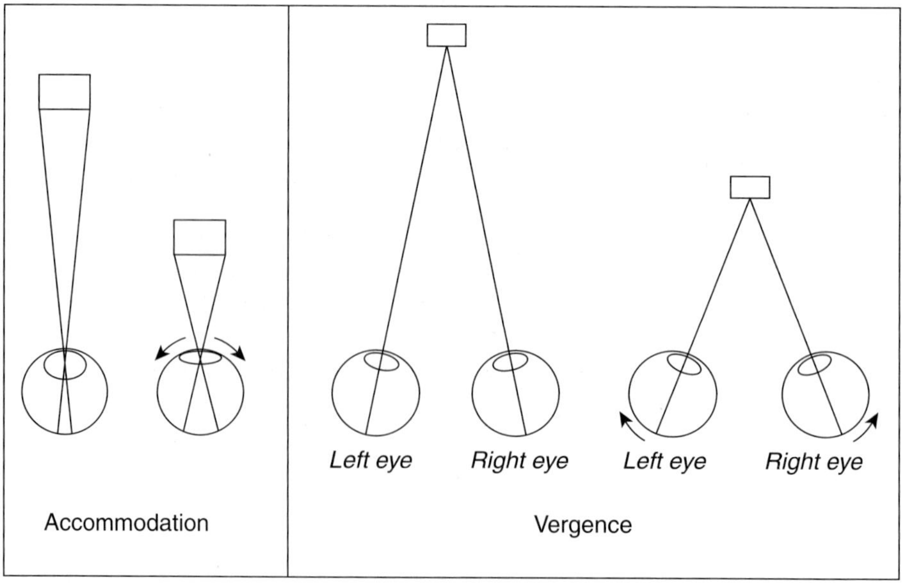

Figure 3.6 Accommodation (left image) and vergence (right image): the arrows indicate the stretching of the eye lens for accommodation and the rotating of the eyes for vergence.

Motion parallax

Depth information is conveyed when objects are moving relative to the viewer (i.e., stationary-viewer motion parallax), when the viewer is moving relative to stationary objects (i.e., moving-viewer motion parallax), or when there is a combination of the two. **Motion parallax** causes objects closer to the viewer to move more quickly across the visual field and objects farther away from the viewer to move more slowly (see Figure 3.7). As an example, consider someone in a moving car. As the car moves, objects such as streetlights and telephone poles that are on the side of the road appear to be moving very quickly past the viewer, while objects farther away from the car, such as a tall building or mountain, appear to move much more slowly. Motion parallax is called a **dynamic** depth cue, because it requires a moving image. In an otherwise sparse 3D environment, motion parallax can provide excellent depth information to the viewer.

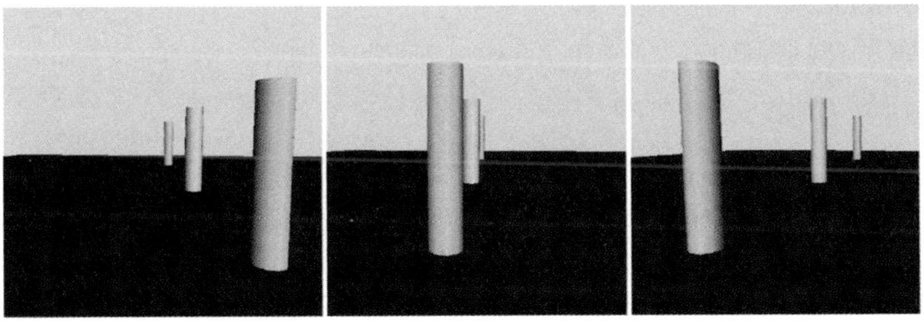

Figure 3.7 A sequence of images illustrating motion parallax. As the viewer moves from left to right, the cylinder closest to the viewer appears to move the most, while the cylinder farthest away from the viewer appears to move the least. (Image courtesy of Joseph LaViola Jr.)

Binocular disparity and stereopsis

Most people view the world with two eyes, and each eye sees a slightly different image. **Binocular disparity** refers to the difference between these two images. A great way to understand binocular disparity is to focus on a near object (such as your finger) and alternate opening and closing each eye. The differences between the two images will be readily apparent.

Binocular disparity tends to be much more pronounced the closer the object is to the viewer (see Figure 3.8). The fusion of these two images (through accommodation and vergence) provides a powerful depth cue by presenting a single stereoscopic image. This effect is referred to as **stereopsis.** Note that if the two images cannot be properly fused (e.g., when an object is very close to the viewer) **binocular rivalry** can occur, which causes the viewer to see one image but not the other or a part of one image and a part of the other.

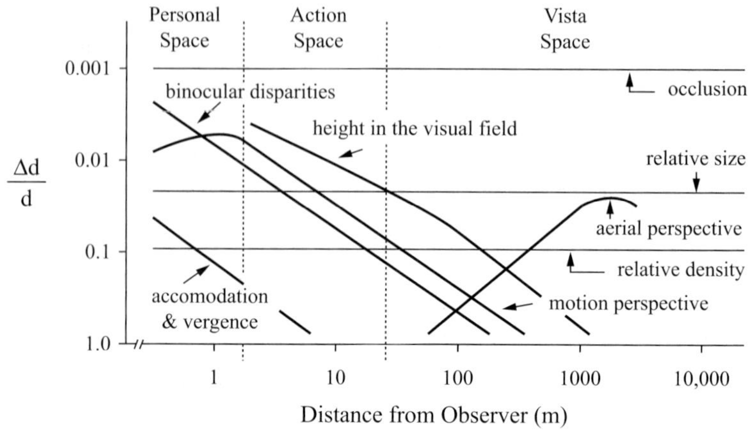

Figure 3.8 The relative importance of depth cues at different distances, adapted from Cutting et al. (1995).

Figure 3.8 compares the relative strength of depth cues at different distances for comparing the depth of two objects (Cutting et al. 1995). As the figure shows, occlusion is the most useful cue for this sort of comparison, as it acts equally well at any distance and can provide a precise comparison of two objects' depths even when the difference between the depths is a thousand times smaller than the distance to the objects. Note, however, that occlusion and many other depth cues only provide relative depth information. Only accommodation, vergence, stereopsis, and motion parallax provide information about absolute depth.

3.3.2 The Auditory System

We now turn to the auditory system and associated cues.

Foundations

The auditory sensory system is probably the second-most used sensory channel after the visual channel. The auditory system consists of the outer, middle, and inner ear. The outer ear collects the sound and directs it to the eardrum, which vibrates, mimicking the sound waves it receives. The eardrum produces a reaction in the three bones of the middle ear (malleus, incus, stapes), which causes the fluid in the inner ear to move. This affects the hair cells, or receptors, in the cochlea (the inner ear), causing them to bend back and forth. Similar to our optical nerves, these receptors send electric signals to the acoustic nerve, which carries them to the brain.

The ear can process frequencies between approximately 20 and 20,000 Hz (hearing of the higher frequencies decreases with age) and detects loudness, pitch, and timbre. Sounds that are not audible to the ear (infrasonic and ultrasonic sounds) may not be detected by the human ear but may have other effects on the human body, including nausea. Humans are good at localizing sound sources through the intensity difference between the ears, especially when sound comes from the frontal hemisphere—we will discuss this further in the next section. Sound is rapidly detected and can have an alerting functionality, which can be powerful as a feedback mechanism. We are also able to focus on specific sounds (applying attention, see section 3.2.2), filtering out others (Goldstein 2014).

The "wrong" usage of infrasound (low frequency) can result in discomfort—potentially nausea (Kruijff and Pander 2005). Another aspect that may deserve further attention is the connection between audio frequencies and haptic sensations, as the human body reacts to low-frequency sound with haptic-like sensations. Cavities such as the stomach, the lungs, and certain bones also sense sound waves and vibrate at specific resonances, especially in the lower frequencies (Altmann 2011; Kruijff and Pander 2005). As such, they can also sense audio and deliver sensations like "feeling" low frequencies. However, the understanding of the effects of other parts of the body on audio perception is still limited (Kruijff et al. 2015).

Auditory Cues

As with the visual system, the auditory system provides listeners with a number of different localization cues that allow them to determine the direction and distance of a sound source. Although there are many different localization cues (Vorländer and Shinn-Cunningham 2015), we will discuss the main ones that apply to 3D UIs here. More details on localization cues and spatial hearing can be found in Gelfand (1998) and Yost (1994).

Binaural Cues

Binaural cues arise from a comparison of the sound waves received by each ear. Depending on the location of the sound source, one ear may receive a sound earlier than another. The difference in time between the arrival of the sound to each ear is known as the interaural time difference (ITD) and is an important cue for determining the sound source's lateral location (i.e., whether the sound source is to the left or the right of the listener). Similarly, because the ears are separated by the listener's head, higher-frequency sound waves (above 2 kHz) are reflected and diffracted by the head so that less acoustic energy reaches the far side of the head, causing an acoustic shadow. Therefore, the relative intensity of the sound varies for each ear depending on the lateral location of the sound source. The difference in sound intensities arriving at each ear is called the interaural intensity difference (IID) and is another important cue for determining a sound source's lateral location.

The fundamental problem with binaural cues is that there are locations relative to the listener's head where ambiguous situations occur (in the absence of any other cues). These situations occur whenever two different sound-source locations provide similar values for the ITD and IID. This phenomenon occurs primarily in two cases. First, when the sound source is directly in the sagittal plane (the anatomical plane dividing a human being into left and right halves), the sound waves will reach each ear at approximately the same time, and the sound's intensity will be approximately the same for both ears, resulting in IIDs and ITDs that are close to zero. This can result in front-back confusion. Second, for sound sources that are more than about three feet from the listener, there are a set of points that provide roughly the same ITD and IID values (Kendall 1995). In these situations, other cues are needed to localize sound sources. For a more detailed discussion on these issues, please refer to Vorländer and Shinn-Cunningham (2015).

One of the ways a listener can deal with ambiguous binaural cues is with dynamic movement of the listener's head or the sound source itself. For example, if the sound source was directly in front of the listener, a leftward rotation of the head would result in the ITD and IID favoring the right ear, thus helping to break the ambiguity. However, investigations into moving sound sources have shown that dynamic movement is still a fairly weak cue (Shilling and Shinn-Cunningham 2002).

Head-Related Transfer Functions

Head-related transfer functions (HRTFs) are the spatial filters that describe how sound waves interact with the listener's torso, shoulders, head, and particularly the outer ears. The outer ears are relatively complex anatomical structures with many notches and grooves that heighten or suppress sound waves at mid and high frequencies depending on the location and frequency content of the sound source. Therefore, HRTFs modify the sound waves from a sound source in a location-dependent manner. These modified sound waves provide a localization cue to the listener.

One of the interesting properties of HRTFs is that they can contain much of the spatial information contained in real-world listening conditions. ITD and IID cues are encoded within the relative phase and magnitude of filters for the left and right ears. In addition, spectral information and sound intensity is present in the absolute frequency-dependent magnitudes of the two filters (Vorländer and Shinn-Cunningham 2015). HRTFs also provide cues that help listeners deal with the ambiguous cases for binaural cues. However, HRTFs have their limitations in that they are often listener-specific, making them difficult to generalize, and they generally do not contain any reverberation information, which is another important cue for localizing sound sources. HRTFs can be measured using a special apparatus and used to produce high-quality spatial sound for individual users. Promising work has also been performed on non-user-specific HRTFs, an example of which can be found in Wenzel et al. (1993).

Reverberation

In natural environments, many different factors may affect the sound waves emanating from a sound source, including atmospheric properties (such as temperature and humidity) and various objects, which can absorb the waves and reflect them in different directions. Therefore, sound waves emanating from a sound source can reach the listener both directly and indirectly (e.g., off the walls, furniture, or ceiling). **Reverberation** is the collection of these reflected waves from various surfaces within a space and acts as an important acoustical cue for localizing sound sources.

Reverberation as a cue does little if anything to aid the listener in the perception of a sound source's direction, but it does aid in the perception of source distance (Shilling and Shinn-Cunningham 2002). In addition, it also provides information about the size and configuration of a listening environment, including geometry and surface properties.

Sound Intensity

A sound's intensity (which is perceived as loudness) is a primary cue for determining a sound source's distance, because intensity will decrease as the distance to the source increases. Because of the simplicity of simulating this cue, it has often been used in 3D auditory displays (Begault 1994).

Vestibular Cues

While not strictly a system processing auditory cues, the vestibular system is closely tied to the ear and the auditory nerves, which is why we will introduce these cues here. The vestibular sense can be best understood as the human balance system. Its structure is situated behind the ear and consists of the otolith organs and three semicircular ducts (also known as canals). The otolith organs (the utricule, also called the vestibule, and the saccule) contain small hairs that are stimulated by movement of fluid within the organs, thereby delivering information on the direction of gravity and linear acceleration. The three semicircular ducts are placed in three mutually perpendicular planes and, just like the otolith organs, also contain fluid that can stimulate the hair cells inside. The semicircular ducts provide information on angular acceleration and deceleration. As you can probably guess, the otolith organs deal with linear movement, while the semicircular ducts register rotational movement, thereby contributing to the human sense of balance.

The system also provides cues for bodily motion, having both a static and a dynamic function. The otolith system monitors the position of the head in space, contributing to the control of human posture. The semicircular ducts track the rotation of the head in space, affecting vestibular eye movements, which allow people to keep visual focus fixed on an object while the head is moving. Altogether, the vestibular system affects the control of the eyes, neck, and trunk/limbs (Goldstein 2014).

One of the side effects of the vestibular system is its influence on cybersickness. It is believed that cybersickness can be caused by a mismatch between visual and vestibular cues. These conflicts can be extreme, as for example is the case when riding a virtual rollercoaster without experiencing any physical movement whatsoever. Methods for avoiding cybersickness via the contribution of vestibular cues can be found in the literature (Harris et al. 1999). Some methods (Kruijff et al. 2015, 2016) specifically look into the provision of a minimal amount of vestibular information to improve self-motion perception that may aid in resolving the conflict.

Vision and Environmental Familiarity

In many cases, the visual system can be used in conjunction with the auditory system to form spatial percepts (Welch and Warren 1986), which can be used to determine a sound's location. Of course, these percepts are useful only if the sound source is within the user's field of view (FOV). In addition, a listener's prior experience with a particular sound and environment can affect the listener's ability to determine the sound source's location. This can be very important in 3D and VE applications where wayfinding (see Chapter 8, "Travel") is needed.

3.3.3 Somatosensory

The somatosensory, or haptic, system is an important perceptual system dealing with what we feel when touching or grasping objects and how we perceive the location and movement of the parts of our bodies.

Foundations

The human somatosensory system is a complex integration of perceptual receptors in the joints, tendons, muscles, and skin that receive various forms of stimulation. It handles haptic sensations—those that relate to touch and force. The somatosensory system is generally subdivided into the cutaneous, proprioceptive, and kinesthetic senses, with the latter two being frequently described as just the kinesthetic sense (Goldstein 2014). The system perceives cutaneous (skin) and subcutaneous (below skin) sensations, the position of the body and limbs, and mechanical sensations in the joints and muscles. According to Loomis and Lederman (1986), the cutaneous sense provides awareness of stimulation of the outer surface of the body by means of receptors within the skin and the associated nervous system, while the kinesthetic sense provides the observer with an awareness of static and dynamic body posture (relative positioning of the head, torso, limbs, and end effectors). These sensations are also known as haptic feedback, and they provide the human with information such as geometry, roughness (touch), and weight and inertia (force).

Within the skin, various types of so-called mechanoreceptors provide haptic cues. In contrast to all other sensory systems, these receptors are distributed throughout the whole body. Similar to other receptors, nerve signals travel to the brain along two major pathways. One pathway (lemniscal) carries signals related to sensing the position of limbs and perceiving touch over large fibers—these signals are transmitted at high speed to support control of movement and reactions to touch. The other pathway (spinothamalic) consists of smaller fibers and transmits signals related to temperature and pain.

An important characteristic of the somatosensory cortex in the brain is that it is organized in a map-like form correlating to locations of the human body. Experiments by Penfield and Rasmussen described the homunculus, showing that some areas of the skin occupy a disproportionately large area in the brain (Penfield and Rasmussen 1950). We will refer to this issue again in section 3.5.1.

Other types of receptors in the skin include thermoreceptors, which send temperature information to the hypothalamus, and nociceptors, which deal with pain. Nociceptors sense more intense chemical, mechanical, or thermal stimulation, sending signals over the spinal cord to the brain, and they reside not only in the skin, but also in the joints, bones, and other organs.

Proprioception, the sense of the position of one's own body and limbs, is based on information from so-called proprioceptors. These proprioceptors are found in muscle spindles, tendons

(Golgi organs), and the fibrous capsules in joints. Proprioceptive cues are believed to be handled in sync with vestibular cues provided by the inner ear (providing orientation and motion cues), to build up an overall sense of body posture (Sherrington 1907). Proprioceptive cues are separated into conscious and unconscious cues that travel to the brain via different pathways (lemniscus pathway, or dorsal or ventral spinocerebellar tracts). An example of an unconscious reaction is the human reflex to level the eyes to the horizon regardless of body orientation (Siegel and Sapru 2010). The kinesthetic sense is strongly tied to the proprioceptive sense, as it deals with the sensation of movement of body and limbs.

Haptic Cues

In this section we take a closer look at all somatosensory cues, as an understanding of them is important to design or evaluate tactile and haptic interfaces. The quality of somatic stimulation depends on both the resolution of the stimulus and certain ergonomic factors. Spatial resolution refers to the diversity and sensitivity of areas in the human body that can be stimulated—some parts, like fingertips, are more sensitive than others. On the other hand, temporal resolution refers to the refresh rate of the stimulus.

Tactile Cues

Tactile cues (taction) are perceived by a variety of cutaneous mechanoreceptors that produce information about surface texture and pressure. This is mainly achieved by skin depression and deformation—without any movement of the skin, the mechanoreceptors will not fire their information to the brain. The events we can sense using mechanoreceptors can be classified by their temporal and physical nature. Gibson (1962) provides us with a good insight on the variety of events we can sense:

- Brief events: pressure, push, slap, pat, tap, prick
- Prolonged events without displacement: vibration, stretching, kneading, pinching
- Prolonged events with displacement: scratching, scraping, rubbing, sliding, brushing, rolling

This variety of events allows us to sense a variety of object properties, including rigidity or plasticity, friction, texture, and resistance. We mainly perceive texture as a product of vibration (Loomis and Lederman 1986), an effect that is widely used in vibro-tactile interfaces (Kontrarinis and Howe 1995; Kruijff et al. 2006). Some cutaneous areas are more sensitive than others. For example, the temporal refresh rate of a stimulus humans can still sense at certain parts of the body can be up to 1000 Hz (Massie 1993). Sensitivity is referred to as tactile acuity and differs for each person. Two methods used for testing differences between people are two-point thresholds (sensing if one or two points are stimulated) and grating (sensing if a surface is smooth or has grooves, Goldstein 2014). For more details on tactile cues, see Gibson (1962) and Loomis and Lederman (1986).

Thermal Cues and Pain

A thermoreceptor senses relative changes in temperature through both warm and cold receptors. Sometimes cold receptors also may respond to higher temperature, which may result in paradoxical responses to heat. On the other hand, a nociceptor responds to stimuli that may potentially damage the body, causing the sensation of pain. Nociceptors handle various forms of danger, including thermal, mechanical, and chemical, leading to different perceptions of pain. More recent research has indicated that pain can be influenced by what a person expects and can direct attention (Goldstein 2014).

Kinesthetic and Proprioceptive Cues

Proprioceptive cues provide people with information about the position and angle of body joints, which humans are able to understand well without direct visual contact. That is, even blind people are easily able to understand the relative location and angle of, for example, hands and feet. It is easy to understand why proprioception is important to drive human motion (Dickinson 1976)—consider having to look at your feet continuously while climbing a staircase (which actually makes many people unsteady). Proprioceptive cues have received a reasonable amount of attention in 3D UI research, as they are useful for many manipulation actions we perform, especially those that are performed out of sight (Mine et al. 1997). Kinesthetic cues help to determine the relationship between the body and physical objects through muscular tension. They can be both active and passive, where active kinesthetic cues are perceived when movement is self-induced, and passive kinesthetic cues occur when the limbs are being moved by an external force (Stuart 1996).

Effects of Tactile and Kinesthetic Cues on Haptic Perception

Both tactile and kinesthetic cues are important in haptic perception. In many simple tasks, one cue is more important than another. For example, feeling the surface texture or determining the relative temperature of an object uses taction as the dominant cue. On the other hand, determining the length of a rigid object using a pinching grasp would predominantly use kinesthetic cues (Biggs and Srinivasan 2002). In more complex tasks, both kinesthetic and tactile cues are fundamental. As an example, consider a handshake between two people. In this case, both kinesthetic and tactile cues play an important role. The tactile cues provide information about the temperature of the other person's hand as well as pressure from the handshake. The kinesthetic cues provide information about the position and movement of each person's hand, arm, elbow, and shoulder, plus information about any forces that the other person is applying. Thus, the role of tactile and haptic cues is dependent on the way we touch or explore an object. Lederman and Klatzky (1987) summarize exploratory procedures, as depicted in Figure 3.9, for understanding objects and their properties. For an extensive discussion on the role of tactile and kinesthetic cues, please refer to the discussion on haptic exploration by Lederman and Klatzky (1987).

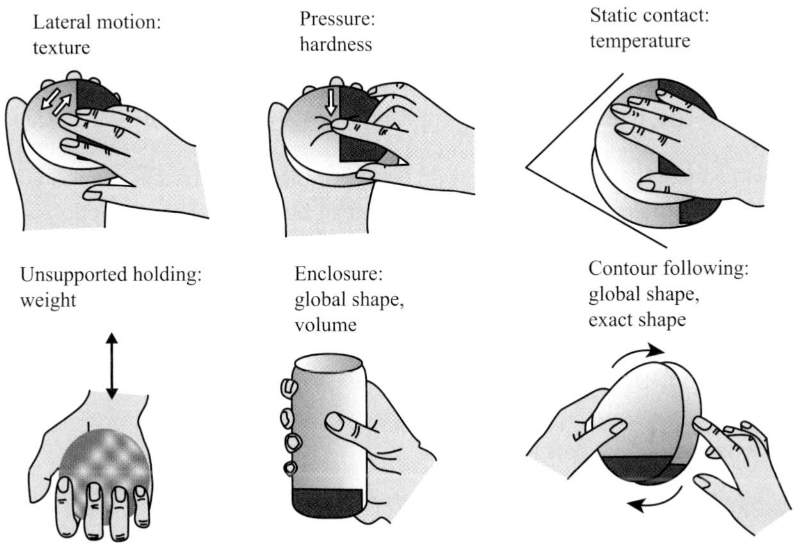

Figure 3.9 Exploratory procedures for understanding object properties. Redrawn from Lederman and Klatzky (1987)

3.3.4 Chemical Sensing System

While taste and smell are somewhat underrepresented in most 3D UIs, they can enrich the overall user experience in realistic environments. In this section we take a brief look at the chemical senses and their interplay.

Foundations

The human chemical system handles both smell (olfaction) and taste (gustation) sensations. Both systems are functionally linked—taste sensations are more difficult to register when no olfactory information is received. Also, smell and taste are seen as the gatekeepers to the human body, as they signal things a person's body needs for survival or detect things that could be bad for the body: think about smelling (or even tasting) a rotten piece of fruit.

An olfactory sensation is triggered by molecules in the air that are released by substances in the environment. Inhaled through the nasal cavity, nose, and mouth, they stimulate different receptor cells, each sensing a different chemical bond. The chemical receptors in the nasal cavity send signals over the olfactory nerve to the olfactory bulb, an area in the brain above the nose. To discriminate a scent, multiple receptor cells are active. A particularity of these receptors is that they are directly connected to the brain. As such, the olfactory perception cycle is much faster than that of other human input systems. In addition to the sensation of scents, so-called trigeminal sensations can be perceived. The trigeminal system connects to nociceptors at multiple places, including the lips, tongue, tooth, oral, and nasal cavities. Thus, humans can also sense burning sensations (like hot pepper) or temperature via the nose and other body parts, like itching sensations on the skin (Goldstein 2014). These sensations are more closely related to tactile sensations and, therefore, cannot necessarily be categorized as purely chemical.

On the other hand, the receptors dealing with taste send signals that occur mainly in the facial nerve system in the brain, in particular two areas in the frontal lobe. The perception of taste is performed via approximately 10,000 taste buds in the tongue, mouth cavity, and throat. The taste buds can adapt extremely fast to new tastes and are most active in the temperature range of 22–32 degrees Celsius.

Olfactory and Gustatory Cues

In this section, we look closer at the various olfactory and gustatory cues, as well as their interplay that leads to the percept of flavor.

Olfactory Cues

Olfactory stimuli mainly provide us with a range of odor cues. Many people have tried to classify the range of odors, but no successful or generally accepted categorization exists. Even when we receive various olfactory cues, we are able to separate and group these cues through perceptual organization (Goldstein 2014). For example, in making breakfast we are still able to distinguish between coffee, orange juice, and fried bacon. In practical terms, scent is primarily used for smelling food or for detecting danger (like fire); due to the speed of perception, smell is especially well suited for danger detection. How many scents humans detect varies widely, and complex scents are easier to remember (Kaye 1999). Finally, olfactory cues have been shown to trigger emotional events or memories. Both unconsciously and consciously, smells affect our emotions, for example when we smell another person, and they can connect to memories or experiences, a sensation called the Proust effect (Goldstein 2014).

Gustatory Cues

Just as with smells, there is no standard classification of tastes. Still, the five basic tastes—sweet, sour, salty, bitter, and umami (savory or meaty flavor, coming from a Japanese categorization)—seem to be generally accepted (Goldstein 2014). However, while these categories define the main tastes we may perceive, our taste system is able to sense several more sensations, such as coolness, numbness, metallic sensations, fattiness, and spiciness (or pungency).

Flavor

The chemical senses are highly interlinked. Flavor sensations are triggered by combined olfactory and gustatory cues. What most people often describe as taste is actually flavor (Shepherd 2012), the experience of nasal and oral stimulation. Flavor sensations are easily combined, as the mouth and nasal cavities are not only functionally but also physically linked. Flavor can be influenced by a person's expectations and satiety (Goldstein 2014).

3.3.5 Sensory Substitution and Multisensory Processing

When designing 3D UIs, we often combine different perceptual channels or substitute information from one perceptual channel into another one. In addition, when we combine different perceptual channels, we often see interplay between the channels, known as cross-modal effects. In this section we look more closely at these issues.

Sensory Substitution

When designing a 3D UI, it often happens that a specific sensory channel cannot be used, because it is somehow blocked on the user side or on the technical side. For example, an environment might be too loud to hear audio cues clearly, or a high-quality force feedback device might not be available. In such cases, interface designers often try to "translate" the missing information over another sensory channel, a process called sensory substitution. This process—which largely originated in the design of interfaces for disabled people—can occur between sensory channels (for example, translating visual into auditory information), but also within sensory systems. The best-known example of within-system sensory substitution is substitution within the somatic system, which has a multitude of receptors that work together at a cognitive level, as we saw in section 3.3.3. Thus, vibrotaction is often used to simulate haptic touch/force feedback (Massimino and Sheridan 1993; Kontrarinis and Howe 1995).

Sensory substitution makes use of the *plasticity of the brain*. This refers to the human ability to change neural pathways and synapses due to changes in behavior, neural processes, or thinking (Shimojo and Shams 2001). This ability is highly useful, for example in those who have experienced a brain injury, as specific abilities can be relearned. Hence, as discussed by Lenay et al. (2003), when we exchange one sensory channel with another, we are not simply making a change at the receptor level. The whole information-processing loop is reordered: the central nervous system needs to learn a new mode of perception. A clear example is substituting visual information with auditory information for the blind. The blind person needs to learn to "see by hearing," and, thus, needs to create a new cognitive model of the world she is dealing with. Therefore, when exchanging sensory channels, we need to consider the metaphor of communication and the influences the new sensory channel has on the interpretation of the information.

Multisensory Processing and Cross-Modal Effects

Another way to use different sensory channels is to add or integrate them, thus creating *multisensory interfaces*. For example, a combination of visual and auditory cues may convey information more effectively than a purely visual representation. However, it is important to note that in research the focus is moving away from traditional multisensory techniques towards multisensory interfaces that differ at the level of human information processing. The sensory channels are no longer seen as separate channels, because they may affect each other. Multisensory processing of this sort occurs more often than is regularly believed (Ernst and Banks 2002). The multisensory processing theory builds upon the integration of sensory signals in so-called multimodal association areas within the brain (Pai 2003).

Research on multisensory factors is ongoing, but many *cross-modal effects* can already be identified. These effects include bias (stimuli from two or more sensory systems can differ and affect each other, leading to modified or even incorrect perception), enrichment (a stimulus from one sensory system can enhance the perception of another sensory system), and transfer (stimulation of one sensory system may trigger perception in another system). For example, vision can alter other modalities (McGurk and MacDonald 1976; Lederman et al. 1986), sound can alter temporal effects of vision (Shimojo and Shams 2001) and can dominate in temporal tasks (Sekuler et al. 1997), tactility can alter vision (Blake et al. 2004, Lederman et al. 1986), and audio can alter tactility (Weisenberger and Poling 2004; Kruijff et al. 2006; Bresciani et al. 2004). For more details, please refer to Shimojo and Shams (2001) and Ernst and Banks (2002).

3.3.6 Evaluating Perceptual Issues

Understanding perceptual issues is important for designing effective 3D UIs, and often new data is needed in order to gain this understanding. In this section, we look at important issues, and methods for evaluating perceptual issues in user studies or experiments.

Typical Issues in 3D UIs

Providing a complete overview of all perceptual problems that may occur in 3D UIs is virtually impossible, as the issues span numerous dimensions. Many of the issues relate to problems in the replication of reality, as the vividness (Steuer 1992) and correctness of perceptual stimuli experienced in real life are currently difficult to reproduce by technical means. While some technical advancements may come near to our human abilities (for example, large displays have been produced that have a resolution similar to that of the human eye), most technologies have their limitations. A general discussion of human factors limitations related to perception can be found in Stanney et al. (1998).

With respect to vision, numerous issues may occur in VR and AR systems. For a good introduction to perceptual issues in AR, refer to Kruijff et al. (2010). In VR systems, some of the main issues may be caused by limited display fidelity (McMahan et al. 2012) and include the provision of adequate motion cues (Kalawsky 1993), lack of appropriate stereopsis cues (Mon-Williams et al. 1993), inadequate visualization of one's own body (Phillips et al. 2012), and depth underestimation and overestimation (Interrante et al. 2006; Jones et al. 2008; Loomis and Knapp 2003). In AR systems, some of the main problems include depth ordering, visibility and legibility issues, object segmentations, and scene abstraction (Kruijff et al. 2010). These problems may be caused not only by such issues as occlusion (Ellis and Menges 1988; Livingston et al. 2003), layer interferences and layout (Leykin and Tuceryan 2004), and rendering and resolution mismatches (Drascic and Milgram 1996), but also by issues that are related to the display and capturing device or the environment itself (Kruijff et al. 2010).

With respect to nonvisual systems, problems are often related to the limitations in reproducing realistic cues. Unfortunately, these issues receive less attention than the visual system. Solving these issues may result in higher fidelity systems that would aid interaction, while potentially also solving inter-sensory conflicts (see section 3.3.5). Regarding auditory system, the main issues are the limits in localizing a cue or drawing the user's attention—often this problem is caused by environmental noise (Biocca 1992). With respect to the **somatosensory** system, problems are often caused by technological limitations, as in many cases interface designers have to make use of sensory substitution to translate haptic information into predominantly vibrotactile cues. This will result in lower accuracy feedback that spans all the different cues we receive, including texture roughness, friction, and force misinterpretations (Lenay et al. 2003; Burdea 1996). Even grounded and nongrounded haptic display devices have similar limitations, especially when haptic feedback needs to be provided to more than a single finger (Burdea 1996). Finally, the **chemical** system is affected by both technological and human limitations: as humans have widely different capabilities for taste and smell (see section 4.3.4) and chemical stimuli are very difficult to produce (and get rid of) in synthetic environments, correct recognition of chemical stimuli is by definition limited.

Evaluation Methods

The majority of measures used to evaluate perception issues are also used in general evaluation settings—you will find an overview in Chapters 4 and 11; also refer to Stanney et al. (1998).

Subjective Measures

User-preference scales can provide insights not only into the overall preference of the user but also into the quality of specific cues. Much of this is in line with normal user study methodology. However, there are a number of perceptual constructs that can be assessed using specific methods. Probably the most dominant for 3D systems is cybersickness, which is thought to be caused by conflicting cues from different perceptual systems. Kennedy et al. (1993), LaViola (2000), and Chapter 11 describe some methods for evaluating cybersickness. Subjective measures of presence are also of interest for 3D UIs. For the various measures that can be used, please refer to Hendrix and Barfield (1995), Singer et al. (1994), Slater and Usoh (1993), and Regenbrecht et al. (1998). We will further discuss many of these methods in Chapter 11.

Performance Measures

Some performance measures relate to information processing and are used to analyze information quality and accuracy. While some of these measures involve cognition (memory recall), there are also other measures that deal with perceptual performance. For example, visual search is a popular method in which users must find specific targets in between distracters, and researchers analyze the time to find the target in relation to visual angle (Wolfe 1998). Furthermore, perceptual issues are of interest in the analysis of motor action performance, which is mostly addressed through Fitts's law—refer to section 3.2.3 for more information. There have also been various efforts to isolate the specific effects of certain perceptual stimuli, in particular in the area of visual perception. Issues that have been addressed include visual acuity and contrast sensitivity, depth ordering, and color perception (Livingston et al. 2012; Hua et al. 2014; Singh et al. 2012). Finally, there are methods to analyze multisensory processing (Shimojo and Shams 2001), including those used to analyze the interplay between audio and visual cues (Storms and Zyda 2000; Ernst and Bülthoff 2004; Burr and Alais 2006); audio, vestibular and haptic cues (Riecke et al. 2009); and the potential interplay between multiple sensory channels and attention (Driver and Spence 1998).

Psycho-Physiological Methods

Finally, psycho-physiological methods have been used to address perceptual issues, in particular for visual perception. The predominant method is eye tracking, which refers to the process of measuring the point of gaze of a user. Eye tracking hardware and software allows the analysis of different kinds of eye movements, including eye fixations and saccades. Analysis can reveal areas of interest and the number of visits to specific areas. These areas are generally visualized using so-called heat maps that place a color-coded layer over the image content, but plots have also been used for this purpose. Eye tracking can provide highly valuable feedback, but it may require careful calibration and may not always be accurate in dynamic environments. For more information on eye tracking methods, please refer to Holmqvist et al. (2011).

3.4 Cognition

Perceived stimuli are processed by cognition in order to initiate a task to be performed. As such, cognition is a key aspect when looking at user interaction, in particular when tasks involve an obvious cognitive component, like finding your way through an environment. In this section, we examine key cognitive issues and discuss the evaluation of cognition.

3.4.1 Foundations

When we think about cognition (no pun intended!), we often think about the knowledge that is somewhere and somehow stored in our brain. What exactly is knowledge, and how does it contribute to cognition? From a user perspective, knowledge is generally regarded as information about the world that is believed to be true, can be justified, and is coherent (Lehrer 1990). Cognition—the driving force behind the generation and usage of knowledge—is the key to many processes, as can be seen in Figure 3.1. It governs processes in memory, language, and thought, but is also directly linked to our perception and attention.

Our knowledge depends on representations, a topic which has been hotly debated by cognitive scientists without reaching a consensus. For the sake of simplicity, we follow the definition by Smith and Kosslyn; a *representation* is a physical state that stands for an object, event, or concept and must be constructed intentionally and carry information (Smith and Kosslyn 2013). Representations may encode information in different formats, including those that are similar to images, feature records, amodal symbols, and statistical patterns in neural networks. These different formats work together to represent and simulate objects (Smith and Kosslyn 2013). Individual memories of a specific category often become integrated to establish so-called *category knowledge*. Interestingly, these category representations bring together representations from different sensory channels and can be adapted through emotion (Cree and McRae 2003).

Category knowledge is stored in long-term memory, where other kinds of memories also reside. According to Kandell et al. (2000), long-term memory consists of declarative (or explicit) and nondeclarative (or implicit) memory. Our declarative knowledge mainly consists of facts and events, while our nondeclarative knowledge holds priming, procedural (like skills and habits), associative, and nonassociative memory. The latter two categories relate to conditioning, including emotional responses (associative), and habituation and sensitization memory (nonassociative).

How do we actually make use of long-term memory? Recalling information from long-term memory requires specific memory traces to be reactivated through pattern completion and recapitulation (Smith and Kosslyn 2013). Recall is affected by cues and context; memory is highly associative. Unfortunately, our memory recall is far from perfect. Not only can it be biased, but misattribution may occur while matching cues, and memory can be triggered by suggestion, leading to skewed recall. Moreover, certain memories can be blocked or suppressed, or simply not be matched due to an overload of cues (Kandell et al. 2000), similar to the cognitive load we will discuss in section 3.4.3.

In contrast, our working memory is temporary (Baddeley 1986). Working memory is used for short-term memory storage and performs manipulations or transformation actions on bits and pieces of information. Research has shown that the working memory span, the amount of information that can be stored, differs between people (Daneman and Carpenter 1980) and gives a general indication of intelligence. Working memory decays fast. For example, verbal item recall decays quickly after only six seconds (Peterson and Peterson 1959), which can be extended through rehearsal. Memory span also affects how effectively working memory and long-term memory can be linked (Kane and Engle 2000). Some of the models that describe working memory include the Atkinson-Shiffrin model (Atkinson and Shiffrin 1971) and the Baddeley-Hitch model (Baddeley and Hitch 1974). Readers who are interested are recommended to read more details in the provided references.

3.4.2 Situation Awareness

Now that we have a theoretical foundation of cognition, let us take a deeper look at how cognition affects our interaction in spatial environments, beginning with situation awareness. Situation awareness, which has been widely studied in aviation, is generally characterized as the internalized model of the current state of the user's environment (Endsley 2012). As such, it is the perception of elements in the environment within a volume of time and space, the comprehension of their meaning, and the projection of their status in the near future (Endsley 1988). This state model can include information from different sources and can describe spatial relationships, fellow users, and task states. It is directly related to decision-making, as the integrated information base is used to take decisions and plan for actions.

In a 3D user interface, situation awareness affects how we interact with the objects around us, as we continuously need to keep track of the spatial setting in which we operate. A particular area of interest in 3D UI navigation (see Chapter 8), is *wayfinding*. Wayfinding is a decision-making process (Figure 3.10) in which a user makes decisions (where am I? which direction should I go?) by mentally processing "input" (information obtained from the environment) and producing "output" (movement along a trajectory). For those interested in more details about cognition and wayfinding, Golledge (1999) provides a good overview. Here, we will discuss the main cognitive issues that affect wayfinding, including cognitive mapping, different kinds of spatial knowledge, and reference frames.

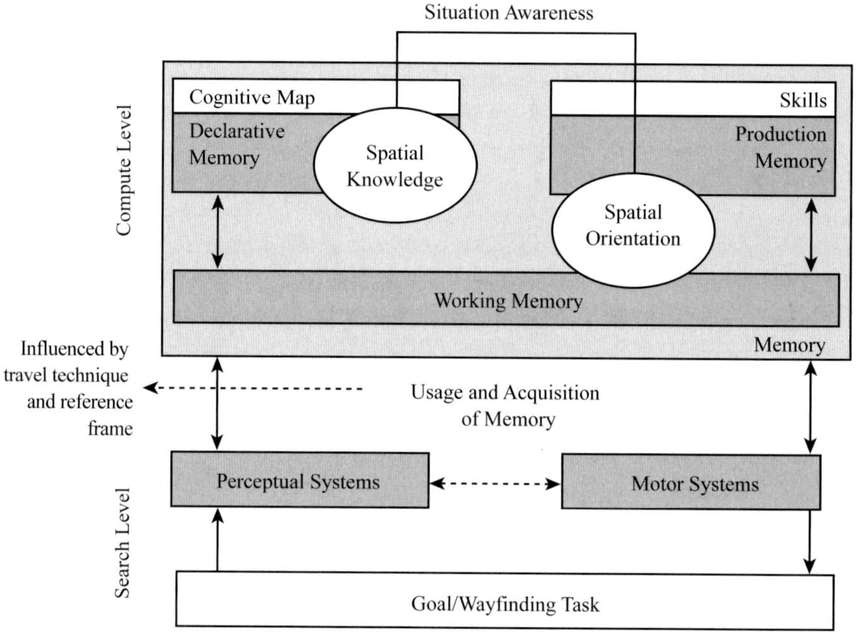

Figure 3.10 A representation of wayfinding as a decision-making process.

Cognitive Mapping

Navigation in a 3D environment involves the processing of multiple sources of sensory information that we receive from the environment and the use of this information to execute a suitable travel trajectory. The environmental information is stored in our long-term memory and is generally referred to as the *cognitive map***,** the body of spatial knowledge we obtain from our environment. To be more precise, the cognitive map is a mental hierarchical structure of information that represents spatial knowledge (Stevens and Coupe 1978; Downs and Stea 1977). When we perform a wayfinding task, we make use of existing spatial knowledge, acquire new spatial knowledge, or use a combination of both. The process of accessing, using, and building the tree-like structures in the cognitive map is also called *cognitive mapping*. Navigation is based on a tight feedback loop that continuously defines the relationship between the information we perceive and our cognitive map of the environment, which enables us to understand our position and orientation. The knowledge of our location and viewing direction is called *spatial orientation*, while the combination of spatial orientation and spatial knowledge (cognitive map) contributes to what we previously labeled *situation awareness*.

Types of Spatial Knowledge

Search strategies and movement parameters influence the effectiveness of spatial knowledge acquisition. These factors affect not only the efficiency of building a cognitive map but also the qualitatively different kinds of spatial knowledge that are acquired. During wayfinding, people obtain at least three different kinds of spatial knowledge (Thorndyke and Hayes-Roth 1982; Lynch 1960). *Landmark knowledge* consists of the visual characteristics of the environment. Visually prominent objects (landmarks) form part of this information, but other visual features such as shape, size, and texture also play a role. In London, for example, Big Ben and the London Eye are locations that many visitors immediately add to their landmark knowledge. *Procedural knowledge* (or *route knowledge*) describes the sequence of actions required to follow a certain path or traverse paths between different locations. Only sparse visual information is needed for procedural knowledge to be used properly (Gale et al. 1990). For example, a visitor to London will quickly memorize the route between her hotel and the nearest underground station. Finally, *survey knowledge* can be described as the configurational or topological knowledge of an environment, consisting of object locations, interobject distances, and object orientations. This kind of knowledge is map-like and can therefore also be obtained from a map, even though the acquired knowledge from the map tends to be orientation-specific (Darken and Cevik 1999). Of the three kinds of spatial knowledge, survey knowledge represents the (qualitatively) highest level of knowledge and normally also takes the longest to mentally construct.

Reference Frames and Spatial Judgments

During real-life motion, we feel as if we are in the center of space, a phenomenon that is called *egomotion*. During such motion, we need to match *egocentric* (first-person) information to the cognitive map, which typically stores *exocentric* (third-person) information (Thorndyke and Hayes-Roth 1982). An egocentric reference frame is defined relative to a certain part of the human body, whereas an exocentric reference frame is object- or world-relative. During egocentric tasks, judgments are made according to the egocentric reference frame (Figure 3.11), which consists of the station point (nodal point of the eye), retinocentric (the retina), headcentric (focused solely on the head), bodycentric (the torso), and proprioceptive subsystems (visual and nonvisual cues from our body parts, such as hands and legs; see section 3.3.3). Details on these reference frames can be found in Howard (1991).

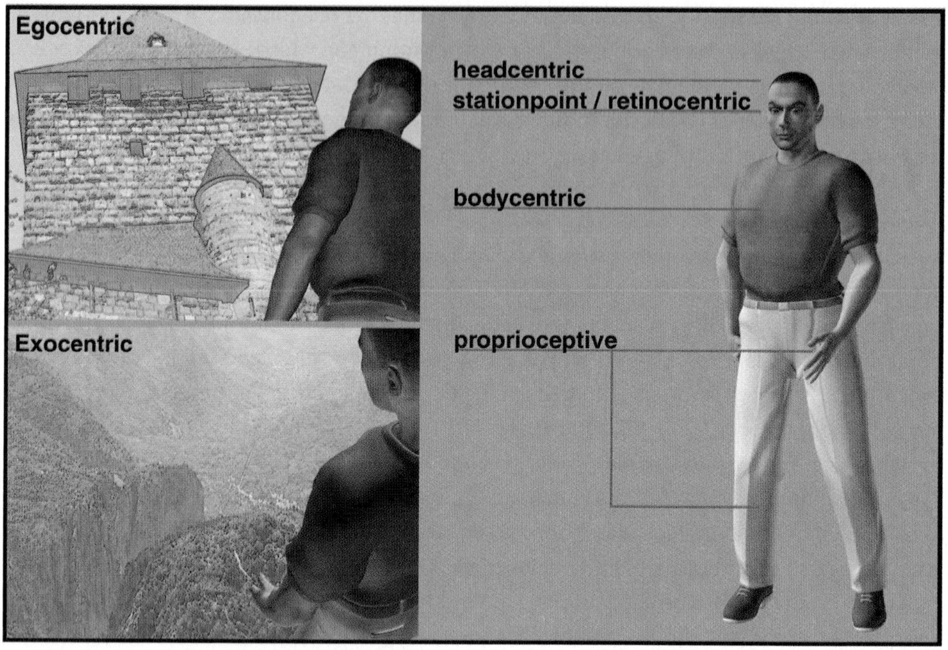

Figure 3.11 Human reference frames (right) and associated views (left). In an egocentric view (top left), the user is inside the environment, while in exocentric view (bottom left), the user is outside the environment, looking in (Image courtesy of Ernst Kruijff).

The *egocentric reference frame* provides us with important information such as distance (obtained from physical feedback like a number of strides or an arm's length) and orientation (obtained from the direction of the eyes, head, and torso). An object's position, orientation, and movement are related to the position and orientation of the eyes, head, and body. During exocentric tasks, the position, orientation, and movement of objects are defined in coordinates external to the body. Namely, they are defined by an object's shape, orientation, and motion. *Exocentric* attributes are not affected by our orientation or position.

In 3D UIs, multiple reference frames can be used with different viewpoints. The egocentric reference frame corresponds to first-person viewpoints, while exocentric reference frames are related to third-person (bird's-eye or outside-in) viewpoints. For example, in many video games, users typically see a first-person (egocentric) view of the environment during navigation but can also access an overview map of the environment showing their current location (exocentric).

When we find our way through an environment, we build up an exocentric representation (survey knowledge). However, when we enter an environment for the first time, we basically depend on egocentric information (landmark and procedural knowledge). Therefore, we often depend on landmarks at first, then develop routes between them, and eventually generalize that egocentric spatial information into exocentric survey knowledge. It remains unclear, however, how the human brain determines the relationship between egocentric and exocentric spatial knowledge.

3.4.3 Evaluating Cognitive Issues

Analyzing cognitive issues can be an important yet also difficult task to better understand user performance in a 3D UI. In this section, we unravel typical issues that can be analyzed, as well as the methods that can be used to evaluate those issues.

Typical Issues

Two primary issues in analyzing cognition are mental load and errors.

Mental load, also referred to as cognitive load, refers to the amount of cognitive work or effort required by a task or situation. The amount of mental load is affected by two main determinants (Vidulich and Tsang 2012): exogenous and endogenous demands. Exogenous demands are defined by the task being performed, and include the task difficulty, priority, and situational contingencies. Endogenous demands are characterized by attention and processing resources that underlie our information processing. Some researchers also consider so-called germane processes to have an effect; these refer to the mental work used to process, construct, and automate schemas. A schema is an organized pattern of thought or behavior that organizes categories of information and the relationships among them (Dimaggio 1997). User abilities and skills contribute to task effectiveness and as such can reduce mental load.

Assessing mental load, as we will show in the next section, can occur at a subjective, performance, or psycho-physiological level. Studies to evaluate mental load and performance are often coupled (Paas and van Merriënboer 1993). For example, it has been shown that performance increases with increasing allocation of mental resources up to the limit of resource availability (Norman and Bobrow 1975), while the usage of resources can be affected by voluntary or strategic allocation processes (Proctor and Vu 2010).

The different stages in the information-processing pipeline can be used to define the various dimensions in which resource allocation takes place. Wickens (2008) defined four such dimensions:

- The *stages of processing* dimension shows that perceptual and cognitive tasks use different resources than those used for the selection and execution of action.
- The *codes of processing* dimension indicates that spatial activity uses different resources than verbal activity.
- The *modalities* dimension indicates that auditory perception uses different resources than does visual perception.

- The *visual channels* dimension distinguishes between focal and peripheral vision, where resources are applied for object recognition (focal) or perception or orientation and movement (peripheral).

These dimensions are useful for analyzing performance issues in 3D UIs more closely, especially those that deploy multisensory input and output methodologies. While user interface designers will not often use methods that can differentiate exactly between these dimensions and processes, it is well worth considering that interprocess effects occur that affect performance.

Human error refers to a lack of success in task performance. We adopt the definition by Sheridan (2008), who defines human error as failing to meet an arbitrary implicit or explicit criterion. While we mainly focus on the cognitive dimension, human error can also occur because of sensory or motor limitations (Sharit 2012). Human error ties into the complete cycle of human information processing, as defined in section 3.2.1. Just as in long-term memory (section 3.4.1), bias, misattribution, and suggestion can be major sources of human error in general. Similar to mental load, human error is strongly tied to our abilities and skills and depends on attention mechanisms.

Human error and mental load are also related, as the unavailability of mental resources can produce erroneous behavior. Not surprisingly, these dimensions are closely related to performance studies as performed in human–computer interaction evaluations (McKenzie 2013).

Evaluation Methods

Evaluation of cognitive issues is an important aspect of iterative design cycles of 3D UIs, as interfaces increasingly deal with more complex data and tasks. In this section, we will mostly focus on methods for evaluating mental load, while only briefly handling error assessment.

One particular issue that needs to be addressed is whether one wants to assess cognitive issues overall or at a task level. The latter is notably more complex, as the workload of primary and secondary tasks needs to be assessed separately. For a more complete methodology that addresses this issue, please refer to Vidulich and Tsang (2012).

Subjective Measures

Subjective measures (based on the user's perception and experience) are the most frequently applied category of cognitive load measurements. Although they only provide a subjective measure of cognitive processes, they often help to explain separately measured performance issues. Thus, they should be understood as an additional measurement, not a primary way of explaining the effectiveness of a user interface. The measures introduced below are mostly used to address issues related to user spatial abilities and mental load. The two most popular and frequently interconnected methods are SBSOD and NASA TLX.

SBSOD, short for Santa Barbara Sense of Direction (Hegarty et al. 2002), is a self-report measure for measuring people's judgments about environmental spatial abilities. It is not an objective measure of a user's spatial ability, yet it is often correlated with other subjective or objective measures of performance. The questionnaire includes rating-scale items such as "I am very good at giving directions," "I am very good at judging distances," or "I don't have a very good 'mental map' of my environment." The overall score on the questionnaire indicates the (potential) spatial ability of the user.

The NASA TLX (task load index) was introduced in the 1980s and has had a huge impact. It has been widely applied in many areas, ranging from aviation to health care to user interface experiments (Hart and Staveland 1988). NASA TLX consists of two parts. Total workload is divided into six subscales that encompass mental demand, physical demand, temporal demand, performance, effort, and frustration. Hence, it not only covers mental load but also physical effort. There is a description for each of the subscales that study participants should read carefully. Ratings are performed on a 100-points range with 5-point steps, and the ratings are combined to calculate the task load index.

The second part of TLX is used to create an individual weighting of the subscales. Participants are asked to perform pair-wise comparisons of the subscales based on perceived importance. This captures the participant's view of the relevance of each measurement with respect to perceived workload. However, as reported by Hart (2006), using the second part of TLX might actually decrease experimental validity. For this reason, most often the first part is used by itself. Using NASA TLX is quite convenient for evaluating workload, as it is time-effective, well supported by online tools, and well established.

Examples of other workload assessment techniques include Task Analysis/Workload scale TAWL (Bierbaum et al. 1991), the Cooper Harper Rating Scale (Harper and Cooper 1984), and the Subjective Workload Assessment Technique SWAT (Reid and Nygren 1988).

Performance Measures

Performance measures of cognitive load are used far less often in the domain of user interface validation, yet there are some powerful methods that have been used in other domains.

SAGAT (Situation Awareness Global Assessment Technique) is a query technique developed by Endsley (1988). As its name implies, it focuses on situation awareness. Endsley considers situation awareness to be an internal model that is derived prior to decision-making and action planning and performance (see section 3.4.2 for more information). SAGAT is a so-called freeze online probe technique, designed for human-in-the-loop simulations. The simulation is frozen at randomly selected times while subjects are queried on their perception of the situation at the time. Endsley reports that the freezing aids in overcoming certain limitations normally encountered when users are queried after the experiment, such as memory limitations and the tendency to overgeneralize. The technique provides diagnostic information on how well the system supports the users' various situation awareness requirements and has been shown to be both reliable and valid (Endsley 2000). Some of the alternatives to SAGAT are GIM and SPAM (Vidulich and McMillan 2000).

Some other methods can also be used after the experiment to assess spatial knowledge acquisition performance. In particular, the drawing of maps has been used to assess the memory recall of participants, looking into the amount and accuracy of spatial knowledge obtained (Billinghurst and Weghorst 1995). However, interpretation of user-drawn maps has been shown to be difficult (Veas et al. 2010; Siegel 1981). Other methods include dead reckoning (Gallistel 1990) and homing (Adler 1971).

Finally, at a cognitive level human errors have been assessed through a variety of methods. The assessment of human errors has a long history and initially was often used to address the probability of human failures to perform a risk analysis, represented in tree-like structures (fault and event trees). As such, task analysis is a critical part of human error analysis (Senders and Moray 1991). These methods are often referred to as human reliability analysis and have been used in particular for risk assessment of human behavior in potentially critical tasks. While these tasks may not always be comparable to tasks performed in a more "safe" 3D UI, the methodologies can be of interest to assess errors. For an overview, refer to Sharit (2012).

Psycho-Physiological Methods

Based on the assumption that mental workload is essentially physiological, various techniques have been used, including those measuring heart rate, pupil dilation, and eye movements, and brain activity using electroencephalography (EEG). EEG has shown promising results to address mental load, but gathering good data and interpreting results are not easy. EEG is used to sense so-called event-related potentials (P300) that are responsive to discrete events (Gopher and Donchin 1986). However, EEG measures can also be recorded in the absence of such events, which can be useful when an operator is monitoring slowly changing content (Kramer and Parasuraman 2007). Unfortunately, EEG can be sensitive to numerous artifacts, including head, eye, and body movements, which can make analysis cumbersome. A good overview of brain-based measures can be found in Teplan (2002).

It is also worth mentioning is that various physiological methods have been used to measure stress and anxiety. It has been shown that emotional stress can be related to mental load (Staal 2004). Methods that have been deployed include galvanic skin response (Villarejo et al. 2012; Yamakoshi et al. 2008), heart rate (Choi and Gutierrez-Osuna 2010; Jongyoon and Gutierrez-Osuna 2011), and EEG (Hosseini et al. 2010; Khosrowabadi et al. 2011).

3.5 Physical Ergonomics

While perception and cognition often receive the most attention when designing and analyzing 3D UIs, physical ergonomics are an important factor that enable us to design systems that can be used comfortably and effectively.

3.5.1 Foundations

Physical ergonomics is related primarily to the human musculoskeletal system, so it's important to understand basic human anatomy and physiology. While we address key issues in this section, we recommend referring to Chiras (2012), who provides details on human anatomy, and Hall (2015), who deals in depth with physiology, including neurological processes.

Muscles, Bones, and Lever Systems

Physical ergonomics depends on the anatomical capacities of the different parts of the human body, which defines how and how well we can perform a specific task. There are about 600 different muscles in the human body. Every muscle is made up of a mixture of fast and slow muscle fibers. The latter can often be used for prolonged contraction (Hall 2015). Muscles function by applying tension to their points of insertion into the bones, while the bones form a lever system. As we will see in the next section, the human body affords a wide range of motions, some which require more strength, some which require longer distance of motion. These actions are matched by the lever systems as well as the length of the muscles (Hall 2015).

An important aspect of muscle contraction is whether it is isometric or isotonic; this is critical for understanding various 3D input devices as well (Zhai 1995). As illustrated in Figure 3.12, muscle contraction is isometric when there is no movement and the muscle does not shorten during contraction. In contrast, during isotonic contraction the muscle does shorten. Isotonic contraction can be concentric or eccentric. In a concentric contraction, the muscle tension rises to meet the resistance, after which it remains the same as the muscle shortens. In eccentric contractions, the muscle lengthens due to the resistance being greater than the force the muscle is producing.

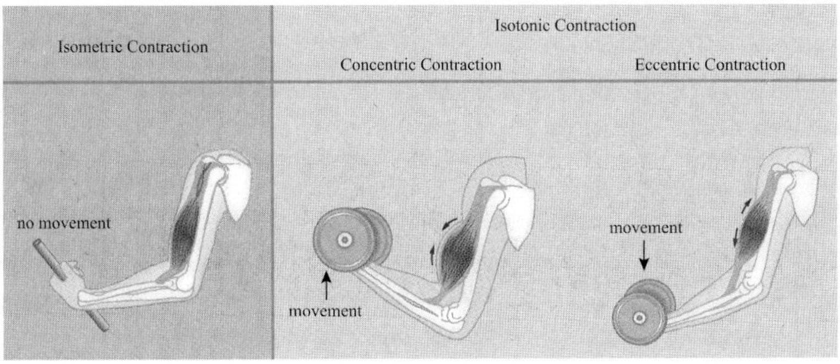

Figure 3.12 Isometric versus isotonic contraction

Human Motion Types

Human motion is produced by our joints and muscles and is often a response to a stimulus, as we discussed in section 3.3.3. The peripheral nervous system triggers effectors via electric signals, that can result in both voluntary (motor) and involuntary actions. Most human output can be defined as a control task that can take the form of interaction tasks such as manipulation or navigation. These tasks couple the body to some kind of controller, thereby creating a *control-body linkage* between the human and a computer input device. This control-body linkage can be based on physical contact or on monitoring techniques (e.g., when hand movements are detected by a camera). The control task can be characterized by its accuracy, speed and frequency, degrees of freedom, direction, and duration, and it is highly affected by the anatomical capabilities of the human body. Thus, task characteristics directly affect the choice of how to map control to the human body.

Some tasks may be performed with only a certain body part (e.g., fine-grained actions are mainly possible with the hands, due to the dependency of many devices on the opposition of the fingers), while other tasks may be possible via multiple body parts. The ability to perform a task with alternative body parts can lead to control substitution: exchanging one body output channel with another one, under the premise that the task can be mapped to both output channels (Lenay et al. 2003; Loomis 2003). For example, flexion can be performed by various joints, including the shoulder, forearm, wrist, fingers, hip, and knee. Control substitution has been the basis for a large number of unconventional interfaces (Kruijff 2007). Hence, it is useful to take a closer look at the different possibilities of the joints of the human body (see Figure 3.13).

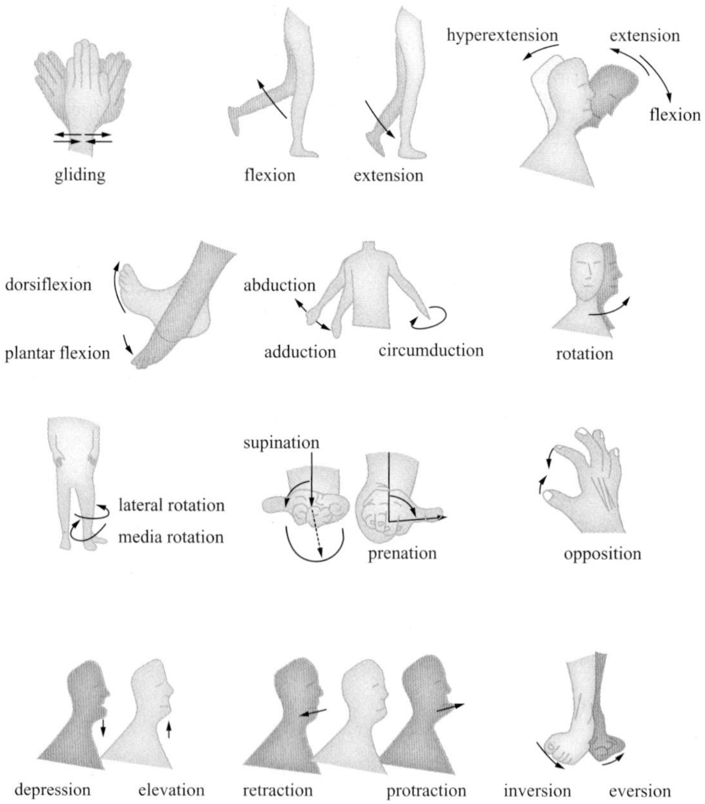

Figure 3.13 Selected physical motion types.

It is important to note, though, that control actions can also be mapped to other human systems, such as the eyes or brain. These systems, known as biocontrol or biofeedback systems, allow for the performance of tasks that are not necessarily based on motor actions.

Sensory-Motor Distribution

The sensory-motor distribution of the cortex is of importance for the performance for the different body parts. As we noted in section 3.3.3, the mapping of the different body parts to the areas in the cortex was pioneered by Penfield and Rasmussen (1950). One of the outcomes is the famous homunculus, representing the mapping of the body parts (in particular the skin) to the cortex (Figure 3.14). In interaction studies, the map is generally used to show the possible precision with which tasks can be performed: the larger the body part is presented, the more likely it is that more precise actions are afforded. Now, let us take a look at the body parts that are mainly used for or affected by user interaction, to understand their strengths and limitations.

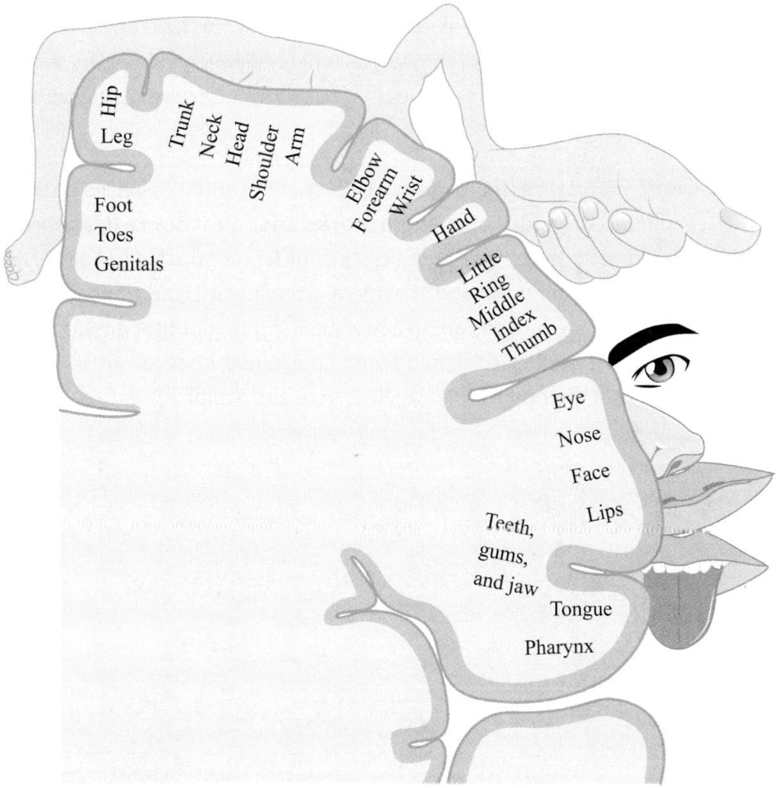

Figure 3.14 The sensory homunculus. Redrawn from OpenStax College - Anatomy & Physiology, Connexions Web site. http://cnx.org/content/col11496/1.6/

Hands and Arms

The hand is the most dominant human control channel and allows a user to perform a tremendous number of actions, using diverse devices. In our daily life, the hand is used for a virtually endless number of different tasks, including grasping and holding, squeezing or bending, pushing and pulling, gestures and postures, hitting or knocking, and throwing. The musculoskeletal configuration of the hand consists of three bone segments: the wrist (carpus), the palm (metacarpus), and the fingers (phalanges). The hand contains three muscle groups, found in the thumb, the little finger, and the palm. The musculoskeletal system affords numerous movements, including gliding movements of the wrist, angular movements (abduction, adduction, flexion, extension) of the fingers and the wrist, and pinching of the fingers via opposition. Altogether, the constellation of the hand, wrist, and arm is a lever system and allows for a large number of control dimensions. Nonetheless, not all the configurations are comfortable. Based on factors like force, duration, and repetition, task performance may be limited (Marras 2012).

The hand allows both coarse and fine motor actions. Depending on the hand-device coupling, humans can perform actions using a power grip of or a precision grip (see Figure 3.15). A power grip refers to holding a device within the palm of the hand, whereas a precision grip allows fine motor control when a device, or a part of the device, is held between the fingers. A good source for the different musculoskeletal effects on the usage of 3D input devices is the work of Zhai et al. (1996).

One particular issue of importance is grip design. Grip opening and shape have been shown to have a great effect on grip strength. For strength (power grip), most device designers revert to the so-called pistol grip. In contrast, for a precision grip, different grip and handle designs are necessary. For example, consider the shape of a micro-screwdriver. Handle and grip shapes are important factors to consider when designing a handheld input or output device; not doing so can lead to issues such as the device slipping out of the hands, unnecessary regrasping of devices, or fatigue and user discomfort (Marras 2012; Veas and Kruijff 2010).

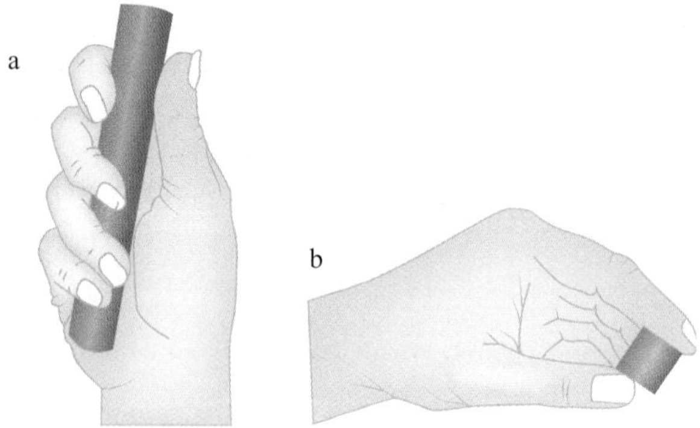

Figure 3.15 Power (a) and precision (b) grip. Redrawn from Castiello 2005.

The hands can be used for unimanual and bimanual tasks. Depending on hand preference, one hand (the dominant hand) is more sensitive than the other hand. In bimanual action, the non-dominant hand forms the frame of reference for the dominant hand (Guiard 1987; Figure 3.16). Bimanual (asymmetric) interaction can be found in many 2D and 3D interfaces. For a thorough discussion of bimanual interaction, please refer to Balakrishnan and Hinckley (1999) or Buxton and Meyers (1986).

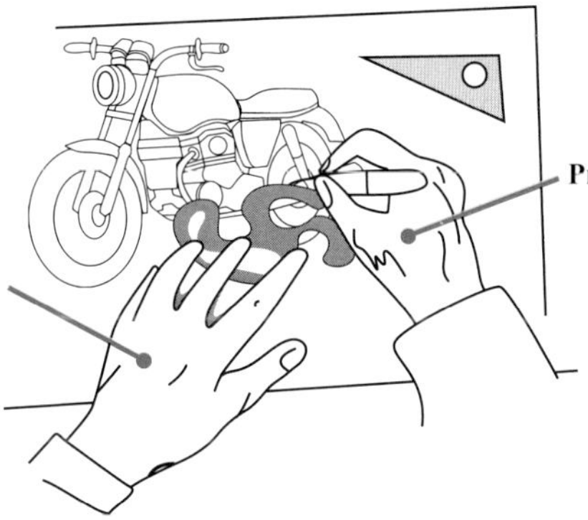

Figure 3.16 Bimanual interaction.

Feet and Legs

Feet and legs are also often used during interaction. The primary purpose of this interaction is physical motion through the environment (i.e., walking), but feet have also been used to control other application actions, as a substitute for the hands (Pakkanen and Raisamo 2004). The foot consists of three bone segments: the tarsus, the metatarsus, and the phalanges or toes. Several muscular structures run over the feet, including the fibrous bands from the ankle, the dorsal muscle on top of the feet, and multiple layers of plantar muscles under the feet. The musculo-skeletal construction of the feet (ankle and toes) allows several movements that partly resemble the movements of the hand: plantar flexion, dorsiflexion, inversion, eversion, flexion, extension, and gliding. Hence, some tasks performed by the hands could potentially be performed by the feet. Not surprisingly, the leg-ankle musculoskeletal construction is—just like the hand-wrist-arm construction—a lever system. The main purpose of this system is to support an upright posture and the control of human motion. Generally, the feet only allow coarse control actions (Bullinger et al. 1997; Goldstein 2002).

Posture

When 3D UIs are designed, it is important to consider not only the control-body linkage but also the general posture users need to take. With the availability of many whole-body interfaces as well as the usage of handheld augmented reality applications, posture is an important factor that affects user comfort and fatigue, up to the point of being unable to interact any longer

(Veas and Kruijff 2010). The field of workplace design has long focused on the human-factors-driven design of machinery being used while standing and also specific types of furniture to let the user perform actions while being seated.

Since most 3D UIs use hand-coupled devices or gestures, the relationships between arms and the rest of the body are critical. As we will describe in more detail in the next section, shoulder and arm fatigue (also nicknamed the "Gorilla arm syndrome" by HCI researchers) will occur when users need to operate with an uncomfortable or unsupported arm pose for a prolonged time. This kind of fatigue is affected by the height and distance of the hands (and arms) in relation to the body. The farther away and higher the hands, the less time users can interact comfortably. As described by Chaffin and Anderson (1991), the duration of user comfort (the *endurance time*) can often be doubled or tripled by lowering the hands (see Figure 3.17) or moving them closer to the body by 10 centimeters. Thus, interacting with faraway objects (reaching far) or controlling a menu at eye-height can quickly become tiring. For more details on workplace design, please refer to Marras (2012).

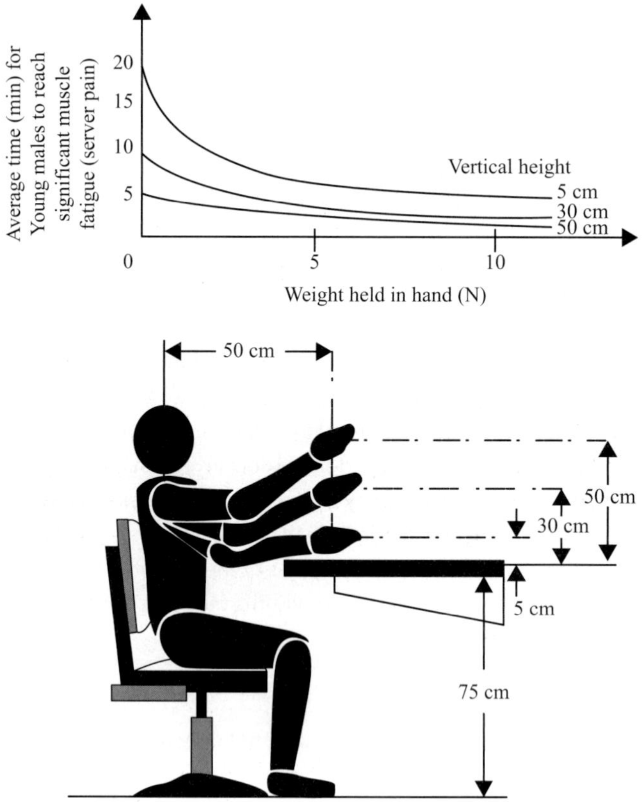

Figure 3.17 Expected time to reach shoulder muscle fatigue, redrawn from Chaffin and Anderson (1991).

3.5.2 Evaluating Physical Ergonomic Issues

While the analysis of physical ergonomics can cover many aspects, most studies will primarily look into fatigue and user comfort. In this section, we take a closer look at these two issues and how they can be evaluated.

Typical Issues

When addressing physical ergonomics in evaluation, UI designers are mainly faced with two highly interlinked or even inseparable issues: fatigue and user comfort.

Fatigue

Humans experience fatigue when load tolerance is surpassed, which depends not just on the user's muscles, bones, and ligaments, but also pain tolerance. Fatigue is often related to the pose a user needs to take to maintain a specific lever system. Fatigue may occur in the shoulder and back as well as in the arms and wrists. Typical signs of fatigue include change of pose, lowering of arms and hands, or the regrasping of an input device. Research has shown that over time, physical fatigue can also affect mental stress. As a result of not just physical but also psychological factors, fatigue can result in errors during task performance, as well as increased performance time (Barker 2009).

User Comfort

Related to fatigue, user comfort spans both physical and psychological dimensions. Comfort refers to a state of ease, which may include the absence of pain. In relation to physical ergonomics, user comfort generally refers to taking and maintaining a comfortable pose over potentially prolonged durations or keeping a comfortable grip on a specific device. The latter can include both physical comfort as well as design factors such as surface texture or shape of devices.

Evaluation Methods

While user comfort may be challenging to evaluate, there are numerous methods to assess fatigue, as it is similar to widely studied health and safety issues in work situations. With all methods, it is important to measure the user-specific physiological boundaries, as comfort and fatigue depend on the musculoskeletal characteristics and capabilities of individual users. This also means that it is important to include a wide variety of users during evaluation. Furthermore, to obtain a good impression of fatigue and user comfort, it often is not enough to make use of subjective methods only; it is highly recommended to compare/correlate the results of different methods (e.g., subjective measures and user observations).

Subjective Measures

Assessing user comfort often requires customized questionnaires for your specific system and application. You will need to reflect on the specific kind of task and task duration and address the different poses the user will take to perform the task. Furthermore, it is useful to ask the users' opinion about the physical aspects of any of the input devices used. Measures of user comfort and fatigue will be mixed, as both are interrelated and often difficult for users to separate. It is often useful to ask for fatigue levels in different body parts. For questions regarding fatigue, a good place to start is Neuberger (2003), where various questionnaires designed for people with some physical deficiency are compared. Furthermore, Marras (2012) offers a good overview of the various muscle-related fatigue issues.

Performance Measures

While it is difficult to evaluate the relationship between performance and fatigue or user comfort, some methods can be used. Task performance analysis, including error analysis, can be correlated with other methods of fatigue over time; that is, does performance decrease or stay stable over time, even when fatigue is noted or measured? While performance over time can be affected by multiple factors (e.g., learning), indications of fatigue-related performance decreases may be clear. As we noted above, sometimes users regrasp a device or take a brief break by lowering their arms before continuing a task. Such indications can be tagged in video observations and compared with the time to perform tasks.

Psycho-Physiological Methods

Finally, various physiological methods have been used to assess fatigue. These methods are often coupled to specific models that define biomechanical principles. Such models are mostly specialized for specific tasks, such as lifting or push-and-pull tasks. As a more general approach, EMG (electromyography, sensing muscle activity) has been applied to address muscle tension and fatigue. While EMG can be cumbersome to deploy, it provides valuable information that cannot yet be achieved predictably using the aforementioned models only. Finally, there are some physical devices that measure specific muscle and joint groups. For example, devices exist that measure the motion of the spine. For an-depth discussion, please refer to Marras (2012).

3.6 Guidelines

In this chapter, we have discussed numerous human factors issues that affect the analysis, design, and evaluation of 3D interaction techniques and devices. In this section, we provide some high-level guidelines.

> **Tip**
>
> Analyze, design, and evaluate interfaces with human factors in mind.

Human factors issues can greatly affect the design of well-performing techniques and devices. As such, designing interfaces with human factors in mind can often aid in addressing issues that would remain unrevealed in a more general user-centered design.

> **Tip**
>
> Refer to the general human factors literature.

3D UI design is often affected by higher-level human factors issues. Many of these issues have been studied before in other domains. Hence, it often makes sense to consider what the underlying human factors are that may affect your interfaces and to search, for example, in medical literature databases or refer to one of the human factors standard references we mention at the end of this chapter.

> **Tip**
>
> Try to isolate human factors issues.

Many human factors are highly interconnected. Try to avoid designing studies that target too many human factors issues; instead, isolate issues through careful study design.

> **Tip**
>
> Assess the true potential of the human body to design alternative interfaces.

Instead of looking at human factors limitations, another view may also be highly fruitful for designing novel interfaces: designing with the sensory and control potential of the human body in mind (Beckhaus and Kruijff 2004; Kruijff 2013).

> **Tip**
>
> Consider longitudinal studies.

As we mentioned several times throughout this chapter, usage duration often affects the extent of the effect of certain human factors issues. A clear example is fatigue over time, but this is true in other areas as well, from the learning of skills to effects such as habituation. Longitudinal studies are typically the only way to obtain data on such effects.

3.7 Conclusion

In this chapter, we introduced key human factors topics to provide a solid foundation for addressing perceptual, cognitive, and physical ergonomic issues in user-centered design processes. An understanding of these factors is important to design effective interaction techniques and devices. As we progress through the upcoming chapters, we will refer to the foundations laid here.

Recommended Reading

Further reading on the foundations of human factors and human potential driven design can be found in:

Salvendy, G. (ed.). 2012. *Handbook of Human Factors and Ergonomics,* 4th ed.

Kruijff, E. 2013. "Human-potential driven design of 3D user interfaces." *Proceedings of the IEEE International Conference on Artificial Reality and Telexistence* (ICAT 2013). Tokyo, Japan.

Further reading on perception and attention can be found in:

Goldstein, E. 2014. *Sensation and Perception,* 9th ed., Wadsworth.

Posner, Michael I. and Boies, Stephen J. 1971. "Components of attention." *Psychological Review* Vol. 78(5), pp 391–408.

Further reading on the basics of cognition including learning and memory, situation awareness and cognitive load can found in:

Smith, E. and Kosslyn, S. 2013. *Cognitive Psychology.* Pearson Education.

Kandell, E., Kupfermann, I., and Iversen, S. 2000. "Learning and memory." In Kandell, E., Schwartz, J., and Jessell, T. (eds.), *Principles of Neuroscience*, 4th ed. McGraw-Hill, pp 1127–1246.

Endsley, M. 2012. "Situation awareness." In Salvendy, G. (ed.), *Handbook of Human Factors and Ergonomics,* 4th ed.

Wickens, D. 2001. "Workload and situation awareness." In Hancock, P. and Desmond, P. (eds.), *Stress, Workload and Fatigue*. Erlbaum, pp 443–450.

More details on ergonomics and control can be found in:

Marras, W. 2012. "Basic biocmechanics and workstation design." In Salvendy, G. (ed.), *Handbook of Human Factors and Ergonomics.*

MacKenzie, I. 1992. "Fitts' Law as a research and design tool in human computer interaction." *Human Computer Interaction* Vol. 7, pp 91–139.

CHAPTER 4

GENERAL PRINCIPLES OF HUMAN–COMPUTER INTERACTION

This chapter serves as an introduction to general principles underlying the design of human–computer interfaces. Standard design and evaluation methods and guidelines are covered and linked to 3D UI design.

4.1 Introduction

In the previous chapter, we focused on the low-level perceptual, cognitive, and ergonomic capabilities of humans. In this chapter, we discuss how humans use those capabilities to interact with computers. We offer a broad overview of the HCI field, ranging from low-level human processor models to the high-level principles of activity theory, and include design guidelines and UX engineering processes for HCI practitioners.

While most of this book discusses specific issues related to the design and evaluation of 3D UIs, we recognize that it is critical to have foundational knowledge in HCI before building the 3D UI–specific knowledge on top of that foundation. Since readers may come to the topic of 3D UIs from a wide variety of backgrounds, not everyone will be familiar with general principles and processes used in HCI. Thus, we offer this chapter for readers needing an introduction to these foundational topics before diving into the particulars of 3D interaction. In this chapter, we offer an overview of the HCI field while highlighting topics of particular relevance to 3D UIs and providing pointers to additional readings that will strengthen this foundation.

4.1.1 What Is HCI?

Human–Computer Interaction (HCI) is a field that seeks to understand the relationship between human users and digital technological artifacts and to design new, effective ways for humans to use computer technologies for all sorts of purposes. Putting the "H" at the beginning of HCI is no coincidence; HCI focuses primarily on the human users and their needs. Thus, it is rooted in an understanding of human perception (sensing), cognition (thinking), and acting in the world coming from psychology, anatomy, biomechanics, and related human-centric fields (many of these topics were discussed in the previous chapter).

The word "computer" in HCI is typically construed very broadly. This word should conjure images not only of desktop and laptop computers but also of phones, watches, microwaves, automobiles, and video games—indeed, anything that contains digital computational elements. While HCI has played a vital role in designing and understanding users' interaction with traditional computers, one could argue that most interaction today, and certainly the more interesting research in HCI, takes place off the desktop, including interaction with 3D UIs.

Another nuance of the definition of HCI is that while the term focuses on the interaction between people and computers, it also includes interaction among multiple people (e.g., couples, colleagues, workgroups, online communities) that is *mediated* by computer technology. So designing effective HCI is not just about how to get the computer to do what you want it to do but also about how to enable effective human–human communication and collaboration.

So what is effective HCI? The answer can depend to a large extent on the purpose of the interaction. HCI encompasses any application of computer technologies, with many different purposes. While serious work is an important computer application category, with its associated measure of task performance, HCI is also concerned with how to make video games more fun and challenging, online chats more engaging and deep, calendar notifications less annoying and more timely, and interactive art more thought-provoking.

Whatever the purpose, HCI is not simply about understanding our current interaction with computers. It is just as much, if not more, about *designing* new forms of interaction. This might take the form of developing a new input device or display, designing a set of gestures to be used in an application, or repurposing existing technology in imaginative new ways. Thus, HCI can be approached both from a scientific perspective (understanding the world of human–computer interactions), and from engineering or art perspectives (creating and designing new human–computer interactions).

Because of this emphasis on design, many practitioners of HCI have traditionally focused on user interfaces (UIs); that is, on designing the parts of a computer system that users see and interact with. More recently, UI design has come to be seen as part of user experience (UX) design, which encompasses not only the specifics of the interface but also the social context of the system, the ecology of tools and technologies in which the system lives, and everything that the user brings to the table (e.g., training, cultural background, emotional state) when using the system. UX also puts particular emphasis on a broad definition of effectiveness, including the emotional impact of using a system.

Interaction techniques are particular elements of a UI. They are the methods by which a user accomplishes a task or part of a task, and they are primarily concerned with the form of the input given by the user (although they also involve display elements that give feedback to the user) and the mapping between that input and its result in the system. In most parts of the HCI world, interaction techniques are no longer of primary importance for designers or researchers, since the techniques that work well for interaction via a mouse, keyboard, or joystick are well understood and standardized. In certain segments of HCI, however (including 3D UIs, touch-based gestural interfaces, and brain–computer interfaces), the input devices being used are so different, widely varied, and nonstandard that the design of interaction techniques becomes a very interesting topic. That's why a large chunk of this book (Part III, "3D Interaction Techniques") is devoted to the design of 3D interaction techniques, although you won't see this topic addressed very deeply in typical HCI books.

One fact that every UX designer comes to terms with early on is that design in HCI is a series of *tradeoffs*. In other words, questions of design are not typically questions that have an unambiguous answer. There is not usually an optimal design (but some designs are demonstrably better than others). In making a design choice (and implicitly rejecting other choices), there are both benefits and disadvantages, and the benefits of one choice must be traded off against those of other choices. As a first principle of any sort of UX design (and of 3D UI design in particular), then, we encourage the reader to recognize these tradeoffs and then analyze them to determine the best course of action.

4.1.2 Chapter Roadmap

In this chapter, we give a summary and high-level overview of some of the key topics in HCI that are most relevant to 3D UIs. Again, this chapter and the previous one are meant for those readers without a background in human factors and HCI.

Since HCI is concerned with both *understanding* how humans interact with computers and *designing* such interactions, we organize the chapter around these ideas. Section 4.2 describes some of what we know from years of research that has sought to understand and explain human–computer interaction. This knowledge has been gathered and synthesized into some overarching *theories* of HCI that are highlighted in this section.

Sections 4.3 and 4.4 address the design side of HCI. In section 4.3, we explain how the knowledge and understanding of HCI, as seen in the theories, has been turned into actionable guidance for designers. We discuss high-level principles and guidelines for designing systems that provide effective user experiences. Since our knowledge is incomplete and even the best set of guidelines is insufficient to guarantee a good user experience, section 4.4 covers the key stages and elements of the UX engineering process.

4.2 Understanding the User Experience

HCI emerged in the early 1980s as a specialty area in computer science that embraced cognitive science and human factors engineering (Carroll 2012). Since then, HCI has attracted researchers from many other disciplines. As a result, HCI has evolved to incorporate many different types of user experiences and many different approaches for better understanding those experiences. In this section, we discuss some of the most prominent UX models and theories that HCI researchers have developed.

We begin in section 4.2.1 by discussing the low-level human processor models, which consider humans as computing entities with processors and memories that handle the atomic actions of interacting with computers. We then discuss user action models in section 4.2.2. Instead of focusing on atomic actions, these models focus on higher-level interactions, such as forming goals for interaction and perceiving whether those goals have been achieved within the system. In section 4.2.3, we describe conceptual models and affordances. In particular, we discuss how different types of affordances help to communicate the designer's conceptual model of a system to the user. In section 4.2.4, we expand our focus beyond just the user and the computer to discuss activity theory and how the real-life settings that HCI occurs in can affect the user experience. Finally, in section 4.2.5, we discuss the notion of embodied interaction and how it incorporates less-traditional user experiences, such as tangible computing, social computing, and ubiquitous computing.

4.2.1 Human Processor Models

Modeling humans as complex computer systems was one of the earliest approaches to understanding human–computer interaction. As first described by Card et al. (1983), the **Model Human Processor** regards humans, their capabilities, and memories to be analogous to computers, processing units, and storage disks, as seen in Figure 4.1. The model consists of three processors. First, a perceptual processor handles the sensory stimuli perceived by the user and stores the translated information into working memory. A cognitive processor then leverages information from both working memory and long-term memory to make decisions. Finally, a motor processor carries out the decisions through physical actions. We provided a similar representation in Chapter 3 (Figure 3.1). In Chapter 3, we looked at these processes from a low-level perspective focusing on human capabilities. In this chapter, we consider the same processes, but look at how they affect the human–computer interaction loop and how they can be formally represented through interaction models.

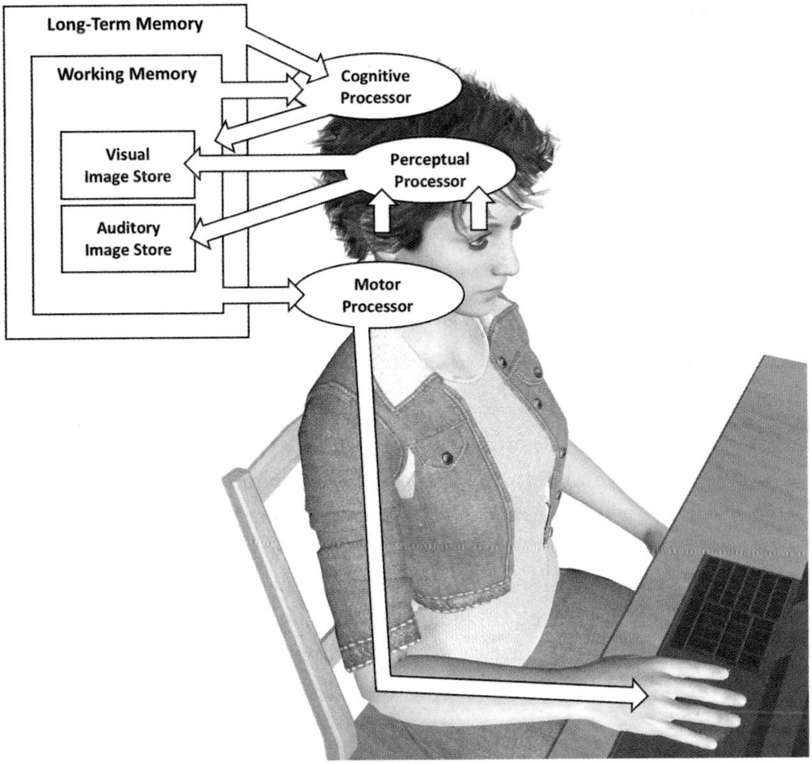

Figure 4.1 The Model Human Processor. (Image adapted from Card et al. 1983)

The Model Human Processor can be used to account for various perceptual, cognitive, and motor processes. Each processor has an estimated cycle time and associated memories with estimated capacities and decay times. For example, Card et al. (1983) estimated that the perceptual processor had a minimum cycle time of 50 milliseconds, a maximum capacity for visual images equal to 17 letters, and an average visual decay half-life of 200 milliseconds. Using such estimates, they were able to calculate the limitations of human capabilities, such as the maximum time interval for an object seen in successive images to be perceived as moving, the amount of time required to determine if two strings match, and the number of words per minute a user can type. These examples demonstrate the Model Human Processor's robust ability to model most perceptual, cognitive, and motor processes at a low level.

Keystroke-Level Model

Some human processor models sacrifice such robustness to be easier to use. For example, the **Keystroke-Level Model** (**KLM**) was one of the first human processor models to become popular. Card et al. (1980) developed it to predict the time that it takes an expert user to perform a given task without errors while using an interactive system. The KLM consists of a system response operator (which enables perception), a cognitive operator, and four possible motor operators. The **R** operator represents the time that the user must wait for the system to respond to a motor operator. The **M** operator represents the time that the user must spend to mentally prepare one or more of the motor operators. The four motor operators focus on handling the input devices, pressing keys or buttons, pointing at a target, and drawing a line. In particular, the **H** operator represents the time required to home the hands on the keyboard or to another device, such as a mouse. The **K** operator represents the time that it takes for a user to perform the motor skills required to press keys and buttons. The **P** operator represents the time that it takes to point to a target on a display and is normally calculated according to Fitts's Law. Finally, the **D** operator represents the time needed to draw a set of straight-line segments, which is applicable to hierarchical menus and can be estimated with the steering law (Accot and Zhai 1999). See Chapter 3, "Human Factors Fundamentals," section 3.2.4, for details on both Fitts's Law and the steering law.

In contrast to the Model Human Processor, the KLM offers the advantage of being easy to use without requiring in-depth knowledge of human factors or psychology. Task times can be predicted using previously established estimates for the operators (Card et al. 1980). This allows designs to be evaluated without recruiting subjects as representative users, and even without building a prototype. However, there are several limitations of the KLM. First, it only measures time, which is only one aspect of user performance. It also only considers expert users and error-free task executions. The mental operator also simplifies all of the user's cognitive actions (and some perceptual actions) to a single value, which cannot represent the depth and diversity of those actions.

GOMS

A more-complex version of the KLM is the **Goals, Operators, Methods, and Selection (GOMS)** model, also created by Card et al. (1983). **Goals** represent what the user wants to accomplish with the system and are often represented as symbolic structures that define the desired state. **Operators** are the elementary perceptual, cognitive, and motor actions required to accomplish each goal, similar to those of the KLM. **Methods** are specific sequences of operators that can be used to accomplish a particular goal. **Selection** rules indicate which method the user should take when multiple methods are available for accomplishing the same goal. Figure 4.2 provides a visual representation of the GOMS model.

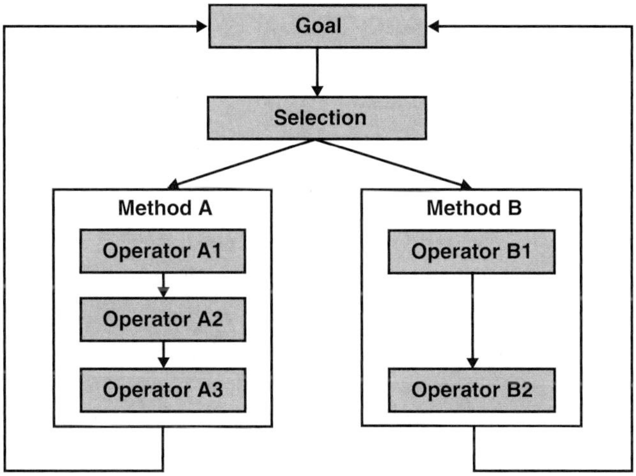

Figure 4.2 A visual representation of the GOMS model. (Image courtesy of Ryan P. McMahan)

Touch-Level Model

Despite being one of the first HCI models, human processor models are still being studied today. Recently, Rice and Lartigue (2014) defined the **Touch-Level Model (TLM)**, which extends the KLM to touchscreen and mobile devices. The TLM retains the original response time (**R**), mental act (**M**), homing (**H**), and keystroke (**K**) operators. It also includes several new operators. The distraction (**X**) operator is a multiplicative operator that adds time to the other operators, as it represents the time lost to distractions that naturally occur in the real world. Common touch gestures are represented by the tap (**T**), swipe (**S**), drag (**D**), pinch (**P**), zoom (**Z**), and rotate (**O**) operators. Specialized gestures requiring one or more fingers are represented by the gesture (**G**) operator. The tilt (**L**) operator represents the time required to physically tilt or rotate the device. Finally, the initial act (**I**) operator models the actions required for preparing the system for use, such as unlocking the device.

Human Processor Models for 3D UIs

A human processor model has yet to be designed specifically for 3D UIs, but researchers have used the concepts of human processor models to design and analyze various 3D interactions. McMahan and Bowman (2007) established several perceptual-motor operators for selecting various 3D objects and system control components in one of their user studies. They then used those operators to estimate the cognitive load of various system control task sequences (e.g., action-first or object-first tasks). Chun and Höllerer (2013) have also used a human processor model to informally compare a flicking gesture to a similar swiping gesture for touchscreen interfaces. Hence, human processor models can be used to design and analyze 3D UIs.

4.2.2 User Action Models

While human processor models represent the discrete atomic events that occur when the user performs certain operations, **user action models** portray the high-level interactions between the human and the system. These models consist of four distinct aspects: (i) the user's goal, (ii) the user's execution of physical actions, (iii) the outcomes of those actions within the system, and (iv) the user's evaluation of those outcomes. For example, consider a user with the goal of moving a virtual object. The user decides upon an action plan, reaches out with a tracked handheld device to virtually touch the object, and presses a button to execute a grab (see Chapter 7, "Selection and Manipulation," section 7.4.1 for details on the virtual hand technique). The system responds by attaching the object so that it now follows the movements of the tracked device. The user sees this outcome and comprehends that the goal of moving the object is in progress.

Seven Stages of Action

Norman's seven stages of action was the first well-known user action model for human–computer interaction. In order to understand what makes interfaces difficult to use, Norman set out to define what happens when someone interacts with a system. His idea was to study the structure of actions. In doing so, he identified four considerations: "the goal, what is done to the world, the world itself, and the check of the world" (Norman 2013). Within these considerations, Norman defined seven stages of action.

The first stage of action is the formation of the user's goal (e.g., the idea to move the virtual object). The second stage involves the formation of the user's intention, which involves identifying a specific action that is expected to accomplish the goal (e.g., grabbing the object). The third stage yields the specification of an action plan, or sequence of actions, that will accomplish the intention (e.g., reach out with handheld device, virtually touch the object, and press the grab button). In the fourth stage, the user executes the action plan by performing the necessary physical actions. In response to the physical actions, the system determines the outcomes of the given input (e.g., attach the virtual object to the device's position). In the fifth stage, the user perceives the stimuli generated by the system (e.g., displayed visuals of the object following the handheld device). The sixth stage involves the cognitive processing of the perceived sensory stimuli to interpret the current system state (e.g., the object is attached to the virtual hand). In the final stage, the user evaluates the outcome by comparing it to the intention and recognizes that the goal is in progress (e.g., the object is being moved). See Figure 4.3 for a visual representation of the seven stages of action.

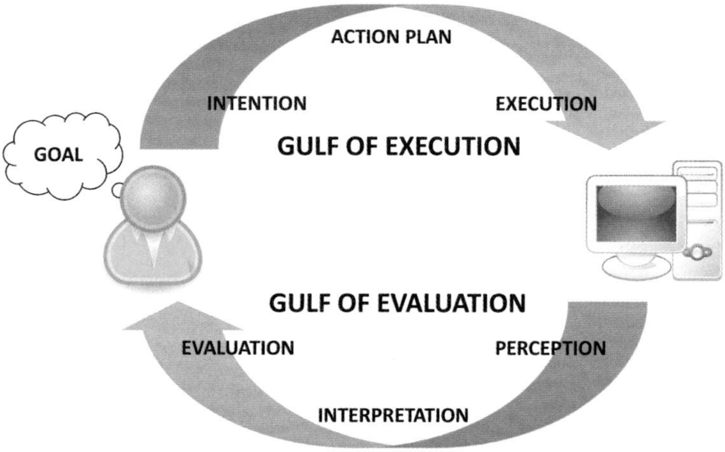

Figure 4.3 Norman's seven stages of action and the Gulfs of Execution and Evaluation. (Image courtesy of Ryan P. McMahan)

Gulfs of Execution and Evaluation

Along with the seven stages of action, Norman identified two major phases of interactions between the user and the system. The first phase involves what the user does to affect the system. The second phase involves how the system informs the user of its state. Norman described both of these phases as "gulfs" to represent the conceptual distance between the user's mental model of the system and the truth about the system.

The **Gulf of Execution** represents the gap between the user's idea of what to do and the actual cognitive and motor actions that must be performed for the user's goal to be realized in the world. A user can achieve a goal by forming intentions, devising an action plan, and physically executing those actions required by the system to accomplish the goal. However, if the actions required by the system do not match the user's intentions, the user's goal will not be obtained. Consider the example goal of moving a virtual object. If the user expects a particular button to be pressed in order to grab the virtual object but the system requires a different button to be pressed, the system will not begin moving the object with the tracked device. Hence, the user has not accomplished the goal.

The Gulf of Execution essentially represents the potential failures of aligning the user's mental model and expectations to the actual workings of the system and its requirements. Given enough time and experience with a particular system, users will develop **procedural knowledge**—the action sequences and routines required to achieve their goals and intentions (Cohen and Bacdayan 1994). However, when first interacting with a new system, the user must rely on **semantic knowledge**—general knowledge of objects, word meanings, facts, and relationships (Patterson et al. 2007). If the user's semantic knowledge does not adequately match the system's interface, the user will be forced to close the Gulf of Execution through trial and error. The designer, therefore, should present a user interface that makes it clear to the user (e.g., through affordances, labels, metaphors, or, if all else fails, instructions) how the system works and how goals can be achieved.

On the other hand, the **Gulf of Evaluation** represents the gap between the actual state of the system, and what the user perceives the state of the system to be through perception and cognition. In order to evaluate whether a goal has been accomplished, the user must perceive available stimuli, interpret those stimuli as outcomes, and assess whether those outcomes match the expected outcomes of the action plan. If the stimuli provided by the system cannot be perceived or are not easily interpreted, it can be difficult for the user to evaluate whether the intentions and goal have been accomplished. Reconsider our virtual hand example and assume that the system waits until the object is released to display its new position, instead of moving the object continuously with the tracked device. It is not possible for the user to confirm that the object is moving until releasing the object, at which point the object is no longer moving. Hence, it would be nearly impossible for the user to move the object to a target position. The designer, therefore, must carefully consider how to present sensory feedback to the user that makes the actual state of the system clear, providing information the user needs to evaluate progress towards goals.

User Action Framework

Another user action model is the **User Action Framework (UAF)**, which is a structured knowledge base of usability concepts and issues that was built upon Norman's seven stages of action model (Andre et al. 2001). At the core of the UAF is the Interaction Cycle, which is a representation of user interaction sequences (Hartson 2003). The Interaction Cycle essentially partitions Norman's seven stages into five phases: (i) planning, (ii) translation, (iii) physical actions, (iv) outcomes, and (v) assessment (Hartson and Pyla 2012). Planning involves the formation of the user's goal and the intention. Translation is the process of devising an action plan. Physical actions cover the motor aspects of executing the action plan. The outcomes (system responses) are entirely internal to the system and include the feedback generated by the system. Finally, the assessment phase covers perceiving the state of the system, interpreting that state, and evaluating the outcomes.

While very similar to the seven stages of action, Hartson and colleagues developed the Interaction Cycle to emphasize the importance of translation during human–computer interactions, in comparison to assessment (Hartson and Pyla 2012). This can be seen in Figure 4.4. Additionally, the Interaction Cycle provides a hierarchical structure for organizing design concepts. The UAF uses this structure along with several established design guidelines to provide a knowledge base of usability concepts and issues. See *The UX Book* by Hartson and Pyla (2012) for more details about this knowledge base.

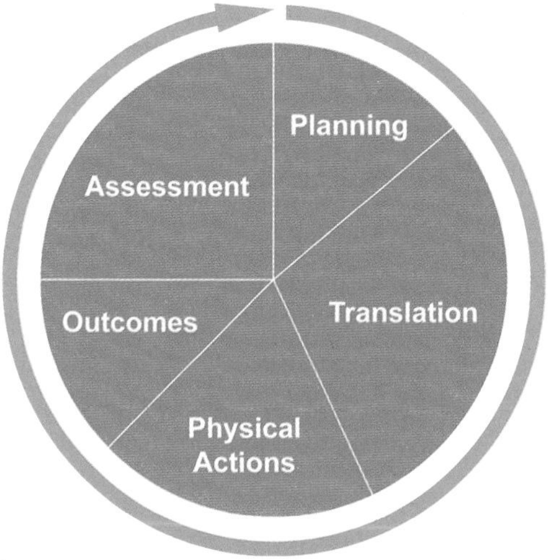

Figure 4.4 Hartson's Interaction Cycle emphasizes the importance of translation. (Image adapted from Hartson and Pyla 2012)

User-System Loop

One user action model that has been developed specifically for 3D UIs is the **User-System Loop** of McMahan et al. (2015), which is a system-centric adaptation of Norman's seven stages of action. In the User-System Loop, every interaction begins with user actions that input devices sense or are manipulated by, which are then interpreted by transfer functions as meaningful system effects. Those effects alter the data and models underlying the simulation's objects, physics, and artificial intelligence. Rendering software then captures aspects of the simulation's updated state and sends commands to output devices to create sensory stimuli for the user to perceive. This essentially models the flow of information between a user and a system (see Figure 4.5).

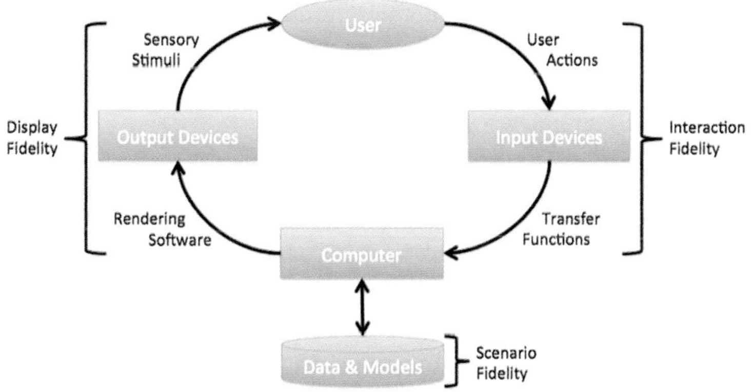

Figure 4.5 The User-System Loop models the flow of information between a user and a computer system from a system-centric point of view. See Chapter 11, section 11.6.3 for a discussion of how different types of fidelity impact the User-System Loop. (Image courtesy of Ryan P. McMahan)

Consider our virtual hand example. The user's actions include reaching out to virtually touch the object and pressing a button. The tracked handheld device acts as the input device. Transfer functions process the position of the device to determine if it is collocated with the virtual object and the button state to determine if a grab is being executed. The simulation updates its state by modeling the movement of the virtual object after the movements of the handheld device. Rendering software generates a 2D image of the object's updated position to the system's visual display, which generates light for the user's eyes to perceive. As seen from this example, the User-System Loop model includes more focus on system actions and less focus on user actions than the seven stages of action or the UAF. However, like the user-centric models, the stages modeled by the User-System Loop can be useful to consider when designing and analyzing user experiences. In particular, the choice of input devices and the design of transfer functions is critical to the usability of many 3D interaction techniques.

4.2.3 Conceptual Models and Affordances

While user action models portray the interactions that occur between a user and the system, conceptual models can be used to understand how the user's expectations match the system's (or designer's) expectations. A **conceptual model** is an understanding of the information and tasks that constitute a system (Norman 2013). Because these models are based on an individual's understanding of a system, and not what actually constitutes the system, conceptual models can be incomplete and informal representations of the system (Rosson and Carroll 2001).

Designer's Model versus User's Model

There are two important conceptual models. The first is the **designer's model**, which represents how the designer understands the system from a development perspective. This model should be a relatively complete and systematic representation of the implemented system. While the designer's model will include a mental representation of the system, technical representations such as task analyses, flow diagrams, and usage models also compose the designer's model of a system (Rosson and Carroll 2001). The second important conceptual model is the **user's model**, which represents how the user understands the system based on experiences with it. Unlike the designer's model, the user's model is formed through ad hoc interactions with the system. This can result in an incomplete and simplistic understanding of what constitutes the system and how it works.

Ideally, for the system to have high levels of usability, the user's model should match the designer's model (Norman 2013). During the development process, designers spend a great deal of time expanding and refining their conceptual models of the system. However, users only have their own experiences and interactions with the system to form their models of it. As the designers do not talk directly with the users in most cases, the system is responsible for communicating the designer's model to the users. If the system and UI do a poor job at making the designer's model clear and consistent, the users will end up with incorrect conceptual models.

For example, consider a detailed virtual environment in which only a couple of objects can be manipulated. There's a good chance that the user's first attempts to interact with the environment may include noninteractive objects. Based on these failed interactions, the user may quickly form the conceptual model that all of the objects are noninteractive. Hence, it is the responsibility of the designer to ensure that the system sufficiently conveys to the user that the two objects can be manipulated.

Affordances

To increase the likelihood of the user's model matching the designer's, HCI researchers have studied affordances of systems. In basic terms, an **affordance** is something that helps the user do something (Hartson and Pyla 2012). The term "affordance" originated from perceptual psychology, where Gibson (1977) introduced the term to refer to a property of an animal's environment that offers or provides the animal with something. Norman (1988) later popularized the concept within the HCI community to refer to the physical and perceived properties of an object that determine how it could possibly be used. Consider, for example, a door push bar, which is often found on the interior side of exterior building doors. Physically, the push bar affords no other action than to push the door open, as pulling on the bar is difficult without a place to grasp it. This affordance (i.e., the door must be pushed and not pulled) is easily perceived and understood by anyone who has prior experience with door push bars. Affordances of a system can help users better understand how it works, which improves their conceptual model of the system.

While the concept of an affordance is simple, there has been some confusion over what the term exactly refers to. This is primarily due to several researchers defining affordances in different ways (Norman 1988; Gaver 1991; McGrenere and Ho 2000). We believe Hartson (2003) addresses the confusion in a logical way with his four categories of affordances—cognitive, physical, functional, and sensory.

A cognitive affordance is a system property that helps the user with cognitive actions, such as deciding upon an action plan. For example, the user is likely to understand that removing objects from the virtual environment is possible with the provision of an eraser in a virtual tool belt (see Chapter 9, "System Control," section 9.8.1 for details on the "tool belt" technique). A physical affordance is a property of the system that helps the user perform the necessary physical actions. In the tool belt example, if the eraser tool is near the extent of the user's reach, it may be difficult for the user to select the eraser without making a conscious effort to reach for it. However, if the eraser and tool belt are located closer, the user should be able to select the eraser with little thought or effort. A functional affordance is a system property that helps the user to accomplish a high-level task. The eraser tool described affords the functionality of removing objects from the virtual environment. Finally, a sensory affordance is a property of the system that helps the user with sensory actions, such as recognizing that a goal has been accomplished. For example, it may be difficult for a user to see whether the eraser tool is touching the object to be erased because of a lack of haptic feedback. If the system highlights objects whenever they are touched by the eraser, the user's perception of "touching" will be improved.

Note how cognitive, physical, functional, and sensory affordances correspond to the four primary aspects of user action models—the user's goal, the user's execution of physical actions, the outcomes of those actions within the system, and the user's evaluation of those outcomes. With traditional UIs, designers are primarily concerned with cognitive and sensory affordances. These types of affordances relate directly to interaction design and information design (see section 4.4.3), respectively. However, for 3D UIs, physical affordances can sometimes be more important than cognitive and sensory affordances. For example, if users cannot physically perform the gesture required to travel within a virtual environment, it is irrelevant that they know what the intended travel gesture is or perceive that they are not traveling due to the gesture not working as expected. Finally, all systems are expected to provide some sort of functional affordances. Why else would people use them? Hence, it is important for 3D UI designers to consider all four types of affordances when creating systems.

4.2.4 Activity Theory

All of the previous models for understanding the user experience have focused primarily on the user and the system. However, humans do not interact with systems in a vacuum. Instead, these interactions occur in the real world, which includes other humans, systems, objects, and activities. Because of this, HCI researchers have looked at the bigger picture—how do humans interact with computers within real-world contexts? This is sometimes called the ecological perspective of UX (Hartson and Pyla 2012). This has led HCI researchers to adopt and develop new theories as tools for analyzing and designing user experiences for specific real-life contexts. One such theory is activity theory.

Activity theory is a framework for helping researchers to orient themselves in complex real-life contexts (Kaptelinin and Nardi 2012). Unlike prior UX models, it did not originate from within the HCI community. Instead, it was adopted from a movement within Russian psychology that originated in the 1920s. The main thrust of this movement was to overcome the conceptual divide between the human mind and aspects of society and culture (Kaptelinin and Nardi 2012). Several researchers contributed fundamental ideas to the movement, including Rubinshtein (1946) and Vygotsky (1980). However, Leont'ev (1978) is considered the chief architect of activity theory (Nardi 1996).

In activity theory, an **activity** is a relationship between a subject and an object, which is commonly represented as "S < – > O" (Kaptelinin and Nardi 2012). A **subject** is a person or a group engaged in an activity while an **object** represents a motive, something that can meet a need of the subject (Nardi 1996). For example, a user (the subject) can use a visual display (the object) to view a virtual environment (the activity). However, it is important to note that objects do not have to be physical things (Kaptelinin and Nardi 2012). If an artist needs a virtual 3D model for communicating a new car design, the virtual model itself serves as the object for the communication activity.

Principles of Activity Theory

Activity theory includes several basic principles (Kaptelinin and Nardi 2012). **Object-orientedness** is the principle that all activities are directed toward their objects and are differentiated from one another by their respective objects (Kaptelinin and Nardi 2006). For example, when users 3D-print a thing, they are 3D-printing some object. Additionally, the activity of 3D-printing a dinosaur model is different from the activity of 3D-printing a sphere.

Another principle of activity theory is that activities are hierarchical structures. Activities are composed of actions, and actions are in turn composed of operations (Kaptelinin and Nardi 2012). **Actions** are the steps necessary to accomplish the activity. Each step corresponds to a goal that the subject must consciously work toward. On the other hand, **operations** are routine processes that bring about the conditions necessary to complete a specific action. For example, in the activity of reviewing a virtual architectural design, an architect will consciously decide to perform the actions of reviewing every space, room by room. However, during this process, the architect is likely not paying attention to the navigation operation, unless the travel technique is poorly designed.

Internalization and externalization are two other basic principles of activity theory (Kaptelinin and Nardi 2012). **Internalization** is the concept that external operations can become internal. For example, when first learning to use a touchpad interface, many users may need to watch their fingers move on the touchpad. However, over time, most users can interact with these interfaces seamlessly, without watching their fingers. On the other hand, **externalization** is the transformation of internal operations into external ones. For example, the artist must externalize her design for a new car into a 3D model before she can share it with others.

The principle of **mediation** is the concept of a third entity that changes the original relationship between a subject and an object (Kuutti 1996). For example, modern GPS systems mediate the activity of humans navigating to their desired locations. A principle closely related to mediation is development. **Development** is the realization that activities will transform over time (Kaptelinin and Nardi 2006). While early humans had to observe the sun and stars in attempts to reach target destinations, the activity of navigation has changed over time due to mediating tools, such as maps, compasses, and GPS.

Activity System Model

Engeström (1987) proposed the **Activity System Model** as an extension of activity theory that accounts for activities carried out by collective subjects. The Activity System Model redefines the notion of an activity to include community as a third element, to represent the three-way interaction between subjects, their communities, and objects. Additionally, Engeström (1987) noted that a special type of entity mediates each of the three distinct interactions. **Instruments** mediate the subject-object interaction. **Rules** mediate the subject-community interaction. And, the **division of labor** mediates the community-object interaction. Finally, the **outcome** of the activity system represents the transformation of the object produced by the interactions and the mediating aspects, as seen in Figure 4.6.

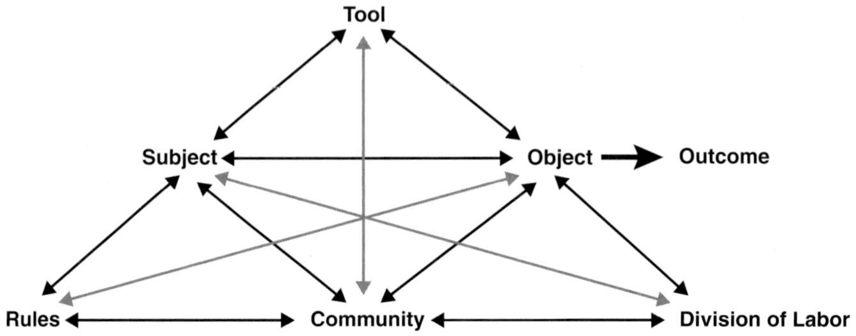

Figure 4.6 Engeström's Activity System Model. (Image adapted from Engeström 1987)

See *Activity Theory in HCI* by Kaptelinin and Nardi (2012) for an in-depth discussion of activity theory and the Activity System Model.

Activity Theory and 3D UIs

In addition to traditional interfaces, activity theory has also been used to understand user experiences in 3D UIs. Roussou et al. (2008) explored using activity theory as a tool for analyzing user interactions within virtual environments. The researchers categorized aspects of the interactions based on their effect within the activity system. For example, they categorized the virtual environment as the tool that mediated the user's ability to accomplish her goal. Additionally, they categorized changes in the user's conceptual model as changes to the rules that mediate the subject and community. As the researchers suggest, there are many other opportunities for using activity theory in the design and evaluation of 3D UIs.

4.2.5 Embodied Interaction

Another concept closely related to activity theory is **Embodied Interaction**, which is defined as "interaction with computer systems that occupy our world, a world of physical and social reality, and that exploit this fact in how they interact with us" (Dourish 2001). In other words, Embodied Interaction exploits our familiarity with the real world, including experiences with physical artifacts and social conversations. Dourish (2001) identifies these familiar real-world aspects as **embodied phenomena**, which by his descriptions are things that exist and are embedded in "real time and real space." He further explains that Embodied Interaction is "the creation, manipulation, and sharing of meaning" through engaged interaction with these embodied phenomena.

In his book *Where the Action Is: The Foundations of Embodied Interactions*, Dourish (2001) primarily discusses the concept of Embodied Interaction in the contexts of tangible computing and social computing. We describe each of these HCI fields below and how Embodied Interaction relates to each.

Tangible Computing

Tangible computing is an HCI field that focuses on users interacting with digital information through the physical environment (Ishii 2008). Specifically, **tangible user interfaces** (TUIs) use physical objects to seamlessly and simultaneously integrate physical representations of digital information and physical mechanisms for interacting with them (Ullmer and Ishii 2001). A key aspect to TUIs is that computation is distributed across a variety of physical objects that are aware of their location and their proximity to other objects (Dourish 2001). This allows for concurrent access to and manipulation of these spatially aware computational devices (Kim and Maher 2008).

By their nature, TUIs provide Embodied Interaction (Dourish 2001). The physical objects used in tangible computing are great examples of embodied phenomena. They are embedded into the physical world and exist in real time and real space. Additionally, these physical objects provide the ability to take advantage of highly developed skills for physically interacting with real-world objects (Dourish 2001). Furthermore, they allow users to create, manipulate, and share meaning through physical interactions, as each physical object represents digital information.

TUIs are highly relevant to the 3D UI community. From an Embodied Interaction perspective, the tangible components are viewed as physical representation of digital information. However, from an AR perspective, the tangible components can be considered enhanced or augmented by the digital information. Hence, they are essentially a subset of AR interfaces (Azuma et al. 2001).

Social Computing

Social computing describes any type of system that serves as a medium or focus for a social relation (Schuler 1994). As media, computer systems can facilitate social conventions and contexts (Wang et al. 2007). Consider, for example, how email has largely replaced conventional paper-based mail. Alternatively, as the focus, a computer system can create new opportunities and types of social interactions (Dourish 2001). For example, massively multiplayer online role-playing games (MMORPGs) have enabled new opportunities for online gamers to socialize in a way not possible in the real world.

Social computing is closely related to **Computer-Supported Cooperative Work (CSCW)**, which addresses how "collaborative activities and their coordination can be supported by means of computer systems" (Carstensen and Schmidt 1999). One of the primary concerns of CSCW is in what context a system is used. To help categorize contexts for CSCW systems, Johansen (1989) introduced the CSCW Matrix, which can be seen in Figure 4.7. This matrix categorizes CSCW contexts based on time and location. With regard to time, individuals can collaborate synchronously at the same time or asynchronously at different times. For location, social interactions can occur collocated in the same place or remotely in different places.

	Same Time	Different Time
Same Location	**Face-to-Face Collaborations** • Conference room • Interactive whiteboard • Shared display	**Ongoing Collaborations** • Public display • Shift work groupware • Team rooms
Different Location	**Remote Collaborations** • Instant messaging • Video conferencing • Virtual worlds	**Coordinated Collaborations** • Email • Group calendar • Project management software • Version control • Wikis

Figure 4.7 The CSCW Matrix categorizes the contexts of social computing according to time and location. (Image adapted from Johansen 1989)

By their nature, social conventions and conversations are embodied phenomena that create, manipulate, and share meaning. Hence, social computing and CSCW applications that facilitate such social interactions provide Embodied Interaction by definition (Dourish 2001). Additionally, CSCW applications that serve as the focus for social relations can provide new opportunities for creating, manipulating, and sharing meaning. Dourish (2001) terms this development of opportunities as "appropriation," which is essentially the emergence and evolution of new practices within real-life settings, both physical and social.

Social computing and CSCW are highly relevant concepts in the 3D UI field. One of the earliest goals within the field was to create systems that enabled **telepresence**, the sharing of task space and person space in collaborative work (Buxton 1992). Since then, researchers have developed a number of systems that allow users to interact in the same virtual 3D space while present in different physical 3D spaces. Researchers have even developed group-to-group telepresence, in which two groups of remote users can meet within a virtual environment and engage in 3D social interactions (Beck et al. 2013). In addition to telepresence, researchers have investigated using 3D UIs as collaborative visualization systems, with multiple systems having been developed (Pang and Wittenbrink 1997; Lascara et al. 1999; Sawant et al. 2000).

4.2.6 Evolving Understanding

In the previous sections, we covered a number of models and theories that attempt to understand and describe the user experience. However, these are just a small sample of the contributions that have been made to the HCI and UX fields. Yet, even if we were able to take the plethora of UX models and theories into account as a whole, we would still not fully understand every user experience. This is mainly due to the fact that HCI is constantly changing. As it evolves and new UIs emerge, it is up to HCI and UX researchers to continue attempting to better understand the user experience.

4.3 Design Principles and Guidelines

Through understanding the user experience, HCI researchers have extracted and elucidated numerous principles and guidelines for designing UIs. In this section, we present some common ones that are repeatedly discussed. We organize these principles and guidelines according to the four distinct aspects of the user action models: (i) goal, (ii) execution, (iii) outcome, and (iv) evaluation.

4.3.1 Goal-Oriented Design Rules

It is important that UX designers create UIs that facilitate the formation of the user's goals. If a UI is overly complex, it may take the user extra time to form a goal. If the UI must be complex due to the system's wide range of functions, the corresponding components should be organized in a sensible manner. Finally, if the purpose of a UI component is not clear, the user may waste time discerning what it does. Hence, in this section, we discuss the design principles of simplicity, structure, and visibility.

Simplicity

Simplicity is the design principle that the UI should be kept "as simple as possible and task focused" (Johnson 2014). Based on the human processor models of HCI, we know that a complex UI will require more perceptual and cognitive processing time in order to form a goal than a simpler UI with fewer components. The Hick-Hyman Law (Hick 1952; Hyman 1953) formally explains that an increase in the number of choices increases decision times logarithmically. Hence, it is important that the design of a UI remains simple, with as few components as possible to achieve tasks within the system.

There are a number of guidelines that UX designers can follow to keep their UIs simple. Nielsen (1994) explains that UIs should not contain information or components that are irrelevant or rarely needed. An example use of this guideline is region-based information filtering, which reduces information clutter in AR applications (Julier et al. 2000). Another guideline to keep the UI simple is to avoid extraneous or redundant information (Constantine and Lockwood 1999). For example, Tatzgern et al. (2013) used compact visualization filters to reduce redundant information in AR applications, like the one seen in Figure 4.8. Finally, if a UI is still complex after removing irrelevant and redundant components, a third design guideline is to provide the user with the capability to customize a default subset of controls (Galitz 2007). For example, smartphones allow users to rearrange the icons representing apps so that their most frequently used apps are visible on the first screen.

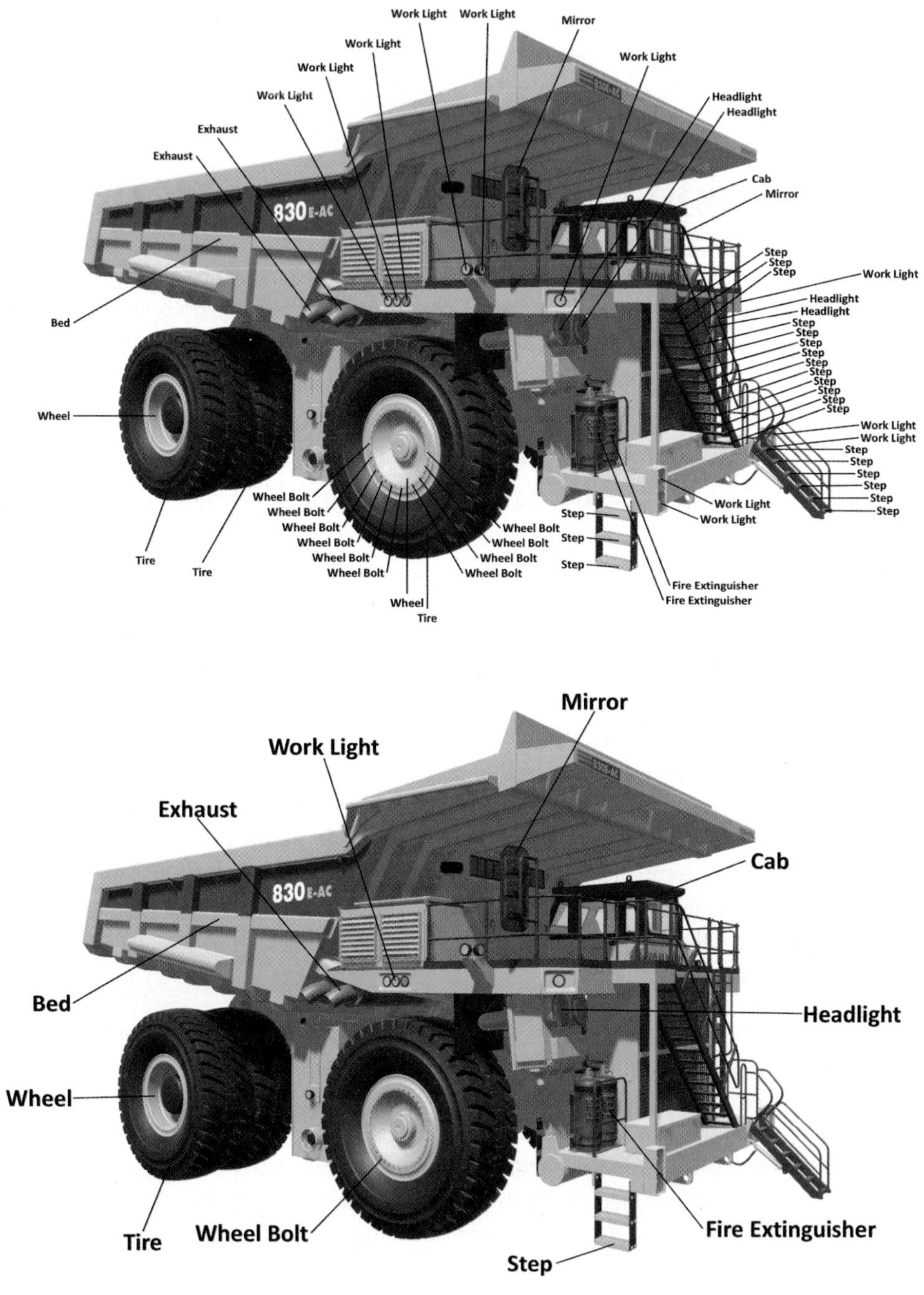

Figure 4.8 The top image shows a truck annotated with numerous labels with a small font that is difficult to read. The bottom image of the truck uses compact visualization filters to remove redundant information, support larger font sizes and to keep the UI simple. (Image courtesy of Ryan P. McMahan)

Structure

Structure is the design principle that the UI should be organized "in a meaningful and useful way" (Stone et al. 2005). In particular, the structure of the UI should match the user's conceptual model of the task (Rosson and Carroll 2001). The structure should facilitate the identification of specific actions that are expected to accomplish the user's goal. To accomplish this, the UI's components should be structured to "appear in a natural and logical order" (Nielsen 1994).

UX designers can rely on some guidelines when structuring their UIs. First, complex tasks should be broken down into simpler subtasks (Stone et al. 2005). A relevant 3D UI example of this guideline is the HOMER technique developed by Bowman and Hodges (1997). HOMER distinctly splits the complex task of manipulating a virtual object into two subtasks—selecting the object and positioning the object in 3D space. Many desktop 3D UIs go even further by breaking down the act of positioning the object into separate controls for each DOF. See Chapter 7, sections 7.9.1 and 7.7.3, for more details on HOMER and desktop-based manipulations, respectively.

Another structure-oriented design guideline is that every sequence of actions should be organized into a group or technique with a beginning, middle, and end (Shneiderman and Plaisant 2010). The SQUAD technique developed by Kopper et al. (2011) is an example of such a technique. It starts with casting a sphere to select a small group of objects and then uses a quad menu to refine the selection through a series of menu selections until the desired target is confirmed (see Chapter 7, section 7.10.3). Lastly, a similar guideline is to group any related or comparable functions. For example, in their rapMenu system, Ni et al. (2008) organized sets of related content into hierarchical pie menus (see Figure 4.9).

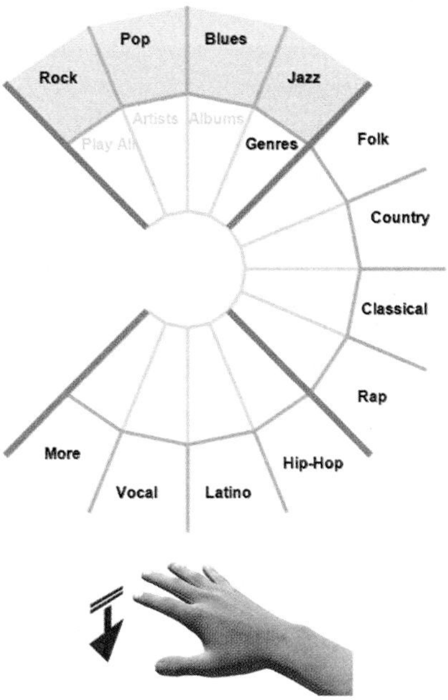

Figure 4.9 Similar controls or content can be grouped in hierarchical menus, such as this radial menu, to provide structure to the UI. (Image courtesy of Ryan P. McMahan)

Visibility

Stone et al. (2005) define **visibility** as the design principle that "it should be obvious what a control is used for." In order for the user to form an intention and corresponding action plan, the user must understand what functions and options are currently available. From these, the user will decide upon a single feature or series of commands to accomplish her current goal.

The first design guideline to ensuring visibility is that UX designers must make certain that their controls are perceivable. This is also known as discoverability. In web-based interfaces, designers should ensure that important UI components do not appear "below the fold" (i.e., below the part of the page that will be initially visible (Nielsen 1999). For 3D UIs, designers have even more placement issues to be concerned with. First, UI components may initially be outside of the user's field of view. Second, controls may be occluded by parts of the virtual environment or other UI components. In general, head-referenced and body-referenced placements are recommended for 3D UI components because they provide a strong spatial reference frame. See Chapter 9, section 9.5.2, for more discussion on placing 3D UI components.

A second visibility guideline is to employ visual icons and symbols to represent UI features in a familiar and recognizable manner (Shneiderman and Plaisant 2010). By doing so, UX designers can leverage users' perceptual processors instead of relying solely on cognitively demanding labels and descriptions. Many 3D UIs can leverage icons and symbols found in traditional desktop UIs. For instance, Moore et al. (2015) provided a recycle bin for removing notes and chords from their virtual musical interface (see Figure 4.10). However, as with traditional UIs, text can be more comprehensible than nonintuitive icons or indirect symbolism (Shneiderman and Plaisant 2010). Hence, 3D UI designers should also be familiar with using labels to make it obvious what their controls are used for.

Figure 4.10 The recycle bin in the Wedge musical interface (Moore et al. 2015) is a visible method for removing notes and chords from the composition environment. (Image courtesy of Ryan P. McMahan)

4.3.2 Execution-Oriented Design Rules

In addition to supporting the formation of the user's goals, UX designers must be concerned with how the user specifies and executes an action plan. If the user does not know *how* to use a UI component, he will have difficulty specifying an action plan, even if he knows *what* the purpose of the UI component is. Additionally, it is futile to specify an action plan if the user cannot physically execute the plan. Finally, UX designers should help users avoid committing errors when executing action plans. Correspondingly, we discuss the design principles of affordance, ergonomics, and error prevention in this section.

Affordance

Affordance is the design principle that "it should be obvious how a control is used" (Stone et al. 2005). Note that a user may understand what the purpose of a UI component is (i.e., it has visibility), but the user may not understand how to use the control (i.e., it lacks affordance). For example, a user may understand that a ray-casting technique is provided for making selections, but the user may not know which button is required to confirm a selection. The clarity of how to use a control will depend on its cognitive, physical, functional, and sensory affordances, which are discussed in section 4.2.3.

While creating affordances may not be intuitive for all UX designers, there are design guidelines that will generally help in that process. One guideline is to leverage the user's familiarity with other UIs, as an interface that has already been mastered is the easiest to learn (Constantine and Lockwood 1999). This can be challenging for 3D UI designers, as many users have yet to experience, let alone master, another 3D UI. However, some aspects of traditional UIs can be leveraged within 3D UIs, such as the case of adapting 2D menus for system control (see Chapter 9, section 9.5.1, for more details).

A second design guideline is to provide **direct manipulation**, which is Shneiderman's concept of creating a visual representation of the world of action that users can directly manipulate and interact with (Shneiderman 1998). Originally, direct manipulation was used to refer to graphical UIs, such as the desktop interface, which provided visual representations for direct interactions, as opposed to command-line interfaces. However, it is easy to see that many 3D UIs, especially VR ones, inherently rely on the concept of direct manipulation. Hence, 3D UI designers should be cognizant of the degree of direct manipulation that their interfaces provide. In particular, the realism or fidelity of the system should, when possible, be kept extremely high (see Figure 4.11 for an example and Chapter 11, "Evaluation of 3D User Interfaces," section 11.6.3, for a discussion of fidelity).

A final design guideline for affordance is consistency. Uniformity in the appearance, placement, and behavior of components within the user interface will make a system easy to learn and remember (Stone et al. 2005). Similar situations should require consistent sequences of actions (Shneiderman and Plaisant 2010). Essentially, consistency builds familiarity within a system. For 3D UI designers, one concern is that many input devices have multiple buttons. As much as possible, the same button should be used for the same type of action (e.g., trigger button for selection, thumb button for navigation).

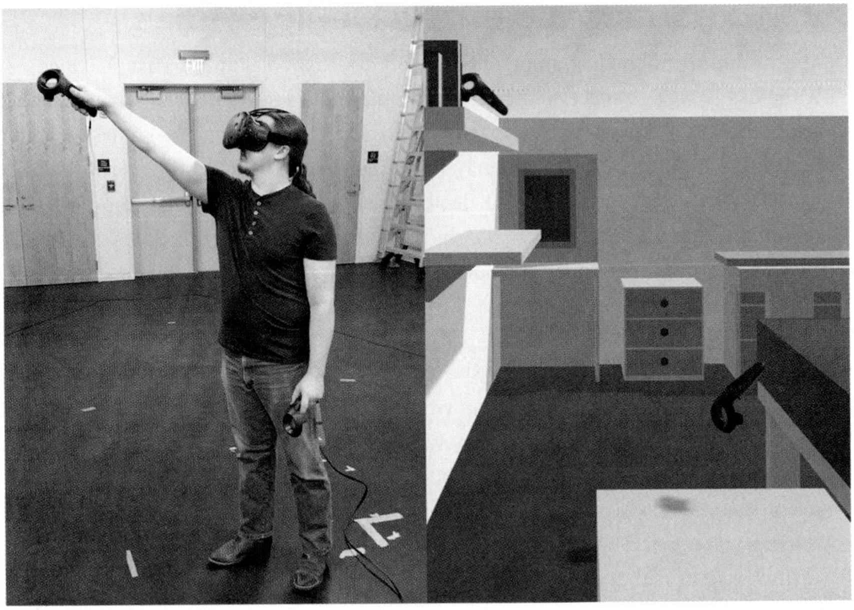

Figure 4.11 Providing realistic, high-fidelity interactions, such as the virtual hand technique, is one design guideline for affordance. (Image courtesy of Ryan P. McMahan)

Ergonomics

Ergonomics is "the science of fitting the job to the worker and the product to the user" (Pheasant and Haslegrave 2005). As a UX design principle, ergonomics is concerned with the physical execution of action plans (see Chapter 3, "Human Factors Fundamentals," section 3.5 for a discussion of the anatomical and physiological foundations of physical ergonomics). Can the user physically execute the motor actions required for the plan without injury or fatigue? If not, the UI is a failure, regardless of whether other design guidelines were closely adhered to.

There are four design guidelines for fitting the UI to the user: (i) clearance, (ii) reach, (iii) posture, and (iv) strength (Pheasant and Haslegrave 2005; Tannen 2009). As a guideline, clearance ensures there is adequate room between objects to move around without inadvertently colliding with something. For traditional UIs, a common clearance issue is the "fat finger" problem, in which users struggle to press a target button due to their fingers also touching nearby buttons. A similar issue for some 3D UIs is attempting to select a small object but struggling to do so because of colliding with other nearby small objects. However, selection technique enhancements can be used to alleviate these issues (see Chapter 7, sections 7.4.3 and 7.5.3).

The reach design guideline is focused on ensuring that the user has the ability to touch and operate controls (Pheasant and Haslegrave 2005). A common reach issue is that users struggle to operate certain smartphones with one hand due to touchscreens larger than their hands.

Reach issues also exist in 3D UIs, particularly with body-referenced controls. If a user is shorter than average and a control is placed at the average extent of a user's arm length, the shorter user will struggle to reach the control.

Another design guideline is to ensure that the user's body posture does not deviate from a natural and comfortable position (Tannen 2009). Postural problems are often the result of other clearance and reach issues (Pheasant and Haslegrave 2005). However, the form factor, or shape, of an input device can also directly cause postural problems, such as contorting the wrist posture to hold a controller (Tannen 2009). Because 3D UIs usually involve and require a broader range of body movements than traditional UIs, UX designers should carefully consider a comfortable posture as a design requirement. Both sitting and standing postures can be comfortable, although standing might lead to fatigue if usage durations are long, and sitting might be uncomfortable if users have to physically turn to look in all directions.

Strength is the focus of the final ergonomics design guideline and pertains to the amount of force required to operate a control (Pheasant and Haslegrave 2005). There are two issues relating to strength. First, there is the issue of the minimum amount of force required to use a control. This is especially important for weaker or smaller users. Second, there is the issue of the maximum amount of force that a control can handle. Some heavy-handed users may exert more force than an interface component can handle, which may result in a broken system or device. For example, many force-feedback devices have a maximum force resistance (see Chapter 5, "3D User Interface Output Hardware," section 5.4.1). If a user exerts more than this, these devices are prone to break.

Error Prevention

One of the most important design principles is the **prevention** of user errors (Shneiderman and Plaisant 2010). User errors occur for a number of reasons (see section 3.4.3 for a definition of human error). Due to poor visibility, the user may have confused a paste icon and functionality for a copy feature. Due to poor affordance, users might misuse an eraser feature and delete entire images. Alternatively, due to poor ergonomics, the user may routinely press the wrong UI component by accident. Errors are time consuming and frustrating for users. More importantly, some errors are difficult or even impossible to reverse. Hence, it is important for UX designers to prevent users from committing errors during execution, when possible.

There are design principles that help to prevent user errors. The first of these is to permit only valid actions (Shneiderman and Plaisant 2010). In systems with many features, it is unlikely that all of the options are valid given the system's current state. Hence, invalid options should be disabled and shown as disabled to the user (Hartson and Pyla 2012). For example, in most applications, the copy menu item is disabled and grayed out unless something is currently selected and can be copied. In 3D UIs, constraints are often used to enforce correct actions. For example, if a large virtual object should only be slid about the floor and not picked up, the 3D UI designer can apply a vertical constraint to the object to keep it on the floor. See Chapter 10, "Strategies in Designing and Developing 3D User Interfaces," section 10.2.2 for more information about constraints.

A second design guideline for preventing errors is to confirm irreversible actions (Shneiderman and Plaisant 2010). UX designers should create most actions to be reversible or easy to recover from (see section 4.3.4 for more discussion on error recovery). However, some actions are difficult or impossible to reverse, such as saving the current state of a file over its previous state. In these cases, UX designers should require users to confirm irreversible actions before executing those actions. This is often achieved through confirmation dialog boxes. However, in some 3D UIs, voice commands (see Chapter 9, section 9.6) can be used to confirm actions without interfering with the user's current physical interactions.

Another error prevention guideline is to offer common outcomes to users based on their current actions. For example, Google's autocomplete feature will suggest search terms based on what the user has typed thus far (Ward et al. 2012). Similarly, when making a repeating event, most calendar applications will offer options to repeat the event every day, week, month, or year, in addition to the capability to specify particular days. The SWIFTER speech widget developed by Pick et al. (2016) is an example of a 3D UI offering common outcomes to prevent errors. With SWIFTER, the user can correct misrecognized speech by selecting the correct word from a provided list of likely alternatives.

4.3.3 Outcome-Oriented Design Rules

The primary reason that the User Action Framework (see section 4.2.2) includes outcomes is that system outcomes have a huge impact on the user experience. Computers are supposed to perform work for humans, not the other way around. If the user initiates a fairly common high-level action, the computer should process that action with as little input as possible from the user. However, the computer must not take complete control of the action and prohibit user input on the outcome. In this section, we discuss the design principles of automation and control.

Automation

The design principle of **automation** is to have the computer and UI automatically execute low-level actions that commonly occur as part of a high-level task (Shneiderman and Plaisant 2010). For example, cascading style sheets (CSS) allow the user to change the font size of all headers across an entire website with a single edit, instead of finding and modifying each individual header instance. This type of automation reduces user work and decreases the likelihood that the user will make a mistake in editing each individual header.

There are three guidelines that UX designers should consider for automation. First, a UI should be designed to avoid tedious input from the user (Hartson and Pyla 2012). Many 2D UIs, particularly Internet browsers and websites, will automatically fill in common information, such as the user's name and street address. This helps avoid typing errors, which could result in less-than-desirable outcomes, such as paying for a pizza to be delivered to a neighbor. For 3D UIs, which already present many challenges with regard to symbolic input, voice recognition can be used to simplify user input and avoid tedious interactions.

Second, UX designers should design interfaces to complete common sequences of actions (Shneiderman and Plaisant 2010). For example, many applications provide a simple installation feature with a default set of options. This allows the user to initiate the installation process with a few clicks, instead of requiring a sequence of inputs to specify the options. Target-based travel techniques, which automate travel to a target location without requiring the user to specify a path (see Chapter 8, "Travel," section 8.6.1), are examples of automating a sequence of actions in 3D UIs.

Third, UX designers should provide interaction methods for completing a series of similar actions in parallel. For example, to delete a sentence in most word processors, the user does not have to delete each character individually by repeatedly pressing the backspace key. Instead, the user can use the mouse cursor to select the entire sentence and then delete it with a single press of the backspace key. Another example would be providing a technique that allows the user to select multiple objects at once (see Chapter 7, section 7.10.2, for some 3D UI examples of multiple-object selection).

Control

Another design principle that is closely related to automation is control. **Control** is the principle of ensuring that the computer and UI respond to the actions of the user (Shneiderman and Plaisant 2010). Users should feel that they are in charge. Hence, the UI should not make decisions that contradict the actions of the users. If UX designers are not careful with automation, they may alienate users by giving too much control to the system. Also, if an interface is not correctly implemented, users may experience a loss of control due to missing or incorrect functionality that fails to produce their desired outcomes (Hartson and Pyla 2012).

One design guideline for providing control to the users is to avoid too much automation (Hartson and Pyla 2012). This guideline may seem to contradict the earlier automation guidelines, but it directly addresses the balance of automation. UX designers must be careful not to create UIs with too little automation or too much automation. Additionally, UX designers should provide mechanisms for easily disengaging automation (Shneiderman and Plaisant 2010). For example, most autocorrect techniques will automatically replace misspelled words with commonly intended ones. However, these techniques often include a simple confirm feature that allows the user to override the automation and accept a non-dictionary word. Similarly, in 3D UIs, some target-based travel techniques allow users to disengage travel toward the target location in order to look around their current positions.

Another control design guideline is to provide features that facilitate both novices and experts (Shneiderman and Plaisant 2010). For instance, novices will be more dependent upon the affordances of a UI, such as a menu item for copying, while experts will benefit from more efficient features, such as a keyboard shortcut for copying. A 3D UI example of facilitating both novices and experts is marking points along a path to control travel, as shown in Figure 4.12 (see Chapter 8, section 8.6.2). Novices can use this technique to specify a single point at their desired destination, and then the technique automates travel to that point. However, experts can use the same technique to specify multiple points and control the path of travel.

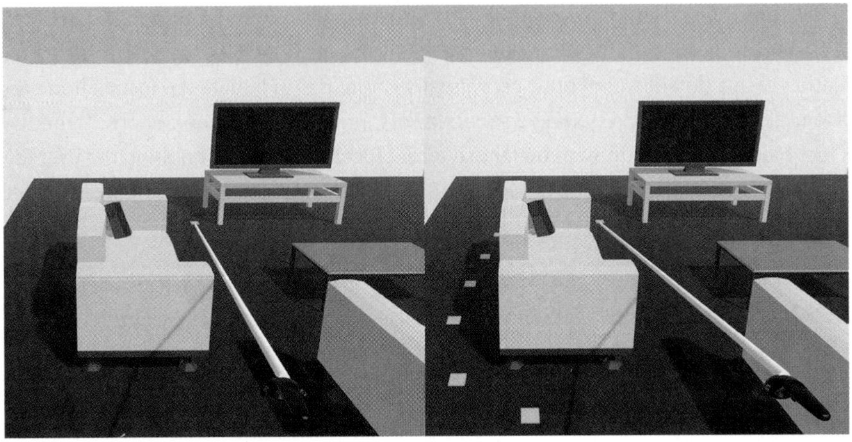

Figure 4.12 The travel technique of marking points along a path is an example of providing control to both novices and experts. Novices can use the technique to specify a single destination (left). Alternatively, experts can specify multiple points to control the path of travel (right). (Image courtesy of Ryan P. McMahan)

A control design guideline that may seem quite obvious is to avoid missing or incorrect functionality (Hartson and Pyla 2012). Such issues usually arise due to UI or backend software bugs. However, these issues can also be caused by incomplete or overly complex designs that do not account for the range and potential sequences of user input. For example, consider a 3D UI in which a virtual hand technique can be used to manipulate and move objects within a virtual environment. If the UX designer does not consider the possibility that the user may attempt to move normally stationary objects, the user may be surprised when he accidentally moves an architectural wall while using the virtual hand technique near it.

4.3.4 Evaluation-Oriented Design Rules

UX designers must also be concerned with how the user perceives, interprets, and evaluates the system's outcomes. If the desired outcome is not obvious, the user may think that he incorrectly used a UI component or that the system is not functioning properly. If an outcome is obvious but incorrect, the system should provide the user with the ability to quickly recover from the error. In this section, we discuss the design principles of feedback and recovery.

Feedback

Feedback is the design principle that "it should be obvious when a control has been used" (Stone et al. 2005). There should be system feedback for every user action (Shneiderman and Plaisant 2010). Feedback for frequent or minor actions can be modest to avoid interrupting the user's workflow. However, feedback for infrequent or major actions should be prominent, in order to get the user's attention.

One guideline for providing feedback is to respond immediately to every user action to avoid a perceived loss of control. Hardware limitations and network communications are usually the cause of delayed responses; in these cases, there is little that UX designers can do to respond immediately with the desired outcome (Hartson and Pyla 2012). However, UX designers can create interfaces to notify users that the outcome is delayed by using warning messages and progress bars. Such notifications can also be useful in 3D UIs, as in the cases of loading a new environment or handling a global effect that takes time to process.

Another design guideline is to provide *informative* feedback (Shneiderman and Plaisant 2010). This may sound intuitive, but it can be challenging to deliver the appropriate amount of information back to the user. Too little information may be unhelpful to the user and quickly disregarded, such as displaying an error code in place of a useful error message. However, too much information may be overwhelming and also quickly disregarded. For instance, consider the "blue screen of death" that would occasionally plague users on older versions of the Microsoft Windows operating system. The screen would include a "wall" of text, including a notification that there is an issue, a short description of the issue, what the user should immediately do, what the user should do if the immediate action does not work, and then a technical error message for debugging the problem.

The concept of informative feedback also extends beyond textual information. For example, consider the ray-casting technique (Chapter 7, section 7.5.1). The results of some early research studies differed on the usability of the technique due to varying feedback regarding the direction of the ray. Poupyrev, Weghorst et al. (1998) used a short line segment attached to the user's hand to represent the direction of the ray and found that users struggled to use their implementation of the technique when additional feedback was not provided. On the other hand, Bowman and Hodges (1997) used a dynamic line segment that would extend out to touch the virtual object being pointed to and found that users were able to easily perform selections with it (see Figure 4.13).

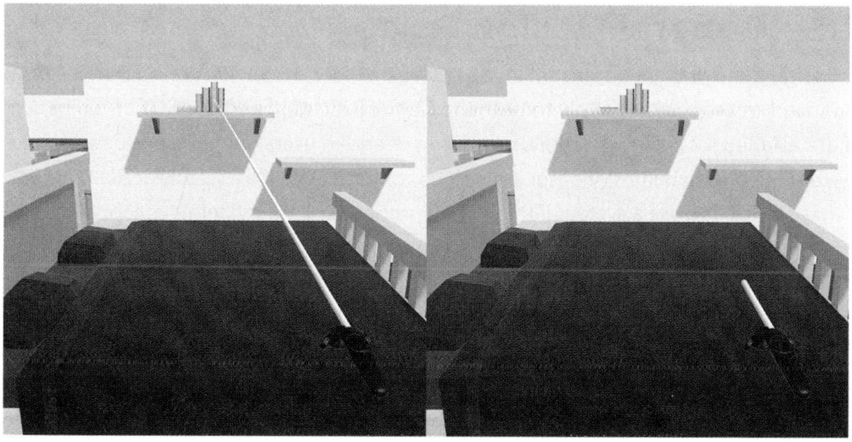

Figure 4.13 The ray-casting technique on the left provides better informative feedback than the ray-casting technique on the right. (Image courtesy of Ryan P. McMahan)

Error Recovery

The design principle of **error recovery** is that the system should help the user recognize, diagnose, and recover from errors (Nielsen 1994). In section 4.3.2, we discussed prevention, which helps prevent the user from committing errors. However, recovery is focused on helping the user after an error has already been committed. This also applies to outcomes that were originally desired by the user but then evaluated as not satisfying the user's goal.

We'll discuss two design guidelines for providing recovery. The first of these is to provide easy-to-reverse actions (Shneiderman and Plaisant 2010). When possible, actions should be able to reverse their own outcomes, and this should be easy to perform. If this is the case, the user will be able to reuse the same knowledge of the control that caused the error to reverse the error. For example, if the user mistakenly moves an image to the wrong position in a photo-editing application, the user can simply move the image back to its original position or to a new desired position. Many 3D interaction techniques with one-to-one correspondences between input and output afford easy-to-reverse actions. However, nonisomorphic mappings can result in difficult-to-reverse outcomes. See Chapter 7, section 7.3.1 for more details on isomorphism.

When actions cannot be used to reverse their own outcomes, UX designers should consider the guideline of providing additional controls that can reverse the outcomes. The undo and redo features provided in many word processors and photo-editing applications are great examples of this guideline. These additional controls allow users to easily reverse the latest outcomes, whether the unit of reversibility is a single action, a data-entry task, or a complete group of actions (Shneiderman and Plaisant 2010). A 3D UI example of providing additional controls for reversing outcomes is the ZoomBack technique (see Chapter 8, section 8.6.1). With the ZoomBack travel technique, the user can move to a new location with one control and then return to the previous position with a second control.

4.3.5 General Design Rules

Some design principles are important at every stage of user action. We consider these design rules general, as they usually apply to both the Gulf of Execution and the Gulf of Evaluation. If a UI is not designed for a diverse set of users, some intended users might be excluded from using the system due to disabilities or other limiting conditions. Even if a UI is physically accessible, users may struggle to use a system if they do not understand the system's vocabulary. Finally, systems that require a great deal of memory recall to use can be imposing and frustrating for users. Below, we discuss the design principles of accessibility, vocabulary, and recognition.

Accessibility

Accessibility is the design principle that an interface is usable by all intended users, despite disabilities or environmental conditions (Johnson 2014). This principle echoes Shneiderman and Plaisant's (2010) concept of providing "universal usability" by recognizing the needs of diverse users and facilitating the transformation of content. This includes facilitating users with disabilities, such as vision-impaired, hearing-impaired, and mobility-impaired users. The United States Access Board provides several guidelines for users with disabilities, including keyboard and mouse alternatives, color settings, font settings, contrast settings, alternative text for images, webpage frames, links, and plug-ins (http://www.access-board.gov/508.htm).

Accessibility has been and continues to be a major problem for many 3D UIs. Users that require glasses for vision correction are excluded from using many HMDs, as the visual displays provide little room for glasses between the eyes and display optics. 3D UI designers often fail to provide transformations of tones into visual signals for hearing-impaired users. Mobility-impaired users are perhaps the most excluded group, as the inherent nature of 3D UIs requires more physical movements than traditional interfaces.

However, strides have been made to improve accessibility to 3D UIs. Some HMDs, such as the Samsung Gear VR, provide a focus adjustment for nearsighted users. Bone-conduction headphones similarly help users with ear drum damage to hear sounds. Researchers have even found evidence that a crosshair always rendered in the same position on the user's display will significantly improve stability for users with balance impairments (Shahnewaz et al. 2016). See Figure 4.14 for an example. UX designers will need to continue exploring solutions for users with disabilities and other limiting conditions to ensure the accessibility of 3D UIs.

Figure 4.14 A static reference frame has been shown to significantly improve accessibility for users with balance impairments. (Image adapted from Shahnewaz et al. 2016)

Vocabulary

Another general design principle is to use the **vocabulary** of the intended users (Johnson 2014). UX designers are sometimes guilty of using their own jargon and terminology instead of those used by their users. Asking about and documenting terminology during the contextual inquiry process (see section 4.4.2) can help remedy this issue. UX designers should also inquire about vocabulary differences among all their stakeholders. For example, if a system is to be used by accountants and non-accountants, the designers should not use the term "general ledger" to refer to the collection of all accounts. Instead, they should consider using "all accounts" or similar terminology for the feature.

Vocabulary is not usually an issue when designing 3D UIs because visual representations and virtual objects are normally preferred to text. However, vocabulary is important for some 3D UIs, especially those designed to facilitate learning or training. For example, Greunke and Sadagic (2016) had to observe the vocabulary of landing signal officers in order for their voice recognition system to support the commands issued by the officers during VR-based training (see Chapter 9, section 9.6 for more details on using voice commands). In a similar situation, Eubanks et al. (2016) used the same terminology as the Association of Surgical Technologists to ensure that their intended users would understand their VR system for training on personal protective equipment protocols (see Figure 4.15).

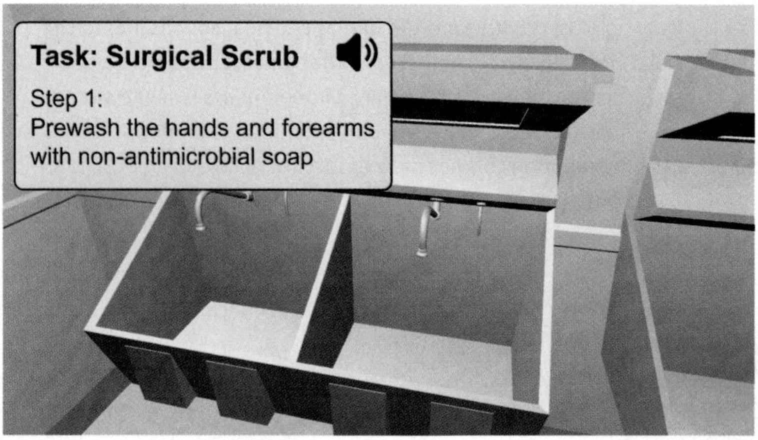

Figure 4.15 Vocabulary can be very important for some 3D UIs, particularly those focused on learning and training. (Image courtesy of Ryan P. McMahan)

Recognition

The design principle of **recognition** is that a UI should provide the knowledge required for operating the UI in the UI instead of requiring users to recall it from memory (Nielsen 1994). Recognition is essentially the activation of a memory given the perception of sensory stimuli similar to those present when the memory was encoded. On the other hand, **recall** is the activation of a memory in the absence of similar stimuli. Recalling information is much more difficult than recognizing information (Johnson 2014). This is why users should not be required to recall information from one screen to another, and instead, UIs should be designed to minimize the memory load on the user (Shneiderman and Plaisant 2010). Norman (2013) characterized this distinction as "knowledge in the world" (recognition) as opposed to "knowledge in the head" (recall).

Let's review three design guidelines for facilitating recognition over recall. First, information likely required by the user should be placed in the context of its use. For example, most databases use associative tables to represent many-to-many relationships by referencing the primary keys of other data tables (e.g., "customer with ID 4 purchased product with ID 8"). However, when displaying these relationships, the UI should fetch the relevant information of each association to avoid requiring the user to recall what every ID refers to (e.g., "John Doe purchased coffee filters"). This guideline is also applicable to 3D UIs. For example, maps and signs can be used to avoid requiring users to recall spatial knowledge during wayfinding tasks (see Chapter 8, section 8.9.2 for more details).

A second design guideline for recognition is to let users know what their options are. Graphical UIs and their menu systems have demonstrated that it is easier to see and choose functions than to recall and type commands, as command-line interfaces require (Johnson 2014). This guideline is highly relevant for voice commands (Chapter 9, section 9.6) and gestural commands (Chapter 9, section 9.7). Both of these interfaces are by default invisible to the user, unless an overview of the available functions is displayed for the user. Hence, users are by default required to recall verbal commands and specific gestures instead of recognizing their options. However, researchers have demonstrated that "feedforward" mechanisms that provide information about commands prior to their execution should be employed (Bau and Mackay 2008).

A third design guideline for promoting recognition over recall is to use pictures and visual representations when possible (Johnson 2014). This directly relates to the principle of visibility and using icons and symbols to represent controls in a recognizable manner (see section 4.3.1). However, it also applies to easily recognizing feedback. For example, most operating systems have distinct symbols for error, warning, and information messages. 3D UI designers can leverage real-world objects in a similar way. For example, Nilsson et al. (2014) used a stop sign to help users recognize that they were unintentionally moving within the physical tracking space while using a walking-in-place technique.

4.3.6 Other Design Rules

While the design principles and guidelines above cover a broad range of issues that designers should be concerned with, they are by no means complete or exhaustive. There are numerous design guidelines that researchers have proposed and validated through user studies. This chapter simply provides an organized overview of the most commonly cited design rules. For those readers interested in learning about other design rules, we have recommended some additional readings at the end of this chapter.

4.4 Engineering the User Experience

Despite being armed with the best set of design principles and guidelines, even experienced UX designers cannot guarantee an optimal user experience for every one of their designs. This is largely because many systems have their own unique purpose, and even those with similar purposes may be intended for use in contrasting real-life settings. As a result, general design principles and guidelines, and even years of UX experience, may be insufficient to foresee the nuances of a system's use and potential pitfalls of a particular UX design. Instead, delivering a system that enables an excellent user experience requires an explicit engineering process (Macleod et al. 1997). In this section, we discuss engineering the user experience and will speak of UX engineering, as opposed to UX design.

The key to UX engineering is the process itself. A process acts as a guiding structure that keeps the UX team members on track with checklists that ensure complex details are not overlooked. In UX engineering, the term **lifecycle** is used to refer to this structured process, which often consists of a series of stages and corresponding activities (Hartson and Pyla 2012). A number of lifecycles have been proposed and investigated for usability and UX engineering (e.g., Hartson and Hix 1989; Mayhew 1999; Helms et al. 2006; and Kreitzberg 2008). However, in this section, we discuss the stages and activities involved in the Wheel lifecycle originally proposed by Helms et al. (2006).

The Wheel lifecycle employs four primary stages for UX engineering: (i) Analyze, (ii) Design, (iii) Implement, and (iv) Evaluate. The **Analyze** stage is about understanding the user's current activities and needs. The **Design** stage involves designing interaction concepts. The **Implement** stage involves realizing the design concepts in the form of prototypes or fully functioning systems. Finally, the **Evaluate** stage serves to verify and refine the interaction design.

In addition to the four stages, a key aspect of the Wheel lifecycle is that it is an iterative process. After the Evaluate stage is completed, the UX engineering process can continue by iterating back through the four stages, starting with the Analyze stage. Additionally, each individual stage can be immediately repeated if its outcomes were unsatisfactory, as seen in Figure 4.16. In our experiences with employing the Wheel lifecycle for UX engineering, we have found these iterative opportunities to be extremely important.

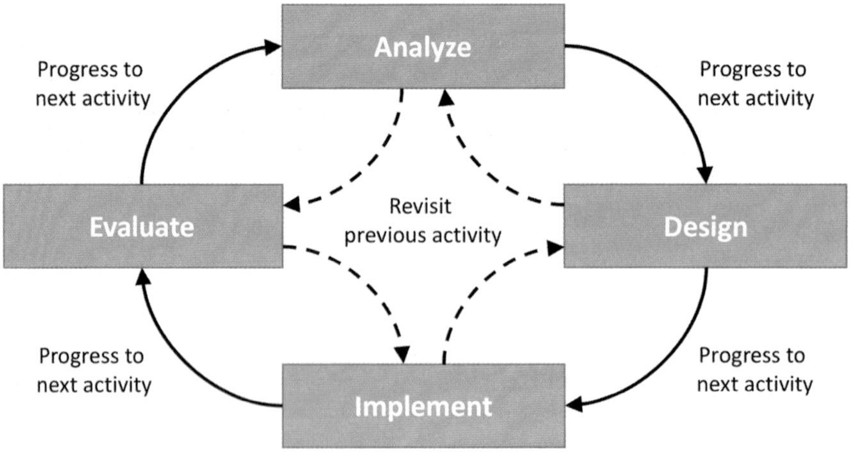

Figure 4.16 An illustration of the Wheel lifecycle process and its opportunities for iteration. (Image adapted from Hartson and Pyla 2012)

4.4.1 System Goals and Concepts

Before the UX engineering process, there must be a reason for developing a UI. Perhaps users consistently complain about a poorly designed system that wastes their time and frustrates them. Or maybe the upper management of a large company has decided to create a new product to better compete in the market. Or possibly a moment of inspiration has spurred an individual to pursue a revolutionary idea that will change the world. Regardless of its origins, there is always a reason behind starting the UX engineering process.

Improving Usability

One of the most common goals of UX engineering is to improve usability. The term **usability** refers to the qualities of a system that impact its effectiveness, efficiency, and satisfaction (Hartson and Pyla 2012). The **effectiveness** of a system depends on the completeness and accuracy with which users can achieve their intended goals. For example, if a user intends to create a 3D building model, the 3D UI would be ineffective if it could not save the model to a common 3D file format (incomplete outcome) or if it was not expressive enough to allow a user to translate the building design in his head to the system (inaccurate outcome). The **efficiency** of a system depends on the resources expended in order to accomplish a goal. If the user must spend a great amount of time and effort maneuvering around a virtual object in order to carefully manipulate a 3D widget, the 3D UI would be extremely inefficient. Finally, **satisfaction** with a system depends on whether users and other people affected by the system consider it comfortable and acceptable to use.

While the effectiveness of a system can be clearly determined based on outcomes, its efficiency and satisfaction qualities are dependent upon several other factors (Shneiderman and Plaisant 2010; McMahan et al. 2014). **Learnability** is an important aspect of a system's usability that refers to how quickly a novice user can comprehend the state of the system and determine what to do in order to complete a task. **Retainabilty** is similar to learnability but concerns how well users maintain their knowledge of the system after not using it for a period of time. **Ease of use** regards the simplicity of a system from the user's point of view and how much mental effort the user must exert every time to use the system. **Speed of performance** is how long it takes the user to carry out a task. **Rate of errors** concerns how many and what types of errors the user makes while attempting to complete a task. **User comfort** often depends on the ergonomics of a system (see Chapter 3, section 3.5) and the amount of physical exertion required of the user. These are some of the common factors that affect a system's usability, but this is certainly not a complete list.

Striving for Usefulness

Another common goal of UX engineering is to create a useful system. Hartson and Pyla (2012) describe **usefulness** as the capacity of a system to allow users to accomplish the goals of work or play. It is important to distinguish usefulness from usability. A system can be highly usable (e.g., easy to learn, easy to use), but if its function serves little purpose in a user's life, it is not useful to that user. Therefore, a useful system is one that provides needed functionality and serves a purpose. Lund (2001) has identified several qualities of useful systems, including aiding in productivity, providing control over daily activities, making it easier to get things done, and saving the user time when tackling a task.

Emotionally Impacting the User

More recently, UX design has focused not only on usability and usefulness but also on the emotional aspects of the user experience. **Emotional impact** refers to the affective aspects of a user experience that influence the emotions of the user (Hartson and Pyla 2012). As Shih and Liu (2007) point out, users are no longer satisfied with usability and usefulness; they want "emotional satisfaction" from systems. Emotional impact helps to explain why some products are extremely popular despite not differing much from other products in terms of usability and usefulness. Characteristics such as novelty, elegance, sleekness, beauty, or coolness of a product can influence the reaction of users, rather than functionality.

There are several ways that a system can emotionally impact a user. Kim and Moon (1998) have identified seven dimensions to describe emotional impacts—attractiveness, awkwardness, elegance, simplicity, sophistication, symmetry, and trustworthiness. Hartson and Pyla (2012) also include pleasure, fun, joy, aesthetics, desirability, novelty, originality, coolness, engagement, appeal, self-expression, self-identity, pride of ownership, and a feeling of contributing to the world. Norman (2004) presents a model of emotional impact including three types of emotional processing—behavioral, visceral, and reflective. **Behavioral processing** concerns pleasure and a sense of effectiveness (stemming from a system's usability and usefulness). **Visceral processing** involves the "gut feelings" and emotions that are evoked by a system's appearance, attractiveness, and aesthetics. Finally, **reflective processing** involves the user's self-image and identify while using a system.

As 3D UIs become more commonplace in consumer products, designers will need to pay careful attention to emotional impact, not just usability and usefulness. Emotional impact may be especially relevant to 3D UIs because of the powerful and visceral experiences that can be provided by technologies such as VR. We recommend reading Kruijff et al. (2016) for an overview of the challenges and methodologies for emotionally impacting users in 3D UIs.

The System Concept

Regardless of the goal behind engineering a user experience, every UX engineering process should begin with a system concept. A **system concept** is a concise summary of the goals of an envisioned system or product (Hartson and Pyla 2012). It is essentially a mission statement for the system that includes the usability, usefulness, and emotional impacts that the engineering process should strive to achieve. It represents the user experience that the system will provide.

4.4.2 Requirements Analysis

Once the system concept and goals of a project have been identified, the first step of the UX engineering process is to analyze the needs of the intended users of the system. This is referred to as **requirements analysis** (Rosson and Carroll 2001). It involves analyzing the users' work domain, work activities, and needs in order to understand the current situation before embarking on a new design. Note that by the term "work," we are referring not only to tasks performed in a job, but also to any activities that help fulfill the purpose of the envisioned system, including things like learning, play, and creative activities. By better understanding the intended users, UX designers can better identify the requirements that the new system should address to support the users' work (or play). In the sections below, we will discuss the subactivities of contextual inquiry, contextual analysis, and requirements extraction.

Contextual Inquiry

Contextual inquiry is the process of planning for and conducting interviews and observations of the work tasks being performed in the field, in order to gather detailed descriptions of the routines and procedures that occur within the work domain (Shneiderman and Plaisant 2010; Hartson and Pyla 2012). The purpose of contextual inquiry is to gain an understanding of how work activities are completed using the current system (computerized, physical, or process-based) within the target work context. There are many details and steps to conducting a proper contextual inquiry (Hartson and Pyla 2012), but the following is a high-level list of the main activities:

- Learn about the organization and work domain before the visit
- Prepare an initial set of goals and question before the visit
- Make arrangements to observe and interview key individuals
- Establish a rapport with the users during the visit
- Take notes and recordings (video and audio) during observations and interviews
- Collect work artifacts (e.g., copies of paper forms and photos of physical items)

Contextual Analysis

After completing the contextual inquiry, the next step of UX engineering is to analyze the collected data. **Contextual analysis** is the process of systematically organizing, identifying, interpreting, modeling, and communicating the data collected from a contextual inquiry (Hartson and Pyla 2012). The purpose of contextual analysis is to understand the work context that the new system is being engineered for. This involves three primary aspects of work—the *people* themselves, their current work *activities*, and the *environment* that they work in (Rosson and Carroll 2001).

One aspect of contextual analysis is to identify and model the stakeholders involved. A **stakeholder** is a person that is either involved in or impacted by the current work practices (Rosson and Carroll 2001). Most stakeholders have a **work role**, which is a collection of responsibilities that accomplish a job or work assignment (Beyer and Holtzblatt 1998). Additionally, since stakeholders do not work in a vacuum, the **social context** of the work place should be accounted for, such as how individuals and groups are organized into larger structures, and how people depend on each other to accomplish their jobs (Rosson and Carroll 2001). **User models**, such as organizational charts and stakeholder diagrams, can be used to represent stakeholders, their work roles, and their work relationships (Hartson and Pyla 2012).

Another aspect of contextual analysis is to identify, interpret, and model the current work activities. A popular approach to accomplish this is a **hierarchical task analysis** (Rosson and Carroll 2001), in which individual tasks and subtasks are identified and organized into a hierarchy to capture the details and relationships of the work activities (Diaper and Johnson 1989). Such task analyses are also known as **task models** (Hartson and Pyla 2012).

Finally, a contextual analysis should also capture and represent the work environment through **environment models**. There are two common approaches to modeling the environment—artifact models and physical models. An **artifact model** represents how stakeholders use physical or electronic elements during work activities (Hartson and Pyla 2012). Artifact models are particularly important for engineering systems that are meant to replace physical elements with electronic ones, such as the electronic receipts that many restaurants and taxis use now. A **physical model** is basically an artifact model that depicts the artifacts, stakeholders, and activities in a physical setting (Hartson and Pyla 2012). Physical models show the placement and movements of people and objects within the physical setting. Such models are important for designing systems that are meant to change the work environment. For example, some restaurants use electronic kiosks for placing orders to reduce wait lines.

Though the purpose of contextual analysis is to understand the user, task, and environment, it also requires systematic steps to capture those models and communicate them. Otherwise, incomplete or inaccurate models may be derived, which can misguide the engineering process. Like contextual inquiry, there are many details and steps to conducting a proper contextual analysis, but we only present high-level activities here.

The first step is to review the data collected from the contextual inquiry and to synthesize work activity notes. A **work activity note** is a simple and concise statement about a single concept, topic, or issue observed during the contextual inquiry (Hartson and Pyla 2012). These notes should capture the key points and issues discussed by the engineering team while reviewing and drawing conclusions from the contextual inquiry data (Shneiderman and Plaisant 2010).

The next step is to organize the work activity notes into an affinity diagram. An **affinity diagram** is a hierarchical representation of the work activity notes (Shneiderman and Plaisant 2010). It serves to sort and organize work activity notes by their similarities and common themes to highlight important concepts, patterns, and issues (Hartson and Pyla 2012). Once organized, an affinity diagram can be used to inform the creation of user, task, and environment models, like the ones discussed above.

Finally, the affinity diagram and models can be used to construct problem scenarios and claims. A **problem scenario** is a story about one or more personas carrying out an activity in the current work practice (Rosson and Carroll 2001). A **persona** is a hypothetical person with a specific work role and personality (Cooper 2004). The purpose of writing problem scenarios is to reveal aspects of general stakeholders, their work activities, and their work environment that should be considered during design. Because of this, problem scenarios are often accompanied by a list of claims. A **claim** is an aspect of a scenario that has important effects on the personas involved and is expressed as a tradeoff of its hypothesized positive and negative effects (Rosson and Carroll 2001). Claims are especially important for extracting requirements.

Requirements Extraction

Contextual analysis is not enough to proceed to the design process. Design requirements are the bridge between analysis and interaction design (Hartson and Pyla 2012). Hence, the UX team must extract requirements from the outcomes of the contextual analysis.

A **requirement** is a statement of something the system must provide in order to fulfill some need of the users. Shneiderman and Plaisant (2010) identify three types of requirements: (i) functional, (ii) performance, and (iii) interface. A **functional requirement** states what the system is required to do, such as "the system shall permit the user to save the current state of the virtual environment." On the other hand, a **performance requirement** states how the system should do what it is supposed to do (e.g., "the system shall provide three file slots for saving the current state"). Finally, an **interface requirement** states what characteristics are required of the UI. An example is "the system shall display a progress bar while saving the current state."

The various types of requirements should be extracted from the models, diagrams, scenarios, and claims created during the contextual analysis. This process involves identifying functions that the system must provide, acceptable or desired qualities of those functions, and how those functions will be represented in the interface. For each identified requirement, the UX team should create a requirement statement.

A **requirement statement** is a structured description of what shall be required of the system and includes categories for each requirement. Requirement statements can also include a rationale that justifies the requirement and other notes that clarify or document any specifics regarding the requirement. The UX team can create a requirements document by organizing all of their requirement statements by the major and minor categories.

Finally, it is important to note that requirements and the requirements document can and should be updated as UX engineering progresses. While most requirements will be identified during requirements analysis, new requirements will likely be identified during the design, prototyping, or evaluation phases. Every new requirement should be formalized and added to the requirements document.

4.4.3 The Design Process

After requirements have been extracted and documented, the design process can begin. It involves using design tools, perspectives, and approaches to explore and identify good design ideas. These ideas are captured and communicated to the rest of the UX team and the stakeholders via design representations. Finally, design production tools are used to refine the design and its complete specification.

Design Tools

Three important tools for exploring design options are ideation, sketching, and critiquing. **Ideation** is the process of quickly brainstorming ideas for designs in a creative and exploratory manner, and **sketching** is "the rapid creation of free-hand drawings expressing preliminary design ideas" (Hartson and Pyla 2012). Both ideation and sketching should be used in a collaborative group process to generate potential designs. **Critiquing** is then used to review and judge those designs, in order to filter and avoid wasting time on poor ideas. However, it is important that ideation and critiquing occur at separate times to avoid stifling creativity and suppressing potentially great ideas during ideation (Hartson and Pyla 2012).

Design Perspectives

There are also three design perspectives or mindsets that are commonly used to guide ideation, sketching, and critiquing (Hartson and Pyla 2012). The first is the **interaction perspective**, which is concerned with how users interact with the system. Usability is the primary focus of the interaction design perspective. As such, the user action models (see section 4.2.2) provide a foundation for the perspective. The second is the **ecological perspective**, which is concerned with how the system is used within its surrounding environment. It primarily focuses on the usefulness of the system and is informed by activity theory (see section 4.2.4). Finally, the third is the **emotional perspective**, which is concerned with the emotional impact of the system and what users value about it. The emotional design perspective focuses on the three types of emotional processing (see section 4.4.1).

Design Approaches

There are a number of approaches that UX designers can take when designing a new system or UI. **Activity design** is the approach of focusing on the system's functionality and the activities that it will support (Rosson and Carroll 2001). An ecological perspective is often kept during activity design, as the UX designers generate ideas to address the functional and performance requirements identified in the requirements document. Outcome-oriented design rules (section 4.3.3) should be taken into consideration during activity design.

While activity design generally addresses the big picture, information design and interaction design are both concerned with the interface requirements. **Information design** is the design approach of focusing on the representation and arrangement of the UI (Rosson and Carroll 2001). It is directly concerned with the Gulf of Evaluation and how users evaluate whether their goals have been accomplished. As such, goal-oriented and evaluation-oriented design rules (sections 4.3.1 and 4.3.4) are carefully adhered to during information design. On the other hand, **interaction design** is the approach of focusing on the mechanisms for accessing and controlling the UI (Rosson and Carroll 2001). It is concerned with the Gulf of Execution and how users plan and execute their action plans. As such, UX designers should consider execution-oriented design rules (section 4.3.2) during interaction design. Both information design and interaction design are normally conducted with an interaction perspective in mind.

Another design approach is **participatory design**, which is "the direct involvement of people in the collaborative design of the things and technologies they use" (Shneiderman and Plaisant 2010). The fundamental concept of participatory design is that users should be involved in the designs that they will be using and should have equal inputs into the design process (Hartson and Pyla 2012). However, extensive user involvement can be costly and can lengthen the design process (Shneiderman and Plaisant 2010). Additionally, users are unlikely to be familiar with design perspectives and guidelines, which may force UX designers to compromise on subpar ideas generated by the users (Ives and Olson 1984). Nevertheless, UX teams interested in participatory design should consider various approaches, such as the PICTIVE approach developed by Muller (1991). In PICTIVE, users sketch and create low-fidelity prototypes that are then recorded during scenario walkthroughs for presentation to other stakeholders. The UX designers then use these videos and their associated feedback to inform the design process.

Design Representations

Throughout the design process, it is important for UX designers to document their conceptual models of the new system. Perhaps more importantly, they need to be able to represent and communicate their conceptual models to each other, the users, and the stakeholders. Design representations can fulfill these needs.

There are various ways to represent and communicate a design. One of the simplest ways is through a **metaphor**—a known concept used to communicate and explain a new concept by analogy (Rosson and Carroll 2001). Perhaps the most well-known UI metaphor is the computer desktop. As personal computers were becoming popular tools for businesses, UX designers used the desktop metaphor to help users understand how to interact with the computers. The computer desktop provided a space to place and organize virtual files and folders. Users could throw away the files and folders by moving them to the virtual trashcan. Additionally, some systems provided email functionality through a virtual inbox positioned on the desktop. As seen with the desktop example, a single metaphor can lead to other related metaphors as the design process unfolds. Together, they can greatly help users understand how to use a system.

Other design representations include the design scenario and the storyboard. A **design scenario** is a story about one or more personas carrying out an activity with the new system (Rosson and Carroll 2001). The purpose of a design scenario is to represent and communicate how users will interact with a system. Design scenarios can be written from an interaction, ecological, or emotional perspective. Some scenarios may include all three perspectives for a holistic view of the new system. Closely related to the design scenario is the storyboard. A **storyboard** is a sequence of drawings illustrating how the envisioned system will be used (Hartson and Pyla 2012). While a design scenario is a written representation of a system's design, a storyboard visually depicts a scenario of users interacting with the system.

A **physical mockup**—a 3D tangible prototype or model of a device or product—is another type of design representation (Hartson and Pyla 2012). Physical mockups are essentially physical and embodied sketches that can be touched and held. They allow UX designers to act out design scenarios. Additionally, they help in identifying potential issues with the ergonomics of a device or system. Physical mockups have traditionally been created with paper, cardboard, and tape, but with the advent of 3D printers, plastic mockups can also be easily created. Physical mockups are especially relevant to the design of special-purpose input devices for 3D UIs.

4.4.4 Prototyping the Design

The implementation stage of the Wheel lifecycle is about bringing the design to life. It is the realization of the interaction design. During the UX engineering process, implementation often takes the form of a **prototype**, an early representation of the design built to model, evaluate, and iterate on the design of a product (Hartson and Pyla 2012). Below, we discuss various characteristics and aspects of prototypes, including their benefits and drawbacks, breadth and depth, fidelity, and level of interactivity.

Benefits and Drawbacks

There are several benefits to using prototypes. They provide a concrete representation of a design that can be communicated to others. They allow for "test drives" and evaluations of designs. For the stakeholders, prototypes provide project visibility and help in transitioning from an old system to the new one. However, there are also some drawbacks to prototypes. Some stakeholders may associate the limited functionality of many prototypes with a poor design, though the design has yet to be fully implemented. On the other hand, some stakeholders may assume "magic" (simulated) functionality is real and expect the final product to deliver more than what is feasible. For the UX team, it is important that the purpose and functionality of each prototype is clearly communicated to the stakeholders before it is presented.

Breadth and Depth

The purpose of each prototype should be identified before it is created, as a prototype can serve many different purposes. The **breadth** of a prototype concerns how many features are implemented, while its **depth** represents how much functionality the features provide (Hartson and Pyla 2012). Different combinations of breath and depth yield different types of prototypes. For example, a **horizontal prototype** is a prototype very broad in features but with less depth in functionality. As such, horizontal prototypes are great for evaluating how users will navigate a design. On the other hand, a **vertical prototype** is one that contains as much depth of functionality as possible for one feature. Vertical prototypes are beneficial for exploring the design of a particular feature in detail.

Another type of prototype is the **T prototype**, which realizes much of the design at a shallow level (the horizontal top of the T) but covers one or a few features in depth (the vertical part of the T) (Hartson and Pyla 2012). T prototypes essentially combine the advantages of both horizontal and vertical prototypes by allowing users to navigate the system and explore some features in detail. Finally, a **local prototype** is a prototype limited in breadth and depth that is focused on a particular isolated feature of the design (Hartson and Pyla 2012). Local prototypes are normally used to evaluate design alternatives for specific portions of the UI.

Prototype Fidelity

The **fidelity** of a prototype refers to how completely and closely a prototype represents the intended design (Hartson and Pyla 2012). A **low-fidelity prototype** provides impressions of the intended design with little to no functionality. A paper prototype made with paper, pencil, and tape is an example of a low-fidelity prototype that can be rapidly implemented to explore design decisions. A **medium-fidelity prototype** provides the look and feel of the intended design with rudimentary functionality. There are numerous software applications that can facilitate the development of medium-fidelity prototypes for desktop, web, and mobile systems, including OmniGraffle, Balsamiq Mockups, PowerPoint, and basic HTML. However, tools for 3D UI prototyping are much less mature. Finally, a **high-fidelity prototype** is a prototype that closely resembles the final product. The aesthetics of a high-fidelity prototype should be nearly identical to the final product's look and feel. Additionally, a high-fidelity prototype should have most, if not all, features fleshed out with full functionality. Due to their functional demands, high-fidelity prototypes are often programmed in the same language as the final product. In general, the fidelity of a prototype will increase with each of its iterations.

Prototype Interactivity

The **interactivity** of a prototype is the degree to which interactions are realized (Hartson and Pyla 2012). There are four common levels of interactivity that prototypes are developed for. At the lowest level, **animated prototypes** visualize predetermined interactions, and therefore offer no interactivity to the user. A video depicting how a user would interact with an interface design is an example of an animated prototype. This form of prototyping is useful to communicate the vision of a 3D UI without investing in full-scale development and is often used in early marketing, such as crowdfunding campaigns. **Scripted prototypes** offer more interactivity than animated prototypes, but they require that the user follows a scripted sequence of interactions. Vertical and T prototypes are most often used for scripted prototypes, as the scripted interactions are used to explore the depth of a particular feature. **Fully programmed prototypes** that implement all interactive features and backend functionality offer the highest level of interactivity. However, these prototypes are costly to develop.

An alternative to pursuing a fully programmed prototype is to create a **Wizard of Oz prototype**. Wizard of Oz prototypes can provide deceptively high levels of interactivity with little functionality actually implemented. These prototypes rely on a hidden UX team member that observes the user's actions and then causes the interface to respond appropriately (like the wizard behind the curtain in the famous film). For 3D UIs, this prototyping method can be quite useful because the actual implementation of many 3D interaction techniques and UI metaphors can be very complex. For example, a 3D UI designer may not want to go to the trouble of implementing a speech or gesture recognition interface, if it is just one of the options being considered. Instead, a Wizard of Oz prototype can allow an evaluator to mimic the actions that the system would take when a user issues a gesture or voice command (Hayes et al. 2013).

4.4.5 Evaluating Prototypes

Once a prototype has been created, it is time to evaluate it to understand how well the underlying design meets its goals with respect to usability, usefulness, and emotional impact. There are a number of methods that can be used to evaluate prototypes. In Chapter 11, "Evaluation of 3D User Interfaces," we discuss several methods for evaluating 3D UIs. However, here we discuss some qualities of evaluation methods that the reader should be familiar with before reading Chapter 11.

Formative versus Summative Evaluations

As discussed above, the Wheel UX lifecycle is an iterative process. During this process, **formative evaluations** will inform the process and the design of the system. These evaluations help identify bad design choices and usability issues before the design is finalized. In other words, formative evaluations help to "form" the design. On the other hand, **summative evaluations** usually occur during the final iteration of the UX engineering process and focus on collecting data to assess the quality of the design. Summative evaluations help to "sum up" the design. Both types of evaluations are important to the UX engineering process.

Rapid versus Rigorous Evaluations

A major consideration in choosing an evaluation method is whether it is rapid or rigorous (Hartson and Pyla 2012). **Rapid evaluations** are fast evaluation methods that are usually inexpensive to conduct. Examples of rapid evaluation methods include cognitive walkthroughs and heuristic evaluations (see Chapter 11, section 11.2, for details on these two methods). On the other hand, **rigorous evaluations** are more formal systematic methods that attempt to maximize the information gained from an assessment while minimizing the risk of errors or inaccuracies involved. However, rigorous evaluations tend to be relatively expensive in terms of both time and resources. Hence, UX evaluators must decide between conducting rapid evaluations, which are less expensive to conduct, or conducting rigorous evaluations, which are more informative. Usually, rapid evaluations are used during the early iterations of the UX lifecycle, and rigorous evaluations may be conducted during the later iterations. As a result, many rapid evaluation methods tend to be formative, while most rigorous evaluation methods tend to serve summative purposes. However, these relationships are not exclusive, and it is possible to have a rigorous formative evaluation method or a rapid summative evaluation method.

Analytic versus Empirical Evaluations

Another consideration to account for when choosing an evaluation method is whether it is analytic or empirical. **Analytic evaluations** are focused on analyzing the inherent attributes of a design, as opposed to observing the system in use (Hartson and Pyla 2012). Analytic evaluations are usually conducted by UX experts and guided by heuristics or guidelines (see Chapter 11, section 11.2, for more details). On the other hand, **empirical evaluations** are based on data collected while observing participants using the system. Due to their nature, analytic evaluations also tend to be rapid evaluation methods while empirical evaluations tend to be more rigorous. However, there are rapid empirical evaluation methods, such as the Rapid and Iterative Testing and Evaluation (RITE) method presented by Medlock et al. (2005).

4.5 Conclusion

In this chapter, we have reviewed the foundations and theories of HCI, from which many design rules have been derived. We have also discussed those design principles and guidelines in detail, including 3D UI examples of their application. Finally, we covered the UX engineering process. With this background, we now turn to the main topics of the book: the design and evaluation of user experience in 3D UIs.

Recommended Reading

We have relied heavily on several well-known HCI books in compiling this overview of the field, and we recommend these books to the reader who wants to learn more. In particular, we recommend three books as excellent resources:

Hartson, R., and P. Pyla. (2012). *The UX Book: Process and Guidelines for Ensuring a Quality User Experience*. Waltham, MA: Morgan Kaufmann Publishers.

Shneiderman, Ben and Catherine Plaisant (2005). *Designing the User Interface, 4th edition.* Addison-Wesley.

Rosson, M., and J. Carroll (2001). *Usability Engineering: Scenario-Based Development of Human Computer Interaction.* Morgan Kaufmann Publishers.

PART III

HARDWARE TECHNOLOGIES FOR 3D USER INTERFACES

One way to describe human–computer interfaces is as a means of communication between a user (or users) and a system. The user must communicate commands, requests, questions, intent, and goals to the system. The system in turn must provide feedback, requests for input, information about the system state, and so on. We can think of this communication process as a series of translations. The user and the system do not speak the same language, so the interface must serve as a translator or intermediary between them. In fact, there are multiple translation steps involved (Figure III.1): the user first translates her goals into actions; next, the input device translates those actions into an electronic form for the system; finally, the system deciphers those signals based on the current system state. Typically, the system responds in some way to the input of the user, and so there must be some transformation of the input to produce the output—this is called a **transfer function**. To communicate this output to the user, the system translates the information into a digital display representation that is again translated by output devices into a form the user can perceive (e.g., light or sound), and finally, the user translates those perceptions into a meaningful semantic representation. The translations that occur between input devices and output devices are also known as **control-display mappings**.

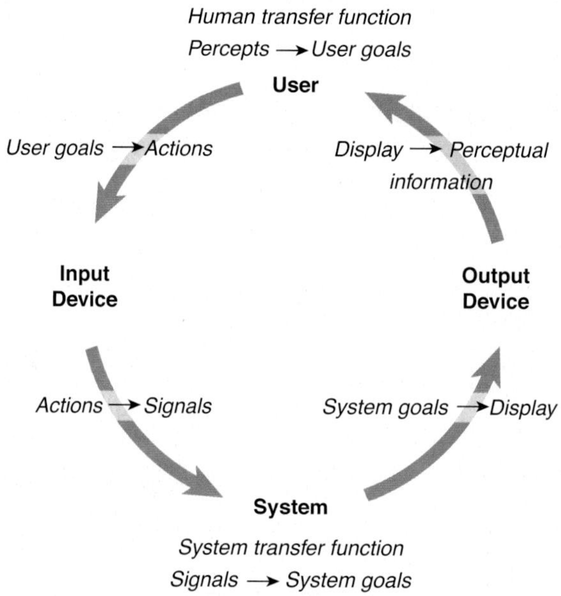

Figure III.1 Human–computer communication through devices and translations.

In the end, though, all of this communication must use physical devices—hardware that serves as the medium of communication between the parties. This part of the book provides an overview of the hardware devices used to realize 3D UIs. Chapter 5, "3D User Interface Output Hardware," covers **output devices**, which present or display information to the user's perceptual system. Although visual displays are the most prominent type of output device for 3D UIs, we also cover auditory and haptic displays. Other displays including olfactory (i.e., smell) and gustatory (i.e., taste) have also been developed. In Chapter 6, "3D User Interface Input Hardware," we discuss **input devices**—the means by which the user gives information to the system. The goal of these chapters is to give you an idea of the types of technologies commonly used in 3D UIs and to help you choose devices for your applications, not to provide an exhaustive survey of current devices or to discuss the design of 3D input/output devices.

CHAPTER 5

3D USER INTERFACE OUTPUT HARDWARE

This chapter begins our discussion of the hardware commonly used in 3D UIs. We examine visual, auditory, and haptic display devices and see how they affect 3D UI design and development. Additionally, we describe the characteristics of different output devices and develop some general strategies for choosing appropriate hardware.

5.1 Introduction

A necessary component of any 3D UI is the hardware that presents information to the user. These hardware devices, called **display devices** (or **output devices**), present information to one or more of the user's senses through the human perceptual system; the majority of them are focused on stimulating the visual, auditory, or haptic (i.e., force and touch) senses. In some cases, they even display information to the user's olfactory system (i.e., sense of smell; Nakamoto 2013), gustatory system (i.e., taste; Narumi et al. 2011), or vestibular system (i.e., sense of self-motion; Cress et al. 1997). Of course, these output devices require a computer to generate the information through techniques such as rendering, modeling, and sampling. The devices then translate this information into perceptible human form. Therefore, we can think of displays as actually consisting of the physical devices *and* the computer systems used in generating the content the physical devices present. Although the focus of this chapter is on display devices, we do provide references to relevant material on topics such as graphical and haptic rendering, as well as material on 3D sound generation.

Display devices need to be considered when designing, developing, and using various interaction techniques in 3D UIs, because some interaction techniques are more appropriate than others for certain displays. Therefore, an understanding of display device characteristics will help the 3D UI developer make informed decisions about which interaction techniques are best suited for particular display configurations and applications.

In this chapter, we explore different display device types (specifically visual, auditory, and haptic devices) and styles that are commonly found in 3D UIs. This is the first of two chapters that deal specifically with hardware technology (see Chapter 6, "3D User Interface Input Hardware"). Recall that in Chapter 3, "Human Factors Fundamentals," we discussed fundamental concepts of the human visual, auditory, and haptic systems, and this information is useful for illustrating the differences among various display types in this chapter. See Hale and Stanney (2014), Sherman and Craig (2003), and Durlach and Mavor (1995) for more details on the human sensory system and its relationship to display technology.

5.1.1 Chapter Roadmap

In section 5.2, we begin by looking at visual display devices. We first examine visual display device characteristics, then present the many different types of visual display devices commonly found in 3D UIs and discuss how they affect 3D UI design. In section 5.3, we examine auditory displays by first describing how 3D sound is typically generated. Next we present the pros and cons of different sound system configurations and discuss the benefits of sound in 3D UIs. In section 5.4, we discuss haptic display devices, beginning with a discussion of different haptic display device characteristics, the different types of haptic display devices, and their use in 3D UIs. In section 5.5, we use the concept of level of fidelity to characterize different displays. Finally, in section 5.6, we present some general guidelines and strategies for choosing display devices for particular systems or applications, followed by section 5.7 which presents the specific display configurations that we will use in each of our running case studies.

5.2 Visual Displays

Visual displays present information to the user through the human visual system. Visual displays are by far the most common display devices used in 3D UIs. As stated in the introduction to this chapter, display devices require the computer system to generate digital content that the display device transforms into perceptible form. For visual display devices in 3D UIs, real-time computer graphics rendering techniques are used to produce the images that the display device presents to the user. Many different real-time rendering techniques have been developed over the years. The details of these techniques are beyond the scope of this book; however, Akenine-Möller et al. (2008), Angel and Shreiner (2011), and Hughes et al. (2013) all provide comprehensive treatments for interested readers.

5.2.1 Visual Display Characteristics

A number of important characteristics must be considered when describing visual display devices. From a 3D UI perspective, we discuss a visual display's

- field of regard and field of view
- spatial resolution
- screen geometry
- light transfer mechanism
- refresh rate
- ergonomics
- effect on depth cues

Other characteristics include brightness, color contrast, and gamma correction.

Field of Regard and Field of View

A visual display device's field of regard (FOR) refers to the amount of the physical space surrounding the user in which visual images are displayed. FOR is measured in degrees of visual angle. For example, if we built a cylindrical display in which a user could stand, the display would have a 360-degree horizontal FOR.

A related term, field of view (FOV), refers to the maximum number of degrees of visual angle that can be seen instantaneously on a display. For example, with a large flat-projection screen, the horizontal FOV might be 80 or 120 degrees depending on the user's position in relation to the screen, because the FOV varies with the user's position and orientation relative to the screen. A display device's FOV must be less than or equal to the maximum FOV of the human visual system (approximately 180 degrees) and will be lower than that if additional optics such as stereo glasses are used.

A visual display device can have a small FOV but still have a large FOR, as in the case of a tracked head-worn display (see section 5.2.2). For a head-worn display, the FOV might be 50 degrees, but because the device is attached to the user's head, with the display always in front of the user's eyes, the FOR is 360 degrees. This is because the synthetic imagery is always perceived by the user regardless of her position or orientation (i.e., the user could make a 360-degree turn and always see the visual images). Thus, the FOV α is always less than or equal to the FOR β. In general, the user at each instant can view α degrees out of the full β degrees available to her.

Spatial Resolution

The spatial resolution of a visual display is related to pixel size and is considered a measure of visual quality. This measure is often given in dots per inch (dpi). The more pixels displayed on the screen, the higher the resolution, but resolution is *not* equivalent to the number of pixels (a common misuse of the term). Instead, resolution depends on both the number of pixels and the size of the screen. Two visual display devices with the same number of pixels but different screen sizes will not have the same resolution, because on the large screen, each individual pixel takes up a larger portion of the screen than on the small screen, and so the large screen has fewer dots per inch.

The user's distance to the visual display device also affects the spatial resolution on a perceptual level. Pixel size can be measured in absolute units such as dots per square inch based on the size of the screen. However, pixel size can also be measured in degrees of solid angle subtended relative to the viewer. Thus, the further the user is from the display, the higher the *perceived* resolution, because individual pixels are not distinguishable. This is similar to the effect of viewing paintings from the pointillist movement (Kieseyer 2001). As the viewer gets close to the painting, she can see the individual dots on the canvas, but as she moves away from it, the dots disappear and the individual dots fuse together to form a cohesive image. This phenomenon can be a problem with lower-quality head-worn displays, because the user's eyes must be very close to the display screens (although optics are typically used to place the virtual image a bit farther away), causing degradation in the perceived spatial resolution.

Screen Geometry

Another visual display characteristic that plays a role in visual quality is screen shape. Visual displays come in a variety of different shapes (see section 5.2.2), including rectangular, circular, L-shaped, hemispherical, and hybrids. In fact, using projectors coupled with projective texturing (also called projection mapping) can create a visual display on almost any planar or nonplanar surface. However, these irregular screen shapes coupled with the projection surface require nonstandard projection algorithms, which can affect visual quality. For example, hemispherical displays can suffer from visual artifacts such as distortion at the edges of the display surface, resulting in lower overall visual quality. In another example, using a part of the body as a projected visual display can produce distortion and color balancing issues based on the body part geometry and its color. With irregular screen shapes, the source images are often predistorted to accommodate the screen's particular geometric shape.

Light Transfer

There are a number of different ways to transfer light, including through a monitor or television, front projection, rear projection, laser light directly onto the retina, and through the use of special optics. A variety of different technologies such as liquid crystals, light-emitting diodes, digital light processing, and organic light-emitting diodes (Hainich and Bimber 2011) can also be used. The light transfer method sometimes dictates what types of 3D UI techniques are applicable. For example, when using a front-projected display device, 3D direct manipulation techniques often do not work well, because the user's hands can get in the way of the projector, causing shadows to appear on the display surface. Using a short-throw projector mounted close to the projection surface can alleviate this problem (Blasko et al. 2005).

Refresh Rate

Refresh rate refers to the speed with which a visual display device refreshes the displayed image from the frame buffer. It is usually reported in hertz (Hz, refreshes per second). Note that refresh rate is not to be confused with frame rate or frames per second (fps), the speed with which images are generated by the graphics system and placed in the frame buffer (Hughes et al. 2013). Although a graphics system could generate images at a rate higher than the refresh rate, the visual display can show them only at its refresh rate limit. The refresh rate of a visual display is an important characteristic because it can have a significant effect on visual quality. Low refresh rates (e.g., below 50–60 Hz) can cause flickering images depending on the sensitivity of a particular user's visual system. Higher refresh rates are important because they help to reduce latency, the start to finish time of taking a user's pose in a virtual or augmented environment and rendering the graphics from said user's unique perspective on a visual display device (so-called "motion to photon" latency). Latency can cause a variety of side effects, from poor interaction performance to cybersickness (LaViola 2000a). Other factors besides refresh rate contribute to latency, including tracking and rendering speeds. All else being equal, however, higher refresh rates lead to lower latency, which results in a better interactive experience.

Ergonomics

Visual display ergonomics is also an important display characteristic. We want the user to be as comfortable as possible when interacting with 3D applications, and we want the visual display device to be as unobtrusive as possible. Comfort is especially important when a user has to wear the display. For example, the weight of a head-worn display can cause a user discomfort, such as muscle strain, when wearing the device for long periods of time. See Chapter 3, "Human Factors Fundamentals," section 3.5 for background on physical ergonomics.

Depth Cue Effects

Finally, an important characteristic of a visual display is its ability to support various depth cues (see Chapter 3, "Human Factors Fundamentals"), especially with stereopsis. A visual depth cue's strength varies depending on visual circumstances. Stereopsis is a very strong visual depth cue with objects in close proximity to the viewer (no more than 30 feet away), because there is very little binocular disparity with objects that are farther away. Because the oculomotor cues are linked to binocular disparity, they are also effective only for objects that are at short distances from the viewer. In contrast, motion parallax can be a very strong visual cue, perhaps stronger than stereopsis, when objects are viewed at a wide range of depths. Of the monocular static cues, occlusion is the strongest.

The monocular depth cues, aside from true accommodation, can be synthetically generated with almost any visual display device, assuming appropriate rendering hardware or software. In addition, motion parallax cues can be generated when the viewer and/or objects move through the world, using either physical or virtual movement. Stereopsis usually requires special-purpose visual display devices, and the display system must produce a left- and a right-eye image with correct geometric properties (i.e., varying binocular disparity depending on object depth).

As for oculomotor cues, visual display devices that allow for stereo viewing also provide a proper vergence cue. However, accommodation cues are generally not present in stereoscopic displays, because graphically rendered objects are always in focus at the same focal depth—the depth of the screen (Cruz-Neira et al. 1993). In fact, the lack of accommodation cues with the majority of stereo visual display devices causes the accommodation-vergence mismatch illustrated in Figure 5.1. Because the graphics are displayed on a fixed screen, the user must focus at that depth to see the graphics sharply. However, the left- and right-eye images are drawn so that the user's eyes will converge to see the object at its virtual depth. When the virtual object depth and the screen depth are different, the user's oculomotor system sends conflicting signals to the brain about the distance to the object.

In general, only "true 3D" displays like volumetric, holographic, and 3D retinal projection devices (see the next section) do not have this cue conflict. Additionally, light-field displays, which depict sharp images from out-of-focus display elements by synthesizing light fields that correspond to virtual scenes located within the viewer's natural accommodation range, can alleviate the accommodation-vergence mismatch (Lanman and Leubke 2013). However, these devices are still in their early stages of development.

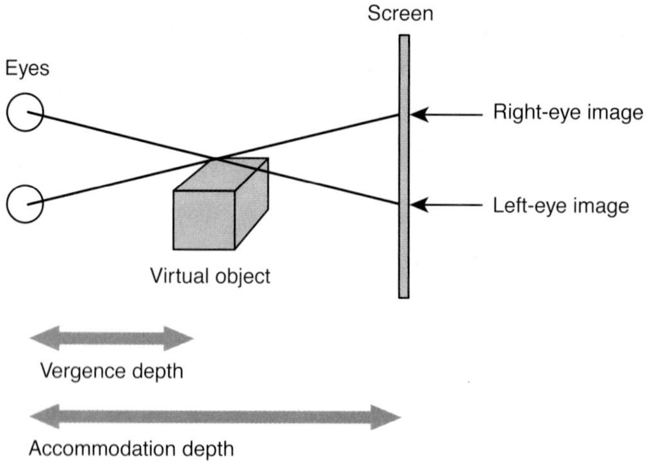

Figure 5.1 Accommodation-vergence mismatch.

5.2.2 Visual Display Device Types

We now examine many different types of visual displays used in 3D UIs, which include the following:

- single-screen displays
- surround-screen and multiscreen displays
- workbenches and tabletop displays
- head-worn displays
- arbitrary surface displays
- autostereoscopic displays

We look at specific examples and identify the advantages and disadvantages of each visual display type with respect to 3D interaction.

Single-Screen Displays

Single-screen displays are commonly used in many different kinds of 3D applications, including video games, modeling, and scientific and information visualization. These displays include conventional monitors, high-definition and higher resolution televisions, and front- or rear-projection displays using a wall or screen material as the projection surface. Smartphone and tablet displays for use in mobile AR (Veas and Kruijff 2010) and VR applications also fall into this category. These displays are relatively inexpensive compared with other, more complex displays and can provide monocular and motion parallax depth cues. Stereopsis can also be achieved using a single-screen display and some additional hardware (stereo glasses and a stereo-capable graphics card, or special optics for using cell phones as head-worn displays). Note that some single-screen displays do not need any special hardware for stereopsis. These monitors are autostereoscopic in nature (discussed later in this section).

Besides an appropriate single-screen display, a pair of stereo glasses is also needed to achieve stereoscopic viewing. These glasses can be either active or passive. Active stereo glasses, often called shutter glasses, are synchronized to open and close their shutters at a rate equal to the refresh rate of the visual display, a technique known as **temporal multiplexing**. An example of active stereo glasses is shown in Figure 5.2. The images for the left and right eye are rapidly alternated on the screen, and the shutter glasses block one eye's view in a coordinated sequence to prevent it from seeing the other eye's view. Infrared or radio signals are sent to the glasses to maintain this synchronization. If the signal is blocked, the shutter glasses stop working and the stereo effect is disrupted. As a general guideline, 3D UIs should discourage the user from moving his hands or other physical objects into the line of sight between the glasses and emitters so as not to disrupt a user's 3D stereoscopic experience. In order to achieve high active stereo quality, a single-screen display must have a high refresh rate, because the display of the two images (one for each eye) effectively halves the refresh rate. As a rule of thumb, a single-screen display with a refresh rate of 120 Hz or better is usually acceptable for obtaining well-perceived stereo images.

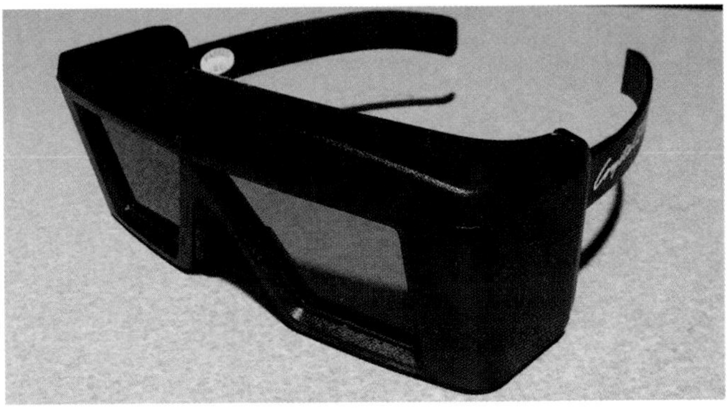

Figure 5.2 Active stereo glasses for viewing stereoscopic images. (Photograph courtesy of Joseph J. LaViola Jr.)

Passive stereo glasses use either polarization or spectral multiplexing. **Polarization multiplexing** filters the two separate, overlaid images with oppositely polarized filters. For example, one filter could be horizontally polarized and the other vertically polarized so that each eye sees only one image. **Spectral multiplexing** (also called anaglyphic stereo) displays the two separate, overlaid images in different colors. The glasses use colored filters so light from any color other than the filter's color is effectively blocked out. For example, cyan and red anaglyph stereo glasses would allow only cyan light to pass through the cyan filter and red light to pass through the red filter, so that each eye sees only its own image. Anaglyph stereo is relatively inexpensive to produce, but it obviously has color limitations. Another type of spectral multiplexing is known as interference filtering, where specific wavelengths of red, green, and blue are used for the left eye, and a slightly different set of red, green, and blue wavelengths are used for right eye. This approach supports full color 3D stereo but is a more expensive solution compared to standard polarization.

In general, active stereo is considered to achieve the highest stereo quality. Active stereo glasses have the advantage that they can make use of the full color spectrum, in contrast to spectral multiplexed stereo glasses that use colored filters. However, passive stereo glasses are inexpensive compared to shutter glasses; they do not need double the refresh rate; and they present a slightly brighter image than active glasses, since they do not need to shutter out the light half of the time. Additionally, there are no synchronization issues between the glasses and the generated images (i.e., no synchronization emitter is needed). A more comprehensive discussion of 3D stereo display methods can be found in Lueder (2012).

A single-screen display coupled with a pair of stereo glasses (see Figure 5.3) makes for a simple yet effective visual display for 3D spatial applications. When a user's head is also tracked (see Chapter 6 for information on user tracking), moving-viewer motion parallax becomes even easier to achieve. Such a setup is commonly referred to as fish-tank virtual reality (Ware et al. 1993). These configurations are relatively inexpensive compared to surround-screen devices (see descriptions later in this section), and they provide excellent spatial resolution at relatively large sizes. For example, a 60-inch 3D HDTV running at 1080p resolution can offer a compelling 3D stereo experience. They also allow the use of virtually any input device and can take full advantage of the keyboard and mouse. This flexibility provides the 3D UI developer with more input-device-to-interaction-technique mappings than do other visual display systems, because the user can see the physical world and is usually sitting at a desk.

On the other hand, single-screen displays are not very immersive, and the user has a very limited range of movement due to their small FOR. This limitation prohibits the use of many physically based travel techniques (see Chapter 8, "Travel") and restricts the user's ability to use her peripheral vision. Additionally, because of the visual display's size, physical objects used for interaction may occlude the visual display, which can break any stereo illusion.

Figure 5.3 A monitor equipped with stereo glasses. (Photograph courtesy of Joseph J. LaViola Jr.)

Surround-Screen Displays

A surround-screen display is a visual output device that increases the FOR for a user or group of users by incorporating either a set of display screens (Figure 5.4 shows a canonical example), a large curved display screen, or some combination of curved and planar screens that makes use of one or more light projection devices. The key characteristic of a surround-screen display is that it tries to "surround" the user with visual imagery in order to provide a large FOR, with the surround level varying based on different device configurations. Over the years these output devices have had numerous configurations from simple multi-monitor displays to large surround multi-projection screens that completely envelop the user.

One of the first surround-screen displays used for 3D interaction was developed at the Electronic Visualization Laboratory at the University of Illinois at Chicago. This system was called the CAVE (Cruz-Neira et al. 1993) or Cave Automatic Virtual Environment, and consisted of four screens (three walls and a floor). This particular display configuration has had many variations and typically has three or more large planar projection-based display screens (often between 8 and 12 feet in width and height) that surround the human participant. The screens are arranged orthogonally so the device looks like a large box. Typically, the screens are rear-projected so users do not cast shadows on the display surface. However, in some cases, the floor of these surround-screen devices can use front-projection as long as the projector is mounted such that the user's shadow is behind the user (e.g., as in Figure 5.4). In more sophisticated configurations, six screens are used to provide a 360-degree FOR, and all screens are rear-projected, including the floor (requiring a lot of extra space to house the device). Regardless of the number of screens, either a single PC with powerful graphics cards capable of handling many screens at once or a PC cluster is typically used to generate the images.

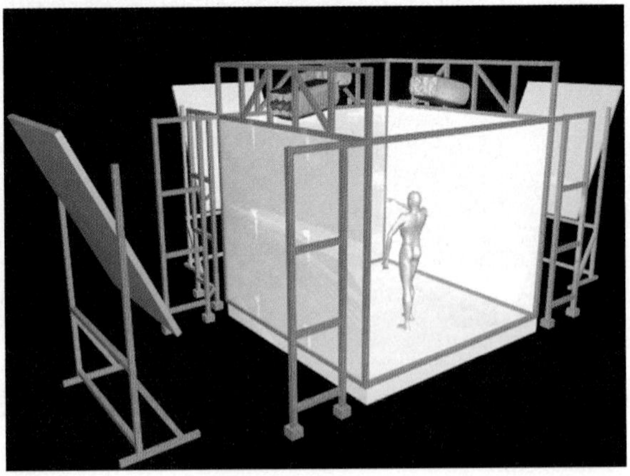

Figure 5.4 An example of a surround-screen VR system. The image shows a four-sided device (three walls and a floor). A projector mounted above the device projects images onto the floor (not pictured). (3D model courtesy of Mark Oribello, Brown University Graphics Group)

There have been a number of interesting variations on the basic structure of a surround-screen display. These variations are based on a number of factors, such as display size, FOV and angle between screens, and number of displays or projectors. For example, the screens do not have to be orthogonal, as shown in Figure 5.5. Here, three large screens are used, and the angle between them is approximately 120 degrees. This type of surround-screen display configuration still provides a large FOV but has a more limited FOR. Smaller versions of the surround-screen display concept have also been developed. The Computer-driven Upper Body Environment (CUBE) is a 360-degree display environment composed of four 32- by 28-inch rear-projected Plexiglas screens. Users stand inside the CUBE, which is suspended from the ceiling, and physically turn around to view the screen surfaces. The screens are approximately one foot from the user's face and extend down to his or her midsection. It was developed at the Entertainment Technology Center at Carnegie Mellon University and represents a small, personalized version of a display that completely surrounds the user.

Other examples of these smaller devices make use of inexpensive LCD panels (see Figure 5.6). As the number of panels increase, the user's FOV and FOR will increase as long as the number of added panels increases the amount of visible screen space. Of course, using collections of LCD panels often results in the presence of perceptible barriers between screens, reducing the seamlessness of the surround-screen display. Many displays of this sort attempt to surround the user in an arc or cylindrical pattern.

Figure 5.5 A variation on the traditional, orthogonal surround-screen display system. This device uses 3 large planar screens where the angle between them is 120 degrees. (Photograph courtesy of Joseph J. LaViola Jr.)

Figure 5.6 A surround-screen display using a collection of display panels.
(Photograph courtesy of Chris North, Department of Computer Science, Virginia Tech)

Up until now, we have examined surround-screen displays that make use of planar screen geometry. However, surround-screen displays also can utilize curved screens, the most common being hemispherical (see Figure 5.7), cylindrical, or some combination of the two (see Figure 5.8). These types of displays typically use either front or rear projection. Curvature can be approximated by either making the angle between planar display screens greater than 90 degrees, like the display in Figure 5.5, or by using a collection of display panels, as in Figure 5.6. However, we do not consider these configurations to be true curved surround-screen displays.

For true curved surround-screen displays that make use of either front or rear projection, special software and/or optics are required to support projection diameters of varying sizes. In the case of front projection for a hemispherical display, a wide-angle lens is attached to the projector, which distorts the output image. Spherical mapping software is used to predistort the image so that it appears correctly on the curved screen. In Figure 5.7, the user sits in front of a small table and can interact with 3D applications using a keyboard and mouse or 3D input devices. Hemispherical displays with much larger projection diameters have also been developed to accommodate multiple users. Similar approaches are taken for rear-projected curved surround-screen displays like the one in Figure 5.8, with the distinction that the predistorted image conforms to the exact geometry of the display surface.

Figure 5.7 A hemispherical display used for interactive molecular visualization. (Photograph courtesy of Paul Bourke)

Figure 5.8 An example of a curved, rear-projected surround-screen display that combines both hemispherical and cylindrical geometry. (Photograph courtesy of Digital Projection)

There are a number of advantages to using a surround-screen display system. They typically provide high spatial resolution and a large FOR. In addition, such devices also have a large FOV, allowing the user to utilize his peripheral vision. Like a single-screen display, surround-screen displays provide monocular depth cues and motion parallax, and when the user is tracked and wears stereo glasses, the device also provides additional motion parallax cues and stereopsis respectively. In contrast with fish-tank VR, a tracked user in a large surround-screen display has much better moving-viewer motion parallax, because she can actually walk around in the device. For example, a user could walk around a virtual chair projected in the center of the display and see the sides and back of the chair. The user would not have this capability with a fish-tank VR setup. Stereopsis issues with surround-screen devices are also similar to those found with a stereo single-display configuration. Surround-screen stereo can be done actively with shutter glasses or passively with, for example, polarized glasses and special polarized lenses for the projectors. Additionally, real and virtual objects can be mixed in the environment. For example, a tractor's cockpit could be brought into the display so an operator could test out its controls while driving through virtual farmland.

One of the biggest disadvantages of large surround-screen display devices is that they are expensive and often require a large amount of physical space. For example, a 10- by 10- by 10-foot CAVE with three walls and a floor can require a room at least 30 feet long, 22 feet wide, and 12 feet high to handle the display screens and the mounted projectors. However, using shorter throw projectors or even clusters of LCD panels can reduce the required room size considerably. The expense is not as much of a problem with smaller surround-screen displays like multi-monitor configurations.

Another problem with these systems, as well as any projection-based display system, is that users can have difficulty seeing objects in stereo under certain conditions. When the user gets close to the display or when objects appear to be right in front of the user, it becomes increasingly difficult to use the visual system's accommodation and vergence capabilities to fuse the two images together. Eye strain is a common problem in these situations.

When more than one person occupies a surround-screen display, they all view the same screens. However, images are typically rendered from only one tracked user's perspective. If an untracked viewer moves in the device, there will be no response from the virtual environment (i.e., the images will be distorted). As the tracked user moves, all non-tracked users effectively see the environment through the tracked user's perspective, which can cause cue conflicts and lead to cybersickness (LaViola 2000a). This problem is a fundamental limitation of surround-screen displays, as well as any visual display device that claims to accommodate multiple users, and is a disadvantage compared to the unlimited number of active viewpoints (user viewpoints that are head tracked to ensure the correct viewing perspective) when using multiple head-worn displays. If non-tracked users stay close to and look in the same direction as the tracked user, they can get a rough approximation of the correct viewpoint, but this is not a completely satisfactory solution.

Over the years, several techniques have been developed to increase the number of active viewpoints. One approach is to use shutter glass synchronization to support two active stereoscopic viewpoints (Agrawala et al. 1997) or four monoscopic viewpoints (Blom et al. 2002). The basic approach to adding more than one active viewpoint is to render images from two or more tracked users and then synchronize the images with the shutter glasses. For example, to allow two active stereoscopic viewpoints, the graphics must be rendered and displayed four times (once for each eye of the two viewers) per frame. The shutter glasses then must be modified so that for one viewer, the left and right eyes switch between the ON/OFF and OFF/ON states while the second viewer's glasses are turned completely off. Then, the second viewer's glasses are in the ON/OFF and OFF/ON states while the first viewer's glasses are turned completely off. Of course, when using this approach, the refresh rate for each eye is cut in half because each eye will see only one of four images displayed; this may cause flicker problems. The frame rate will also be affected, because the rendering engine must perform twice as many computations. More sophisticated approaches have been developed that support stereo for up to six tracked users (Kulik et al. 2011). This approach uses six customized DLP projectors for fast time-sequential image display coupled with polarization techniques. High-speed shutter glasses running at 360 Hz are required and can be programmed from the application to adapt to different scenarios. This approach was initially designed for a large single display screen but could be extended to surround-screen display configurations.

Although physical objects (including the user's body) do not have to be represented as graphical objects in surround-screen display systems, an important issue with using physical objects in this type of display device is the physical/virtual object occlusion problem. The problem arises when the user tries to move a physical object behind a virtual object. Visually, the physical object will appear in front of the graphical object because the graphical object is actually being projected on the screen. This is a common problem with any projection or panel-based display device, and it can lessen the immersive experience and break the stereo illusion.

For those surround-screen displays that use front projection (which makes the display brighter than most rear-projected devices), direct 3D selection, manipulation, and navigation techniques may not work well, because moving too close to the display surface casts shadows on the screen, breaking the stereo illusion and possibly occluding virtual objects. For these types of devices, indirect techniques such as virtual laser pointers, gestures, or keyboard- and mouse-based video game style controls work best. Finally, if the surround-screen display has curvature, spatial resolution and image quality are usually not uniform across the display. For example, the center of the hemispherical display may have higher resolution and quality, while these values decrease toward the display's edges. However, work by Majumder and Sajadi (2013) has begun to address this issue with automatic screen calibration methods.

Workbenches and Tabletop Displays

Another type of display is like a workbench or tabletop. One of the original displays of this type was the Responsive Workbench, developed by Krüger and Fröhlich (1994). These display devices are used to simulate and augment interaction that takes place on desks, tables, and workbenches. Figure 5.9 shows two workbench displays with differing characteristics. The picture on the left shows a standard single workbench where the display can be rotated to be completely horizontal or almost vertical, designed primarily for 3D stereo and interaction. The image on the right shows a small workbench that has a pressure-sensitive display surface for 2D input, which lets users write on the screen surface and makes it easier to utilize both 2D and 3D interaction techniques.

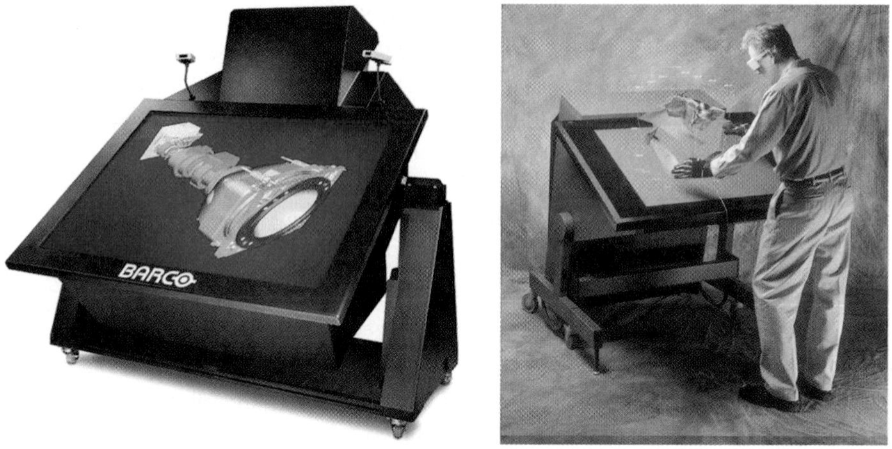

Figure 5.9 Workbench style displays. (Photographs courtesy of Barco and Fakespace Systems)

The example displays shown in Figure 5.9 have evolved in recent years with technology advancements. Workbenches like the one in the left image of Figure 5.9 have become smaller and more personalized as shown in Figure 5.10. With the advent of low-cost multi-touch input technology such as frustrated total internal reflection (Han 2005) and capacitive touch screens, the workbench on the right in Figure 5.9 has evolved into horizontal, multi-touch, table-based non-immersive 2D displays. However, coupling 3D UI technologies (3D stereo and user tracking) with these displays has provided even more powerful technology for 3D spatial interaction, since multi-touch input can be combined with 3D UI techniques to create rich interaction experiences (Steinicke et al. 2013). Figure 5.11 shows an example of a table-based display that uses both multi-touch and 3D spatial input (Jackson et al. 2012).

Figure 5.10 A personalized workbench display that supports tracked 3D stereo and interaction. (Photograph courtesy of Joseph J. LaViola Jr.)

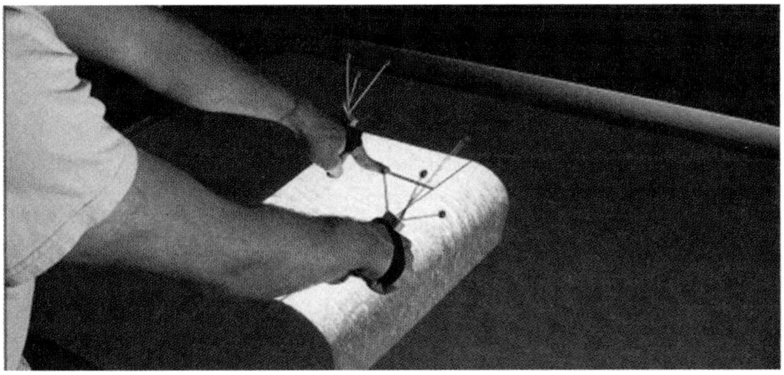

Figure 5.11 A table-based workbench style display that combines multi-touch and 3D spatial input. (Photograph courtesy of Bret Jackson)

In general, workbenches and table-based displays provide relatively high spatial resolution and make for an intuitive display for certain types of applications. For example, a horizontal display configuration is ideally suited to a surgical training application, while a display with a 35-degree orientation would be useful in a drafting or 3D modeling application. Relative to large surround-screen displays, workbench screen sizes are smaller, which improves visual quality. Workbenches and table-based displays also can provide the same visual depth cues that surround-screen and single-screen displays do (assuming appropriate stereo and user-tracking hardware).

As with a large surround-screen or single-screen display, the device can accommodate multiple users, but with the same viewpoint constraints described in the previous section. In general, users have limited mobility when interacting with a workbench because the display is stationary, rather than head-coupled like a head-worn display (discussed later in this section) and does not enclose them like a large surround-screen display. Therefore, as with single-screen displays, the range of viewpoints from which a user can see 3D imagery is restricted, because from some viewpoints, all or part of the screen is not visible. For example, it would not be possible for a user to see the bottom of a stationary graphical object with a completely horizontal table display, because the display surface would no longer be in the user's FOV. From a 3D interaction perspective, then, physically based travel techniques are not appropriate when using a workbench, because the user has little maneuverability compared to other display devices. However, most direct selection and manipulation techniques (see Chapter 7, "Selection and Manipulation") work well because most of the screen real estate is within arm's reach.

Head-Worn Displays

Our discussion of visual display devices has so far focused on stationary displays (i.e., displays that do not move with the user). In this section, we examine visual displays in which the device is attached (coupled) to the user's head. A head-coupled display device used for 3D applications is typically called a head-mounted display (HMD) or a head-worn display (HWD), or more colloquially, a "headset," "goggles," or "glasses." Although it is not yet a common term except in some academic circles, we have chosen to use the term "head-worn display (HWD)" throughout this book. This term emphasizes the fact that such displays are wearable—they can be put on and taken off like a watch, a necklace, or a piece of clothing. The term "HMD," while very common in the literature, is a holdover from the days when displays were attached permanently to pilots' helmets; we no longer "mount" displays to people's heads! An HWD is a sophisticated piece of equipment, because it requires the complex integration of electronic, optical, mechanical, and even audio components (some HWDs support 3D spatial sound). As such, many different HWDs have been designed and developed over the years, with a variety of design choices and tradeoffs. Regardless of internal design, an HWD's main goal is to place images directly in front of the user's eyes using one or two small screens (e.g., LCD, OLED). In some cases, a smartphone's high-resolution screen can be used as the display engine for an HWD (see Figure 5.12). A combination of refractive lenses and/or mirrors (depending on the optical technique used) is used to present and sometimes magnify the images shown on the screens (see Melzer and Moffitt [2011] for more details on the physical design of HWDs). An example of a HWD that has screens and optics embedded in the device is shown in Figure 5.13.

Figure 5.12 An example of a head-worn display that uses a cell phone as the display engine. (Photograph courtesy of Samsung)

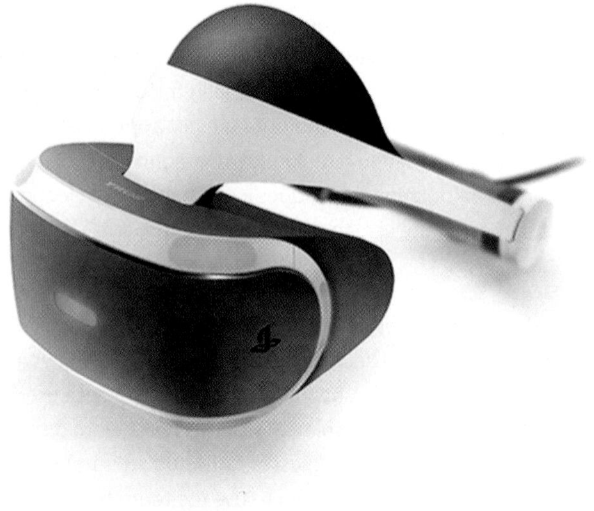

Figure 5.13 A head-worn display for virtual reality. (Photograph courtesy of Sony)

There have been a variety of different head-coupled display designs that make use of the basic HWD concept. In the early 1990s, Bolas (1994) developed an arm-mounted display that applied a counterweight on the opposite side of the display to make it easier to manipulate (see Figure 5.14). This counterweight made it possible for this device to use better optics and heavier, higher-quality display screens (i.e., CRTs), providing greater resolution. This device also made use of mechanical tracking technology (see Chapter 6) to track the user's head position and orientation. Tsang and colleagues (2002) used this idea to create an arm-mounted device that attached a flat panel display to an armature. This display enables the metaphor of a window into the 3D virtual world. Given display and optics technology miniaturization and improvement, the same or better resolution can be achieved in a small and lighter form factor. For example, today's HWDs achieve high-definition quality or better resolution and can weigh less than one pound, making HWD-based arm-mounted displays less relevant for 3D spatial interfaces.

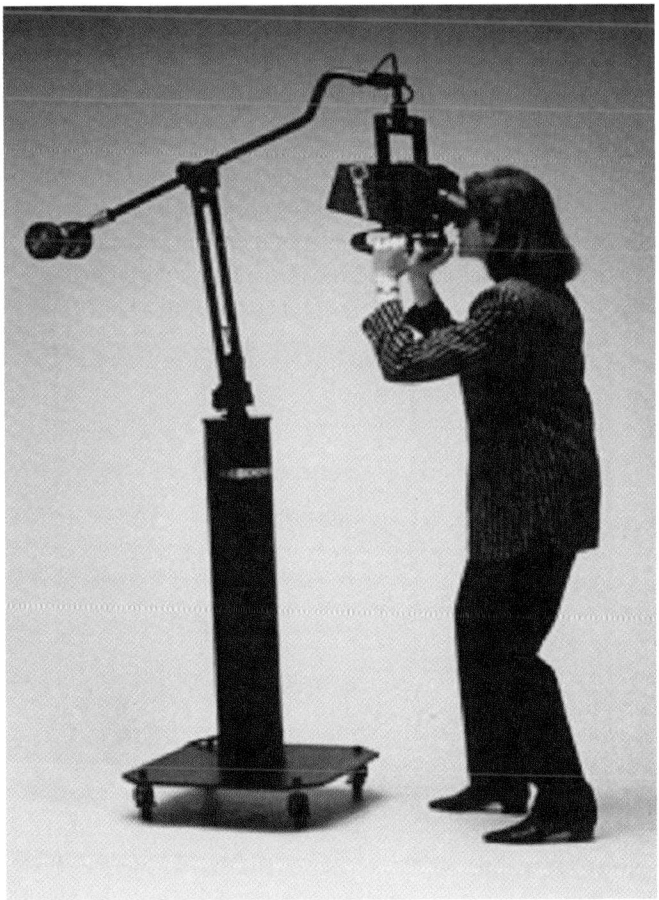

Figure 5.14 An arm-mounted display called the Binocular Omni-Orientation Monitor. (Photograph of the Boom 3C courtesy of Fakespace Labs, Mountain View, California)

Another HWD design variation is the head-mounted projective display (HMPD). In HMPDs, small projectors are attached to the head-coupled device, and these project the graphical images into the real environment. Retroreflective material (a special bendable material that reflects light back in the direction it came from, regardless of its incident angle with the screen surface) is placed strategically in the environment so that the user sees the graphics reflecting off the material. HMPDs thus are a hybrid between conventional HWDs and projection displays (Hua et al. 2001). HMPDs are ideally suited to collaborative applications in mixed and augmented reality, because using retroreflective screens provides correct occlusion cues for both virtual and real objects and because all participants have their own individually correct viewpoints (Hua et al. 2002). With projector miniaturization, microprojectors can be used in HMPDs giving them a form factor on par with sunglasses, making them extremely lightweight with high resolution (see Figure 5.15).

HWDs that project images directly onto a user's retina are known as virtual retinal displays. The virtual retinal display (VRD), also called the light-scanning display, was invented at the Human Interface Technology Lab (Tidwell et al. 1995). With a VRD, photon sources are used to generate coherent beams of light (e.g., lasers, LEDs), which allow the system to draw a rasterized image onto the retina. In order to generate full-color images, three light sources are needed (red, green, and blue), while monochrome versions of the VRD require only one. These light beams are intensity-modulated to match the intensity of the image being rendered, meaning that is possible to produce fully immersive and see-through display modes for AR applications. The light beams then scan across the retina to place each image point, or pixel, at the proper position.

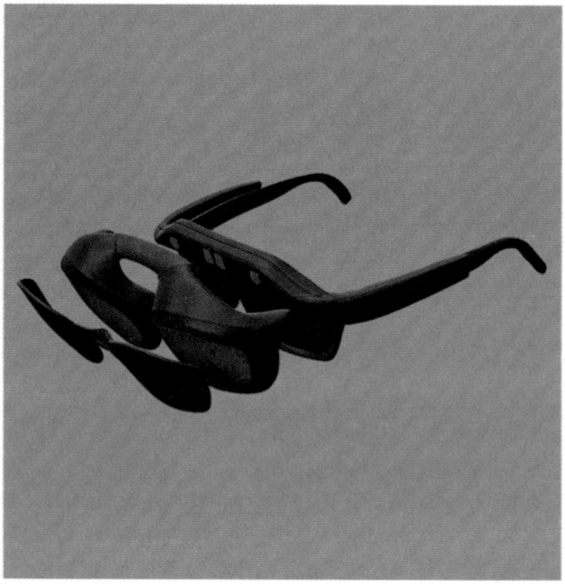

Figure 5.15 An example of a head-mounted projective display that supports both virtual and augmented reality applications by using an attachment that makes it project onto an integral opaque or see-through surface, instead of onto surfaces in the environment. (Image courtesy of CastAR)

Another variation on the traditional HWD is a design that supports seeing both virtual and real imagery. These types of HWDs support augmented and mixed reality applications. There are three main HWD designs that support the ability to see both real and virtual imagery simultaneously (Billinghurst 2014). *Optical see-through displays* place optical combiners in front of the user's eyes; the combiners are partially transparent, so that the user can see the real world through them, and partially reflective, so that the user can see virtual images reflected from small head-mounted screens. The advantage of optical see-through displays is that they provide a direct view of the real world with full resolution and no time delay. However, it is more difficult to get wide FOVs and it is much easier to see registration problems with the superimposed virtual imagery.

Video see-through displays work by streaming real-time video from head-mounted cameras to the graphics subsystem, which renders virtual computer graphics images into the video buffers in real time, blending the virtual and real. The result is displayed to the user in a traditional closed-view HWD (Azuma 1997). Video see-through displays provide a digitized image of the real world, making wide FOVs easier to support as well as providing more registration and calibration strategies between virtual imagery and the real world. In addition, they provide the full gamut of compositing technologies to combine real and virtual imagery. On the other hand, a video image of the real world is almost always of lower visual quality than a direct optical view. It is important to note that with video see-through displays the views must be orthoscopic (Drascic and Milgram 1996), which is crucially dependent on the optical path to the cameras that must be typically folded (State et al. 2005). Figure 5.16 presents an example of an early AR video see-through display, while Figure 5.17 shows a modern optical see-through display.

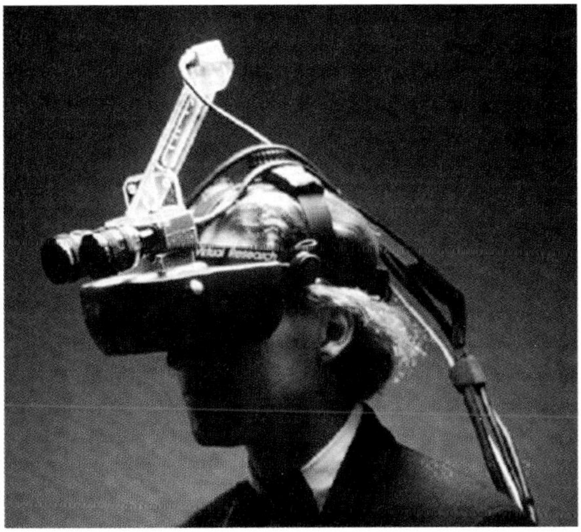

Figure 5.16 Early video see-through AR. (Included by permission from UNC Department of Computer Science)

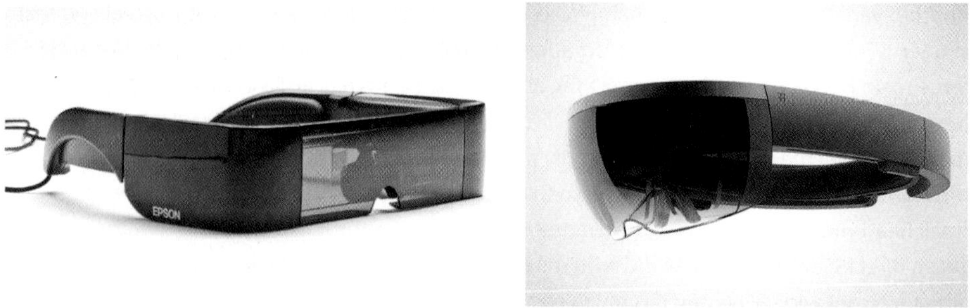

Figure 5.17 Modern optical see-though AR displays. (Photographs courtesy of Epson and Microsoft)

Finally, a third design is to use head-worn projector-based displays (including ones that don't use retroreflective surfaces). These HWDs support combining real and virtual in the actual physical environment, rather than in the optics or the computer. Of course, one of the many challenges with this type of display is ensuring that there is correct color correction and perspective viewing since the images are projected onto arbitrary objects. This type of design is further discussed the "Arbitrary Surface Display" section below.

In terms of visual depth cues, as with other display systems, tracked HWDs allow for all the monoscopic and motion parallax depth cues. Stereoscopy is produced differently with HWDs than with projection-based displays and monitors. With non-head-coupled devices, active stereo is produced often using temporal multiplexing (i.e., drawing images for the left and right eye on the same screen sequentially). With an HWD, stereopsis is achieved by drawing two separate images on one screen or two separate screens—one for each eye—at the same time.

One of the biggest advantages of HWDs is that the user can have complete physical visual immersion (i.e., a 360-degree FOR), because the user always sees the virtual world regardless of head position and orientation. Even though tracked HWDs have a 360-degree FOR, the FOV will vary depending on the device construction and cost. HWDs with small FOVs can cause perception and performance problems. Even high-end HWDs can have limited FOVs when compared to surround-screen displays. According to Neale (1998), restricted FOVs can impede a user's ability to acquire spatial information and develop spatial cognitive maps of unfamiliar spaces. Small FOVs may also produce distortions in perception of size and distance and reduce performance on some visual tasks. However, better optics and display technology have helped to improve HWD FOVs with low-cost designs achieving 100-degree FOVs or more, reducing these perceptual issues.

HWDs have other benefits when compared to projection and single-screen displays. HWDs do not suffer from the active viewpoint problem that plagues projection and single-screen displays, because each user can have his own HWD with his own tracked view of the virtual world. Of course, multiple HWDs require more graphical computing power to drive them, and multiple viewers also cannot see each other directly when wearing non-see-through HWDs.

HWDs have both pros and cons when it comes to stereoscopic viewing. Because they use one display per eye, HWDs eliminate the need to do temporal multiplexing. A potential problem with stereoscopic HWDs is that each person has a different interocular distance (the distance between the two eyes), meaning that stereo images have to be separated by that distance for correct binocular stereopsis. However, many HWDs provide a way to adjust the screens and optics for a range of interocular distances, improving stereo viewing. In addition, the interocular distance should be changed by setting the distance between the virtual cameras used in the 3D application. Tracking the position of the user's eyes relative to a HWD's optics can also help to maintain proper interocular distance (Itoh and Klinker 2014).

In many HWD designs, the images the user sees are always in focus and have the same focal depth, causing accommodation and vergence cue conflicts when users look at objects with different virtual depths, leading to eye strain and discomfort. This phenomenon also occurs with projection-based and single-screen displays but may be more pronounced with HWDs and VRDs, because the displays are close to the user's eyes. Omura et al. (1996) developed a system to alleviate this problem by incorporating movable relay lenses into an HMD. The lenses are continuously adjusted, based on gaze direction. The virtual screen surface appears to be at the same distance as the user's vergence point, creating a display with matched accommodation and vergence cues. Research by McQuaide and colleagues (2002) developed something similar for a VRD using a deformable membrane mirror (a microelectromechanical system) to dynamically change the focal plane, which would enable the viewer to see 3D objects using the natural accommodative response of the visual system cues.

Eye tracking (see Chapter 6) appears to be a useful approach for dealing with accommodation-vergence problems. Using eye tracking will also significantly benefit VRDs, because when users move their eyes while using a VRD, they can lose all or part of the image, since the images from retinal displays are sent to a fixed location. Work by Chinthammit et al. (2002) demonstrated how an eye-tracking system can be used to let VRD images be coupled to a user's eye movements. These types of eye-tracking-coupled display systems are still in the early stages of development, but low-cost eye-tracking technology is making this approach more practical and will enable HWDs to support all the visual depth cues.

HWDs have the advantage of being more portable and often less expensive as compared to surround-screen and single-screen displays. However, surround-screen and single-screen displays generally have higher spatial resolutions than HWDs, because the display screens have to be small and lightweight to keep the overall weight of the HWD low. Even though HWDs can achieve high resolution, their projection and single-screen counterparts tend to always be ahead of the resolution curve, and this trend is likely to continue until we reach the limits of the human visual system.

Ergonomically, the weight and weight distribution of an HWD must be considered, because a heavier HWD can cause strain in neck muscles from extended use. HWDs may not fit every user, because everyone has a different head size and shape. The HWD's center of gravity is also an essential part of maintaining user comfort (Melzer 2014). Another ergonomic consideration for many HWDs is the cabling that connects the display to the computer. Users of non-see-through HWDs may trip over cables or get wrapped up in them as they move around. Approaches to address this problem include moving computation into the display itself, having the user carry or wear the computer, or using wireless technology to transmit display and input signals between the computer and the HWD.

Because the real world may be completely blocked from the user's view, interaction while wearing an HWD often requires some type of graphical representation of either one or both hands, or the input device used. These graphical representations can be as simple as a cube or as sophisticated as a high fidelity hand model. Non-see-through HWDs also limit the types of input devices that can be used because the user cannot physically see the device in order to use it. It's also important to graphically represent the boundaries of the physical space and any physical obstacles, so that the user avoids injury.

Arbitrary Surface Displays

Thus far, we have examined displays that use simple planar or curved screens. Another display approach is to project imagery directly on arbitrary surfaces of any shape or size. Creating visual displays out of everyday objects and surfaces is known as projection mapping or spatial augmented reality (Bimber and Raskar 2005).

Projecting imagery onto arbitrary surfaces presents many challenging problems, and the level of difficulty is often dependent on the complexity of the geometrical surface and its color and texture characteristics. Other issues include whether 3D stereo is needed, how to deal with shadows, and display area restrictions. A common approach to creating these types of displays from a hardware perspective is to use one or more projector-camera pairs. In some cases, projector-camera pairs are placed onto steerable motorized platforms that can move in real time to project imagery to increase the display surface size (Wilson et al. 2012). Using more than one projector helps to alleviate many issues due to shadows and display size. The camera is used to perform display surface estimation, including the display surface's geometry, color, and texture. Calibration of the camera and the projector is also required to ensure that the images are displayed correctly. Another approach is to use optical overlays, such as mirror beam combiners or transparent surfaces. More details on these approaches can be found in Bimber and Raskar (2005). Some examples of arbitrary surface displays are shown in Figures 5.18 and 5.19.

In terms of 3D stereo, one of the advantages of arbitrary surface displays is that projecting onto 3D objects supports appropriate depth, since the images are directly placed onto the 3D surface. However, if images need to appear in front of or behind the display surface, view-dependent stereoscopic projection is required (Raskar et al. 1998). Depending on the display configuration, support for multiple head-tracked viewers is also possible. For example, a version of the Virtual Showcase (Bimber et al. 2001) makes use of four mirrors so each user can have their own view. With these displays, 3D spatial interaction is often limited to passive viewing, but they do support various selection and manipulation techniques. As with surround-screen displays, if front projection is used, more indirect methods of interaction are needed (see Chapter 7, "Selection and Manipulation") since direct manipulation can cause shadows, breaking the display illusion.

Figure 5.18 The Illumroom, an example of projection mapping to create an extended display in a living room. The projector-camera pair correctly projects onto the various surfaces in the room. (Photograph courtesy of Microsoft)

Figure 5.19 The Virtual Showcase, an augmented surface display that projects virtual information onto a physical 3D artifact, presenting a seamless integration of the physical object and virtual content. (Photograph courtesy of Oliver Bimber)

Autostereoscopic Displays

In this last section on visual displays, we discuss **autostereoscopic** display devices, which generate 3D imagery without the need for special shutters or polarized glasses. These displays mainly use lenticular, volumetric, or holographic display technology, which we mention below. However, other techniques for creating autostereoscopic displays exist as well, including compressive light fields, diffractive-optical elements, integral imaging, parallax illumination, and barrier grids. A discussion of these techniques goes beyond the scope of this book, but Holliman et al. (2011) and Wetzstein et al. (2012) provide nice surveys of these autostereoscopic display technologies.

Parallax barrier displays use a vertical grating where one eye sees odd pixels through the grating, while the other eye sees even pixels to support stereopsis. Lenticular displays (see Figure 5.20) typically use a cylindrical lens array in front of the display screen. The cylindrical lens array approach directs different 2D images into different subzones, and these zones are projected out at different angles. When the viewer's head is positioned correctly in front of the display, each eye sees a different image, allowing for binocular disparity. These lenses effectively replace the vertical grating in the parallax barrier approach. These techniques have the drawback that the user must be in a stationary position. Extensions to the basic approach do allow for user movement and the maintaining of motion parallax (see Dodgson 2005, Perlin et al. 2000, and Schwerdtner and Heidrich 1998 for examples).

According to Blundell and Schwarz (2000), a volumetric display device permits the generation, absorption, or scattering of visible radiation from a set of localized and specified regions within a physical volume (holographic displays can also fit into this definition). In other words, volumetric displays create "true" 3D images by actually illuminating points in 3D space. This is in contrast to other stereoscopic displays, which provide the illusion of 3D images but are actually projected onto a 2D surface.

Figure 5.20 A lenticular display. (Photograph courtesy of Joseph J. LaViola Jr.)

Volumetric displays generate 3D imagery using a number of different methods. Two of the most common use either a swept- or a static-volume technique (Blundell 2012). Swept-volume techniques sweep a periodically time-varying 2D image through a 3D spatial volume at high frequencies. Displays using swept-volume techniques (see Figure 5.21) have a mechanical component, because they spin a 2D screen within the viewing volume to create the 3D image. Static-volume techniques create 3D images without the need of mechanical motion within the viewing volume. One static-volume approach uses two intersecting invisible laser beams to create a single point of visible light. This allows the drawing of voxels (3D pixels) inside the volume by controlling when and where the lasers intersect (Downing et al. 1996). Rapidly scanning these intersection points in a predefined way enables the drawing of a true 3D image (Ebert et al. 1999). Other static-volume approaches use a high-speed projector with a stack of air-spaced liquid crystal scattering shutters (multiplanar optical elements), which act as an electronically variable projection volume. The high-speed projector projects a sequence of slices of the 3D image into the stack of scattering shutters, and each slice is halted at the proper depth (Sullivan 2003). Figure 5.22 shows a display using this static-volume approach.

One display system that provides a rough approximation of what a volumetric display looks like is known as pCubee (see Figure 5.23). Although it does not create "true 3D," the use of LCD panels placed in a box configuration coupled with a head-tracked perspective rendering and a physics simulation gives users the impression that they are looking into a cubic volume (Stavness et al. 2010). This approach is a less expensive alternative to true volumetric displays. Brown et al. (2003) did something similar to pCubee, using a head-mounted projective display and a retroreflective cube.

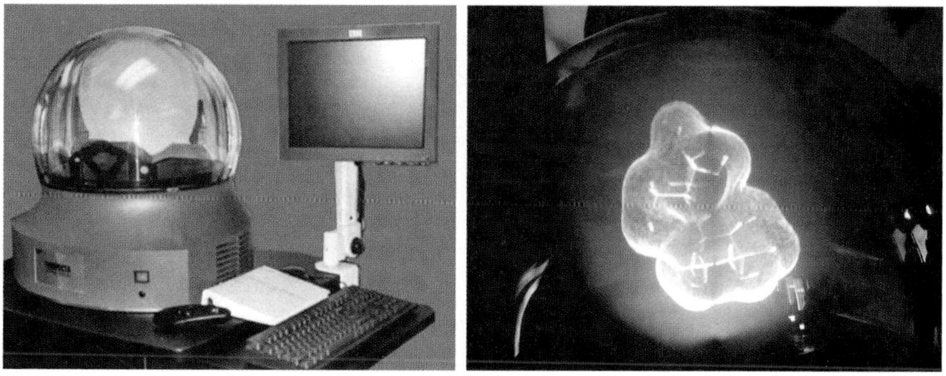

Figure 5.21 A volumetric display system that uses the swept-volume technique. On the left is the display device and on the right a volumetric image. (Photographs courtesy of Actuality Systems)

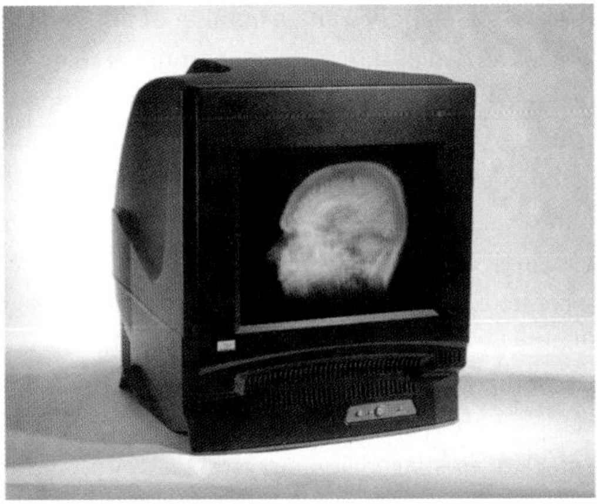

Figure 5.22 A volumetric display that uses a multiplanar, static-volume approach to generate 3D images. (Photograph courtesy of LightSpace Technologies)

Figure 5.23 pCubee, a simulated volumetric display that puts five LCD panels in a box configuration. (Photograph courtesy of Dr. Ian Stavness)

Holographic displays are similar to volumetric displays in that they both produce true 3D images, but the two categories use different techniques to generate the imagery. Holographic displays produce 3D imagery by recording and reproducing the properties of light waves (amplitude, wavelength, and phase differences) from a 3D scene. The process involves a computational step in which a 3D description of a scene is converted into a holographic fringe pattern (a diffraction pattern that captures light from different directions) and an optical step that modulates the fringe pattern and turns it into a 3D image. Lucente (1997) provides a detailed introduction to the steps involved in generating 3D images using holographic displays, and more information on approaches to creating holographic displays can be found in Yaras et al. (2010).

An important concept to understand about volumetric and holographic displays is that because they produce true 3D imagery, they do not suffer from the active viewpoint problem that plagues projection-based displays and monitors. Therefore, the number of viewers with the correct perspective is basically unlimited. In addition, with these devices no trackers are needed to maintain moving-viewer motion parallax. They also do not suffer from the accommodation–vergence cue conflicts that accompany more traditional stereoscopic displays. However, current volumetric displays have the problem that they cannot provide many monocular depth cues, such as occlusion and shading, unless coupled with head tracking. Additionally, both volumetric and holographic displays generally can display images only within a small working volume, making them inappropriate for immersive VR or AR.

There has been little 3D UI research with lenticular and holographic displays (Bimber 2006). However, the same interfaces that work for rear-projected displays should also work for lenticular displays. Volumetric displays have an interesting characteristic in that many of them have an enclosure around the actual 3D imagery, meaning that users cannot physically reach into the display space. Balakrishnan et al. (2001) built volumetric display prototypes to explore these issues. They developed a set of UI design options specific to these displays for performing tasks such as object selection, manipulation, and navigation (Balakrishnan et al. 2001). Grossman and Balakrishnan extended this work using multi-finger gestures (Grossman et al. 2004) to interact with volumetric displays; they also designed selection (Grossman and Balakrishnan 2006) and collaboration techniques (Grossman and Balakrishnan 2008).

5.3 Auditory Displays

Auditory displays are another important aspect of presenting sensory information to the user, but they are overlooked in many 3D UIs (Cohen and Wenzel 1995). One of the major goals of auditory displays for 3D UIs is the generation and display of spatialized 3D sound, enabling the human participant to take advantage of his auditory localization capabilities. **Localization** is the psychoacoustic process of determining the location and direction from which a sound emanates (Sherman and Craig 2003). Having this feature in a 3D application can provide many important benefits to the 3D UI designer.

Note that the topic of auditory displays and 3D sound generation is a very large and active field, and going into great detail on the subject is beyond the scope of this book. For more details on 3D sound and audio displays, Blauert (1997), Begault (1994), Vorländer and Shinn-Cunningham (2015), and Xie (2013) all provide comprehensive introductions. Chapter 3, "Human Factors Fundamentals," describes the human auditory system and spatial sound perception in section 3.3.2.

5.3.1 3D Sound Generation

Before 3D sound can be used in a 3D UI, it must be generated in some way. This generation process is important because it can have an effect on the quality of the interface and the user's overall experience with the application. There are many different techniques for generating 3D sound, and we briefly describe two of the most common. The first is 3D sound sampling and synthesis, and the second is auralization.

3D Sound Sampling and Synthesis

The basic idea behind 3D sound sampling and synthesis is to record sound that the listener will hear in the 3D application by taking samples from a real environment. For example, with binaural audio recording, two small microphones are placed inside a person's ears (or in the ears of an anthropomorphic dummy head) to separately record the sounds heard by left and right ears in the natural environment. All of the 3D sound cues discussed in section 3.3.2 are present in these recordings, which are capable of producing very realistic results. However, the main problem with this type of sound generation is that it is specific to the environmental settings in which the recordings were made. Therefore, any change in the sound source's location, introduction of new objects into the environment, or significant movement of the user would require new recordings. Unfortunately, these changes will occur in most 3D applications, making this basic technique impractical for the majority of situations.

An alternative approach, which is one of the most common 3D sound-generation techniques used in 3D applications today, is to simulate the binaural recording process by processing a monaural sound source with a pair of left- and right-ear head-related transfer functions (HRTFs, discussed in section 3.3.2), corresponding to a desired position within the 3D environment (Kapralos et al. 2003). With these empirically defined HRTFs, real-time interactivity becomes much more feasible, because particular sound sources can be placed anywhere in the environment and the HRTFs will filter them accordingly to produce 3D spatial audio for the listener.

As with binaural recording, there are some important issues that need to be considered with the HRTF approach. In general, HRTF measurements are taken in echo-free environments, meaning that they will not produce reverberation cues. Additionally, as with binaural recording, one pair of HRTFs applies to only one position in the environment, which means that many HRTF pairs are needed in order to have spatial audio in the whole space. Ideally, HRTF measurement should be done for all possible points in the space, but this is highly impractical because of time and resource constraints. One approach to dealing with this problem is to use interpolation schemes to fill in the HRTF measurement gaps (Kulkarni and Colburn 1993). The other major issue with using HRTF measurements for generating spatialized sound is that there is a large variation between the HRTFs of different subjects. These differences are due to variations in each listener's outer ears, differences in measurement procedures, and perturbations in the sound field by the measuring instruments (Carlile 1996). One method for dealing with these variations is to use generic HRTFs. These HRTFs are constructed in a number of ways, including using an anthropomorphic dummy head or averaging the responses of several listeners

(Xie 2013). Another method is to build personalized HRTFs that are specific to a particular user by capturing a 3D model of the user's head and ears that can then be fed into a numeric sound propagation solver (Meshram et al. 2014).

Auralization

Auralization is the process of rendering the sound field of a source in space in such a way as to simulate the binaural listening experience through the use of physical and mathematical models (Kleiner et al. 1993). The goal of auralization is to recreate a listening environment by determining the reflection patterns of sound waves coming from a sound source as they move through the environment. Therefore, this process is very useful for creating reverberation effects.

There are several computer-based approaches to creating these sound fields, including wave-based modeling, ray-based modeling, ambisonics, and wave-field synthesis. With wave-based modeling techniques, the goal is to solve the wave equation so as to completely re-create a particular sound field. In many cases, there is no analytical solution to this equation, which means that numerical solutions are required. In the ray-based approach, the paths taken by the sound waves as they travel from source to listener are found by following rays emitted from the source. The problem with the ray-based approach is that these rays ignore the wavelengths of the sound waves and any phenomena associated with them, such as diffraction. This means this technique is appropriate only when sound wavelengths are smaller than the objects in the environment but larger than the roughness of them (Huopaniemi 1999).

Ambisonics is a directional recording approach that can capture a full sphere-based sound field with a minimum of four microphones, based on the idea that a sound source in relation to a listener can be represented by its orthogonal components and a nondirectional component measured with an omnidirectional microphone. Note that higher order ambisonics adds more microphones to the configuration to increase localization accuracy. One of the advantages of this approach is that it provides flexible output and will work with a variety of external speaker configurations. However, four-channel ambisonics can only create an accurate localization for a single centered listener.

Finally, wave-field synthesis is a technique that can, in theory, completely capture an acoustic environment so that sounds can be made to sound like they originate anywhere within or beyond the listening area. This approach is based on the notion that a virtual sound source can be approximated by overlapping sources originating from actual sources at other positions. The major drawback of this approach is that many loudspeakers that are placed close together are needed to adequately display the sound field. Other material on auralization and its use in 3D applications can be found in Vorländer (2007), Dobashi et al. (2003), Naer et al. (2002), Manocha et al. (2009), and Funkhouser et al. (2004).

5.3.2 Sound System Configurations

The 3D sound generated using any of the many techniques available can then be presented to the user. The two basic approaches for displaying these signals are to use headphones or external speakers, and there are advantages and disadvantages to each.

Headphones

A common approach to the display of 3D sound is to use stereophonic headphones that present different information to each ear. Note that if 3D sound is not required in the 3D UI, monophonic (presenting the same information to each ear) headphones will work just as well, but for the purposes of this discussion, when we refer to headphones, we are referring to the stereophonic variety. Headphones coupled with HRTFs have many distinct advantages in a 3D UI. They provide a high level of channel separation, which helps to avoid crosstalk, a phenomenon that occurs when the left ear hears sound intended for the right ear, and vice versa. They also isolate the user from external sounds in the physical environment (i.e., noise-cancellation headphones), which helps to ensure that these sounds do not affect the listener's perception. They are often combined with visual displays that block out the real world, such as HWDs, helping to create fully immersive experiences. Additionally, headphones allow multiple users to receive 3D sound (assuming that they are all head-tracked) simultaneously, and they are somewhat easier to deal with, because there are only two sound channels to control.

The main disadvantage of headphones is a phenomenon called inside-the-head localization (IHL). IHL is the lack of externalization of a sound source, which results in the false impression that a sound is emanating from inside the user's head (Kendall 1995). IHL occurs mainly because of the lack of correct environmental information, that is, lack of reverberation and HRTF information (Kapralos et al. 2003). The best way to minimize IHL is to ensure that the sounds delivered to the listener are as natural as possible. Of course, this naturalness is difficult to achieve, as shown in our previous discussions on the complexity of 3D sound generation. At a minimum, having accurate HRTF information will go a long way toward reducing IHL. Including reverberation can basically eliminate IHL at a cost of reduced user localization accuracy (Begault 1992). Two other minor disadvantages of headphones are that they can be cumbersome and uncomfortable to wear for extended periods of time, and they can make it difficult to hear and talk with collaborators. However, according to Begault (1994), other than the IHL problem and possible comfort issues, headphone displays are superior devices for conveying 3D spatialized sound.

External Speakers

The second approach to display 3D sound is to use external speakers placed at strategic locations in the environment. This approach is often used with visual displays that are not head worn. With the exception of external speakers that use wave-field synthesis, the main limitation with this approach is that it makes it difficult to present 3D sound to more than one head-tracked user (external speakers work very well for nonspatialized sound with multiple users). On the other hand, with external speakers, the user does not have to wear any additional devices.

The major challenge with using external speakers for displaying 3D sound is how to avoid crosstalk and make sure the listener's left and right ears receive the appropriate signals. The two main approaches for presenting 3D sound over external speakers are transaural audio and amplitude panning. **Transaural audio** allows for the presentation of the left and right binaural audio signals to the corresponding left and right ears using external speakers (Kapralos et al. 2003). Although transaural audio overcomes IHL, it requires some type of crosstalk cancellation technique, which can be computationally expensive, to ensure that the ear does not receive unwanted signals. See Gardner (1998), Mouchtaris et al. (2000), Garas (2000), and Li and colleagues (2012) for details on different crosstalk cancellation algorithms. **Amplitude panning** adjusts the intensity of the sound in some way to simulate the directional properties of the interaural time difference and the interaural intensity difference (see section 4.3.2). In other words, by systematically varying each external speaker's intensity, a phantom source is produced in a given location. Although amplitude panning produces a robust perception of a sound source at different locations, it is very difficult to precisely control the exact position of the phantom source (Vorländer and Shinn-Cunningham 2015). See Pulkki (2001) and Pulkki and Karjalainen (2014) for details on many different amplitude panning techniques.

A final issue when using external speakers is speaker placement, because sounds emanating from external speakers can bounce or be filtered through real-world objects, hampering sound quality. For example, in a surround-screen system, placing the speakers in front of the visual display could obstruct the graphics, while placing them behind the display could muffle the sound. Some surround-screen displays use perforated screens to allow placement of speakers behind the screens without significant audio degradation.

5.3.3 Audio in 3D Interfaces

There are several different ways 3D UIs can use audio displays, including

- localization
- sonification
- ambient effects
- sensory substitution and feedback
- annotation and help

Localization

As stated at the beginning of section 5.3, the generation of 3D spatial sound creates an important audio depth cue, providing the user with the ability to use her localization skills and giving her an aural sense of the 3D environment. Three-dimensional sound can be used in a variety of ways in 3D interfaces, including audio wayfinding aids (see Chapter 8), acoustic cues for locating off-screen objects (such as enemies in games and training applications), and an enhanced feeling of moving through a virtual space.

Sonification

Sonification is the process of turning information into sounds (the audio equivalent of visualization) (Hermann et al. 2011). It can be useful when trying to get a better understanding of different types of data. For example, in a 3D scientific visualization application for examining fluid flow, a user could move her hand through a portion of the dataset, and sounds of varying frequency could be generated to correspond to varying flow speeds.

Ambient Effects

Ambient sound effects can provide a sense of realism in a 3D application. For example, hearing birds chirping and the wind whistling through the trees helps to augment an outdoor wilderness environment, and hearing cars traveling down city streets could make a city environment more compelling. Ambient effects can also be used to mimic real-world feedback. For example, if a door opening and closing in the real world makes a distinct sound, playing such a sound for virtual door would improve realism and let the user know the door opened or closed without seeing it visually.

Sensory Substitution

In the case of audio displays, **sensory substitution** (discussed in section 3.3.5) is the process of substituting sound for another sensory modality, such as touch. This substitution can be a powerful tool in 3D UIs when haptic feedback (see section 5.4) is not present. For example, a sound could substitute for the feel of a button press or physical interaction with a virtual object, or it could let the user know an operation has been completed.

Annotation and Help

Recorded or synthesized speech can play a role as an annotation tool in collaborative applications, such as distributed model viewers, and as a means to provide help to users when interaction in the 3D environment is unclear. For example, the 3D environment could inform the user that they are navigating in the wrong direction or provide information from other users about the design of a new engine.

5.4 Haptic Displays

The last type of display device that we examine in this chapter is the haptic display. Haptic displays provide the user with the sense of touch and proprioception by simulating the physical interaction between virtual objects and the user. The word **haptics** comes from the Greek word *haptein*, meaning "to touch," but is used to refer to both sensations of force or kinesthesia when nerve endings in joints and muscles are stimulated and tactile feedback when nerve endings in the skin are stimulated (Burdea 1996). Therefore, depending on the design of the haptic display, these devices can provide the user with a sensation of force, touch, vibration, temperature, or a combination of any of these. Haptic displays are often coupled with input devices so that they can provide a fast feedback loop between measuring user motion and haptic feedback communicated back to the user. Ensuring a very low latency between human motion and haptic feedback is one of the major requirements in creating effective haptic displays. Chapter 3, "Human Factors Fundamentals," provides an overview of the human haptic system in section 3.3.3.

An important component of a haptic display system (besides the actual physical device) is the software used to synthesize forces and tactile sensations that the display device presents to the user: **haptic rendering**. Haptic rendering is based on a large variety of generic algorithmic techniques, such as physics-based modeling and simulation, but can also be based on psychophysical modeling of human haptic perception, an approach particularly popular in tactile rendering (Israr and Poupyrev 2011). Haptic rendering is an active research field; however, in this chapter, we focus on the physical output devices instead of the haptic display system as a whole. See Burdea (1996), Basdogan and Srinivasan (2002), and Lin and Otuday (2008) for more details on haptic rendering algorithms, haptic devices, and the human haptic system.

5.4.1 Haptic Display Characteristics

Haptic displays have many different characteristics that influence the use of haptic devices in 3D UIs. In this section, we discuss three of the most common characteristics, including

- perceptual dimensions
- resolution
- ergonomics

See Sherman and Craig (2003) for more information on haptic display characteristics.

Perceptual Dimensions

The most important characteristic of a haptic display is its capability to present information to the user. The majority of haptic displays require direct physical contact between devices and the human body; the user has to "feel" the device. There are a few exceptions to this rule, including special-purpose heat or wind displays, or more general-purpose ultrasonic systems (i.e., powerful and directed sound waves a user can feel).

Unlike visual or auditory displays, in haptics there are multiple parallel physiological and perceptual mechanisms that evoke human haptic sensations. Therefore, numerous techniques are used to create haptic sensations, and there is no one single "best" haptic display. The design of a haptic display and its specific applications depend on the perceptual dimensions that we would like to evoke. On the most basic level, a display might provide tactile or kinesthetic cues, or both. If the device provides tactile cues, the actuation mechanisms can target different skin receptors by using vibrations at different frequencies and amplitudes, static relief shapes, or direct electrical stimulation, where the electrical charge directly interacts with the tactile nerve endings. If the device is designed to output kinesthetic cues, the actuation mechanisms can target different muscle groups in the limb and either actively modify forces that apply to the human body (as in classic force feedback displays) or modulate the perceived resistance of the device to human actuation, which can be done either actively using haptic brake displays or passively using simple physical props.

Body location that is used for haptic actuation is another important perceptual dimension. The density and distribution of nerve endings in skin, muscle, and tendons differ across body locations. For example, the tactile spatial resolution in the tip of the finger was measured with the two-points threshold test to be ~1mm, while the resolution on the back increases to more than 20mm (Cholewiak and Collins 1991). Additionally, the size of the activation area that the display can support affects both perception and display design: a full-body tactile display is perceived very differently than a single vibrating motor. Considering all these perceptual dimensions is essential in designing the haptic display and the display's application compatibility.

Resolution

The **spatial resolution** of a haptic display refers to the minimum spatial proximity of the stimuli that the device can present to the user. It should correspond to perceptual spatial resolution in those body locations where the haptic display is applied. For example, the forearm is less sensitive to closely placed stimuli than are the fingertips (Sherman and Craig 2003); therefore, a tactile device designed for the fingers should have much higher spatial resolution than one designed for the forearm.

The **temporal resolution** of a haptic display refers to the minimal temporal proximity of the tactile stimuli generated by haptic displays; it is often referred to as the refresh rate of the haptic displays. Temporal resolution of displays is very important in delivering high-quality haptic sensations. For example, in force displays a low temporal resolution can cause unintended vibrations, making virtual objects feel softer than intended. Therefore, force displays usually require refresh rates at a minimum of 1000 Hz to provide quality haptic output (Massie 1993).

Ergonomics

In order to generate haptic sensations and communicate information via tactile and force representations, haptic displays need a close physical coupling to the user. Therefore, ergonomics and safety play a vital role in designing and characterizing these displays. For example, some tactile displays use direct electrical stimulation to stimulate tactile receptors. Therefore, care must be taken not to exceed the amount of current that might cause uncomfortable sensations or injury. Similarly, high-fidelity force displays may exert forces that are unsafe for the participant. Errors in haptic display design may cause discomfort or even injury.

In addition to safety, user comfort and convenience are also important concerns when designing haptic displays. For example, it takes time and effort for the user to attach or put on many haptic devices, especially with multiple force contacts. Designing attachment mechanisms that make this process easy and convenient is important for haptic device acceptance by the end users. Furthermore, once the device is attached to the user, its weight can be burdensome, and the device could restrict the user's ability to move around or to perform anything but the intended haptic tasks. Regardless of the haptic display used, the user's comfort and safety must be a primary concern.

5.4.2 Haptic Display Types

A wide variety of haptic displays have been developed through the years in both research and industrial settings; many of them have evolved from work done in telerobotics and teleoperation (Biggs and Srinivasan 2002). There have also been a number of attempts to classify haptic displays. For example, they are often categorized based on the types of actuators, i.e., the active components of the haptic display that generate the force or tactile sensations (see Hatzfeld and Kern (2014) for a comprehensive introduction to actuator technology).

In this discussion we group haptic displays from a user-centric perspective, placing them into one of six categories:

- ground-referenced
- body-referenced
- tactile
- in-air
- combination
- passive

In this section, we briefly describe some devices that provide examples for these categories.

Ground-Referenced Haptic Devices

Ground-referenced feedback devices (also called world-grounded) create a physical link between the user and a ground point in the environment, such as a desktop, wall, ceiling, or floor. Note that because these devices are fixed to the physical environment, their range is limited. Different types of ground-referenced displays include force-reflecting joysticks, pen-based force-feedback devices, stringed devices, motion platforms, and large articulated robotic arms. Ground-referenced displays typically use electric, pneumatic, or hydraulic actuator technology.

Force-reflecting joysticks as well as force-feedback steering wheels are commonly available, relatively inexpensive, and often used in computer games, such as driving and flight simulators. Pen-based haptic displays add haptic feedback to a familiar pointing device (e.g., a stylus). An example of such a display is shown in Figure 5.24. String-based feedback devices use thin steel cables to apply forces to the user's hand; they are lightweight and can also support a large workspace (Ishii and Sato 1994). On a larger scale, there are large articulated arms that are grounded to the floor or ceiling. They can generate much higher levels of force, which means safety is a much more critical issue. The advantage of these devices is that they can provide a fairly large range of motion for the user. Examples of this type of device are the Argonne Remote Manipulator (Brooks et al. 1990) and the SARCOS Dextrous Arm Master (Burdea 1996): arm exoskeleton force displays that can apply forces to the hand, elbow, and shoulder.

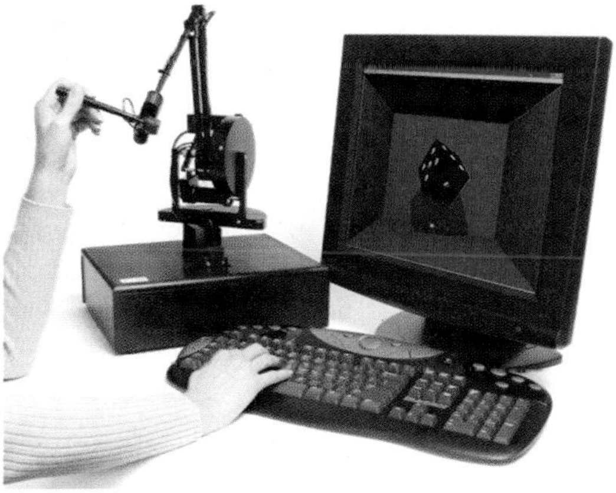

Figure 5.24 A ground-referenced force-feedback device. (Photograph courtesy of SensAble Technologies)

In addition to haptic devices designed to enhance manual control and manipulation, ground-referenced haptic displays also include devices such as treadmills, motion platforms, and other locomotion devices for traveling through 3D environments (see Chapter 8 for more details).

Body-Referenced Haptic Devices

In contrast to ground-referenced haptic displays, body-referenced feedback places the haptic device on some part of the user's body—the haptic display is "grounded" to the user. The main benefit of body-referenced displays is that they provide the user with much more freedom of motion in the surrounding environment than do ground-referenced displays (i.e., the user can walk around and is not constrained to workspaces instrumented with haptic displays). The disadvantage, however, is that the user has to bear the entire weight of the device. Therefore, ergonomic factors such as weight and size are critical in designing usable and effective devices, which is a significant engineering challenge. This type of display typically uses electrical or pneumatic actuator technology.

One promising approach that reduces the weight of body-referenced devices, making it more ergonomic, is to use electrical muscle stimulation to send electrical signals to different muscle groups causing involuntary muscle movements to generate haptic forces (Kruijff et al. 2006). This approach typically uses electrodes, connected to a transcutaneous electrical nerve stimulation (TENS) device, strategically placed on different muscles to invoke movement. For example, placing electrodes on forearm muscles can make a user's hand move up and down with the right amount of stimulation. This type of haptic system has been used in a virtual reality boxing game (Lopes et al. 2015).

Body-referenced displays can be further classified by the body locations that are actuated by the devices. One popular type is the arm-based exoskeleton, which is similar to a ground-referenced arm exoskeleton force display, except that they are grounded to the user's back rather than the floor, ceiling, or wall. The second type of body-referenced display is the hand-force-feedback device. Such devices are grounded to the user's forearm, palm, or back of the hand, depending on the design. These displays typically use cables, tendons, and pulleys to transmit forces to the hand and fingers, with the actuators placed remotely. An example of such a device is shown in Figure 5.25; this device can produce forces that prohibit the user from bending the fingers (e.g., if the user is grasping a virtual ball). An alternative approach to designing hand force-feedback devices involves putting the actuators in the user's palm, which reduces the overall complexity of the devices (Burdea et al. 1992). Full-body mobile exoskeletons have been also demonstrated recently, although their purpose is usually to amplify user mobility and strength rather than provide haptic feedback per se. Regardless of the type of body-referenced haptic displays, because the user wears them, they require setup time to be put on the user and calibrated for specific body size.

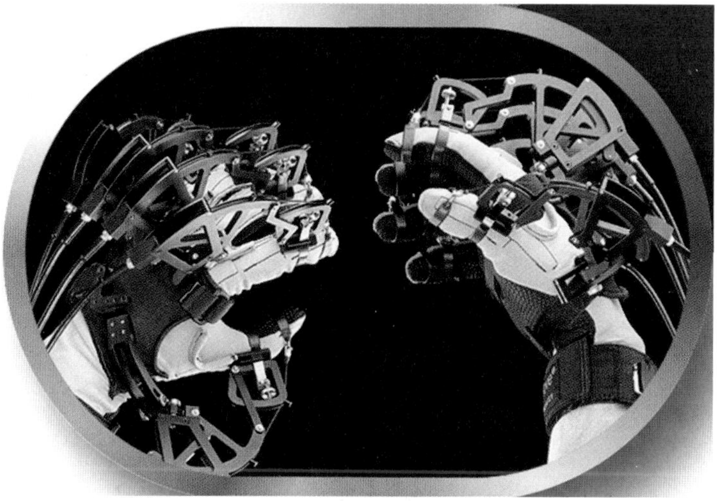

Figure 5.25 A body-referenced force-feedback device. (Photograph reproduced by permission of Immersion Corporation, © 2004 Immersion Corporation. All rights reserved)

Tactile Displays

Tactile displays aim to present haptic information by stimulating the user's tactile sense. Because human skin is highly sensitive, significantly less energy is required to produce strong and recognizable tactile sensations. Therefore, these displays are generally much smaller and more lightweight than the force displays that we discussed above. All tactile displays are based on producing tactile sensations by applying physical stimuli on human skin. Therefore, tactile displays can be categorized by the physical principles of the stimulation. They include mechanical displacement-based displays, vibrotactile displays, electrocutaneous displays, electrovibration displays, surface friction displays, and thermoelectric displays.

Examples of mechanical displacement-based displays include inflatable bladders and relief-style displays, where an array of pins creates a physical shape display or "tactile picture" that can be both observed by the user and felt by the hand (see Figure 5.26; Follmer et al. 2013). Vibrotactile displays (see Figure 5.27) communicate tactile sensations by placing vibrating actuators on the fingertips and hands; the most typical actuator used in vibrotactile displays is a vibrating motor. Vibrotactile displays are commonly used in game controllers and mobile phones. Electrocutaneous displays directly stimulate tactile receptors in human skin with electric charges passing through the skin (Kaczmarek et al. 1991). This sensation is not familiar to the user and feels like tingling. In another type of electrotactile stimulation, a current stimulates the eighth cranial nerve located behind the wearer's ear. These electrical signals provide the user not with a tactile sensation, but with vestibular stimulation, which can create a sensation of motion.

Figure 5.26 InForm is a mechanical displacement display that is able to produce tactile haptic shapes (Follmer et al. 2013). (Photograph courtesy of MIT Media Lab)

Figure 5.27 A tactile device that puts vibrating actuators on the fingertips and the palm of the hand. (Photograph reproduced by permission of Immersion Corporation, © 2004 Immersion Corporation. All rights reserved)

Electrovibration-style tactile displays create tactile sensations by controlling electrostatic friction between instrumented surfaces and sliding fingers (Bau et al. 2010). An alternating voltage applied to the conductive surface produces an attraction force between the finger and the conductive surface. This force modulates friction between the surface and the skin of the moving hand, creating a friction-like sensation as the finger slides on the surface. This friction can be combined with a visual representation, allowing the user to feel the surface of virtual 3D images as demonstrated in Figure 5.28 (Kim et al. 2013). Note that any surface can be augmented with such tactile sensations, including surfaces of everyday objects, input devices, and physical props (Bau et al. 2012).

Surface friction tactile displays are similar to electrovibration displays in that they control friction between the human hand and a surface, but the tactile effect is based on vibrating a surface at ultrasonic frequency and creating a squeeze film of air between the human hand and the touch surface. The thin layer of air reduces the friction between the hand and display, making it more "slippery" (Winfield et al. 2007). The friction can further be manipulated by modulating the amplitude of the ultrasound vibration. Finally, thermoelectric displays produce the sensation of heat and are usually developed using various thermoelectric devices, such as Peltier modules (Jones 2008).

All the technologies that we discussed above allow for design of actuation technologies and control techniques needed to produce tactile sensations. The higher-level goal of designing tactile displays is the construction of high-order tactile percepts that can communicate complex meanings, expressions, and experiences to the user. This second category includes tactile languages to communicate symbolic information, display images and sounds, communicate alerts and messages, and present spatial information such as directions and shapes (Israr and Poupyrev 2011).

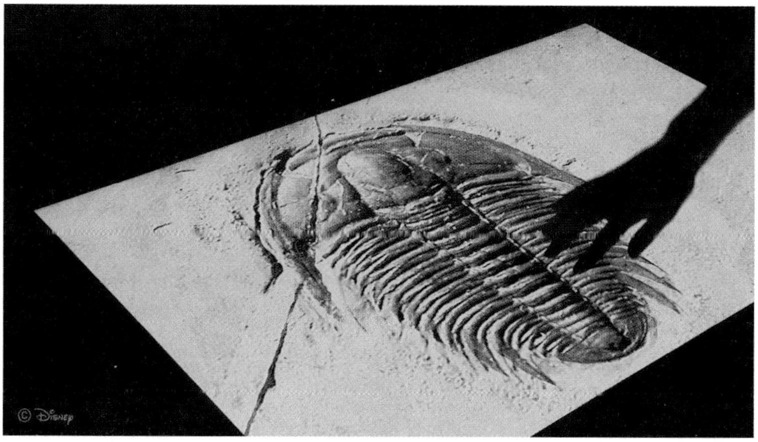

Figure 5.28 Electrovibration displays allow the user to feel the bumps and ridges on the 3D rendering projected on the surface of the display (Kim et al. 2013). (Photograph courtesy of Ivan Poupyrev, copyright Disney, printed with permission)

In-Air Haptics

With all the haptic and tactile feedback technologies discussed so far in this chapter, in order to feel virtual objects, users have to have direct physical contact with the haptic apparatus, either by touching some physical objects equipped with haptic devices or wearing tactile feedback devices in the form of haptic gloves, belts, vests, etc. Requiring users to wear physical devices significantly impedes natural user interaction and may limit the overall range of applications that employ tactile feedback. Consequently, a more recent approach in haptic displays are haptic devices that create tactile sensations in "mid-air" without the need for direct physical contact with the haptic apparatus. Most of the devices for creating in-air tactile sensations are based on using air to stimulate human skin.

The earliest approach to creating in-air tactile sensations was introduced in Sensorama, invented by cinematographer Morton Heilig in the 1960s. Sensorama combined stereoscopic graphics with smell, stereo sound, a vibrating seat, and wind blowing into the user's face to increase the sense of immersion. Similar air-blowing techniques have also been used for decades in location-based entertainment (e.g., Walt Disney World's "Soarin'" attraction, which simulates flying in a glider). Similarly, coarse-grained heat sensations can be created using heat lamps as displays (Dinh et al. 1999).

In ultrasound-based in-air haptics displays (Iwamoto et al. 2008), a two-dimensional array of hundreds of miniature ultrasonic transducers forms a beam of ultrasonic radiation pressure using a phased array focusing approach (Wilson et al. 2014). Because of the low ultrasound frequency, 99.9% of the incident acoustic energy will reflect from the human skin, creating a pressure field that provides perceivable tactile sensations. By modulating the ultrasound beam at approximately 200 Hz, the perceived intensity of tactile sensations increases due to the high sensitivity of skin to vibratory stimuli at this frequency. However, the disadvantage of this approach is the short effective distance of such displays.

An alternative approach to creating in-air tactile sensations using concentrated air pressure fields is based on using air vortices (Kruijff and Pander 2005). Here, the tactile sensations are produced by a pressure differential inside of an air vortex (Sodhi et al. 2013), providing effective tactile sensations over relatively large distances (over one meter in length). Also, this approach allows for an efficient, relatively inexpensive, and scalable design of in-air haptic devices. In one implementation, standard miniature speakers driven synchronously can consistently create a vortex that can be further directed by using a flexible nozzle (see Figure 5.29).

In-air tactile sensations are not currently able to provide the highly detailed and responsive tactile sensations that are possible with electromechanical devices. However, they offer new interactive modalities when designing 3D UIs in both desktop and room-scale settings.

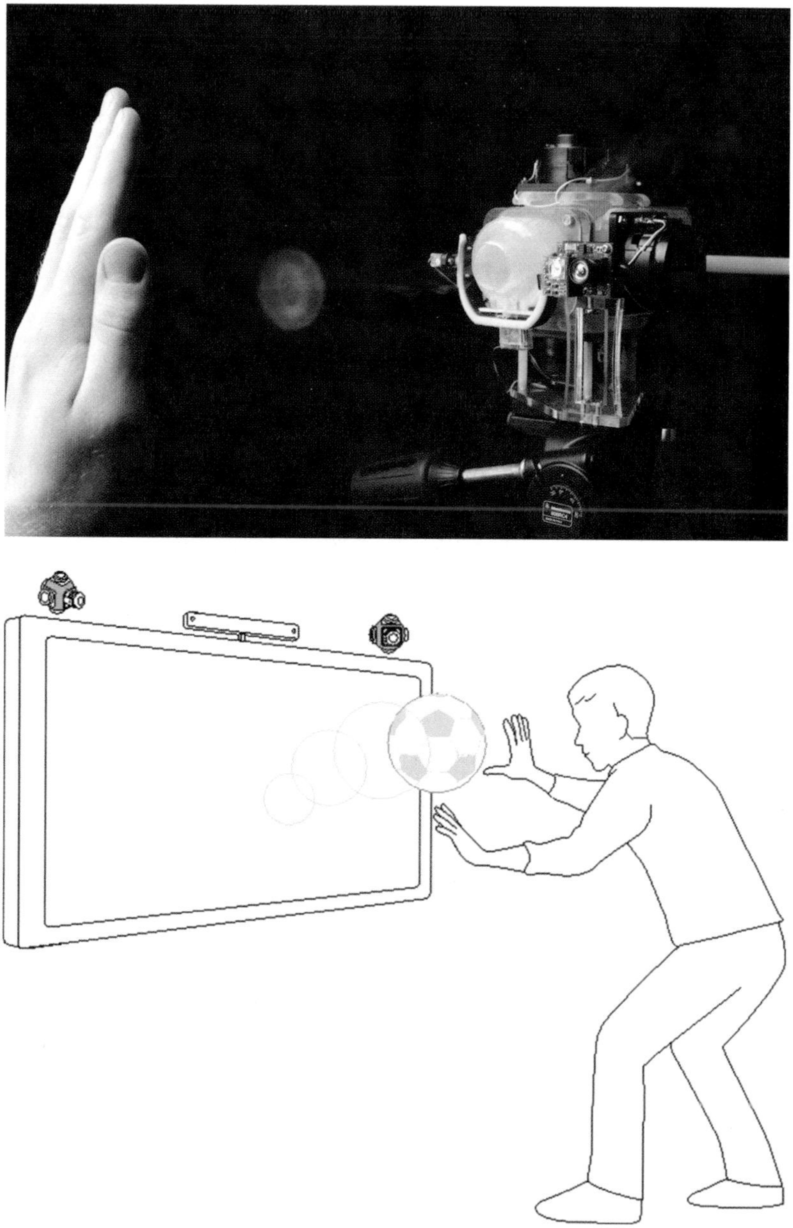

Figure 5.29 Vortex-based in-air tactile display (Sodhi et al. 2013). (Photographs courtesy of Ivan Poupyrev, copyright Disney, printed with permission)

Combination Devices

Because of the complexities of simulating force and touch sensations, most haptic and tactile devices focus on producing feedback within one of the four haptic display categories above. However, combining different types of feedback can create more believable and recognizable haptic sensations. Figure 5.30 is an example of such a device that combines ground-referenced and body-referenced feedback styles. Another example of a combination display uses a body-referenced hand-force device coupled with tactile feedback for the user's fingertips (Kramer 1993).

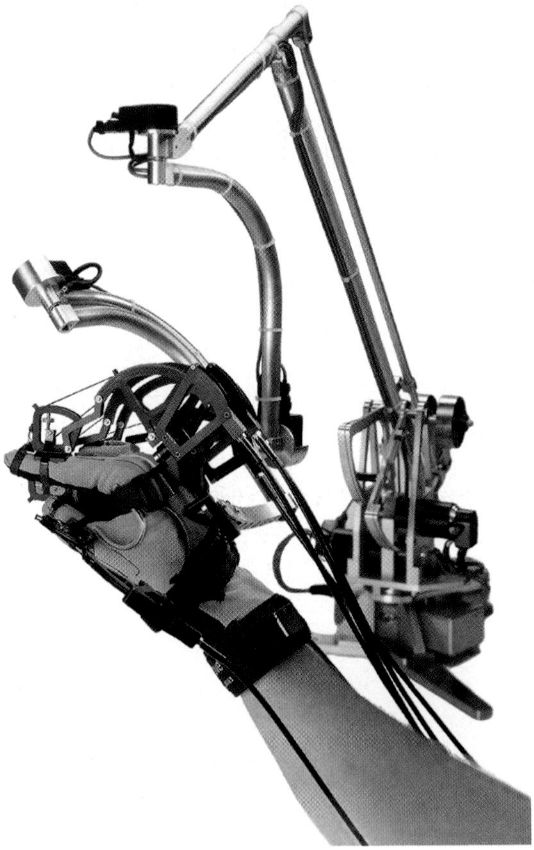

Figure 5.30 A haptic device that combines ground-referenced and body-referenced force feedback. (Photograph reproduced by permission of Immersion Corporation, © 2004 Immersion Corporation. All rights reserved)

Passive Haptics

The haptic devices we have seen thus far have all been active devices that generate forces or tactile sensations using some type of actuator technology controlled with haptic rendering techniques. Another class of haptic interfaces are those that are based on using passive physical representations of virtual objects to communicate their physical qualities. Their unique characteristic is that they convey a constant force or tactile sensation based on the geometry and texture of the particular object. For example, a real cup or hammer can be used to provide a fully realistic haptic sensation when the virtual world contains a virtual cup or hammer. Passive haptic devices are not necessarily restricted to handheld objects and can include tabletops, walls, and the floor, as well as providing basic input capabilities, e.g., touch input and position tracking (Poupyrev, Tomokazu et al. 1998).

Passive haptic devices (or "props") are very specific in that they are solid physical objects that directly mimic the virtual objects that they are used to represent. Not surprisingly, they have been shown to be effective in improving the perceived realism of VEs (Insko 2001). Of course, their underlying limitation is their specificity and the need for exact registration between virtual objects and their passive representations. Refer to Chapter 9, "System Control," section 9.4, and Chapter 10, "Strategies in Designing and Developing 3D User Interfaces," section 10.2.1, for a thorough discussion of passive haptic devices used in 3D UIs.

5.4.3 Haptic Displays in 3D Interfaces

The ability to present haptic feedback to the user in a 3D UI is a powerful tool in developing more effective, efficient, and immersive experiences. In particular, from an immersive standpoint, haptic displays can help to improve the realism of a 3D UI (Biggs and Srinivasan 2002), which is particularly important in applications such as entertainment and gaming. Of course, realistically simulating the haptic cues of real-world objects is currently difficult to do—"getting it right" is quite challenging, and a poorly designed haptic display can in fact hinder the immersive experience. Even worse, strong forces from a haptic display can be dangerous, potentially harming the user.

From a 3D UI perspective, one natural use of haptic feedback is to provide feedback when grabbing and manipulating virtual objects using direct manipulation. Ground-referenced devices like the one shown in Figure 5.24 have been used in surgical training (Körner and Männer 2003), molecular docking (Brooks et al. 1990), and 3D modeling and painting applications (Foskey et al. 2002). Tactile feedback can be used to simulate the texture of physical surfaces (e.g., a designer might want to explore the surface textures of different objects in an industrial design application), as shown in Figure 5.28. In another example, a tactile display could be used to help a firefighter determine a doorknob's temperature in the context of a training simulation. Haptic feedback can also be used to signal the user that an interaction task has been invoked or completed, successfully or not. Finally, passive haptic devices can also be used in 3D interfaces as props that provide weight and texture and represent an inexpensive way to display haptic cues to the user.

5.5 Characterizing Displays by Level of Fidelity

Choosing a specific display for a 3D UI can be overwhelming, given the number of different displays and configurations available. In the sections above we have described various characteristics of visual, auditory, and haptic displays as a way to think about them more abstractly and systematically. Thinking about characteristics like FOV, stereoscopy, resolution, and overall quality, we can see that all of these characteristics are related to the realism, or *fidelity*, of the display.

To be more precise, a display's level of fidelity is the degree to which the sensory stimuli produced by a display correspond to those that would be present in the real world (Bowman and McMahan, 2007; McMahan et al. 2012). For example, in a real-world environment, a typical human would be able to see the world all around her (360-degree FOR), would have a more than 180-degree horizontal FOV, would perceive a spatial resolution limited only by the receptors on the retina, and would have stereoscopic vision with no crosstalk and a perfect accommodation-vergence match. Auditory and haptic stimuli would be similarly perfect. In a typical HWD, however, while the 360-degree FOR would still be present, the FOV would be much lower (perhaps 100 degrees), the spatial resolution would be significantly less, and stereoscopic vision would be compromised by an accommodation-vergence mismatch.

Why do we care about a display's fidelity? First, much of the research on displays is aimed at ever-increasing realism. Display manufacturers and their customers want higher and higher resolutions (witness the current trend of "retina" displays in which individual pixels are said to be undetectable at normal viewing distances), wider and taller FOVs, better stereo and other depth cues, more lifelike color reproduction, and so on. Talking about a display's fidelity allows us to benchmark it with respect to the real world and to compare it to other displays in a standard way.

Second, a display's fidelity can have significant effects on the user's experience with the display. For example, a wider FOV may lead to faster performance on a visual search task (Arthur 2000), and higher overall fidelity may result in a greater sense of engagement (McMahan et al. 2012). Again, thinking about these findings in terms of fidelity is more general and more useful than a comparison of specific displays.

It should be clear from this discussion that display fidelity is not a single thing or a number that captures everything about the sensory realism of a display. Rather, it's made up of a number of components, each of which has its own level. A nonexhaustive list of *visual* display fidelity components includes:

- field of regard (FOR)
- field of view (FOV)
- stereoscopy quality

- refresh rate
- spatial resolution
- color reproduction quality
- display latency

Similar lists apply to auditory and haptic displays, although it's more difficult to nail down all of their components. Auditory display fidelity would include components related to auditory quality, spatiality, and latency, while haptic display fidelity components would include latency, resolution, and other haptic quality aspects.

Sometimes we can state outright that display A has higher fidelity than another display B. For this to be true, all display fidelity components of A would need to be at a level greater than or equal to the respective components of B. Another way of saying this is that it would be possible to simulate display B perfectly using display A (Slater et al. 2010). For example, a four-screen surround-screen display has higher fidelity than a single-screen display using one of the screens/projectors from the surround-screen display.

More often, however, the comparison of fidelity levels between two displays is more mixed, with one display having higher levels of certain components of fidelity and the other having higher levels for other components. For example, a HWD can provide a 360-degree FOR, while a three-screen surround-screen display has an FOR of only 270 degrees. However, the surround-screen display might provide a 120-degree FOV (with stereo glasses on), while the HWD might provide only 90 degrees. In a case like this, to decide which display is most appropriate for a given user task, it would be important to look at empirical results on the effects of FOR and FOV for that task to determine which one is most important to optimize.

For further reading on display fidelity and its effects on 3D UI user experience, see Bowman and McMahan (2007), McMahan et al. (2012), and Ragan et al. (2013, 2015).

5.6 Design Guidelines: Choosing Output Devices for 3D User Interfaces

Choosing the appropriate output devices for a 3D application is a difficult task, and unfortunately there is no single rule of thumb telling developers which output devices to use.

Tables 5.1–5.3 present summaries of the advantages and disadvantages of the output devices we have discussed in this chapter; these can be used as a quick and general guide for starting the process of choosing an appropriate output device for a 3D UI. Note that new and more powerful display devices are becoming available all the time, so these guidelines should be considered general rules of thumb, as there can always be exceptions to these pros and cons.

Table 5.1 Visual display devices: pros and cons, visual depth cues supported.

Visual Display Types	Pros and Cons	Visual Depth Cues Supported
Single-screen displays (e.g., monitors, wTVs, projection screens, tablets)	+ Relatively inexpensive + High spatial resolution + Can use virtually any input device – Small FOR/FOV – No peripheral vision – Not very immersive – Physical/virtual object occlusion problem	• Monocular • Stereopsis if using stereo-capable display • Limited motion parallax when tracked because of limited mobility • Vergence if using stereo • Accommodation only in plane of display
Surround-screen displays, planar geometry (e.g., CAVE-like displays)	+ Large FOV/FOR when display is large + Makes use of peripheral vision + Real and virtual objects easily mixed in 3D application – Requires large amount of physical space – Can be expensive – Typically limited to one active tracked viewer; limited to six tracked viewers in stereo with special equipment – Physical/virtual object occlusion problem	• Monocular • Stereopsis • Full motion parallax when tracked with large display but limited with smaller displays • Vergence if using stereo • Accommodation only in plane of display
Surround-screen displays, nonplanar geometry (e.g., hemispherical, cylindrical displays)	+ Often uses front projection for brighter images + Large FOR/FOV when display is large – Spatial resolution not always uniform across display surface – Front projection makes direct manipulation difficult – Typically limited to one active tracked viewer; limited to six tracked viewers in stereo with special equipment – Physical/virtual object occlusion problem	• Monocular • Stereopsis • Full motion parallax when tracked with large display but limited with smaller displays • Vergence if using stereo • Accommodation only in plane of display

Visual Display Types	Pros and Cons	Visual Depth Cues Supported
Workbenches and tabletop displays	+ Good spatial resolution + Devices can be tilted to mimic desks and easels + Some devices permit 2D input on display surface, such as stylus and multitouch – No peripheral vision – Typically limited to one active tracked viewer; limited to six tracked viewers in stereo with special equipment – Physical/virtual object occlusion problem	• Monocular • Stereopsis • Limited motion parallax when tracked because of limited mobility • Vergence if using stereo • Accommodation only in plane of display
Head-worn displays, traditional VR (non-see-through)	+ 360-degree FOR + Portable + No physical/virtual object occlusion problems + Inexpensive + Good spatial resolution + Unlimited tracked number of users in stereo (one display per user) – Medium FOV compared to surround-screen displays – Have to wear the device – Limited peripheral vision – Weight and cables cause ergonomic issues – Unable to see other users or the real world directly	• Monocular • Stereopsis if using stereo-capable HWD • Full motion parallax when tracked • Vergence if using stereo • Accommodation possible in research prototypes
Head-worn displays, traditional AR (optical- or video-see-through)	+ 360-degree FOR + Portable + Inexpensive + Good spatial resolution + Unlimited tracked number of users in stereo (one display per user) – Physical/virtual object occlusion problems unless combined with scene mapping – Small FOV compared with traditional VR HWDs – Have to wear the device – Limited peripheral vision – Weight and cables cause ergonomic issues	• Monocular • Stereopsis if using stereo-capable HWD • Full motion parallax when tracked • Vergence if using stereo • Accommodation only for real world with optical see-through HWD

Visual Display Types	Pros and Cons	Visual Depth Cues Supported
Head-worn displays, virtual retinal displays	+ Bright, high-resolution images + Potential to have FOV matching human visual system + 360-degree FOR – Needs eye tracking – Little work done with 3D UIs	• Monocular • Stereopsis if using stereo-capable VRD • Full motion parallax when tracked • Vergence if using stereo • Accommodation possible in research prototypes
Arbitrary surface displays	+ Use any object or surface to present visual information + Good spatial resolution + Can create simulated true 3D imagery + FOV and FOR can be large, depending on projection area – Color correction needed to ensure a correct image – Physical/virtual object occlusion problem – 3D UI can be limited due to front projection	• Monocular • Stereopsis • Full motion parallax when tracked • Vergence if using stereo • Accommodation possible
Autostereoscopic displays (lenticular and parallax barrier)	+ No glasses required to see stereo + High spatial resolution – Limited sweet spot – Limited FOV and FOR – Physical/virtual object occlusion problem	• Monocular • Stereopsis • Limited motion parallax when tracked • Vergence • No accommodation
Autostereoscopic displays (volumetric and holographic)	+ Produce true 3D imagery + Unlimited active viewers (all will see correct perspective) + No accommodation–vergence cue conflicts + No trackers needed – Limited FOV, FOR, and display area – Occlusion difficult with holographic displays – Little work done with 3D UIs	• Monocular (only with some devices) • Stereopsis • Motion parallax • Vergence • Accommodation

Table 5.2 Pros and cons of using headphones or external speakers in a 3D sound display.

Auditory Display Types	Pros and Cons
Headphones	+ High level of channel separation + Isolate users from external sounds + Multiple users can hear 3D sound (provided they are tracked) – Inside-the-head localization – Uncomfortable to wear for extended periods of time
External speakers	+ User does not need to wear any additional devices – 3D sound generation more difficult – Need to worry about crosstalk

Table 5.3 Pros and cons of different haptic display device types.

Haptic Display Types	Pros and Cons
Ground-referenced	+ Can produce high levels of force if needed + Don't have to wear them + Accurate trackers – Limited movement when using them – Safety concerns
Body-referenced	+ More freedom of motion than ground-referenced + Provide more control with direct manipulation of virtual objects – User has to bear weight of device – Can be burdensome to put on
Tactile	+ Smaller and more lightweight when compared to force displays + Useful for simulating touch + Can produce vestibular sensations – Difficult to get sensations correct – Often stimulate only a small area of skin
In-Air	+ Do not have to wear a device + Sensations can be located anywhere – Does not provide precise force or tactile information – Limited range
Combination	+ Useful for combining tactile and force feedback – More complex – Can be burdensome to wear

Haptic Display Types	Pros and Cons
Passive	+ Useful when haptics is required for a specific object or physical proxy + Easy to design and use + Increases sense of realism – Constant force and tactile sensations – Limited by specificity

Although there are many factors to consider when choosing output devices, such as finances, restrictions from available input devices, and ergonomics, the most important consideration is the application itself.

> **Tip**
>
> Analyze the application's goals and its underlying operations and tasks to obtain direction in choosing an appropriate output device.

As an example, consider a medical visualization tool that allows doctors to teach medical students about various surgical procedures. Because of the collaborative nature of this application, a single HWD or simple monitor would probably not be appropriate, since several people need to see the display simultaneously. In this case, using a large-screen display or having each person wear their own HWD is probably the better choice. In contrast, an application used in phobia treatment (Hodges et al. 1999) or to reduce pain (Hoffman et al. 2008) requires an individual user to be completely immersed in the environment with the real-world blocked out. Clearly, an HWD or six-sided surround-screen display is the best choice for this application. As a final example, a holographic or volumetric display might be the best choice for an exhibit in a museum, because users do not need to wear any special glasses for the 3D stereo effect and because an unlimited number of viewers can get correct views simultaneously.

Choosing an audio display is a somewhat easier task, because it often enhances an application's effectiveness. Of course, choosing the appropriate audio configuration, whether it is headphone-based or a multiple speaker system, still depends on the type of application and on the other devices used.

With haptics, the display choice often depends on the type and accuracy of the feedback required. In some applications, a tactile sensation is enough to give the user a sense that there is something tangible about the objects they see and interact with. However, if the application requires a real force, such as a molecular docking application (Brooks et al. 1990) in which users try to fit different molecules together, a ground-referenced force-feedback device is more appropriate.

The examples presented thus far are more about common sense than any scientific discovery. However, another approach to determining the most appropriate display device for a given application is through empirical study. Bowman et al. (2002) developed guidelines for choosing appropriate display devices by examining interaction techniques across different display platforms. For example, they compared users' preferences for real and virtual turns during navigation in an HWD and a four-sided surround-screen display. The results showed that users had a preference for real turns in the HWD and for virtual turns in the surround-screen display because of its limited FOR.

Tip

Visual display devices with a 360-degree FOR should be used in applications in which users perform frequent turns and require spatial orientation.

In another set of empirical studies, Swan and colleagues compared a monitor, surround-screen display, workbench, and a large wall display for the task of navigating in a battlefield visualization application. For this particular application, the results showed that users were faster at performing the navigation tasks on the desktop than with the other display devices, perhaps because of the higher spatial resolution and brightness achievable on a conventional monitor. For more details on the study, see Swan et al. (2003).

Kasik et al. (2002) also performed empirical evaluations on different visual display devices. They compared a high-resolution 20-inch monitor, a hemispherical display, and a large 50-inch flat screen panel by testing how quickly and accurately users found objects of interest in sophisticated 3D models. Users performed better with the monitor than with the flat panel or the hemispherical display, indicating that higher spatial resolution was an important factor in their search tasks. Other evidence from subjective studies (Demiralp et al. 2006) indicates that higher spatial resolution and crispness is important to users in scientific visualization. Other studies that have compared different display devices empirically include Johnsen and Lok (2008), Qi et al. (2006), Schulze et al. (2005), and Sousa Santos et al. (2009).

Tip

For visual search and pattern identification tasks in 3D environments, choose a display with high spatial resolution.

Although these empirical studies are quite powerful, their results should be used with caution because these studies are often designed for specific tasks and applications, making them difficult to generalize. In addition, as technologies continue to improve, results from older studies need to be reevaluated. Nevertheless, the development of guidelines based on empirical results should continue to be an important area of 3D UI research and will help to make it easier to determine the best display devices for given applications.

5.7 Case Studies

The following sections discuss the output device considerations for our two case studies. If you are not reading the book sequentially, you may want to read the introduction to the two case studies in Chapter 2, section 2.4.

5.7.1 VR Gaming Case Study

For our VR first-person action-adventure game, there are two obvious visual display types to consider: HWDs and surround-screen displays. We want users to be able to turn around physically to view different parts of the world around them, because that enhances the sense of presence and makes the environment seem more like a real physical place. So single screens are not an option.

HWDs have the advantages of being relatively inexpensive, easy to obtain and set up, usable in any sort of physical space, and good for inspection of and interaction with nearby objects. The advantages of surround-screen displays are their lighter headgear (simple stereo glasses) and the ability for the player to see her own body in the space. For a VR game targeted at home use, cost and convenience trump all, so HWDs are the clear choice. We might consider a surround-screen display, however, if the game was set up in a dedicated space like a VR arcade. For the remainder of the case study, we'll assume the use of a typical consumer HWD.

In choosing an HWD, several issues arise that we'll have to handle. First, ergonomics becomes a concern. HWDs can still be bulky, heavy, and uncomfortable. We will want to choose a display that is as light and comfortable as possible. The HWD should also have a comfortable accommodation distance and allow for adjustment of the distance between the optics/displays (interocular distance) to avoid eyestrain and provide for correct stereo viewing.

Since the player will not be able to see the real-world directly, we should also address safety. Preferably, the HWD can be used wirelessly or with an all-in-one backpack system, so that players won't become tangled in cables or have a tripping hazard. We also want the real world to "bleed through" when the user is in danger of running into a real-world object. A system like the HTC Vive's chaperone feature can display the boundaries of the physical space (walls) when the user approaches or reaches out close to them. It's also possible to use a depth camera to detect other obstacles in the play area, such as furniture or people/pets walking through the room (Nahon et al. 2015).

The fidelity of the display is moderately important for a game of this type. The virtual world will not be intended to look just like a real-world environment, so it's possible for the game to be effective even without the highest levels of fidelity. At the same time, we do want players to feel present in the game world, so it's important to have a reasonable FOV (100 degrees horizontal, which is currently the standard for many consumer HWDs, should be fine) and to provide a good spatial resolution.

So far, we've only discussed a single player, which is ideal for an HWD. But in most games, even if they're not explicitly multiplayer, it's desirable to allow nonplayers to watch the action in real time. This could be accomplished with support for multiple HWDs, but nonplayers with HWDs might just get in the way, and this solution is not scalable to a larger audience (most people won't have ten HWDs sitting around). A better solution is a green screen compositing solution, where a video camera captures the player in front of a green screen and then composites this with a view of the virtual world, so that viewers can see the player immersed in the game world from a third-person point of view. This approach was popularized by the game *Fantastic Contraption* (Figure 5.31) and works great for both in-person viewers and posting or streaming of gameplay videos online.

Figure 5.31 Mixed reality compositing in *Fantastic Contraption*, allowing viewers to see both the player and the virtual world she inhabits. (Photograph courtesy of Northway Games)

Finally, we need to consider nonvisual displays. For this game, spatial sound will certainly add to the realism and experience of the game (e.g., hearing monsters sneak up behind you), so we'll want to ensure that the player has a good pair of headphones. Using physical props to provide haptic feedback is not really an option, since the same physical space will be used for a variety of virtual rooms. We can provide some level of haptic feedback through the handheld controllers—both the passive feedback created by holding the controllers themselves and the rumble/vibration feedback they can produce.

Key Concepts

- Choose a visual display that will be both effective and practical for your end users.
- Carefully consider human factors issues related to VR displays.
- Don't forget to account for social aspects such as non-users viewing the VR experience.

5.7.2 Mobile AR Case Study

While creating the HYDROSYS outdoor AR application, we had to design a suitable platform to meet various physical and technical requirements. The devices used for analysis of environmental processes not only had to withstand outdoor environments, but they also had to be comfortable to hold and make clear visibility of content possible. Moreover, the device setup had to enable high tracking accuracy and real-time rendering of the augmented content. Providing an accurate platform turned out to be a true challenge. In this section we unravel the various issues and derive useful recommendations.

The type and specifications of the visual display itself was not a primary concern for this application. We needed a low-cost AR display that could be tracked outdoors and used by multiple users in harsh conditions. A handheld, video-see-through AR display was really the only reasonable choice. More difficult, however, were the physical requirements of the entire platform, including issues of form factor, sensor integration, and ruggedness.

Let us first go into the physical requirements of the platform. The platform had to be **robust** to withstand the harsh external conditions, as the platform would be used in low temperatures, snow, and rain—not something most electronic devices will withstand. While interacting, the device needed to be comfortable to hold to enable **ergonomic** usage of the system over potentially long periods of time. Users would often perform analyses for half an hour or more, and sore arm muscles would not be acceptable! Even more so, the setup had to be **compact** so as to be transported, for example tucked away in a small backpack. Finally, the setup had to be **modular** such that users could adjust the setup based on the usage conditions.

Now, you may ask yourself why a waterproof smartphone could not have been used, as it would have met many of the requirements. Unfortunately, the built-in quality of smartphone sensors at the time was not good enough to provide adequate tracking, for which reason external sensors such as a high-quality GPS sensor, a good camera, and a precision inertial sensor for rotation measurement had to be used. While this situation has changed somewhat, there are still cases in which developers will prefer to use these higher-quality sensors.

We based the design of a suitable platform on prior experiences with another handheld AR platform used for visualization of an underground infrastructure (Schall et al. 2009). The usage environment was less harsh than for HYDROSYS, yet many of the same requirements applied. This prior platform, called Vesp'r (Figure 5.32), consisted of a central unit that held a Sony UMPC mobile computer and the sensors, as well as all the needed cabling. Sensors included a high-quality camera, a high-precision GPS, and an inertial measurement unit. The device afforded both single- and two-handed usage by mounting either one grip below or two grips at the sides of the setup. The grips enabled a power grip (see section 3.5.1), important for holding the slightly heavier setup firmly. (Note an inappropriate grip would limit ergonomic usage.) This was especially important when the device had to be held at eye height, a pose that eases the

Figure 5.32 Vesp'r handheld AR device setup. (Image courtesy of Ernst Kruijff and Eduardo Veas).

match between augmented content and the real world, yet normally is quite tiring. While the single-handed setup was slightly less comfortable to hold, it did enable interaction with the screen directly. With the two handles mounted at the sides, the interaction was performed through controllers embedded in the handles. We elaborate further on the input structure in the next chapter.

Through various studies we found that the shape and balance of the setup, as well as controller allocation, can greatly help in supporting ergonomic usage. Very interestingly, a heavier device is not necessarily a worse device; a heavier but well-balanced and ergonomically formed device may outperform an ill-designed lighter platform (Veas and Kruijff 2008). Support for specific body poses extended the duration for ergonomic usage. We noticed users would often rest their elbows against their waists when using the device two-handed, which would stabilize the grip and distribute the weight better. Based on this, we chose the angle at which the display was mounted on the support structure so that users could clearly observe screen content from multiple poses. A different screen angle could lead to uncomfortable poses, as outdoor lighting and reflection limit the angle at which screen content is visible.

In HYDROSYS, we targeted a robust setup that could withstand even rougher conditions. We used a weather-resistant tablet and a MIL-standard Panasonic UMPC that was heavier than the Sony UMPC used for the Vesp'r yet had an outdoor-visible screen and a strong battery. The latter was very useful for driving the additional sensors over time while reducing the need for an additional battery pack. Similar to Vesp'r, we used a high-precision GPS, inertial sensors, and a high-quality camera.

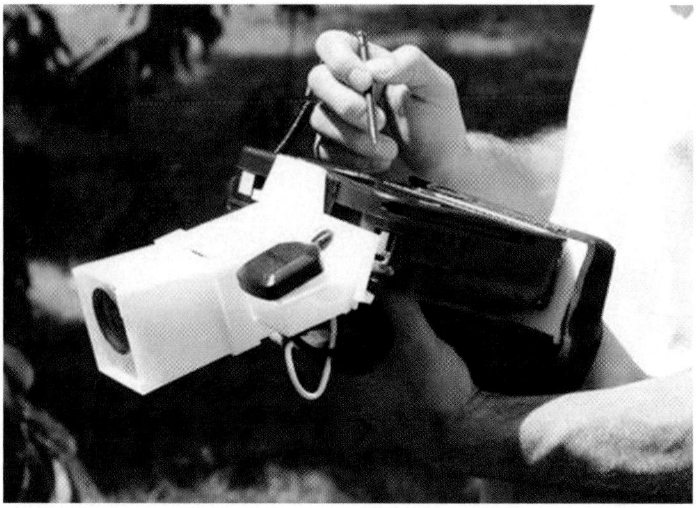

Figure 5.33 HYDROSYS handheld AR device setup. (Image courtesy of Ernst Kruijff and Eduardo Veas)

Figure 5.33 shows the final setup achieved after three iterations. The setup contained an x-like mount behind the UMPC that was made out of a composite of 3D-printed plastic and aluminum. To the mount we connected a neoprene (a light but robust material) hull that could be compressed to limit the space cables and sensor control boxes would take up. The neoprene construction could be held comfortably by one hand. To the plastic frame, various 3D-printed units could be mounted to hold the preferred sensors. While the previous iterations also included a tripod mount, the final prototype included a camera belt connected to the setup to relieve the user of some of the weight, important when holding the device single-handed while controlling the application. The final prototype was a good balance between robustness, ergonomics, modularity, and compactness. For more details, see Veas and Kruijff (2010). We also revisit ergonomic considerations in Chapter 11, "Evaluation of 3D Interfaces."

Key Concepts

While the development of the described prototype at first blush seems limited to the described domain, many of the lessons learned actually apply to a wide range of handheld AR setups.

- Support a comfortable power grip to hold the system firmly, especially when the user is required to hold the device at eye height.
- Allow users to vary their poses, and look into the potential of resting the arms against the body to extend usage duration.
- Closely analyze the relationship between display angle and pose, as changing pose to see content clearly may result in nonergonomic usage.

- Look closely at the balance of the setup—if the device tips in the wrong direction, even a good pose or grip may not be sufficient to hold the system for long. Balance may be more important than overall weight.
- Try to limit the need for additional batteries for operation and compress additional cables, as they tend to take up a lot of space.

5.8 Conclusion

In this chapter, we have examined a variety of different output devices including different types of visual displays, auditory displays, and haptic and tactile feedback devices. We have also examined some strategies for choosing an appropriate output device and discussed the effects of display fidelity. However, output devices are not the only important hardware components used in 3D UIs. Input devices, the devices used to perform actions and tasks within the applications, are equally important. The choice of input device can affect the choice of output device, and vice versa. In the next chapter, we continue our examination of hardware used in 3D UIs by exploring the many different input device varieties and how they affect 3D UI design.

Recommended Reading

For thorough expositions on computer graphics rendering, we recommend the following:

Akenine-Möller, T., E. Haines, and N. Hoffman (2008). *Real-Time Rendering*, 3rd ed. Wellesley, MA: AK Peters.

Angel, E. and D. Shreiner (2011). *Interactive Computer Graphics: A Top-Down Approach with Shader-Based OpenGL*, 6th ed. Boston: Addison-Wesley.

Hughes, J., A. van Dam, M. McGuire, D. Sklar, J. Foley, S. Feiner, and K. Akeley (2013). *Computer Graphics: Principles and Practice*, 3rd ed., Upper Saddle River, NJ: Addison-Wesley Professional.

A thorough discussion of the design of head-worn displays can be found in the following:

Melzer, J., and K. Moffitt (2011). *Head-Mounted Displays: Designing for the User.* Create Space Independent Publishing Platform. New York: McGraw-Hill.

Details on autostereoscopic techniques and true 3D displays can be found in the following:

Blundell, B. G. (2012). "Volumetric 3D Displays." In J. Chen, W. Cranton, and M. Fihn (eds.), *Handbook of Visual Display Technology,* 1917–1931. Berlin: Springer.

Holliman, N., N. Dodgson, G. Favalora, and L. Pockett (2011). "Three-Dimensional Displays: A Review and Applications Analysis." *IEEE Transactions on Broadcasting* 57(2): 362–371.

Wetzstein, G., D. Lanman, M. Hirsch, W. Heidrich, and R. Raskar (2012). "Compressive Light Field Displays." *IEEE Computer Graphics and Applications* 32(5): 6–11.

Comprehensive introductions to 3D spatialized audio displays can be found in the following:

Begault, D. R. (1994). *3D Sound for Virtual Reality and Multimedia.* Boston: Academic Press.

Blauert, J. (1997). *Spatial Hearing: The Psychoacoustics of Human Sound Localization.* Cambridge, MA: MIT Press.

Kapralos, B., M. Jenkin, and E. Milios (2003). "Auditory Perception and Virtual Environments" Dept. of Computer Science, York University, CS-2003-07.

Vorländer, M. and B. Shinn-Cunningham (2015). "Virtual Auditory Displays." In K. Hale and K. Stanney (eds.), *Handbook of Virtual Environments: Design, Implementation, and Applications*, 2nd ed., 87–114., Boca Raton, FL: CRC Press.

Xie, B. (2013). *Head-Related Transfer Function and Virtual Auditory Display.* Plantation, FL: J. Ross Publishing.

Information on 3D spatialized sound rendering can be found in the following:

Manocha, D., P. Calamia, M. Lin, L. Savioja, and N. Tsingos (2009). "Interactive Sound Rendering." *ACM SIGGRAPH 2009 Courses* (SIGGRAPH '09). ACM, New York, NY, USA, Article 15, 338 pages.

Vorländer, M. (2007). *Auralization: Fundamentals of Acoustics, Modelling, Simulation, Algorithms and Acoustic Virtual Reality.* Berlin: Springer.

Details of haptic display device technology and haptic cues can be found in the following:

Biggs, S. J. and M. A. Srinivasan (2002). "Haptic Interfaces." In K. Stanney (ed.), *Handbook of Virtual Environments*, 93–115. Mahwah, NJ: Lawrence Erlbaum Associates.

Burdea, G. (1994). *Force and Touch Feedback for Virtual Reality.* New York: Wiley Interscience.

Hatzfeld, C. and T. A. Kern (2014). *Engineering Haptic Devices: A Beginner's Guide*, 2nd ed. Berlin: Springer-Verlag.

Information on haptic and tactile rendering algorithms can be found in the following:

Basdogan, C. and M. A. Srinivasan (2002). "Haptic Rendering in Virtual Environments." In K. Stanney (ed.), *Handbook of Virtual Environments: Design, Implementation, and Applications,* 117–134. Mahwah, NJ: Lawrence Erlbaum Associates.

Lin, M. C. and M. Otaduy (2008). *Haptic Rendering: Foundations, Algorithms and Applications. Wellesley*, MA: AK Peters, Ltd.

Finally, two interesting papers that exemplify the nuances of empirical studies for display device evaluation are these:

Pausch, R., D. Proffitt, and G. Williams (1997). "Quantifying Immersion in Virtual Reality." *Proceedings of SIGGRAPH '97*, 13–18.

Robertson, G., M. Czerwinski, and M. van Dantzich (1997). "Immersion in Desktop Virtual Reality." *Proceedings of the 1997 ACM Symposium on User Interface Software and Technology (UIST '97)*, 11–19.

CHAPTER 6

3D USER INTERFACE INPUT HARDWARE

This chapter continues our discussion of the hardware commonly used in 3D UIs. We examine a variety of input devices that are used in immersive, mobile, and desktop applications and their effect on 3D UIs. We also discuss how to choose input devices for different 3D applications by looking at some important device attributes, taxonomies, and evidence from empirical studies.

6.1 Introduction

As we saw in Chapter 5, "3D User Interface Output Hardware," choosing appropriate output devices is an important component of designing, developing, and using a 3D application, because they are the primary means of presenting information to the user. An equally important part of 3D UI design is choosing an appropriate set of input devices that allow the user to communicate with the application. For example, we might need to track the user's head or let him interact with the application using his voice. Perhaps our 3D UI has specific needs, such as letting users throw 3D virtual paint around using a paint bucket or providing a way to record handwritten notes. As with output devices, there are many different types of input devices to choose from when developing a 3D UI, and some devices are more appropriate for certain tasks than others.

This chapter is meant as a guide to the types of input devices available and how they are used in 3D UIs. As with the previous chapter, this chapter is not meant to be a fully exhaustive discussion on all the input devices ever developed or the technical details of input device design; rather, it presents a representative sample of devices commonly found in 3D applications. See Schmalstieg and Höllerer (2016), Sherman and Craig (2003), and Burdea and Coiffet (2003) for other expositions on 3D input hardware.

We encourage you to think about the content in this chapter while exploring the rest of the book and especially when thinking about interaction techniques. The connection between interaction techniques and input devices is important because of the distinction and the dependencies between the two. Input devices are just the physical tools that are used to implement various interaction techniques (Foley and Wallace 1974). In general, many different interaction techniques can be mapped onto any given input device. The question is how natural, efficient, and appropriate the mapping between a given input device and a given technique will be.

6.1.1 Input Device Characteristics

Many different characteristics can be used to describe input devices. One of the most important is the degrees of freedom (DOF) that an input device provides. A degree of freedom is simply a specific, independent way that a body moves in space. A device such as a tracker generally captures three position values (x, y, z) and three orientation values (yaw, pitch, roll) for a total of six DOF. To a large extent, a device's DOF gives an indication of how complex the device is and the power it has in accommodating various interaction techniques.

Another way to characterize input devices is by the input type and frequency of the data they generate. Input device data frequency can be either discrete, continuous, or a combination of the two. Discrete input devices typically generate a single data value (e.g., a Boolean value or an element from a set) based on the user's action. They are often used to change modes in an application, such as changing the drawing mode in a desktop 3D modeling program, or to indicate the user wants to start performing an action, such as instantiating a navigation technique. Continuous input devices generate multiple data values (e.g., real-valued numbers, pixel coordinates, etc.) in response to a user's action and, in many cases, regardless of what the user is doing (tracking systems and bend-sensing gloves are examples). In many cases, input devices consist of both discrete and continuous data components (e.g., game motion controllers that are tracked in space coupled with several buttons), providing a larger range of device-to-interaction technique mappings.

Input devices can also be described based on the types of sensors they use to capture data. For example, **active sensors** require the user to wear, hold, or manipulate the device to generate useful data. In other words, these input devices will not provide any useful information to the computer unless they are manipulated in some way. Otherwise, the device just sits there and does nothing. Input devices with active sensors can generate both discrete (e.g., buttons) and continuous data (e.g., acceleration and velocity). For example, trackballs, sliders, and dials are examples of input devices with active sensors because the user has to manipulate them to generate sequences of continuous data in a given range. In another example, a video game motion controller with active sensor–based buttons and acceleration sensors can generate discrete data to issue commands (when the user presses appropriate buttons) and continuous data for tracking user motion (this data is automatically generated when the device is on).

Input devices that make use of **passive sensors** do not require the user to hold or wear any input hardware to generate useful data. These types of devices are decoupled from the user and are typically placed in a strategic location in the physical environment so the user can interact with a 3D application unobtrusively. A classic example of an input device that uses passive sensors is the video camera. Note that a video camera could be placed on a user as part of an input device, but this would effectively make it an active sensor because the user would need to wear/manipulate the device. The key distinction between active and passive sensors is the level of manipulation required to generate useful data from them. With active sensors, manipulation is required. With passive sensors, no device manipulation is needed.

In the context of 3D spatial input devices, both active and passive sensor–based devices are often required to continuously monitor (Sherman and Craig 2003) the user's movements. For example, a tracker is a device that will continually output position, orientation, and/or motion information about the user's pose so it can be relayed to the 3D application. These devices are useful when we want to know where something is in space and we do not want to have to keep asking for it. A perfect example of this is head tracking, which is a requirement for 3D audio displays and active viewer motion parallax in visual displays. With these monitoring devices, the data often needs to be segmented into distinct sequences. These sequences are commonly used in 3D gesture recognition (LaViola 2013). With active sensor–based devices, data segmentation is often done manually. For example, a user presses a button on a game motion controller to tell the 3D application to start and stop data monitoring for a specific segment. However, with passive sensor–based input devices, the 3D application itself typically has to determine when a specific data segment begins and ends, which can be more challenging.

Finally, input devices can be categorized by their intended use. For example, some devices are designed to specifically determine position and/or orientation information (locators), while others are designed to produce a real number value (valuators) or to indicate a particular element of a set (choice). Other input device characteristics include whether the device measures relative (i.e., the difference between the current and past measurement) or absolute (i.e., measurements based on a constant point of reference) values, or allows for position or rate control (Jacob 1996).

6.1.2 Chapter Roadmap

The bulk of this chapter contains a discussion of different input devices used in 3D UIs and how they affect interaction techniques.

In section 6.2, we discuss traditional input devices, which are typically used on the desktop for 2D interaction, but can be applied in some cases to 3D interaction in both desktop and immersive settings.

Section 6.3 examines 3D spatial input devices. First, we explore the active and passive sensing devices that track the user or an object's pose. Second, we discuss how to use the sensing technologies for tracking the user. Third, we discuss the most common 3D input device, the 3D mouse, which combines sensing technologies with other physical input components.

Section 6.4 covers nonspatial input technologies (speech and brain input) that are complementary to the use of 3D spatial input devices in 3D UIs. In section 6.5, we present examples of special-purpose input devices that are designed for specific tasks and that do not fit well into other categories.

To conclude the chapter, section 6.6 provides valuable information on strategies for building custom input devices, while in section 6.7, we present some ideas and guidelines for choosing input devices for a particular task or application. Finally, section 6.8 discusses the input devices chosen for our running case studies.

6.2 Traditional Input Devices

There are many input devices that are used in desktop 3D UIs. Many of these devices have been used and designed for traditional 2D desktop applications such as word processing, spreadsheets, and drawing. However, with appropriate mappings, these devices can also work well in 3D UIs and in 3D applications such as modeling and computer games. Of course, most of these devices could also be used in more immersive 3D UIs that use surround-screen displays or HWDs, although some would be more appropriate than others.

In this section, we discuss

- keyboards
- 2D mice and trackballs
- pen- and touch-based tablets
- joysticks
- desktop 6-DOF input devices

In general, these are active sensing devices because the user must physically manipulate them to provide information to the 3D application.

6.2.1 Keyboards

The keyboard is a classic example of a traditional active sensing desktop input device that contains a set of discrete components (buttons). They are commonly used in many desktop 3D applications from modeling to computer games. For example, the arrow keys are often used as input for simple travel techniques in first-person shooter computer games. Unfortunately, using the standard keyboard in most 3D application domains such as immersive VR or mobile AR is not practical due to the size of a traditional keyboard and the need for a supporting surface. In the case of fully immersive 3D environments, when users are wearing an HWD, the real world is completely blocked out of the user's view, making a traditional keyboard challenging to operate. However, when using some less immersive displays, such as a single-screen display or table, users can still make use of traditional keyboards.

Because entering alphanumeric characters is important in many 3D applications that use HWDs and surround-screen displays, other, less conventional devices are needed in these environments (see Chapter 9, section 9.2.2). Since the development of the standard keyboard, there have been a variety of different keyboard layouts and designs to make it easier to enter alphanumeric information when traditional keyboards are not appropriate. A thorough exposition of different keyboard designs and text entry can be found in MacKenzie and Tanaka-Ishii (2007).

Perhaps the easiest way to bring a keyboard into a 3D UI is to miniaturize it so it can be carried or worn. This technique also has the advantage that it can retain the familiar QWERTY layout so that users do not have to relearn the keys' positions (see Figure 6.1). However, miniature keyboards are not generally large enough to allow touch typing (or ten-finger typing), so users must type with one or two fingers and cannot use the muscle memory built up from years of keyboard usage.

In a 3D UI, a miniature keyboard may be held in one hand while the other hand types (similar to a palmtop computer), or the keyboard may be worn by or attached to the user. An experiment comparing several text input devices for wearable computers found that a miniature keyboard strapped to the forearm of the nondominant hand produced the best performance and user satisfaction (Thomas et al. 1998).

Figure 6.1 An example of a miniature keyboard (Used with permission from Microsoft).

A second way to make the keyboard small enough to be held in one hand is to reduce the number of physical keys. For example, the keypads on some mobile phones can easily be used with one hand by pressing the 12 to 15 keys with the thumb. Because today's mobile phones contain so many features requiring text input (e.g., entering names into a list of contacts), many different symbolic input mechanisms have been developed for them, some of which could be applied in 3D UIs. One phone–based text-input technique uses the standard layout of letters on the numeric phone keypad (a, b, and c are mapped to the 2 key; d, e, and f to the 3 key; and so on). Users press the key with the desired letter and disambiguate the letter by pressing the key multiple times. Another type of handheld keyboard is known as a chord keyboard, first introduced by Englebart and English (1968). This device is held in one hand, and the user presses combinations of keys as a single chord for alphanumeric input (see Figure 6.2). A chord keyboard aims to provide all the functionality of a full-sized keyboard while using many fewer keys. In order to provide more symbols than there are keys on the device, the user presses multiple keys simultaneously to produce some symbols. The set of keys that are pressed together is called a chord, a name taken from the method of producing a musical chord on the piano by striking multiple keys at once. Figure 6.2 shows a commercially available chord keyboard (the Twiddler2) that has 12 keys and requires that no more than two keys be pressed at once to produce any letter, number, or standard punctuation symbol.

Figure 6.2 A 12-key chord keyboard. (Photograph courtesy of Doug Bowman)

Chord keyboards have been studied extensively in other contexts (Noyes 1983), particularly mobile and wearable computing, and many different layouts and form factors have been tried. In general, users need a great deal of training to become proficient with chord keyboards, since the layout is not related to the standard QWERTY keyboard, but the advantage of one-handed symbolic input may make this training worthwhile in some situations.

Miniature keyboards like the ones described in the previous paragraph are not as popular as they once were. Instead, "soft" and gesture keyboards, virtual devices implemented entirely in software, have become more prominent. With these keyboards, users either press virtual keys instead of physical ones to enter symbols, or they make gestures over the virtual keys to enter words (Zhai and Kristensson 2012). Most smartphones and tablets include a soft keyboard that is displayed on the screen. Users tap the virtual keys with a stylus or finger to simulate pressing the key. Soft keyboards have the advantages that they can easily be reconfigured for different layouts or alphabets and that they don't require a specialized input device. However, the major disadvantages of soft keyboards are the limitation of single-point input (one finger or pen at a time) and their lack of active and passive haptic feedback. Even if the virtual keyboard lies on a physical surface, the user cannot feel the contours of the keys to help her find a key without looking or hear the click of the key being depressed to help her know a symbol was entered. Rapid text entry with a soft keyboard usually relies on word prediction, word completion, and automatic correction.

An example of a different take on a soft keyboard is a novel virtual keyboard device called the Senseboard (see Figure 6.3). The concept is that a full-sized QWERTY keyboard can exist virtually on any surface, and users can type with all ten fingers on this virtual keyboard. This

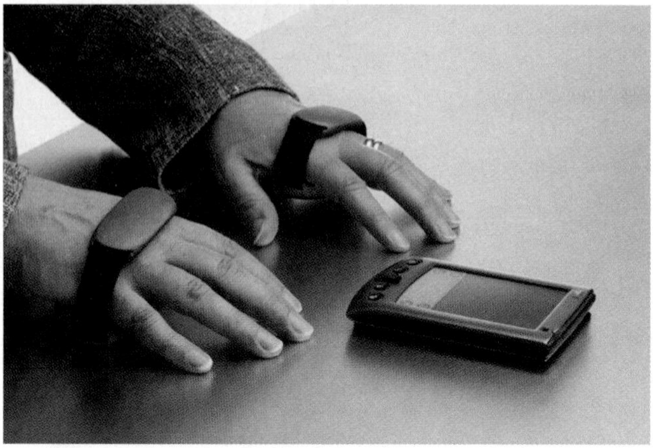

Figure 6.3 Senseboard virtual keyboard prototype. (Photograph courtesy of Senseboard Technologies AB)

is accomplished by the use of muscle sensors to determine finger movement plus pattern recognition to determine the probable word in ambiguous situations.

Note that virtual keyboards need not be limited to the standard QWERTY layout. In fact, for tapping of a soft keyboard by a pen or single finger, the QWERTY layout is certainly suboptimal (although it will allow better performance by novices). For example, Zhai et al. (2000) developed the Metropolis keyboard, a layout for soft keyboards based on quantitative analysis of letter frequency, distance between keys, and so on.

6.2.2 2D Mice and Trackballs

Two-dimensional mice and trackballs are another classic example of traditional active sensing input devices made popular by the Windows, Icons, Menus, and Pointers (WIMP) interface metaphor (van Dam 1997). The mouse is one of the most widely used devices in traditional 2D input tasks and comes in many different varieties. The trackball is basically an upside-down mouse. Instead of moving the whole device to move the pointer, the user manipulates a rotatable ball embedded in the device. One of the advantages of the trackball is that it does not need a flat 2D surface to operate, which means that it can be held in the user's hand and will still operate correctly. Regardless of the physical design of the mouse or trackball, these devices have two essential components. The first is a continuous 2D locator for positioning a cursor and generating 2D pixel coordinate values. The second is a set of discrete components (usually one to three buttons). Mice and trackballs are relative devices that report how far they move, rather than where they are in a fixed space. As with keyboards, they are commonly used in many different 3D applications and provide many different choices for mapping interaction technique to task.

For example, they are often combined with keyboards in computer games to enable more complex travel techniques. The keyboard may be used for translation while the mouse or trackball is used to rotate the camera so the user can see the 3D environment (e.g., look up, look down, turn around). More details on how mice and trackballs (and 2D locators in general) are used in 3D interaction techniques can be found in Chapter 7, "Selection and Manipulation," and Chapter 8, "Travel."

Mice and trackballs have the same problem as the keyboard in that they are not designed to be brought into more immersive 3D, mobile, or AR environments. Because a mouse needs to be placed on a supporting surface in order for the locator to function properly, it is difficult to use with these displays. Since the trackball can be held in one hand (see Figure 6.4), it can be used in immersive 3D, mobile, and AR environments, and it has also been successfully incorporated into a 3D interface using a workbench display (Forsberg et al. 1997). However, in most cases, 3D mice are used in these types of 3D interfaces because they are tracked and provide additional DOF. Section 6.3.3 discusses 3D mice.

Figure 6.4 An example of a handheld wireless trackball device that could be used in AR, mobile, and immersive 3D environments.

6.2.3 Pen- and Touch-Based Tablets

Pen- and touch-based tablets (see Figure 6.5) and handheld smartphones can generate the same types of input that mice do, but they have a different form factor. These devices have a continuous component (a 2D locator) for controlling a cursor and generating 2D pixel coordinate values. These values can be generated in several ways. Depending on the particular hardware, the stylus can move on or hover over the tablet surface to generate coordinate values. Touching the surface of the screen can also provide 2D coordinate information. Additionally, the stylus or the tablet itself can have various buttons for generating discrete events. In contrast to mice, pen- and touch-based tablets are absolute devices, meaning that the device reports where the stylus or touch is in the fixed reference frame of the tablet surface.

Large pen- and touch-based tablets are not appropriate for most fully immersive, mobile, and AR visual displays because of their weight. However, smaller tablets and smartphones (and personal digital assistants (PDAs) in the past) have been integrated successfully into 3D UIs in immersive environments (Forsberg et al. 2006; Poupyrev, Tomokazu et al. 1998; Watsen et al. 1999) as well as in mobile and AR settings (Lee et al. 2009; Steed and Julier 2013). Larger pen-based tablets can be used in 3D applications where the user is sitting, such as with desktop 3D displays, some workbench and single-wall displays, and small hemispherical displays. These types of devices are popular in both desktop 3D and immersive VR applications, because they give the user the ability to interact with a "pen and paper" style interface, and they allow the user to bring 2D interaction techniques such as handwriting and menu-based techniques (see Chapter 9, section 9.5) into 3D environments (Cao et al. 2006; Chuah and Lok 2012; Lee et al. 2009; Forsberg et al. 1998; Poupyrev, Tomokazu et al. 1998; Watsen et al. 1999).

Figure 6.5 A large pen- and touch-based LCD tablet allowing the user to draw directly on the screen. (Photograph courtesy of Wacom Technology.)

6.2.4 Joysticks

Joysticks are another example of input devices traditionally used on the desktop and in video games and with a long history as computer input peripherals. These devices are similar to mice and pen-based tablets in that they use active sensing and have a combination of a continuous 2D locator and a set of discrete components such as buttons and other switches. However, there is an important distinction between the mouse and the joystick. With a mouse, the cursor stops moving as soon as the mouse stops moving. With a joystick, the cursor typically continues moving in the direction the joystick is pointing. To stop the cursor, the joystick's handle must be returned to the neutral position. This type of joystick is commonly called an **isotonic joystick,** and the technique is called rate control (i.e., the position of the device is mapped to the cursor's speed, as opposed to position control, in which the position of the device is mapped to the cursor's position). Many console video game systems make use of different joystick designs (both analog and digital) in their game controllers (see Figure 6.6). Joysticks can also be augmented with haptic actuators, making them haptic displays as well (Burdea 1996).

Isometric joysticks have also been designed. Isometric devices have a large spring constant so they cannot be perceptibly moved. Their output varies with the force the user applies to the device. A translation isometric device is pushed, while a rotation isometric device is twisted. A problem with these devices is that users may tire quickly from the pressure they must apply in order to use them. Figure 6.7 shows an example of such a device.

Figure 6.6 Simple joysticks have evolved into sophisticated game controllers. (Photograph courtesy of Joseph J. LaViola Jr.)

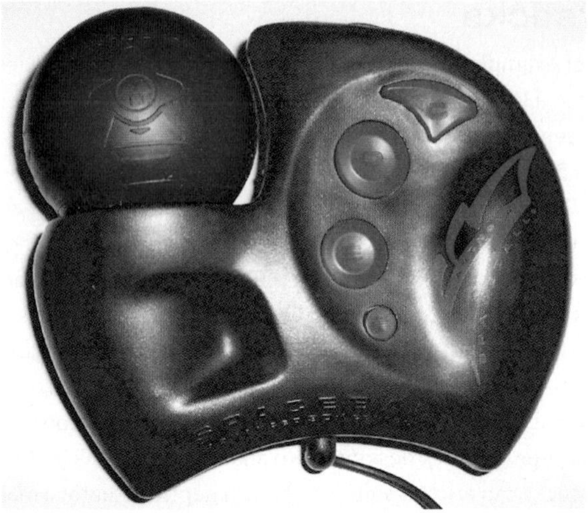

Figure 6.7 An isometric 3D input device. (Photograph courtesy of Andrew Forsberg, Brown University Graphics Group)

Joysticks have been used as input devices in computer games for many years. They are frequently used in driving and flight simulation games, and when integrated into game controllers, they are the input device of choice with console video game systems. Additionally, they are sometimes used in CAD/CAM applications. Joysticks by themselves were designed primarily for desktop and console video game systems. However, when integrated as part of game controllers, they can be used in 3D UIs to support several types of 3D interfaces. For example, the two analog joysticks in Figure 6.6 can be used to translate and rotate the user's viewpoint in a similar way to using the keyboard and mouse. However, these traditional game controllers are often not tracked (position and orientation), reducing their utility in 3D spatial interfaces in VR, AR, and mobile environments. More details on tracked game controllers can be found in section 6.3.3.

6.2.5 Desktop 6-DOF Input Devices

A derivative of the joystick is a 6-DOF input device that uses isometric forces to collect 3D position and orientation data. Figure 6.8 shows an example of a 6-DOF input device that was developed specifically for 3D interaction on the desktop. Slight push–and–pull pressure of the fingers on the cap of the device generates small deflections in *x*, *y*, and *z*, which moves objects dynamically in the three corresponding axes. With slight twisting and tilting of the cap, rotational motions are generated along the three axes. Figure 6.9 shows how such a device is manipulated to obtain 3D position and orientation information.

Figure 6.8 A desktop 6-DOF input device that captures 3D position and orientation data. (Photograph courtesy of 3Dconnexion)

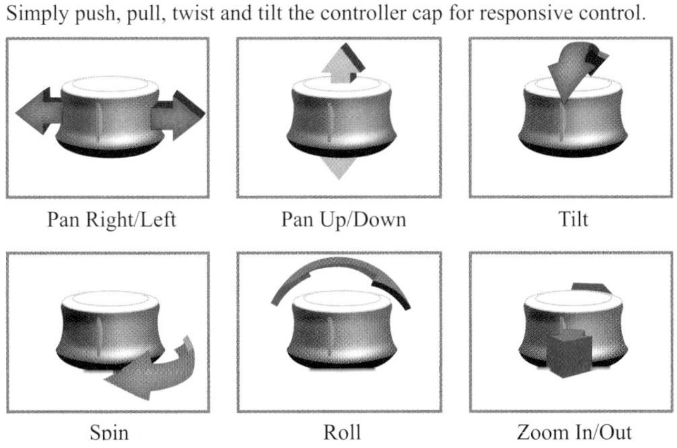

Figure 6.9 Example interactions with a ground-referenced isometric 6-DOF device.

Unlike some of the other devices in this section, which were designed for 2D desktop interaction but can be used in immersive 3D UIs, this type of device is designed for 3D interaction, but only in a desktop computing setting. Desktop 6-DOF input devices are commonly used in 3D applications for manipulating virtual objects. They were originally developed for telerobotic manipulation and are used today by 3D designers and artists with CAD/CAM and animation applications. They do not replace the mouse; rather, they are used in conjunction with it. One hand on the motion controller positions the objects in 3D space, while the other hand with the mouse can simultaneously select menu items and edit the object. These devices are rarely used in more immersive environments because they work best when grounded and not carried in the user's hands. However, when coupled with additional tracking hardware this type of device can be carried by the user for both one and two handed control (Simon and Doulis 2004). Additionally, they can be difficult to use when trying to make fine manipulations, and it takes practice to become proficient with them.

6.3 3D Spatial Input Devices

In many 3D applications, it is important for the UI to provide information about the user or a physical object's position, orientation, or motion in 3D space. For example, an application might need the user's head position and orientation so that full motion parallax and stereoscopic depth cues can be included in the application. Another UI might require information about the bending of the user's fingers so that a virtual hand corresponding to the user's physical hand can be rendered. In most cases, we want this information sent to the 3D application automatically without the user having to signal the computer system to collect it. This information will support fundamental tasks such as real-time rendering with the proper perspective or continuously understanding the location of a user's hand or body position.

We can categorize these devices based on whether they use active (i.e., handheld or worn) or passive (i.e., completely unobtrusive) sensing and what part of the body they focus on. In this section, we first examine different sensing technologies and then explore how these technologies can be used to track different parts of the user (e.g., body, eyes, fingers) as well as physical objects. In addition, we will explore their relationships to 3D UIs.

6.3.1 Sensing Technologies for 3D Tracking

One of the most important aspects of 3D interaction is providing an understanding of a user's position, orientation, and/or motion to maintain a proper correspondence between physical and virtual content. As a result, having accurate tracking is a crucial part of making interaction techniques usable within 3D applications. In fact, the ability to track and understand the location of a user in 3D space is fundamental to many interaction techniques described in Part IV of this book. The critical characteristics of trackers include the sensor technology used, their range, latency (delay between the time a motion occurs and when it is reported), jitter (noise or instability), and accuracy. Currently, there are a number of different sensing technologies in use, which include

- magnetic sensing
- mechanical sensing
- acoustic sensing
- inertial sensing

- optical sensing
- radar sensing
- bioelectric sensing
- hybrid sensing

These sensing methods represent the main technologies used in tracking systems to find user and object position and orientation. However, other methods can be used, especially for eye and finger tracking, which we describe in section 6.3.2. See Zhou and Huosheng (2008), Foxlin (2002), Welch and Foxlin (2002), and Allen et al. (2001) for more details on motion sensing and tracking technology.

Magnetic Sensing

Magnetic sensors use a transmitting device that emits a low-frequency magnetic field. A small sensor, the receiver, determines its position and orientation relative to this magnetic source. The range of these sensors varies, but they typically work within a radius of 4 to 30 feet. Figure 6.10 shows an example of a magnetic tracking system. The figure shows several different sizes for the magnetic source, each supporting different ranges. The smaller the magnetic source transmitter, the smaller the acceptable range of the tracking system. For example, the smallest magnetic source transmitter in Figure 6.10 has a range of up to 5 feet, while the large ball has a range of up to 15 feet. A system with a 5-foot range would clearly not be appropriate for large display environments such as surround-screen visual displays or HWDs where the user needs a lot of space to roam. Such a system would be primarily used with conventional monitors (for fish-tank VR) and small workbench displays, where the range of the device is not a critical factor.

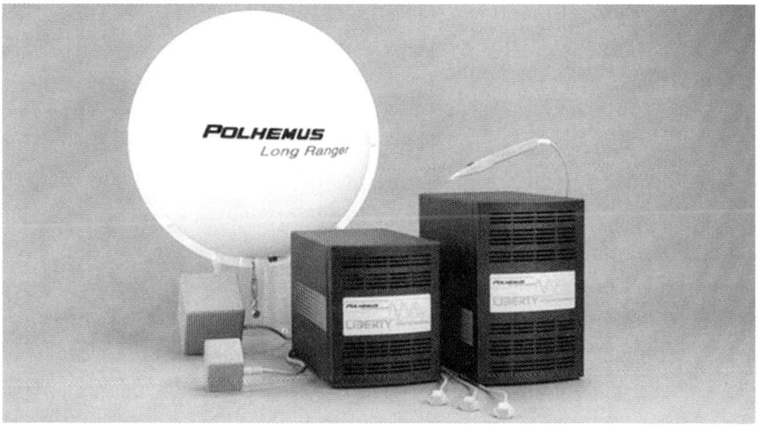

Figure 6.10 A magnetic sensor consists of an electronics unit, a magnetic field generator, and receivers that track the user or object. The image shows three different-sized magnetic field generators that support different-sized tracking ranges, two different electronic units that support different numbers of receivers, and a set of receivers. Note the receiver shown above the larger electronics unit is embedded in a stylus-like device. (Photograph courtesy of Polhemus Inc.)

Since magnetic sensors have a limited tracking range, they are not appropriate for outdoor and mobile AR applications. However, there have been attempts to use a lightweight magnetic tracking system for mobile 3D applications by having the user wear the magnetic source on the body to get relative position information of the user's head and hands (Basu et al. 2012).

Magnetic sensors tend to be accurate to within 0.01 inch in position and 0.01 degree in orientation, and their accuracy tends to degrade the farther away the receiver is from the source. Their main disadvantage is that any ferromagnetic or conductive (metal) objects present in the room with the transmitter will distort the magnetic field, reducing the accuracy. These accuracy reductions can sometimes be quite severe, making many interaction techniques, especially gesture-based techniques, difficult to use. Distortions can be handled with calibration routines and filtering algorithms (Hagedorn et al. 2007; Kindratenko 2000), but doing so can increase start-up time and online computational overhead. In some cases, these filtering and distortion algorithms are directly embedded into the magnetic tracking system.

Mechanical Sensing

Mechanical sensors have a rigid structure with a number of interconnected mechanical linkages combined with electromechanical transducers such as potentiometers or shaft encoders. One end is fixed in place, while the other is attached to the object to be tracked (usually the user's head or hand). As the tracked object moves, the linkages move as well, and measurements are taken from the transducers to obtain position and orientation information. Arm-mounted visual displays use this type of sensor technology. Additionally, many ground-referenced force-feedback devices (see section 5.4.2 in Chapter 5) are mechanically based, making them trackers as well as force displays. Mechanical sensors are very accurate and transmit information with very low latencies. However, they are often bulky, limiting the user's mobility and making it difficult to interact in mobile 3D and AR applications.

Acoustic Sensing

Acoustic sensors (see Figure 6.11) typically use high-frequency sound emitted from source components and received by microphones. The source may be on the tracked object, with the microphones placed in the environment (an **outside-in** approach), or the source may be in the environment, with the microphones on the tracked object (an **inside-out** approach). The dominant approach to determining position and orientation information with acoustic tracking is to use time-of-flight duration of ultrasonic pulses. In other words, the distance between emitter and receiver can be determined by the time it takes for an ultrasonic pulse to travel from source to destination, multiplied by the speed of sound. From this distance, position can be estimated, and with more receivers, a set of three points can be used to determine orientation using triangulation. More recent approaches to acoustic sensing include using standard speakers and a microphone found in most commodity laptops and devices to sense user motion (Gupta et al. 2012). An inaudible tone is sent through the speaker and gets frequency-shifted when it reflects off moving objects like a user's hand. This frequency shift is then measured by the microphone, which does not have to be placed on the tracked object. This approach cannot track objects precisely but can sense motion well enough to support simple gestures.

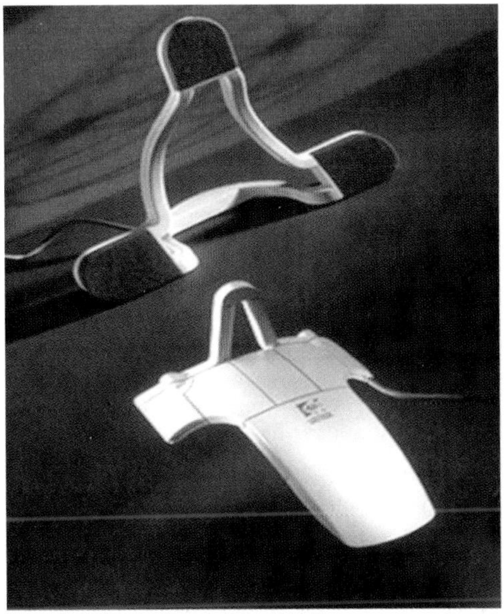

Figure 6.11 An acoustic sensing device (the Fly Mouse). The mouse-like device generates the acoustic signals from which the receiver determines position and orientation information. (Photograph courtesy of Logitech International)

The advantages of acoustic sensing systems are that they are relatively inexpensive and lightweight. However, these devices often have a short range and low sampling rates (compared with mechanical and inertial sensors, which can have sampling rates above 1 kHz). In addition, their accuracy suffers if acoustically reflective surfaces are present in the room. Another disadvantage of acoustic sensing is that external noises, such as jingling keys or a ringing phone, can cause interference in the signal and thus significantly reduce accuracy. As with any tracking system that has accuracy problems, many interaction techniques are difficult to use if an ultrasonic sensor loses signal, has significant jitter, or suffers from distortions anywhere within the tracking range (distortions usually increase significantly as the user moves toward a tracking boundary).

Inertial Sensing

Inertial sensors (see Figure 6.12) use a variety of inertial measurement devices, such as angular-rate gyroscopes, linear accelerometers, and magnetometers. Typically, these sensors are combined into a single package called an inertial measurement unit (IMU). These devices provide derivative measurements of position and orientation (i.e., gyroscopes provide angular velocity, and linear accelerometers provide linear acceleration), so their data must be integrated to obtain position and orientation information. When data is integrated, the result is a relative measurement (e.g., angular velocity is integrated to obtain change in position). The one exception to this rule is that a three-axis linear accelerometer can be used to determine the direction of gravity directly (and therefore the pitch and roll of the device), since gravity is an acceleration.

Figure 6.12 An inertial tracker. The inertial sensors are located in the cube shown in the picture. (Photograph courtesy of InterSense, Inc.)

Because the tracking system is in the sensor, its range is limited only by the length of the cord that attaches the sensor to the electronics unit. Wireless sensing is also common with these systems. In fact, inertial sensing components are commonly found in mobile devices such as smartphones and tablets. Since the electronics unit is embedded within the device, its range is effectively unlimited. In addition, these sensors can produce measurements at high sampling rates. Inertial sensors were originally used in large tracking systems on ships, submarines, and airplanes in the 1950s (Welch and Foxlin 2002). However, the weight of these devices prohibited their use in tracking for 3D UIs until they became small enough to fit in microelectronic mechanical systems (MEMS).

The major limitation of inertial sensors is that they suffer error accumulation from sensor biases, noise, and drift (see Foxlin [2002] for a detailed discussion on error accumulation). Error accumulation can be severe with linear accelerometers, which is why most purely inertial tracking systems track only orientation. Although there are inertial navigation systems that can track position and orientation, they are used on ships and submarines, where tracking error within a mile is often acceptable, in contrast to the sub-centimeter accuracy required in 3D UIs. Gyroscopes also suffer from error accumulation, but this is less severe, and there are methods for compensating for this problem by making use of sensor fusion techniques such as Kalman filtering to improve the orientation estimates (Azuma and Bishop 1994; Williamson et al. 2010). For example, inertial sensors often handle error accumulation by including magnetometer measurements to prevent accumulation of gyroscopic drift.

Common 3D interaction techniques are difficult to implement without position tracking. However, orientation-only tracking systems can be used for head tracking where the user will basically stand in one place and look around. In addition, low-latency inertial orientation tracking is often combined with another form of position tracking (see the discussion of hybrid sensing below). A virtual travel technique (see Chapter 8, "Travel") can be used in this case to allow translation through the environment. In addition, the data produced by these inertial sensors works well for 3D gesture recognition when coupled with heuristics

(Wingrave et al. 2010) and machine learning-based recognizers (Hoffman et al. 2010). These 3D gestures can be used in a variety of different ways, especially in system control (see Chapter 9, "System Control").

Optical Sensing

Another approach to position and orientation tracking of users and physical objects is from measurements of reflected or emitted light. These types of trackers use computer vision techniques and optical sensors such as cameras. A variety of different cameras can be used, from simple desktop webcams, to stereo and depth cameras, to sophisticated high-resolution cameras with high sampling rates and pixel densities.

Depth cameras provide more information than a traditional single camera, because they support extraction of a 3D representation of a user or object. Three different technologies are typically used in depth cameras: time of flight, structured light, and stereo vision (Bhowmik 2014). Time-of-flight depth cameras determine the depth map of a scene by illuminating it with a beam of pulsed light and calculating the time it takes for the light to be detected on an imaging device after it is reflected off of the scene. Structured-light-depth cameras use a known pattern of light (often infrared) that is projected into the scene. An image sensor is then able to capture this deformed light pattern based on the shapes in the scene and finally extract 3D geometric shapes using the distortion of the projected optical pattern. Finally, stereo-based cameras attempt to mimic the human visual system using two calibrated imaging devices laterally displaced from each other. These two cameras capture synchronized images of the scene, and the depth for image pixels is extracted from the binocular disparity. More information on how depth cameras are used in optical tracking can be found in Chen et al. (2013).

Since the first edition of this book, optical sensors and optical tracking techniques have become more powerful and more common for 3D interaction. Optical sensing systems can be categorized, like acoustic sensors, as either outside-in or inside-out, and they can either use markers or markerless configurations.

Marker-based outside-in systems have their sensors mounted at fixed locations in the environment, and tracked objects are marked with active or passive landmarks such as retroreflective markers (see Figure 6.13) or colored gloves (Wang and Popovic 2009; Figure 6.14). The number and size of these landmarks vary depending on the type of optical tracking system and how many DOF are required.

Markerless outside-in systems still have the optical sensor or sensors mounted at fixed locations in the environment, but no landmarks are required, making the tracking completely unobtrusive (Starner et al. 1998). Depth cameras often provide a markerless outside-in configuration (Wang et al. 2011).

Figure 6.13 An example of a marker-based outside-in optical tracking system. Multiple camera sensors are placed strategically in the environment, and the user wears several retroreflective markers to track the body and face. (Photograph courtesy of Vicon Motion Systems Ltd.)

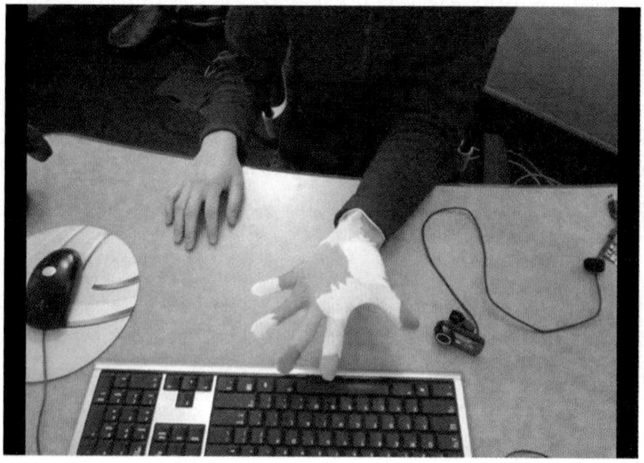

Figure 6.14 An example of a marker-based outside-in optical hand tracking system where a single camera sensor is used and the markers are colored gloves with unique patterns. (Photograph courtesy of Robert Wang)

Marker-based inside-out systems place optical sensors on the user or tracked object while the landmarks are placed in the environment. There are many different landmarks that can be used, such as active LED beacons or passive fiducials such as cards with recognizable patterns (Foxlin and Naimark 2003; Hogue et al. 2003). These passive fiducials were first developed as part of an AR conferencing system (Kato and Billinghurst 1999), which later evolved into the ARTookKit tracking library. Figure 6.15 shows an example of a marker-based inside-out tracking system known as the HiBall, composed of a set of small, high-speed cameras, which are aligned in a self-contained housing and that can be affixed to the user's head (Welch et al. 2001). A set of LEDs are placed in the environment, and their positions are surveyed. The LEDs are flashed at high speed in a specific known sequence, and providing the camera can see enough LEDs, the position and orientation of the tracker can be calculated directly through triangulation. Figure 6.16 shows another example of a marker-based inside-out tracking system where fiducials with known patterns are used as landmarks for tracking. The Lighthouse tracking system used with the HTC Vive HWD is another interesting example of marker-based inside-out tracking. It uses optical sensors on the HWD to detect laser light that is swept horizontally and vertically across the scene by two emitters.

Markerless inside-out systems still place the optical sensors on the user or tracked object, but instead of having known fiducials or beacons placed in the physical environment, the underlying tracking algorithms attempt to make use of the physical environment itself

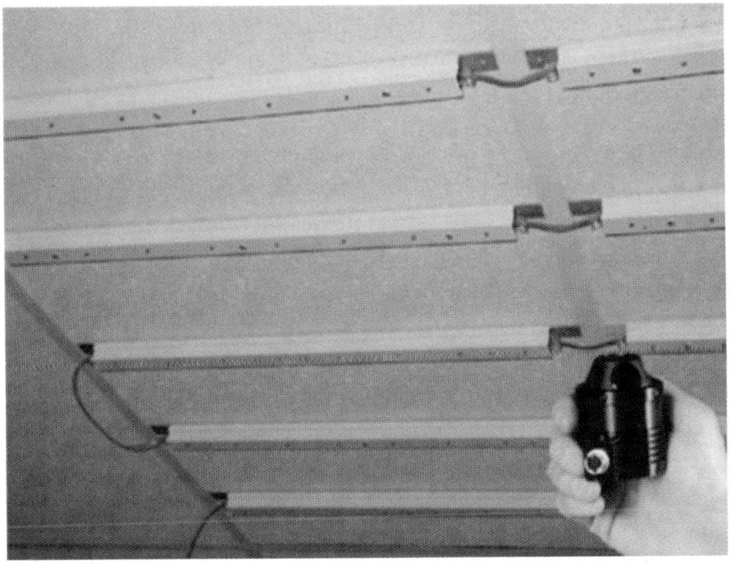

Figure 6.15 The HiBall Tracking System. The LED beacons are mounted on the ceiling, and the camera sensors are located in the handheld object. (Photograph of the HiBall-3000 Tracker courtesy of 3rd Tech, Inc.)

Figure 6.16 An example of a marker-based inside-out tracking system that uses several fiducial markers with known unique patterns placed strategically on the walls and ceiling of a room. (Photograph courtesy of Valve)

(e.g., everyday objects and structures) to determine position, orientation, or motion. There are two main approaches to markerless optical tracking (Billinghurst et al. 2015). First, the feature-based approach finds the correspondence between 2D image features and their 3D world coordinate equivalents. User position and orientation can then be found by projecting the 3D coordinates of the features into the observed 2D image coordinates and performing a minimization operation. SIFT (Lowe 2004), SURF (Bay et al. 2008), and FREAK (Alahi et al. 2012) represent examples of algorithms that perform natural feature detection and description.

Second, the model-based approach extracts pose information based on tracking known or acquired models of real-world objects. Early approaches would model the real-world 3D objects using a CAD program, and object structure was approximated with simple primitives such as lines, circles, and spheres. Edge filters were then used to extract pose based on a matching between filter data and the primitives (Wuest et al. 2005). Instead of modeling the real world beforehand, another approach is to create and update a map of the physical environment while simultaneously determining pose within it. This method is known as SLAM (Simultaneous Localization and Mapping). Originally used in the robotics domain (Dissanayake et al. 2001), there have been many SLAM variations developed for tracking with optical sensors (Fuentes-Pacheco et al. 2015). One example using a standard monocular camera breaks up the SLAM idea, having separate components for camera tracking and map building (Klein and Murray 2007, 2008). This approach is known as PTAM (Parallel Tracking and Mapping; see Figure 6.17). SLAM can be used with depth cameras or depth cameras that also contain RGB sensors (Lieberknecht et al. 2011). Methods that use iterative closest points (ICP) have also used depth sensors to create maps of a 3D scene that can be used for tracking (Izadi et al. 2011). With these sensors, depth information can be extracted to create meshes that can be used as part of the mapping process (see Figure 6.18). In some cases, tracking may be lost as the camera sensor moves about the environment, requiring some form of relocalization (Glocker et al. 2013).

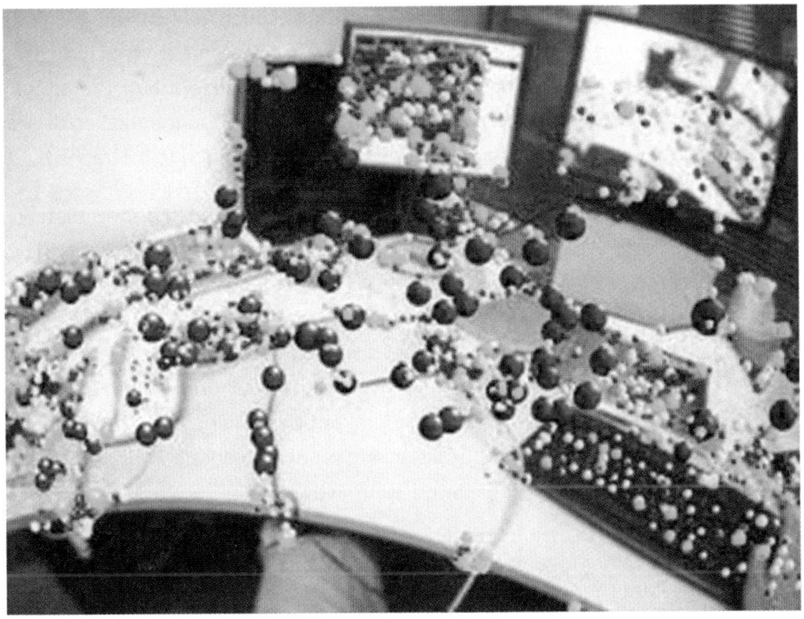

Figure 6.17 Tracking using the PTAM algorithm. Real-world feature points are used in conjunction with the SLAM concept. (Photograph courtesy Georg Klein and David Murray, University of Oxford)

Figure 6.18 A 3D model of an indoor physical environment using a depth sensor and RGB sensor. This model can then be used during SLAM or for user tracking once the model is created. (Image courtesy of Raphael Favier and Francisco Heredia, VCA Lab, Eindhoven University of Technology)

Setting up vision-based tracking systems can be difficult, because many parameters must be set in order to track the user or physical objects properly. These parameters include the number of cameras, the placement of the cameras, what visual background is put up, the design and placement of landmarks—whether they are in the environment or on the tracked user or object—as well as what parts of the body and how many people need to be tracked.

Vision-based sensor systems have a clear advantage in that the user can be completely untethered from the computer. However, except in markerless outside-in tracking, the user still needs to wear markers or wear/hold optical sensors. The major disadvantage of vision-based trackers is occlusion. In many cases, the camera cannot pick up information about parts of the user's body that are occluded by other parts. For example, it is difficult to extract information from all of the fingers when the hand is oriented in certain ways. Adding more cameras and landmarks can help to reduce the occlusion problem, but this can increase the complexity of the tracking algorithm. In addition, optical tracking is not as accurate as high-precision mechanical or electromagnetic tracking-based approaches.

Radar Sensing

Radar sensing is an established sensing technique using modulated electromagnetic waves sent toward moving or static targets that scatters transmitted radiation, with some portion of the energy redirected back toward the radar where it is intercepted by a receiving antenna. The time delay, phase or frequency shift, and amplitude attenuation capture rich information about the target's properties, such as distance, velocity, size, and orientation. However, traditional radar sensing is designed to detect large objects such as ships and aircraft where precise sensing is not required, making it impractical for sensing in 3D UIs, where precise knowledge of a user's body or object pose or motion is required. However, recent work by Lien et al. (2016) has led to radar sensing that can be utilized for detecting 3D hand gestures with high accuracy.

The approach of Lien et al. (2016) uses millimeter wave radar to illuminate the user's hand with a 150-degree-wide radar beam with pulses repeated at very high frequency (1–10 kHz). The reflected signal represents a superposition of reflections from multiple dynamic scattering centers (see Figure 6.19). These collections of scattering centers represent dynamic hand configurations. This data is then processed into multiple abstract representations, which are used to extract both instantaneous and dynamic characteristics of a moving hand and its parts. These representations can be used to train machine learning algorithms to classify subtle finger and hand movement gestures.

The main advantage of millimeter wave radar for 3D UIs is that subtle hand movements can be detected, which can lead to a wide variety of different interface controls for all facets of 3D selection and manipulation, navigation, and system control. However, the fundamental limitation is that this sensing approach does not actually capture the skeletal structure of a hand. Thus, it does not actually track the hand's position and orientation in space.

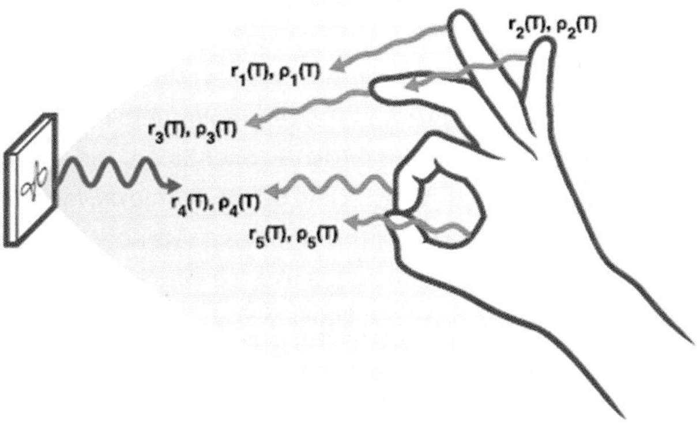

Figure 6.19 Millimeter wave radar sends a wide radar beam at high frequencies to gather dynamic scattering centers of a user's hand that can be then used for 3D hand gesture recognition. (Image courtesy of Ivan Poupyrev, Google)

Bioelectric Sensing

Bioelectric sensors aim to measure electrical activity in the body. These active sensors have primarily been used in the medical field for various diagnostic procedures, but they can also be used to gather information about the human body to support 3D interaction. The main bioelectric sensor technology used in 3D spatial input is electromyography (EMG). EMG detects the electrical potential generated by the muscles when electrically or neurologically activated. Figure 6.20 shows an example of using these sensors to detect finger gestures (Saponas et al. 2008, 2010). The data generated by EMG is often noisy, making it difficult to use for precise 3D interaction techniques. They often require sophisticated signal processing and machine learning algorithms to process the data. As such, bioelectric sensors are often more useful for 3D gestural input (LaViola 2013).

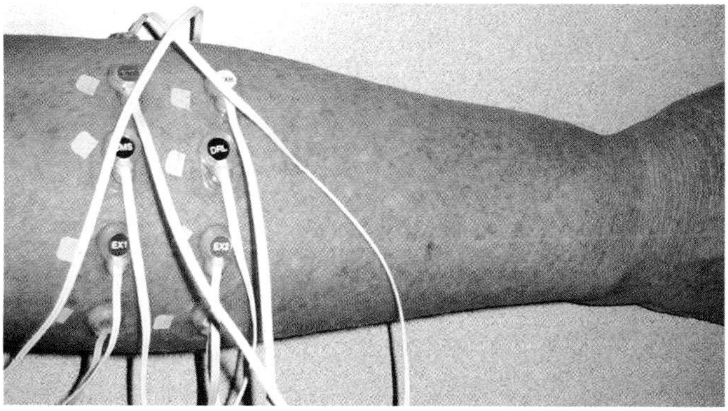

Figure 6.20 An example of EMG sensors applied to a user's forearm. (Photograph courtesy of Desney Tan, Microsoft Research)

Hybrid Sensing

Hybrid trackers put more than one sensing technology together to help increase accuracy, reduce latency, and provide a better overall 3D interaction experience. In general, the individual sensing technologies are used to compensate for each other's weaknesses. An example of such a tracking system is shown in Figure 6.21. This example combines inertial and ultrasonic sensing technologies. The inertial component measures orientation, and the ultrasonic component measures position, enabling the device to attain 6-DOF. Moreover, information from each component is used to improve the accuracy of the other. As a side note, this tracking system has the added advantage of being wireless, with the user wearing a small battery-powered electronics box on her belt (Wormell and Foxlin 2003).

One common approach to is to combine vision and inertial sensing together to support more robust user tracking (You et al. 1999; Williamson et al. 2010). Inertial sensors can provide low-latency orientation and position estimates, and the slower but more accurate optical sensors can be used to provide an absolute reference frame and to correct drift from the inertial sensors. Global positioning systems (GPS) are often used in conjunction with accelerometers or gyroscopes for tracking in large-scale, outdoor, augmented reality environments, where it is impossible to fix sources or receivers to the environment (Honkamaa et al. 2007).

The major difficulty with hybrid trackers is that combining more than one sensor technology produces more complexity. The extra complexity is warranted, however, if tracking accuracy is significantly improved. Sensor fusion algorithms (e.g., Kalman filters) are often required to combine the different sensors together seamlessly to ensure that each sensor type is used properly (You and Neumann 2001; He et al. 2014).

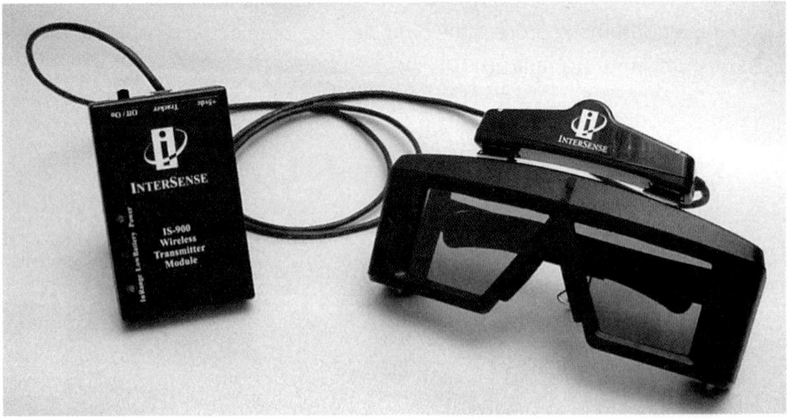

Figure 6.21 A wireless inertial/ultrasonic hybrid tracker. (Photograph courtesy of InterSense, Inc.)

6.3.2 Tracking the Body for 3D User Interfaces

As we have seen at the beginning of section 6.3, 3D UIs often require information about a user's position, orientation, or motion in 3D space to support the variety of 3D spatial interaction techniques discussed in the next part of this book. Various parts of the body (head, hands, limbs, fingers, eyes, or the whole body) can be tracked to gather data to support various 3D UIs. In this section, we examine how the sensor technologies described in section 6.3.1 are used for tracking different parts of the user's body and discuss their implications for 3D UIs.

Tracking the Head, Hands, and Limbs

Head and hand tracking can be considered the cornerstones of 3D interaction. Head tracking is important to ensure that any computer-generated imagery is displayed in the correct perspective in both VR and AR applications. Head tracking also supports motion parallax, which is an important depth cue. Hand tracking is important because the hands are the primary mechanism for performing different 3D interaction tasks. As full-body interaction and motion capture has become more popular in several different application areas, tracking the limbs and other parts of the body (e.g., the torso or feet) is also useful in the context of 3D interaction.

Tracking the head, hands, and limbs can be done with both active and passive sensors. With active sensors such as magnetic or hybrid ultrasonic/inertial sensors, a small device is placed on the area or areas that need tracking. For example, in head tracking the tracker is often placed on a pair of 3D stereo glasses or embedded directly into an HWD. Sensors can also be placed on the backs of the user's hands for hand tracking, which makes it easier for users to perform different hand-based gestures and other movements (e.g., making a fist). When many sensors are needed, as in the case of full-body tracking, body suits are often worn to ensure the sensors are all placed properly, making the suit itself one large sensing device.

Using marker-based outside-in optical sensors for head, hand, and body tracking is similar. For full-body tracking, markers can be placed on a body suit (see Figure 6.13). This approach can also be used for head (see Figure 6.22) or hand tracking by placing the markers in those specific areas.

The major limitation with these tracking approaches is that the user needs to wear the sensors or the markers, which can often be cumbersome. Passive sensors such as depth cameras provide an unobtrusive approach to head, hand, and limb tracking. Users simply need to interact in front of the passive sensor, and the device, coupled with recognition software, can extract a skeleton representation of the user's head, hands and other joints (Shotten et al. 2011) that can be used in the 3D application. Since the passive sensor is usually located in one place with a finite range, user mobility is often limited, which represents a disadvantage of using this approach, especially in the case of mobile AR.

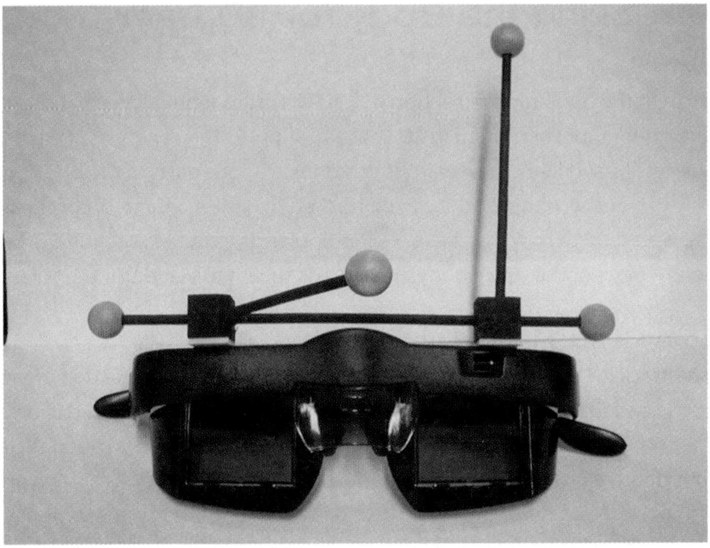

Figure 6.22 Using marker-based outside-in vision sensing to support head tracking. The markers are strategically placed on the 3D stereo glasses to obtain a coordinate system for the head. (Photograph courtesy of Oliver Kreylos)

Tracking the Fingers

In some cases, it is useful to have detailed tracking information about the user's fingers, such as how the fingers are bending or whether two fingers have made contact with each other. This information can be gathered using both active and passive sensing devices. Data gloves are an example of an active sensing approach that can provide this information. For passive sensing, vision-based approaches are typically used. In this section, we examine both of these approaches and discuss tradeoffs in terms of 3D user interface design.

Active sensor–based data gloves typically use bend-sensing technology to track the fingers and to detect hand postures (static configurations) and certain gestures (a series of postures). For example, data gloves can distinguish between a fist, a pointing posture, and an open hand. The raw data from the gloves is usually given in the form of joint angle measurements, and software is used to detect postures and gestures based on these measurements.

Many data gloves have been developed over the years. Some of the earliest used light-based sensors, which are rudimentary vision–based sensors that use flexible tubes with a light source at one end and a photocell at the other (Defanti and Sandin 1977). As the fingers are bent, the amount of light that hits the photocells varies, producing a measurement of the amount of bending. Another light-based approach uses optical goniometer sensors consisting of flexible tubes with a reflective interior wall, a light source at one end, and a photosensitive detector on the other, which detects both direct and reflected light rays (Zimmerman et al. 1987). Depending on the bending of the tubes, the detector changes its electrical resistance as a function of light intensity. These types of light-based sensors were used in older, first-generation data gloves.

Today, more sophisticated sensor technology is used, such as fiber-optic sensors, resistive ink sensors, strain-gauge bend sensors (Kramer 1991), and inertial measurement units (IMUs) Figure 6.23 shows an example of a glove that captures acceleration and gyroscopic information for each finger. Dipietro et al. (2008) provides a thorough overview of different types of bend-sensing data gloves.

Data gloves typically have between 5 and 22 sensors. For example, a glove that has 5 sensors will usually measure one joint in each finger, while a glove with 18 sensors could measure at least two joints in each finger, abduction between fingers, wrist roll and yaw, and others. An example of an 18-senor glove that uses bend sensors is shown in Figure 6.24.

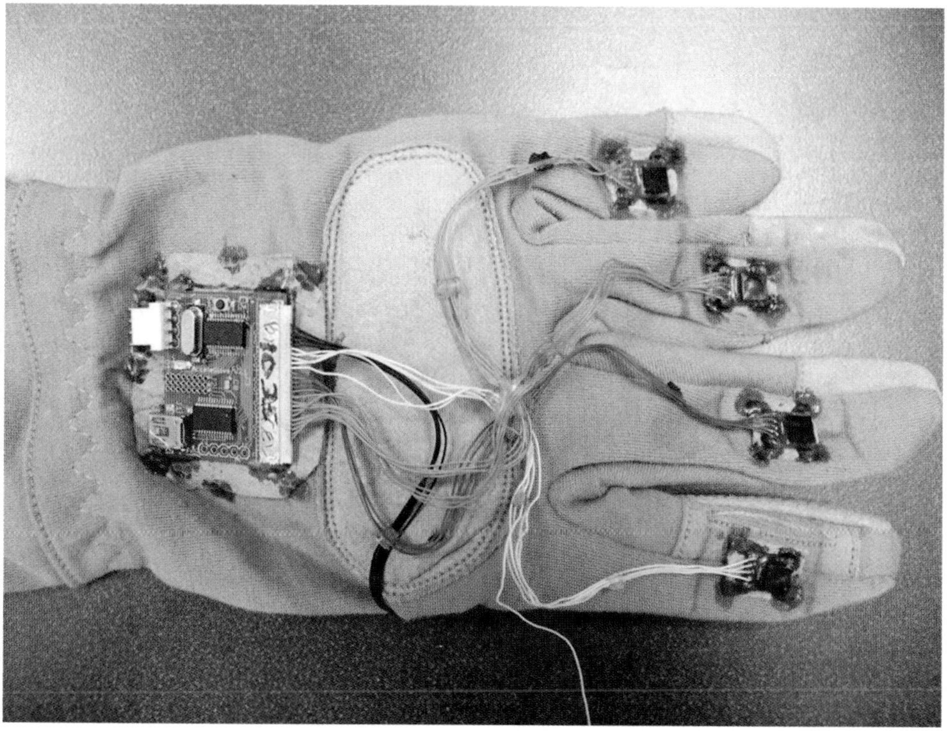

Figure 6.23 A data glove that uses accelerometers, gyroscopes, and magnetometers to capture information about each finger. (NuGlove Photograph courtesy of AnthroTronix)

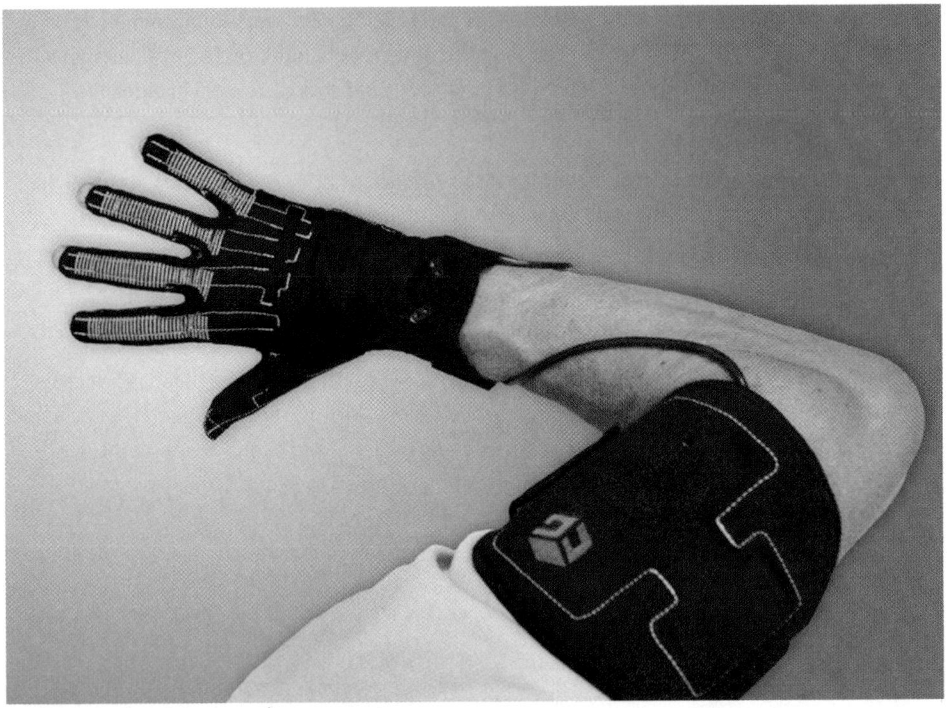

Figure 6.24 A bend-sensing data glove that can track the fingers. (CyberGlove Model III photograph courtesy of CyberGlove Systems)

From a 3D UI perspective, data gloves are commonly used for hand gesture and posture recognition (LaViola 2013), which can be applied to a variety of different interaction techniques. For example, a flick of the wrist could indicate that the user wants to delete an object. A pointing posture could indicate a travel technique such as steering (see Chapter 8). Often, hand postures and gestures are used as system commands in the context of system control techniques (see Chapter 9). Note that to recognize some gestures (such as a waving hand), a motion tracker must be attached to the data glove.

In some 3D UIs, a virtual representation of a user's hand or hands is required. Data gloves with an associated tracking system can provide such a representation. In general, these types of representations are useful when the real world is completely blocked from the user's view (e.g., when using an HWD) and the user needs to see her hands in the scene with other virtual objects. For instance, a user might wish to get an understanding of where her hands are in relation to various dials and controls in a virtual car's interior.

One of the major advantages of bend-sensing gloves is that they provide a large number of DOF, making it possible to recognize a variety of hand gestures and postures as well as providing a representation of the user's hand in the 3D application. However, the user does have to wear the device, and there will always be a significant portion of the population for which the glove does not fit well. In addition, bend-sensing gloves sometimes need calibration on a user-by-user basis.

As an alternative to bend-sensing gloves, Pinch Gloves (see Figure 6.25) determine only whether a user is touching two or more fingertips together. These gloves have a conductive material at each of the fingertips, so that when the user pinches two fingers together, an electrical contact is made. These devices are often used for performing grabbing and pinching gestures in the context of object selection, mode switching, and other techniques (see Bowman et al. [2002] for details).

The conductive cloth can also be placed in other locations besides the finger tips. For example, if the conductive cloth is on the back of the glove along the user's fingers and thumb, as shown in Figure 6.25, and if a finger is tracked, the user can make gestures that can be interpreted as simple sliders by simply making a cloth contact with the tracked fingertip and one of the cloth strips on the back of the other glove. When contact is made, the system can determine the location of the tracked fingertip as the user slides it up and down the cloth strip. If a tracker is attached to the other glove, it is trivial to determine if the user's finger is moving toward the wrist or away from the wrist when making the gesture. This simple technique has been used to adjust object size or increase and decrease parameter values (LaViola 2000b). Pinch Gloves were popular in the late 1990s and early 2000s, but they are rarely used today. However, they do still have advantages in 3D UI design and can easily be built from scratch with today's maker and DIY technology.

Figure 6.25 A Pinch Glove is a user-worn input device that uses conductive cloth at each of the fingertips. (Photograph courtesy of Joseph J. LaViola Jr.)

Both pinch gloves and bend-sensing gloves have limitations. Although it is possible to determine if there is finger contact (e.g., index finger to thumb) with a bend-sensing glove, some form of hand gesture recognition is required, which will not be as accurate as the Pinch Glove (which has essentially 100% accuracy, assuming the device is functioning properly). Conversely, one can get an idea of how the fingers are bent when using Pinch Gloves, but they provide only very rough estimates. Ideally, a data glove should have the functionality of both bend-sensing gloves and Pinch Gloves. A system that combined both bend-sensing and pinch-based input, Flex and Pinch (LaViola 1999b), helped to make certain interaction techniques easier to perform, such as locking during a scaling operation or starting and stopping an object selection operation.

Finally, another example of using active sensors is to track the fingers using EMG. NASA Ames Research Center developed a bioelectric input device that reads muscle nerve signals emanating from the forearm (see Figure 6.26). These nerve signals are captured by a dry electrode array on the arm. The nerve signals are analyzed using pattern recognition software and then routed through a computer to issue relevant interface commands. Figure 6.26 shows a user controlling a virtual 757 aircraft (Jorgensen et al. 2000). This type of device could also be used to mimic a real keyboard in a VE or mobile setting. Recently, this approach has resurfaced in the form of gesture-sensing armbands that use EMG.

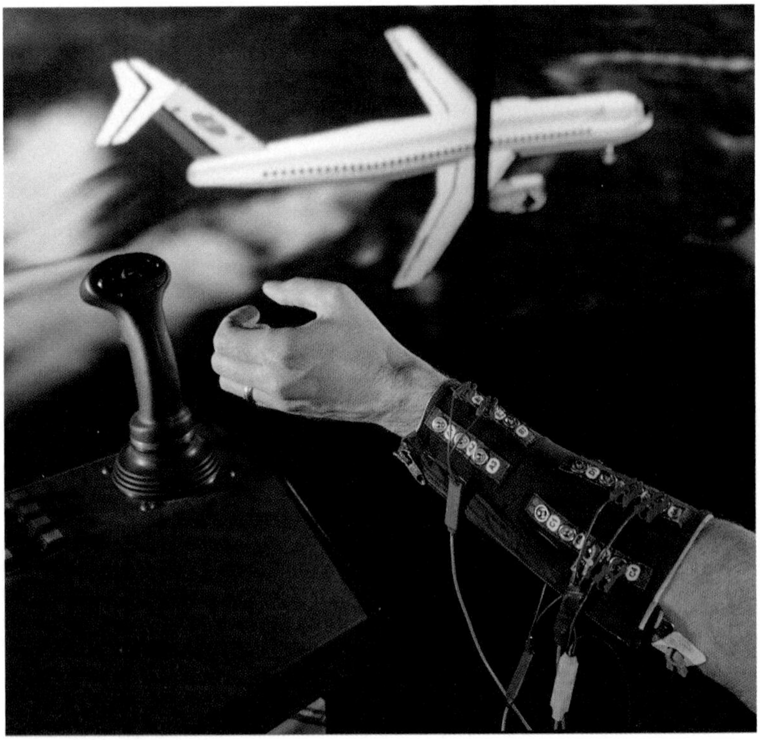

Figure 6.26 An example of a device that tracks finger movements and gestures by using EMG sensors to detect muscle activity in the forearm. (Photograph courtesy of NASA Ames Research Center)

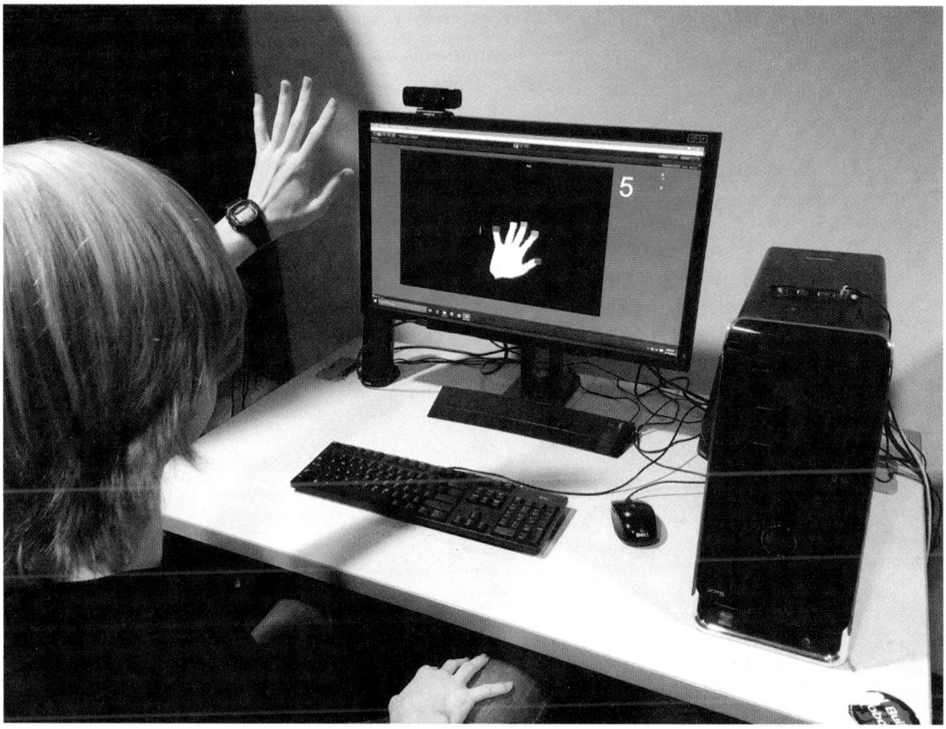

Figure 6.27 An example of tracking the fingers using a depth camera, making use of passive sensing. (Photograph courtesy of Arun Kulshreshth)

Using active sensors such as gloves is not the only way to track a user's fingers. Passive sensing devices (e.g., depth cameras like the example in Figure 6.27) are also viable alternatives and have been shown to be robust (Qian et al. 2014; Sridhar et al. 2015) in terms of accuracy and speed. Relying on computer vision algorithms rather than more direct measurements finger tracking can be completely unobtrusive. However, line of sight issues still remain, and passive sensors do not offer the range that an instrumented glove can achieve. Depth camera devices are sometimes used on the desktop, but they can also be mounted on the front of an HWD to provide hand and finger tracking in VR and AR systems. Millimeter wave radar (see Figure 6.19) is also a viable alternative as a passive sensing device for tracking subtle movements of both the hand and fingers.

Tracking the Eyes

Eye trackers are input devices used to determine where the user is looking. Eye-tracking technology is based primarily on optical sensing: the device tracks the user's pupils using corneal reflections detected by a camera. Devices can be worn (Figure 6.28) or attached to a computer screen (Figure 6.29). Thus, eye trackers are an example of devices that primarily make use of passive sensing but can be considered either active or passive devices, depending on their physical relationship to the user. Other eye-tracking techniques include electrooculography, which measures the skin's electric potential differences using electrodes placed around the eye, and embedding mechanical or optical reference objects in contact lenses that are worn directly on the eye (Duchowski 2009).

Figure 6.28 An example of a user-worn eye-tracking device that performs pupil tracking to determine eye gaze. (Photograph courtesy of SensoMotoric Instruments, GmbH(SMI), www.smivision.com)

Figure 6.29 An example of a passive eye-tracking device that does not require the user to wear anything. (Photograph courtesy of Joseph J. LaViola Jr.)

From a generic interaction perspective, eye-tracking systems have been used both as an evaluation tool and to interact with an application. For example, these devices are used to collect information about a user's eye movements in the context of psychophysical experiments, to get application usage patterns to help improve the interface, or for training in visual inspection tasks (Duchowski et al. 2001). Eye-tracking systems are also used as input devices. For example, a menu system could allow selection of menu items by gaze fixations with a certain dwell time. In the context of 3D UI design, eye-tracking systems have the potential to improve upon many existing 3D interaction techniques. For example, there are numerous techniques based on gaze direction (e.g., gaze-directed steering, gaze-directed manipulation) that use a head-tracker as an approximation to where the user is looking. Because the gaze vector in these techniques is accurate only if the user is looking straight ahead, usability problems can occur if the user looks in other directions while keeping the head stationary. Eye-tracking devices might help improve these gaze-directed techniques, because the actual direction of the gaze from the user can be obtained. See Duchowski (2009), Wang and Winslow (2015), Jacob (1995), Stellmach and Dachselt (2012), Sidorakis et al. (2015), and Sundstedt (2010) for more information on eye-tracking systems and their use in 3D applications.

6.3.3 3D Mice: Combining Spatial Tracking with Physical Device Components

In the last section, we described different approaches to tracking the body for 3D UIs, based on the different sensing technologies described in section 6.3.1. In many cases, we need to couple these tracking systems, specifically trackers that can provide 3D position, orientation, and/or motion information, with other physical device components, such as buttons, sliders, knobs, dials, joysticks, and touchpads, to create more functionally powerful input devices. We call these devices **3D mice** and define them broadly as handheld or user-worn input devices that combine position, orientation, and/or motion tracking with physical device components.

The distinguishing characteristic of 3D mice, as opposed to regular 2D mice, is that users physically move them in 3D space instead of just moving the device along a flat surface collecting 2D movement data. Therefore, users hold 3D mice or, in some cases, wear them. Additionally, with orientation information present, it is trivial to determine where the device is pointing (the device's direction vector), a function used in many fundamental 3D interaction techniques (see Chapters 7 and 8). Because of their generality, they can be mapped to many different interaction techniques, and in one form or another they are often the primary means of communicating user intention in 3D UIs for a variety of VR, AR, and mobile applications.

Handheld 3D Mice

A common design approach for 3D mice is to place a motion tracker inside a structure that is fitted with different physical interface widgets. Actually, one of the first 3D mice to be developed used no housing at all. The "bat" (Ware and Jessome 1988), so named because it is a mouse that flies, was developed by Colin Ware in the late 1980s. It was simply a 6-DOF tracking device with three buttons attached to it. Such a device is rather easy to build with a few electrical components (provided you have the tracking device). A more sophisticated and elegant version of the bat is shown in Figure 6.30. This device houses a motion tracker in a structure that looks like a simple remote control. It has been used in conjunction with surround-screen displays for both navigation and selection of 3D objects.

The physical structure that houses the motion tracker is often shaped like an input device used in the real world. For example, the 3D mouse shown in Figure 6.31 is modeled after an air force pilot's flight stick. Some 3D mice have also been developed to look like their 2D counterparts. For example, the Fly Mouse (see Figure 6.11) looks similar to a conventional 2D mouse, but it uses acoustic tracking, has five buttons instead of two, and can also be used as a microphone for speech input.

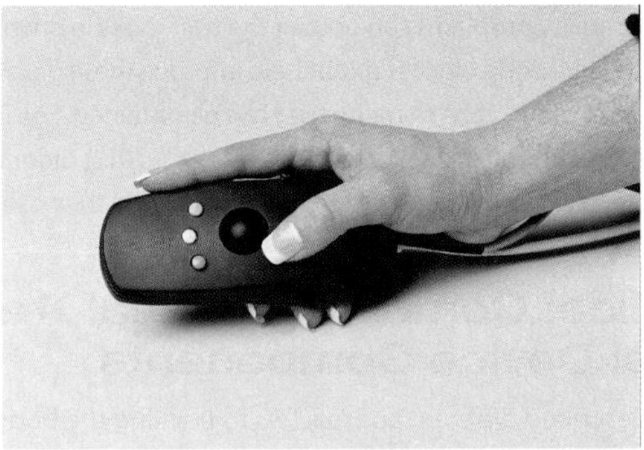

Figure 6.30 The Wanda input device. (Photograph courtesy of Ascension Technology Corporation)

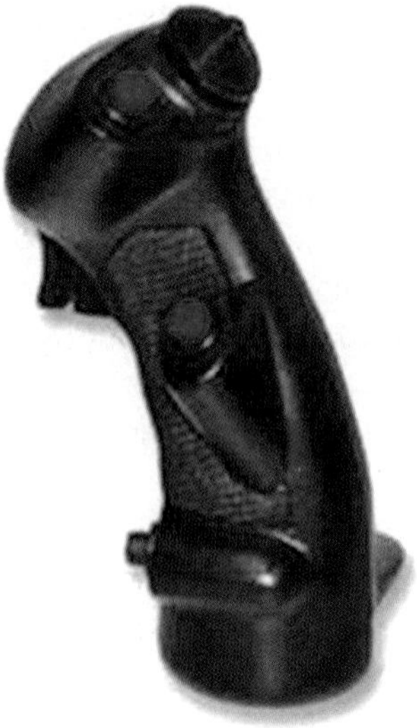

Figure 6.31 A 3D joystick modeled after a flight stick. (Built by VP Integrated Solutions as a large-scale visualization device)

Figure 6.32 The Cubic Mouse. (Photograph courtesy of Fakespace Systems)

The Cubic Mouse (shown in Figure 6.32), originally developed at Fraunhofer IMK, is a 3D mouse designed primarily as an interactive prop for handling 3D objects. It was ideally suited for examining volumetric data because of its ability to intuitively map to the volume's coordinates and act as a physical proxy for manipulating it (Fröhlich and Plate 2000). The device consists of a box with three perpendicular rods passing through the center, an embedded tracker, and buttons for additional input. The Cubic Mouse does have a disadvantage in that the three orthogonal rods can get in the way when the user is holding the device in certain configurations.

Aside from the Fly Mouse (Figure 6.11), the 3D mice we have shown thus far have all been tethered. Many current 3D mice, however, are completely wireless, often making use of 6-DOF optical sensing. For example, the Bug (Stefani and Rauschenbach 2003) is an ergonomically designed wireless device with two buttons and a slider. It looks similar to a desktop mouse but features three spherical markers (used by the optical tracking system to measure position and orientation) protruding from the device. Other wireless 3D mice have been developed in the console gaming and VR markets by combining optical and inertial sensors (see Figure 6.33) together with different combinations of buttons and analog controllers. Regardless of the configuration of any of these handheld 3D mice, their roots can be traced back to the bat in that their intended purpose is to provide position, orientation, and/or motion data of the hand in 3D space with the ability to initiate and end 3D interactions via a button press.

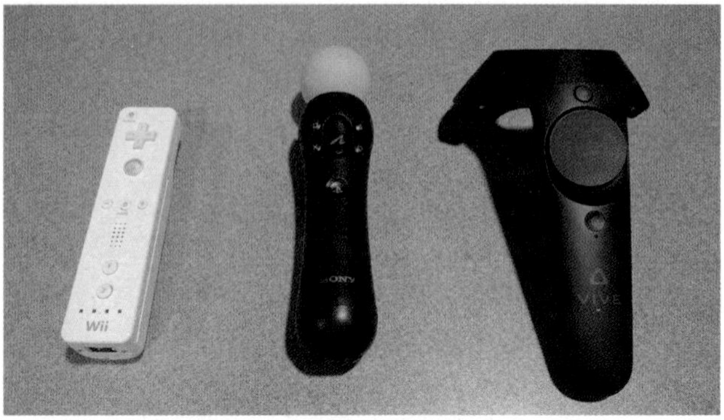

Figure 6.33 Examples of modern 3D mice that make use of optical and inertial sensing to produce 3D position, orientation, and motion data. Since users hold a 3D mouse, their hands are effectively tracked in 3D space, and coupled with buttons, analog controllers, dials, etc., these 3D mice provide for a variety of mappings from device to 3D interaction technique. (Photograph courtesy of Joseph J. LaViola Jr.)

User-Worn 3D Mice

Another approach to the design of 3D mice is to have the user wear them instead of hold them. Assuming the device is light enough, having the device worn on the user's finger, for example, makes the device an extension of the hand. Figure 6.34 shows the Ring Mouse, an example of such a device. It is a small, two-button, ring-like device that uses ultrasonic tracking that generates only position information. One of the issues with this device is that it has a limited number of buttons because of its small form factor.

The FingerSleeve, shown in Figure 6.35, is a finger-worn 3D mouse that is similar to the Ring Mouse in that it is small and lightweight, but it adds more button functionality in the same physical space by using pop-through buttons (Zeleznik et al. 2002). Pop-through buttons have two clearly distinguished activation states corresponding to light and firm finger pressure.

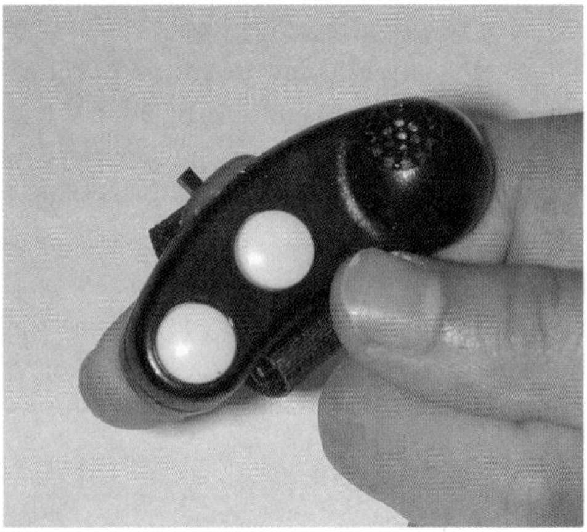

Figure 6.34 The Ring Mouse input device uses acoustic tracking and is worn on a user's index finger. (Photograph courtesy of Joseph J. LaViola Jr.)

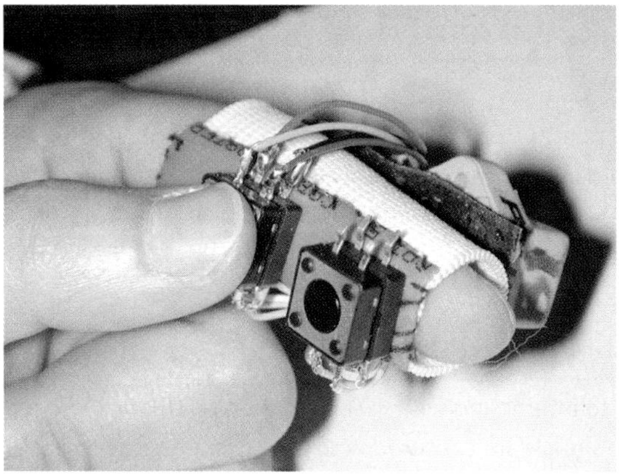

Figure 6.35 A user pressing one of the multilevel buttons on the FingerSleeve. (Photograph reprinted from Zeleznik et al. (2002), © 2002 IEEE Press)

The device can be worn on the index finger of either the left or right hand and is made of an elastic fabric and a small piece of flexible plastic that can be found at any arts and crafts store. The fabric is sewn into a sleeve with a varying diameter that fits snugly for most users. The plastic is sewn onto the front of the sleeve to provide a solid mount for pop-through buttons, and the buttons are glued into place a few millimeters apart on top of the plastic. A 6-DOF tracker is secured to the back of the sleeve using Velcro. See Zeleznik et al. (2002) for more details.

A more recent device looks more like an actual ring (see Figure 6.36) and is designed to support 3D gestural interaction among other interaction metaphors that include touch input. Other examples of finger-worn 3D mice are the EyeRing (Nanayakkara et al. 2013), PickRing (Wolf and Willaredt 2015), and uTrack (Chen et al. 2013).

Figure 6.36 An example of a finger-worn 3D mouse that supports gesture-based interaction. (Photograph courtesy of Nod, Copyright © 2016 Nod Inc www.nod.com)

6.4 Complementary Input for 3D User Interfaces

Not all input in 3D UIs comes from 3D spatial input devices. Some complementary input technologies are often used in 3D interaction. Sometimes these input technologies are used alone, but more often they are used in conjunction with 3D spatial input. In this section we discuss two important complementary input modalities: speech and brain input.

6.4.1 Speech Input

A powerful approach to interacting with 3D applications is to track and recognize signals from human speech. These signals are captured with acoustic sensing devices such as a single microphone or array of microphones. These signals are then taken and run through speech or spoken dialogue recognizers to interpret the content of the speech.

Speech input provides a nice complement to other input devices. It is a natural way to combine different modes of input (i.e., multimodal interaction) to form a more cohesive and intuitive interface (Lucente et al. 1998). When functioning properly, speech input can be a valuable tool in 3D UIs, especially when both of the user's hands are occupied. Beyond choosing a good speech recognition engine, there are many other important issues to consider when using speech for a 3D interface (LaViola 1999a).

One important issue is where the microphone is to be placed. Ideally, a wide-area microphone is used so that the user need not wear a headset. Placing such a microphone in the physical environment could be problematic, however, because it might pick up noise from other people or machines in the room. One of the big problems with using speech input is having the computer know when to and when not to listen to the user's voice. Often, a user is conversing with a collaborator with no intention of issuing voice commands, but the application "thinks" the user is speaking to it. This misinterpretation can be very troublesome.

One of the best ways to avoid this problem is to use an implicit or invisible push-to-talk scheme. A traditional push-to-talk scheme lets the user tell the application when he or she is speaking to it, usually by pushing a button. In order to maintain the naturalness of the speech interface, we do not want to add to the user's cognitive load. The goal of implicit push-to-talk is to embed the "push" into existing interaction techniques, so the user does not have the burden of remembering to signal the application that a voice command is about to be issued. As an example, consider a furniture layout application in which a user wants to place different pieces of furniture into a room. The user wishes to put a table into a kitchen. To accomplish this task, the user must create the object and then place it in the room. The user shows where the table should be placed using a laser pointer and then says, "Give me a table, please." The act of picking up the laser pointer signals the application that the user is about to ask for an object.

This action "piggybacks" the voice command onto the placement task, making the push-to-talk part of the technique implicit.

More recently, speech recognition has matured enough to use a different approach, in which the user simply says the name of the speech recognition agent followed by the speech command (e.g., "Recognizer, place the red cube on the table"). The system simply listens for its name, and listens for other commands only after its name has been spoken. This works well enough to reduce many problems with users giving inadvertent commands. More information on speech input can be found in LaViola et al. (2014) as well as Chapter 9.

6.4.2 Brain Input

The goal of brain–computer interfaces (BCIs) in the context of 3D UIs is to use neuronal activity of the brain to control devices and issue commands in both the physical and virtual worlds (Millán 2003). Additionally, BCI devices can be used to track the user's cognitive load, emotional state, and alertness, among other things, to adapt UIs and experiences as needed.

A brain–computer input device monitors brainwave activity primarily through electroencephalogram (EEG) signals. EEG records electrical activity of the brain along the scalp by measuring voltage fluctuations resulting from ionic current within the neurons of the brain. The user simply wears a noninvasive headband or a cap with the integrated electrodes.

Other types of technologies such as functional magnetic resonance imaging (fMRI), positron emission tomography (PET), and functional near-infrared spectroscopy (fNIRS) have also been used. A more invasive approach would be to surgically implant microelectrodes in the motor cortex. Of course, this approach is still not practical for common use, but it can be acceptable for severely disabled people who cannot interact with a computer in any other way. Early research showed that a monkey with microelectrodes implanted in its motor cortex could move a mouse cursor to desired targets (Serruya et al. 2002), and this research has extended to humans as well in many reported studies (Dornhege et al. 2007). BCIs are still in their infancy, but the underlying potential of such an interface is immense, not only for 3D UIs but for all other types of computer interaction.

An example of a portable BCI device using active EEG sensors is shown in Figure 6.37. This device has 14 EEG channels that can be used in conjunction with signal processing software and machine learning algorithms to detect emotional states, allowing the user to directly interact with virtual or physical objects via the brain. From a 3D UI perspective, such a BCI device could be used to translate and rotate 3D objects or move a robotic arm. Although these devices are still rudimentary and can be challenging to use, they show the potential of this technology. More information on brain–computer interfaces can be found in Dornhege et al. (2007) or Wolpaw and Wolpaw (2012).

Figure 6.37 An example of a head-worn brain–computer input device that reads EEG information from strategically placed points on the scalp. (Photograph courtesy of Emotiv)

6.5 Special-Purpose Input Devices

Many other types of devices are used in 3D UIs. These devices are often designed for specific applications, used in conjunction with specific output devices, or with specific user populations. In this section, we present some examples of these special-purpose devices. A more thorough discussion of special-purpose devices can be found in Kruijff (2007).

Special-purpose 3D input devices have been used in the context of 3D modeling. For example, ShapeTape (shown in Figure 6.38) is a flexible, ribbon-like tape of fiber-optic curvature sensors that comes in various lengths and sensor spacing. Because the sensors provide bend and twist information along the tape's length, it can be easily flexed and twisted in the hand, making it an ideal input device for creating, editing, and manipulating 3D curves (Grossman et al. 2003). In addition, the device can be used in system control (see Chapter 9) by recognizing different gestures made by the tape (e.g., quickly moving the endpoints of the tape together or apart). Note that in some cases, other input devices (the bat, for example) can be attached to the tape to increase functionality (Balakrishnan et al. 1999).

Another example of a specially designed 3D input device for character animation is shown in a Figure 6.39. This device is an articulated doll that has embedded sensors across 16 different joints so users can configure the doll into different poses as part of animating characters in software. The use of this device is analogous to bending action figures into various poses; only in this case the pose information is used to drive a virtual 3D character.

The iSphere (see Figure 6.40) is a 3D input device specifically designed for 3D modeling of parametric surfaces. The device has 24-DOF, two for each face of a dodecahedron that uses capacitive sensors to support proximity sensing and touch sensing for push-and-pull operations on 3D surfaces (Lee et al. 2005).

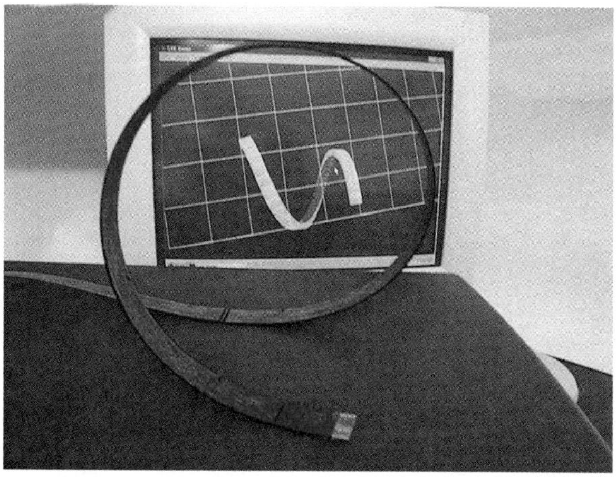

Figure 6.38 ShapeTape being used to manipulate 3D curves. (Photograph courtesy of Measurand, Inc., www.measurand.com)

Figure 6.39 A 3D input device used for posing 3D characters. The device uses 32 sensors across 16 body joints so users can manipulate the mannequin to create particular poses that are translated to virtual characters. (Photograph courtesy of Clip Studio)

Figure 6.40 The iSphere, a 24-DOF device for 3D modeling of parametric surfaces. This 12-sided capacitive 3D input device was designed and tested with Maya in Ted Selker's Context aware computing group at MIT Media lab. The goal was to create and explore a more intuitive physical 3D input and manipulation approach. (Photograph courtesy of Jackie Lee and Ted Selker)

In many cases, a particular output device will drive or inspire the development of specific 3D input devices. For example, many surround-screen display configurations use a floor that is actually a display surface, so users must either remove their shoes or wear slippers when they enter the device to avoid making scuff marks and tracking in dirt. An input device called Interaction Slippers (Figure 6.41) takes advantage of the need for slippers in these environments.

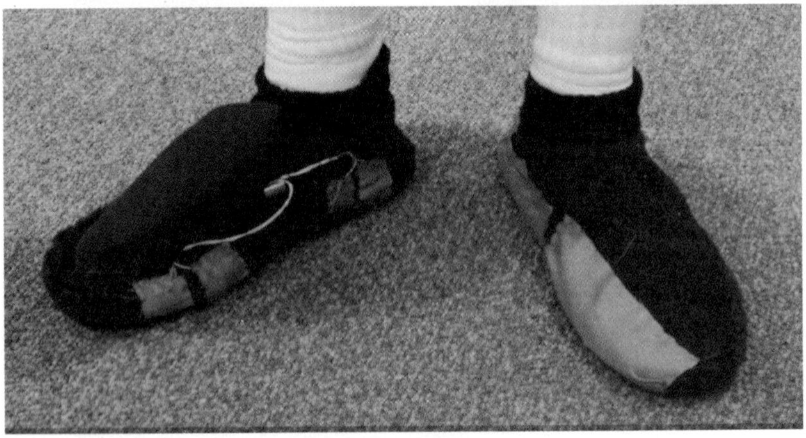

Figure 6.41 A user wearing Interaction Slippers. (Photograph reprinted from LaViola et al. 2001, © 2001 ACM Press)

The Interaction Slippers (LaViola et al. 2001) embed a wireless trackball device (the Logitech Trackman) into a pair of common house slippers. The slippers use wireless radio technology to communicate to the host computer. The Trackman is inserted into a handmade pouch on the right slipper and rewired. Two of the Trackman's three buttons are connected to a pair of conductive cloth patches on the instep of the right slipper. On the instep of the left slipper, two more conductive cloth patches are attached (as shown in Figure 6.41). Touching a cloth patch on the left slipper to a cloth patch on the right slipper completes the button press circuit. This design enables two gestures corresponding to heel and toe contacts respectively. The slippers were designed for interacting with the Step WIM navigation technique, in which a miniature version of the world is placed on the ground under the user's feet, allowing him to quickly travel to any place in the VE. LaViola et al. (2001) describes the slippers in more detail.

An example of an input device that was specifically developed for a particular 3D application is the CavePainting Table (see Figure 6.42), used in CavePainting (Keefe et al. 2001), a system for painting 3D scenes in a VE. The CavePainting Table uses a prop-based design that relies upon multiple cups of paint and a single tracked paintbrush. These paint cup props stay on a physical table that slides into the surround-screen device and also houses knobs and buttons used for various interaction tasks. In conjunction with the table, a real paintbrush is augmented with a single button that turns the "paint" on and off. The bristles of the brush are covered with conductive cloth, and users can dip the brush into the paint cups (which are lined with conductive cloth as well) to change brush strokes. A tracked bucket is used to throw paint around the virtual canvas.

Figure 6.42 The CavePainting Table used in the CavePainting application. (Photograph reprinted from Keefe et al. 2001, © 2001 ACM; reprinted with permission)

In some cases, making a simple addition to a simple prop or an existing input device can create a powerful tool for interacting in 3D applications. For example, when interacting with 3D applications that utilize workbench-style displays, attaching a motion tracker to a piece of Plexiglas can create a useful tool for interacting in 2D and 3D. In addition, these devices can have touch-sensitive screens (see Figure 6.43). Such a device allows the user to perform 2D interaction techniques, such as writing, selection of objects, and selection of commands from 2D palettes, as well as 3D interaction techniques, such as volumetric selection via sweeping the device through the virtual world (Schmalstieg et al. 1999; Coquillart and Wesche 1999; Williams et al. 1999). Adding a motion tracker to or using the existing tracking system in a handheld tablet or smart phone can support even more powerful interactions that combine 2D and 3D techniques because the device would also provide computational power and output from the display.

The Control Action Table (CAT) is another device designed for use in surround-screen display environments (Hachet et al. 2003). This freestanding device (shown in Figure 6.44) looks like a circular tabletop. The CAT uses angular sensors to detect orientation information using three nested orientation axes. The device also has an isometric component; the tabletop is equipped with a potentiometer that detects forces in any 3D direction. Thus, the user can push or pull on the device for translational movement. Additionally, the CAT has a tablet for 2D interaction mounted on the tabletop, which makes it unique because it supports both 6-DOF and 2D input in the same device. Other advantages of the CAT include the ability to control each DOF individually and its location persistence or "parkability" (meaning that its physical state does not change when released). The CAT does have some inherent limitations, because the nature of the nested orientation axes can make some orientations hard to specify, and in certain configurations (e.g., when the tabletop is vertical), translational movement can be difficult to perform.

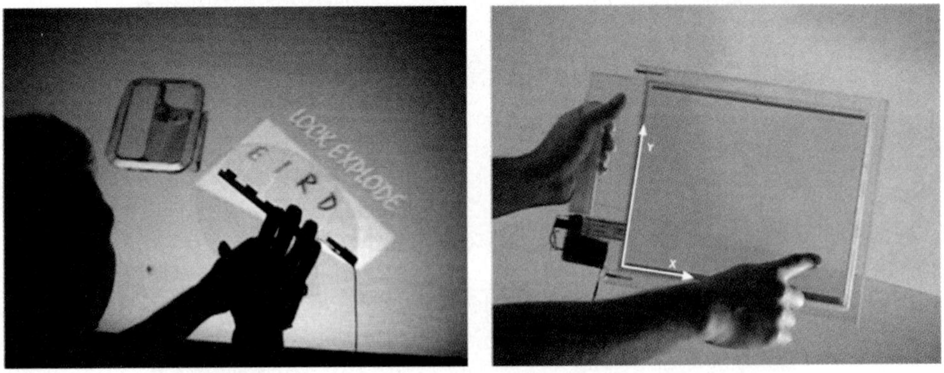

Figure 6.43 Transparent palettes used for both 2D and 3D interaction. (Williams et al. 1999; photographs courtesy of Fakespace Labs, Mountain View, California)

Figure 6.44 The CAT is designed for surround-screen display environments. It combines 6-DOF input with 2D tablet interaction. (Photograph courtesy of the Iparla Team [LaBRI–INRIA])

As a final example of special-purpose input devices for 3D UIs, the device shown in Figure 6.45 is designed specifically for children with cerebral palsy. The device is a stick that has a control unit and uses a combination of LED lighting and vibration feedback coupled with an inertial tracking system to determine the stick's balance. Balancing the stick is a very important activity for cerebral palsy patients, as it is a part of their exercise routines. The device can be connected to video games to improve their overall user experience when performing everyday balancing exercises (Darrah et al. 2003).

Figure 6.45 A 3D input device used specifically for children with cerebral palsy. It can be connected to games to better engage these children when they perform various exercises. (Photograph courtesy of Hariraghav Ramasamy)

6.6 Do It Yourself (DIY) Input Devices

3D UI researchers and practitioners are not limited to commercially available input devices. They can instead choose to develop novel and useful devices for 3D UIs using simple electronic components, sensors, and household items. Since the first edition of this book, we have seen a revolution in terms of the number of DIY projects for input devices, robotics, and other applications. This revolution is often referred to as the Maker Movement (Hatch 2013) or the new industrial revolution (Anderson 2014). DIY input device designs and prototypes have resulted in several of the commercial input devices sold today. We have already seen devices such as the bat, the Cubic Mouse, the FingerSleeve, and the CAT, all of which were designed and built by researchers in small academic research labs. In this section, we briefly discuss some strategies for making custom input devices by first presenting some ideas on building the physical devices and then discussing methods for creating the interface between devices and the computer.

6.6.1 Strategies for Building Input Devices

There are a variety of strategies for constructing DIY input devices. One of the first things to consider is the device's intended functionality, because doing so helps to determine what types of physical device components will be required. For example, the device might need to sense forces, 3D motion, or simply button presses. Based on the intended device functionality, the device developer can choose appropriate sensors, whether they are digital or analog. These sensors can easily be found in electronics stores or on the Internet. Examples include pressure sensors, bend sensors, potentiometers, thermistors (for sensing temperature), photocells (for sensing light), simple switches, and many others (see Figure 6.46). These sensors come in a variety of styles and configurations, and the appropriate choice is often based on trial and error. This trial-and-error approach is especially important with buttons, because buttons and switches come in many different shapes, sizes, and force thresholds—the amount of force the user needs to activate the button or switch.

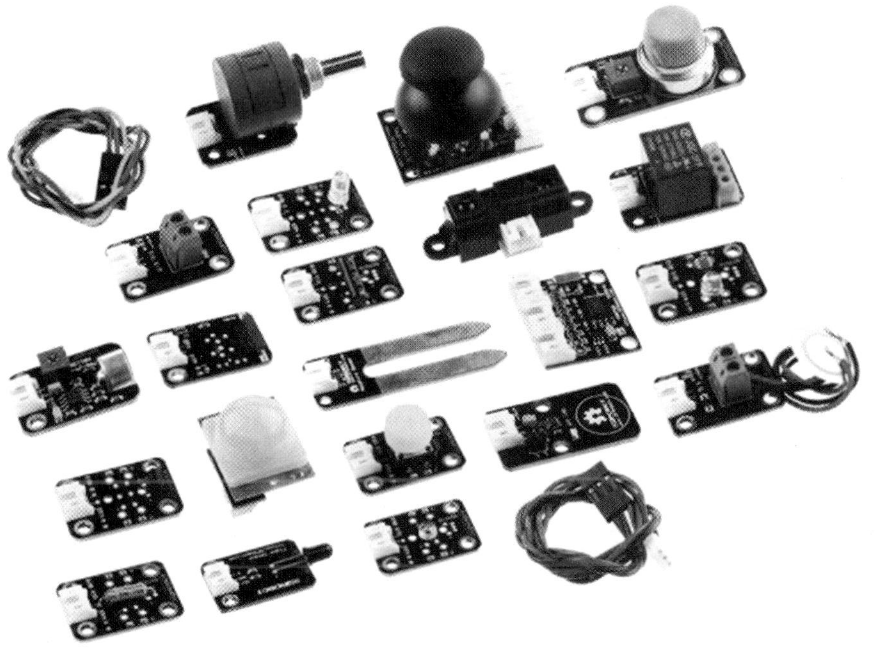

Figure 6.46 A variety of different sensors that can be used to for DIY input devices. The image shows light, sound, distance, magnetic, accelerometer, vibration, touch, and gas sensors. (Photograph courtesy of RobotShop, Inc.)

In many cases, building the sensors is a feasible option, especially if they are switches or buttons. One approach used successfully in the past for building simple switches is to use conductive cloth. Conductive cloth is just fabric with conductive material sewn into it, and it has many advantages for building custom input devices. In fact, the input devices shown in Figures 6.25, 6.41, and 6.42 all use conductive cloth as part of their designs. Conductive cloth is an inexpensive and fairly robust material. Because it is cloth, it is flexible, so it can be used just about anywhere, in many different sizes and geometric configurations. Additionally, conductive cloth is easily sewn onto other fabrics so that devices can be constructed on clothing.

Another important consideration when making DIY input devices is how the sensors are housed in the physical device. Positioning sensors in the device housing is especially important when they are active components such as buttons, dials, and sliders, because the user must be able to interact with them comfortably (i.e., support proper ergonomics such as grip) to manipulate the device. For example, if a homemade 3D mouse is being constructed with several buttons, these buttons should be placed so that the user does not have to experience any undue strain in order to press any of the buttons. Sensor placement in homemade input devices is also affected by the geometry of the device itself. See Veas and Kruijff (2008) and Veas and Kruijff (2010) for a more detailed discussion on sensor housing and ergonomics.

Initially, one of the reasons many 3D UI designers did not build homemade devices is that they do not have the ability or equipment to construct the physical housing the sensors were placed in and on. Milling machines and vacuum forming devices (a device that heats plastic and stretches it over a mold) were not commonplace, making it a challenge for anyone to construct a reasonably robust physical housing for the 3D input device. However, with 3D printing technology becoming commonplace, the construction of the physical housing is no longer an impediment to DIY input device design. You can get access to a 3D printer easily or own one for the price of a moderately powered desktop computer. With a 3D printer, constructing the device housing is based on a model developed in 3D modeling software.

Using a 3D printer can still be challenging for a novice user. One approach that makes it easier to fabricate the physical housing for an input device is called Makers' Marks, a system based on physically authoring assemblies with sculpting materials and annotation stickers. Device developers physically sculpt the shape of an object and attach stickers to place existing parts or high-level features. The tool then extracts the 3D pose of these annotations from a scan of the design and synthesizes the geometry needed to support integrating desired parts using a library of clearance and mounting constraints (Savage et al. 2015).

Another approach for developing the physical housing for a 3D input device is to use Lego bricks. The Lego Interface Toolkit (Ayers and Zeleznik 1996), a rapid prototyping system for creating physical interaction devices, uses this approach. It utilizes Lego bricks along with push buttons and rotational and linear sensors that support a variety of physical configurations. This component-based approach enables the input device developer to quickly snap together different device components. Designers can easily iterate in their designs and then move to a more permanent physical housing solution.

Another approach is to use modeling clay to create input device housings. The advantage of using modeling clay is that it can be molded into any shape the designer wants and can be quickly changed to try out different geometries. Both of these approaches are useful for rapid prototyping of the device to support iterative 3D input device design and development.

6.6.2 Connecting the DIY Input Device to the Computer

The other important part of constructing DIY input devices is choosing how to connect them to the computer. In the majority of cases, homemade input devices require some type of logic that the user needs to specify in order for the computer to understand the data the input device produces. The one exception is when existing devices are taken apart so that the sensors in them can be used in different physical configurations. An example of this is the Interaction Slippers shown in Figure 6.41. Because the device uses the rewired components of a wireless mouse, it can use a standard USB port to transmit information to the computer, thus requiring no additional electronics or device drivers.

The main approach for connecting a DIY input device to the computer so it can be used in 3D interfaces is to use a microcontroller. A microcontroller is just a small computer that can interface with other electronic components through its pins. There are many different varieties to choose from, depending on price, power, ease of programming, and so on. Two of the most commonly used microcontrollers today are the Arduino and Raspberry Pi (see Figure 6.47). The designer can connect an input device to a microcontroller on a circuit board, which in turn communicates to the computer through a serial or USB port or wirelessly though Bluetooth, Wi-Fi, RF, or other technologies.

Typically, the designer first builds the electronics on a prototyping board (breadboard), which is an easy way to establish electrical connections between the device and the microcontroller without the need to solder. In many cases, debugging the circuits developed on a breadboard can be challenging, especially for novice users. Drew et al. (2016) developed the Toast board, a tool that provides immediate visualization of an entire breadboard's state, meaning users can diagnose problems based on a wealth of data instead of having to form a single hypothesis and plan before taking a measurement.

Using any of the many software packages (many of which are free and use Basic or C) for writing microcontroller code, the developer can write a program for controlling the input device and download it to the microcontroller. After the prototyping and testing stage, the microcontroller and any associated electronics can be attached to an appropriate circuit board. The homemade input device then has its own electronics unit for sending information from the device to the computer and, with appropriate software such as device drivers, to the 3D UI. Note that many software packages that are used in 3D applications (i.e., Unity 3D and Unreal Engine) have plugins for easy integration of DIY input devices. Using microcontrollers does require some effort and has a slight learning curve, but the approach gives the input device developer a lot of freedom in choosing how the input device/computer interface is made. A nice introduction to using microcontrollers to build input devices can be found in Forman and Lawson (2003). More specifically, Hughes (2016) provides a comprehensive introduction to using Arduino, while Monk (2016) provides an excellent reference on how to use the Raspberry Pi.

Figure 6.47 Example of two of the most common microcontroller boards for DIY 3D input devices. (Photograph courtesy of Joseph J. LaViola Jr.)

One way to still use microcontrollers but sidestep many of the issues involved in using them is to use Phidgets (Greenberg and Fitchett 2001). Phidgets are physical input device widgets that can be combined through a toolkit, which essentially encapsulates the implementation and construction details of connecting input devices to computers. In effect, they provide the ability to create homemade input devices without the need to program microcontrollers and design circuit boards. More details on how Phidgets are used can be found in Greenberg and Boyle (2002).

6.7 Choosing Input Devices for 3D User Interfaces

With knowledge of the wide range of input devices and sensors available, 3D UI designers must choose appropriate input devices that are best suited to the needs of a particular application. The designer needs to examine the various tasks the 3D UI needs to support, find (or develop) the appropriate interaction techniques, and ensure that the chosen input devices are mapped to these techniques appropriately. In this section, we first examine some important factors to consider when choosing input devices. We then discuss two important tools, input device taxonomies and empirical evaluations, that can aid the designer in choosing input devices for 3D applications.

6.7.1 Important Considerations

Many factors must be considered when choosing an input device for a particular 3D UI. Device ergonomics, the number and type of input modes, the available technique-to-device mapping strategies, and the types of tasks the user will be performing all play a role in choosing suitable input devices. The problem is amplified because of the variety of possible operations the user might perform within the context of a given 3D application. A particular device might be perfect for one task but completely inappropriate for another.

Device ergonomics is clearly an important consideration when choosing an input device for a 3D application. We do not want to put undue strain on the user's body (see Chapter 3, "Human Factors Fundamentals," section 3.5). Such strain can lead to repetitive stress injuries and make it difficult for the user to perform common tasks. Devices should be lightweight, require little training, and provide a significant transfer of information to the computer with minimal effort.

A particular device's input modes must be considered when choosing an input device for a 3D application. The types of input required for the application help to reduce the possible device choices. For example, a conventional 3D modeling system uses a keyboard and other 2D devices such as a mouse or a tablet. However, these devices in an immersive 3D modeling system are not appropriate, because they are difficult to use while standing and do not provide the appropriate DOF needed to track the user's head and hands. In contrast, a desktop 3D computer game does not necessarily require a complicated 6-DOF tracking device, because, in most cases, the keyboard and a mouse or game controller will suffice. To take another example, a simple immersive architectural walkthrough requires the user to be head-tracked and have a way to navigate through the environment. In such an application, although a bend-sensing glove could be used to navigate (using some collection of gestures), it would probably not be appropriate, given the complexity of the device. A simpler device such as a Wanda, shown in Figure 6.30, is much easier to use because the application does not need all of the extra DOF that a bend-sensing glove gives the user.

An input device can handle a variety of interaction techniques depending on the logical mapping of the technique to the device. The major issue is whether that mapping makes the device and the subsequent interaction techniques *usable*. Therefore, an important consideration when choosing an input device in a 3D application is how the device will map to the interaction techniques required to perform application tasks. There is a bit of a chicken-and-egg problem here; one should choose the input device to match the interaction techniques, but one should also design the interaction techniques to fit the chosen input device. In practice, the choice of devices, techniques, and device-to-technique mappings must be made together.

It is in these mappings where tradeoffs are usually made, because often a device will have a natural mapping to one or two of the interaction techniques in the application but relatively poor mappings to the others. For example, in the context of an immersive scientific visualization application, a 3D tracker may be attached to the user's hand and used for selection and manipulation of a tool for examining the dataset. The user can simply move the tool within the space of the dataset to explore it, and this represents a natural mapping from device to interaction technique. However, using the 3D tracker to input parameter values to change the rendering style has a less natural mapping from device to interaction technique. If the scientific visualization application were on the desktop, the keyboard would provide a much more natural mapping for changing rendering styles but would also make object selection and manipulation much more difficult.

This example makes the point that there is often a tradeoff when choosing an input device for a 3D application. In many cases, input devices have been designed for general use, which means that although they can be used for a variety of interaction techniques, they may not provide the best mapping for any one of them. Sometimes, several specialized devices may provide better usability than a single general-purpose device.

> **Tip**
>
> It is sometimes better to have a series of specialized devices that work well for a specific group of interaction techniques rather than one or two generic input devices for all of the techniques in a 3D application.

Examples of this type of approach can be found in the work of Hinckley et al. (1994); Forsberg et al. (1998); and Keefe et al. (2001).

6.7.2 Input Device Taxonomies

Input device taxonomies can be a useful tool for determining which input devices can be substituted for each other, and they can also help in making decisions about what devices to use for particular tasks. In addition, they are an important part of 3D UI design, because they provide a mechanism for understanding and discussing the similarities and differences among input devices. In this section, we briefly review some of these input device taxonomies from a historical perspective to show the evolution of these tools. Additionally, we discuss how they can be used to help make decisions about choosing appropriate devices in 3D UIs.

One of the first input device taxonomies was developed by Foley and Wallace (1974). Their approach was to separate the input device from the interaction technique. They created a set of four virtual devices, which at the time covered most input devices. These virtual devices were the pick, locator, button, and valuator. A **pick** device is used to designate a user-defined object. A **locator** is used to determine position and/or orientation. A **button** is used to designate a system-defined object. Finally, a **valuator** is used to input a single value within a set of numbers. Two additional virtual devices, stroke and string, were added to this set by Enderle et al. (1984). A **stroke** is a sequence of points, and a **string** is a sequence of characters.

This virtual device taxonomy proves useful in many different situations. For example, the 3D UI developer can use this taxonomy as a tool for quickly reducing the number of possible input devices to choose from by simply examining which virtual devices fit the application best and selecting the devices that fit in those categories. If a 3D locator is required in an application, then we can automatically eliminate all of the physical devices that do not map to this virtual device. However, this taxonomy does have a fundamental flaw, because devices that appear to be equivalent in the taxonomy can be dramatically different both physically and practically. For example, a mouse and a stylus are very different devices, yet they are both considered to be 2D locators and stroke devices.

Other taxonomies were developed to take different input device characteristics into account. For example, Foley et al. (1984) improved upon the virtual device taxonomy by mapping elementary interaction tasks (e.g., select, position, orient) to the devices that perform those tasks. Based on task requirements, only a limited set of devices could be used for any particular task. However, because the taxonomy is task-based, an input device can appear for more than one task. Although this taxonomy can help to reduce the set of possible input devices even further than the virtual device taxonomy, it still has the problem that the structure of the device space and any pragmatic differences that distinguish input devices from one another are hidden.

To compensate for the pragmatic deficiencies of earlier taxonomies, Buxton (1983) developed a taxonomy that organizes continuous input devices into a 2D space, the dimensions of which are DOF and properties sensed (i.e., motion, position, pressure). Additionally, a subclassification is used to distinguish for devices that have a mechanical intermediary between the hand and the sensing mechanism and those that are touch-sensitive. An example of how this taxonomy classifies input devices is shown in Figure 6.48. We note two issues with this taxonomy. First, it was not developed to handle discrete input devices. Second, although it can determine if it is incorrect to substitute one input device for another, it cannot tell us why that substitution is inappropriate.

Mackinlay et al. (1990b) extended Buxton's taxonomy in two ways. First, they distinguished between absolute and relative quantities. Second, they separated translational and rotational movement. In addition, they distinguished between the different translational and rotational axes instead of using DOF. For example, a 6-DOF position-tracking device would be labeled a device for sensing position in *x*, *y*, and *z* Cartesian coordinates and orientation in *rX*, *rY*, and *rZ* rotational coordinates with an infinite number of possible values sensed for each axis (see Figure 6.49). Their taxonomy allows for the description of both discrete and continuous devices, as well as simple devices that can be combined into complex controls. This taxonomy was one of the first that recognized that human performance issues are important to understanding how devices work for given tasks. It could be used for choosing input devices in a similar manner to previous taxonomies—as a tool to help narrow down device choices by examining device pragmatics and mappings to interaction tasks.

Card et al. (1991) further refined their taxonomy to analyze devices morphologically. They explore how devices could be examined as points in a parametrically designed design space. They used two metrics, footprint and bandwidth, to illustrate how different parts of the design space could be explored in order to illustrate where parts of the space would be interesting for further prototyping and engineering efforts.

		Number of Dimensions					
		1		2		6	
Property Sensed	Position	Bend Sensor	Linear Slider	Tablet and Stylus	Isotonic Joystick	Trackers (Position & Orientation)	M
				Touch Tablet			T
	Motion		Treadmill	Mouse	TrackBall		M
	Pressure	Torque Sensor			Isometric Joystick	SpaceBall & SpaceMouse	T

Figure 6.48 Buxton's input device taxonomy, based on pragmatic attributes of devices, categorizes devices based on DOF, properties sensed, and whether the device uses an intermediary between the user and sensing mechanism (M) or is touch-sensitive (T). (Adapted from Buxton (1983))

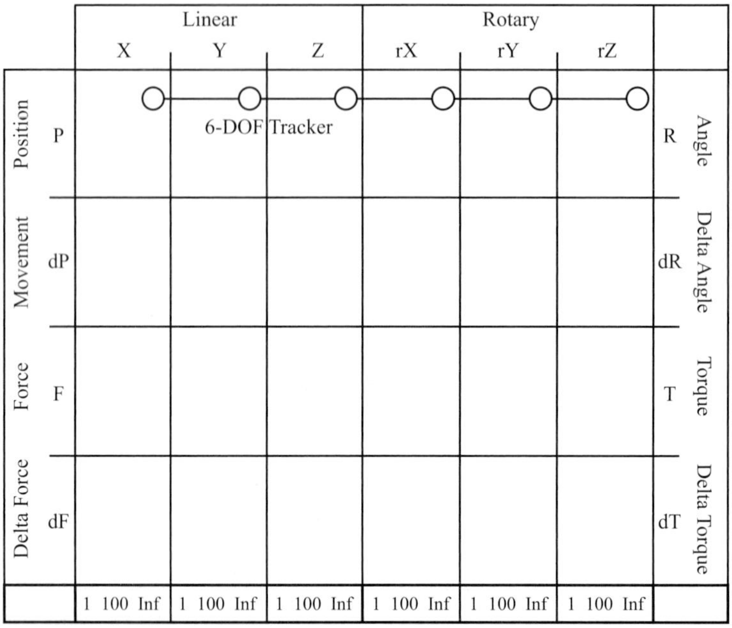

Figure 6.49 Mackinlay et al.'s (1990b) input device taxonomy categorizes a 6-DOF tracker. The circles indicate that the device senses one of the properties shown along the vertical axis. The placement of these circles within a column shows how many values are sensed.

Although the taxonomies we have discussed thus far provide frameworks for characterizing and understanding different input devices, they are limited in that they can reduce the number of possible input device choices but not determine which specific device is preferable. Jacob and Sibert (1992) took these flaws into account by realizing that perceptual and cognitive issues were ignored. They developed a theoretical model to address these issues. Their approach is based on the idea that observers perceive multidimensional spaces based on their perceptual structures (Garner 1974). The theory breaks these structures into two distinct components. Single composite perceptions are *integrally* related, while distinct perceptions are *separably* related. A multidimensional input device can be considered integral or separable based on whether it is a device that considers DOF together (a single composition) or that treats DOF individually (distinct compositions). The argument for this approach is that two 3D tasks may seem equivalent but have different perceptual spaces, implying that different input devices should be used.

For example, users perceive the task of positioning and orienting an object as integral (all six DOF are controlled at once to set the object's pose), so an integral 6-DOF device like a tracker is the best choice. On the other hand, users may perceive the task of selecting a color as separable (three parameters like hue, saturation, and value are controlled independently), so the best device would be one that lets users control a single DOF at a time. This model was not designed for characterizing devices but rather to indicate when 3D input devices should be used instead of 2D devices for a given task. It has been used in different input device evaluations, such as those of Hinckley et al. (1997) and Balakrishnan et al. (1997).

6.7.3 Empirical Evaluations

In general, the taxonomies we discussed in the last section are useful for narrowing down the choice of input device for a particular task or 3D UI. However, in order to get concrete information about which devices are appropriate for given tasks, empirical studies are often required. In contrast to the lack of empirical work done on choosing appropriate output devices for 3D applications (see Chapter 5), there has been a good amount of research evaluating input devices for interacting in 3D. Performing empirical analyses of input devices is somewhat easier than performing comparisons of output devices, because it is easier to obtain quantitative measurements of device performance. Characteristics such as speed, accuracy, and ease of learning are often used to measure how a device will perform in a certain task. In addition, tools such as Fitts's law and the steering law (see Chapter 3, "Human Factors Fundamentals," section 3.2.4) provide a basis for quantitative analysis.

Studies have been conducted to determine the effectiveness of 3D input devices compared to traditional desktop devices such as the mouse. For example, Hinckley et al. (1997) compared the mouse with a 6-DOF tracking device for performing 3D object rotation tasks. Their results showed that the tracking device performed 36% faster than the 2D mouse without any loss of accuracy. In another study, Ware and Jessome (1988) compared the mouse and the bat (see section 6.3.3) for manipulating 3D objects. These results indicated that 3D object manipulation was easier to perform with the bat than with the mouse. Although these are only two studies, they do suggest that 3D input devices with three integral DOF or more are better than a mouse for handling freeform 3D object manipulation.

Zhai conducted a number of interesting studies specifically on 3D input devices (Zhai 1998) and came up with guidelines for choosing appropriate 3D input devices. For example, in Zhai and Milgram (1998), 6-DOF flying mice were shown to be easy to learn and to outperform many other 3D input devices in terms of speed. However, flying mice, such as the ones described in section 6.3.3, do have disadvantages in that they cause fatigue easily and lack persistence in position when released. In contrast, desktop 6-DOF devices (see Figure 6.8) were shown to reduce user fatigue, increase device persistence, and provide smoother pointer movement, but with slower performance. This is a specific instance of the classic speed–accuracy tradeoff.

Tip

When speed and a short learning curve are of primary concern (e.g., for video games or location-based entertainment), free-moving 6-DOF devices are most suitable. When comfort, trajectory control, and coordination are most important (e.g., for 3D modeling or teleoperation), a desktop-based 6-DOF input device should be used.

Other interesting early empirical studies of 3D input devices can be found in Zhai and Woltjer (2003), Balakrishnan et al. (1997), Kessler et al. (1995), and Zhai (1995). There have been a variety of empirical studies on 3D input devices since the first edition of this book, and to discuss them all goes beyond the scope of the text. However, several studies that are worth mentioning include Dang et al. (2009), Teather and Stuerzlinger (2008), Schultheis et al. (2012), and Siegl et al. (2014).

Empirical work for determining appropriate input devices for specific tasks in 3D UIs can be difficult because of the many variables that are involved, but it continues to be an important area of research as 3D UIs continue to evolve. As new devices are developed, scientific studies must be conducted to determine how these devices can be used most effectively.

6.8 Case Studies

In this section we discuss the input requirements and design for our two case studies. Again, if you are not reading the book sequentially, you will want to go back to Chapter 2, section 2.4, to understand the context for these case studies.

6.8.1 VR Gaming Case Study

For our VR action-adventure game, full 6-DOF tracking of the player's head is a given. The player needs to be able to look in all directions, lean, crouch, and walk, using only head and body movements. Given the selection and manipulation techniques we will propose (see Chapter 7, "Selection and Manipulation," section 7.12.1), we will also need 6-DOF tracking of both the player's hands. The most important tracking requirement for us is low latency. The visual response to head movements must feel almost instantaneous to provide a good user experience, especially during rapid movements such as reacting to a monster's presence. A secondary consideration is jitter. If the scene or the virtual hands seem to be vibrating due to tracking noise, this will distract the player and diminish the sense of presence. Fortunately, several consumer-level tracking systems that are packaged with high-quality HWDs achieve both of these requirements.

Besides tracking, we have to consider what other input devices the player will use to interact with the VR system to play the game. There are three primary categories of hand-based input we can consider: 3D mice, gloves, and bare hands. Of course, this choice can't be made in isolation—input device choice and interaction technique design can't be fully separated.

It's tempting to say that bare-hand interaction, through a vision-based hand- and finger-tracking system, will always be preferable because it is the most like real-world interaction and the least cumbersome. But naturalism is not always the best design choice for VR (Bowman et al. 2012). In addition, such approaches often have significant limitations. Consider using a bare-hand tracking system to pick up a virtual object. The user can move his hand into position and grasp with his fingers, but since there is no haptic feedback, the user has no clear indication when the fingers are touching the object. A "natural" hand going through a virtual object may be more uncanny than a less "natural" technique. Dropping the object is similarly problematic: how does the user know how far he has to spread his fingers before the object is released?

Due to this ambiguity and since game players are used to interacting through devices, we will not choose bare-hand input for our VR game. But what about gloves? They can provide a similar level of natural hand and finger movements, can be tracked even when the user is not looking at them, and can incorporate vibrotactile haptic feedback. Gloves also have significant downsides, however. Putting them on and taking them off can be tedious. Sensors can be damaged as the gloves are stretched and pulled. And gloves are seen as less sanitary when multiple users use the same pair.

Overall, for durability, cleanliness, and unambiguous immediate response, it's still tough to beat 3D mice. For our game, then, we will use two equivalent ergonomically designed controllers that can be held in the players' hands, can be tracked with six DOFs, and can provide buttons and touchpads for input. The device on the far right in Figure 6.33 is an example.

But don't handheld 3D mice limit us to 3D versions of traditional "point and click" interactions? Not necessarily. Tracked controllers can also be used for certain forms of gesture input based on the 3D pose of the controller (e.g., tilting a controller to specify speed), the motion of the controller (e.g., drawing a circle in the air to cast a spell), and even the way the user is grasping the device (e.g., the Oculus Touch device can detect when the user is touching the buttons, allowing a form of simple grasp/release gestures).

Controllers themselves can also be incorporated into the design of our game directly, by using the physical controller as a handle for a virtual tool. This can be really interesting for a puzzle game where players have to use a variety of virtual tools to progress through the game world. Having made the choice to use handheld 3D mice, we can design the game and its interactions to incorporate novel and interesting tools rather than direct hand interaction. Of course, if we were designing a simulation of the real world rather than a fantasy game world, we might make this choice differently.

Key Concepts

- Completely natural interaction is not always possible or desirable, and this should be considered when choosing input devices.
- Handheld 3D mice provide a familiar bridge between traditional desktop/console interaction and VR.
- Buttons are more reliable than vision-based gesture tracking—gestures are not recognized every time.
- Gesture-based interaction can be incorporated into systems using many different types of input, not just bare-hand tracking.

6.8.2 Mobile AR Case Study

HYDROSYS required accurate tracking of the handheld device in outdoor settings. We decided to deploy a special tracking installation (an Ubisense ultra-wideband tracking system) mounted on a 4 x 4 vehicle that could be taken into the field. This allowed us to track the handheld device with high accuracy at close range to enable detailed environmental analyses. When moving away from the vehicle to perform more general analyses, users instead would use the embedded GPS and inertial sensors.

With respect to direct user input, the majority of handheld AR applications make use of a tablet or phone to visually explore data. In doing so, users can theoretically work directly with the available touchscreen. In practice, this is not always as simple as it sounds. In particular, with setups that are extended with additional sensors and controllers—as in the setup used in HYDROSYS—the screen might not be readily usable. Users may be required to hold the device with two hands, which limits control of the touchscreen to thumb presses on a limited part of the screen.

Fortunately, we designed the HYDROSYS handheld unit to support single-handed usage, but even so, touch-based control was still hard. Most users would be using gloves due to the cold operational conditions. While the touchscreen could handle finger presses, we noticed "fat finger" problems would occur as the area touched by the glove would be large, and certain functions could not be properly selected as a trade-off of the system control design (see Chapter 9 for more detail). Thus, we needed either to adjust the system control interface to support larger selection areas or look for other possibilities.

While designing HYDROSYS, we carefully considered two-handed usage with an earlier prototype, called Vesp'r (see section 5.7.2), as single-handed usage was possible but not always the preferred mode of operation (Veas and Kruijff 2008). In Vesp'r, we integrated controls into the power grip handles, to keep a firm grip on the setup while controlling the application. We embedded micro-joysticks, based on familiar controllers and usable for 2D interaction by the index finger and thumb respectively, next to several buttons accessible by the index or middle finger. Another option with a slightly different control mapping was an additional handle in which we included a scroll wheel with middle, left, and right clicks (see Veas and Kruijff (2008) for more details).

For the initial HYDROSYS design iteration, we followed a similar control scheme. While the deployed UMPC actually includes a range of buttons and a micro-joystick at the side that could theoretically be used while holding the device with both hands, these controls are small. They were simply too difficult to use, so we avoided them completely.

In the end, we decided to simply make use of the accompanying pen to interact with the screen (see Figure 6.50), as this could be done reasonably well with gloves, and the accuracy and performance speed of using the pen was much higher. A pen is simple to hold even with gloves and performs remarkably well!

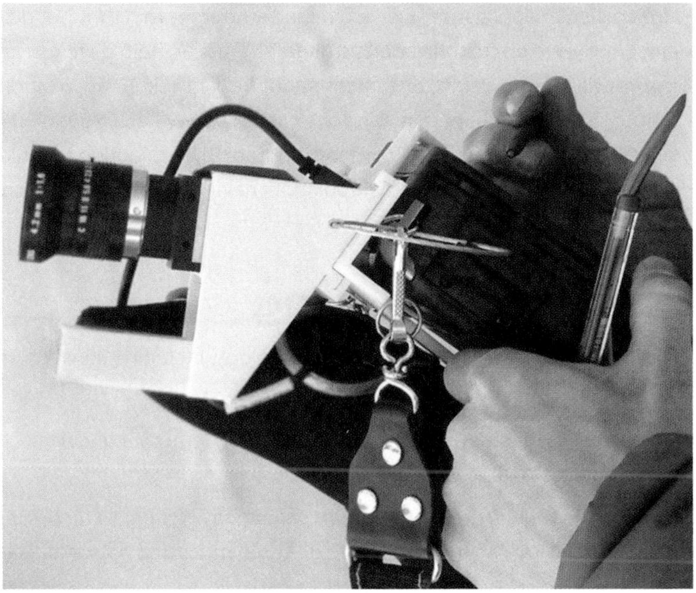

Figure 6.50 Pen input while using the handheld setup. (Image courtesy of Ernst Kruijff)

The specific platform used in HYDROSYS differs considerably from handheld AR applications that are used only occasionally and for shorter usage durations. For those applications, you should consider the most straightforward input to the system, without having to worry about ergonomics too much.

Key Concepts

- For mobile AR, provide easily accessible controllers that perform well if direct touchscreen–based control is not possible.
- Integrate all devices without destroying ergonomics, in particular considering how controllers are operated while holding the device in a certain grip.

6.9 Conclusion

In this chapter, we have presented a variety of different input and device types that can be and have been used in 3D UIs. We have discussed input device characteristics and use those characteristics to help classify different input devices, based primarily how the devices collect data and whether they need to be held or worn to be useful. We looked briefly at traditional input devices such as the keyboard and mouse, but have focused our discussion on 3D spatial input devices that capture a user or object's position, orientation, or motion in space. We have also looked at complementary input technologies and special-purpose input devices that have been designed for particular applications. We examined strategies for DIY input device design and development. Finally, we discussed various strategies that can help developers decide what the most appropriate input device or devices might be for their 3D application. With the material from Chapter 5 and this chapter in mind, we can now move on to the next part of the book, which provides a detailed discussion of many different 3D interaction techniques for common 3D UI tasks such as selection and manipulation, navigation, and system control.

Recommended Reading

For a more detailed discussion of motion-tracking technology, including sensor fusion, we recommend the following:

Schmalstieg, D., and T. Höllerer (2016). *Augmented Reality: Principles and Practice.* Addison-Wesley Professional.

Zarchan, P., and H. Musoff (2015). *Fundamentals of Kalman Filtering: A Practical Approach,* Fourth Edition. Reston, VA: American Institute of Aeronautics and Astronautics.

Foxlin, E. (2002). "Motion Tracking Requirements and Technologies." In K. Stanney (ed.), *Handbook of Virtual Environments: Design, Implementation, and Applications,* 163–210. Mahwah, NJ: Lawrence Erlbaum Associates.

Welch, G., and E. Foxlin (2002). "Motion Tracking: No Silver Bullet, but a Respectable Arsenal." *IEEE Computer Graphics and Applications, Special Issue on "Tracking"* 22(6): 24–38.

Allen, D., G. Bishop, and G. Welch (2001). "Tracking: Beyond 15 Minutes of Thought." *SIGGRAPH Course #11.*

A comprehensive discussion of computer vision techniques used in optical tracking can be found in the following:

Forsyth, D., and J. Ponce (2011). *Computer Vision: A Modern Approach*, Second Edition. Pearson.

Szeliski, R. (2011). *Computer Vision: Algorithms and Applications*. Springer.

A thorough discussion of eye tracking can be found in these texts:

Duchowski, A. T. (2009). *Eye Tracking Methodology: Theory and Practice*, Second Edition. London: Springer.

Wang, X., and B. Winslow (2014). "Eye Tracking in Virtual Environments." In K. Hale and K. Stanney (eds.), *Handbook of Virtual Environments: Design, Implementation, and Applications*, Second Edition, 197–210. Boca Raton, FL: CRC Press.

Comprehensive surveys on data gloves and glove-based input can be found in the following:

Dipietro, L., Sabatini A., and P. Dario (2008). "A Survey of Glove-Based Systems and Their Applications." *IEEE Transactions on Systems, Man, and Cybernetics, Part C (Applications and Reviews)* 38(4): 461–482.

LaViola, J. (1999). "Whole-Hand and Speech Input in Virtual Environments." Master's Thesis, Department of Computer Science, Brown University.

More information on using modern day microcontrollers can be found in the following:

Hughes, J. M. (2016). *Arduino: A Technical Reference: A Handbook for Technicians, Engineers, and Makers*. O'Reilly Media.

Monk, S. (2016). *Raspberry Pi Cookbook: Software and Hardware Problems and Solutions*, 2nd Edition. O'Reilly Media.

Finally, an important starting point for anyone interested in 6-DOF device evaluation is the following:

Zhai, S. (1995). "Human Performance in Six Degree of Freedom Input Control." PhD Dissertation, Department of Computer Science, University of Toronto.

PART IV

3D INTERACTION TECHNIQUES

In Part III, we presented information about the input and output device technologies that make 3D interaction possible. However, choosing or designing good interaction devices is not sufficient to produce a 3D UI that enables a good user experience. In Part IV, we discuss interaction techniques for the most common 3D interaction tasks. Remember that interaction techniques are methods used to accomplish a given task via the interface and that they include both hardware and software components. The software components of interaction techniques are also known as *control-display mappings* or *transfer functions*, and they are responsible for translating information from the input devices into associated system actions that are then displayed to the user (see the introduction to Part III). Many of the techniques we present can be implemented using a variety of different devices; the interaction concept and the implementation details are what make them unique.

We organize Part IV by user interaction task. Each chapter describes a task and variations on that task. Techniques that can be used to complete that task are discussed, along with guidelines for choosing among the techniques. We also provide implementation details for some important techniques.

The implementation details are described in plain English. We decided not to provide mathematical equations, code, or pseudocode. Today, many of this machinery is directly supported by the functionality of modern game engines and development kits. Equations that are needed can usually be found in the papers referenced in our discussions. We decided not to provide code or pseudocode for several reasons. Code would have been extremely precise, but we would have had to choose a language and a toolkit or game engine on which the code would be based. Pseudocode would have been more general, but even with pseudocode, we would be assuming that your development environment provides a particular set of functionality and uses a particular programming style. Thus, we decided to use natural language to describe the interaction techniques. This choice ensures descriptiveness and allows each reader to translate the implementation concepts into his or her own development environment.

Chapter 7, "Selection and Manipulation," covers the closely related tasks of selection and manipulation. We begin with these tasks because they have been widely studied, they are fundamental aspects of 3D interaction, and techniques for these tasks form the basis for many other 3D interaction techniques.

Chapter 8, "Travel," relates to the task of navigation, which is movement in and around an environment—a fundamental human task. Navigation includes both travel and wayfinding. Travel is the motor component of navigation—the low-level actions that the user takes to control the position and orientation of his viewpoint. In the real world, travel is the more physical navigation task, involving moving feet, turning a steering wheel, letting out a throttle, and so on. In the virtual world, travel techniques allow the user to translate and/or rotate the viewpoint and to modify the conditions of movement, such as the velocity. Wayfinding is the cognitive component of navigation—high-level thinking, planning, and decision-making related to user movement. It involves spatial understanding and planning tasks, such as determining the current location within the environment, determining a path from the current location to a goal location, and building a mental map of the environment. In virtual worlds, wayfinding can also be crucial—in a large, complex environment, an efficient travel technique is of no use if the traveler has no idea where to go. When we speak of wayfinding techniques, we refer to wayfinding aids included as part of the interface or in the environment. Unlike travel techniques or manipulation techniques, where the computer ultimately performs the action, wayfinding techniques support the performance of the task only in the user's mind.

System control tasks and symbolic input are the topics of Chapter 9, "System Control." System control addresses changing the mode or state of the system, often through commands or menus. Symbolic input, the task of entering or editing text, numbers, and other symbols, is often interwoven with system control tasks. These two tasks have not been as heavily researched as manipulation, travel, and wayfinding, but they are nonetheless important for many 3D UIs.

CHAPTER 7

SELECTION AND MANIPULATION

The quality of the interaction techniques that allow us to manipulate 3D virtual objects has a profound effect on the quality of the entire 3D UI. Indeed, manipulation is one of the most fundamental tasks for both physical and virtual environments: if the user cannot manipulate virtual objects effectively, many application-specific tasks simply cannot be performed. Therefore, we start our discussion of 3D interactions with techniques for selecting and manipulating 3D objects.

7.1 Introduction

The human hand is a remarkable tool; it allows us to manipulate physical objects quickly and precisely, with little conscious attention. Therefore, it is not surprising that the design and investigation of manipulation interfaces are important directions in 3D UIs. The goal of manipulation interface design is the development of new interaction techniques or the reuse of existing techniques that facilitate high levels of user-manipulation performance and comfort while diminishing the impact from inherited human and hardware limitations (Knight 1987).

7.1.1 3D Manipulation

This chapter is devoted to interaction techniques for 3D manipulation: software components that map user input captured by input devices (Chapter 6, "3D User Interface Input Hardware"), such as the trajectory of the user's hand and button presses, into the desired action in the virtual world (such as selection or rotation of a virtual object). We demonstrate that there is an astonishing variety of 3D interaction techniques for manipulation—the result of the creativity and insight of many researchers and designers. They provide a rich selection of ready-to-use interface components or design ideas that can inspire developers in implementing their own variations of manipulation interfaces.

7.1.2 Chapter Roadmap

We start by answering the question, "What is a 3D manipulation task?" (section 7.2). Understanding the details of manipulation tasks is important, because it does not make sense to design and evaluate interaction techniques for the manipulation task in general. The design, analysis, and deployment of interaction techniques depend heavily on the details of the specific task for which a technique was developed. Although input devices are discussed in Chapter 6, we mention some of their properties that directly affect the design of manipulation techniques.

In section 7.3, we discuss various classifications of manipulation techniques and provide a general overview of the techniques. We then discuss many techniques for selection and manipulation, classified by their metaphors:

- grasping (section 7.4)
- pointing (section 7.5)
- surface (section 7.6)
- indirect (section 7.7)
- bimanual (section 7.8)
- hybrid (section 7.9)

Section 7.10 completes the discussion of selection and manipulation by discussing other aspects of 3D interaction design. Finally, we present several design guidelines for selection and manipulation in section 7.11 and conclude with our case studies in section 7.12.

7.2 3D Manipulation Tasks

The effectiveness of 3D manipulation techniques greatly depends on the manipulation tasks to which they are applied. The same technique could be intuitive and easy to use in some task conditions and utterly inadequate in others. For example, the techniques needed for the rapid arrangement of virtual objects in immersive modeling applications could be very different from the manipulation techniques used to handle surgical instruments in a medical simulator. Therefore, before discussing interaction techniques, it is important to define what we actually mean by *manipulation*.

In everyday language, manipulation usually refers to any act of handling physical objects with one or two hands. For the practical purpose of designing and evaluating 3D manipulation techniques, we narrow the definition of the manipulation task to *spatial rigid object manipulation*—that is, manipulations that preserve the shape of objects. This definition is consistent with an earlier definition of the manipulation task in 2D UIs (Foley et al. 1984) as well as earlier human and motion analysis literature (McCormick 1970; Mundel 1978).

However, even within this narrower definition there are still many variations of manipulation tasks characterized by a multitude of variables, such as application goals, object sizes, object shapes, the distance from objects to the user, characteristics of the physical environment, and the physical and psychological states of the user. Designing and evaluating interaction techniques for every conceivable combination of these variables is not feasible; instead, interaction techniques are usually developed to be used in a *representative subset* of manipulation tasks. There are two basic approaches to choosing this task subset: using a *canonical* set of manipulation tasks or using *application-specific* manipulation tasks.

7.2.1 Canonical Manipulation Tasks

The fundamental assumption of any task analysis is that all human interactions of a particular type are composed of the same basic tasks, which are building blocks for more complex interaction scenarios (Mundel 1978). Consequently, if we can distill 3D manipulation into a number of such basic tasks, then instead of investigating the entire task space of 3D manipulation, we can design and evaluate interaction techniques only for this small subset. The results can be then extrapolated to the entire space of 3D manipulation activities. This section develops one of the possible sets of canonical manipulation tasks.

Tasks

Virtual 3D manipulation imitates, to some extent, general target acquisition and positioning movements that we perform in the real world—a combination of reaching/grabbing, moving, and orienting objects. Virtual 3D manipulation also allows users to do that which is not possible in the real world, such as making an object bigger or smaller. Therefore, we designate the following tasks as basic manipulation tasks:

- **Selection** is the task of acquiring or identifying a particular object or subset of objects from the entire set of objects available. Sometimes it is also called a target acquisition task (Zhai et al. 1994). The real-world counterpart of the selection task is picking up one or more objects with a hand, pointing to one or more objects, or indicating one or more objects by speech. Depending on the number of targets, we can distinguish between *single-object selection* and *multiple-object selection*.
- **Positioning** is the task of changing the 3D position of an object. The real-world counterpart of positioning is moving an object from a starting location to a target location.
- **Rotation** is the task of changing the orientation of an object. The real-world counterpart of rotation is rotating an object from a starting orientation to a target orientation.
- **Scaling** is the task of changing the size of an object. While this task lacks a direct real-world counterpart, scaling is a common virtual manipulation for both 2D and 3D UIs. Hence, we include it as a basic manipulation task.

This breakdown of the tasks is compatible with a well-known task analysis for 2D GUIs (Foley et al. 1984) and several task analyses for VEs (Mine 1995a; Bowman and Hodges 1997; Poupyrev et al. 1997). Although some also include object deformation (changing the shape of an object), we do not include it, because 3D object deformations are often accomplished via manipulation of 3D widgets using the canonical above. Additionally, selection processes might be preceded by an exploratory task. As we discussed in section 3.5, sometimes users explore the physical characteristics of an object (such as texture or shape) before selecting it. This may, for example, occur when an object is occluded or an interface is used eyes-off, and the actual characteristics of the object are unknown before selection.

Parameters of Canonical Tasks

For each canonical task, there are many variables that significantly affect user performance and usability (Foley et al. 1984). For example, in the case of a selection task, the user-manipulation strategy would differ significantly depending on the distance to the target object, the target size, the density of objects around the target, and many other factors. Some of the task variations are more prominent than others; some are stand-alone tasks that require specific interaction techniques. For example, object selections within arm's reach and out of arm's reach have been often considered two distinct tasks (Mine 1995a).

Therefore, each canonical task defines a **task space** that includes multiple variations of the same task defined by **task parameters**—variables that influence user performance while accomplishing this task (Poupyrev et al. 1997). Each of these parameters defines a design dimension, for which interaction techniques may or may not provide support. Table 7.1 outlines some of the task parameters for canonical tasks that have been often addressed in the 3D UI literature.

Table 7.1 Tasks and their parameters.

Task	Parameters
Selection	Distance and direction to target, target size, density of objects around the target, number of targets to be selected, target occlusion
Positioning	Distance and direction to initial position, distance and direction to target position, translation distance, required precision of positioning
Rotation	Distance to target, initial orientation, final orientation, amount of rotation, required precision of rotation
Scaling	Distance to target, initial scale, final scale, amount of scale, required precision of scale

7.2.2 Application-Specific Manipulation Tasks

The canonical tasks approach simplifies manipulation tasks to their most essential properties. Because of this simplification, however, it may fail to capture some manipulation task aspects that are application-specific. Examples of such application-specific manipulation activities include positioning of a medical probe relative to virtual 3D models of internal organs in a VR medical training application, moving the control stick of the virtual airplane in a flight simulator, and exploring the intricacies of an object's surface such as a mountain range. Obviously, in these examples, generalization of the manipulation task does not make sense—it is the minute details of the manipulation that are important to capture and replicate. This chapter only briefly considers such application-specific tasks; it concentrates instead on interaction techniques for performing generic manipulation tasks. The design of application-specific techniques is discussed in the special literature related to these applications. Chen and Bowman (2009) provide a discussion of the application- and domain-specific approaches to designing 3D interaction techniques.

7.2.3 Manipulation Techniques and Input Devices

There is a close relationship between the properties of input devices that are used to capture user input and the design of interaction techniques for a manipulation task: the choice of devices often restricts which manipulation techniques can be used. We discussed input devices in Chapter 6; here we briefly review some of the important device properties that relate to manipulation techniques.

Just like input devices, visual display devices and their characteristics (supported depth cues, refresh rate, resolution, etc.) can significantly affect the design of 3D manipulation techniques. Haptic displays could also have a pronounced effect on the user performance of manipulation tasks. We restrict our discussion to input devices, however, because they are intimately linked to interaction techniques for manipulation. Some discussion of the effect of display devices on manipulation tasks can be found in Chapter 10, "Strategies in Designing and Developing 3D User Interfaces."

Control Dimensions and Integrated Control in 3D Manipulation

Two characteristics of input devices that are key in manipulation tasks are, first, the *number of control dimensions* (how many DOF the device can control), and second, the *integration* of the control dimensions (how many DOF can be controlled simultaneously with a single movement). For example, a mouse allows for 2-DOF integrated control, and magnetic trackers allow simultaneous control of both 3D position and orientation (i.e., 6-DOF integrated control). Typical game controllers, on the other hand, provide at least 4-DOF, but the control is separated—2-DOF allocated to each of two joysticks, where each has to be controlled separately (refer to Figure 6.6).

The devices that are usually best for 3D manipulation are multiple DOF devices with integrated control of all input dimensions (Zhai et al. 1997). Integrated control allows the user to control the 3D interface using natural, well-coordinated movements, similar to real-world manipulation, which also results in better user performance (Crowford 1964; Hinckley, Tullio et al. 1997; Zhai and Senders 1997a, 1997b). Although early studies (Ellson 1947; Senders et al. 1955) found that human performance was poor in multidimensional control, recent studies suggest that this conclusion was due mostly to the limited input device technology that was available for multiple DOF input at the time when those experiments were conducted. Indeed, the input devices that were used did not allow users to control all degrees of freedom simultaneously (Zhai and Senders 1997a, 1997b). For example, in one experiment, subjects were required to manipulate two separate knobs to control the 2D position of a pointer (Senders et al. 1955).

Some 3D manipulation techniques also rely on more than one device with multiple integrated DOF. Such techniques usually employ two handheld devices and allow the user to complete a task by coordinating her hands in either a symmetric or an asymmetric fashion. These types of techniques are referred to as bimanual interactions. In section 7.8, we cover several techniques that employ a bimanual metaphor.

Most of the techniques discussed in this chapter assume that advanced input devices (such as 6-DOF trackers) are available. The reality of real-world 3D UI development, however, is that the device choice often depends on factors besides user performance, such as cost, device availability, ease of maintenance, and targeted user population. Therefore, even though 6-DOF devices are becoming less expensive and increasingly accessible, a majority of 3D UIs are still designed for input devices with only 2-DOF, such as a mouse, or those that separate degrees of freedom, such as game controllers. Thus, we discuss some 3D interaction techniques for desktop devices later in this chapter.

Force versus Position Control

Another key property of input devices that significantly affects the design of interaction techniques is whether the device measures position or motion of the user's hand, as motion trackers and mice do (isomorphic control), or whether it measures the force applied by the user, as joysticks do (elastic or isometric control ; see Chapter 3, section 3.5.1, and Figure 3.12 for more details). Studies led by Zhai (Zhai and Milgram 1993) found that in 6-DOF manipulation tasks, position control usually yields better performance than force control. Force control is usually preferable for controlling rates, such as the speed of navigation. Most 3D manipulation techniques discussed in this chapter assume that devices provide position control.

Device Placement and Form Factor in 3D Manipulation

The importance of device shape in manual control tasks has been known for a long time. Hand tools, for example, have been perfected over thousands of years, both to allow users to perform intended functions effectively and to minimize human wear and tear (McCormick 1970).

In 3D UIs, these objectives are also highly relevant; furthermore, the shape of the input device strongly influences the choice of 3D manipulation interaction techniques. Two popular device configurations used in 3D UIs are presented in Figure 7.1: on the left, the device is attached to the hand, sometimes called a power grip, and on the right, the device is held in the fingers, a so-called precision grip. The choice of approach influences the choice of interaction techniques, as they involve different muscle groups in manipulation (Zhai et al. 1996). When the device is directly attached to the hand, all translation and rotation operations are carried out by larger muscle groups of the user's shoulder, elbow, and wrist. In contrast, with the precision grip, the user can use smaller and faster muscle groups in the fingers. The results of experimental studies demonstrate that a precision grip usually results in better user performance, particularly in 3D rotation tasks. See Chapter 3, section 3.5.1, and Figure 3.15 for more information about power and precision grips.

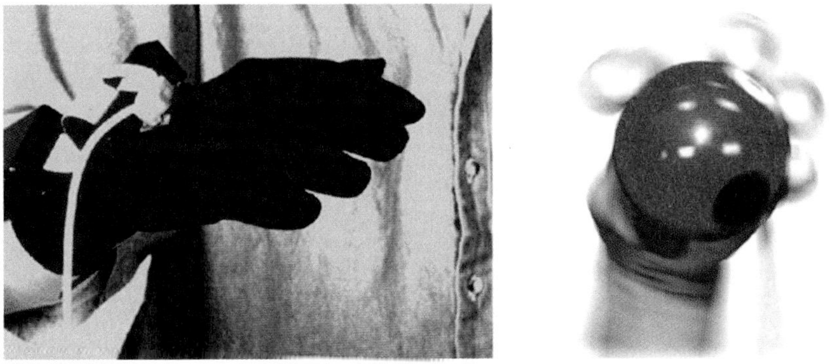

Figure 7.1 Two strategies for handling the input device: attached to the hand (power grip) and rolled in the fingers (precision grip). (Photograph courtesy of Ivan Poupyrev)

Precision-grip devices also decrease the effect of "clutching" on user manipulation (Zhai et al. 1996). Clutching occurs when a manipulation cannot be achieved in a single motion—the object must be released and then regrasped in order to complete the task. A familiar real-world example of clutching is using a traditional wrench to tighten a bolt in a small space. The operator must continually remove the wrench from the bolt, rotate it, and then place it back on the bolt, which is inconvenient and frustrating. Precision-grip devices allow the user to roll the device in his fingers, thus allowing an infinite amount of spatial rotation without the need for clutching. Devices that are attached to the hand require clutching after a small amount of rotation.

So, as long as the design of the device promotes using fingers for 3D manipulation, user performance benefits. Because a spherical shape is easier to rotate in the user's hand, ball-shaped devices (Figure 7.1) are preferable when precise and efficient manipulation is required. It would also be reasonable to think that shaping the device to replicate the shape of virtual objects would also improve user performance (a so-called "physical props" technique). This, however, was not found to be true: shaping the device like a virtual object does not yield a significant benefit for manipulation performance; in fact, devices with generic shapes usually perform better (Hinckley et al. 1997; Ware and Rose 1999). However, the physical props technique can be beneficial in applications when speed of learning, sense of immersion, or user enjoyment is more important than manipulation performance. We discuss the physical props approach in more detail in Chapter 10.

7.3 Classifications for 3D Manipulation

The design of effective 3D manipulation techniques is an important research problem. The challenge was very well defined by Sheridan (cited in Zhai 1995):

> *How do the geometrical mappings of body and environmental objects, both within the VE and the true one, and relative to each other, contribute to the sense of presence, training, and performance? In some cases there may be a need to deviate significantly from strict geometric isomorphism because of hardware limits or constraints of the human body. At present we do not have design/operating principles for knowing what mapping . . . is permissible and which degrades performance.*

As the next section describes, a vast variety of 3D manipulation techniques has been invented in an attempt to meet this challenge. Their variety might be somewhat overwhelming; therefore, we start with basic classifications of interaction techniques.

7.3.1 Classifications of Manipulation Techniques

Many 3D manipulation techniques relate to one another, and many share common properties. Classifying them according to common features is useful in understanding the relations between different groups of techniques and can help us to grasp a larger picture of the technique design space. Certainly, there is more than one way to group techniques together; here we discuss only some that have been proposed in the literature.

Isomorphism in Manipulation Techniques

The design of 3D manipulation interfaces has been strongly influenced by two opposing views. The **isomorphic view** suggests a strict, geometrical, one-to-one correspondence between hand motions in the physical and virtual worlds on the grounds that it is the most natural and therefore is better for users. The results of early human factors studies indicate that although isomorphism is, indeed, often more natural (overview in Knight 1987), it also has important shortcomings. First, these mappings are often impractical because of constraints in the input devices. For example, the tracking range may be restricted, which is one of the most common limitations. Second, isomorphism is often ineffective because of the limitations of humans. For example, our arm length naturally limits our reaching distance. Finally, it has been argued that 3D UIs can be more effective, intuitive, and rich if, instead of trying to imitate physical reality, we create mappings and interaction techniques that are specifically tailored to 3D environments, providing in some sense a "better" reality (Stoakley et al. 1995).

Hence, the **nonisomorphic** approach deviates significantly from strict realism, providing users with "magic" virtual tools such as laser beams, rubber arms, voodoo dolls (Poupyrev et al. 1996; Pierce et al. 1999), and others. These nonisomorphic mappings and techniques can allow users to manipulate objects quite differently than in the physical world, while maintaining usability and performance (Bowman and Hodges 1997; Poupyrev, Weghorst et al. 1998).

The relative advantage of isomorphic versus nonisomorphic techniques depends on the application: when strict realism of manipulation is *not* the major requirement of the application, nonisomorphic mappings might be effective and engaging for the user. In fact, the majority of 3D direct manipulation techniques today are nonisomorphic techniques.

Classification by Task Decomposition

We can also observe that all manipulation techniques consist of the same basic components that serve similar purposes (Bowman et al. 1999). For example, in a selection task, the interaction technique should provide the user with a means to indicate an object to select and to confirm the selection and provide visual, haptic, or audio feedback while performing the task (Figure 7.2). Manipulation and rotation tasks can be decomposed in a similar way.

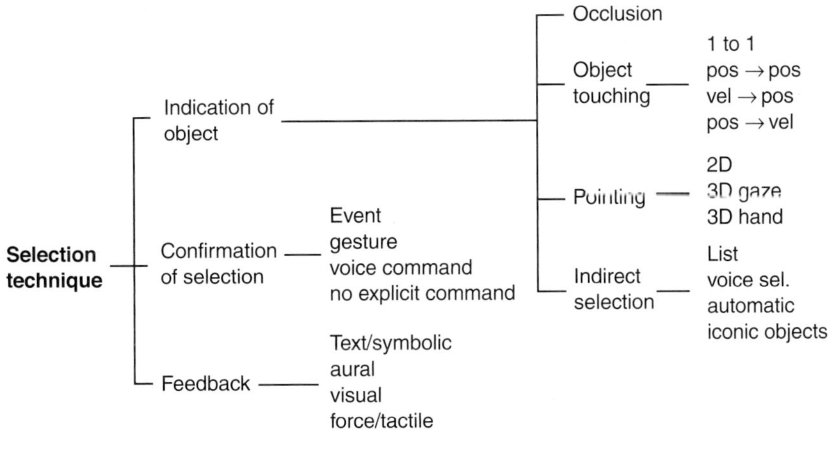

Figure 7.2 Classification of selection techniques by task decomposition.

Hence, we can consider 3D manipulation techniques as being constructed out of several "building blocks" (technique components), where each block allows accomplishing a single suboperation. The entire "construction kit" can include a variety of different components for each suboperation. The advantage of this approach is that we can structure the interaction technique design space so that new techniques can be constructed out of basic elements simply by picking the appropriate components and putting them together. More information on the use of task decomposition classifications for interaction technique design and evaluation can be found in Chapter 11, "Evaluation of 3D Interfaces."

Classification by Metaphor

Most current 3D UI manipulation techniques are based on a few basic interaction metaphors or a combination of metaphors. Each of these metaphors forms the fundamental mental model of a technique—a perceptual manifestation of what users can do by using the techniques (**affordances**) and what they cannot do (**constraints**). Particular techniques can be considered as different implementations of these basic metaphors.

In this chapter, we present a metaphor-based taxonomy for classifying 3D manipulation techniques. This taxonomy is based on six common metaphors used for 3D manipulation: grasping, pointing, interacting with a surface, indirectly manipulating objects, bimanual interactions, and combining metaphors to create hybrid techniques. Sections 7.4–7.9 cover these six metaphors. We cover other issues relating to 3D manipulations, such as 3D rotations, multiple-object selections, and progressive refinement, in section 7.10.

7.4 Grasping Metaphors

The most natural technique for interacting in a 3D world is to grasp and manipulate objects with one's hands. Many first-time users of 3D UIs will attempt to reach out and grasp virtual objects, whether the system supports this capability or not. For those systems that do support such interactions, we have identified two distinct approaches to providing the ability to grasp virtual objects—hand-based techniques and finger-based techniques. **Hand-based grasping** techniques take a simplified approach to implementing grasping interactions by representing the user's virtual hand as a single-point effector (i.e., all interaction calculations are based on a single transform that usually corresponds to the 6-DOF position of the user's physical hand). Alternatively, **finger-based grasping** techniques take the more realistic, and much more complex, approach of modeling the user's virtual hand as a hierarchy of finger segments that are normally directly controlled by the positions of the user's physical fingers. In addition to discussing these two categories of grasping techniques, we also discuss ways that researchers have found to enhance the usability of grasping.

7.4.1 Hand-Based Grasping Techniques

Hand-based techniques are the most common approach to implementing grasping metaphors because most 3D UI systems do not support the ability to track the user's physical fingers.

However, many 3D UI systems employ at least one tracker to capture the position and orientation of the user's dominant hand. Hand-based grasping techniques use this 6-DOF information to provide a virtual representation of the user's physical hand within the 3D UI. In turn, the user can select and directly manipulate virtual objects with her hands.

Typically, a 3D cursor is used to visualize the current locus of user input; for example, the cursor can be a 3D model of a human hand (Figure 7.3). Semitransparent volumetric cursors have also been investigated: their advantage is that transparency adds an additional depth cue, aiding selection of the 3D virtual objects (Zhai et al. 1994). The position and orientation of the input device are mapped onto the position and orientation of the virtual hand. To select an object, the user simply intersects the 3D cursor with the target of selection and then uses a trigger technique (e.g., button press, voice command, or hand gesture) to pick it up. The object is then attached to the virtual hand and can be easily translated and rotated within the 3D UI until the user releases it with another trigger.

We discuss the following hand-based grasping techniques in this section:

- simple virtual hand
- Go-Go

Figure 7.3 Virtual hand. (Poupyrev et al. 1996, © 1996 ACM; reprinted by permission)

Simple Virtual Hand

The simple virtual hand technique is a direct mapping of the user's hand motion to a virtual hand's motion in a VE, typically (but not always) a one-to-one mapping to establish a direct correspondence between the device and VE coordinate systems. Mappings such as this are also called transfer functions or control-display gain functions. They are often classified by the number of integrations applied to the measured user input (Knight 1987; Zhai 1995). For example, in zero-order mappings, displacement of the input device results in displacement of the controlled element, while in first-order mappings, it results in a change of the velocity. Note that although in most cases the orientation of the input device is mapped directly to the orientation of the virtual hand, in some cases it is useful to scale 3D device rotations similar to the way we scale translations. Scaling rotations is not a trivial problem, and we discuss how this can be done in section 7.10.1.

Simple virtual hand techniques are isomorphic interaction techniques. They are rather intuitive because they directly simulate our interaction with everyday objects. The fundamental problem with such techniques is that only objects within the area of the user's reach can be selected and manipulated (even when using a scaled mapping, the user will have a finite reach). In order to select objects located further away, the user must employ a travel technique (Chapter 8, "Travel") to move to the object, which in many cases is inconvenient and increases the complexity of the 3D UI. In fact, the difficulty of selecting objects located outside of the user's reach has been reported as one of the major problems in 3D UIs (Durlach and Mavor 1995), and this has prompted the development of a number of manipulation techniques that attempt to overcome this problem.

Go-Go

The "Go-Go" technique (Poupyrev et al. 1996) attempts to improve on the simple virtual hand by providing an unobtrusive technique that allows the user to interactively change the length of the virtual arm. When the user's real hand is close to the user, Go-Go uses a one-to-one mapping like simple virtual hand, and the movements of the virtual hand correspond to the real hand movements. However, when the user extends her hand beyond a predefined distance threshold, the mapping becomes nonlinear and the virtual arm "grows," thus permitting the user to access and manipulate remote objects.

The Go-Go technique therefore provides a simple way to interactively control the length of the virtual arm—simply by stretching the real hand out or bringing it closer. A small model is usually rendered in the position of the real hand to provide a visual reference for the user's hand position. Different mapping functions (see Figures 7.4 and 7.5) can be used to achieve a different control-display gain between the real and virtual hands (Bowman and Hodges 1997), which allows designers to adjust the mapping for the needs of a particular application.

The Go-Go technique provides direct, seamless, 6-DOF object manipulation both close to the user and at a distance. It allows users to both bring faraway objects near and move near objects farther away. The maximum afforded reaching distance, however, is still finite. Furthermore, as the distance increases, the technique maps small movements of the user's hand into large movements of the virtual hand, which complicates precise positioning at a distance. A number of experimental studies (Bowman and Hodges 1997; Poupyrev, Weghorst et al. 1998) have evaluated the Go-Go technique in a subset of manipulation tasks, and all found that users did not have any difficulties understanding it. However, in selection tasks Go-Go is usually less effective than ray-casting (see section 7.5), as it requires 3-DOF control as opposed to 2-DOF.

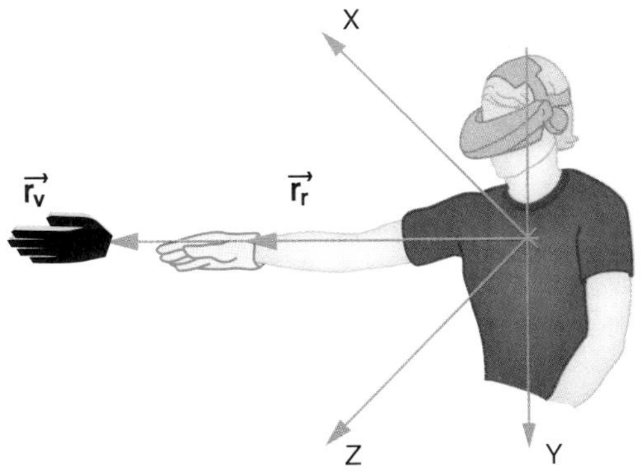

Figure 7.4 Go-Go interaction technique: egocentric coordinate system. (Poupyrev et al. 1996, © 1996 ACM; reprinted by permission)

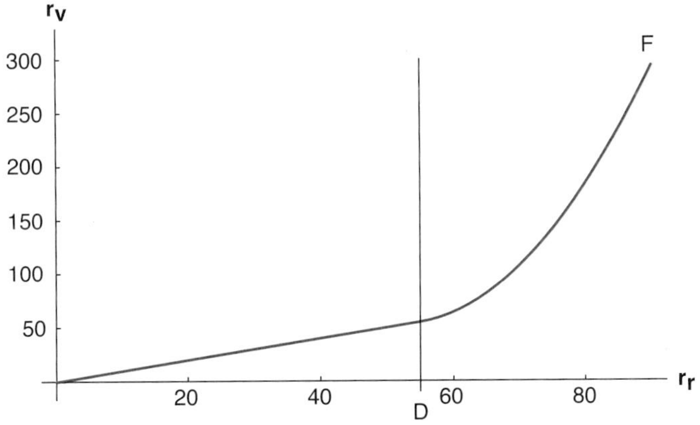

Figure 7.5 Go-Go interaction technique: mapping function *F*. (Poupyrev et al. 1996, © 1996 ACM; reprinted by permission)

7.4.2 Finger-Based Grasping Techniques

Finger-based grasping techniques have been less common in the past, though they have received much more attention lately due to depth-based optical sensors and physics-based computer vision techniques (Hongyong and Youling 2012; Guna et al. 2014). By using such technologies or traditional motion capture systems (Jacobs and Froehlich 2011), finger-based grasping techniques allow the user to interact with and manipulate objects with more precision. This enables new interactions, such as holding a virtual egg by its sides or twirling a virtual pencil between one's virtual fingers. A challenge of all these techniques, however, is that without haptic feedback, it may be difficult for users to determine how to move their fingers to achieve the desired manipulation. In addition, if virtual fingers are not allowed to penetrate the virtual objects, they may be in different positions than a user's real fingers.

The major difference among various finger-based grasping techniques is how they physically simulate the fingers and interactions. In this section, we discuss the following finger-based grasping techniques:

- rigid-body fingers
- soft-body fingers
- god fingers

Rigid-Body Fingers

Borst and Indugula (2005) developed a rigid-body finger-based grasping technique by using bend-sensing gloves to track the user's real hand and fingers and mapping those positions to the user's virtual hand and fingers, which were represented by rigid bodies. To produce realistic physics-based interactions, the researchers employed a system of virtual torsional and linear spring-dampers that dynamically influenced the mappings between the user's real hand and virtual hand (Figure 7.6). Therefore, they referred to the user's real hand as the tracked hand and the virtual hand as the spring hand.

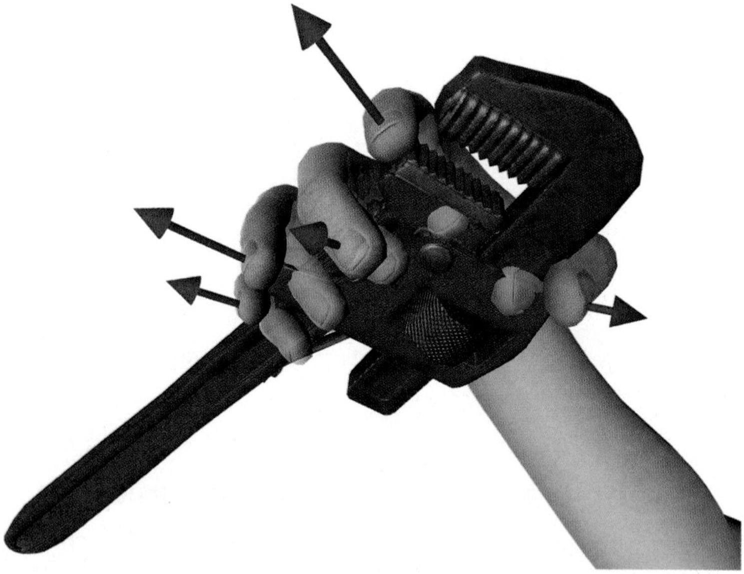

Figure 7.6 Rigid-body fingers use spring-dampers to map the user's tracked physical fingers (green) to the user's virtual fingers and to determine the applied forces for each rigid body (red arrows). (Image adapted from Borst and Indugula 2005)

In most cases, the posture of the spring hand matched that of the tracked hand. However, when the tracked hand would collide with and penetrate the inner space of a virtual object, the spring hand would dynamically prevent visual interpenetration and would produce forces and torques that enabled direct interactions with the virtual object, such as picking it up at a specific point and rotating the object about that point. However, due to the choice of spring-damping coefficients and friction parameters, the rigid-body fingers were prone to being "sticky," which made it difficult to precisely release objects. Prachyabrued and Borst (2012) later developed and evaluated a new spring model that employed a heuristic-based release function to reduce this "sticking object" problem.

Soft-Body Fingers

Jacobs and Froehlich (2011) developed a new hand model for increasing the usability of finger-based grasping techniques. Their approach was to use deformable (i.e., soft-body) representations for the virtual fingers and employ a lattice shape-matching algorithm that deformed the pads of the virtual fingers to dynamically adapt to the shapes of grasped virtual objects. When the user's real fingers initially collided with a virtual object, the virtual finger pads would only deform slightly, resulting in only a few points of collision. When the real fingers penetrated the inner space of the virtual object, the deformation and lattice shape matching of the virtual finger pads would increase and produce many more points of collision. This essentially created an implicit friction model, in contrast to pure rigid-body interactions, which rely on a single friction value per object.

The key to the soft-body fingers technique developed by Jacobs and Froehlich (2011) was the lattice shape-matching algorithm that they employed. The FastLSM algorithm (Rivers and James 2007) was computationally less expensive than previous shape-matching algorithms. Additionally, it was able to simulate both rigid and soft models using a conventional rigid-body physics engine. This afforded simulation of both types of models at similar computational costs.

God Fingers

While algorithms like FastLSM have improved the efficiency of calculating soft-body dynamics, these approaches are still computationally expensive (Talvas et al. 2013). As a result, researchers have investigated the concept of god objects. A **god object** represents a virtual point that adheres to rigid-body physics and thus never penetrates virtual objects; instead, it remains at their surfaces (Zilles and Salisbury 1995). By assigning a god object to a tracked user position, the direction of force can be easily calculated when that physical position penetrates the inner space of a virtual object.

Talvas et al. (2013) employed the god-object concept to develop the god-fingers technique, which simulates the contact area between the user's virtual finger pad and a virtual object. As seen in Figure 7.7, the first step of this simulation is to compute the contact area about the god-object contact point as if the contact surface were flat. The contact area is then fitted to the geometry of the object based on the god-object's force direction. Finally, odd deformations are prevented by using an angular threshold between the god-object's force direction and the normals of the involved faces. Talvas et al. (2013) demonstrated that the god-fingers technique afforded more complex manipulations of virtual objects. However, it is important to note that the technique only simulates soft-body dynamics and does not produce any visual deformations of the user's virtual fingers.

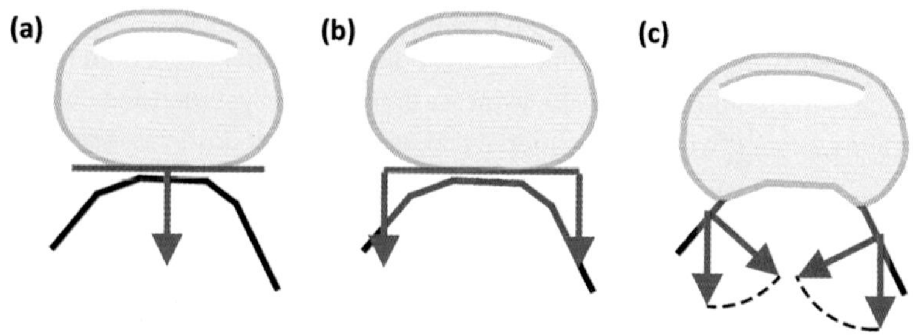

Figure 7.7 The god-fingers technique simulates the contact between the user's virtual finger pad and a virtual object. (a) The contact area is computed as if the finger's surface were flat. (b) The contact area is fitted to the object's geometry based on the god-object's force direction. (c) An angular threshold between the god-object's force direction and the normals of the involved faces is used to filter out odd deformations. (Image adapted from Talvas et al. 2013)

7.4.3 Enhancements for Grasping Metaphors

A number of enhancements have been investigated for hand-based and finger-based grasping metaphors. All of the following enhancements employ more complex transfer functions and interaction logic to increase the efficiency of grasping techniques. Some of the techniques also use additional visual feedback to enhance usability of the techniques. We discuss the following enhancements to grasping metaphors:

- 3D bubble cursor
- PRISM
- Hook
- intent-driven selection

3D Bubble Cursor

A bubble cursor is an area cursor that dynamically changes its radius to always touch the closest target. Grossman and Balakrishnan (2005) originally developed a 2D version of the bubble cursor as an efficient selection technique for sparse and dense environments. Vanacken et al. (2007) extended the concept to 3D virtual environments to create the 3D bubble cursor.

The 3D bubble cursor, a hand-based grasping enhancement, is a semitransparent sphere that dynamically resizes itself to encapsulate the nearest virtual object, which is then highlighted. When the 3D bubble cursor cannot be enlarged anymore without intersecting other nearby virtual objects, the closest object is encapsulated by a second semitransparent sphere and highlighted (see Figure 7.8). Vanacken et al. (2007) compared the 3D bubble cursor to a standard simple virtual hand, implemented as a single 3D point cursor, and found that the bubble cursor provided faster selection times.

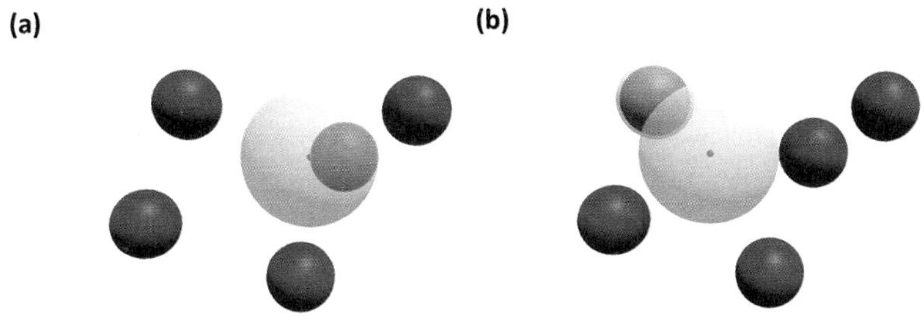

Figure 7.8 The 3D bubble cursor allows efficient selection of the nearest virtual object. (a) The radius of the cursor automatically enlarges to encapsulate the nearest virtual object. (b) To avoid intersecting other nearby objects when enlarging the radius, a second semitransparent sphere is used to encapsulate the nearest virtual object. (Image adapted from Vanacken et al. 2007)

PRISM

Frees and Kessler (2005) developed PRISM (Precise and Rapid Interaction through Scaled Manipulation) as a general enhancement for hand-based grasping metaphors (Figure 7.9). The basic concept of PRISM is to apply a scaled-down motion to the user's virtual hand when the user's physical hand is moving below a specified speed (SC). This results in a decreased control-display gain, which affords increased precision, and a mismatch in the positions of the real hand and virtual hand. To fix this mismatch, Frees and Kessler (2005) implemented an offset recovery, in addition to the normal one-to-one direct mapping, when the user's real hand is moving faster than a specified maximum velocity (Max V). Finally, to account for tracking errors or inadvertent drift, Frees and Kessler (2005) also specified a minimum velocity (Min V) required for motions. If the velocity of the user's real hand is slower than this minimum, the virtual hand will remain still.

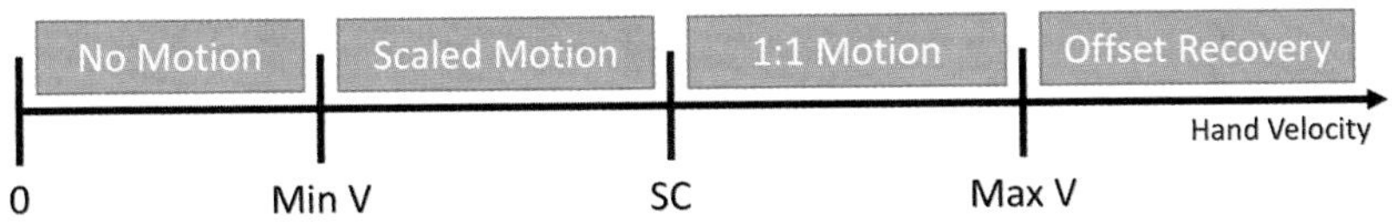

Figure 7.9 PRISM employs four interaction modes to afford precise interactions for grasping metaphors. (Image adapted from Frees and Kessler 2005)

Wilkes and Bowman (2008) applied the PRISM enhancement to the grasping-based manipulations of the HOMER technique (see Section 7.9). Once the user selects an object, the scaled HOMER technique decreases the motion of the virtual hand and object when the velocity of the user's real hand drops below the specified scaling constant. The researchers found that the scaled HOMER technique afforded increased levels of precision for both long- and short-distance manipulation tasks, without compromising speed.

Hook

Standard grasping techniques make it difficult to select moving objects. The Hook enhancement is based on the observation that if a target is moving in an unpredictable but non-Brownian motion, the user must follow the target in order to attempt to overtake it (Ortega 2013). By observing the relation between moving targets and the cursor (or hand) over time, Hook can heuristically estimate which target is being tracked. When the user makes a selection, that estimation can be used to avoid unintended selections.

To heuristically estimate which target the user is tracking, Hook computes the distance from the cursor to each target every frame and orders the targets based on increasing distances. Each target's score is then increased or decreased based on that ordered list. Only a limited number of close targets will have their scores increased. All other targets will have their scores decreased. However, scores cannot decrease below 0. Finally, once a selection is indicated, Hook selects the target with the highest score. Ortega (2013) demonstrated that Hook significantly improved completion times and decreased errors, for both fast and slow targets, when compared to the simple virtual hand technique.

Intent-Driven Selection

Periverzov and Ilies (2015) presented intent-driven selection as an enhancement for finger-based grasping techniques. The concept of intent-driven selection is to use the posture of the virtual fingers as an indication of the user's level of confidence in selecting an object. A proximity sphere is positioned within the grasp of the virtual hand in such a manner that the virtual fingers touch the surface of the sphere (Figure 7.10). Virtual objects within this proximity sphere represent the subset of target objects that the user can make a selection from. As the user becomes more confident in making a selection and closes the virtual hand, additional proximity spheres are placed within the outer sphere to specify a smaller subset of potential targets until only one target is selected. Periverzov and Ilies (2015) demonstrated that the intent-driven selection enhancement enabled users to select objects faster and more efficiently than a conventional finger-based grasping technique, especially for challenging selection tasks.

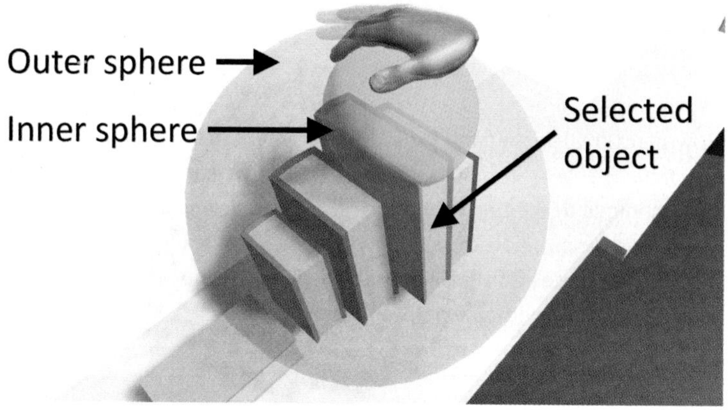

Figure 7.10 Intent-driven selection employs proximity spheres to progressively refine the selection of objects. (Image adapted from Periverzov and Ilies 2015)

7.5 Pointing Metaphors

This section presents another of the fundamental classes of 3D manipulation techniques—**pointing** techniques. The motivation behind the pointing technique is to allow the user to easily select and manipulate objects located beyond the area of reach by simply pointing at them. When the vector defined by the direction of pointing intersects a virtual object, the user can select it by issuing a trigger event that confirms the selection. Examples of triggers are buttons and voice commands. After the object is selected, it can be attached to the end of a pointing vector for manipulation (Figure 7.11).

Pointing is a powerful selection technique. A number of experimental evaluations have demonstrated that it results in better selection performance than grasping-based techniques (see section 7.4), because pointing requires significantly less physical hand movement from the user (Poupyrev, Weghorst et al. 1998; Bowman, Johnson et al. 1999). Pointing, however, is generally a very poor positioning technique: object manipulation can be efficiently accomplished only in radial movements around the user (perpendicular to the pointing direction) when the task does not require changing the distance between the user and objects. Rotations can be effectively accomplished only about one axis: the axis defined by the pointing vector. Expressive 6-DOF manipulation with basic pointing techniques is therefore impossible; enhanced pointing techniques must be used to address this problem.

One of the earliest instances of a pointing technique was described in the "put-that-there" interface, developed by Bolt at MIT in the early 1980s (Bolt 1980). The put-that-there system allowed users to select and manipulate objects by pointing at them, with voice commands used as a trigger. Since then, a number of pointing techniques have been reported (Jacoby et al. 1994; Mine 1995a; Bowman and Hodges 1997). The difference between them is defined mostly by two design variables: first, how the **pointing direction** is defined (i.e., how the input device position and orientation is mapped onto the direction of the ray), and second, by the **type of selection calculation**, which defines the visual feedback provided and how many objects are selected when users point at them. Based on this second variable, we organize pointing techniques in this section into two categories—vector-based and volume-based techniques. We also discuss enhancements for pointing metaphors.

7.5.1 Vector-Based Pointing Techniques

Vector-based pointing techniques require only a vector in order to calculate what object the user intends to select and manipulate. This makes vector-based pointing rather easy to implement. As a result, these techniques are commonly used for pointing in 3D UIs. In this section, we discuss the following vector-based pointing techniques:

- ray-casting
- fishing reel
- image-plane pointing

Ray-Casting

With ray-casting, the user points at objects with a virtual ray that defines the direction of pointing, and a virtual line segment attached to the hand visualizes the pointing direction (Figure 7.11). In immersive environments, the virtual ray can be attached directly to the virtual hand controlled by a 6-DOF sensor. The *pointing vector* in the case of the simple ray-casting technique is estimated from the direction of the virtual ray that is attached to the user's virtual hand and the 3D position of the virtual hand. In cases where the hand's position and orientation cannot be tracked (or cannot be tracked accurately), the ray may emanate from the tracked head position and extend in the direction the head is pointing; this is termed "gaze-based ray-casting." More than one object can be intersected by the ray, but only the one closest to the user should be selected; thus the interaction technique must consider all possible candidates for selection.

In the simplest case of the ray-casting technique, the *shape* of the ray can be a short line segment attached to the user's hand (Figure 7.11). This, however, could be difficult to use when selecting small objects located far away, as it does not provide the user with sufficient visual feedback on whether the ray is actually intersecting the virtual object. An infinitely long virtual ray provides the user with better visual feedback, as it allows the user to select objects simply by touching them with the ray (Bowman and Hodges 1997).

Figure 7.11 Ray-casting technique. (Poupyrev, Weghorst et al. 1998, © 1998 Blackwell Publishing; reprinted by permission)

Virtual ray-casting is a very powerful selection technique, except when a high precision of selection is required, such as when selecting small or faraway objects (Poupyrev, Weghorst et al. 1998; Bowman, Johnson et al. 1999). In such task scenarios, ray-casting selection performance erodes significantly because of the high angular accuracy required and the amplification of hand and tracker jitter with increased distance. This has been observed by a number of researchers (Liang and Green 1994; Forsberg et al. 1996) and supported by results of experimental studies (Poupyrev, Weghorst et al. 1998). At medium range with moderately sized or large objects, ray-casting is perhaps the simplest and most efficient selection technique.

Fishing Reel

The difficulty of controlling the distance to the virtual objects being manipulated is a problem for all pointing techniques. One possible solution is to supply the user with an additional input mechanism dedicated to controlling the length of the virtual ray. Similar to the way a fishing reel works, this technique allows the user to select an object with the simple ray-casting technique, then reel it back and forth using the dedicated input mechanism, which could be, for example, a simple mechanical slider, a joystick, or a pair of buttons added to the tracking device (Bowman and Hodges 1997). Although the fishing reel lets the user control the distance to the object, it separates the manipulation's degrees of freedom—the ray direction is controlled by the spatial movements of the user's hand, while distance is controlled by other means.

Image-Plane Pointing

The image-plane family of techniques (Pierce et al. 1997) simplifies the object selection task by requiring the user to control only 2-DOF. With this technique, the user selects and manipulates 3D objects by touching and manipulating their 2D projections on a virtual image-plane located in front of the user (Figure 7.12).

There are several variations of the image-plane interaction techniques; Figure 7.12 presents the so-called "sticky finger" variation of the image-plane technique. The object underneath the user's finger (or handheld input device) is selected by first casting a vector from the user's eye point through the finger and then finding an object intersecting with this vector. After selection, the 3D object can be manipulated; the object is scaled down and brought within the user's reach for manipulation.

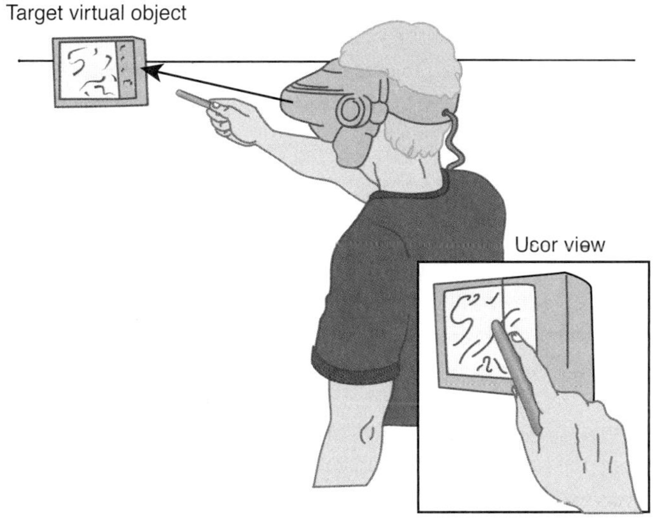

Figure 7.12 The "sticky finger" image-plane pointing technique.

Image-plane techniques simulate direct touch and are therefore intuitive and easy to use for selection. Though this technique allows the user to modify the orientation of 3D objects, their distance from the user cannot be directly controlled, because objects are scaled down for manipulation. The Voodoo dolls technique (see section 7.7.2) and the scaled-world grab technique (see section 7.9) tackle this problem.

7.5.2 Volume-Based Pointing Techniques

Volume-based pointing techniques require the definition of a vector and a volume in order to determine what the user intends to select and manipulate. Usually, the volume is defined in some relation to the vector, such as using a vector to define the axis of a cone. However, in some cases, the vector is used to intersect an object, which then defines the position of a volume given that intersection point. In this section, we discuss the following volume-based pointing examples:

- flashlight
- aperture selection
- sphere-casting

Flashlight

The flashlight technique was developed to provide a "soft" selection technique that does not require precision and accuracy of pointing to virtual objects with the ray (Liang and Green 1994). The technique imitates pointing at objects with a flashlight, which can illuminate an object even when the user does not point at it precisely.

In the flashlight technique, the pointing direction is defined in the same way as in the simple ray-casting technique, but it replaces the virtual ray with a conic selection volume, with the apex of the cone at the input device. Objects that fall within this selection cone can be selected. The technique therefore allows easy selection of small objects even when they are located far from the user.

The obvious problem with the flashlight technique is disambiguation of the desired object when more than one object falls into the spotlight. Two basic rules are usually used for disambiguation (Liang and Green 1994). First, if two objects fall into the selection volume, then the object that is closer to the centerline of the selection cone is selected. Second, if the angle between the object and the centerline of the selection cone is the same for both objects, then the object closer to the device is selected.

The flashlight technique does not require that an entire object fall into the spotlight: even if an object is touched by the side of the selection volume ("illuminated" by the flashlight), it can be considered a selection candidate. Although this makes it very easy to select virtual objects, this ease of selection becomes a disadvantage when selection of small objects or tightly grouped objects is required. In these situations (as well as some others), it is desirable to directly specify the spread angle of the selection cone.

Aperture Selection

The aperture technique makes this possible. The aperture technique (Forsberg et al. 1996) is a modification of the flashlight technique that allows the user to interactively control the spread of the selection volume. The pointing direction is defined by the 3D position of the user's viewpoint in virtual space, which is estimated from the tracked head location and the position of a hand sensor, represented as an aperture cursor within the 3D UI (Figures 7.13 and 7.14a). The user can interactively control the spread angle of the selection volume simply by bringing the hand sensor closer or moving it farther away. The aperture technique thus improves the spotlight technique by providing an efficient interactive mechanism of object disambiguation by interactive control of the selection volume (Figure 7.13).

The aperture technique further simplifies selection of virtual objects by using the orientation of the pointer around a central axis (i.e., its twist) as an additional disambiguation metric. Two small virtual plates are mounted in parallel at the end of the pointer. In a case of selection ambiguity, the user twists the pointer to align the orientation of the plates with the orientation of the object to be selected. This informs the interface which 3D object the user intends to pick up. For example, on the left side of Figure 7.14b, the orientation of the plates indicates that the user intends to pick up the entire 3D object, because the plate orientation corresponds to the orientation of the object; on the right side of Figure 7.14b, the orientation of the plates indicates that the user would like to select only the horizontal disk located in the middle of the 3D object. Selection sensitivity based on the grasp orientation is directly derived from the real experience of grabbing objects with our hands; we always match our hand orientation with the orientation of the object to make it easy to pick up.

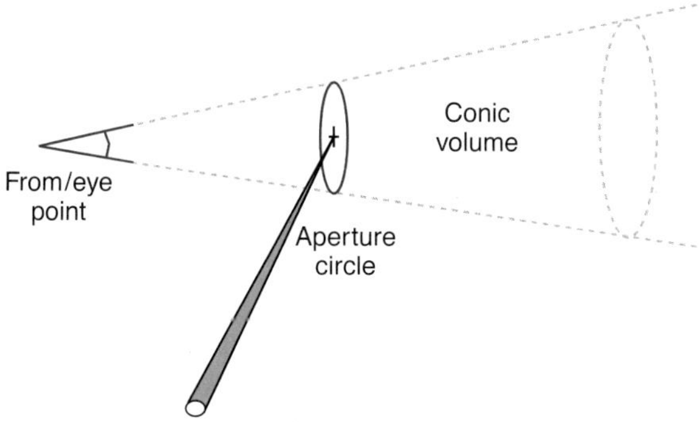

Figure 7.13 Aperture selection technique. (Forsberg et al. 1996, © 1996 ACM; reprinted by permission)

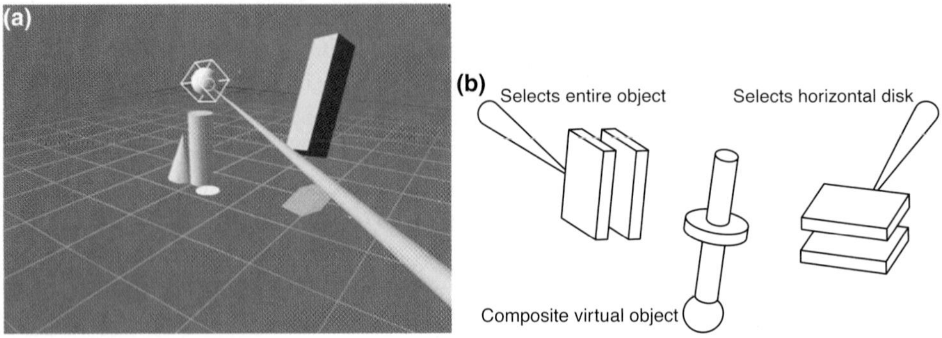

Figure 7.14 Aperture technique: (a) an example of use; (b) selection sensitivity based on grasp orientation. (Reprinted by permission of Brown University)

The fundamental design ideas behind the aperture and flashlight techniques can be easily applied to a wide variety of 3D UI configurations, in both desktop and immersive VEs. Of course, the flashlight and aperture techniques are essentially pointing techniques and therefore inherit all the limitations of ray-casting for object manipulation. This means that the flashlight and aperture techniques would not be effective for freeform 6-DOF manipulations of virtual objects. Nevertheless, these are effective and useful selection techniques. The choice between them depends on the application requirements. In general, if objects are not tightly grouped together, the flashlight is a simple and effective technique. When a higher degree of control is needed, an aperture technique can be effective.

Sphere-Casting

Another approach to volume-based pointing is to define the position of a predefined volume at the intersection of a vector used for pointing and the virtual environment. An example of this approach is the sphere-casting technique. Sphere-casting is essentially a modified version of ray-casting that casts a sphere onto the nearest intersected surface. Objects found within the sphere are considered selectable. Kopper et al. (2011) used this pointing technique for their Sphere-casting refined by QUAD-menu (SQUAD) technique (see section 7.10.3).

7.5.3 Enhancements for Pointing Metaphors

Researchers have investigated several ways to improve the usability and efficiency of pointing metaphors. Some enhancements were intended to simplify the requirement of pointing directly at an object, such as bendcast. However, many of the enhancements have been focused on making it easier to distinguish between multiple objects within the pointing direction or to afford the user a higher level of precision. In this section, we discuss the following enhancements for pointing metaphors:

- Bendcast
- depth ray
- absolute and relative mapping

Bendcast

Bendcast is the pointing analog to the 3D bubble cursor (see section 7.4.3). This enhancement bends the vector used for pointing toward the object closest to the vector's path. To determine the closest object for Bendcast, the point-line distance from each selectable object to the pointing vector must be calculated. Once the closest object is determined, a circular arc can be used to provide visual feedback for the bending of the vector (Riege et al. 2006). Cashion et al. (2013) found that this enhancement is more forgiving than simple ray-casting but works best when only a few objects are located near the pointing vector's path.

Depth Ray

The depth ray is a simple enhancement designed to disambiguate which object the user intends to select when the pointing vector intersects multiple candidate targets. The depth ray enhancement augments the pointing vector with a depth marker that exists along the length of the ray (Grossman and Balakrishnan 2006; Vanacken et al. 2007). At the time of selection, the object closest to the depth marker, and of course intersected by the pointing vector, is selected (see Figure 7.15). In order to change which object is closest to the marker, the user can control the position of the depth marker by moving her hand forwards or backwards to make the marker move in the same manner along the pointing vector.

Figure 7.15 The depth ray enhancement uses a depth marker to determine which object to select when multiple objects are intersected by the pointing vector: (a) the depth ray selected the intersected object closest to the depth marker; (b) the depth marker can be repositioned by moving the hand forwards or backwards. (Image courtesy of Ryan P. McMahan)

Absolute and Relative Mapping

In dense environments, the enhancements discussed above may not be enough to afford fine-grained control and prevent errors associated with selecting the wrong target inadvertently. The absolute and relative mapping (ARM) enhancement, presented by Kopper et al. (2010), provides manual control of the control-display gain ratio of pointing to allow users to increase the effective angular width of targets as needed. Kopper et al. (2010) found that this enhancement clearly increases the ease and precision of selection and placement tasks.

By default, ARM employs the simple ray-casting technique to point at and select targets. When more precision is needed, the user presses a button that turns on relative mapping with a 10:1 control-display gain ratio, which effectively increases the angular width of targets near the pointing vector by a factor of 10. The resulting effect is that a physical wrist rotation causes the pointing vector to virtually rotate only a tenth of the physical change in angle. This gives the impression of a "slow motion" pointer. When the relative mapping button is released, the pointing vector jumps back to its absolute position.

7.6 Surface Metaphors

In the past decade, there has been a proliferation of multi-touch surfaces due to the popularity of smartphones and tablets. As a result, the general population has become experienced with using touch gestures to directly interact with virtual objects, usually in a 2D context. However, multi-touch surfaces can also be used to interact with 3D UIs (Steinicke et al. 2008). Hence, in this section, we distinguish between surface-based 2D interaction techniques and surface-based 3D interaction techniques.

7.6.1 Surface-Based 2D Interaction Techniques

Numerous interaction techniques have been investigated and developed for interacting with 2D contexts on multi-touch displays and surfaces (Wobbrock et al. 2009). For an in-depth discussion of such 2D interactions with surfaces, we recommend reading *Brave NUI World* by Wigdor and Wixon (2011). Here, however, we provide a brief overview of the common 2D interactions used with multi-touch surfaces. In particular, we discuss the following techniques:

- dragging
- rotating

Dragging

Dragging involves directly selecting and translating an object by touching it with one or more fingers and then sliding them across the surface. The most common approach is to use a single finger for this interaction (Hinrichs and Carpendale 2011). Dragging results in the virtual object being translated within a 2D plane coinciding with or parallel to the surface. The distance and direction of the translation is equivalent to the 2D vector defined by the initial contact point and the final contact point, at which the user removes his or her fingers from the surface.

Rotating

A number of surface-based 2D interaction techniques have been investigated for rotating virtual objects. The most commonly used approach is an independent rotation that occurs about the center of the object (Hancock et al. 2006). When the object is touched within a specified area, usually its corners, the user can drag his or her fingers across the surface to rotate the touched area about the center of the virtual object (see Figure 7.16).

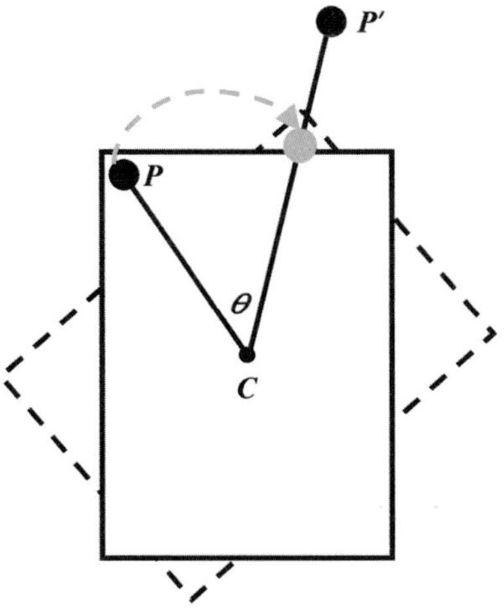

Figure 7.16 An independent rotation involves rotating an object about its center (*C*) at an angle of θ, which is defined by the initial contact point (*P*), the center of the object, and the current contact point (*P′*). (Image adapted from Hancock et al. 2006)

Another common but slightly different approach is to use two contact points to simultaneously translate and rotate a virtual object (Hancock et al. 2006). The first contact point serves to define the translation of the object (exactly as dragging does) and the center of rotation. The amount of rotation is determined by the difference between the initial angle formed by the first and second contact points, and the final angle defined by the two contact points before the fingers are lifted from the surface. See Figure 7.17 for a depiction of a two-point rotation.

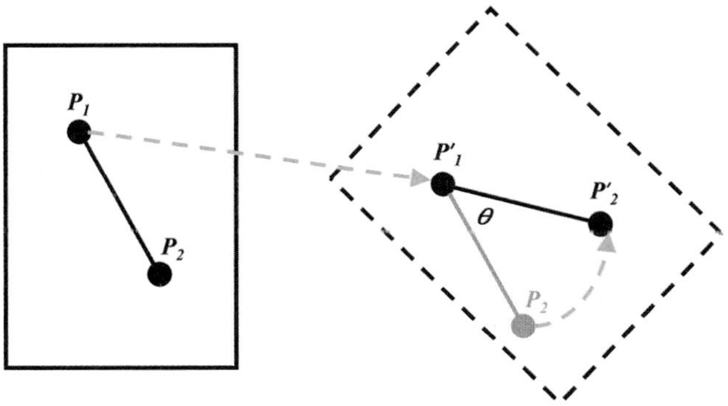

Figure 7.17 A two-point rotation involves translating the object from the first contact's initial position (P_1), to its final position (P'_1), and defining the angle of rotation (θ), by the second contact's initial position (P_2), the first contact's relative position, and the second contact's final position (P'_2). (Image adapted from Hancock et al. 2009)

7.6.2 Surface-Based 3D Interaction Techniques

While dragging and rotating objects have been widely adopted as intuitive techniques for interacting with multi-touch surfaces in 2D contexts, interacting with the third dimension—depth—is not as intuitive. A number of techniques have been investigated to allow users to control the depth of virtual objects relative to the surface. In this section, we discuss the following techniques that support 3D interactions:

- pinching
- void shadows
- balloon selection
- corkscrew widget
- triangle cursor

Pinching

Another common surface-based interaction technique is pinching (or splaying) the fingers to visually shrink (or enlarge), respectively, a virtual object (Wobbrock et al. 2009). This technique visually scales the virtual object based on the distance between two contact points. If the two contact points are being pinched, or dragged toward one another, the distance between them decreases, which results in the object's visual scale decreasing. If the two contact points are being splayed, or spread apart from one another, then as the distance between them increases, the visual scale of the object increases. Pinching and splaying can be accomplished with two fingers on a single hand or with one finger per hand (Hinrichs and Carpendale 2011).

In 2D contexts, pinching essentially modifies the absolute scale of the virtual object based on the changes in the distance between the two contact points. However, in 3D contexts, this interaction technique can also be used to manipulate the depth of an object relative to the surface (Giesler et al. 2014). Hence, we classify it as a 3D interaction technique.

It is important to note that pinching affords easy interactions only with visible objects. If virtual objects are stacked on top of each other, the topmost object is likely to occlude the objects stacked below it. Since the pinching interaction has no mechanism to specify the depth of selection, as it functions similar to vector-based pointing, only the topmost object can be manipulated. Hence, in order to manipulate objects below the topmost object, the user must first move the topmost object to view the object below it. The remaining 3D interaction techniques in this section address this occlusion problem.

Void Shadows

Giesler et al. (2014) developed the concept of void shadows to specifically address the occlusion problem of the pinching technique and other common surface-based interactions. With void shadows, every interactive object below the surface casts a "shadow" up onto the surface. These shadows are calculated based on an unseen shadow plane that resides above the multi-touch surface, as seen in Figure 7.18a. As a result, stacked objects of the same size cast nested shadows of various sizes onto the surface, as seen in Figure 7.18b. A shadow volume is also rendered to highlight the relation between each object and its shadow.

The advantage of void shadows is that the technique allows common surface-based interaction techniques to be used to manipulate objects in 3D space. Dragging a void shadow will result in the corresponding object being moved in its 2-DOF horizontal plane. Rotating a void shadow using the two-point technique will change the yaw of the virtual object. Finally, pinching can be used to change the depth of an object, even if it is not the topmost object in a stack. Giesler et al. (2014) compared void shadows to a simple virtual hand implementation and found that void shadows afforded more precise interactions without increasing completion times.

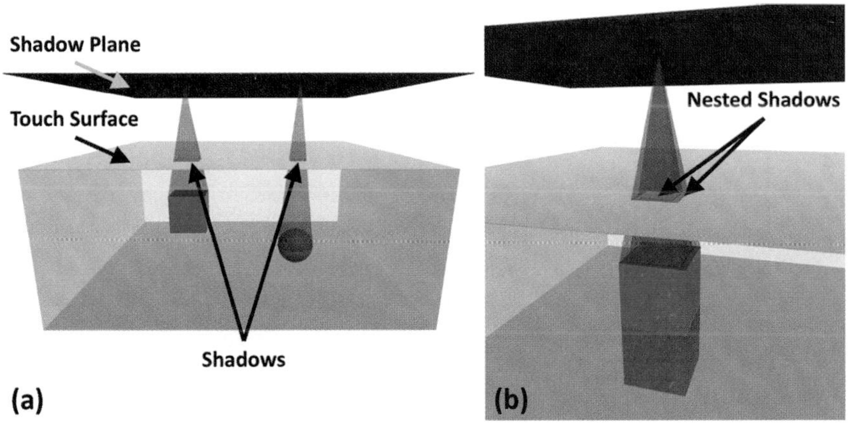

Figure 7.18 The concept of void shadows: (a) the shadow of each object cast upon the surface is calculated based on an unseen shadow plane located above the touch surface; (b) stacked objects of the same size cast nested shadows of various sizes. (Image adapted from Giesler et al. 2014)

Balloon Selection

In order to allow for selections at various depths, Benko and Feiner (2007) developed the balloon selection technique, which is modeled after the metaphor of controlling the height of an anchored balloon by pulling its string away from the anchor. This metaphor decomposes the 3-DOF positioning task into two separable tasks: (1) a 2-DOF horizontal positioning task controlled by the anchor point and (2) a 1-DOF vertical positioning task controlled by the length of the string pulled from the anchor point.

The two separable tasks can be simultaneously defined by and controlled with two contact points on a multi-touch surface. When the user first touches the surface with a finger, the anchor is defined, which controls the horizontal position of the 3D cursor. The user then places a second finger on the surface adjacent to the anchor, to simulate grabbing the string, and drags the second finger away from the anchor to pull the virtual string, effectively lowering the 3D balloon cursor. To raise the cursor, the second finger can be dragged back toward the anchor to shorten the string. See Figure 7.19 for a depiction of the balloon selection technique.

Benko and Feiner (2007) also proposed allowing users to change the size of the balloon selection cursor, effectively changing the size of the selection volume, by employing a third contact point. To adjust the size of the cursor, users would change the distance between this third contact point and the anchor. As the distance between the points increased, the balloon cursor would be scaled up. As the distance decreased, the cursor would shrink. Strothoff et al. (2011) also proposed a modification that would allow the user to manipulate the yaw of the selected object by using the two-point rotation technique described in section 7.6.1.

Benko and Feiner (2007) compared the balloon selection technique to a 3-DOF simple virtual hand technique and a keyboard-based technique. They found that the balloon selection technique was significantly faster than using the keyboard for 3-DOF positioning. Additionally, they found that balloon selection had a significantly lower error rate than simple virtual hand.

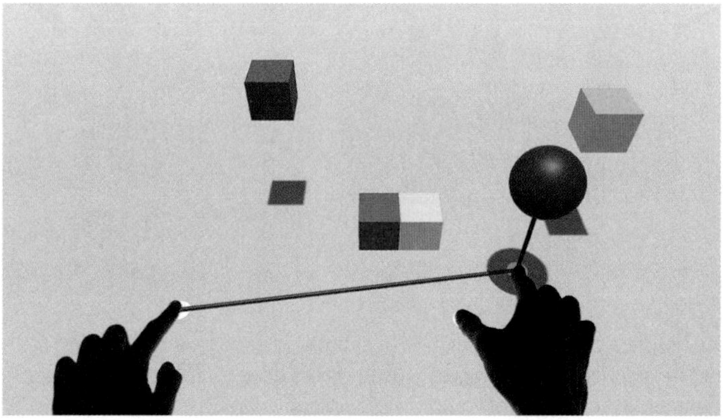

Figure 7.19 The balloon selection technique uses an anchor contact point to define the horizontal position of the cursor, a second contact point to determine the vertical position of the cursor given a virtual string, and a third contact point to change the size of the cursor. (Image courtesy of Ryan P. McMahan)

Corkscrew Widget

As another technique for making selections at various depths, Daiber et al. (2012) developed the corkscrew widget, a circular selection widget displayed at the surface (see Figure 7.20). Dragging this widget along the surface allows the user to change the horizontal position of a selection point. However, the user can also change the depth of the selection point by performing a rotation gesture on the outer portion of the widget. A clockwise rotation on the widget makes the selection point sink while a counter-clockwise rotation raises the selection point, even above the surface's display. In their study, Daiber et al. (2012) found that users performed depth-based interactions faster with the corkscrew widget than the balloon selection technique, but it also resulted in more errors. Hence, the corkscrew widget is best suited for quick and imprecise depth-based selections and manipulations.

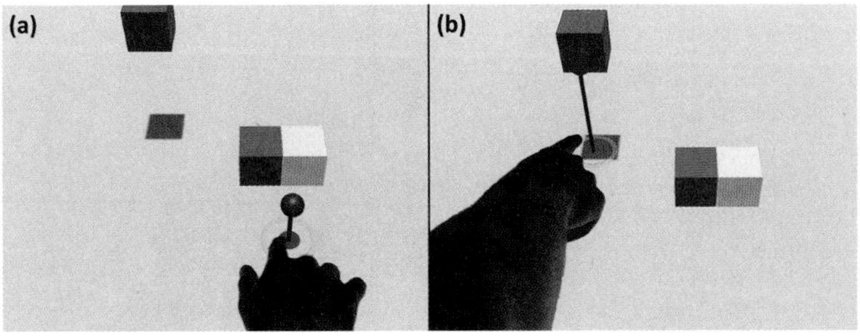

Figure 7.20 The corkscrew widget: (a) dragging the widget changes the horizontal position of the selection point; (b) rotating the widget changes the vertical position of the selection point. (Image courtesy of Ryan P. McMahan)

Triangle Cursor

Strothoff et al. (2011) presented the triangle cursor as an alternative to the balloon selection technique. Like balloon selection, the triangle cursor separates the 3-DOF task of positioning the selection cursor into the two separate tasks of specifying its 2-DOF horizontal position and manipulating its 1-DOF vertical position. With the triangle cursor, the 2-DOF horizontal position is calculated as the midpoint between two contact points, usually the thumb and the index finger. Meanwhile, the 1-DOF vertical position is determined by the distance between the two contact points. As the distance nears zero, the height of the cursor nears the surface. As the distance nears the extent of the user's ability to splay the thumb and finger, the height of the cursor nears the ceiling of the 3D virtual space.

To affect the yaw rotation of a selected object, Strothoff et al. (2011) again used the two-point rotation technique described in section 7.6.1. However, they used the midpoint between the thumb and finger as the center of rotation, as opposed to using either contact point. Visual feedback for the triangle cursor, including its yaw, is provided in the form of an isosceles triangle segmented by its axis (see Figure 7.21).

Strothoff et al. (2011) compared the triangle cursor to the balloon selection technique, and found that the triangle cursor afforded faster completion times, fewer positional errors, and fewer rotational errors. The researchers hypothesized that the better performance could be due to the one-handed aspect of the triangle cursor, while the balloon selection technique requires both hands to position the selection cursor. This hypothesis is supported by the work of Zhai et al. (1996), which indicates that smaller muscle groups, such as the fingers, provide finer-grained control than larger muscle groups, such as the hands. The triangle cursor is therefore well suited for precise, surface-based 3D interactions.

Figure 7.21 The triangle cursor uses the midpoint between two contact points to define the horizontal position of the cursor, the distance between the contact points to determine the vertical position of the cursor, and the angle of the points about their midpoint to change the yaw of selected objects. (Image courtesy of Ryan P. McMahan)

7.7 Indirect Metaphors

In this next section, we discuss a number of interaction techniques that allow the user to manipulate virtual objects without directly interacting with them. Hence these techniques are referred to as indirect interactions.

There are several potential reasons for using indirect metaphors. First, indirect techniques can be used to interact with remote objects without first traveling, similar to how pointing techniques can be used. Second, indirect interactions help to avoid occlusion problems that stem from the user's physical body parts visually blocking interactions, such as the "fat finger" problem (Strothoff et al. 2011). Third, indirect interaction techniques can purposefully constrain manipulations by reducing the degrees of freedom for manipulation tasks. Such constraints have been shown to improve efficiency and precision (see Chapter 10).

We have categorized indirect metaphors into three distinct approaches—control spaces, proxies, and widgets. **Control-space** techniques separate control from the display by allowing the user to interact in a physical space distinct from the apparent location of the virtual environment and mapping those interactions to the environment. **Proxy** techniques have the user directly interact with proxies (i.e., representative copies of objects within the virtual environment) and then map those manipulations onto the original objects. **Widget** techniques place within the virtual environment widgets that the user can directly manipulate. These widgets, in turn, affect their context or associated virtual objects.

7.7.1 Indirect Control-Space Techniques

A number of indirect control-space techniques have been investigated. Many of these techniques provide a control space that is physically separated from the display space and virtual environment. Some of the techniques use a control space that is collocated with the display space, but at an offset, in order to provide remote interactions and avoid occlusions. In this section, we specifically discuss the following control-space techniques:

- indirect touch
- virtual interaction surface
- levels-of-precision cursor
- virtual pad

Indirect Touch

This approach to indirect interaction involves using a multi-touch surface, separate from the primary display, as the control space for manipulating virtual objects seen on the display. Simeone (2016) refers to this approach as **indirect touch**. With indirect touch, the user can initially touch the external multi-touch surface to control a cursor on the primary display, then with a second finger, touch the surface to select an object under the cursor (Knoedel and Hachet 2011). Once an object is selected, conventional surface-based interaction techniques (see section 7.6) or indirect-specific techniques, such as Indirect6 (Simeone 2016), can be used to manipulate the object. See Figure 7.22 for an example of using indirect touch to interact.

An important design decision for indirect touch interactions is whether to use an absolute or relative mapping. With an absolute mapping, the area of the multi-touch surface is directly mapped to the primary display's area. If the user touches the center of the surface and drags the contacting finger down to the center of the lower edge, the cursor will appear at the center of the display and will move down to the center of the display's bottom edge. With a relative mapping, the same touch gesture would result in the cursor moving to the center of the display, if it were originally at the center of the display's top edge. If an absolute mapping is used, the initial contact can be used for selection. However, Simeone (2016) found that this required users to look at the multi-touch surface to mentally map its space to that of the display. If a relative mapping is used, a second contact is required to make selections.

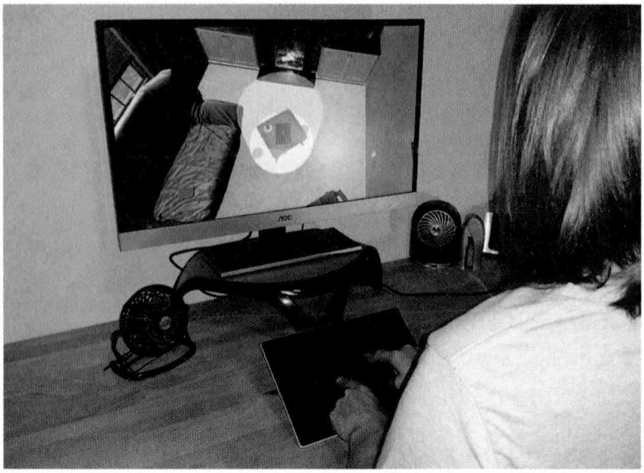

Figure 7.22 An example of an indirect control-space technique. (Image courtesy of Ryan P. McMahan)

In terms of performance, Knoedel and Hachet (2011) found that indirect touch requires significantly more time to manipulate objects than conventional direct-touch interactions. However, they did find that indirect touch improves the efficiency of moving virtual objects along optimal trajectories and the accuracy of placing them in target positions. Simeone (2016) also compared indirect touch to two direct-touch techniques and did not find any significant decreases in performance when using indirect touch. He also found that indirect touch provides a more comfortable viewing experience.

Virtual Interaction Surface

Ohnishi et al. (2012) have extended the concept of indirect touch to nonplanar surfaces located within the virtual environment, which they call virtual interaction surfaces. While the previous indirect touch techniques mapped the 2D plane of an external multi-touch display to the 2D viewing plane of the primary display, virtual interaction surfaces map the same multi-touch gestures to 3D virtual surfaces that exist within the virtual environment. See Figure 7.23 for an example of a virtual interaction surface.

Ohnishi et al. (2012) identified several possible benefits to using virtual interaction surfaces. First, these surfaces allow the user to manipulate objects relative to desired paths or even other objects. For example, translating and rotating an object along a curved surface is normally very difficult with other 3D interaction techniques, but with the appropriate virtual interaction surface, this complex task becomes a trivial dragging task (section 7.6.1), as seen in Figure 7.23. Second, virtual interaction surfaces can be defined to coincide with the surfaces of 3D objects located within the virtual environment. This can allow the user to draw directly on a complex 3D object without worrying about pointing or occlusion issues. Additionally, this would facilitate placing objects on uneven terrain, particularly in the case of occlusions, such as placing a tree behind a hill. Virtual interaction surfaces can also be used to define unique 3D volumes by calculating the projected intersections of the normals created by the multi-touch gestures. Finally, Ohnishi et al. (2012) also discussed how virtual interaction surfaces allow users to complete complex tasks without needing to change their viewing position or direction.

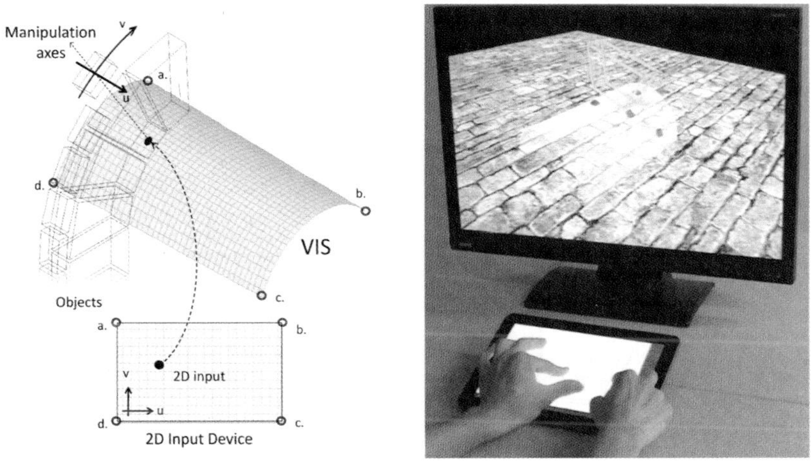

(a) concept of object placement

(b) object placement in action

Figure 7.23 A virtual interaction surface turns the complex 3D task of translating and rotating a box along the surface of a cylinder into a simple 2D action. (Ohnishi et al. 2012, © 2012 IEEE; reprinted by permission)

Levels-of-Precision Cursor

The levels-of-precision (LOP) cursor developed by Debarba et al. (2012) takes the concept of indirect touch and enhances it with physical 3D interactions. With the previously described indirect touch and virtual interaction surface techniques, the external multi-touch surface is usually a larger tablet that is placed on a table in a stationary position. However, the LOP cursor technique uses a smartphone, which can be held and dynamically positioned with one hand. In turn, this affords 3D interactions in addition to the indirect touch gestures.

For 3D interactions, Debarba et al. (2012) used the smartphone's inertial sensors and a sensor fusion algorithm (Madgwick et al. 2011) to determine the absolute orientation of the multi-touch surface, as opposed to using an external tracking system. They used this orientation to map the smaller area of the smartphone onto the larger surface of the display (see Figure 7.24). Indirect selections made on the smartphone are then mapped to this area. This affords the ability to freely point toward the display and select objects.

For additional levels of precision, Debarba et al. (2012) provided two additional modes of interaction. For one mode, the user can hold a thumb on the smartphone and drag it to position the display's cursor within the small projected area. In this holding mode, selections are made when the thumb is lifted off the multi-touch surface. Additionally, the user still has the ability to change the position of the projected area by freely pointing at the display (see Figure 7.24). However, in the second mode, the user can pin the area to the display by using a double tap gesture. While the area is pinned, any touch gestures are mapped directly to the pinned area.

In their research, Debarba et al. (2012) found that the LOP cursor afforded significantly more precise selections than ray-casting without requiring greater interaction times.

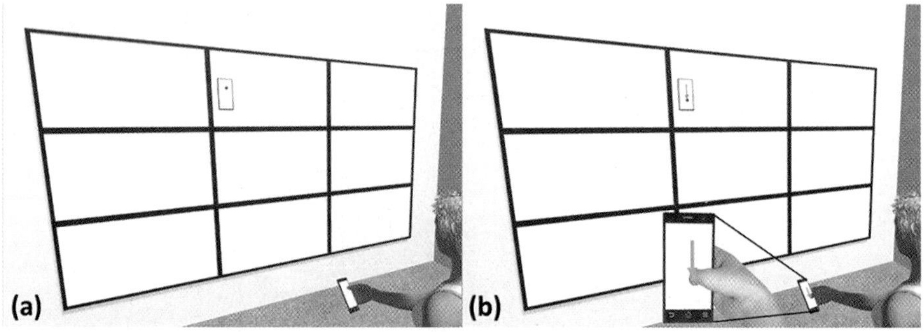

Figure 7.24 The LOP cursor: (a) the user can freely point the smartphone at the display to change the mapping of the smaller indirect surface to the display surface; (b) the user can precisely change the position of the cursor by dragging a thumb on the smartphone screen. (Image adapted from Debarba et al. 2012)

Virtual Pad

Virtual pad is another indirect control-space technique, developed by Andujar and Argelaguet (2007). However, unlike the previously described techniques, the virtual pad technique does not require an external multi-touch surface. Instead, a virtual surface is provided within the virtual environment as an indirect control space. This allows the technique to be used with immersive displays, such as CAVEs and HMDs, to which the prior techniques are not easily adapted.

Andujar and Argelaguet (2007) developed the virtual pad technique for interacting with 2D-adapted menus (see Chapter 9), though it could also be used with the virtual interaction surfaces discussed above. Instead of using ray-casting or another 3D interaction technique to directly select options on a remote graphical window, the user can use the same techniques on a nearby virtual pad to indirectly select options on the graphical window (see Figure 7.25). The advantage of this approach is that the user can customize the control space independently of the 3D UI application by manipulating the size, shape, and position of the virtual pad. Andujar and Argelaguet (2007) demonstrated that the virtual pad technique increased the user's comfort while providing the ability to dynamically trade off speed for accuracy, or vice versa.

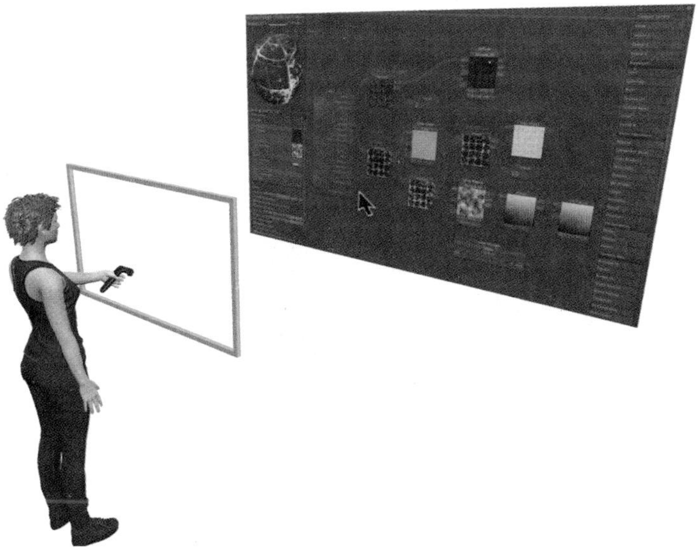

Figure 7.25 Instead of using ray-casting to directly interact with remote objects, the virtual pad technique allows the user to use virtual hand with a local control space to control remote selections. (Image adapted from Andujar and Argelaguet 2007)

7.7.2 Indirect Proxy Techniques

Proxy techniques are interaction techniques that address many of the issues with remote object manipulation (McMahan et al. 2014). By giving the user local proxies, or representations of remote objects, proxy techniques allow the user to use a more natural grasping method to perform direct manipulations. Any manipulations of these local proxies are in turn applied to the remote objects that they represent, circumventing issues such as needing to travel to reach an object or not being able to select an occluded object. We discuss two indirect proxy techniques in this section:

- world in miniature
- Voodoo Dolls

World-in-Miniature

An alternative to using techniques like Go-Go or simple ray-casting to manipulate remote objects is to scale the entire world down and bring it within the user's reach. The world-in-miniature (WIM) technique (Stoakley et al. 1995) provides the user with a miniature handheld model of the virtual environment, which is an exact copy of the VE at a smaller scale (Figure 7.26). The user can indirectly manipulate virtual objects by interacting with their representations in the WIM.

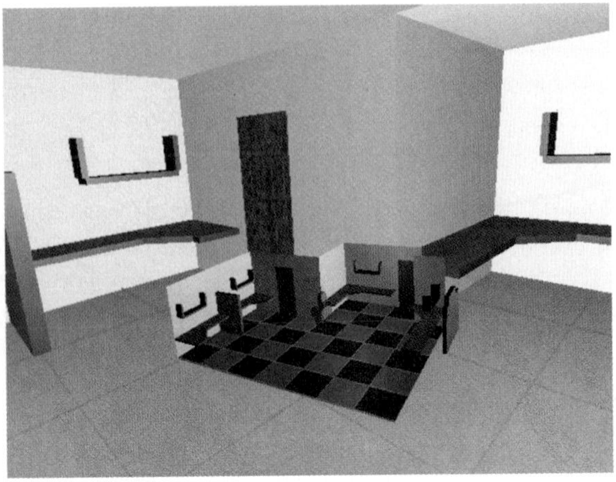

Figure 7.26 WIM technique. (Stoakley et al. 1995, © 1995 ACM; reprinted by permission)

When implementing the WIM technique, it is important to perform the proper transformations between the WIM coordinate system and the global coordinate system of the full-scale VE. WIM also requires the careful use of back-face culling techniques. For example, only the "inside" of the walls of the room model in Figure 7.26 should be rendered, which allows the user to easily see the interior of the WIM from any angle or position.

The WIM is a powerful technique that allows easy object manipulation both within and outside of the area of user reach. It can also combine navigation with manipulation, because the user can also move his or her virtual representation in the WIM (see Chapter 8). There is, however, a downside to this technique: it does not scale well. Although WIM works relatively well for small and medium-sized environments, such as the interior of a virtual building or rooms, using WIM in a very large environment would require an extreme scale factor, resulting in very small object copies in the WIM. This would make accurate selection and manipulation extremely difficult. A technique allowing the user to choose the parts of the environment to be represented, perhaps by scaling and scrolling the WIM (Wingrave et al. 2006), may overcome this problem. In spite of this shortcoming, WIM can be effectively used in many different classes of 3D UIs. It can also be used in desktop 3D UIs; in fact, WIM can be considered a 3D generalization of the traditional overview maps that are often used in 3D games.

Voodoo Dolls

Voodoo Dolls (Pierce et al. 1999) is a two-handed interaction technique that combines and builds upon the image-plane selection and WIM techniques discussed earlier in this chapter. Voodoo Dolls uses a pair of pinch gloves to allow the user to seamlessly switch between different frames of references for a manipulation task, allowing manipulation of objects with widely varying sizes and at different distances.

The technique is based on several key ideas. First, it proposes to manipulate virtual objects indirectly, using temporary, miniature, handheld copies of objects called **dolls** (Figure 7.27). Similar to the WIM, the user manipulates these dolls instead of the virtual objects, which therefore can be at any distance, of any size, and in any state of occlusion.

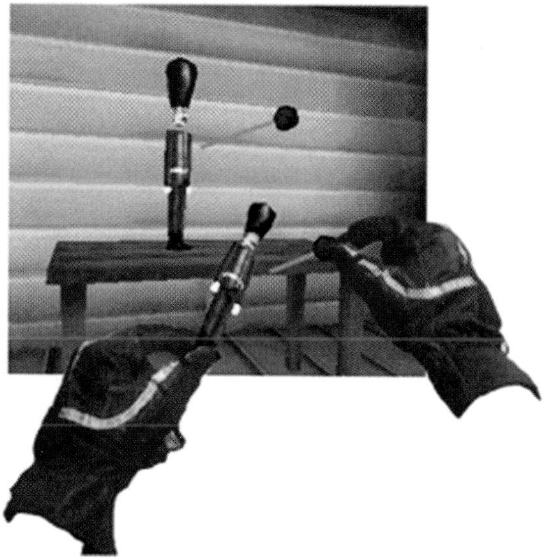

Figure 7.27 Voodoo Dolls interaction technique. (Pierce et al. 1999, © 1999 ACM; reprinted by permission)

Unlike the WIM technique, however, the Voodoo Dolls technique allows the user to decide which objects in the VE will be used in interaction. The user starts the manipulation sequence by selecting the target object (or group of objects) with an image-plane technique, which creates the dolls representing the target objects and places them in the user's hand, as shown in Figure 7.28. Because only a subset of the virtual objects is used in manipulation, Voodoo Dolls can scale the copies to a convenient size to interact with, overcoming one of the limitations of the WIM technique, which lacks a mechanism for setting the scale of the world-in-miniature.

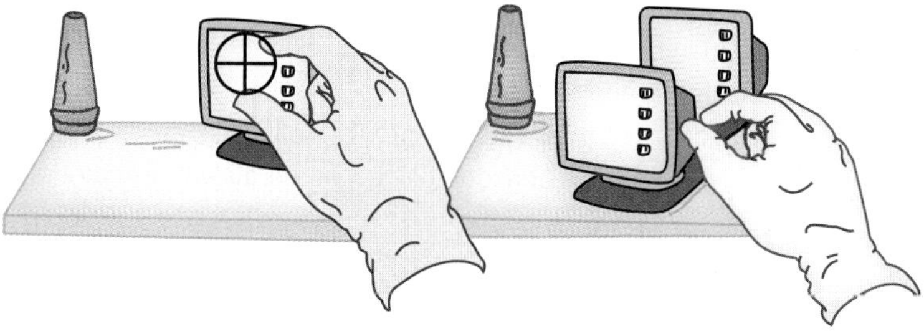

Figure 7.28 Creating a doll in the Voodoo Dolls technique.

Second, the technique allows the user to explicitly and interactively specify a frame of reference for manipulation. The doll that the user holds in her nondominant hand represents a stationary frame of reference, and the corresponding virtual object does not move when the user moves this doll. The doll that the user holds in her dominant hand defines the position and orientation of the corresponding object relative to the stationary frame of reference (Figure 7.28). Because the user can explicitly define the manipulation frame of reference, manipulation can be more convenient. While the user is holding a doll in the nondominant hand, she can easily shift her hands into a more convenient position without affecting the remote objects. To start manipulation, the user simply passes the doll into the dominant hand.

Voodoo Dolls is an interesting and powerful interaction technique that allows users to perform some sophisticated tasks, such as the manipulation of moving, animated objects—which is difficult to accomplish with other interaction techniques. The technique, however, requires the use of two 6-DOF devices, which increases the hardware demands on the application.

7.7.3 Indirect Widget Techniques

Another common indirect interaction metaphor is the use of widgets. Widgets are objects placed within the virtual environment that the user can directly manipulate to indirectly affect other virtual objects or contexts. We discuss various types of widgets in Chapter 9; however, here we describe those widgets that afford indirect interactions, including the following:

- 3D widgets
- virtual sphere
- Arcball

3D Widgets

Widgets are a common technique for manipulating objects in 3D space, especially for desktop-based 3D UIs (Figure 7.29). One of the first examples of using widgets to provide a simple way to rotate and position objects in desktop 3D UIs was reported by Houde (1992), and although there have been further developments and expansions (e.g., Conner et al. 1992), the key ideas behind these techniques have not changed significantly.

The basic approach of using widgets and handles is to put controls directly in the 3D scene with the objects that are being manipulated. When an object is selected, a number of 3D graphical objects (widgets) become visible, and they can be clicked and dragged around (Figure 7.29). Each widget is responsible for only a small set of manipulation DOF. For example, some widgets allow users to translate objects only in a horizontal plane, others allow translations in the vertical direction, and others enable rotation around a central axis. As the user interacts with a widget, the motion of the mouse is "captured" by the widget, and only a subset of the object's total DOF is affected by the mouse. Hence, widgets work as visual manipulation constraints.

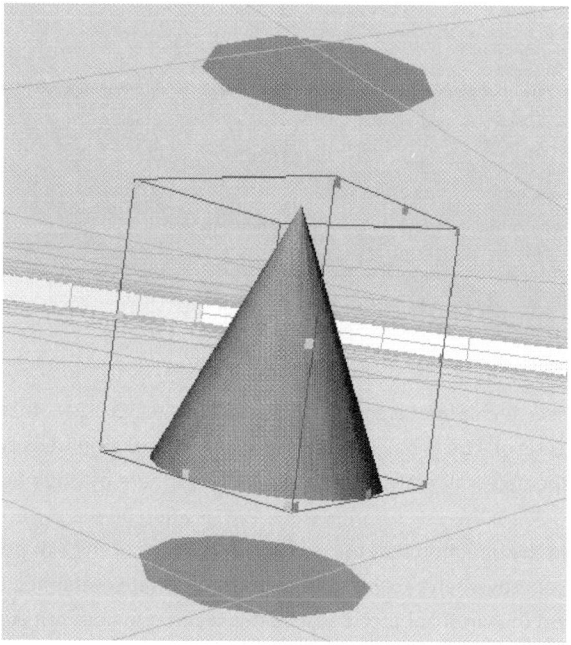

Figure 7.29 3D widgets for object manipulation.

The main advantage of widgets is an easy and seamless transition between different manipulation sequences—the user simply selects another widget to perform another manipulation. The disadvantage of widgets is visual clutter: adding manipulation controls increases the number of graphical interface elements in the 3D scene. In addition, the user needs to learn how each of the widgets responds to mouse input, though through intelligent placement of widgets and careful design of affordances, their functionality can become self-explanatory.

3D widgets have become a standard technique to interact with virtual objects, for both desktop and immersive 3D environments, and they have become a standard part of many 3D computer graphics toolkits and applications as well. See Chapter 9 for more detail on 3D widgets.

Virtual Sphere

A number of interaction techniques have proposed integrated methods of using 2-DOF manipulations to control three-axis rotation of 3D objects. Several variations have been reported, such as the Virtual Sphere (Chen et al. 1988) shown in Figure 7.30, Rolling Ball (Hanson 1992), and Virtual Trackball (Hultquits 1990) techniques. The fundamental approach behind these techniques is similar, and we refer to all of them as Virtual Sphere techniques.

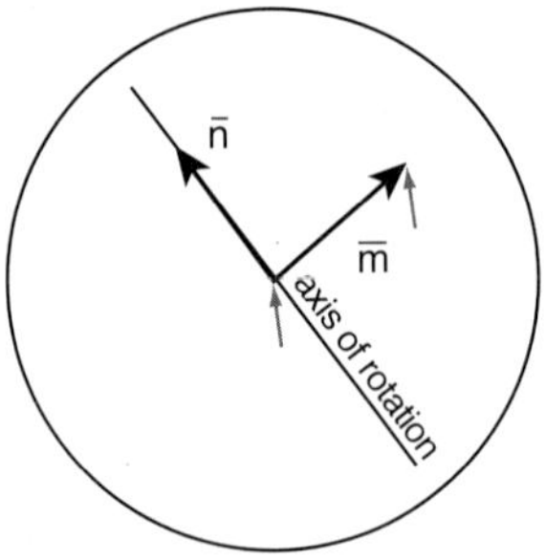

Figure 7.30 Virtual sphere technique.

The basic idea for these techniques is simple: Imagine that the 3D object that we wish to rotate is enclosed inside of a glass ball that can be freely rotated around its center point. Then, instead of rotating the object directly, we rotate this glass sphere by nudging it with the mouse cursor as if the cursor were the user's finger, stuck to a location on the surface of the sphere. The sphere rotates in the direction that the user "pushes" it about the axis perpendicular to the direction of cursor movement. To visualize this virtual sphere metaphor, a circle or sphere is often drawn around the virtual object. Because this technique does not allow rotating the object around the axis pointing out of the screen (depth or *z*-axis), usually mouse movements along the edge of the circle or outside of it produce rotations around this axis.

Arcball

Arcball (Shoemake 1992) is a "mathematically correct" 3D rotation technique designed originally for mouse-based interactions. It is based on the observation that there is a close connection between 3D rotations and spherical geometry. This can be illustrated using a simple physical example. Imagine rotating a pencil fixed at one end. Obviously, the other end would travel on the surface of a sphere, and each orientation of the pencil could be then identified as a **point** on this sphere. **Rotation** of the pencil would draw an **arc** on the sphere. If the pencil has unit length, then the length of the arc is equal to the rotation angle. Thus, in general, the orientation of a body can be represented as a point on a unit sphere, while rotation can be represented as an arc connecting the starting and final body orientations. This example is illustrative, albeit not quite correct: each point on a 3D sphere actually specifies a **family of rotations,** because twisting the pencil would not draw an arc. Therefore, the correct geometric representation of 3D rotations involves using a 4D unit quaternion sphere.

The implementation of Arcball follows from this spherical representation of 3D rotations. Similar to the Virtual Sphere technique, a 3D object is enclosed within a virtual sphere of radius *R*. The user rotates the object by clicking and dragging the mouse on the circle that represents the projection of the sphere on the screen surface (Figure 7.31). The Arcball uses a circle of radius *R* only to provide a visual reference for the user; all computations are made using a normalized unit sphere.

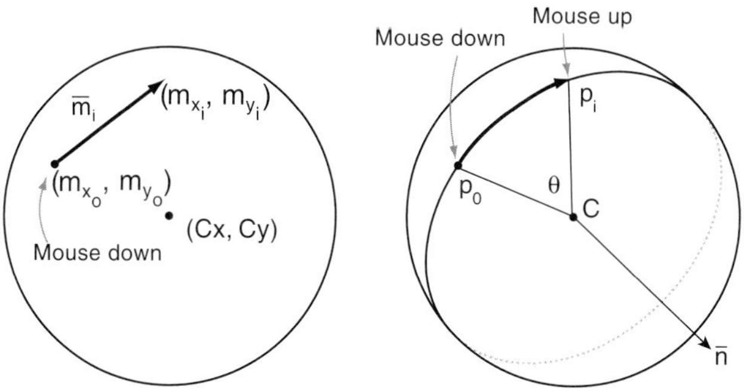

Figure 7.31 Arcball technique. (Image adapted from Shoemake 1992)

As the user drags the mouse, the Arcball technique computes an arc on a unit sphere with starting point p_0, corresponding to the 2D mouse position when the user starts rotating (m_{x_0}, m_{y_0}); and current point p_i corresponding to the current mouse position (m_{x_1}, m_{y_1}) (see Figure 7.31). Having obtained the initial and final points of the arc on the sphere, we can now calculate the rotation corresponding to this arc. There are several techniques to do this, such as the one provided by Shoemake (1992), which uses quaternion notation.

7.8 Bimanual Metaphors

Most of the techniques described earlier in this chapter require only one hand to interact with the 3D UI. Often this is done to avoid potential hardware limitations, such as only having access to a single 6-DOF controller. However, a few techniques have required both hands for interactions, such as the balloon selection, world-in-miniature, and Voodoo dolls techniques. In this section, we take a closer look at bimanual interaction metaphors.

Ulinski et al. (2009) have identified four distinct classes of bimanual interactions—symmetric-synchronous, symmetric-asynchronous, asymmetric-synchronous, and asymmetric-asynchronous. Symmetric-synchronous interactions involve each hand performing identical movements at the same time, while symmetric-asynchronous interactions involve identical movements at different times. We will discuss some symmetric bimanual interaction techniques in this section.

On the other hand, asymmetric interactions involve the hands performing different movements in coordination to accomplish an interaction, either at the same time or different times. For example, the balloon selection technique is an asymmetric-synchronous technique, as one hand defines the anchor position while the other hand simultaneously controls the length of the metaphorical balloon string. However, the Voodoo dolls technique is an asymmetric-asynchronous technique, as the nondominant hand creates the dolls and then the dominant hand manipulates them.

In this section, we discuss symmetric bimanual metaphors and then asymmetric ones (see Chapter 3, section 3.5.1 for more detail on bimanual interaction).

7.8.1 Symmetric Bimanual Techniques

Many of the bimanual interactions discussed in this chapter are asymmetric. However, in this section, we discuss symmetric techniques that involve both hands performing the same actions. In particular, we talk about the following techniques:

- Spindle
- iSith

Spindle

Spindle is a symmetric-synchronous bimanual technique originally developed by Mapes and Moshell (1995). With the technique, two 6-DOF handheld controllers are used to define a virtual spindle that extends from one controller position to the other. The center of this spindle represents the primary point of interaction, which can be used to select and manipulate objects. In order to move a virtual object, both hands must be moved in unison in order for the center of the spindle to move the desired distance. This allows for 3-DOF translations.

In addition to translating objects, the Spindle technique can also be used to simultaneously rotate the yaw and roll of a virtual object. By rotating the hands relative to each other, the user can change the orientation of the spindle, which in turn affects the yaw and roll of the selected object. Finally, the user can also lengthen or shorten the distance between the two handheld controllers to directly manipulate the relative scale of the object.

Schultheis et al. (2012) found that the Spindle technique significantly outperformed a simple virtual hand implementation and a standard mouse interface for manipulating the positions and orientations of virtual objects. However, the researchers acknowledged that the bimanual interaction technique required training and sufficient practice to efficiently use.

iSith

Another symmetric-synchronous technique is the Intersection-based Spatial Interaction for Two Hands, or iSith, developed by Wyss et al. (2006). With iSith, the positions and orientations of two 6-DOF handheld controllers are used to define two separate rays, similar to ray-casting with both hands. The shortest line between these two rays is then calculated by crossing the two vectors to find a vector perpendicular to both. Wyss et al. (2006) referred to the center of this perpendicular vector as the projected intersection point (PIP) and used it as the primary point of interaction, similar to Spindle's center point. However, unlike the Spindle technique, this interaction point can easily be moved by rotating only the handheld controllers, as opposed to physically translating the hands (see Figure 7.32).

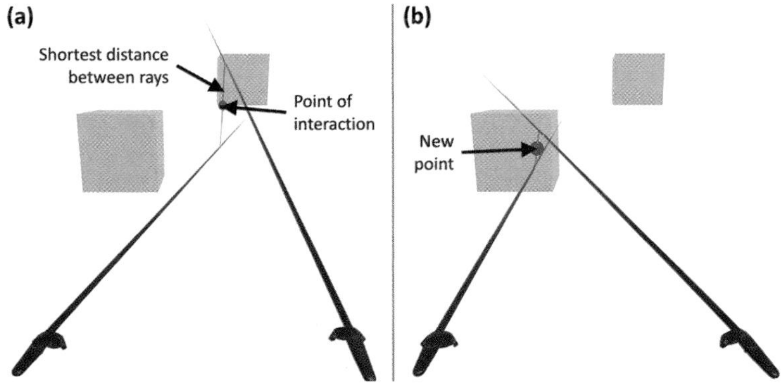

Figure 7.32 With the bimanual iSith technique, (a) the point of interaction can be quickly translated by (b) rotating the two handheld controllers (Image adapted from Wyss et al. 2006)

7.8.2 Asymmetric Bimanual Techniques

We have already discussed a number of asymmetric bimanual techniques, such as balloon selection, world-in-miniature, and Voodoo Dolls; however, we discuss two other asymmetric interactions in this section:

- Spindle + Wheel
- flexible pointer

Spindle + Wheel

Cho and Wartell (2015) extended the original Spindle technique to include an additional feature for rotating the pitch of the selected virtual object. The feature was a virtual wheel collocated with the dominant hand's cursor (see Figure 7.33). The user can twist the dominant-hand controller to rotate this virtual wheel about its axis. The change in rotation is then applied to the pitch of the selected virtual object.

Cho and Wartell (2015) call this approach the Spindle + Wheel technique because it simply extends the original Spindle technique with the wheel feature. Because of the dominant-hand feature, the Spindle + Wheel technique is an asymmetric bimanual interaction, as opposed to the original symmetric technique. In a study, Cho and Wartell (2015) found that the addition of the asymmetric wheel significantly improved user performance compared to the original Spindle technique. Hence, researchers should consider how other symmetric interactions could be improved with asymmetric features.

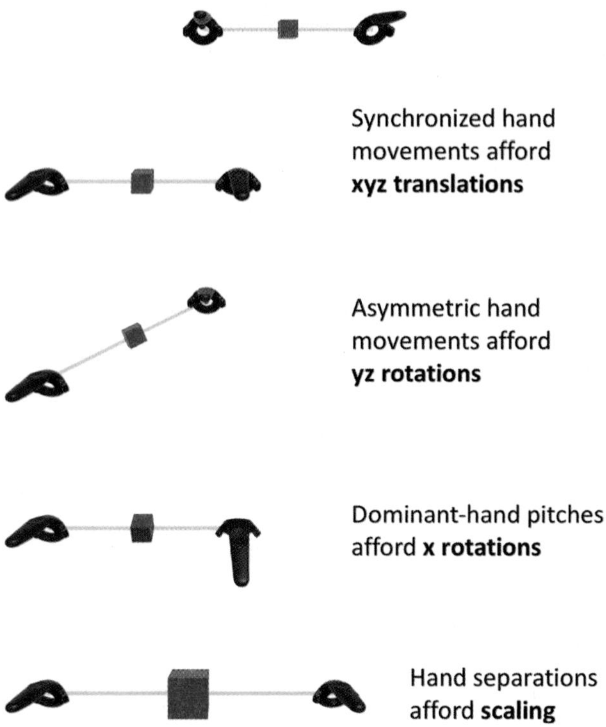

Figure 7.33 The Spindle + Wheel technique affords 7-DOF control (xyz translations + xyz rotations + uniform scaling) by augmenting the original 6-DOF Spindle technique with a dominant-hand wheel feature for pitch rotations. (Image courtesy of Ryan P. McMahan)

Flexible Pointer

Ray-casting uses a virtual hand position and the direction of the virtual ray to define the pointing direction. In cases where both of the user's hands are tracked, the pointing direction can be specified using a two-handed technique: one hand (usually closer to the user) specifies the origin of the virtual ray, while the other hand specifies where the ray is pointing to (Mine et al. 1997). The disadvantage of two-handed pointing is that both hands must be tracked; however, it allows for richer and more effective pointing interaction.

Olwal and Feiner (2003) took advantage of the concept of two-handed pointing to provide the flexible pointer technique. The flexible pointer is a curved ray that can be used to point at partially obscured objects (see Figure 7.34). The pointer is implemented as a quadratic Bézier spline. Three points—the nearest hand, the farthest hand, and a control point—control the position, length, and curvature of the Bézier spline. The nearest and farthest hand points are directly determined from the positions of the two 6-DOF handheld controllers. The control point, however, gravitates closer to the hand with the greatest deviation in orientation from the two-handed axis. In turn, the control point affects the curvature of the flexible pointer, which can allow users to point around occluding objects.

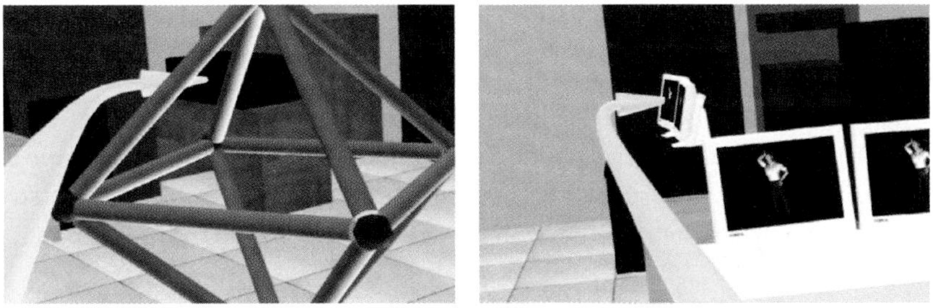

Figure 7.34 A flexible pointer can be used to point at partially obscured objects. (Olwal and Feiner 2003; reprinted by permission of the authors)

7.9 Hybrid Metaphors

It is difficult, perhaps impossible, to design a single best 3D manipulation technique that fits all possible interaction scenarios. Indeed, just as in the real world there is no tool that can do every possible task, in 3D UIs no interaction technique can be effective in every manipulation situation. Therefore, combining manipulation techniques to bring together the best properties of different interaction techniques has been an active research direction. Two basic approaches have emerged: technique aggregation and technique integration.

Aggregation of techniques is the simplest method to combine several techniques together: the user is provided with a manual or automatic mechanism for choosing the desired manipulation technique from a limited set of possible options. This mechanism can be, for example, a 3D menu system that can be displayed on command—a sort of virtual toolbox from which the user can choose manipulation techniques (Mine et al. 1997). Various system control techniques that can be used for this purpose are discussed in Chapter 9.

Technique integration is another approach to combining techniques in which the interface switches transparently between interaction techniques depending on the current task context. This approach is based on the simple observation that all manipulations are based on a repeating task sequence: an object must be selected before it can be manipulated. Hence, different stages of the manipulation sequence can be completed using different techniques.

7.9.1 Integrated Hybrid Techniques

In the simplest case of technique integration, the interface can simply switch from the selection technique to the manipulation technique after the user selects an object, and switch back to the selection mode after the user releases the manipulated object. Theoretically, these techniques can be optimized to achieve the best performance in each mode. The techniques in this section implement various versions of this idea. We discuss the following ones:

- HOMER
- Scaled-World Grab

HOMER

HOMER (Bowman and Hodges 1997) stands for hand-centered object manipulation extending ray-casting. The user selects an object using a ray-casting technique, and instead of the object being attached to the ray, the user's virtual hand instantly moves to the object and attaches to it. The technique then switches to the manipulation mode, allowing the user to position and rotate the virtual object.

To allow the user to position virtual objects within a large manipulation range, the technique linearly scales the user-reaching distance within the user-centered coordinate system. The tracked distance between the user and her real hand is linearly scaled using a constant and then applied to the distance between the user and her virtual hand. The value of the scaling constant is defined at the moment of selection. It depends on the distance between the user and the object and the distance between the user and her real hand at the moment of selection. As with the Go-Go technique, the virtual hand (and thus the object) is placed along a line defined by the user's body and the user's real hand, at the scaled distance. The rotations of the object are controlled independently, using an isomorphic mapping from the real to virtual hand.

HOMER allows a user to easily reposition an object within the area between the virtual object and himself, no matter how far away the object is at the moment of selection. However, the maximum distance at which the user can reposition an object is limited—it depends on the distance between the user and her real hand at the moment of selection. For example, if the user picks a virtual object that is located far away, brings it close, and releases it, then returning the object to its original position would be difficult. Indeed, in this case, the scaling coefficient will be very small because the object is located within the user's reach. Hence, the user would have to move away from the object, use another interaction technique, or perform many consecutive manipulations of the object to move it back to its original position.

Scaled-World Grab

The scaled-world grab (Mine et al. 1997) technique is based on principles similar to HOMER. The user starts by selecting an object using some selection technique. In Mine's implementation, an image-plane selection technique is used (see section 7.5.1). After successful selection, the interface switches into manipulation mode, and the user can position and rotate the virtual object in space. However, instead of scaling the user's hand motion, as in HOMER, the scaled-world grab technique scales down the *entire VE* around the user's virtual viewpoint. The scaling coefficient is calculated so that the manipulated object is brought within the user's area of reach and, therefore, can be manipulated using the simple virtual hand technique. An interesting property of this technique is that as long as the center of the scaling operation is the point midway between the user's eyes, the user will often not even notice that scaling actually took place, because the world does not change visually.

Similar to the HOMER technique, the scaled-world grab technique performs well for operations at a distance, but it may not be effective when the user wants to pick up an object located within arm's reach and move it farther away.

7.10 Other Aspects of 3D Manipulation

In the previous sections, we have covered many different approaches to provide selection and manipulation capabilities to users in 3D UIs. However, there are still other aspects of 3D manipulation that 3D UI designers should be concerned with. These include nonisomorphic 3D rotation mappings, multiple-object selection, and the progressive refinement of selections.

7.10.1 Nonisomorphic 3D Rotation

The 3D interaction techniques discussed above deal only with object selection and translation—rotations are mapped directly from the input device to the virtual object. In some applications, it might also be useful to design and implement other mappings between the rotations of the device and the object—**nonisomorphic 3D rotation techniques**.

For example, by amplifying rotations of the 6-DOF device, we can allow the user to control large ranges of 3D rotations with small rotations of the 3D device. This allows for more effective use of 3D input devices that have an inherently limited rotation range, such as camera-tracked devices (Poupyrev et al. 1999), and can also be used to develop interfaces for users with disabilities. Amplifying virtual rotations also minimizes the need for clutching (see section 7.2.3). It has been demonstrated that clutching significantly hinders user performance in rotation tasks (Zhai et al. 1996).

Alternatively, rotation techniques can also be used to slow down rotation of the device. Such techniques would map large device rotations to smaller rotations of the manipulated object. This allows for very precise 3D rotation control, which can be useful, for example, in teleoperation applications, such as robotic surgery.

The challenge of designing nonisomorphic 3D rotation techniques is the nonintuitive mathematics behind 3D rotations: they do not follow the familiar laws of Euclidean geometry, and they often use quaternions, an alternative to matrices as a representation of 3D rotations (Shoemake 1985). In this section, we discuss how 3D rotation techniques can be designed and implemented; for the basic properties of quaternions and how they are related to 3D rotations, please refer to the recommended readings listed at the end of the chapter.

Absolute and Relative 3D Rotation Mappings

Some interesting and nontrivial properties of 3D rotation mappings must be taken into account when designing 3D rotation techniques. These properties follow from the fundamental difference between the absolute and relative amplifications of 3D device rotations.

Absolute amplification simply means that on each cycle of the simulation loop, we scale the absolute orientation of the 3D device (i.e., its rotation relative to the initial zero orientation). Alternatively, we can amplify only **relative** changes in the device orientation. This means that we calculate how much the device orientation has changed from the orientation that we measured in the previous cycle of the simulation loop. We amplify this difference between the current and previous orientation. The virtual object is then rotated from its current orientation by the amplified difference.

Usability Properties of 3D Rotation Mappings

Unlike translations, relative and absolute mappings of 3D rotations produce completely different rotation paths from the *same* 6-DOF device rotation. More importantly, they also produce an entirely different *feel* of the 3D interface (Poupyrev, Weghorst et al. 2000). First, absolute mappings do not always preserve the direction of 3D rotations. In some cases, the device and virtual object would rotate in different directions, which violates the principle of **directional compliance** (for more information on feedback compliances, see Chapter 10). Relative mappings, on the other hand, *always* preserve the directional correspondence between rotations of the device and virtual object. Directional compliance in 3D rotations is important, as it allows the user to predict and plan the manipulation sequence to bring a virtual object into the desired orientation. Therefore, absolute mappings have only limited applications in 3D interaction.

Although absolute rotations do not provide directional correspondence, they do preserve **nulling correspondence.** In other words, rotating the device into an initial zero orientation will also bring the virtual object into its initial zero orientation. Relative mappings, however, do not preserve nulling correspondence: nulling the device brings a virtual object into some unpredictable orientation.

Nulling preserves a consistent correspondence between the origins of the coordinate systems in both the physical and virtual spaces. Whether or not it is important for usability, however, depends on the input device shape and the tactile cues that the device provides. For devices that provide strong kinesthetic cues so that the user can *feel* the device's orientation, any inconsistency between the zero orientations of the device and virtual object will be easily noticed and may pose a problem. Examples include devices that mount a tracker on a hand, such as a data glove, and other devices that have an easily recognizable shape. If the device does not provide strong kinesthetic cues, such as a ball-shaped device that can be freely rotated in the user's fingers, it is impossible for the user to feel the zero device orientation—in a sense, zero orientation would not exist for such devices. Therefore, the nulling correspondence is not essential, and relative 3D rotation techniques would be effective and usable.

An empirical evaluation (Poupyrev, Weghorst et al. 2000) showed that a relative rotation technique that amplified 6-DOF device rotation was 13% faster than a conventional one-to-one mapping in a 3D orientation matching task, while no effect on accuracy was found. These results demonstrate that linear relative amplification can be an effective tool in designing 3D rotation interfaces.

Note that nonisomorphic rotation also applies in 3D interaction settings beyond object rotation. In particular, it can be used for amplifying rotation of the user's viewpoint based on head tracking as well. We discuss nonisomorphic viewpoint rotation in section 8.8.1.

7.10.2 Multiple-Object Selection

Some 3D UI tasks require multiple objects to be selected, such as grouping two objects together as one. Other 3D interaction tasks would be much faster to complete by executing one action on multiple selected objects, as opposed to repeating the same action over and over for each individual object. For example, it is faster to delete multiple objects from the virtual environment by selecting multiple objects and invoking a single delete command, as opposed to selecting and deleting each individual object.

As a result, researchers have investigated different approaches for selecting multiple objects in 3D UIs. In this section, we discuss the following multiple-object selection techniques:

- serial selection mode
- volume-based selection techniques
- defining selection volumes
- selection-volume widget

Serial Selection Mode

Any of the single-object selection techniques discussed earlier in this chapter can be modified for multiple-object selections by providing a serial selection mode (Lucas 2005). Once activated, a serial selection mode will add any newly selected object to a list of previously selected objects. This is similar to holding the shift key on a desktop computer while clicking on a series of files to select.

A serial selection mode can be implemented in a number of ways. Perhaps the easiest approach is to assume that the mode is active by default. Every valid object selection will be added to the list of currently selected objects. In order to clear the list, the user can make an invalid selection, such as selecting empty space. Another easy approach is to use one device button for single-object selections and one for serial selections. Nearly any system control technique, such as a voice command or menu option, can be used to turn on and off a serial selection mode (see Chapter 9 for more details on system control techniques).

Volume-Based Selection Techniques

In section 7.5.2, we covered a number of volume-based pointing techniques, including flashlight, aperture selection, and sphere-casting. These techniques can be easily modified to select multiple objects at once by either selecting every object completely enclosed by the volume or selecting every object partially overlapped by the volume. The proper choice between these two options depends on the type of 3D UI application and the volume-based selection technique used. If the application is likely to require fewer objects to be selected at once or if many dissimilar objects are collocated within the virtual environment, an interaction designer is likely to choose the full-enclosure approach to reduce the number of selected objects and to allow users to distinguish between fully enclosed objects and partially enclosed ones. However, if the application is likely to require many objects to be selected at once and all of the objects are similar, then the partial-overlap approach may be more attractive.

Defining Selection Volumes

Another approach to multiple-object selection is to dynamically define a selection volume. Unlike the volume-based pointing techniques, in which the volume is predefined or can only be modified in one dimension, this approach allows the user to define a new selection volume for every multiple-object selection task. Additionally, these techniques can provide more control over the shape of the selection volume.

Ulinski et al. (2007) developed and investigated techniques for dynamically defining cubic volumes for selecting multiple points within a volumetric dataset. With the symmetric bimanual Two-Corners technique, the user could define the cubic selection volume with the position of the dominant hand serving as the top back corner of the box and the nondominant hand position defining the bottom front corner. Contrastingly, the asymmetric bimanual Hand-in-Middle technique positioned the center of the cubic selection volume at the nondominant hand, and the user could change the dimensions of the volume by moving the dominant hand toward or away from the nondominant hand in each dimension.

Lucas (2005) investigated a more complex technique for defining a selection volume based on the user's current view of the virtual environment. Using a virtual tablet with a picture of the current view, the user could draw a 2D lasso around the portion of the visible environment that she desired to select. The lasso technique would then define a selection volume based on the projection of that 2D lasso into the virtual environment, from the current camera position.

Selection-Volume Widget

Another multiple-object selection approach is to use a selection-volume widget. Like the volume-based pointing techniques, a selection-volume widget can be positioned away from the user using any remote manipulation technique. It can also be dynamically resized and shaped, similar to the volume-defining techniques above. Hence, a selection-volume widget can provide the best features of the two previous approaches.

Lucas (2005) implemented a selection-volume widget technique called PORT (Pointer Orientation-based Resize Technique). PORT uses a six-sided box as a selection-volume widget and uses the Go-Go technique for manipulating the position of this widget. In order to dynamically resize the widget, he used the orientation of the dominant handheld controller to determine which of the six widget faces to extrude out or collapse in. The user could then press up on the controller's joystick to extrude the face or pull down on the joystick to collapse the face. This orientation-based approach allowed the selection-volume widget to be resized in one particular direction, as opposed to along an entire axis. This feature was important for avoiding the need to repeatedly position and resize the box in order to obtain a specific volume in space.

7.10.3 Progressive Refinement

Many issues can make object selection difficult to nearly impossible, including tracking jitter, hand jitter, small targets, faraway targets, occluded targets, moving targets, and dense virtual environments. To address such issues, Kopper et al. (2011) introduced the concept of **progressive refinement** for selection, which involves gradually reducing the set of selectable objects until only one target remains. The progressive aspect of the approach allows a larger set of objects to be initially considered for selection, which decreases the likelihood that the target object is accidentally omitted. The refinement aspect of the approach affords a more forgiving control space, which decreases the likelihood of the wrong object being selected. Because multiple steps are used for a single selection, each step can use a fast selection technique that does not require precision. Thus, progressive refinement affords more accurate object selections without requiring the user to interact precisely.

Kopper et al. (2011) identified three dimensions for designing progressive refinement techniques—the type of progression, the refinement criteria, and the display of selectable objects. The type of progression can be accomplished through a series of discrete steps or through a continuous process that evaluates selectable objects every frame. The refinement criteria determine how the user will reduce the set of selectable objects, whether by spatially interacting with the virtual environment, specifying desired object attributes like color or shape, or interacting with a subset of "out-of-context" objects, outside of the virtual environment. Finally, for displaying the set of selectable objects, progressive refinement techniques can leave the objects within their original virtual environment context or out of context in another virtual space.

While there are several examples of progressive refinement techniques for 3D UIs, we will discuss the following approaches in this section:

- SQUAD
- Expand
- Double Bubble

SQUAD

Kopper et al. (2011) developed the Sphere-casting refined by QUAD-menu (or SQUAD) technique as a progressive refinement approach for making object selections in dense virtual environments. The technique consists of two phases. During the first phase, the user specifies the initial subset of environment objects to consider selectable by sphere-casting (see section 7.5.2). This initial step uses volume-based selection as a spatial refinement criterion, and the objects are displayed within their original context.

After the initial step of sphere-casting, the set of selectable objects is distributed and displayed in a quad menu that replaces the user's view of the virtual environment. During this out-of-context phase, the user can use ray-casting to select one of the four quadrants. Once a quadrant is chosen, objects in the other quadrants are discarded and the remaining selectable objects are again distributed and displayed among all four quadrants of the menu. This discrete progression continues until a quadrant with only one object is selected.

Kopper et al. (2011) compared SQUAD to traditional ray-casting and found that it was significantly faster for selecting small objects and for making selections in low-density environments. Perhaps more importantly, the researchers also found that SQUAD was significantly better than ray-casting when errors were considered, as the technique afforded near-perfect selection accuracy.

Expand

One of the primary problems with the SQUAD technique is that the user loses the original context for making further selections. To address this issue, Cashion et al. (2012) developed the Expand technique, which also uses two phases for selection. During the first phase, the user uses a large cursor to define an area of selectable objects, similar to SQUAD's sphere-casting step. However, during the second step, Expand zooms the user's view of the virtual environment to this area, as opposed to SQUAD, which replaces the user's view with the quad menu. Along with this zoomed-in view, Expand creates clones of the selectable objects and distributes the clones in a virtual grid in front of the view (see Figure 7.35). To complete the second phase and finalize a selection, the user points to the clone in the grid that matches the original target, which can still be seen in the zoomed-in view.

Cashion et al. (2012) compared Expand to SQUAD for a wide range of selection scenarios. The researchers found that the Expand technique generally performed faster than SQUAD, especially when object density was high. However, they also determined that SQUAD was more accurate and faster for making object selections in dynamic, low-density scenes.

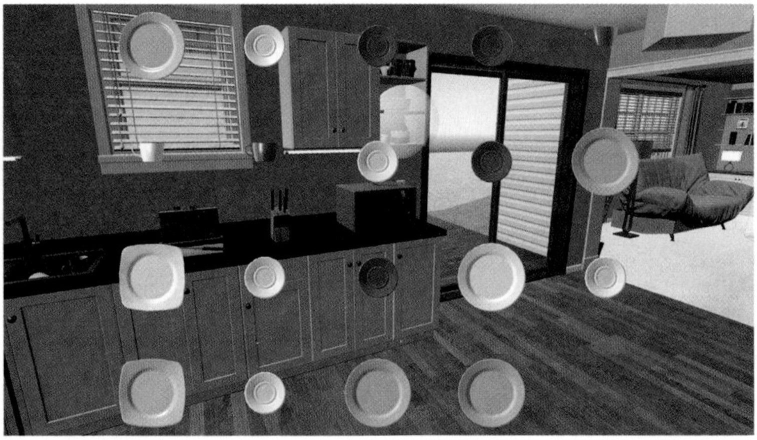

Figure 7.35 With the Expand progressive refinement technique, selectable objects remain in their original context while clones are displayed in a virtual grid for making a final selection. (Image courtesy of Ryan P. McMahan)

Double Bubble

An issue with both SQUAD and Expand is that in dense environments, the initial volume selection step can result in many candidate objects to be refined in the second step. In SQUAD, this causes the user to have to make many QUAD menu selections, while in Expand, this results in a large grid of choices from which it may be difficult to choose the target.

The Double Bubble technique (Bacim 2015) addresses this issue. To reduce the number of items in the initial selection, a 3D Bubble Cursor (see section 7.4.3) is used. However, to make this technique usable in dense environments, the bubble is not allowed to shrink beyond a certain size. If only a single object is in the bubble when the user confirms the selection, it is selected directly. Otherwise, the objects in the bubble are placed into a menu in the image plane, similar to the Expand technique. Objects are laid out in the menu so that they are near to their projected images in the 3D environment. To reduce the difficulty of the menu selection, the 3D Bubble Cursor is also used in this step.

Like SQUAD, both selection steps in Double Bubble are very fast and do not require precision from the user. Like Expand, all selections can be made with only two clicks. This hybrid progressive refinement technique was shown to have excellent speed and accuracy performance compared to ray-casting and to other best-practice techniques (Bacim 2015).

7.11 Design Guidelines

The interaction techniques presented in this chapter can form the basis for a wide variety of 3D UIs for manipulation. Many of these techniques can be combined with interaction techniques for other tasks not directly related to manipulation, such as travel (Chapter 8) and system control (Chapter 9).

We wrap up this chapter with a set of general design guidelines, highlighting some of the important points discussed earlier in the chapter.

> **Tip**
>
> Use existing manipulation techniques unless a large amount of benefit might be derived from designing a new application-specific technique.

Although designing new interaction techniques is important, there is no need to reinvent the wheel. The requirements of many 3D applications can be met by applying and creatively modifying the interaction techniques presented in this chapter.

> **Tip**
>
> Use task analysis when choosing a 3D manipulation technique.

Manipulation is a rich user activity, and some interaction techniques are better for certain conditions of manipulation than for others. The choice and design of manipulation techniques should provide high levels of usability and performance for the most common manipulation tasks in an application. Ask yourself: How precise is the manipulation required to be? Do I need positioning, or is selection sufficient? How far away do users need to manipulate virtual objects? How large are the objects to be manipulated?

> **Tip**
>
> Match the interaction technique to the device.

It is important to consider device properties when choosing manipulation techniques. When 6-DOF devices are used, interaction techniques that allow for integrated manipulation control will perhaps be more intuitive and effective than those that separate control dimensions. Carefully consider the shape of the device. When a high level of manipulation precision is required, it might be preferable to use devices that permit a precision grip and can be manipulated by the fingers.

> **Tip**
>
> Use techniques that can help to reduce clutching.

Clutching is wasted motion: by using techniques that amplify the user hand motion in rotation and positioning tasks, we can decrease the need for clutching and therefore can increase comfort and user performance.

> **Tip**
>
> Nonisomorphic ("magic") techniques are useful and intuitive.

The early notion that interaction in VEs should be an exact imitation of our interaction in the real world does not hold—nonisomorphic techniques are useful and intuitive. In fact, most manipulation techniques depart from real-world interaction to a greater or lesser degree by allowing "magic" interactions with virtual objects.

> **Tip**
>
> Use pointing techniques for selection and grasping techniques for manipulation.

Ray-casting and other pointing techniques provide notably better performance in selection tasks, but they are not as useful in manipulation. Use virtual hand–based techniques for manipulation tasks.

> **Tip**
>
> Consider the use of grasp-sensitive object selection.

Grasp-sensitive object selection, where the user matches the orientation of the device to the orientation of the desired object, is a powerful technique to simplify and improve user selection.

> **Tip**
>
> Reduce degrees of freedom when possible.

Manipulation techniques do not necessarily have to manipulate all 6-DOF. In fact, some very effective selection techniques, such as the image-plane techniques, provide very effective interaction by restricting DOFs—making 3D selection an essentially 2D task. In addition, many applications do not require 6-DOF manipulation. Adding constraints (see Chapter 10) to generic 3D manipulation techniques can help the user be more efficient and precise.

> **Tip**
>
> Consider the trade-off between technique design and environment design.

Two strategies can be used in designing manipulation interfaces. First, you can tune interaction techniques so that they maximize user performance in the target task conditions. Second, you can design your environment so that existing techniques can be used effectively. If the application allows flexible environment design, this second approach might be extremely useful.

> **Tip**
>
> There is no single best manipulation technique.

The ideal 3D manipulation technique has not yet been designed. Each technique has its strengths and weaknesses. The best technique for one application is not necessarily the best for another. Any choice of technique will result in trade-offs. Managing these trade-offs is one of the keys to good 3D UI design.

7.12 Case Studies

In this section, we discuss the design of the 3D manipulation techniques for our case studies. If you have not yet done so, read the introductions to the case studies in Chapter 2, section 2.4.

7.12.1 VR Gaming Case Study

As a puzzle game, our proposed VR game will have a variety of selection and manipulation tasks as users pick up, place, drop, and operate various objects and tools in the world and as they battle monsters. The primary selection tasks will be to pick up items to be collected from the world, pick items out of the inventory, and target monsters. Manipulation tasks will include placing items into the inventory, positioning/orienting/placing items in the world, and operating gadgets such as doorknobs, levers, and buttons.

These selection and manipulation tasks should use techniques that are fun and playful to increase players' engagement. Some of them should be challenging (e.g., can you toss the ball so that it rolls to a stop just on top of the floor switch that unlocks the door?) without being tedious, frustrating, or fatiguing. Especially for selection and manipulation interactions that are part of the gameplay itself, performance (speed and accuracy) is *not* the most important issue. Instead, techniques should be part of a believable story of how things work in the fantasy world of the game. They should be designed not only to have utilitarian efficiency but also to be cool and integral to the game.

We have designed a bimanual interaction concept for selection, based on the handheld controllers we selected in the input device section (section 6.7.1). The nondominant-hand controller acts as a flashlight players can use to light up broad regions of the room around them, while the dominant hand holds a tool that can be used for, among other things, selection of a specific object. The flashlight serves a dual purpose: it illuminates objects that would otherwise be difficult to see in the dimly lit world of our spooky hotel (so it fits naturally into the story), but it also indicates what part of the world and what objects the player is currently interested in, which can aid selection of those objects with the other hand.

In this way, actions of the dominant hand don't have to be very precise. Since only objects illuminated by the flashlight beam are selectable, one of them can be highlighted at all times, and the player only has to make coarse-grained movements of the dominant hand to highlight one of the others. The dominant hand tool can orient itself to point towards the flashlight beam at all times, and movements of the dominant hand are mapped to choices among the directions the tool needs to point to select specific objects within the beam. This progressive refinement approach (rough selection followed by simple actions to refine the selection to a single object) has been shown to provide good performance (Kopper et al. 2011), and in this case it should help players avoid frustrating situations where it might be difficult to point precisely to small objects in cluttered areas of the environment with ray-casting.

To actually collect the objects targeted by the flashlight and tool, whether they are in the world or in the inventory, the user will simply press a button on the dominant hand controller. This is an opportunity to develop a playful tool design. Perhaps the button press shoots a sticky "frog's tongue" out of the tool, which flies out to the object, sticks to it, then brings it back to the tool. Depending on the theme and story of the game, many concepts could be applied, using the same basic interaction.

Targeting monsters can work in a similar way, with the player first illuminating the monster with the flashlight, then pressing a button on the tool. Since the frog tongue is unlikely to be effective against big scary monsters, the player may have to choose a different tool, like a dart gun or a disintegration ray (we address tool choice in Chapter 9, "System Control," section 9.7).

Once items have been picked from the world or inventory, they can be placed in other locations in the world or placed in the inventory. The same button can be used to shoot the frog's tongue back out into the environment, where the object flies outward until it hits something, and a second button can be used to drop it. Alternatively, if the user wants to place the object nearby, they can manipulate the object with the tool and then press the second button to drop it at that location. Thus, we enable both local and remote manipulation.

Operating gadgets like doorknobs or levers is similar: the player targets them with the flashlight, then uses the tool to operate the gadget. Again, various tools may be needed (graspers, cutters, spinners, etc.), and each tool may have slightly different mechanics. This enables the game to keep offering new challenges as the player progresses through the rooms of the hotel, so that there are eventually a wide variety of tools available. The most difficult challenges of the game might require the use of several tools in creative ways. We leave the design of the specifics to your imagination.

Key Concepts

The key concepts that we used for 3D manipulation in our VR gaming case study were:

- Progressive refinement selection techniques can help users avoid fatigue by not requiring precise interactions.
- Basic 3D selection and manipulation techniques can be customized to fit the theme or story of a particular application.

7.12.2 Mobile AR Case Study

Selection and manipulation are important tasks in the majority of VR systems. Yet in many AR applications these tasks are performed far less frequently. Often, the main task is the exploration of information or obtaining guidance by navigating physically through a scene. As more complex applications are starting to appear, however, this situation is changing, and direct interaction with objects in the user's environment is more common.

In HYDROSYS, since the information space includes a multitude of labels, the amount of information per label that could be observed at first glance was limited. Packing too much information in a label would have led to a highly cluttered information space, where labels would overlap each other considerably and in which the actual environment could hardly be observed. To gain access to detailed information, users had to filter data and select labels to get different views of the available sensor data. Furthermore, the multiview navigation system as well as the collaboration components included selection tasks. We go into more detail in upcoming chapters.

Selection of system control items, labels and camera viewpoints in HYDROSYS was strongly connected to the limitations of the input and output devices. In particular, selection depended on the screen size and resolution, because that affected the size of interface elements and thus the selection area. In AR, you want to keep menu items small so as to limit perceptual overlap with the real-world content. However, this obviously comes with a trade-off, as small items will be more difficult to select. In HYDROSYS, either finger- or pen-based selection could be used, depending on the outside temperature and the frequency of action.

If users were exploring a single data set from a first-person perspective, selection frequency would be low. Users would basically explore data by walking around. In this situation, finger-based selection was acceptable, since selection tasks only occurred occasionally. However, if a rich sensor data set was being explored at a larger site, potentially with multiple users, the requirements for selection would be different. Users would frequently change the data visualization (system control) and move between different viewpoints (navigation). Here, the more precise pen was the preferred input method. However, using the pen also meant that users would hold the device with a single-handed grip while performing selections. This illustrates how performance and user comfort often affect each other, leading to interesting trade-offs in 3D UI design.

Key Concepts

The key lessons that we learned from the mobile AR case study for 3D manipulation were:

- Size of selectable items: keep the size of your selectable objects or menu items as small as possible, while reflecting the limitations of your input method and the visibility (legibility) of these items.
- Selection method: depending on the frequency of selection tasks, different input methods could be preferable. Often, there is a direct relationship between input method, selection performance and frequency, and user comfort.

7.13 Conclusion

In this chapter, we have discussed how 3D selection and manipulation techniques affect how users interact with 3D UIs. We have presented six categories of manipulation metaphors, including grasping, pointing, surface, indirect, bimanual, and hybrid techniques. Within these categories, we have covered a broad range of 3D manipulation techniques. Many are applicable to immersive 3D UIs, while some are specifically designed for desktop or surface-based interactions. We have also discussed several design aspects of 3D manipulation techniques, including nonisomorphic 3D rotations, selection of multiple objects at once, and progressive refinement. We presented several design guidelines for choosing and designing 3D manipulation techniques. We now turn to the fundamental 3D interaction task of navigation in Chapter 8.

Recommended Reading

One of the most comprehensive reviews of the physiology and psychology of human grasping and manipulation can be found in this text:

MacKenzie, C. and T. Iberall (1994). *The Grasping Hand.* Amsterdam: North-Holland.

An interesting study that discusses the effect of muscle groups and device shapes on manipulation performance can be found in the following:

Zhai, S. and P. Milgram (1993). "Human Performance Evaluation of Manipulation Schemes in Virtual Environments." *Proceedings of the 1993 IEEE Virtual Reality Annual International Symposium (VRAIS '93),* IEEE Press, 155–161.

An excellent survey of 3D object selection techniques is presented in:

Argelaguet, F. and C. Andujar (2013). "A Survey of 3D Object Selection Techniques for Virtual Environments." *Computers & Graphics* 37: 121–136.

Readers interested in more details on the usability properties of rotation mapping might wish to take a look at this text:

Poupyrev, I., S. Weghorst, and S. Fels (2000). "Non-Isomorphic 3D Rotational Interaction Techniques." *Proceedings of the 2000 ACM Conference on Human Factors in Computing Systems (CHI 2000),* 540–547.

Finally, classifications, overviews, and empirical evaluations of interaction techniques for 3D manipulation can be found in the following two papers:

Poupyrev, I. and T. Ichikawa (1999). "Manipulating Objects in Virtual Worlds: Categorization and Empirical Evaluation of Interaction Techniques." *Journal of Visual Languages and Computing* 10(1): 19–35.

Bowman, D., and L. Hodges (1999). "Formalizing the Design, Evaluation, and Application of Interaction Techniques for Immersive Virtual Environments." *The Journal of Visual Languages and Computing* 10(1): 37–53.

CHAPTER 8

TRAVEL

As we described in the introduction to Part IV, navigation is a fundamental human task in our physical environment. We are also increasingly faced with navigation tasks in synthetic environments: navigating the Web via a browser, navigating a complex document in a word processor, navigating through many layers of information in a spreadsheet, or navigating the virtual world of a computer game. Navigation in 3D UIs is the subject of this chapter.

8.1 Introduction

This chapter discusses both aspects of navigation: travel and wayfinding. In the first edition of this book, we covered these topics in two separate chapters. However, because they are tightly integrated, we have combined the topics in this edition. The emphasis is on interaction techniques for travel, which are supported by wayfinding information.

8.1.1 Travel

Travel is the motor component of navigation—the task of moving from the current location to a new target location or moving in the desired direction. In the physical environment, travel is often a "no-brainer." Once we formulate the goal to walk across the room and through the door, our brains can instruct our muscles to perform the correct movements to achieve that goal. However, when our travel goal cannot be achieved effectively with simple body movements (we want to travel a great distance, or we want to travel very quickly, or we want to fly), then we use vehicles (bicycles, cars, planes, etc.). All vehicles contain some interface that maps various physical movements (turning a wheel, depressing a pedal, flipping a switch) to travel.

In 3D UIs, the situation is similar: there are some 3D interfaces where simple physical motions, such as walking, can be used for travel (e.g., when head and/or body trackers are used), but this is only effective within a limited space at a very limited speed. For most travel in 3D UIs, our actions must be mapped to travel in other ways, such as through a vehicle metaphor, for example. A major difference between real-world travel in vehicles and virtual travel, however, is that 3D UIs normally provide only visual motion cues, neglecting vestibular cues—this visual-vestibular mismatch can lead to cybersickness (see Chapter 3, "Human Factors Fundamentals," section 3.3.2.)

Interaction techniques for the task of travel are especially important for two major reasons. First, travel is easily the most common and universal interaction task in 3D interfaces. Although there are some 3D applications in which the user's viewpoint is always stationary or where movement is automated, those are the exception rather than the rule. Second, travel (and navigation in general) often supports another task rather than being an end unto itself. Consider most 3D games: travel is used to reach locations where the user can pick up treasure, fight with enemies, or obtain critical information. Counterintuitively, the secondary nature of the travel task in these instances actually increases the need for usability of travel techniques. That is, if the user has to think about how to turn left or move forward, then he has been distracted from his primary task. Therefore, travel techniques must be intuitive—capable of becoming "second nature" to users.

8.1.2 Wayfinding

Wayfinding is the cognitive process of determining and following a route between an origin and a destination (Golledge 1999). It is the cognitive component of navigation—high-level thinking, planning, and decision-making related to user movement. It involves spatial understanding and planning tasks, such as determining the current location within the environment, determining a path from the current location to a goal location, and building a mental map of the environment. Real-world wayfinding has been researched extensively, with studies of aids like maps, directional signs, landmarks, and so on (Golledge 1999).

In virtual worlds, wayfinding can also be crucial. In a large, complex environment, an efficient travel technique is of no use if one has no idea where to go. When we speak of "wayfinding techniques," we refer to designed wayfinding aids included as part of the interface or in the environment. Unlike travel techniques or manipulation techniques, where the computer ultimately performs the action, wayfinding techniques only support the performance of the task in the user's mind (see Chapter 3, section 3.4.2 for a discussion of situation awareness, cognitive mapping, and the different types of spatial knowledge).

Clearly, travel and wayfinding are both part of the same process (navigation) and contribute towards achieving the same goals. However, from the standpoint of 3D UI design, we can generally consider them to be distinct. A travel technique is necessary to perform navigation tasks, and in some small or simple environments a good travel technique may be all that is necessary. In more complex environments, wayfinding aids may also be needed. In some cases, the designer can combine techniques for travel and wayfinding into a single integrated technique, reducing the cognitive load on the user and reinforcing the user's spatial knowledge each time the technique is used. Techniques that make use of miniature environments or maps fit this description (see section 8.6.1), but these techniques are not suitable for all navigation tasks.

8.1.3 Chapter Roadmap

In this chapter, we discuss both interaction techniques for travel tasks and the design of wayfinding aids. We begin by describing specific types of travel tasks (section 8.2) and some classifications of travel techniques (section 8.3). We then discuss a wide variety of travel techniques, classified by their metaphors:

- walking (section 8.4)
- steering (section 8.5)
- selection-based travel (section 8.6)
- manipulation-based travel (section 8.7)

Section 8.8 completes the discussion of travel by discussing other aspects of travel technique design. The design of wayfinding aids is presented in section 8.9. Finally, we present design guidelines for navigation interfaces (section 8.10), followed by our case studies (section 8.11).

8.2 3D Travel Tasks

There are many different reasons why a user might need to perform a 3D travel task. Understanding the various types of travel tasks is important because the usability of a particular technique often depends on the task for which it is used. As we describe various techniques in the following sections, we provide guidance (as often as possible) on the task types for which a particular technique is appropriate. Experiments based on travel "testbeds" (e.g., Bowman, Johnson et al. 1999; Lampton et al. 1994; Nabiyouni and Bowman 2015) have attempted to empirically relate task type to technique usability. We classify travel tasks under the headings of **exploration**, **search**, and **maneuvering**.

8.2.1 Exploration

In an exploration or browsing task, the user has no explicit goal for her movement. Rather, she is browsing the environment, obtaining information about the objects and locations within the world and building up knowledge of the space. For example, the client of an architecture firm may explore the latest building design in a 3D environment. Exploration is typically used at the beginning of an interaction with an environment, serving to orient the user to the world and its features, but it may also be important in later stages. Because a user's path during exploration may be based on serendipity (seeing something in the world may cause the user to deviate from the current path), techniques to support exploration should allow continuous and direct control of viewpoint movement or at least the ability to interrupt a movement that has begun. Forcing the user to continue along the chosen path until its completion would detract from the discovery process. Of course, this must be balanced, in some applications, with the need to provide an enjoyable experience in a short amount of time (Pausch et al. 1996). Techniques should also impose little cognitive load on users so that they can focus cognitive resources on spatial knowledge acquisition, information gathering, or other primary tasks.

To what extent should 3D UIs support exploration tasks? The answer depends on the goals of the application. In some cases, exploration is an integral component of the interaction. For example, in a 3D visualization of network traffic data, the structure and content of the environment is not known in advance, making it difficult to provide detailed wayfinding aids. The benefits of the visualization depend on how well the interface supports exploration of the data. Also, in many 3D gaming environments, exploration of unknown spaces is an important part of the entertainment value of the game. On the other hand, in a 3D interface where the focus is on performing tasks within a well-known 3D environment, the interface designer should provide more support for search tasks via goal-directed travel techniques.

8.2.2 Search

Search tasks involve travel to a specific goal or target location within the environment. In other words, the user in a search task knows the final location to which he wants to navigate. However, it is not necessarily the case that the user has knowledge of where that location is or how to get there from the current location. For example, a gamer may have collected all the treasure on a level, so he needs to travel to the exit. The exit may be in a part of the environment that hasn't yet been explored, or the user may have seen it previously. This leads to the distinction between a **naïve search** task, where the user does not know the position of the target or a path to it in advance, and a **primed search** task, where the user has visited the target before or has some other knowledge of its position (Darken and Sibert 1996).

Naïve search has similarities with exploration, but clues or wayfinding aids may direct the search so that it is much more limited and focused than exploration. Primed search tasks also exist on a continuum, depending on the amount of knowledge the user has of the target and the surrounding environment. A user may have visited a location before but still might have to explore the environment around his starting location before he understands how to begin traveling toward the goal. On the other hand, a user with complete survey knowledge of the environment can start at any location and immediately begin navigating directly to the target. Although the lines between these tasks are often blurry, it is still useful to make the distinction.

Many 3D UIs involve search via travel. For example, the user in an architectural walkthrough application may wish to travel to the front door to check sight lines. Techniques for this task may be more goal oriented than techniques for exploration. For example, the user may specify the final location directly on a map rather than through incremental movements. Such techniques do not apply to all situations, however. Bowman, Johnson, and Hodges (1999) found that a map-based technique was quite inefficient, even for primed search tasks, when the goal locations were not explicitly represented on the map. It may be useful to combine a target-based technique with a more general technique to allow for the continuum of tasks discussed above.

8.2.3 Maneuvering

Maneuvering is an often-overlooked category of 3D travel. Maneuvering tasks take place in a local area and involve small, precise movements. The most common use of maneuvering is to position the viewpoint more precisely within a limited local area to perform a specific task. For example, the user needs to read some written information in the 3D environment but must position herself directly in front of the information in order to make it legible. In another scenario, the user wishes to check the positioning of an object she has been manipulating in a 3D modeling system and needs to examine it from many different angles. This task may seem trivial compared to large-scale movements through the environment, but it is precisely these small-scale movements that can cost the user precious time and cause frustration if not supported by the interface.

A designer might consider maneuvering tasks to be search tasks, because the destination is known, and therefore use the same type of travel techniques for maneuvering as for search, but this would ignore the unique requirements of maneuvering tasks. In fact, some applications may require special travel techniques solely for maneuvering. In general, travel techniques for this task should allow great precision of motion but not at the expense of speed. The best solution for maneuvering tasks may be physical motion of the user's head and body because this is efficient, precise, and natural, but not all applications include head and body tracking, and even those that do often have limited range and precision. Therefore, If close and precise work is important in an application, other techniques for maneuvering, such as the object-focused travel techniques in section 8.7.2, must be considered.

8.2.4 Additional Travel Task Characteristics

In the classification of the tasks above, they are distinguished by the user's goal for the travel task. Remember that many other characteristics of the task should be considered when choosing or designing travel techniques:

- **Distance to be traveled:** In a 3D UI using head or body tracking, it may be possible to accomplish short-range travel tasks using natural physical motion only. Medium-range travel requires a virtual travel technique but may not require velocity control. Long-range travel tasks should use techniques with velocity control or the ability to jump quickly between widely scattered locations.
- **Amount of curvature or number of turns in the path:** Travel techniques should take into account the amount of turning required in the travel task. For example, steering (see section 8.5.1) based on torso direction may be appropriate when turning is infrequent, but a less strenuous method, such as hand-directed steering (most users will use hand-directed steering from the hip by locking their elbows in contrast to holding up their hands), would be more comfortable when the path involves many turns.
- **Visibility of the target from the starting location:** Many target-based techniques (section 8.6) depend on the availability of a target for selection. Gaze-directed steering (section 8.5.1) works well when the target is visible but not when the user needs to search for the target visually while traveling.
- **Number of DOF required for the movement:** If the travel task requires motion only in a horizontal plane, the travel technique should not force the user to also control vertical motion. In general, terrain-following is a useful constraint in many applications.
- **Required accuracy of the movement:** Some travel tasks require strict adherence to a path or accurate arrival at a target location. In such cases, it's important to choose a travel technique that allows for fine control and adjustment of direction, speed, or target location. For example, map-based target selection (section 8.6) is usually inaccurate because of the scale of the map, imprecision of hand tracking, or other factors. Travel techniques should also allow for easy error recovery (e.g., backing up if the target was overshot) if accuracy is important.
- **Other primary tasks that take place during travel:** Often, travel is a secondary task performed during another more important task. For example, a user may be traveling through a building model in order to count the number of windows in each room. It is especially important in such situations that the travel technique be unobtrusive, intuitive, and easily controlled.

8.3 Classifications for 3D Travel

With the various types of travel tasks in mind, we turn to the design of interaction techniques for travel. Before discussing the techniques themselves, we present a number of ways to classify travel techniques.

8.3.1 Technique Classifications

A common theme of 3D interaction research has been the attempt to classify and categorize interaction techniques into structures. This is not a pointless academic exercise, but rather an attempt to gain a more complete understanding of the tasks and techniques involved.

For the task of travel, several different classification schemes have been proposed. None of these should be considered the "correct" taxonomy; they each provide different views of the same space. In this section, we discuss four classification schemes

- active versus passive
- physical versus virtual
- using task decomposition
- by metaphor

Active versus Passive Techniques

One way to classify travel techniques is to distinguish between **active** travel techniques, in which the user directly controls the movement of the viewpoint, and **passive** travel techniques, in which the viewpoint's movement is controlled by the system. Most of the techniques we present in this chapter are active, but in some cases it may be useful to consider a technique that is automated or semiautomated by the system (Galyean 1995; Mackinlay et al. 1990a). We discuss this issue in section 8.8.4. This is especially useful if the user has another primary task, such as gathering information about the environment while traveling. Bowman, Davis et al. (1999) studied active and passive techniques and also included a third category called route planning. Route planning is both active *and* passive—users actively plan their path through the environment, then the system executes this path (section 8.6.2).

Physical versus Virtual Techniques

We can also classify travel techniques into those that use **physical** travel, in which the user's body physically translates or rotates in order to translate or rotate the viewpoint, and **virtual** travel, in which the user's body primarily remains stationary even though the virtual viewpoint moves. Desktop 3D systems and gaming consoles utilize virtual translation and rotation. Many VR systems use a combination of physical rotation (via head tracking) and virtual translation, while others use physical translation and rotation via a locomotion device or real walking technique. We discuss physical techniques in section 8.4, while sections 8.5–8.7 present primarily virtual techniques. The active/passive and physical/virtual classifications are orthogonal, so they can be combined to define a 2×2 design space.

Classifications Using Task Decomposition

Bowman et al. (1997) decomposed the task of travel into three subtasks: direction or target selection, velocity/acceleration selection, and conditions of input (Figure 8.1). Each subtask can be performed using a variety of technique components.

- **Direction** or **target selection** refers to the primary subtask in which the user specifies how to move or where to move.

- **Velocity/acceleration selection** describes how users control their speed.
- **Conditions of input** refers to how travel is initiated, continued, and terminated.

This taxonomy covers a large portion of the design space for travel techniques (only a few representative technique components are shown in the figure) and allows us to view the task of travel in more fine-grained chunks (subtasks) that are separable. By choosing a technique component for each of the three subtasks, we can define a complete travel technique. For example, the most common implementation of the pointing technique (see section 8.5.1) uses pointing steering, constant velocity/acceleration, and continuous input (a button held down).

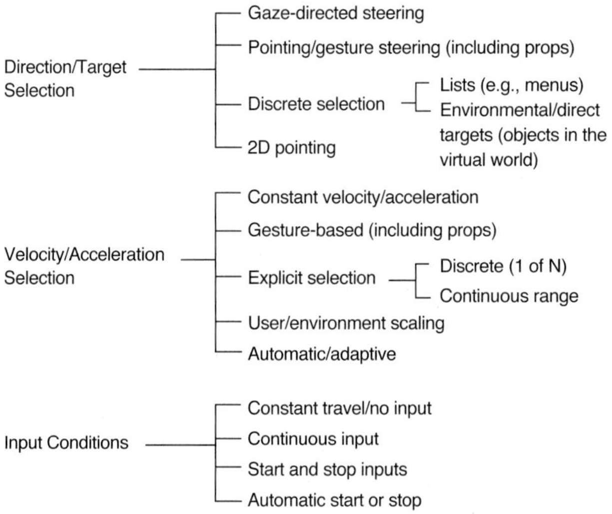

Figure 8.1 Taxonomy of travel techniques focusing on subtasks of travel. (Bowman et al. 1997, © 1997 IEEE)

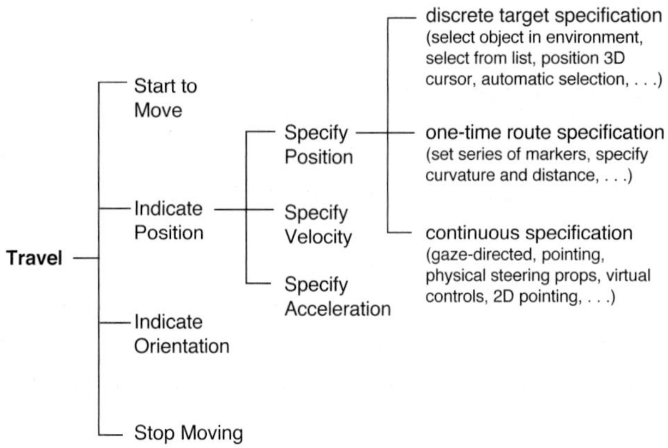

Figure 8.2 Taxonomy of travel techniques focusing on level of user control. (Bowman, Davis et al. 1999; reprinted by permission of MIT Press and *Presence: Teleoperators and Virtual Environments*)

A second task decomposition (Bowman, Davis et al. 1999) subdivides the task of travel in a different, more chronological way (Figure 8.2). In order to complete a travel task, the user first starts to move, then indicates position and orientation, and then stops moving. Of course, this order does not always strictly hold: in some target-based techniques, the user first indicates the target position and then starts to move. One feature of this taxonomy that distinguishes it from the first is the explicit mention of specifying viewpoint orientation, which is an important consideration for 3D UIs without head tracking (see section 8.8.1). As shown in the figure, the taxonomy further decomposes the position specification subtask into position (*xyz* coordinates), velocity, and acceleration subtasks. Finally, it lists three possible metaphors for the subtask of specifying position: discrete target specification, one-time route specification, and continuous specification of position. These metaphors differ in the amount of control they give the user over the exact path (the active/passive distinction). We discuss these metaphors in sections 8.5 and 8.6.

Classification by Metaphor

Finally, we can classify travel techniques by their overall interaction metaphor. In one way, such a classification is not as useful because it does not allow us to look at subtasks of travel separately. However, classification by metaphor is easier to understand, especially from the user's point of view. If someone tells you that a particular travel technique uses an "airplane" metaphor, for example, you can infer that it allows you to move in all three dimensions and to steer using hand motions. In addition, if new metaphors are developed, they can be added to such an informal classification easily. Thus, classification by metaphor is a useful way to think about the design space for interaction techniques.

In this chapter, we provide our own classification based on metaphors. Sections 8.4–8.7 organize travel techniques by four common metaphors: walking, steering, target/route selection, and travel-by-manipulation. These sections consider only the task of controlling the position of the viewpoint and do not consider issues such as specifying viewpoint orientation, controlling the speed of travel, or scaling the world. We cover these issues in section 8.8.

8.4 Walking Metaphors

The most natural technique for traveling in a 3D world is to physically walk around it. However, due to technological and space limitations, real walking is not always practical or feasible. To overcome this, many researchers have designed and developed interaction metaphors based on walking. We have classified those metaphors into three categories based on human gait. We call the first category "full gait" techniques, as those metaphors involve all of the biomechanics of a full gait cycle (see Figure 8.3). In contrast, the second category of walking metaphors mimics only some of the biomechanical aspects of human gait. We refer to these metaphors as "partial gait" techniques. Finally, "gait negation" techniques are designed to keep the user walking within a defined space by negating the user's forward locomotion.

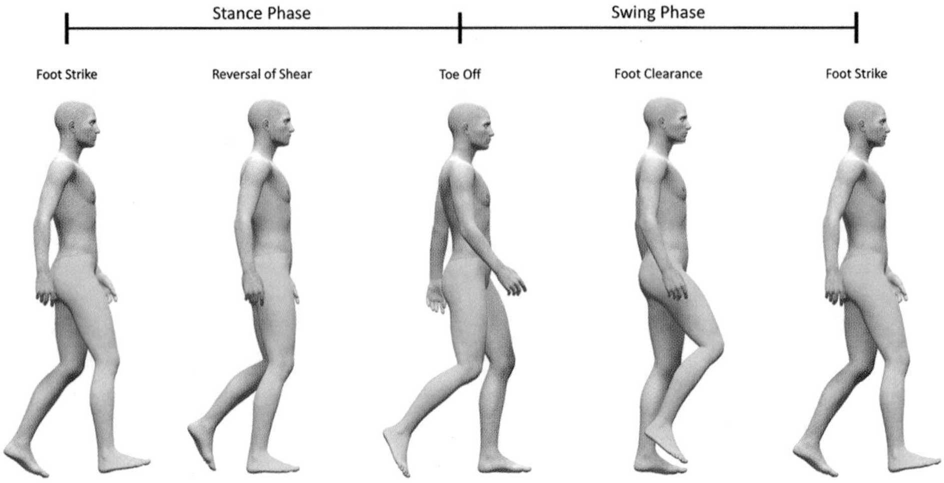

Figure 8.3 Illustration of the human gait cycle. (Image courtesy of Ryan P. McMahan)

8.4.1 Full Gait Techniques

The human gait cycle involves two main phases for each leg—the stance phase and the swing phase (Whittle 1996). The stance phase begins with a heel strike and is immediately followed by the foot flattening on the ground. At this point, the leg is in midstance, supporting the body's weight while the other leg is in its swing phase. The stance phase ends with the heel and toes coming off the ground. At this point, the leg is in its swing phase until the heel strikes the ground again. Full gait techniques are walking metaphors that afford all of the events and biomechanics involved with the stance and swing phases of human gait. We will discuss

- real walking
- redirected walking
- scaled walking

Real Walking

Real walking is the most direct and obvious full gait technique. It is natural, provides vestibular cues (which help the user understand the size of the environment and avoid getting sick), and promotes spatial understanding. However, real walking is not always practical or feasible and can work only when the size of the environment is less than the range of the tracking system, unless combined with another travel technique. Even if a large-area tracking system is available, the physical space must also be free of obstacles.

Real walking also raises issues with cabling: cables for trackers, input devices, and/or displays may not be long enough to allow complete freedom of movement in the tracked area, and unless cabling is carefully handled by another person or managed by a mechanical system, walking users can easily become tangled in cables as they move about the space. Wireless devices, such as wireless video transmitters and receivers, can alleviate these concerns for some systems. Alternatively, in so-called backpack systems, the user carries a portable computer to which all the devices are connected.

Usoh et al. (1999) used a large-area tracking system to determine the effect of a physical walking technique on the sense of presence. They created a small, compelling environment with a virtual pit whose bottom was far below the floor on which the user stood. They found that users who physically walked through the environment felt more present and exhibited greater fear of the virtual pit than users who walked in place (described in section 8.4.2) or used a virtual travel technique. Other researchers have found that real walking leads to a higher level of spatial knowledge in a complex environment (Chance et al. 1998).

Real walking is also becoming more important for other types of 3D applications, especially mobile augmented reality (Höllerer et al. 1999; Nurminen et al. 2011). In these systems, users are free to walk around in very large-area indoor or outdoor environments and have additional graphical information superimposed on their view of the real world (Figure 8.4). These applications often use Global Positioning System (GPS) data for tracking, possibly enhanced with orientation information from self-contained inertial trackers. Most GPS devices only give coarse-grained position information on the scale of meters, which is not sufficiently precise for most 3D UIs. Recent technological developments may lead to increasing the precision of most GPS devices to centimeters (Pesyna et al. 2014), however, most 3D UIs will still require millimeter precision. Another option is to use inside-out optical tracking of the environment using SLAM or one of its variants (see Chapter 6, "3D User Interface Input Hardware," section 6.3.1).

Figure 8.4 Mobile augmented reality: (a) prototype system (© 2002 Computer Graphics and User Interfaces Lab, Columbia University); (b) user's view (© 1999 Tobias Höllerer, Steve Feiner, and John Pavlik, Computer Graphics and User Interfaces Lab, Columbia University)

Real walking can be a compelling travel technique, but its effectiveness is dependent upon the tracking system and tracking area. In most practical 3D UIs, real walking can be used in a small local area, but other techniques are needed to reach other parts of the environment. However, in our experience, when users are allowed to both walk and use a virtual travel technique, they quickly learn to use only the virtual technique because it requires less effort.

Redirected Walking

To overcome the large-area requirements of real walking, researchers have investigated redirecting users away from the boundaries of the tracking space while walking. This is known as redirected walking (Razzaque et al. 2002). The concept behind the technique is to guide users unwittingly along paths in the real world that differ from the path perceived in the virtual world. The perceptual phenomenon that enables redirected walking is that visual stimuli often dominate proprioceptive and vestibular stimuli when there is a conflict among them. Hence, a user can be imperceptibly led away from the tracking boundaries by, for example, rotating the virtual scene and the intended virtual path toward the center of the tracking area as the user turns or walks.

A basic approach to redirected walking is the stop-and-go method (Bruder et al. 2015). With this method, the virtual world is rotated around a stationary user faster or slower than the user is physically turning (i.e., rotation gains are applied). This allows the technique to orient the user's forward direction away from the tracking boundaries. The key to the stop-and-go method is to influence the user to physically turn in the first place. Researchers have investigated a number of ways to accomplish this, including location-oriented tasks (Kohli et al. 2005), visual distractors (e.g., a butterfly; Peck et al. 2009), and verbal instructions (Hodgson et al. 2014).

A more advanced approach to redirected walking is to continuously redirect the user while walking through the virtual environment (Bruder et al. 2015). For example, if the user is walking straight ahead in the virtual world, small rotations of the virtual scene can be used to redirect the user along a circular path within the tracking area (Figure 8.5). If the rotations are small enough, they will be imperceptible and the user will have the impression of truly walking straight ahead in the virtual world.

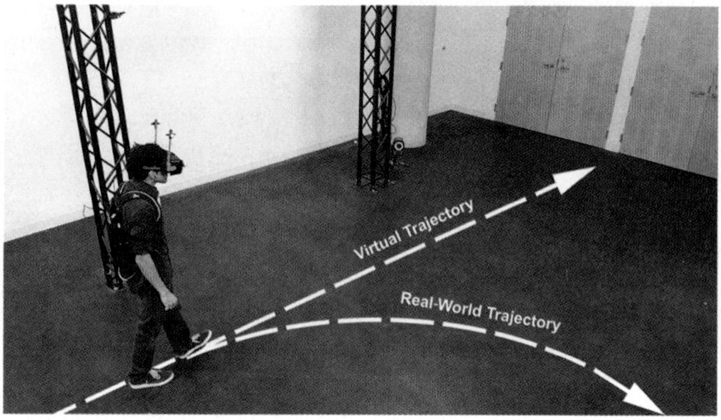

Figure 8.5 With continuous redirected walking, the user is imperceptibly guided away from the boundaries of the tracking area through subtle manipulations of the virtual scene. (Image adapted from Bruder et al. 2015)

When implementing a redirected walking technique, it is important to avoid perceptible visual conflicts with the proprioceptive and vestibular cues. Steinicke et al. (2010) conducted studies to estimate detection thresholds for these conflicts. They found that users could be physically turned about 49% more or 20% less than a displayed virtual rotation. Users can also be physically translated 14% more or 26% less than a displayed virtual translation. Additionally, the researchers found that users will perceive themselves walking straight in the virtual environment while being continuously redirected on a circular arc if the arc's radius is greater than 22 meters.

An important aspect of continuous redirected walking is how to rotate the virtual scene relative to the physical tracking space while the user is walking. Two commonly used algorithms are steer-to-center and steer-to-orbit (Hodgson et al. 2014). The goal of the steer-to-center algorithm is to continuously redirect the user's physical movements through the center of the tracking area while adhering to the detection thresholds. In contrast, the goal of the steer-to-orbit algorithm is to continuously redirect the user's physical movements along a circular arc, as if the user were orbiting the center of the tracking space. Hodgson and Bachmann have shown that the steer-to-center algorithm helps to avoid tracking boundaries better for relatively open-spaced virtual environments (Hodgson and Bachmann 2013), while the steer-to-orbit algorithm performs better for relatively enclosed VEs (Hodgson et al. 2014).

An alternative to rotating the virtual scene is to manipulate the dimensional properties of the scene. Suma et al. (2012) demonstrated that VEs can make use of self-overlapping architectural layouts called "impossible spaces." These layouts effectively compress large interior environments into smaller tracking spaces by showing only the current room to the user despite another room architecturally overlapping it. Vasylevska et al. (2013) have expanded upon the concept of impossible spaces to create flexible spaces, which are created by dynamically generating corridors between rooms to direct the user away from the center of the tracking space when exiting a room and back toward the center when entering the next room.

While redirected walking can overcome some of the tracking limitations of real walking, it has its own challenges. First, continuous redirected walking requires a large tracking space to be imperceptible. Using it in smaller spaces is not very effective. Second, even in large tracking spaces, users can still walk outside of the space if they decide to ignore visual cues, tasks, and distractors. Finally, Bruder et al. (2015) have demonstrated that redirected walking with small arcs demands more cognitive resources than with larger arcs. For those readers interested in more details on redirected walking, we recommend a book on human walking in VEs (Steinicke et al. 2013).

Scaled Walking

Another full gait technique that overcomes the large-area requirements of real walking is scaled walking. With this technique, users can travel through virtual environments larger than the physical space by scaling their movements, so that one physical step equals several virtual steps. A basic approach to scaled walking is to apply a uniform gain to the horizontal components of the user's head tracker data. However, Interrante et al. (2007) have shown that this approach induces significantly more cybersickness and is significantly less natural and easy to use than real walking.

A better scaled-walking approach is the Seven League Boots technique (Interrante et al. 2007). With this technique, only the user's intended direction of travel is scaled. This avoids scaling the oscillatory motions of the user's head that occur during gait, which would result in excessive swaying of the user's viewpoint. Seven League Boots also uses a dynamically changing scaling factor based on the speed of physical walking. When users walk slowly, no scaling is applied, but at faster walking speeds, travel is scaled to be even faster. This is similar to common mouse acceleration techniques in desktop UIs and enables users to explore local areas with one-to-one walking and reach distant areas by quickly walking in their direction.

The user's intended direction of travel must be determined to implement Seven League Boots. Interrante et al. (2007) propose that the best method is to determine the direction of travel as a weighted combination of the user's gaze direction and the direction of the user's horizontal displacement during the previous few seconds. When displacement is minimal, as it is when standing, a weight of 1 is assigned to the gaze direction. However, when displacement resembles walking, a weight of 0 is assigned to the gaze direction to allow the user to look around while walking.

While scaled walking techniques afford the biomechanics of a full gait cycle and circumvent the physical limitations of real walking, they can be unnatural to use. Based on work by Steinicke et al. (2010), scaled walking techniques are perceptible when the scale factor is greater than 1.35 times the user's physical motions. And while scaled walking can increase the size of the area users can reach with natural walking, that area is still finite, meaning that additional travel techniques will be needed to reach other parts of the virtual environment.

8.4.2 Partial Gait Techniques

Not all walking metaphors incorporate both the stance and swing phases of human gait. Some techniques focus on recreating specific aspects of the gait cycle to provide seminatural interactions for travel. These techniques often circumvent the restrictions of using real walking, such as space limitations, by representing only a subset of the gait cycle. For instance, walking in place incorporates the actions associated with the stance phase but not those of the swing phase in order to keep the user in place. The human joystick metaphors incorporate the swing aspects of gait but not the stance aspects. Other techniques focus on recreating the motions of the gait cycle using anatomical substitutions, such as finger walking (Kim et al. 2008). In this section, we cover

- walking in place
- human joystick

Walking in Place

An alternative to real walking is walking in place: users move their feet to simulate walking while actually remaining in the same location. This technique seems like a good compromise because users still physically exert themselves, which should increase the sense of presence, and the limitation on the size of the environment is removed.

However, there are several caveats to be considered. First, walking in place does not incorporate the swing phase of the gait cycle, as real walking does, so the sense of presence or real movement is diminished. Second, the size of the environment, while theoretically unlimited, still has a practical limitation because users exert more energy while using walking in place than real walking (Nilsson et al. 2013).

Several approaches have been used to implement walking in place. Early on, Slater et al. (1995) used a position tracker and a neural network to analyze the motions of the user's head to distinguish walking in place from other types of movements. When the system detects that the user is walking in place, it moves the user through the virtual world in the direction of the user's gaze. Instead of tracking head motions, Templeman et al. (1999) tracked and analyzed leg motions in their Gaiter system to determine when the user was stepping in place and in which direction. In a similar system, Feasel et al. (2008) used a chest tracker and the orientation of the user's torso to determine the direction of virtual motion. They also analyzed vertical heel movements instead of steps to reduce the half-step latency seen in most other implementations.

More recently, Nilsson et al. (2013) investigated the kinematics of walking in place (Figure 8.6). In most implementations, a marching gesture is utilized, in which the user lifts each foot off the ground by raising the thighs. Nilsson et al. (2013) proposed two additional gestures—wiping and tapping. With wiping, the user bends each knee while keeping the thigh relatively steady, similar to wiping one's feet on a doormat. With tapping, the user lifts each heel off the ground while keeping the toes in contact with the ground. In a study of perceived naturalness, the researchers found that tapping was considered the most natural and least strenuous of the three walking-in-place gestures.

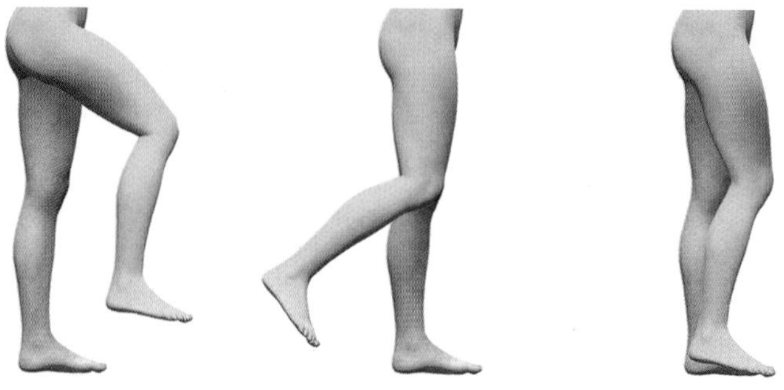

Figure 8.6 Three types of walking-in-place gestures: (a) marching by raising the thighs to lift each foot; (b) wiping by bending the knees to move each foot backward; (c) tapping by lifting the heels while keeping the toes on the ground. (Image adapted from Nilsson et al. 2013)

Studies have shown that walking in place does increase the sense of presence relative to completely virtual travel but that it's not as effective as real walking (Usoh et al. 1999). These techniques also sometimes suffer from the problems of recognition errors and user fatigue. This approach applies to systems where higher levels of naturalism are needed and where the environment is not too large. For applications in which the focus is on efficiency and task performance, however, a steering technique (see section 8.5) is often more appropriate.

Human Joystick

While walking in place excludes the swing phase of gait, the human joystick metaphor incorporates it instead of the stance phase. The concept of this metaphor is that the user's body acts like the handle of a joystick to initiate travel in different directions. One early implementation was the Virtual Motion Controller, or VMC (Wells et al. 1996). This general-purpose device aimed to allow virtual motion by allowing users to perform a subset of the walking motion they would perform in the physical world. The VMC consisted of a platform with embedded pressure sensors beneath the surface (Figure 8.7). The sensors were distributed along the rim of the platform, so that a user standing in the center of the platform placed no pressure on the sensors and so that the pressure sensed would increase the farther the user stepped from the center. By analyzing the pressure sensed at various locations, the device could determine the direction and distance that the user had stepped from the center.

Another implementation of the human joystick technique is to calculate the 2D horizontal vector from the center of the tracking space to the user's tracked head position and then use that vector to define the direction and velocity of virtual travel. McMahan et al. (2012) implemented this technique in a CAVE-like system. They defined a no-travel zone at the center of the tracking volume to avoid constant virtual locomotion due to minute distances between the user's head position and the center of the tracking volume. To initiate travel, the user stepped outside of the neutral zone to define the 2D travel vector. After this initial swing phase, the user simply stood in place to continue the same direction and speed of travel. The user could move closer to or farther from the center to adjust the travel speed. Additionally, the user could move laterally to redefine the direction of travel relative to the tracking center.

In both implementations of the human joystick, the user's gaze direction is independent of the direction of travel, which is defined by either the positions of the user's feet or the position of the user's head. This allows the user to travel backwards, which techniques like walking in place do not allow. The human joystick has also been shown to afford higher levels of presence (McMahan et al. 2012) than purely virtual travel. However, McMahan (2011) also found that the human joystick technique was significantly less efficient than a traditional keyboard and mouse travel technique. He attributed this to the fact that the human joystick technique requires the user to step back to the center of the tracking volume to terminate travel. This is very different from real human gait, which requires little to no effort to stop locomotion.

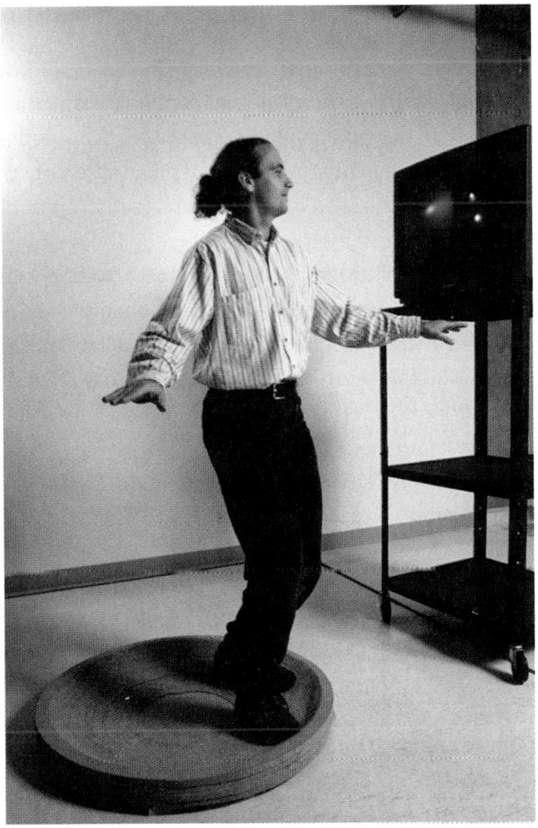

Figure 8.7 Virtual Motion Controller. (Photograph courtesy of HIT Lab, University of Washington)

8.4.3 Gait Negation Techniques

When realism is desired (e.g., in training applications), partial gait techniques can be less than satisfactory because they don't capture the same motion and effort as real walking. However, real walking and full gait techniques are often limited by space and technological constraints. Thus, there is a third type of walking metaphor that uses special locomotion devices to provide a somewhat realistic walking motion and feel while not actually translating the user's body. We refer to these as gait negation techniques, because they negate the forward movement of the user's gait. In this section, we will discuss the following gait negation techniques:

- treadmills
- passive omnidirectional treadmills
- active omnidirectional treadmills
- low-friction surfaces
- step-based devices

Treadmills

The simplest form of gait negation is a common treadmill. Of course, the basic treadmill does not allow the user to turn naturally, so some sort of indirect turning mechanism, such as a joystick, is needed (Brooks 1986). This can be implemented easily but is not appropriate for applications requiring high levels of realism. Researchers have created many different devices to try to solve this problem. One simple idea is to track the user's head and feet on a standard treadmill in order to detect when the user is trying to make a turn. This detection is based on analysis of the direction the feet are pointing, deviation of a foot's motion from the forward direction, and other factors. When the system detects a turn, it rotates the treadmill, which is mounted on a large motion platform (Noma and Miyasato 1998). The motion platform also allows tilting of the treadmill to simulate slopes. Experience with this setup indicates that it works well for slow, smooth turns but has too much latency for sudden or sharp turns. In addition, it does not allow sidestepping.

Passive Omnidirectional Treadmills

Another approach to gait negation is to use a treadmill that is specially constructed to allow walking in any direction. There are two categories of these omnidirectional treadmills. The first category relies on the user's weight and momentum to activate the treadmill's surface. These are known as passive omnidirectional treadmills, which we discuss in this section. The second category actively controls the treadmill's surface in reaction to detecting the user's movements. These are known as active omnidirectional treadmills, which we discuss in the next section.

As explained, passive omnidirectional treadmills rely on the user's weight and momentum to activate their surfaces. In turn, these moving surfaces negate the user's gait and keep the user in the center of the space. An example of a passive omnidirectional treadmill is the

Omnidirectional Ball-Bearing Disc Platform (OBDP) developed by Huang (2003). This prototype uses hundreds of ball bearings arranged in a concave platform to passively react to the user's walking motions. When the user steps forward, the ball bearings roll toward the center of the device due to the curvature and return the user's foot to the center of the platform. Due to the unnaturalness of stepping on a concave surface and the abrupt response of the ball bearings, the OBDP also requires a frame around the user's waist to stabilize the user in the event of a fall.

Another example of a passive omnidirectional treadmill is the Virtusphere (Figure 8.8; Medina et al. 2008). This device serves as a human-sized "hamster ball" that rolls in place while the user walks inside of it. Like the OBDP, the weight of the user's steps initiates the rolling of the Virtusphere's surface. However, once the Virtusphere is rolling, the user must exert reverse forces in order to stop the device without falling. Research conducted by Nabiyouni et al. (2015) shows that the Virtusphere provides a user experience that is significantly worse than a joystick or real walking.

Figure 8.8 The Virtusphere, a human-sized "hamster ball," is an example of a passive omnidirectional treadmill. (Image courtesy of Mahdi Nabiyouni)

Active Omnidirectional Treadmills

While passive omnidirectional treadmills are built to react to the user's weight and momentum, active omnidirectional treadmills are built to detect the user's walking motions and move to negate them. One implementation for such a device is to chain together several belt-based treadmills side to side to create a larger treadmill that can be rotated left and right. While each section supports forward and backward motions, the overall chain supports lateral movements. Hence, the treadmill surface has the ability to move in any arbitrary horizontal direction. The omnidirectional treadmill, or ODT (Darken et al. 1997), the Torus treadmill (Iwata 1999), and the Cyberwalk (Schwaiger et al. 2007) are examples of this type of active omnidirectional treadmill. The ODT was constructed for the military with the hope that it could be used to train infantry naturally in a 3D UI. The device allowed walking or even running in any direction, but also had some serious usability and safety issues that made it less than effective.

The most important issue was that because the ODT continually moved the surface in order to recenter the user on the treadmill and keep the user from walking off the edge of the device, the recentering motion caused the user to lose his or her balance, especially during turns or sidestepping. The ODT was found to support walking at a moderate speed with gradual turns, but not many of the other movements that soldiers would need to make.

Another approach to creating an active omnidirectional treadmill is to use conveyor rollers in a radial pattern (i.e., with all the rollers' direction of motion being toward the center of the device) instead of belts. Some commercial versions consist of 16 sections of rollers surrounding a small stable platform in the center. When the user is detected walking outside of the small platform by an optical tracking system, the relevant rollers are actively controlled to move the user back to the center platform. The speed of the rollers is controlled to match the user's forward momentum. Otherwise, the user may fall if there's a mismatch in inertia and roller speed.

Low-Friction Surfaces

Gait negation can also be implemented by using low-friction surfaces to negate the kinetics or forces of walking. Like omnidirectional treadmills, low-friction surfaces can support virtual travel in any horizontal direction. Iwata and Fujii (1996) implemented an early example of such a device. They used sandals with low-friction film on the soles to allow the user to shuffle his feet back and forth on a floor sheet of low-friction film. The sandals also had rubber soles on the toes to afford braking. Swapp et al. (2010) implemented a similar device called the Wizdish. The major difference between the two devices is that the Wizdish used a concave low-friction surface that not only negated the forces of stepping forward but also brought the user's foot back to the center. In recent years, a number of low-friction surfaces have been developed to target the consumer market (Figure 8.9). These devices often utilize a support frame around the user's waist for balance and safety.

Figure 8.9 A low-friction surface for virtual locomotion in HWD-based VR. (Image courtesy of Virtuix)

There are several fundamental challenges for low-friction surfaces. First, the degree of friction must be properly balanced between the surface and the shoes. If the amount of friction is too high, the user will exert much more energy to move than in real walking. If the amount of friction is too low, the surface will be slippery, and the user is likely to slip or fall. Second, though these devices are designed to simulate real walking, they require biomechanics that are more similar to skating than walking. Finally, based on the authors' personal experiences, low-friction surfaces require time to learn how to use effectively.

Step-Based Devices

The final gait negation technique that we cover here are step-based devices. These devices are developed to detect where the user is about to step and to provide a surface for the user to step on. By "catching" the user's steps, these devices can then recenter the user by moving both steps back toward the center of the space. The GaitMaster (Iwata 2001) is such an approach. Rather than using a treadmill or a frictionless surface, the user straps her feet onto platforms that rest on top of two small motion bases (Figure 8.10). The system attempts to detect the user's walking motion via force sensors embedded in the platforms and move the platforms appropriately so that a hard "ground" surface is felt at the correct location after each step. This device is technically quite complex, and it can have serious safety and usability issues because of the powerful hydraulics involved and the latency in detecting foot motion.

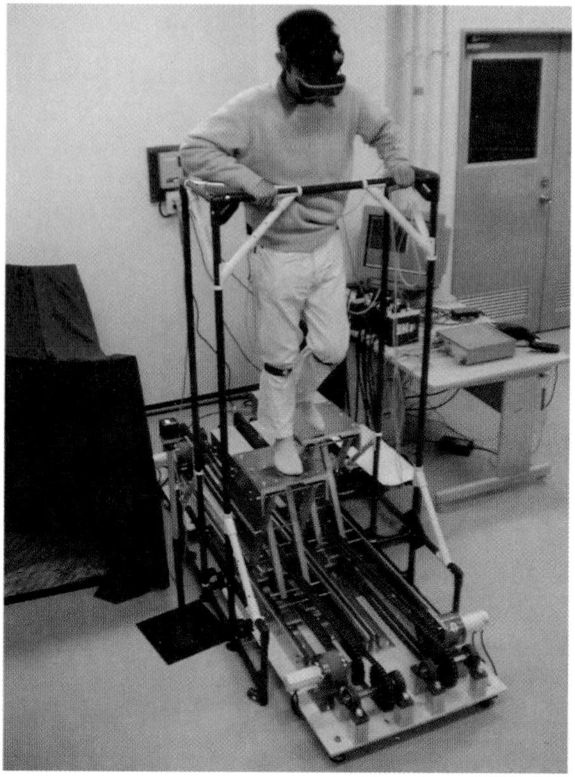

Figure 8.10 GaitMaster2 locomotion device. (Iwata 2001, © 2003 IEEE; reprinted by permission)

Another step-based device example is the CirculaFloor, also developed by Iwata et al. (2005). This system uses multiple omnidirectional robotic vehicles as moveable tiles that are programmed to position themselves under the user's steps. Each tile provides a sufficient area for walking to avoid requiring precise positioning. As the user walks, the vehicles can move in the opposite direction to cancel the user's global movement. Additionally, once the user steps off a tile, it can be circulated back to catch the next step.

In general, gait negation devices have not been as successful as one might hope. This is because they are still too expensive, too susceptible to mechanical failures, and too slow to respond to the user's movements. Most importantly, the devices do not produce the perception of natural walking for the user because of biomechanics and forces that are different from real walking. Therefore, instead of being able to use her natural ability to walk, the user must learn to adapt her walking motion to the device's characteristics. Still, such devices may prove useful in certain applications that require physical locomotion via walking. For a more detailed overview of locomotion devices, see Hollerbach (2002) and Steinicke et al. (2013).

8.5 Steering Metaphors

Although a great deal of work has been focused on natural locomotion techniques such as those described in section 8.4, most 3D UIs, from video games to immersive VR, use some sort of virtual travel technique. Among virtual techniques, by far the most common metaphor is steering, which refers to the continuous control of the direction of motion by the user. In other words, the user constantly specifies either an absolute ("move along the vector (1,0,0) in world coordinates") or relative ("move to my left") direction of travel. In most cases, this specification of travel direction is either achieved through spatial interactions or with physical steering props. Hence, we categorize steering techniques under these two major categories.

8.5.1 Spatial Steering Techniques

Spatial steering techniques allow the user to guide or control the movement of travel by manipulating the orientation of a tracking device. Steering techniques are generally easy to understand and provide the highest level of control to the user. The spatial steering techniques we will describe are

- gaze-directed steering
- hand-directed steering (pointing)
- torso-directed steering
- lean-directed steering

Gaze-Directed Steering

The most common steering technique—and the default travel technique in many 3D toolkits (Kessler et al. 2000)—is gaze-directed steering (Mine 1995a). Quite simply, this technique allows the user to move in the direction toward which he is looking. In a tracked environment, the gaze direction is obtained from the orientation of a head tracker (although true gaze-directed steering would use an eye tracker); in a desktop environment, the gaze direction is along a ray from the virtual camera position (assumed to be one of the user's eye positions) through the center of the viewing window. Once the gaze direction vector is obtained, it is normalized, and then the user is translated along this vector in the world coordinate system. The vector may also be multiplied by a velocity factor to allow for different rates of travel (see section 8.8.2 for velocity specification techniques). Some discrete event (e.g., a button press or joystick movement) is needed to start and stop the motion of the user.

The basic concept of gaze-directed steering can be extended by allowing motion along vectors orthogonal to the gaze vector. This gives the user the ability to **strafe**—to move backward, up, down, left, and right (Chee and Hooi 2002). This ability is especially important for desktop systems, where setting the gaze direction may be more cumbersome than in a head-tracked VE. Additionally, strafing is often used for maneuvering (see section 8.2.3).

From the user's point of view, gaze-directed steering is quite easy to understand and control. In a desktop 3D environment, it seems quite natural to move "into" the screen. In an immersive 3D UI with head tracking, this technique also seems intuitive, especially if motion is constrained to the 2D horizontal plane. In addition, the hardware requirements of the technique are quite modest; even in an immersive system, the user needs only a head tracker and a button. However, if complete 3D motion is provided (i.e., "flying"), gaze-directed steering has two problems. First, when users attempt to travel in the horizontal plane, they are likely to travel slightly up or down because it's very difficult to tell whether the head is precisely level. Second, it's quite awkward to travel vertically up or down by looking straight up or down, especially when wearing an HWD.

But perhaps the most important problem with gaze-directed steering is that it couples gaze direction and travel direction, meaning that users cannot look in one direction while traveling in another. This may seem a small issue, but consider how often you look in a direction other than your travel direction while walking, cycling, or driving in the physical world. Studies have shown that pointing (see below) outperforms gaze-directed steering on tasks requiring motion relative to an object in the environment (Bowman et al. 1997).

Hand-Directed Steering (Pointing)

To avoid the coupling of gaze direction and travel direction, the pointing technique (Mine 1995a) uses the orientation of the user's hand (or tracked controller) to specify the direction of travel. Hence, pointing is also known as hand-directed steering. The forward vector of the hand tracker is first transformed into a world coordinate vector (this forward vector depends on the specific tracking system, method of mounting the tracker on the hand, and 3D UI toolkit used). The vector is then normalized and scaled by the velocity, and the user is moved along the resulting vector. The same concept could be implemented on the desktop, for example, by using the keyboard to set the travel direction and the mouse to set the gaze direction. In this case, however, well-designed feedback indicating the direction of travel would be necessary. In the case of an immersive 3D UI, the user's proprioceptive sense (i.e., the sense of one's own body and its parts) can tell her the direction in which her hand is pointing. Once the travel vector is obtained, the implementation of the pointing technique is identical to that of the gaze-directed steering technique.

An extension of the pointing concept uses two hands to specify the vector (Mine 1997). Rather than use the orientation of the hand to define the travel direction, the vector between the two hands' positions is used. An issue for this technique is which hand should be considered the "forward" hand. In one implementation using Pinch Gloves (Bowman, Wingrave et al. 2001), the hand initiating the travel gesture was considered to be forward. This technique makes it easy to specify any 3D direction vector and also allows easy addition of a velocity-control mechanism based on the distance between the hands.

This pointing technique is more flexible but also more complex than gaze-directed steering, requiring the user to control two orientations simultaneously. This can lead to higher levels of cognitive load, which may reduce performance on cognitively complex tasks like information gathering (Bowman, Koller et al. 1998). The pointing technique is excellent for promoting the acquisition of spatial knowledge because it gives the user the freedom to look in any direction while moving (Bowman, Davis et al. 1999).

Torso-Directed Steering

Another simple steering technique uses the user's torso to specify the direction of travel. This torso-directed technique is motivated by the fact that people naturally turn their bodies to face the direction in which they are walking. A tracker is attached to the user's torso, somewhere near the waist (for example, the tracker can be mounted on a belt that the user wears). If the tracker is attached much higher than this, undesirable rotations may occur when the user looks away from the direction of travel. After the travel direction vector is obtained from this tracker, the technique is implemented exactly as gaze-directed steering. The torso-directed technique does not apply to desktop 3D UIs.

The major advantage of the torso-directed technique is that, like pointing, it decouples the user's gaze direction and travel direction. Unlike pointing, it does this in a natural way. The user's cognitive load should be lessened with the torso-directed technique, although this has not been verified experimentally. The torso-directed technique also leaves the user's hands free to perform other tasks. However, the torso-directed technique also has several disadvantages. The most important of these is that the technique applies only to environments in which all travel is limited to the horizontal plane, because it is not practical to point the torso up or down. The technique also requires an additional tracker beyond the standard head and hand trackers for tracking the user's torso.

Lean-Directed Steering

A slightly more complex steering technique allows the user to define the direction of travel by leaning. This metaphor uses the natural motion of leaning towards something to view it but interprets the leaning direction as a direction for travel. Lean-directed steering is similar to the Human Joystick techniques we described in section 8.4.2, except that the user does not take any steps in lean-directed steering.

One example is the PenguFly technique developed by von Kapri et al. (2011). With PenguFly, both of the user's hands are tracked in addition to the head. The direction of travel is then specified by the addition of the two vectors defined from each hand to the head. The travel speed is defined by half of the length of this lean-directed vector (Figure 8.11). Lean-directed steering has been shown to be more accurate for traveling than pointing due to its higher granularity of control over the travel speed (von Kapri et al. 2011). However, it also induces a significant increase in cybersickness, likely due to the large body motions required.

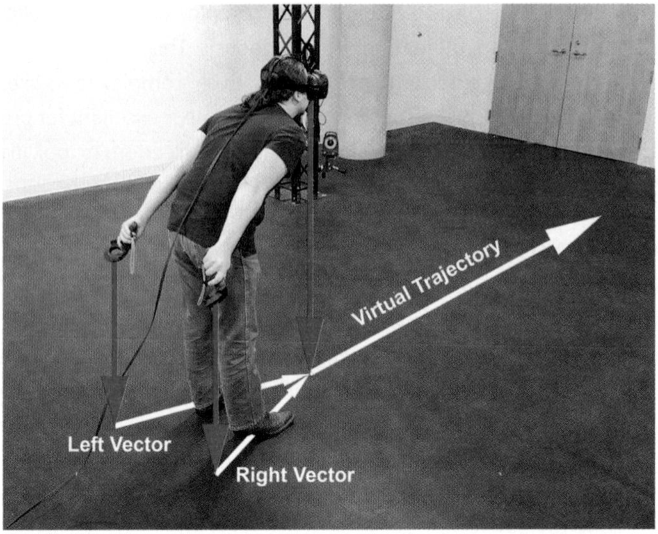

Figure 8.11 PenguFly is a lean-directed steering technique that defines travel direction as the vector created by adding the two vectors created from the hands to the head. The length of this vector also defines the velocity of travel. (Image adapted from von Kapri et al. 2011)

Another lean-directed steering implementation is the ChairIO interface developed by Beckhaus et al. (2007). The interface is based on an ergonomic stool with a rotating seat and a spring-based column that can tilt and even allow the user to bounce up and down. With magnetic trackers attached to the seat and the column, the ChairIO allows the movements of the user to be tracked as she leans and turns in the seat. This tracking information can then be used for steering. Similarly, Marchal et al. (2011) developed the Joyman interface, which consisted of essentially a trampoline, a rigid surface, an inertial sensor, and a safety rail to prevent falling. While holding onto the rail, the user could lean extremely far in any direction, which would cause the rigid surface to also lean toward one side of the trampoline's structure. The inertial sensor detects the orientation of the lean and then translates it into a direction and speed for steering.

All of the lean-directed steering techniques integrate direction and speed into a single, easy-to-understand movement. These techniques allow the user to rely on natural proprioceptive and kinesthetic senses to maintain spatial orientation and understanding of movement within the environment. Additionally, Kruijff et al. (2016) found that adding walking-related sensory cues, such as footstep sounds, head-bobbing camera motions, and footstep-based vibrotactile feedback, can all enhance the user's senses of vection and presence. The major disadvantage to these techniques is that they are limited to 2D locomotion unless another technique or feature is added to allow for vertical motion.

8.5.2 Physical Steering Props

Steering techniques for travel can also be implemented with a variety of physical props (specialized devices designed for the task of steering). In general, steering props are useful when a certain type of vehicle is being simulated, when the interface must be usable by anyone without any training, or when steering is an important part of the overall user experience. Additionally, automobile steering wheels may be a good choice for some general-purpose applications because they are understandable by anyone who has driven a car. Props provide users with appropriate affordances and feedback—telling them what can be done, how to do it, and what has been done. A potential pitfall is that props may create unrealistic expectations of realistic control and response in users accustomed to using the same steering interface in a real vehicle. Additionally, most physical steering props facilitate only 2D horizontal travel.

We discuss the following types of steering props in this section

- cockpits
- cycles

Cockpits

The most obvious steering prop is a simple steering wheel similar to that found in a car, which of course can be combined with a typical accelerator and brake for virtual driving. These devices generally require that the user be seated but can be quite effective to implement a simple vehicle metaphor. They are also usable in either immersive or desktop VEs and are understandable by almost any user.

Other specialized steering props can be used to simulate real or imaginary vehicles for particular application domains. For example, realistic ship controls can be used to pilot a virtual ship (Brooks 1999), or an actual cockpit from a tractor can be used to control a virtual tractor (Deisinger et al. 2000). Of course, this near-field haptics approach (Brooks 1999) has been used in aircraft simulators for years. Disney used steering props in several of its VR-based attractions (Pausch et al. 1996; Schell and Shochet 2001). For example, the virtual jungle cruise ride at DisneyQuest in Orlando allows several guests to collaboratively steer and control the speed of a virtual raft using physical oars, and the Pirates of the Caribbean attraction includes a steering wheel and throttle for the virtual ship. In addition, many arcade games use such props—motorcycle handlebars, steering wheels, skateboards, skis, and the like.

Cycles

If physical exertion is desired but walking is not necessary, a bicycle or other pedal-driven device can be used. A typical exercise bicycle setup (Brogan et al. 1998) is the easiest to implement, because these devices usually already report the speed of pedaling. Some of them also report the degree of handlebar turning or user leaning, allowing natural steering.

Figure 8.12 Uniport locomotion device. (Photograph courtesy of Sarcos)

The Uniport is a unicycle-like device that allows travel through virtual worlds seen through an HWD (Figure 8.12); it was designed for infantry training (as one of the precursors to the omnidirectional treadmill). It is obviously less effective at producing a believable simulation of walking, and users may also have difficulty steering the device. However, it is mechanically much less complex and produces significant exertion for the user, which may be desired for some applications.

8.6 Selection-Based Travel Metaphors

Another major category of travel metaphors depends on the user selecting either a target to travel to or a path to travel along. These selection-based travel metaphors often simplify travel by not requiring the user to continuously think about the details of travel. Instead, the user specifies the desired parameters of travel first and then allows the travel technique to take care of the actual movement. While these techniques are not the most natural, they tend to be extremely easy to understand and use.

8.6.1 Target-Based Travel Techniques

In some cases, the user's only goal for a travel task is to move the viewpoint to a specific position in the environment. For example, the user may want to inspect a virtual piece of art by moving next to it. The user in these situations is likely willing to give up control of the actual motion to the system and simply specify the endpoint. Target-based travel techniques meet these requirements.

Even though the user is concerned only with the target of travel, this should not necessarily be construed to mean that the system should move the user directly to the target via teleportation. An empirical study (Bowman et al. 1997) found that teleporting instantly from one location to another in a 3D UI significantly decreases the user's spatial orientation (users find it difficult to get their bearings when instantly transported to the target location). Therefore, continuous movement from the starting point to the endpoint is recommended when spatial orientation is important. On the other hand, continuous movement that's not under the user's control can increase cybersickness. For this reason, a compromise is often used in which the user is not teleported instantaneously but instead is moved *very* quickly through virtual space to the target. This "blink" mode of travel gives users enough visual information to help them understand how they have moved, but is so short that it's unlikely to make users feel sick.

There are many ways to specify the target of travel. In this section, we describe two techniques:

- representation-based target techniques
- dual-target techniques

Many other target-based travel techniques specify the target using interaction techniques designed for another task. We call this type of technique a **cross-task** technique because the technique implementation has crossed from one task to another. Cross-task target-specification techniques include

- selecting an object in the environment as the target of travel using a selection technique (see Chapter 7, "Manipulation")
- placing a target object in the environment using a manipulation technique (see Chapter 7)
- selecting a predefined target location from a list or menu (see Chapter 9, "System Control")
- entering 2D or 3D coordinates using a number entry technique or a location name using a text entry technique (see Chapter 9)

Representation-Based Target Techniques

A 2D map or 3D world-in-miniature can be used to specify a target location or object within the environment (Figure 8.13). A typical map-based implementation of this technique (Bowman, Wineman et al. 1998) uses a pointer of some sort (a tracker in an immersive 3D UI, a mouse on the desktop) to specify a target and simply creates a linear path from the current location to the target, then moves the user along this path. The height of the viewpoint along this path is defined to be a fixed height above the ground.

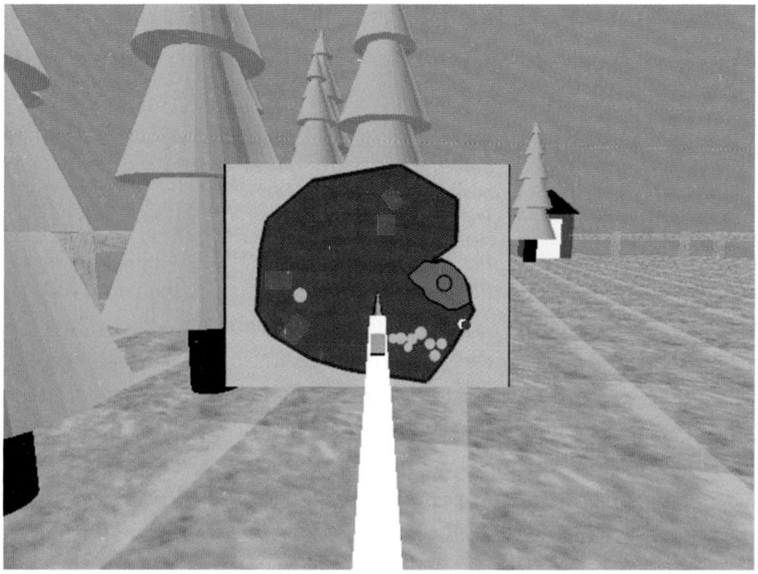

Figure 8.13 Map-based target specification. The darker dot on the lower right of the map indicates the user's current position and can be dragged to a new location on the map to specify a travel target in the full-scale environment. (Bowman, Johnson et al. 1999; reprinted by permission of MIT Press and *Presence: Teleoperators and Virtual Environments*)

Dual-Target Techniques

Dual-target travel techniques allow the user to travel easily between two target locations. Normally, the user directly specifies the first target location by using a selection technique while the second target location is implicitly defined by the system at the time of that selection. For example, the ZoomBack technique (Zeleznik et al. 2002) uses a typical ray-casting metaphor (see Chapter 7) to select an object in the environment and then moves the user to a position directly in front of this object. Ray-casting has been used in other 3D interfaces for target-based travel as well (Bowman, Johnson et al. 2001). The novel feature of the ZoomBack technique, however, is that it retains information about the previous position of the user and allows users to return to that position after inspecting the target object.

Zeleznik and colleagues used this technique in the context of a virtual museum. The technique allowed users to select a painting on the wall, examine that painting up close, and then return to the original location where multiple paintings could be viewed. Their implementation used a specialized pop-through button device (see Chapter 6, "3D User Interface Input Hardware"). Users moved to the target object with light pressure on the button and could choose either to remain there by pressing the button firmly or to return to their previous location by releasing the button. This technique could also be implemented using two standard buttons, but the pop-through buttons provide a convenient and intuitive way to specify a temporary action that can then be either confirmed or canceled. This general strategy could be applied to other route-planning and target-based techniques as well.

8.6.2 Route-Planning Travel Techniques

A second category of selection-based travel techniques, called route planning, allows the user to specify a path or route through the environment, then moves the user along that path. The essential feature of the route-planning metaphor is this two-step process: the user plans, and then the system carries out the plan. This type of technique is much less common than continuous steering or target-based travel but has many uses. The techniques can allow the user to review, refine, or edit the path before its execution. For example, the user might want to define a camera path to be followed in an animation. He could do this with a steering technique, but the result would likely be a more erratic and less precise path.

Route-planning techniques also allow the user to focus on other tasks, such as information gathering, during the actual period of travel. Route-planning techniques still give users at least some degree of control over their motion, but they move that control to the beginning of the travel task. This section contains information on the following route-planning techniques:

- drawing a path
- marking points along a path

Drawing a Path

One way to specify a route is to draw the desired path. A continuous path ensures the highest level of user control. One published technique for desktop 3D UIs allows the user to draw directly in the 3D environment using the mouse by a projection of the 2D mouse path onto the 3D geometry in the environment (Figure 8.14; Igarashi et al. 1998). This technique assumes that the camera should always move at a given height above a surface rather than fly through empty space. The technique includes intelligent mapping of the path: rather than simply projecting the 2D stroke onto the nearest 3D surface in the scene, the algorithm takes into consideration the continuity of the path and the surface the path has followed up to the current point. Thus a path can be drawn that goes through a tunnel even if all of the ground within the tunnel is not visible to the user.

In an immersive 3D UI, the user likely cannot reach the entire environment to draw in it directly, so drawing on a 2D or 3D map of the environment could be used to specify the path. This requires a transformation from the map coordinate system to the world coordinate system, and in the case of a 2D map, an inferred height.

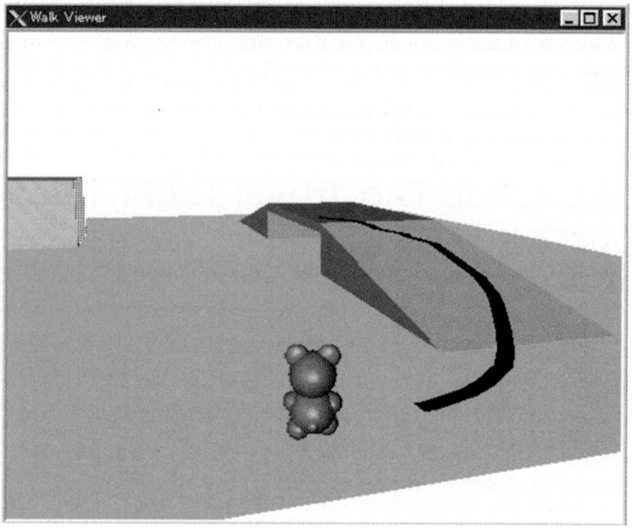

Figure 8.14 Path-drawing system. (Igarashi et al. 1998, © 1998 ACM; reprinted by permission)

Figure 8.15 Route-planning technique using markers on a 3D map. (Bowman, Davis et al. 1999; reprinted by permission of MIT Press and *Presence: Teleoperators and Virtual Environments*)

Marking Points along a Path

Another method for specifying a path in a 3D environment is to place markers at key locations along the path. Again, these markers could be placed in the environment directly (using a mouse on the desktop or perhaps using a manipulation-at-a-distance technique; see Chapter 7) or on a 2D or 3D map of the environment. The system is then responsible for creating a continuous path that visits all of the marker locations. One simple implementation (Bowman, Davis et al. 1999) used a 3D map of the environment and moved the user along a straight-line path from one marker to the next (Figure 8.15). The path might also be more complex; the markers could be used as control points for a curve, for example. One advantage of this type of technique is that the user can vary the level of control by placing more (increased user control) or fewer (increased system control) markers. A key issue with marker placement techniques is feedback: how does the user know what path will be traversed? A well-designed technique will include interactive feedback to show the user the path in the environment or on the map.

8.7 Manipulation-Based Travel Metaphors

Manipulation-based travel techniques are another type of cross-task technique that can be quite effective in some situations. These techniques use hand-based object manipulation metaphors, such as HOMER, Go-Go, and so on (see Chapter 7), to manipulate either the viewpoint or the entire world.

Manipulation-based travel techniques for travel should be used in situations where both travel and object manipulation tasks are frequent and interspersed. For example, consider an interior layout application, where the user's goal is to place furniture, carpets, paintings, and other items in a virtual room. This task involves frequent object manipulation tasks to place or move virtual objects and frequent travel tasks to view the room from different viewpoints. Moreover, the designer will likely move an object until it looks right from the current viewpoint and then travel to a new viewpoint to verify the object's placement. If the same metaphor can be used for both travel and object manipulation, then the interaction with this environment will be seamless and simple from the user's point of view.

8.7.1 Viewpoint Manipulation Techniques

There are several approaches to manipulating the viewpoint to achieve travel. Examples of viewpoint manipulation techniques described below are

- camera manipulation
- avatar manipulation
- fixed-object manipulation

Camera Manipulation

A technique for travel in a desktop VE that still uses position trackers is called the camera-in-hand technique (Ware and Osborne 1990). A tracker is held in the hand, and the absolute position and orientation of that tracker in a defined workspace specifies the position and orientation of the camera from which the 3D scene is drawn. In other words, a miniature version of the world can be imagined in the work area. The tracker is imagined to be a virtual camera looking at this world (see Figure 8.16). Travel then is a simple matter of moving the hand in the workspace.

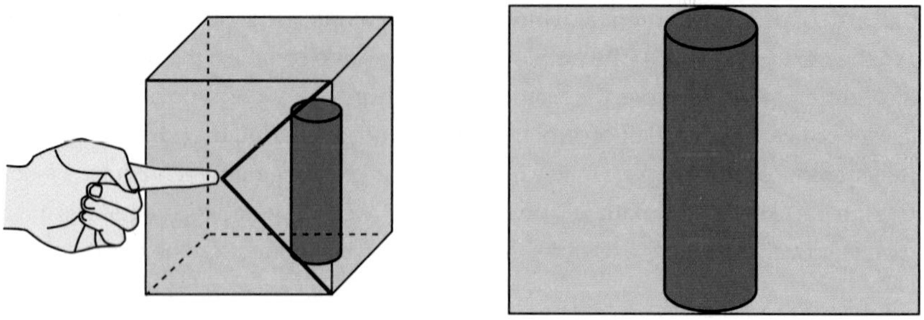

Figure 8.16 Camera-in-hand technique. The user's hand is at a certain position and orientation within the workspace (left), producing a particular view of the environment (right).

The camera-in-hand technique is relatively easy to implement. It simply requires a transformation between the tracker coordinate system and the world coordinate system, defining the mapping between the virtual camera position and the tracker position.

This technique can be effective for desktop 3D UIs (if a tracker is available) because the input is actually 3D in nature, and the user can use her proprioceptive sense to get a feeling for the spatial relationships between objects in the 3D world. However, the technique can also be confusing because the user has an exocentric (third-person) view of the workspace, but the 3D scene is usually drawn from an egocentric (first-person) point of view.

Avatar Manipulation

Instead of manipulating the camera, the user can manipulate a virtual representation of himself in order to plan a route. For example, in the world-in-miniature (WIM) technique (see Chapter 7, section 7.7.2), a small human figure represents the user's position and orientation in the miniature world (Figure 8.17). The user selects and manipulates this object in the miniature environment in order to define a path for the viewpoint to move along or simply a target location; then the system executes this motion in the full-scale environment. Pausch et al. (1995) found that this technique is most understandable when the user's view actually flies *into* the miniature world, having it replace the full-scale world and then creating a new miniature. One major advantage of this technique relative to the other route-planning techniques is that the user representation has orientation as well as position so that viewpoint rotations, not just translations, can be defined.

Similarly, a path can be defined by moving a user icon on a 2D map of the environment, a technique that would apply equally well to desktop and immersive 3D UIs. Because this path is only 2D, the system must use rules to determine the height of the user at every point along the path. A common rule would keep the viewpoint at a fixed height above the ground.

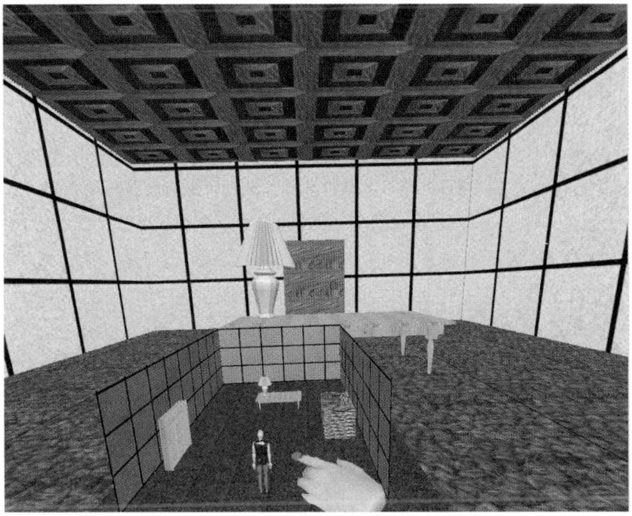

Figure 8.17 WIM (in foreground) held in front of the corresponding full-scale environment. The user icon is at the bottom of the image. (Image courtesy of Doug A. Bowman)

Fixed-Object Manipulation

You can also use a manipulation technique for travel by letting a selected object serve as a focus for viewpoint movement. In other words, the user selects an object in the environment and then makes hand movements, just as he would to manipulate that object. However, the object remains stationary and the viewpoint is moved *relative* to that object. This is called fixed-object manipulation. Although this is hard to understand without trying it yourself, a real-world analogy may help. Imagine grabbing a flagpole. The pole is fixed firmly to the ground, so when you move your hand toward your body, the flagpole doesn't move; rather, *you* move closer to it. Similarly, you might try to rotate the flagpole by turning your hand, but the effect instead will be to rotate your body in the opposite direction around the pole.

Let us consider a specific example of fixed-object manipulation in 3D UIs. Pierce et al. (1997) designed a set of manipulation techniques called image-plane techniques (see Chapter 7, section 7.5.1). Normally, an object is selected in the image plane, then hand movements cause that object to move within the environment. For example, moving the hand back toward the body would cause the selected object to move toward the user as well. When used in travel mode, however, the same hand motion would cause the viewpoint to move *toward the selected object.* Hand rotations can also be used to move the viewpoint *around the selected object.* The scaled-world grab technique (Mine et al. 1997) and the LaserGrab technique (Zeleznik et al. 2002) work in a similar way.

Fixed-object manipulation techniques provide a seamless interaction experience in combined travel/manipulation task scenarios, such as the one described above. The user must simply be aware of which interaction mode is active (travel or manipulation). Usually, the two modes are assigned to different buttons on the input device. The two modes can also be intermingled using the same selected object. The user would select an object in manipulation mode, move that object, then hold down the button for travel mode, allowing viewpoint movement relative to that selected object, then release the button to return to manipulation mode, and so on.

8.7.2 World Manipulation Techniques

An alternative to manipulating the viewpoint to travel is to manipulate the entire world relative to the current viewpoint. A number of techniques take this approach. We categorize them by the number of points used to manipulate the world:

- single-point world manipulation
- dual-point world manipulation

Single-Point World Manipulation

One method for using manipulation techniques for travel tasks is to allow the user to manipulate the world about a single point. An example of this is the "grab the air" or "scene in hand" technique (Mapes and Moshell 1995; Ware and Osborne 1990). In this concept, the entire world is viewed as an object to be manipulated. When the user makes a grabbing gesture at any point in the world and then moves her hand, the entire world moves while the viewpoint remains stationary. Of course, to the user this appears exactly the same as if the viewpoint had moved and the world had remained stationary.

In order to integrate this travel technique with an object manipulation technique, the system must simply determine whether or not the user is grabbing a moveable object at the time the grab gesture is initiated. If an object is being grabbed, then standard object manipulation should be performed; otherwise, the grab gesture is interpreted as the start of a travel interaction. In this way, the same technique can be used for both tasks.

Although this technique is easy to implement, developers should not fall into the trap of simply attaching the world object to the virtual hand, because this will cause the world to follow the virtual hand's rotations as well as translations, which can be quite disorienting. Rather, while the grab gesture is maintained (or the button held down), the system should measure the displacement of the virtual hand each frame and translate the world origin by that vector.

In its simplest form, this technique requires a lot of arm motion on the part of the user to travel significant distances in the VE. Enhancements to the basic technique can reduce this. First, the virtual hand can be allowed to cover much more distance using a technique such as Go-Go (Poupyrev et al. 1996). Second, the technique can be implemented using two hands instead of one, as discussed next.

Dual-Point World Manipulation

Manipulating the world has also been implemented by defining two manipulation points instead of one. The commercial product SmartScene, which evolved from a graduate research project (Mapes and Moshell 1995), allowed the user to travel by using an action similar to pulling oneself along a rope. The interface was simple—the user continuously pulled the world toward him by making a simple grab gesture with his hand outreached and bringing the hand closer before grabbing the world again with his other hand. This approach distributed the strain of manipulating the world between both of the user's arms instead of primarily exerting one.

Another advantage of dual-point manipulation is the ability to also manipulate the view rotation while traveling. When the user has the world grabbed with both hands, the position of the user's nondominant hand can serve as a pivot point while the dominant hand defines a vector between them. Rotational changes in this vector can be applied to the world's transformation to provide view rotations in addition to traveling using dual-point manipulations. Additionally, the distance between the two hands can be used to scale the world to be larger or smaller, as discussed in section 8.8.5.

8.8 Other Aspects of Travel Techniques

In addition to the techniques covered in the previous sections, there are many other aspects of travel techniques that 3D UI designers should be concerned with. These include how to orient the viewpoint, how to specify the velocity of travel, how to provide vertical travel, whether to use automated or semiautomated travel, whether to scale the world while traveling, how to transition between different travel techniques, using multiple cameras and perspectives, and considerations of using nonphysical inputs, such as brain signals.

8.8.1 Viewpoint Orientation

Thus far, we have focused almost exclusively on techniques for changing the position (*xyz* coordinates) of the viewpoint. Travel also includes, however, the task of setting the viewpoint orientation (heading, pitch, and roll). Here we discuss techniques specifically designed to specify the orientation of the viewpoint, including

- head tracking
- orbital viewing
- nonisomorphic rotation
- virtual sphere techniques

Head Tracking

For immersive VR and AR, there is usually no need to define an explicit viewpoint orientation technique, because the viewpoint orientation is taken by default from the user's head tracker. This is the most natural and direct way to specify viewpoint orientation, and it has been shown that physical turning leads to higher levels of spatial orientation than virtual turning (Bakker et al. 1998; Chance et al. 1998).

Orbital Viewing

A slight twist on the use of head tracking for viewpoint orientation is orbital viewing (Koller et al. 1996). This technique is used to view a single virtual object from all sides. In order to view the bottom of the object, the user looks up; in order to view the left side, the user looks right; and so on. However, recent research by Jacob et al. (2016) has indicated that head roll motions, instead of head yaw motions, should be used for horizontal orbital viewing, when interacting with a stationary screen.

Nonisomorphic Rotation

There are certain situations in immersive VR when some other viewpoint orientation technique is needed. The most common example comes from projected displays in which the display surfaces do not completely surround the user, as in a three-walled surround-screen display. Here, in order to see what is directly behind, the user must be able to rotate the viewpoint (in surround-screen displays, this is usually done using a joystick on the "wand" input device). The redirected walking technique (Razzaque et al. 2002) slowly rotates the environment so that the user can turn naturally but avoid facing the missing back wall. Research has produced nonisomorphic rotation techniques (LaViola et al. 2001) that allow the user of such a display to view the entire surrounding environment based on amplified head rotations (for an introduction to nonisomorphic mappings, see Chapter 7, section 7.3.1).

A number of different nonisomorphic mappings could be used for setting the virtual viewpoint orientation. For a CAVE-like display, LaViola et al. (2001) used a nonlinear mapping function, which kicks in only after the user has rotated beyond a certain threshold, dependent on the user's waist orientation vector and position within the CAVE. A scaled 2D Gaussian function has been shown to work well. LaViola et al. (2001) offer more details on nonisomorphic viewpoint rotation.

Virtual Sphere Techniques

For desktop 3D UIs, setting viewpoint orientation is usually a much more explicit task. The most common techniques are the Virtual Sphere (Chen et al. 1988) and a related technique called the Arcball (Shoemake 1992). Both of these techniques were originally intended to be used for rotating individual virtual objects from an exocentric point of view and are described in detail in Chapter 7, "Manipulation," section 7.7.3. For egocentric points of view, the same concept can be used from the inside out. That is, the viewpoint is considered to be the center of an imaginary sphere, and mouse clicks and drags rotate that sphere around the viewpoint.

8.8.2 Velocity Specification

Next, we need to consider techniques for changing the speed of travel. Many 3D UIs ignore this aspect of travel and simply set what seems to be a reasonable constant velocity. However, this can lead to a variety of problems, because a constant velocity will always be too slow in some situations and too fast in others. When the user wishes to travel from one side of the environment to another, frustration quickly sets in if he perceives the speed to be too slow. On the other hand, if he desires to move only slightly to one side, the same constant velocity will probably be too fast to allow precise movement. Therefore, considering how the user or system might control velocity is an important part of designing a travel technique.

The user can control velocity in many different ways. We discuss the following approaches to defining or manipulating velocity:

- discrete changes
- continuous control
- direct input
- automated velocity

Discrete Changes

One way to allow the user to control velocity is through discrete changes based on predefined amounts. A simple example is using two buttons, one to increase the speed and the other to decrease it. These buttons could be on the input device held by the user or displayed on a menu within the 3D UI. While discrete changes in velocity can help alleviate most of the issues with traveling too slow or too fast, the user may not be able to set the velocity to the desired speed if that value falls between two of the discrete steps. An interaction designer may decide to use a smaller step value to decrease that likelihood, but this in turn can cause the user to press a button an unnecessarily large number of times to eventually reach the desired velocity. Hence, interaction designers must be careful in selecting step values for discrete changes.

Continuous Control

Considering the issues with discrete changes, a likely better solution is to afford the user continuous control over velocity. Often, continuous velocity control can be integrated with the direction control technique being used. For example, in gaze-directed steering, the orientation of the head is used to specify travel direction, so the position of the head relative to the body can be used to specify velocity. This is called lean-based velocity (Fairchild et al. 1993; LaViola et al. 2001; Song and Norman 1993). In LaViola's implementation, this involves looking at the absolute horizontal distance between the head and the waist. Once this distance exceeds a threshold, then the user begins to translate in the direction of leaning, and the velocity is some multiple of the leaning magnitude. Similarly, a technique that bases velocity on hand position relative to the body (Mine 1995a) integrates well with a pointing technique.

Other methods for continuously controlling velocity make use of physical devices. A physical prop that includes acceleration and braking pedals can be used to control velocity similar to controlling the speed of a vehicle. Velocity may also be controlled with the use of physical force-based devices, such as a force-feedback joystick. In these cases, velocity is a function of the amount of force applied. For more information on such techniques, see MacKenzie (1995).

An obvious advantage to the continuous control techniques is that the user can achieve his desired travel speed. However, with some implementations, such as the techniques based on relative positions, it can be difficult to sustain a specific speed.

Direct Input

Another method of allowing the user to specify velocity is through direct input. For example, the user can enter a numeric value using a keyboard or specify the velocity through a voice command. While direct input techniques like these allow the user to specify and sustain a desired velocity, they are often inconvenient and distract the user from other tasks.

Automated Velocity

The main drawback to allowing the user to control velocity is that it adds complexity to the interface. In cases where velocity control would be overly distracting to the user, a system-controlled velocity technique may be appropriate. For example, to allow both short, precise movements with a small velocity and larger movements with a high velocity, the system could automatically change the velocity depending on the amount of time the user had been moving. In such techniques, travel starts slowly and gradually gets faster until it reaches some maximum speed. The shape of the velocity curve and the maximum velocity might depend on the size of the environment, the need for precise travel, or other factors. Of course, this technique decreases the precision of longer movements. Another potential technique uses the concept of "slow-in, slow-out" from animation (Mackinlay et al. 1990a), meaning that travel begins slowly, gets faster, and then slows again as the destination comes near. This implies that the destination is known, so this can be fully automated only with a target-based travel technique (section 8.6.1).

8.8.3 Vertical Travel

Many of the techniques presented in this chapter are restricted to traveling within the horizontal plane (e.g., the walking metaphors and physical steering props). Some of the techniques afford traveling in vertical directions, such as the spatial steering metaphors, but this is often due to the ability to travel in all three dimensions, as opposed to only vertical movements. However, there have been a few techniques focused on vertical travel.

Slater, Usoh, and Steed (1994) used the walking-in-place technique and collisions with virtual ladders and stairs to provide vertical travel via climbing. The direction of climbing was determined by whether the user's feet collided with the bottom step of a ladder or staircase (climbing up) or with the top step (climbing down). While on a ladder or staircase, the user could reverse the climbing direction by physically turning around.

More recently, researchers have developed other techniques for climbing ladders. Takala and Matveinen (2014) created a technique based on reaching for and grabbing the rungs of a virtual ladder. Once a rung is grabbed, users can travel up or down by moving the grabbed rung in the opposite direction (e.g., moving the rung down to climb up). To provide a more realistic technique for climbing ladders, Lai et al. (2015) developed the march-and-reach technique, in which the user marches in place to virtually step on lower ladder rungs while reaching to virtually grab higher rungs. While users found the technique more realistic, it was more difficult to use than walking in place or Takala's technique of reaching and grabbing.

8.8.4 Semiautomated Travel

In certain applications, particularly in the areas of entertainment, storytelling, and education, the designer wants to give the user the feeling of control while at the same time moving the user toward an eventual goal and keeping her attention focused on important features of the environment. For example, in Disney's Aladdin attraction (Pausch et al. 1996), the user needs to feel as if she is controlling her magic carpet, but the experience must be limited to a certain amount of time, and every user needs to reach the end of the story. In such applications, semiautomated travel techniques are needed.

The basic concept of semiautomated travel is that the system provides general constraints and rules for the user's movement, and the user is allowed to control travel within those constraints. This idea is of course applicable to both immersive and desktop 3D UIs. A particular implementation of this concept is Galyean's river analogy (Galyean 1995). He used the metaphor of a boat traveling down a river. The boat continues to move with the current whether the user is actively steering or not, but the user can affect the movement by using the rudder. In particular, he designed an application in which the designer defined a path through the environment (the river). The user was "attached" to this path by a spring and could move off the path by some amount by looking in that direction (Figure 8.18).

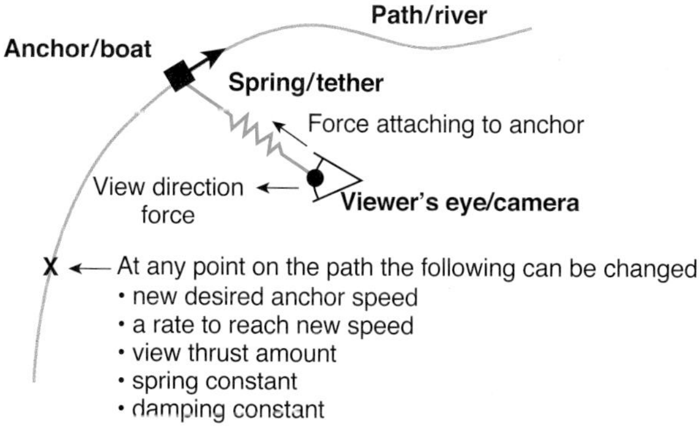

Figure 8.18 Galyean's (1995) guided navigation technique. (© 1995 ACM; reprinted by permission)

8.8.5 Scaling the World

In section 8.4.1, we noted that the most natural and intuitive method for traveling in a 3D virtual world is real walking, but real walking is limited by the tracking range or physical space. One way to alleviate this problem is to allow the user to change the scale of the world so that a physical step of one meter can represent one nanometer, one kilometer, or any other distance. This allows the available tracking range and physical space to represent a space of any size.

There are several challenges when designing a technique for scaling the world and traveling. One is that the user needs to understand the scale of the world so that he can determine how far to move and can understand the visual feedback he gets when he moves. Use of a virtual body (hands, feet, legs, etc.) with a fixed scale is one way to help the user understand the relative scale of the environment. Another issue is that continual scaling and rescaling may hasten the onset of cybersickness or discomfort (Bowman, Johnson et al. 2001). In addition, scaling the world down so that a movement in the physical space corresponds to a much larger movement in the virtual space will make the user's movements much less precise.

There are two common approaches to designing scaling-and-traveling techniques:

- active scaling
- automated scaling

Active Scaling

The most common approach to scaling and traveling is to allow the user to actively control the scale of the world. Several research projects and applications have used this concept. One of the earliest was the 3DM immersive modeler (Butterworth et al. 1992), which allowed the user to "grow" and "shrink" to change the relative scale of the world. The SmartScene application (Mapes and Moshell 1995) also allowed the user to control the scale of the environment in order to allow rapid travel and manipulation of objects of various sizes. The interface for changing the environment's scale was simple—users wore Pinch Gloves (see Figure 6.23), made a simple pinch gesture, and either brought the hands together to signify scaling the world down or moved the hands apart to scale the world up. The scaled-world grab technique (Mine, Brooks, and Séquin 1997) scales the user in an imperceptible way when an object is selected (Figure 8.19). The user sees the same scene (disregarding stereo) before and after the selection, although the world has actually been scaled. Although this technique is meant for object manipulation, the scaling also allows the user to travel larger distances using physical movements.

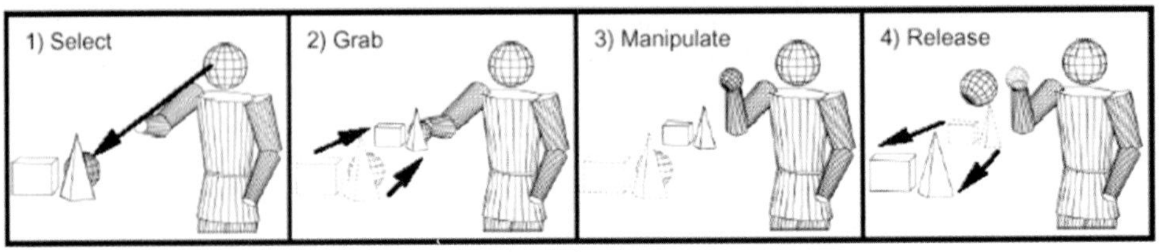

Figure 8.19 Scaling in the scaled-world grab technique. (Mine et al. 1997, © 1997 ACM; reprinted by permission)

Automated Scaling

While active scaling allows the user to specify the scale of the world, it requires additional interface components or interactions to do so. Alternatively, 3D UIs can be designed to have the system change the scale of the world based on the user's current task or position. This automated approach affords scaling and traveling without requiring the user to specify the scale. An example of automated scaling is the multiscale virtual environment (MSVE) interface developed by Kopper et al. (2006). Each MSVE contains a hierarchy of objects, with smaller objects nested within larger objects. As the user travels from a larger object to a smaller object, the system detects that the user is within the smaller object's volume and scales the world up. For example, a medical student learning human anatomy could travel from outside the body and into an organ. During this travel, the system detects the travel and scales the world up to make the organ the same size as the medical student. Alternatively, when the student travels from the organ to outside the body, the system scales the world back down.

MSVEs allow the user to concentrate on traveling instead of scaling while still gaining the benefits of having the world scaled up or down. However, such VEs require careful design, as the hierarchy of objects and scales need to be intuitive and usable for the user.

8.8.6 Travel Modes

Most of the travel techniques discussed in this chapter use a single mode for travel. However, some techniques require additional modes to transition among different travel methods. For example, many 3D desktop applications require several travel modes, since the user can control only two or three of the camera's six DOF with a standard mouse and keyboard. When providing a number of travel modes like this, it is important that the modes are well integrated to allow easy transition from one to another. At the same time, travel modes must be clearly distinguished to avoid the user moving the camera in unintentional DOF.

An early novel approach to transitioning among travel modes was Zeleznik and Forsberg's (1999) UniCam, a 2D camera-control mechanism (Figure 8.20) originally derived from the SKETCH camera-control metaphor (Zeleznik et al. 1996). In UniCam, the user controls travel through the 3D scene by making 2D gestural commands, using a mouse or stylus with a button, to manipulate the virtual camera. To facilitate camera translation and orbiting, the viewing window is broken up into two regions, a rectangular center region and a rectangular border region. If the user clicks within the border region, a virtual sphere rotation technique is used to orbit the viewer about the center of the screen. If the user clicks within the center region and drags the pointer along a horizontal trajectory, image-plane translation is invoked. If the user drags the pointer along a vertical trajectory, the camera zooms in or out. The user can also invoke orbital viewing about a focus point by making a quick click to define a dot and then clicking again elsewhere.

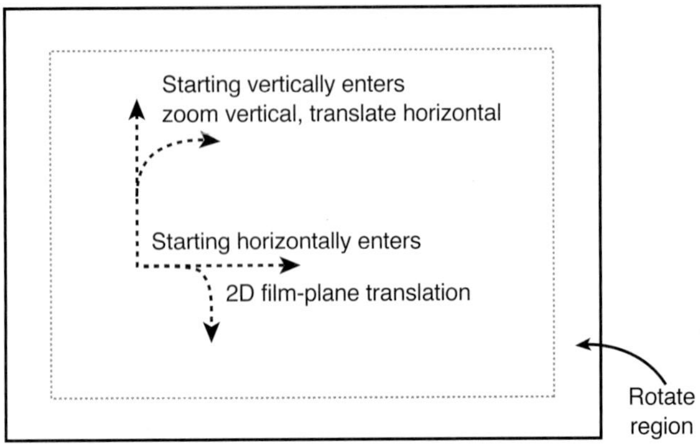

Figure 8.20 Gesture-based controls for camera translation and rotation. (Zeleznik and Forsberg 1999; © 1999 ACM; reprinted by permission)

A similar but more recent approach to integrating travel modes is the Navidget travel widget (Hachet et al. 2008). With the Navidget technique, the user can first zoom in by encircling, with a pointer or stylus, the area to keep within the camera's field of view. If the user holds the input button after sketching a circle, instead of zooming, a virtual sphere appears to provide orbital viewing. Upon release of the input button, the camera moves to the final viewing position. Four additional widgets are attached to the virtual sphere and can manipulate the size of the sphere, which in turn controls the viewing distance that the camera is placed at. Finally, an outer region allows the user to orbit between the front and back of the virtual sphere by moving into the region and then back into the sphere.

8.8.7 Multiple Cameras

While most of the techniques described in this chapter rely on a single (usually virtual) camera, some travel techniques have been designed to specifically incorporate different perspectives of multiple cameras. An early example of such a technique is the through-the-lens metaphor developed by Stoev and Schmalstieg (2002). This metaphor provides two different viewpoints that can be used to simultaneously explore the virtual world. The primary viewpoint is a standard immersive view of the world surrounding the user. The secondary viewpoint is a sort of magic lens (Bier et al. 1993) that is seen within the surrounding world but displays a different perspective of the world, as if positioned elsewhere or viewing the same world in an alternate dimension. Kiyokawa and Takemura (2005) expanded upon the through-the-lens metaphor by adding the capability to create an arbitrary number of viewing windows with their tunnel-window technique.

Multi-camera techniques have also been used with AR. Veas and colleagues (2010) investigated techniques for observing video feeds from multiple cameras within an outdoor environment. They developed three techniques for transitioning to remote camera feeds with visible viewpoints of the same scene—the mosaic, the tunnel, and the transitional techniques. The mosaic and tunnel techniques provide egocentric transitions to the remote camera while the transitional technique provides an exocentric transition. Veas et al. (2012) later developed a multiview AR system by combining different views of remote cameras, views generated by other users' devices, a view of 2D optical sensors, cameras on unmanned aerial vehicles, and predefined virtual views—more on these techniques can be found in the mobile AR case study below (section 8.11.2).

In a different multi-camera approach, Sukan et al. (2012) stored snapshots of augmented scenes that could later be virtually visited without physically returning to their relative locations. Along with still images of the real world, the researchers also stored the position of the camera. This allowed for virtual augmentations and objects to be dynamically updated when the snapshots were virtually viewed later. This approach enabled users to quickly switch between viewpoints of the current scene.

8.8.8 Nonphysical Input

All of the techniques discussed in this chapter require some form of physical input, whether physically walking within a tracked space or using a mouse for orbital viewing. However, not all travel techniques require physical (motor) input. Researchers have recently begun investigating brain–computer interfaces (BCIs) for navigating VEs. In an early study, Pfurtscheller et al. (2006) used an electroencephalogram (EEG) device to determine when the user was thinking about walking forward, and in turn, moved the user's view down a virtual street. More recently, Larrue et al. (2012) used an EEG device to provide the ability to turn left or right by thinking, in addition to walking forward by thought. While BCI techniques can be used to enable travel without physical actions, these techniques currently require a great deal of time to train the BCI system. Generically trained signal-processing algorithms can be used to reduce this time, but these algorithms can be unresponsive and induce false positives.

8.9 Wayfinding in 3D Environments

We now turn to the cognitive aspect of navigation—wayfinding. In general, the effectiveness of wayfinding depends on the number and quality of wayfinding **cues** or **aids** provided to users. The following sections on user-centered and environment-centered wayfinding cues will present a number of different wayfinding aids. These sections will address wayfinding in practice, such as how to include cues, when to include cues, and how the design of the VE affects wayfinding. See Golledge (1999) for a discussion of the theoretical foundations of wayfinding.

8.9.1 User-Centered Wayfinding Cues

User-centered wayfinding cues make use of the characteristics of human perception and can draw upon multiple human senses. Thus, most user-centered support is display-oriented. Because output devices still cannot deliver information that fully matches the capabilities of the human perceptual system (see Chapter 3, "Human Factors Fundamentals"), they can have a negative impact on wayfinding. However, there are certain strategies that developers can use to lessen these negative effects. In this section, we discuss various user-centered wayfinding cues:

- field of view
- motion cues
- multisensory output
- presence
- search strategies

Field of View

A small **field of view** (**FOV**) may inhibit wayfinding. Because a smaller portion of the VE is visible at any given time, the user requires repetitive head movements to comprehend the spatial information obtained from the viewpoint. Using a larger FOV reduces the amount of head movement and allows the user to understand spatial relationships more easily. Some studies, such as Péruch et al. (1997) and Ruddle et al. (1998), do not fully support these claims, showing little difference in the orientation capabilities of a user between several small FOVs (40, 60, and 80 degrees, or in desktop environments). However, they have demonstrated the usefulness of larger FOVs when environments become more detailed and complex. Furthermore, wide FOVs closer to the FOV of the human visual system (like those in some surround-screen displays) were not considered in these studies.

Another negative side effect of a small FOV is the lack of optical-flow fields in users' peripheral vision. Peripheral vision provides strong motion cues, delivering information about the user's direction, velocity, and orientation during movement. In addition, it has been shown that small FOVs may lead to cybersickness (Stanney et al. 1998).

Motion Cues

Supplying **motion cues** enables the user to judge both the depth and direction of movement and provides the information necessary for dead reckoning (backtracking of the user's own movement). Motion cues can be obtained from peripheral vision, as discussed above, but motion cues are not purely visual—it is important to supply the user with additional vestibular (inertia and balance) cues if possible. These cues generally fall in the category of embodied self-motion cues (Riecke et al. 2012). A lack of vestibular cues causes an intersensory conflict between visual and physical information. This may cause cybersickness and can affect judgments of egomotion, thus negatively impacting the formation of the cognitive map.

The effect of vestibular cues on the orientation abilities of users in VEs has been the subject of a range of studies. Usoh et al. (1999) compared real walking (section 8.4.1) against walking in place (section 8.4.2) and hand-directed steering (section 8.5.1). The two walking metaphors, which included physical motions, were found to be better than the steering technique, which only included virtual motions. Other studies of virtual and physical travel have shown positive effects of real motion on spatial orientation (Klatzky et al. 1998; Chance et al. 1998).

Our understanding of the proper balance between visual and vestibular input is still being formed. Harris et al. (1999) performed tests matching visual and vestibular input and concluded that developers should support vestibular inputs corresponding to at least one-quarter of the amount of visual motion. However, statically tilting the user's body has been shown to have a positive effect on self-motion perception in some cases. In a small study, Nakamura and Shimojo (1998) found that vertical self-motion increases as the user is tilted further back in a chair. In a more recent study, Kruijff et al. (2015) found that statically leaning forward increased perceived distances traveled, likely due to an increase in perceived speed of self-motion. Additionally, Kruijff et al. (2016) found that dynamically leaning enhanced self-motion sensations.

Multisensory Output

In addition to the visual and vestibular systems, developers might want to experiment with **multisensory output** (i.e., adding auditory, tactile, or other multimodal stimuli) to deliver wayfinding cues. Audio can provide the user with useful directional and distance information (Davis et al. 1999). For example, the sound of trains can indicate the direction to the station, whereas the volume allows the user to estimate the distance to the station. Audio for wayfinding support is still a largely open question. Another form of multisensory support is the tactile map—a map whose contours are raised so they can be sensed by touch as well as sight. Initial experiments used tactile maps to fill in gaps in the spatial knowledge of visually impaired people. The tactile map was used as an additional cue, not as a substitute for another cue type (Jacobson 1996). Tan et al. (2002) showed that tactile cues can aid in the formation and usage of spatial memory, so tactile wayfinding aids are another area of great potential.

Presence

The sense of **presence** (the feeling of "being there") is a much-explored but still not well-understood phenomenon that is assumed to have an impact on spatial knowledge. Briefly, the idea is that if the user feels more present in a virtual world, then real-world wayfinding cues will be more effective. Many factors influence the sense of presence, including sensory immersion, proprioception, and the tendency of the user to become immersed. For example, in the study conducted by Usoh et al. (1999), real walking increased the sense of presence considerably compared to walking in place. The inclusion of a **virtual body**—the user's own virtual representation may also enhance the sense of presence, which in turn has a positive effect on spatial knowledge acquisition and usage (Draper 1995; Usoh et al. 1999). See Chapter 11, "Evaluation of 3D User Interfaces," for more discussion of presence.

Search Strategies

A final user-centered wayfinding technique is to teach the user to employ an effective **search strategy**. Using a search strategy often depends on user skill. More skilled users, such as professional aviators, use different strategies than users with limited navigation experience. Not only do skilled users depend on other kinds of spatial knowledge and therefore on other cues in the environment, but they often use different search patterns as well. Whereas novice users depend largely on landmarks, skilled users make use of cues like paths (e.g., a coastline).

Using a search strategy inspired by navigation experts can increase its effectiveness. For example, search patterns such as those used during aviation search-and-rescue missions may aid a user during wayfinding (Wiseman 1995). The basic line search follows a pattern of parallel lines. The pattern search starts at a specific central point and moves further away from it, using quadratic or radial patterns. The contour search is designed to follow contours in a landscape, like a river or a mountain. Finally, the fan search starts from a center point and fans out in all directions until the target is found. Of course, the use of these search strategies is dependent on the content of the environment—they might work well in a large outdoor environment but would not make sense in a virtual building.

Another important search strategy is to obtain a bird's-eye view of the environment rather than performing all navigation on the ground. Users can be trained to employ this strategy quite easily, and it results in significantly better spatial orientation (Bowman et al. 1999). This can even be automated for the user. In the "pop-up" technique (Darken and Goerger 1999), users can press a button to temporarily move to a significant height above the ground, and then press the button again to go back to their original location on the ground.

We assume that novice users can learn search techniques, even if the described pattern search strategies are seen primarily in expert navigators. Placing a rectangular or radial grid directly in the environment provides a visual path along which users can search. Although these grids may supply directional and depth cues, they do not force users to employ a good search strategy.

8.9.2 Environment-Centered Wayfinding Cues

Environment-centered wayfinding cues refer to the conscious design of the virtual world to support wayfinding. Beyond the technology and training support described above, most wayfinding aids for virtual worlds can be directly related to aids from the real world. These range from natural environmental cues, like a high mountain, to artificial cues, such as a map. In this section, we discuss several environment-centered wayfinding cues:

- environment legibility
- landmarks
- maps
- compasses
- signs
- trails
- reference objects

Environment Legibility

Just as urban planners design cities in the real world to be navigable, virtual worlds can be designed to support wayfinding. In his book, Lynch (1960) describes several **legibility techniques** that serve as principles for urban design. These techniques allow the user to quickly obtain an understanding of an environment by understanding its basic structural elements.

Lynch identified five basic building blocks that can be applied to design a legible environment: paths, edges, districts, nodes, and landmarks. **Paths** are elements or channels for linear movement, like streets or railways. People often view a city from the perspective of such paths. **Edges** are related to paths, but are focused on bordering spaces rather than on movement. These edges can be natural, like a river, or artificial, like a walled structure. **Districts** are areas that are uniquely identifiable because of their style (e.g., type of buildings), color, or lighting. **Nodes** are gathering points, such as a major intersection of streets, or the entrance to a certain district. Finally, **landmarks** are static objects that are easily distinguished and often placed near a node (Darken and Sibert 1996). Landmarks are crucial enough to wayfinding that we discuss them in further detail below.

Landmarks

Landmarks are easily distinguishable objects that can be used to maintain spatial orientation, develop landmark and route knowledge, and serve as foundations for distance and direction estimation. Although landmarks are naturally part of a legible environment design, artificial landmarks may be added to any environment to support wayfinding. When a landmark is being placed, it is important that the landmark can be easily spotted, such as on a street corner, as opposed to placing it within a city block. It is also important to consider whether the landmark will serve as a global or local landmark. Global landmarks are visible from practically any location, so they provide directional cues. Local landmarks help users in the decision-making process by providing useful information when a decision point is reached (Steck and Mallot 2000). Finally, users should be able to distinguish a landmark from other surrounding objects within the environment. This can be accomplished by altering its visual characteristics, such as using a different color, texture, light, shape, or size.

Maps

One of the most common wayfinding aids is the **map**. Although simple in concept, the design of maps for wayfinding in 3D UIs is surprisingly complex. First, the designer should realize that the map can be dynamic because it is virtual. This means that you-are-here markers can be continuously displayed. The map can be updated if the environment changes. Paths to the next destination can be overlaid on the map (or the world itself). The map can even be rotated to face the direction the user is facing or zoomed to show only the local area.

With all this added flexibility come some difficult design choices, as clutter and confusion should be avoided. In general, it is recommended to use you-are-here markers and to show an up-to-date version of the environment on the map. However, designers should be careful about automatically rotating or zooming the map, as this can cause confusion, depending on the user's task, or even inhibit the formation of survey knowledge (Darken and Cevik 1999).

Another design choice is where and when to display the map. On small AR or VR displays, a legible map may take up a large percentage of the display area. At the least, a mechanism to display or hide the map should be provided. One effective technique is to attach the virtual map to the user's hand or a handheld tool, so that the map can be viewed or put away with natural hand motions. Figure 8.21 illustrates a map attached to the user's hand in this way. Unlike most maps, this map is not a spatial representation of the 3D environment, but rather a hierarchical representation showing objects at different levels of scale (Bacim et al. 2009).

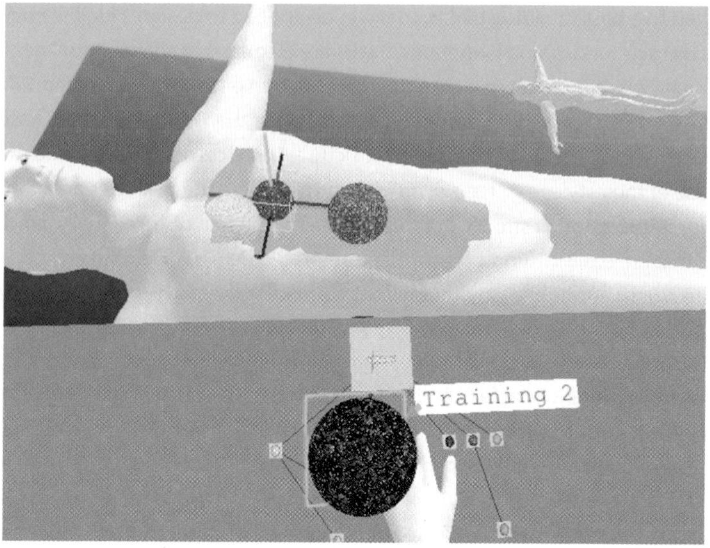

Figure 8.21 A hierarchical map used as a wayfinding aid in a multiscale 3D environment. (Image courtesy of Felipe Bacim)

Compasses

A **compass** primarily serves to provide directional cues. For a trained navigator, a compass in combination with a map is an invaluable wayfinding tool. However, most users of 3D UIs will not be familiar with effective methods for using compass information. As a VE wayfinding aid, compasses are typically found in navigation training tools, such as those used in the military.

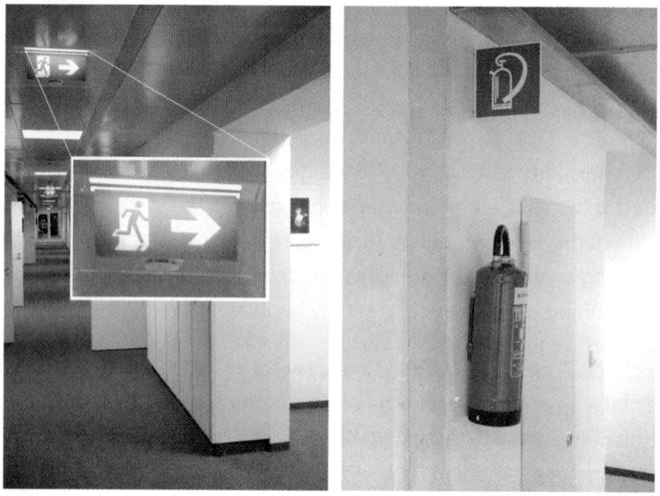

Figure 8.22 Examples of signs (left) and local landmarks (right) from the real world. (Photograph courtesy of Ernst Kruijff)

Signs

Signs are used extensively in real-world environments to provide spatial knowledge and directions (Figure 8.22), but surprisingly there is little research on the use of signs as a wayfinding cue in VEs. Signs can be extremely effective because of their directness, but signs can also become confusing in complex environments (think about badly designed airports). Signs should be placed in an easily observable location, should supply clear directions, and should be spaced far enough apart that multiple signs do not confuse the user.

Trails

In order to help the user "retrace his steps" in an environment or to show which parts of the world have been visited, **trails** can be included as an artificial wayfinding aid. A trail can be made up of a simple line or by using markers that include directional information, just like footprints in the real world. A trail can be placed directly into the environment but can also be shown on a map (Darken and Peterson 2002; Grammenos et al. 2002).

Reference Objects

Reference objects are objects that have a well-known size, such as a chair or a human figure, and aid in size and distance estimation. Users often have difficulty judging distances in large, mostly empty environments, and VR systems have well-known deficiencies in distance perception (Renner et al. 2013). Distances are highly under or overestimated. When reference objects are placed in such a space, estimation of sizes and distances becomes easier.

8.9.3 Combining Travel and Wayfinding Techniques

Since travel and wayfinding are intimately linked, techniques for these two tasks should be integrated if possible. In some cases, hardware can provide this directly. For example, a treadmill couples a method of travel with a vestibular feedback component. Other techniques have inherent proprioceptive cues. Gaze-directed steering, for example, supplies directional information via head-centric cues. Wayfinding aids may actually be part of the travel technique. For example, the World-in-Miniature technique combines a 3D map with a route-planning travel metaphor (section 8.7.1). Finally, wayfinding aids can be placed in the environment near the focus of the user's attention during travel. For example, a small compass can be attached to the (real or virtual) tip of a stylus when the pointing technique (section 8.5.1) is used.

8.10 Design Guidelines

This chapter has provided a large number of potential techniques for travel in 3D environments. One reason there are so many techniques for this and other 3D interaction tasks is that no single technique is best for all applications and situations. Therefore, as in the other chapters in Part IV, we present some general guidelines to help the designer choose an appropriate travel technique for a given application.

Tip

Match the travel technique to the application.

The authors are of the opinion that no set of 3D interaction techniques is perfect for all applications. Designers must carefully consider the travel tasks that will be performed in the application (section 8.2), what performance is required for travel tasks, in what environment travel will take place, and who will be using the application.

Example: A visualization of a molecular structure uses an exocentric point of view and has a single object as its focus. Therefore, an object-inspection technique such as orbital viewing is appropriate.

Tip

Consider both natural and magic techniques.

Many designers start with the assumption that the 3D interface should be as natural as possible. This may be true for certain applications that require high levels of realism, such as military training, but many other applications have no such requirement. Nonisomorphic "magic" travel techniques may prove much more efficient and usable.

Example: The task of furniture layout for an interior design application requires multiple viewpoints but not natural travel. A magic technique such as scaled-world grab (section 8.8.5) will be efficient and will also integrate well with the object manipulation task.

Tip

Use an appropriate combination of travel technique, display devices, and input devices.

The travel technique cannot be chosen separately from the hardware used in the system.

Example: If a personal surround-screen display is used, a vehicle-steering metaphor for travel fits the physical characteristics of this display. If a pointing technique is chosen, then an input device with clear shape and tactile orientation cues, such as a stylus, should be used instead of a symmetric device, such as a ball.

Tip

Choose travel techniques that can be easily integrated with other interaction techniques in the application.

Similarly, the travel technique cannot be isolated from the rest of the 3D interface. The travel technique chosen for an application must integrate well with techniques for selection, manipulation, and system control.

Example: A travel technique involving manipulation of a user representation on a 2D map suggests that virtual objects could be manipulated in the same way, providing consistency in the interface.

Tip

Provide multiple travel techniques to support different travel tasks in the same application.

Many applications include a range of travel tasks. It is tempting to design one complex technique that meets the requirements for all these tasks, but including multiple simple travel techniques is often less confusing to the user. Some VR applications already do this implicitly, because the user can physically walk in a small local area but must use a virtual travel technique to move longer distances. It will also be appropriate in some cases to include both steering and target-based techniques in the same application. We should note, however, that users will not automatically know which technique to use in a given situation, so some small amount of user training may be required.

Example: An immersive design application in which the user verifies and modifies the design of a large building requires both large-scale search and small-scale maneuvering. A target-based technique to move the user quickly to different floors of the building plus a low-speed steering technique for maneuvering might be appropriate.

Tip

Make simple travel tasks easier by using target-based techniques for goal-oriented travel and steering techniques for exploration and search.

If the user's goal for travel is not complex, then the travel technique providing the solution to that goal should not be complex either. If most travel in the environment is from one object or well-known location to another, then a target-based travel technique is most appropriate. If the goal is exploration or search, a steering technique makes sense.

Example: In a virtual tour of a historical environment, the important areas are well known, and exploration is not required, so a target-based technique such as choosing a location from a menu would be appropriate. In a visualization of weather patterns, the interesting views are unknown, so exploration should be supported with a steering technique such as pointing.

> **Tip**
>
> Use a physical locomotion technique if user exertion or naturalism is required.

Walking or redirected walking require large tracked areas, and physical locomotion devices can have serious usability issues. However, for some applications, especially training, where the physical motion and exertion of the user is an integral part of the task, such a device is required. First, however, consider whether your application might make do with something simpler, like walking in place.

Example: A sports training application will be effective only if the user physically exerts himself, so a locomotion device should be used.

> **Tip**
>
> The most common travel tasks should require a minimum amount of effort from the user.

Depending on the application, environment, and user goals, particular types of travel are likely to be common in a specific system, while others will only be used infrequently. The default navigation mode or controls should focus on the most common tasks.

Example: In a desktop 3D game in an indoor environment, most travel will be parallel to the floor, and users very rarely need to roll the camera. Therefore, a navigation technique that uses left and right mouse movement for camera yaw, up and down movement for camera pitch, and arrow keys to move the viewpoint forward, backward, left, and right would be appropriate for this application.

> **Tip**
>
> Use high-speed transitional motions, not instant teleportation, if overall environment context is important.

Simply providing a smooth path from one location to another will increase the user's spatial knowledge and keep her oriented to the environment (Bowman et al. 1997). The movement can be at high speed to help avoid cybersickness. This approach complements the use of wayfinding aids. Teleportation should only be used in cases where knowledge of the surrounding environment is not important.

Example: Unstructured environments, such as undeveloped terrain or information visualizations, can be quite confusing. Give users spatial context by animating their target-based travel with a brief, high-speed motion.

Tip

Train users in sophisticated strategies to help them acquire survey knowledge.

If spatial orientation is especially important in an application, there are some simple strategies that will help users obtain spatial knowledge (Bowman, Davis et al. 1999). These include flying up to get a bird's-eye view of the environment, traversing the environment in a structured fashion (see section 8.9.1), retracing paths to see the same part of the environment from the opposite perspective, and stopping to look around during travel. Users can easily be trained to perform these strategies in unfamiliar environments.

Example: Training soldiers on a virtual mockup of an actual battlefield location should result in increased spatial knowledge of that location. If the soldiers are trained to use specific spatial orientation strategies, their spatial knowledge in the physical location should improve.

Tip

If a map is used, provide a you-are-here marker.

You-are-here (YAH) maps combine a map with a YAH-marker. Such a marker helps the user to gain spatial awareness by providing her viewpoint position and/or orientation dynamically on the map. This means that the marker needs to be continuously updated to help the user match her egocentric viewpoint with the exocentric one of the map.

8.11 Case Studies

In this section, we discuss the design of the travel techniques and navigation interfaces for our two case studies. For background on the case studies, see Chapter 2, section 2.4.

8.11.1 VR Gaming Case Study

Navigation in our VR game is simultaneously the simplest and most complicated interaction to design. We want the primary navigation technique to be real walking, to give the user a heightened sense of presence in the world of the game. Of course, the tricky part is giving users the impression of a vast virtual space, when in reality, they may only have access to a small tracked physical play area. In addition, we don't want users to constantly be reminded that they are having to avoid the physical boundaries of the space, since that would distract them from being engaged with the story.

The most common solutions to this problem are less than satisfactory. Walking in place is simply not realistic or controllable enough for the game we envision. Redirected walking isn't possible in tracked areas the size of most people's living rooms. Applying a scale factor to walking so that the physical space maps directly to the virtual space doesn't make sense when the virtual space is so much larger (and when it contains multiple floors), and it's also difficult to use for fine-grained maneuvering tasks. Teleportation, while popular in many VR games, can be jarring and disorienting. Players have to plan for where to teleport so that they will be able to move away from a physical boundary (wall) once they arrive, which is cognitively demanding and reminds players of the real world, breaking presence. So the typical behavior with teleportation is to always stand in the center of the space and teleport every time you need to move even a little bit.

Let's break the problem down a bit. First, consider navigating within a single virtual room. Assume that the game requires a minimum play area of 2x2 meters but that virtual rooms can be bigger than that. To allow players to physically walk around the entire virtual room, we could use many of the travel techniques described in the chapter, all of which come with tradeoffs. In general, purely virtual techniques would cause users to become reliant on virtual travel, so that they rarely perform physical walking. Scaled walking techniques could work within a single room, but could lead to sickness and lack of control.

In the end, we decided on a modified form of teleportation that still encourages (actually, requires) physical walking. We will design our virtual rooms to be composed of multiple cells, with each cell being the size of the tracked play area. Obstacles on the floor (chasms, debris, etc.) will indicate that the user can't walk beyond the border of the cell. To get to a different cell, users will gaze at a special object in the cell and perform some trigger action (a gesture or button press) that will cause a rapid movement to that cell.

The key is that the movement will start at the current location in the current cell and end at the *corresponding location* in the target cell. In this way, the mapping of the physical play area to the cell boundaries is still correct, and users can reach the entire cell by physically walking around it. Since users don't get to choose the exact target location of the movement, they have to walk within the cell to get access to the virtual objects therein.

How does this technique fit into the story of the game? Many narratives are possible. For example, we could say that you have a bird as a companion, and when you raise your hand the bird comes and picks you up and takes you to the part of the room you're looking at. This would explain how you get past the barriers and also why you're not in complete control of where you end up.

So what about moving from room to room? Since doors will by definition be near the boundaries of the physical space, moving through a virtual door will put players in a position where they can't move any further into the new room without running into the wall. Again, we could use teleportation to move from the center of one room to the center of an adjoining room, but we think a more creative solution that could actually enhance the story is possible.

Imagine that all the doors in our fictional hotel have been sealed shut by the bad guys. But the designers of the hotel, envisioning just such a scenario, included some secret passages that we can use. These take the form of those fake bookshelves you've seen in dozens of bad spy flicks, where pressing a hidden lever causes the bookcase to spin around into the room on the other side of the wall. So to go through a wall, players have to stand on a semicircular platform next to the bookshelf and activate it somehow. Then the bookshelf and platform rotates them into the room on the other side. In this way, the user-room relationship is correct, and the user can physically walk back into the play area (Figure 8.23). This should also be fun and engaging. Sound effects will also help.

Figure 8.23 Rotating the virtual game environment relative to the physical tracking space, illustrated by the blue volume, using the bookshelf metaphor. (Image courtesy of Ryan P. McMahan)

When using the rotating bookshelf technique, we want to avoid making the user feel sick due to visual-vestibular mismatch. We suggest providing a clear view not only of the current room but also the room behind the bookshelf. For example, we could cut a couple of holes through the bookshelf so users can see the room beyond before they activate the technique. If the user knows where she's about to go and sees the rotation through the holes (with the bookshelf as a fixed frame of reference), that should reduce feelings of sickness.

The last piece we have to consider is vertical navigation from one floor to the next. In a play area with only a flat floor, it would be very difficult to do believable stairs, although there are some interesting techniques for climbing virtual ladders (Lai et al. 2015; see section 8.8.3). In a hotel environment, however, virtual elevators are the obvious choice.

Like all of the designs we've presented in our case study, this is only one of many possible ways to interact effectively in our VR game. But it does provide some unique ways to navigate the large environment of this virtual hotel in a way that should seem natural and fluid, despite the challenges of a limited physical play area.

Key Concepts

The key concepts that we used for travel in the virtual reality gaming case study were:

- Natural physical movements for navigation can enhance the sense of presence.
- Even with a limited tracking area, consider ways to allow and encourage the use of a physical walking metaphor.
- If the application allows, use story elements to help users make sense of travel techniques.

8.11.2 Mobile AR Case Study

On-site exploration of environmental data implies that users may explore sites of different scales. In HYDROSYS, the scales varied widely, from small sites of a couple hundreds of meters to sites spanning several kilometers in length. While you can certainly walk across such sites, larger sites come with inherent issues that may limit the awareness and understanding of the available augmented data. For example, consider a site with changes in elevation: it is unlikely you can see the whole environment from a single perspective due to occlusion. Furthermore, the cameras used for handheld AR often narrow the view of the site.

We tried solving these limitations by developing a multiview camera navigation system. In other words, we deployed multiple cameras to allow users to take different viewpoints at the site, rather than limiting them to the view from their own physical location. The system included the cameras of the handheld units, but also a pan-tilt unit and several cameras mounted underneath a large blimp. Our system not only enabled the user to view the site from different perspectives to gain a better awareness, but also to share viewpoints with other users at the site, supporting collaborative work.

Implementing the right techniques to support multiview navigation encompasses both cognitive (wayfinding) and performance issues. To advance spatial awareness, we had to develop techniques that enhance overview possibilities and deal with occlusion issues, while conveying correct spatial relations (Veas et al. 2012). Users had to clearly understand the spatial features of the site to be able to interpret the augmented information correctly. We assumed that multiple camera viewpoints could provide a better overview of the site that could aid in creating a more accurate mental map of the environment. This principle is well known from the area of surveillance systems, but our system approach differs from such systems. In surveillance systems, the cameras are mostly static, while the observer is expected to have good knowledge of the site and the location of the cameras around the site. In contrast, the HYDROSYS setup also consisted of dynamic cameras and thus dynamic viewpoints, which may not easily be processed by the user, as she may not know the site, and the information displayed in a camera image might be difficult to match to the mental map.

Processing of the spatial information into the mental map is affected by discrepancies between the camera view and the user's own first-person view (Veas et al. 2010), including the camera position and orientation, and the visibility of objects and locations. Clearly, cameras that are not from or in the user's point of view and that are looking at another part of the scene are more difficult to process mentally. The key to an effective navigation technique is the approach used for traversing between the local and remote views. Such an approach might provide additional data such as maps or 3D models that convey the spatial configuration of a site, but that information might not always be readily available, or it might be difficult to match map/model data to ad hoc views.

In an initial evaluation (Veas et al. 2010), we showed that users prefer a technique that imposes lower workload if it allows them to perform reasonably well. Still, the evaluation also showed room for improvement in our initial techniques.

In the final system, we took a hybrid AR and 3D model exploration approach (Veas et al. 2012). Users could assess the locations of the different cameras by either looking through the lens of the selected camera or by switching to a 3D exploration mode. In the latter, the user could freely explore the underlying 3D model of the site at hand, similar to exploring Google Maps in 3D. This offers the advantages of resolving occlusion more easily and providing a good overview, since users do not need to stick to the available camera viewpoints. However, the 3D model has the disadvantage of being a static and potentially outdated model of the environment.

The interface showed the camera viewpoints (Figure 8.24) with regularly updated thumbnails of their video footage, and a mini-map could also be displayed. The user could switch to another camera's viewpoint by selecting it directly or in a menu.

We also experimented with a method called variable perspective. This mode is an AR visualization technique (Figure 8.25) developed to combine views from different perspectives in a single image. It seamlessly blends between two different cameras: the first-person point of view and a second camera that can be rotated to visually "flip" the scene at further distances. This effect is similar to a famous scene from the movie *Inception*, in which the world is bent towards the user. The environment simply "curls upwards" at the switch point between first- and third-person perspective, thus presenting a gradual transition between both viewpoints. If the third-person view comes from a bird's-eye view, this helps users see parts of the site that might be occluded from the first-person view.

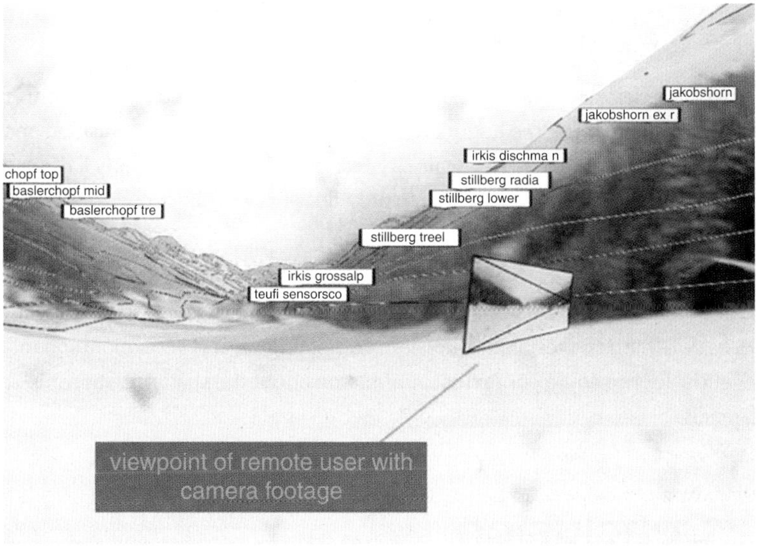

Figure 8.24 A viewpoint and corresponding video footage from a remote user is displayed in the 3D model. The user can travel to the remote viewpoint by clicking on the camera. (Image courtesy of Eduardo Veas and Ernst Kruijff)

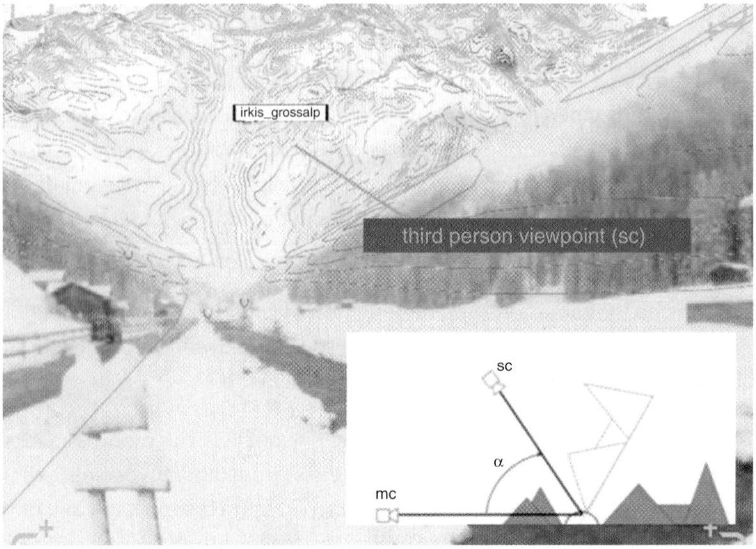

Figure 8.25 Variable perspective visualization. The first-person viewpoint (mc in the diagram) is shown on the bottom, and the remote viewpoint (sc) is shown on the top. The remote viewpoint can be moved and "flipped" to define the (exocentric) angle at which the distant parts of the site can be viewed. (Image courtesy of Eduardo Veas and Ernst Kruijff)

Key Concepts

The key lessons that we learned from the mobile AR case study for travel were:

- Situation awareness: creating a good mental map of the observed environment is crucial to adequately making use of the augmented information within. The acquisition and processing of spatial knowledge at larger-scale sites can be an issue, particularly if users have not visited the site before. The 3D UI needs to provide users with an overview, using techniques such as mini-maps and multi-camera setups.
- Multiview: the use of multi-camera systems can help by providing an overview and resolving occlusions. However, we need to carefully consider how users switch between viewpoints, as switching can result in confusion. Combining AR and 3D exploration modes can be beneficial for providing contextual information about the spatial relationships between the cameras.

8.12 Conclusion

In this chapter, we have discussed how both 3D travel techniques and wayfinding affect navigation in 3D UIs. We have presented four categories of travel metaphors, including walking, steering, selection-based travel, and manipulation-based travel. Within each of these categories, we have presented multiple techniques, each with its own approach to realizing its travel metaphor. We have also discussed several design aspects of travel techniques, including viewpoint orientation, velocity specification, vertical travel, semiautomated travel, scaling the world, travel modes, handling multiple cameras, and nonphysical input. We then discussed how wayfinding affects navigation in 3D environments, including user-centered and environment-centered wayfinding cues. Finally, we discussed several guidelines for designing navigation interfaces for 3D UIs and how those guidelines influenced our two case studies. The upcoming chapter concludes part IV with an in-depth treatment of system control in 3D UIs.

Recommended Reading

For an excellent overview of locomotion devices, we recommend the following:

Hollerbach, J. (2002). "Locomotion Interfaces." In K. Stanney (ed.), *Handbook of Virtual Environments: Design, Implementation, and Applications*, 239–254. Mahwah, NJ: Lawrence Erlbaum Associates.

Steinicke, F., Y. Visell, J. Campos, and A. Lécuyer (2013). *Human Walking in Virtual Environments: Perception, Technologies, and Applications*. New York: Springer.

An informative presentation on the implementation of travel techniques for desktop 3D interfaces can be found in this text:

Barrilleaux, J. (2000). *3D User Interfaces with Java 3D.* Greenwich, CT: Manning.

Readers interested in more details on the empirical performance of common travel techniques should take a look at the following:

Bowman, D., D. Johnson, and L. Hodges (2001). "Testbed Evaluation of VE Interaction Techniques." *Presence: Teleoperators and Virtual Environments* 10(1): 75–95.

For an introduction to the effects of sense of presence on wayfinding, we recommend reading:

Regenbrecht, H., T. Schubert, and F. Friedman (1998). "Measuring the Sense of Presence and Its Relations to Fear of Heights in Virtual Environments." *International Journal of Human-Computer Interaction* 10(3): 233–250.

Usoh, M., K. Arthur, M. Whitton, R. Bastos, A. Steed, M. Slater, and F. Brooks Jr. (1999). "Walking > Walking-in-Place > Flying in Virtual Environments." *Proceedings of SIGGRAPH '99*, 359–364.

For an example of a study on the effects of wayfinding in training transfer, we recommend reading:

Darken, R., and W. Banker (1998). "Navigating in Natural Environments: A Virtual Environment Training Transfer Study." *Proceedings of the 1998 IEEE Virtual Reality Annual International Symposium (VRAIS '98)*, 12–19.

CHAPTER 9

SYSTEM CONTROL

On a desktop computer, we input text and commands using 2D UI elements such as pull-down menus, pop-up menus, or toolbars on an everyday basis. These elements are examples of system control techniques—they enable us to send commands to an application, change a mode, or modify a parameter. While we often take the design of such techniques in 2D UIs for granted, system control and symbolic input are not trivial in 3D applications. Simply adapting 2D desktop based widgets is not the always the best solution. In this chapter, we discuss and compare various system control and symbolic input solutions for 3D UIs.

9.1 Introduction

The issuing of commands is a critical way to access any computer system's functionality. For example, with traditional desktop computers we may want to save a document or change from a brush tool to an eraser tool in a painting application. In order to perform such tasks, we use system control techniques like menus or function keys on a keyboard. Designers of desktop and touch-based system control interfaces have developed a plethora of widely used and well-understood graphical user interface (GUI) techniques, such as those used in the WIMP (Windows, Icons, Menus, Point and Click) metaphor (Preece et al. 2002). While quite a few techniques exist, designing a 3D UI to perform system control can be challenging. In this chapter, we will provide an overview of system control methods, and review their advantages and disadvantages.

Although much of the real work in a 3D application consists of interaction tasks like selection and manipulation, system control is critical because it is the glue that lets the user control the interaction flow between the other key tasks in an application. In many tasks, system control is intertwined with symbolic input, the input of characters and numbers. For example, users may need to enter a filename to save their work or specify a numeric parameter for a scaling command. In this chapter, we will focus on system control and symbolic input concurrently instead of handling these tasks separately.

To be sure, 2D and 3D applications differ with respect to symbolic input. For example, in writing this book with a word processor, the core activity is symbolic input, accomplished by typing on a keyboard. This activity is interspersed with many small system control tasks—saving the current document by clicking on a button, inserting a picture by choosing an item from a menu, or underlining a piece of text by using a keyboard shortcut, just to name a few. Yet, within most 3D applications the focus is the opposite: users only input text and numbers occasionally, and the text and numbers entered usually consist of short strings. While this may change in the future with more effective techniques, the current state of affairs is centered on limited symbolic input to support system control tasks.

We can define system control as the user task in which commands are issued to

1. request the system to perform a particular function,
2. change the mode of interaction, or
3. change the system state.

The key word in this definition is **command**. In selection, manipulation, and travel tasks, the user typically specifies not only *what* should be done, but also *how* it should be done, more or less directly controlling the action. In system control tasks, the user typically specifies only *what* should be done and leaves it up to the system to determine the details.

In this chapter we consider system control to be an explicit instead of an implicit action. Interfaces from other domains have used methods to observe user behavior to automatically adjust the mode of a system (e.g., Celentano and Pittarello 2004; Li and Hsu 2004), but we will not focus on this breed of interfaces.

In 2D interfaces, system control is supported by the use of a specific **interaction style**, such as pull-down menus, text-based command lines, or tool palettes (Preece et al. 2002). Many of these interaction styles have also been adapted to 3D UIs to provide for a range of system control elements (see section 9.4), which may be highly suitable for desktop-based 3D UIs. 2D methods may also be appropriate in handheld AR applications, where the application often also relies on screen-based (touch) input. But for immersive applications in particular, WIMP-style interaction may not always be effective. We cannot assume that simply transferring conventional interaction styles will lead to high usability.

In immersive VR, users have to deal with 6-DOF input as opposed to 2-DOF on the desktop. These differences create new problems but also new possibilities for system control. In 3D UIs it may be more appropriate to use nonconventional system control techniques (Bullinger et al. 1997). These system control methods may be combined with traditional 2D methods to form hybrid interaction techniques. We will talk about the potential and implications of merging 2D and 3D techniques at several stages throughout this chapter.

9.1.1 Chapter Roadmap

Before describing specific techniques, we will consider two categories of factors that influence the effectiveness of all techniques: human factors and system factors. We then present a classification of system control techniques for 3D UIs (section 9.3). Next, we describe each of the major categories in this classification (sections 9.4–9.8). In each of these sections, we describe representative techniques, discuss the relevant design and implementation issues, discuss specific symbolic input issues, and provide guidance on the practical application of the techniques. In section 9.9, we cover multimodal system control techniques, which combine multiple methods of input to improve usability and performance. We conclude the chapter, as usual, with general design guidelines and system control considerations in our two case studies.

9.2 System Control Issues

In this section, we discuss higher-level characteristics of the human and of the system that influence the design and user experience of system control interfaces.

9.2.1 Human Factors

3D UI designers have to deal with a number of **perception** issues that can limit the user experience of a system control interface. Issues include visibility, focus switching, and the choice of feedback modalities.

Visibility is probably the most prevalent issue in 3D applications. In both VR and AR, system control elements (such as menus or buttons) can occlude the content of the environment. Scaling down system control elements could be an option if supported by the screen resolution, but this may result in (further) reduction of legibility. Another approach is to use semitransparent system control elements. While this may make content more visible, it may come at the cost of reduced visibility and readability of the system control element itself. Visibility issues particularly effect graphical widgets (see section 9.5).

Focus switching occurs when a system control element is visually decoupled from the area where the main interaction is performed. For example, if you are using a tablet to display menus while modeling in an immersive environment, you will need to switch focus between the tablet screen and the object you are working on. The visual system may literally have to adjust its focus (accommodation) when using the separate displays. In addition, if system control actions occur frequently, this may interrupt the flow of action. And especially when multiple displays are used, the sequence of actions in a task may influence performance (Kruijff et al. 2003; McMahan 2007). Collocated menus (see section 9.5.1) are one way to avoid this sort of switching.

In a 2D desktop GUI, mode change feedback is often a combination of haptic, auditory, and visual events: the user presses the mouse or touchpad and may feel a click (haptic), hear a click generated by the input device or operating system (auditory), and observe how the appearance of, for example, a button may change (visual). While it may seem straightforward to port the same feedback to a 3D application, this is often not the case. Visual button press feedback may easily remain unnoticed, while auditory feedback may be drowned out by ambient noise. Multimodal feedback is often a good choice to deal with these issues; we will take a closer look at this type of interface in section 9.9.

The main **cognitive** issue in system control is the functional breadth and depth of the system. Depending on the complexity of an application, a varying number of options (functions) may be available. These options are likely structured in different categories (breadth). Each category may have several options that may be further structured in subcategories (depth). Complex functional structures may cause users to be cognitively challenged to understand which options are available and where they can be found, and designers should be careful to create understandable classifications of functions and to hide rarely used functionality.

Ergonomic issues in system control interfaces include control placement, and the pose, grip, and motion types a particular device is used with. Shape, size, and location of controls can highly affect system control. For example, the button to trigger a system control action may not be easily reachable while a device is held with a particular grip, and thus pressing the button may require regrasping the device in a grip that is not optimal for other tasks. This is often the case in handheld AR setups: holding the device for accessing system controls with the thumbs, for example, is not compatible with the grasp used for viewing the augmented scene.

Designers should investigate the relationship between different grips and the accessibility of buttons. For more information, refer to Veas and Kruijff (2008, 2010), as well as standard industrial reference guides (Cuffaro 2013).

The motion required to perform a specific system control action is another ergonomic issue. For example, for a 1-DOF menu (see section 9.4.1), we need to consider how a user can rotate his wrist, as well as the placement and size of the menu items that will lead to comfortable and efficient selection.

Finally, when multiple devices are used for system control and other actions, designers should consider how switching between devices is accomplished, where devices may get stored ("pick up and put away"), and how the tasks are matched to specific devices. For example, while using a tablet with a pen might improve the control of detailed menus within an immersive environment, the flow of action can be disrupted when users need to switch frequently between the tablet and, for example, a 3D mouse for other tasks.

9.2.2 System Factors

As we noted above, system control is often the glue that holds together the application. High-level characteristics of the system are important to consider when designing system control interfaces. System characteristics can even dictate specific choices for system control. The main issues are the visual display devices, the input devices, and ambient factors.

Visual displays will impose specific perceptual boundaries, such as resolution, size, and luminance, that will affect what system control methods may be used and how well they will perform. For example, more complex applications can force the use of a secondary screen (such as a tablet) for system control, as system control would otherwise clutter and occlude the main screen.

The choice of input devices defines the possibilities for control mappings. General-purpose devices such as a stylus or joystick may work with a number of system control techniques. In other cases, you may need to introduce a secondary device or physically extend the primary input device to provide controls that are well suited for system control methods. Extending an existing device or designing a completely new device is not trivial, but it is certainly possible because of the wide availability of DIY approaches (see Chapter 6, "3D User Interface Input Hardware," section 6.6).

Ambient system factors such as noise, device constraints (e.g., no tethered devices possible, nowhere to place additional devices), or the motion range of a user may also affect the design of system control techniques and system control task performance. For example, ambient noise may cause recognition errors in speech interfaces, and such errors can reduce user performance and perceived usability.

9.3 Classification

Although there is a broad diversity of system control techniques for 3D UIs, many draw upon a small number of basic types or their combination. Figure 9.1 presents a classification of techniques organized around the main interaction styles. This classification was influenced by the description of nonconventional control techniques in McMillan et al. (1997). There is a device-driven logic underneath most styles: often, available devices drive the selection of a specific system control technique. We use the classification as the organizing structure for the next five sections.

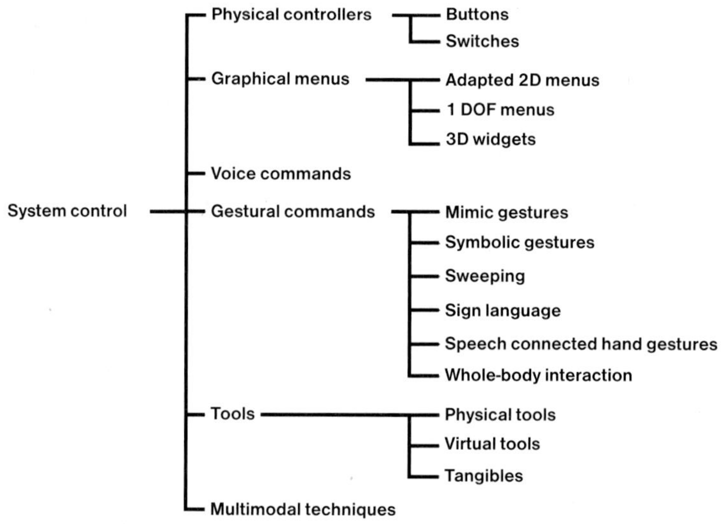

Figure 9.1 Classification of system control techniques.

As is the case in the other chapters on 3D interaction techniques, our classification is only one of many possibilities, and slightly different alternatives have been proposed (Lindeman et al. 1999; Dachselt and Hübner 2007).

9.4 Physical Controllers

Physical controllers such as buttons and switches offer a lightweight solution for performing system control, analogous to function keys in desktop systems.

9.4.1 Techniques

Buttons and switches are a direct way of changing a mode in an application. In contrast to using a pointing device to select, for example, an item from a menu, the physical controller allows the user to directly switch the mode between different states. Examples of well-known techniques are the function keys on a keyboard or buttons on a gaming device to which functions can be assigned. Gamers, for instance, often toggle between weapons in first-person shooters by pressing specific buttons.

9.4.2 Design and implementation issues

Buttons and switches can provide a useful and straightforward system control method; however, there are a number of issues that should be noted.

Placement and Form

When built-in controllers are used, you should carefully validate their placement and the potential need for regrasping a device to access the button, as discussed in section 9.2.1. While some devices are designed carefully from this perspective (e.g., Figure 9.2), other devices may have controllers placed at locations that are less accessible. Furthermore, devices such as tablets or phones often have very flat buttons that may be difficult to reach and control, making system control in handheld AR applications tricky to perform. Thus, it is not only the placement but also the physical form and quality (robustness) of buttons and switches that should be considered carefully.

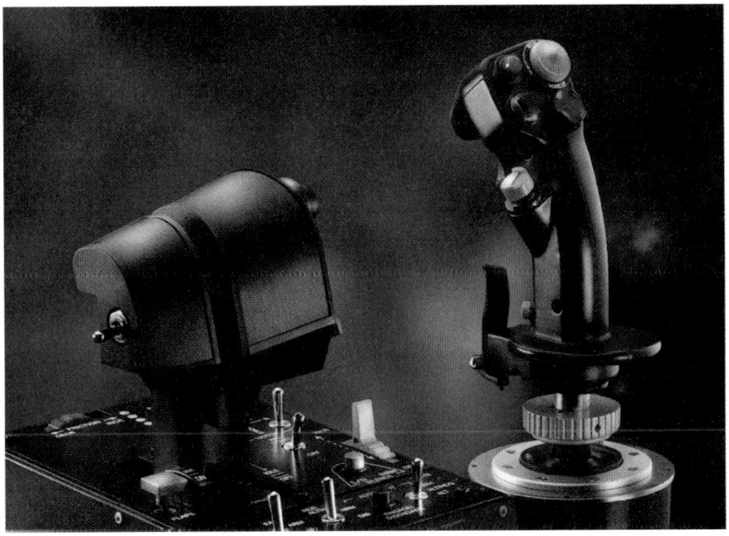

Figure 9.2 A Thrustmaster flight joystick deploying numerous switches and buttons. (© Guillemot Corporation S.A. All rights reserved. Thrustmaster® is a registered trademark of Guillemot Corporation S.A.)

These controllers are often used eyes-off: finding the right controller can be achieved using proprioceptive feedback but also through the feel of a button when different controllers are located close to each other. When designing new devices or extending existing devices, it is important to carefully evaluate different variants.

Representation and Structure

Buttons and switches are not connected to any menu-like structure. Rather, their structure is based on the placement of buttons and their interrelationship. Button locations on many devices are more often defined by accessibility (ergonomic placement) than by functional structure. This means that mode feedback changes should be clearly communicated to the user, possibly through multiple sensory modalities. It may also make sense to place a small label or pictogram on the button itself to indicate its usage, allowing the user to visually explore the functionality of the buttons before operation.

9.4.3 Practical Application

Buttons and switches are highly useful in a number of situations, in particular when users need to switch frequently between functions. These function keys can be lightweight, quick, and straightforward if users know where to find each button and what it does. However, they can be a burden too when mode change is not clearly communicated, buttons are badly positioned, or there is an unknown functional mapping. In applications that are used for short durations by inexperienced users, function keys may be very useful, but only with a small functional space. For example, for public systems in theme parks, a very limited number of buttons can be easily understood and matched to simple tasks in the system. If users have the time and motivation to learn more complicated sets of functions, this may come with a great increase in performance. Game interfaces are a great example: gamers with prolonged experience with specific button layouts can achieve incredible speeds in performing system control actions. Finally, physical controllers can also be used for symbolic input, as buttons can be directly assigned to certain letters or numbers.

9.5 Graphical Menus

Graphical menus for 3D UIs are the 3D equivalent of the 2D menus that have proven to be a successful system control technique in desktop UIs. Because of their success and familiarity to users, many developers have chosen to experiment with graphical menus for 3D UIs. However, the design of graphical menus for 3D UIs comes with some unique challenges.

9.5.1 Techniques

Graphical menus used in 3D UIs can be subdivided into three categories:

- adapted 2D menus
- 1-DOF menus
- 3D widgets

Adapted 2D Menus

Menus that are simple adaptations of their 2D counterparts have, for obvious reasons, been the most popular group of 3D system control techniques. Adapted 2D menus basically function in the same way as they do on the desktop. Some examples of adapted 2D menus are pull-down menus, pop-up menus, floating menus, and toolbars. These menus are a common choice for more complex sets of functions. Menus are well suited for providing good structure for larger numbers of functions, and most users are familiar with the underlying principles (interaction style) of controlling a menu. On the other hand, these menus can occlude the environment, and users may have trouble finding the menu or selecting items using a 3D selection technique.

Figure 9.3 shows an example of an adapted 2D menu used in a Virtual Museum application in a surround-screen display. It allows a user to plan an exhibition by finding and selecting images of artwork. The menu is semitransparent to reduce occlusion of the 3D environment. Another example can be seen in Figure 9.4, showing a pie menu in a virtual environment. Pie menus can often be combined with marking-menu techniques (see section 9.7; Gebhardt et al. 2010)

Figure 9.3 A floating menu in the Virtual Museum application. (Photograph courtesy of Gerhard Eckel, Fraunhofer IMK)

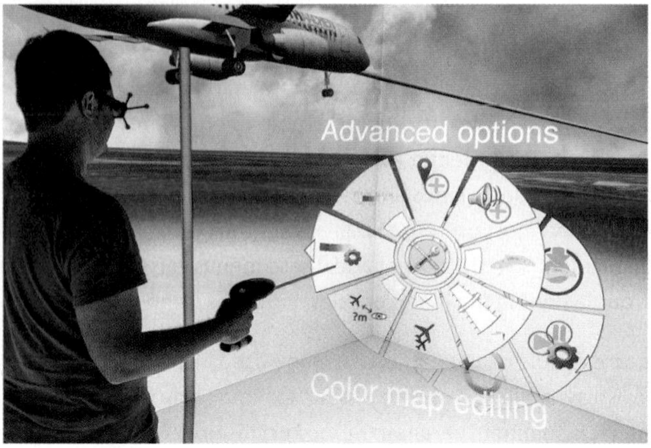

Figure 9.4 Pie menu in immersive virtual environment. (Photograph courtesy of Thorsten Kuhlen, Virtual Reality & Immersive Visualization Group, RWTH Aachen)

There are numerous ways of adapting 2D menus by tuning aspects such as placement or input technique. For example, one adaptation of 2D menus that has been successful in 3D UIs is to attach the menus to the user's head. This way, the menu is always accessible, no matter where the user is looking. On the other hand, head-coupled menus can occlude the environment and potentially reduce the sense of presence.

Another method is attaching a menu to the user's hand in a 3D UI, assigning menu items to different fingers. For example, Pinch Gloves (see Chapter 6, Figure 6.25), can be used to interpret a pinch between a finger and the thumb on the same hand as a menu selection. An example of a finger-driven menu in AR is depicted in Figure 9.5 (Piekarski and Thomas 2003). Using Pinch Gloves, a typical approach is to use the nondominant hand to select a menu and the dominant hand to select an item within the menu. However, in many applications there will be more options than simple finger mapping can handle. The TULIP (Three-Up, Labels In Palm) technique (Bowman and Wingrave 2001) was designed to address this problem by letting users access three menu items at a time and using the fourth finger to switch to a new set of three items.

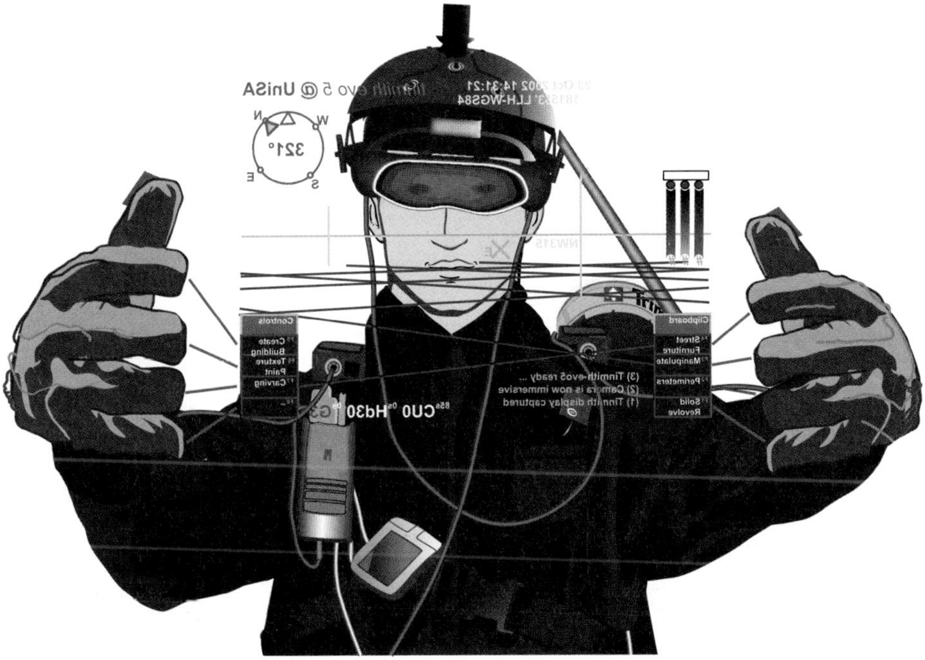

Figure 9.5 TINMITH menu using Pinch Gloves. (Adapted from Piekarski and Thomas 2003)

Another powerful technique is to attach the menu to a physical surface, which could be not just a phone or a tablet but also any other kind of surface. Figure 9.6 shows an example. These devices are often tracked. Finding the menu is then as easy as bringing the physical tablet into view. The physical surface of the tablet also helps the user to select the menu items, and the menu can easily be put away as well. However, the structure and flow of action may change considerably if the tablet is used for menus while a different input device is used for primary tasks.

Figure 9.6 Tablet control of interactive visualizations layered on top of surround-view imagery in the UCSB Allosphere. Photograph shows left-eye view of stereo content viewed and controlled by the user. (Image courtesy of Donghao Ren and Tobias Höllerer)

1-DOF Menus

Selection of an item from a menu is essentially a one-dimensional operation. This observation led to the development of **1-DOF menus.** A 1-DOF menu is often attached to the user's hand, with the menu items arranged in a circular pattern around it; this design led to the name **ring menu** (Liang and Green 1994; Shaw and Green 1994). With a ring menu, the user rotates his hand until the desired item falls within a "selection basket." Of course, the hand rotation or movement can also be mapped onto a linear menu, but a circular menu matches well with the mental expectation of rotation. The performance of a ring menu depends on the physical movement of the hand and wrist, and the primary axis of rotation should be carefully chosen.

Hand rotation is not the only possible way to select an item in a 1-DOF ring menu. The user could also rotate the desired item into position with the use of a button or buttons on the input device: a dial on a joystick is one example of how this could be achieved. Another method is using tangible tiles, such as those used in the tangible skin cube (Figure 9.7, Lee and Woo 2010). 1-DOF menus can also be used eyes-off by coupling the rotational motion of the wrist to an audio-based menu. These kinds of techniques have also been used in wearable devices (Kajastila and Lokki 2009; Brewster et al. 2003).

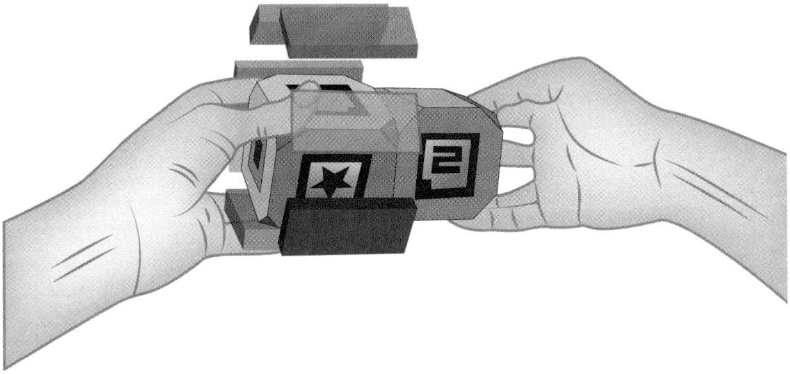

Figure 9.7 Ring menu implemented with tangible skin cubes. (Adapted from Lee and Woo 2010)

Handheld widgets are another type of 1-DOF menu that, instead of using rotation, use relative hand position (Mine et al. 1997). By moving the hands closer together or further apart, different items in the menu can be selected.

In general, 1-DOF menus are quite easy to use. Menu items can be selected quickly, as long as the number of items is relatively small and ergonomic constraints are considered. Because of the strong placement cue, 1-DOF menus also afford rapid access and use. The user does not have to find the menu if it is attached to his hand and does not have to switch his focus away from the area in which he is performing actions.

3D Widgets

The most exotic group of graphical menu techniques for system control is 3D widgets. They take advantage of the extra DOF available in a 3D environment to enable more complex menu structures or better visual affordances for menu entries. We distinguish between two kinds of 3D widgets: collocated (context-sensitive) and non-context-sensitive widgets.

With collocated widgets, the functionality of a menu is moved onto an object in the 3D environment, and geometry and functionality are strongly coupled. Conner and colleagues (1992) refer to widgets as "the combination of geometry and behavior." For example, suppose a user wishes to manipulate a simple geometric object like a box. We could design an interface in which the user first chooses a manipulation mode (e.g., translation, scaling, or rotation) from a menu and then manipulates the box directly. With collocated 3D widgets, however, we can place the menu items directly on the box—menu functionality is directly connected to the object (Figure 9.8). To scale the box, the user simply selects and moves the scaling widget, thus combining the mode selection and the manipulation into a single step. The widgets are context-sensitive; only those widgets that apply to an object appear when the object is selected. As in the example, collocated widgets are typically used for changing geometric parameters and are also often found in desktop modeling applications.

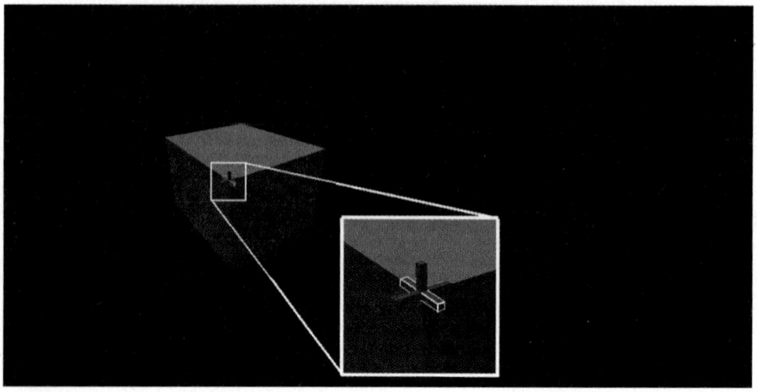

Figure 9.8 A 3D collocated widget for scaling an object. (Image courtesy of Andrew Forsberg, Brown University Computer Graphics Group)

The command and control cube, or C^3 (Grosjean et al. 2002), is a more general-purpose type of 3D widget (non-context-sensitive). The C^3 (Figure 9.9) is a $3 \times 3 \times 3$ cubic grid, where each of the 26 grid cubes is a menu item, while the center cube is the starting point. The user brings up the menu by pressing a button or making a pinch on a Pinch Glove; the menu appears, centered on the user's hand. Then the user moves his hand in the direction of the desired menu item cube relative to the center position and releases the button or the pinch. This is similar in concept to the marking menus (Kurtenbach and Buxton 1991) used in software such as Maya from Autodesk.

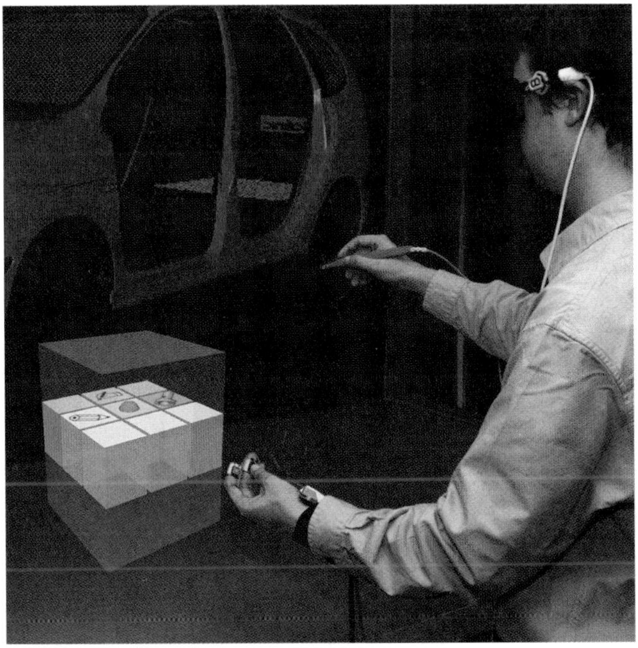

Figure 9.9 The command and control cube. (i3D-INRIA. Data © Renault. Photograph courtesy of Jerome Grosjean)

9.5.2 Design and Implementation Issues

There are many considerations when designing or implementing graphical menus as system control techniques in a 3D UI. In this section we will discuss the main issues that relate to placement, selection, representation, and structure.

Placement

The placement of the menu influences the user's ability to access the menu (good placement provides a spatial reference) and the amount of occlusion of the environment. We can consider menus that are **world-referenced**, **object-referenced**, **head-referenced**, **body-referenced**, or **device-referenced** (adapted from the classification in Feiner et al. 1993).

World-referenced menus are placed at a fixed location in the virtual world, while object-referenced menus are attached to an object in the 3D scene. Although not useful for most general-purpose menus, these may be useful as collocated 3D widgets. Head-referenced or body-referenced menus provide a strong spatial reference frame: the user can easily find the menu. Mine et al. (1997) explored body referenced menus and found that the user's proprioceptive sense (sense of the relative locations of the parts of the body in space) can significantly enhance menu retrieval and usage. Body-referenced menus may even enable eyes-off usage, allowing users to perform system control tasks without having to look at the menu. Head- and body-referenced menus are mostly used in VR—while they may be applied in AR too, for example in an HWD setup, this is done infrequently. The last reference frame is the group of device-referenced menus. For instance, on a workbench, display menus may be placed on the border of the display device. The display screen provides a physical surface for menu selection as well as a strong spatial reference. Handheld AR applications often make use of device-referenced designs: while the user moves the "window on the world" around, the menus stay fixed on the display plane.

Handheld AR systems often use hybrid interfaces, in which 2D and 3D interaction methods are used in concert to interact with spatial content. Both due to familiarity and the fact that 2D techniques (such as menus) are frequently optimized for smaller screens, these methods are often an interesting option. Just because an application contains 3D content does not mean that all UI elements should be 3D. Nonetheless, hybrid interaction may introduce some limitations, such as device or context switching.

Non-collocated menus also result in focus switching, since menus are often displayed at a different location than the main user task. This problem can be exacerbated when menus are deliberately moved aside to avoid occlusion and clutter in an environment. Occlusion and clutter are serious issues; when a menu is activated, the content in the main part of the interaction space may become invisible. It is often hard to balance the issues of placement, occlusion, and focus switching. An evaluation may be needed to make these design decisions for specific systems.

Menu usage in AR may be even more challenging—with HWDs, the screen real estate can be limited by a narrow FOV. An even bigger problem is occlusion: even when handheld AR displays offer a wide FOV, placement of menus can still clutter the space and occlude the environment. Thus, AR system controls often need to be hidden after usage to free up the visual space.

Selection

Traditionally, desktop menus make use of a 2D selection method (mouse-based). In a 3D UI, we encounter the problem of using a 3D selection method with these 2D (or even 1D) menus. This can make system control particularly difficult. In order to address this problem, several alternative selection methods have been developed that constrain the DOF of the system control interface, considerably improving performance. For example, when an adapted 2D menu is shown, one can discard all tracker data except the 2D projection of the tracker on the plane of the menu. 2-DOF selection techniques such as image-plane selection also address this issue (see Chapter 7, "Selection and Manipulation"). Still, selection will never be as easy as with an inherently 2D input method. Alternatively, the menu can be placed on a physical 2D surface to reduce the DOF of the selection task, or a phone or a tablet can be used for menus.

Representation and Structure

Another important issue in developing a graphical menu is its representation: how are the items represented visually, and if there are many items, how are they structured?

The size of and space between items is very important. Do not make items and inter-item distances too small, or the user might have problems selecting the items, especially since tracking errors may exacerbate selection problems.

Application complexity is often directly related to the number of functions. Make sure to structure the interface by using either functional grouping (items with similar function are clustered) or sequential grouping (using the natural sequence of operations to structure items). Alternatively, one could consider using context-sensitive menus to display only the applicable functions.

Control coding can give an extra cue about the relations between different items and therefore make the structure and the hierarchy of the items clearer (Bullinger et al. 1997). Methods include varying colors, shapes, surfaces, textures, dimensions, positions, text, and symbols to differentiate items.

Finally, AR applications used in outdoor environments will be limited by visibility issues (Kruijff et al. 2010): both the bright conditions and limits in screen brightness affect visibility and legibility of menus. Color and size should thus be chosen carefully. Often it might help to use more saturated colors and larger sizes to increase visibility and legibility (Gabbard et al. 2007; see Figure 9.10).

Figure 9.10 Legibility with different backgrounds in augmented reality. This mockup image shows several frequently occurring issues: the leader line of label 1 (right) is difficult to see due to the light background, whereas label 2 (left) can be overlooked due to the low color contrast with the blue sign behind and above it. Label 3 can barely be read, as the label does not have a background color. While this reduces occlusion, in this case legibility is low due to the low contrast and pattern interferences of the background. (Image courtesy of Ernst Kruijff)

9.5.3 Practical Application

Graphical menu techniques can be very powerful in 3D UIs when their limitations can be overcome. Selection of menu items should be easy, and the menu should not overlap too much with the user's workspace in which the user is working.

Especially with applications that have a large number of functions, a menu is probably the best choice of all the system control techniques for 3D UIs. A good example of an application area that requires a large set of functions is engineering (Cao et al. 2006; Mueller et al. 2003). Medical applications represent another domain that has large functional sets (Bornik et al. 2006). Both of these can benefit from the hybrid approach: using 2D menus on devices such as tablets. Still, the approach of putting graphical menus on a remote device works only when users can see the physical world. For example, it will be useless in an immersive HWD-based system, except when the tablet is tracked and the menu is duplicated in the HWD. Finally, menus have often been used for symbolic input by showing, for example, a virtual keyboard in combination with a tablet interface to input text and numbers.

9.6 Voice Commands

The issuing of voice commands can be performed via simple speech recognition or by means of spoken dialogue techniques. Speech recognition techniques are typically used for issuing single commands to the system, while a spoken dialogue technique is focused on promoting discourse between the user and the system.

9.6.1 Techniques

A spoken dialogue system provides an interface between a user and a computer-based application that permits spoken interaction with the application in a relatively natural manner (McTear 2002; Jurafsky and Martin 2008).

The most critical component of a spoken dialogue system (and of simple speech recognition techniques) is the **speech recognition engine**. A wide range of factors may influence the speech recognition rate, such as variability among speakers and background noise. The recognition engine can be speaker-dependent, requiring initial training of the system, but most are speaker-independent, which normally do not require training. Systems also differ in the size of their vocabulary. The response generated as output to the user can confirm that an action has been performed or inform the user that more input is needed to complete a control command. In a spoken dialogue system, the response should be adapted to the flow of discourse (requiring a dialogue control mechanism) and generated as artificial speech.

Today's voice recognition systems are advanced and widespread. In particular, phones use voice commands and spoken dialogue. Therefore, as such, phones could be leveraged to allow for voice control in immersive VR and head-worn and handheld AR systems.

Many 3D UIs that use speech recognition also include other complementary input methods (Billinghurst 1998). These techniques are labeled **multimodal** and are discussed in section 9.8.

9.6.2 Design and Implementation Issues

The development of a 3D UI using speech recognition or spoken dialogue systems involves many factors. One should start by defining which tasks need to be performed via voice interfaces. For an application with a limited number of functions, a normal speech recognition system will probably work well. The task will define the vocabulary size of the speech engine—the more complex the task and the domain in which it is performed, the more likely the vocabulary size will increase. Highly complex applications may need conversational UIs via a spoken dialogue system in order to ensure that the full functionality of voice input is accessible. In the case of a spoken dialogue system, the design process should also consider what vocal information the user needs to provide in order for the system to determine the user's intentions.

Developers should be aware that voice interfaces are *invisible* to the user. The user is normally not presented with an overview of the functions that can be performed via a speech interface. In order to grasp the actual intentions of the user, one of the key factors is verification. Either by error correction via semantic and syntactic filtering (prediction methods that use the semantics or syntax of a sentence to limit the possible interpretation) or by a formal discourse model (question-and-answer mechanism), the system must ensure that it understands what the user wants.

Unlike other system control techniques, speech-based techniques initialize, select, and issue a command all at once. Sometimes another input stream (like a button press) or a specific voice command should be used to initialize the speech system. This disambiguates the start of a voice input and is called a push-to-talk system (see also Chapter 6, "3D User Interface Input Hardware," section 6.4.1). Error rates will increase when the application involves direct communication between multiple participants. For instance, a comment to a colleague can easily be misunderstood as a voice command to a system. Therefore, one may need to separate human communication and human–computer interaction when designing speech interfaces. Syntactic differences between personal communication and system interaction might be used to distinguish between voice streams (Shneiderman 2000).

9.6.3 Practical Application

Speech input can be a very powerful system control technique in a 3D UI; it is hands-free and natural. The user may first need to learn the voice commands—which is easy enough for a smaller functional set—before they can be issued. However, most of today's systems are powerful enough to understand complete sentences without learning. Moreover, most of today's phones already include a powerful speech recognition system that can be readily used. As such, for hybrid interfaces or handheld AR, voice recognition may be a good option. Speech is also well suited for symbolic input, as speech can be directly translated into text. As such, it is a lightweight method to dictate text or numbers. Also, as we will talk about in section 9.9, voice can be combined with other system control techniques to form a multimodal input stream to the computer.

In those domains where users need to rely on both hands to perform their main interaction tasks (e.g., a medical operating room), voice might be a useful system control asset. The doctor can keep using his hands, and since there is nothing to touch, the environment can be kept sterile. Still, continuous voice input is tiring and cannot be used in every environment.

Voice interface issues have been studied in many different contexts. For example, using speech commands for controlling a system via a telephone poses many of the same problems as using voice commands in a 3D UI. Please refer to Brewster (1998) for further discussion of issues involved in such communication streams.

9.7 Gestural Commands

Gestures were one of the first system control techniques for VEs and other 3D environments. Ever since early projects like Krueger's Videoplace (Krueger et al. 1985), developers have been fascinated by using the hands as direct input, almost as if one is not using an input device at all. Especially since the seemingly natural usage of gestures in the movie *Minority Report*, many developers have experimented with gestures. Gesture interfaces are often thought of as an integral part of *perceptual user interfaces* (Turk and Robertson 2000) or *natural user interfaces* (Wigdor and Wixon 2011). However, designing a truly well performing and easy-to-learn system is one of the most challenging tasks of 3D UI design. While excellent gesture-based interfaces exist for simple task sets that replicate real-world actions—gaming environments such as the Wii or XBox Kinect are good examples—more complex gestural interfaces for system control are hard to design (LaViola 2013).

Gestural commands can be classified as either **postures** or **gestures.** A posture is a static configuration of the hand (Figure 9.11), whereas a gesture is a movement of the hand (Figure 9.12), perhaps while it is in a certain posture. An example of a posture is holding the fingers in a V-like configuration (the "peace" sign), whereas waving and drawing are examples of gestures. The usability of gestures and postures for system control depends on the number and complexity of the gestural commands—more gestures imply more learning for the user.

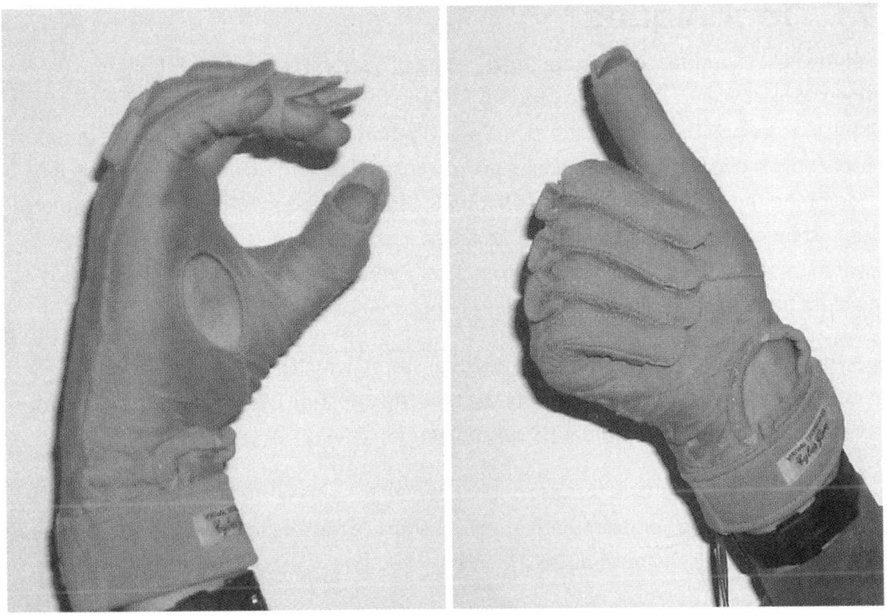

Figure 9.11 Examples of postures using a Data Glove. (Photograph courtesy of Joseph J. LaViola Jr.)

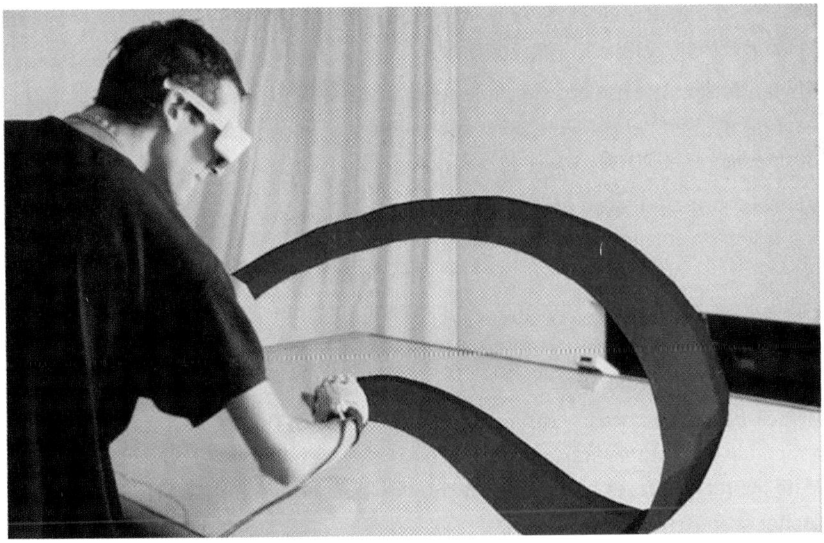

Figure 9.12 Mimic gesture. (Schkolne et al. 2001; © 2001 ACM; reprinted by permission)

9.7.1 Techniques

One of the best examples to illustrate the diversity of gestural commands is Polyshop (later Multigen's Smart Scene; Mapes and Moshell 1995). In this early VE application, all interaction was specified by postures and gestures, from navigation to the use of menus. For example, the user could move forward by pinching an imaginary rope and pulling herself along it (the "grabbing the air" technique—see Chapter 8, "Travel," section 8.7.2). As this example shows, system control overlaps with manipulation and navigation in such a 3D UI, since the switch to navigation mode occurs automatically when the user pinches the air. This is lightweight and effective because no active change of mode is performed.

In everyday life, we use many different types of gestures, which may be combined to generate composite gestures. We identify the following gesture categories, extending the categorizations provided by Mulder (1996) and Kendon (1988):

- **Mimic gestures:** Gestures that are not connected to speech but are directly used to describe a concept. For example, Figure 9.12 shows a gesture in 3D space that defines a curved surface (Schkolne et al. 2001).
- **Symbolic gestures:** Gestures as used in daily life to express things like insults or praise (e.g., "thumbs up").
- **Sweeping**: Gestures coupled to the use of marking-menu techniques. Marking menus, originally developed for desktop systems and widely used in modeling applications, use pie-like menu structures that can be explored using different sweep-like trajectory motions (Ren and O'Neill 2013).
- **Sign language:** The use of a specified set of postures and gestures in communicating with hearing-impaired people (Fels 1994), or the usage of finger counting to select menu items (Kulshreshth et al. 2014).
- **Speech-connected hand gestures:** Spontaneous gesticulation performed unintentionally during speech or language-like gestures that are integrated in the speech performance. A specific type of language-like gesture is the **deictic gesture**, which is a gesture used to indicate a *referent* (e.g., object or direction) during speech. Deictic gestures have been studied intensely in HCI and applied to multimodal interfaces such as Bolt's "put that there" system (Bolt 1980).
- **Surface-based gestures:** Gestures made on multitouch surfaces. Although these are 2D, surface-based gestures (Rekimoto 2002) have been used together with 3D systems to create hybrid interfaces, an example being the Toucheo system displayed in Figure 9.13 (Hachet et al. 2011).

- **Whole-body interaction:** While whole-body gestures (motions) can be mimic or symbolic gestures, we list them here separately due to their specific nature. Instead of just the hand and possibly arm movement (England 2011), users may use other body parts like feet, or even the whole body (Beckhaus and Kruijff, 2004).

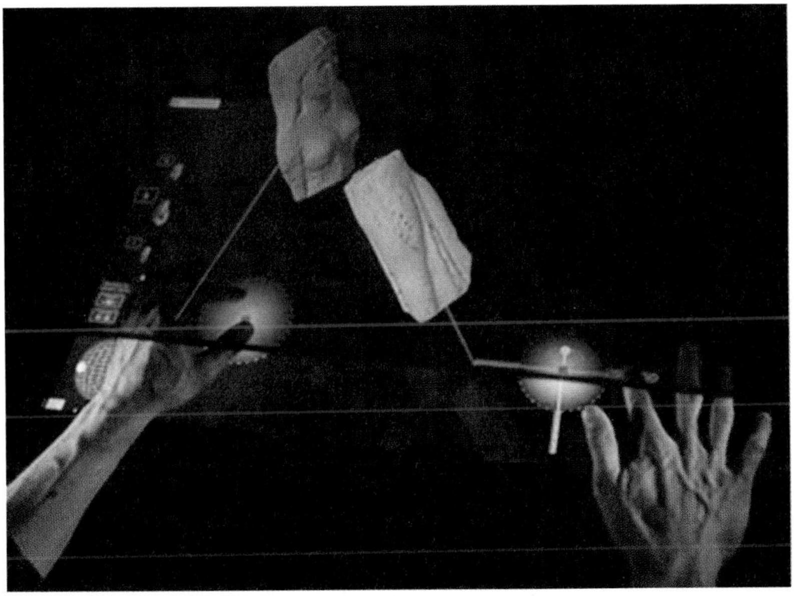

Figure 9.13 TOUCHEO—combining 2D and 3D interfaces. (© Inria / Photo H. Raguet).

9.7.2 Design and Implementation Issues

The implementation of gestural interaction depends heavily on the input device being used. At a low level, the system needs to be able to track the hand, fingers, and other body parts involved in gesturing (see Chapter 6, "3D User Interface Input Hardware," section 6.3.2. At a higher level, the postures and motions of the body must be recognized as gestures. Gesture recognition typically makes use of either machine learning or heuristics.

Gesture recognition is still not always reliable. Calibration may be needed but may not always be possible. When gestural interfaces are used in public installations, recognition should be robust without a calibration phase.

When a menu is accessed via a gestural interface, the lower accuracy of gestures may lead to the need for larger menu items. Furthermore, the layout of menu items (horizontal, vertical, or circular) may have an effect on the performance of menu-based gestural interfaces.

Gesture-based system control shares many of the characteristics of speech input discussed in the previous section. Like speech, a gestural command combines initialization, selection, and issuing of the command. Gestures should be designed to have clear *delimiters* that indicate the initialization and termination of the gesture. Otherwise, many normal human motions may be interpreted as gestures while not intended as such (Baudel and Beaudouin-Lafon, 1993). This is known as the gesture segmentation problem. As with push-to-talk in speech interfaces, the UI designer should ensure that the user really intends to issue a gestural command via some implicit or explicit mechanism (this sometimes is called a "push-to-gesture" technique). One option could be to disable gestures in certain areas, for example close to controllers or near a monitor (Feiner and Beshers, 1990).

The available gestures in the system are typically invisible to the user: users may need to discover the actual gesture or posture language (*discoverability*). Subsequently, the number and composition of gestures should be easy to learn. Depending on the frequency of usage of an application by a user, the total number of gestures may need to be limited to a handful, while the set of gestures for an expert user may be more elaborate. In any case, designers should make sure the cognitive load is reasonable. Finally, the system should also provide adequate feedback to the user when a gesture is recognized.

9.7.3 Practical Application

Gestural commands have significant appeal for system control in 3D UIs because of their important role in our day-to-day lives. Choose gestural commands if the application domain already has a set of well-defined, natural, easy-to-understand, and easy-to-recognize gestures. In addition, gestures may be more useful in combination with another type of input (see section 9.9). Keep in mind that gestural interaction can be very tiring, especially for elderly people (Bobeth et al. 2012). Hence, you may need to adjust your choice of system control methods based on the duration of tasks.

Figure 9.14 A user performing a 3D climbing gesture in a video game application. (Image courtesy of Joseph LaViola).

Entertainment and video games are just one example of an application domain where 3D gestural interfaces are becoming more common. This trend is evident from the fact that all major video game consoles and the PC support devices capture 3D motion from a user. In other cases, video games are being used as the research platform for exploring and improving 3D gesture recognition. Figure 9.14 shows an example of using a video game to explore what the best 3D gesture set would be for a first-person navigation game (Norton et al. 2010). A great deal of 3D gesture recognition research has focused on the entertainment and video game domain (Cheema et al. 2013; Bott et al. 2009; Kang et al. 2004; Payne et al. 2006; Starner et al. 2000).

Figure 9.15 A user controlling an unmanned aerial vehicle (UAV) with 3D gestures (Image courtesy of Joseph LaViola).

Medical applications used in operating rooms are another area where 3D gestures have been explored. Using passive sensing enables the surgeon or doctor to use gestures to gather information about a patient on a computer while still maintaining a sterile environment (Bigdelou et al. 2012; Schwarz et al. 2011). 3D gesture recognition has also been explored with robotic applications in the human-robot interaction field. For example, Pfeil et al. (2013) used 3D gestures to control unmanned aerial vehicles (UAVs; Figure 9.15). They developed and evaluated several 3D gestural metaphors for teleoperating the robot. Williamson et al. (2013) developed a full-body gestural interface for dismounted soldier training, while Riener (2012) explored how 3D gestures could be used to control various components of automobiles. Finally, 3D gesture recognition has recently been explored in consumer electronics, specifically for control of large-screen smart TVs (Lee et al. 2013; Takahashi et al. 2013).

Gesture interfaces have also been used for symbolic input. Figure 9.16 shows an example of such an interface, in which pen-based input is used. These techniques can operate at both the character-level and word-level. For example, in Cirrin, a stroke begins in the central area of a circle and moves through regions around a circle representing each character in a word (Figure 9.16).

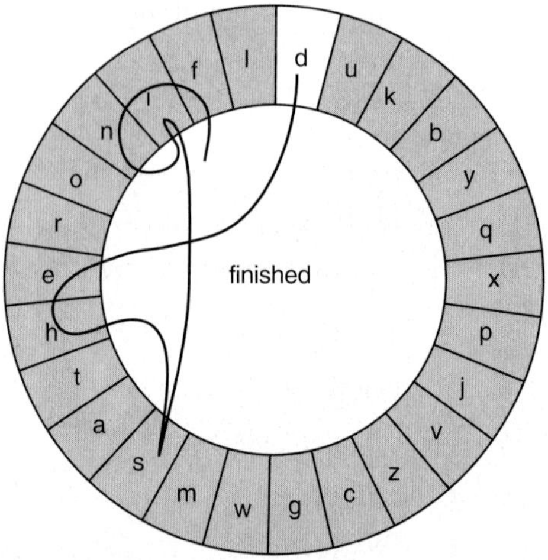

Figure 9.16 Layout of the Cirrin soft keyboard for pen-based input (Mankoff and Abowd 1998, © 1998 ACM; reprinted by permission

9.8 Tools

In many 3D applications, the use of real-world devices for 3D interaction can lead to increased usability. These devices, or their virtual representations, called **tools**, provide directness of interaction because of their real-world correspondence. Although individual tools may be used for selection, manipulation, travel, or other 3D interaction tasks, we consider a *set* of tools in a single application to be a system control technique. Like the tool palettes in many popular 2D drawing applications, tools in 3D UIs provide a simple and intuitive technique for changing the mode of interaction: simply select an appropriate tool.

Figure 9.17 Tool belt menu. Note that the tool belt appears larger than normal because the photograph was not taken from the user's perspective. (Photograph reprinted from Forsberg et al. [2000], © 2000 IEEE)

We distinguish between three kinds of tools: physical tools, tangibles, and virtual tools. Physical tools are a collection of real physical objects (with corresponding virtual representations) that are sometimes called **props.** A physical tool might be used to perform one function only, but it could also perform multiple functions over time. A user accesses a physical tool by simply picking it up and using it. Physical tools are a subset of the larger category of tangible user interfaces (TUI, Ullmer and Ishii 2001). Physical tools are tangibles that represent a real-world tool, while tangibles in general can also be abstract shapes to which functions are connected. In contrast, virtual tools have no physical instantiation. Here, the tool is a metaphor; users select digital representations of tools, for example by selecting a virtual tool on a tool belt (Figure 9.17).

9.8.1 Techniques

A wide range of purely virtual tool belts exist, but they are largely undocumented in the literature, with few exceptions (e.g., Pierce et al. 1999). Therefore, in this section we focus on the use of physical tools and TUIs as used for system control in 3D UIs.

Based on the idea of props, a whole range of TUIs has appeared. TUIs often make use of physical tools to perform actions in a VE (Ullmer and Ishii 2001; Fitzmaurice et al. 1995). A TUI uses physical elements that represent a specific kind of action in order to interact with an application. For example, the user could use a real eraser to delete virtual objects or a real pencil to draw in the virtual space. In AR, tools can also take a hybrid form between physical shape and virtual tool. A commonly used technique is to attach visual markers to generic physical objects to be able to render virtual content on top of the physical object. An example can be found in Figure 9.18, where a paddle is used to manipulate objects in a scene (Kawashima et al. 2000).

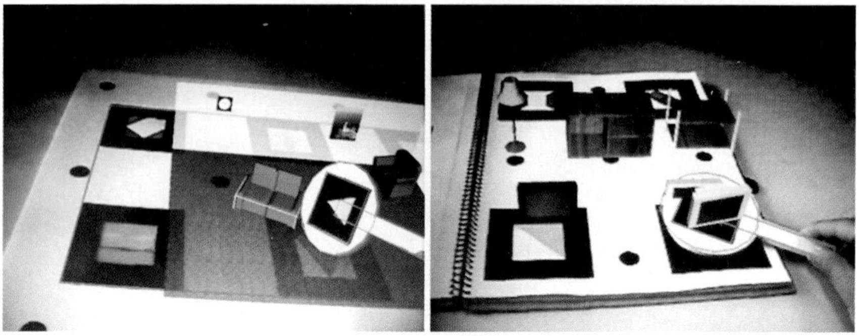

Figure 9.18 Using tools to manipulate objects in an AR scene. (Kato et al. 2000, © 2000 IEEE).

Figure 9.19 Visualization artifacts—physical tools for mediating interaction with 3D UIs. (Image courtesy of Brygg Ullmer and Stefan Zachow, Zuse Institute Berlin)

Figure 9.19 shows a TUI for 3D interaction. Here, Ethernet-linked interaction pads representing different operations are used together with radio frequency identification (RFID)-tagged physical cards, blocks, and wheels, which represent network-based data, parameters, tools, people, and applications. Designed for use in immersive 3D environments as well as on the desktop, these physical devices ease access to key information and operations. When used with immersive VEs, they allow one hand to continuously manipulate a tracking wand or stylus, while the second hand can be used in parallel to load and save data, steer parameters, activate teleconference links, and perform other operations.

A TUI takes the approach of combining representation and control. This implies the combination of both physical representations and digital representations, or the fusion of input and output in one mediator. TUIs have the following key characteristics (from Ullmer and Ishii 2001):

- Physical representations are computationally coupled to underlying digital information.
- Physical representations embody mechanisms for interactive control.
- Physical representations are perceptually coupled to actively mediated digital representations.

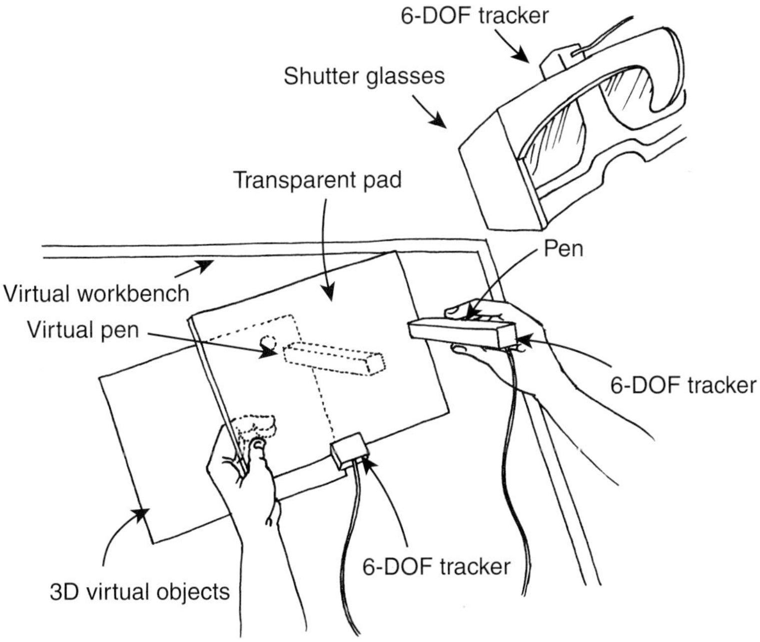

Figure 9.20 Personal Interaction Panel—combining virtual and augmented reality. (Adapted from Schmalstieg et al. 1999)

These ideas can also be applied to develop prop-based physical menus. In HWD-based VEs, for example, a tracked pen can be used to select from a virtual menu placed on a tracked tablet (Bowman and Wingrave 2001), which may also be transparent. An example of the latter approach is the Personal Interaction Panel (Schmalstieg et al. 1999), which combines a semitransparent Perspex plate to display a menu, combining VR and AR principles (Figure 9.20). Tablet computers can also be used; a tablet has the advantage of higher accuracy and increased resolution. The principal advantage of displaying a menu on a tablet is the direct haptic feedback to the user who interacts with the menu. This results in far fewer selection problems compared to a menu that simply floats in the VE space.

9.8.2 Design and Implementation Issues

The form of the tool communicates the function the user can perform with the tool, so carefully consider the form when developing props. A general approach is to imitate a traditional control design (Bullinger et al. 1997). Another approach is to duplicate everyday tools. The user makes use of either the real tool or something closely resembling the tool in order to manipulate objects in a spatial application.

Another important issue is the **compliance** between the real and virtual worlds; that is, the correspondence between real and virtual positions, shapes, motions, and cause-effect relationships (Hinckley et al. 1994). Some prop-based interfaces, like the Cubic Mouse (Fröhlich and Plate 2000), have demonstrated a need for a clutching mechanism. See Chapter 7 for more information on compliance and clutching in manipulation techniques.

The use of props naturally affords eyes-off operation (the user can operate the device by touch), which may have significant advantages, especially when the user needs to focus visual attention on another task. On the other hand, it also means that the prop must be designed to allow tactile interaction. A simple tracked tablet, for example, does not indicate the locations of menu items with haptic cues; it only indicates the general location of the menu.

A specific issue for physical menus is that the user may want to place the menu out of sight when it is not in use. The designer may choose to put a clip on the tablet so that the user can attach it to his clothing, may reserve a special place in the display environment for it, or may simply provide a handle on the tablet so it can be held comfortably at the user's side.

9.8.3 Practical Application

Physical tools are very specific devices. In many cases, they perform only one function. In applications with a great deal of functionality, tools can still be useful, but they may not apply to all the user tasks. There is a trade-off between the specificity of the tool (a good affordance for its function) and the amount of tool switching the user will have to do.

Public installations of VEs (e.g., in museums or theme parks) can greatly benefit from the use of tools. Users of public installations by definition must be able to use the interface immediately. Tools tend to allow exactly this. A well-designed tool has a readily apparent set of affordances, and users may draw from personal experience with a similar device in real life. Many theme park installations make use of props to allow the user to begin playing right away. For example, the Pirates of the Caribbean installation at Disney Quest uses a physical steering wheel and cannons. This application has almost no learning curve—including the vocal introduction, users can start interacting with the environment in less than a minute (Mine 2003).

9.9 Multimodal Techniques

While discussing the various system control techniques, we already mentioned that some techniques could be combined with others. In this section, we go deeper into the underlying principles and effects of combining techniques using different input modalities—**multimodal techniques**. Such techniques connect multiple input streams: users switch between different techniques while interacting with the system (LaViola et al. 2014). In certain situations, the use of multimodal system control techniques can significantly increase the effectiveness of system control tasks. However, it may also have adverse effects when basic principles are not considered. Here, we will shed light on different aspects of multimodal techniques that will help the developer make appropriate design choices for multimodal 3D UIs.

9.9.1 Potential Advantages

Researchers have identified several advantages of using multimodal system control techniques (mostly in the domain of 2D GUIs) that can also apply to 3D UIs:

- **Decoupling:** Using an input channel that differs from the main input channel used for interaction with the environment can decrease user cognitive load. If users do not have to switch between manipulation and system control actions, they can keep their attention focused on their main activity.
- **Error reduction and correction:** The use of multiple input channels can be very effective when the input is ambiguous or noisy, especially with recognition-based input like speech or gestures. The combination of input from several channels can significantly increase recognition rates (Oviatt 1999; Oviatt and Cohen 2000) and disambiguation in 3D UIs (Kaiser et al. 2003).
- **Flexibility and complementary behavior:** Control is more flexible when users can use multiple input channels to perform the same task. In addition, different modalities can be used in a complementary way based on the perceptual structure of the task (Grasso et al. 1998; Jacob and Sibert 1992).
- **Control of mental resources:** Multimodal interaction can be used to reduce cognitive load (Rosenfeld et al. 2001); on the other hand, it may also lead to less effective interaction

because multiple mental resources need to be accessed simultaneously. For example, as Shneiderman (2000) observes, the part of the human brain used for speaking and listening is also the part used for problem solving—speaking consumes precious cognitive resources.

Probably the best-known multimodal technique is the famous "put-that-there" (Bolt 1980). Using this technique, users can perform manipulation actions by combining pointing with speech. Many others have used the same combination of gesture and speech (e.g., Figure 9.21), where speech is used to specify the command and gestures are used to specify spatial parameters of the command, all in one fluid action. In some cases, speech can be used to disambiguate a gesture, and vice versa.

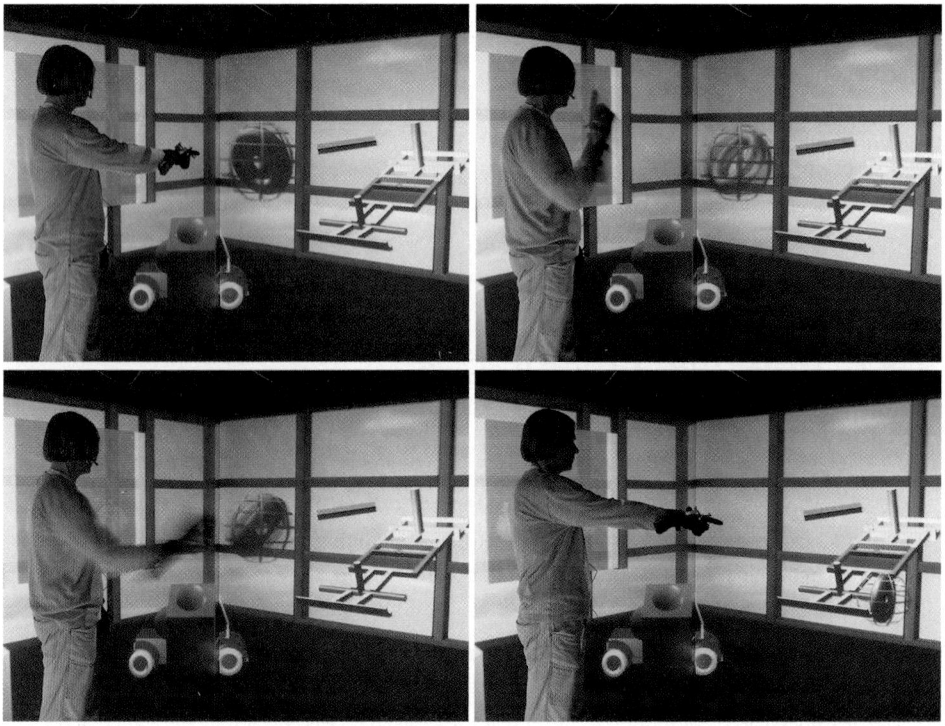

Figure 9.21 A car wheel is selected, rotated, and moved to its correct position using voice and gestures. (Photographs courtesy of Marc Eric Latoschik, AI & VR Lab, University of Bielefeld; Latoschik 2001)

Another possible technique is to combine gesture-based techniques with traditional menus, as in the "marking menus" technique. This means that novice users can select a command from a visual menu, while more experienced users can access commands directly via gestural input. This redundancy is similar to the use of keyboard shortcuts in desktop interfaces.

9.9.2 Design Principles

Designing multimodal system control techniques can be a complex undertaking. On a single technique level, the design guidelines from the various techniques discussed in the previous sections will apply. However, by combining techniques, several new issues come into play.

First, the combination of modalities will depend on the task structure: How can you match a specific task to a specific modality, and how does the user switch between modalities? Switching may affect the flow of action in an application—disturbances in the flow of action may lead to bad performance and lower user acceptance. A good way to verify flow of action is to perform a detailed logging that identifies how much time is spend on specific subparts in the task chain and compares this to single-technique (non-multimodal) performance. When combining two techniques, it can also make sense to do multimapping of tasks to modalities, that is, to allow users to perform a specific task using multiple methods.

Second, while multimodal techniques may free cognitive resources, this is not necessarily the case for all implementations. Cognitive load should thus be evaluated, either through self-assessment by a user (which only provides general indications) or through additional correlation with physiological measures that can assess stress or even brain activity. See Chapter 3, "Human Factors Fundamentals," section 3.4.3, for more information. In direct relation to cognitive load, attention is also an issue to consider: does the user need to pay much attention to using the combined technique (or accompanying visual or non-visual elements), or can the user remain focused on the main task?

9.9.3 Practical application

Using multimodal techniques can be useful in many situations. Complex applications can benefit from the complementary nature of multimodal techniques, allowing for more flexible input and potentially reducing errors. The reduction of errors is especially important for applications with limited or no time for user learning. For example, consider a public space installation: by supporting multiple modes of input, discovering the underlying functionality may become easier for users.

Also, some modalities may be easier to perform by certain classes of users: an elderly user may have difficulties with precise motor input but may be able to control an application by voice instead. This points to the general complementary behavior of multimodal techniques: when one input channel is blocked, either due to external factors or user abilities, another channel can be used. For instance, consider bright daylight limiting text legibility in an AR application or environmental noise limiting voice recognition. Being able to perform the task using another input channel can drastically increase performance.

Finally, multimodal techniques are applicable to scenarios that mimic natural behavior. In both realistic games and in applications that use a natural interaction approach, combinations of input modalities that mirror the ways we interact with other humans can improve the user experience.

9.10 Design Guidelines

Throughout this chapter, we have presented many design guidelines for specific 3D system control techniques. In this section, we summarize some general guidelines. Because there still have not been many empirical evaluations of system control techniques for 3D UIs, however, most of the guidelines should be regarded as rules of thumb.

> **Tip**
>
> Avoid disturbing the flow of action of an interaction task.

System control is often integrated with another 3D interaction task. Such a task structure forms a chain of actions. Because of this integration, system control techniques should be designed to avoid disturbing the flow of action of an interaction task. Lightweight mode switching, physical tools, and multimodal techniques can all be used to maintain the flow of action.

> **Tip**
>
> Prevent unnecessary focus switching and context switching.

One of the major interruptions to a flow of action is a change of focus. This may occur when users have to cognitively and/or physically switch between the actual working area and a system control technique, or even when they must look away to switch devices.

> **Tip**
>
> Design for discoverability.

Especially with "invisible" system control techniques like voice and gesture input, users will need to discover what is possible with the application. Make sure to aid this process by providing cues within the application or (alternatively) introduce a training phase.

> **Tip**
>
> Avoid mode errors.

Always provide clear feedback to the user so that she knows which interaction mode is currently active.

Tip

Use an appropriate spatial reference frame.

Placing your system control technique in the right position can make a big difference in its usability. Users often get distracted when searching for a way to change the mode of interaction or issue a command. If the controls are not visible at all, placed far away from the actual work area, or not oriented toward the user, the result will be wasted time. On the other hand, system controls attached to the user's hand, body, or a device are always available.

Tip

Structure the functions in an application and guide the user.

There are several good techniques for structuring the functionality of an application, including hierarchical menu structures and context-sensitive system control. In cases where the number of functions is so large that these techniques are not effective, it can make sense to place some of the system control functionality on another device, such as a tablet, where resolution and selection accuracy are less of an issue.

Tip

Consider using multimodal input.

Using multimodal input can provide more fluid and efficient system control but can also have its drawbacks.

Tip

3D is not always the best solution—consider hybrid interfaces.

Just because the applications are inherently 3D, 3D system control techniques are not necessarily the best solution. Often a 2D technique is more straightforward, especially if a tablet or phone can be used for controlling the menus. However, take care when designing interfaces that require a great deal of switching between modalities.

9.11 Case Studies

System control issues are critical to both of our case studies. If you have not yet read the introduction to the case studies, take a look at section 2.4 before reading this section.

9.11.1 VR Gaming Case Study

Given the description so far of our VR action-adventure game, you might think that the game is purely about direct interaction with the world and that there are no system control tasks to consider. Like most real applications, however, there are a variety of small commands and settings that the player needs to be able to control, such as saving a game to finish later, loading a saved game, pausing the game, choosing a sound effects volume, etc. Since these actions will happen only rarely and are not part of the game world itself, a simple 3D graphical point-and-click menu such as those described in section 9.5 will be sufficient. Pointing can be done with the dominant hand's controller, acting as a virtual laser pointer.

There are, however, two more prominent system control tasks that will occur often, and are more central to the gameplay. The first of these tasks is opening the inventory, so a collected item can be placed in it or so an item can be chosen out of it. An inventory (set of items that are available to the player) is a concept with a straightforward real-world metaphor: a bag or backpack. We can fit this concept into our story by having the hero (the player) come into the story already holding the flashlight and a shopping bag. The shopping bag can be shown hanging from the nondominant hand (the same hand holding the flashlight).

To open the bag (inventory), the player moves the dominant hand close to the bag's handle (as if he's going to pull one side of the bag away from the other). If the player is already holding an object in the dominant hand, he can press a button to drop it into the bag, which can then automatically close. This is essentially a "virtual tool" approach to system control (section 9.8), which is appropriate since we want our system control interface to integrate directly into the world of the game.

If the player wants to grab an item out of the inventory, it might be tricky to see all the items in the bag from outside (especially since, like many games of this sort, the inventory will magically be able to hold many items, some of which might be larger than the bag itself). To address this, we again draw inspiration from the game *Fantastic Contraption*, which provides a menu that's accessed when the player grabs a helmet and puts it over his head, placing the player in a completely different menu world. Similarly, we allow the player to put his head inside the bag, which then grows very large, so that the player is now standing inside the bag, with all the items arrayed around him (a form of graphical menu), making it easy to select an object using the selection techniques described in section 7.12.1. After an item is selected, the bag shrinks back to normal size and the player finds himself standing in the virtual room again.

The second primary in-game system control task is choosing a tool to be used with the tool handle on the player's dominant hand. As we discussed in the selection and manipulation chapter, the user starts with a remote selection tool (the "frog tongue"), but in order to solve the puzzles and defeat the monsters throughout the game, we envision that many different tools might be acquired. So the question is how to select the right tool mode at the right time. Again, we could use a very physical metaphor here, like the virtual tool belt discussed in section 9.8, where the player reaches to a location on the belt to swap one tool for another one. But this action is going to occur quite often in the game and will sometimes need to be done very quickly (e.g., when a monster is approaching and the player needs to get the disintegration ray out NOW). So instead we use the metaphor of a Swiss army knife. All the tools are always attached to the tool handle, but only one is out and active at a time. To switch to the next tool, the player just flicks the controller quickly up and down. Of course, this means that the player might have to toggle through several tool choices to get to the desired tool, but if there aren't too many (perhaps a maximum of four or five), this shouldn't be a big problem. Players will quickly memorize the order of the tools, and we can also use sound effects to indicate which tool is being chosen, so switching can be done eyes-free.

Key Concepts

- Think differently about the design of system control that's part of gameplay and system control that's peripheral to gameplay.
- When there are few options to choose from, a toggle that simply rotates through the choices is acceptable (and maybe even faster), rather than a direct selection.
- System control doesn't have to be boring, but be careful not to make it too heavyweight.

9.11.2 Mobile AR Case Study

While many AR applications tend to have lower functional complexity, the HYDROSYS application provided access to a wider range of functions. The process of designing adequate system control methods revealed issues that were particular for AR applications but also showed similarities to difficulties in VR systems.

As with all 3D systems, system control is highly dependent on the display type and input method. In our case, we had a 5.6" screen on the handheld device, with a 1024 x 600 resolution, and users provided input to the screen using finger-touch or a pen. The interface provided access to four different task categories: data search, general tools, navigation, and collaboration tools. As each category included numerous functions, showing all at once was not a viable approach—either the menu system would overlap most of the augmentations, or the menus would be illegible. Thus, we had to find a screen-space-effective method that would not occlude the environment.

We created a simple but suitable solution by separating the four groups of tasks. We assigned each task group an access button in one of the corners. When not activated, a transparent button showing the name of the task group was shown. We chose a transparent icon to limit occlusion of the augmented content. The icon did have legibility issues with certain backgrounds (see the bottom of Figure 9.22), a problem typical for AR interfaces (Kruijff et al. 2010). This was not a major problem, since users could easily memorize the content of the four icons.

Once a menu button was selected, a menu would appear at one of the four borders of the screen, leaving the center of the screen visible. In this way, users could have a menu open while viewing the augmented content. We used straightforward 2D menus with icons, designed to be highly legible under different lighting conditions that occur in outdoor environments. Menu icons combined visual representations and text, as some functions could not be easily represented by visual representation alone. In some cases, we could not avoid pop-up lists of choices—only a limited number of icons could be shown on a horizontal bar—but most of the menus were space-optimized. One particular trick we used was the filtering of menu options. In the data search menu bar (see the top of Figure 9.22), we used the principle of *guided exploration*. For example, certain types of visualizations were only available for certain types of sensor data: when a user selected a sensor data type, in the next step, only the appropriate visualization methods were shown, saving space and improving performance along the way.

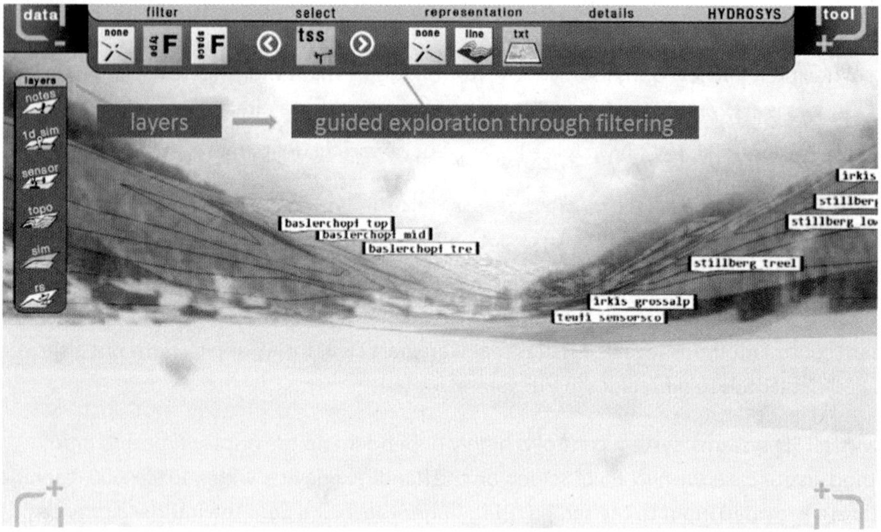

Figure 9.22 Example of a menu bar, in this case the data search menu, using the guided exploration approach. (Image courtesy by Ernst Kruijff and Eduardo Veas).

Key Concepts

- Perceptual issues: Visibility and legibility affect the design methods of AR system control in a way similar to those of general 2D menu design. However, their effects are often stronger, since AR interfaces are highly affected by display quality and outdoor conditions.
- Screen space: As screen space is often limited, careful design is needed to optimize the layout of system control methods to avoid occlusion of the augmentations.

9.12 Conclusion

Though system control methods for 3D UIs have been developed and used extensively, many issues are still open for further research. We have discussed a wide range of techniques, but the design space for such techniques is virtually limitless. We expect to see many new and interesting 3D system control techniques, not only within the categories described here but also in new categories that have not yet been invented. There is also a lack of good empirical evidence for the user experience of various system control techniques at the present time—further UX evaluations are needed in order to validate current design guidelines and develop new ones. Nevertheless, this chapter has served to demonstrate the importance and complexity of system control interfaces and has presented a wide range of existing system control techniques for 3D UIs. This concludes our tour through 3D interaction techniques for the universal tasks. We now move on to general design and evaluation of 3D UIs in part V.

Recommended Reading

For more details on human factors see:

Salvendy, G. (ed.) (2012). *Handbook of Human Factors and Ergonomics*. Hoboken, NJ: John Wiley & Sons.

Kruijff, E., Swan II, E., and Feiner, S. (2010). "Perceptual issues in Augmented Reality Revisited." *Proceedings of the IEEE and ACM International Symposium on Mixed and Augmented Reality,* 3–12.

An introduction to the origins of nonconventional control can be found in this book chapter:

Bullinger, R, H., Kern, P., and M. Braun (1997). "Controls." In G. Salvendy (ed.), *Handbook of Human Factors and Ergonomics,* 697–728. New York: John Wiley & Sons.

More details on graphics widgets can be found in:

Schmalstieg D., and Höllerer, T. (2016). *Augmented Reality: Principles and Practice.* Addison-Wesley.

More details on using voice as an input modality can be found in the following text:

Pieraccini, R. (2012). *The Voice in the Machine: Building Computers That Understand Speech.* Cambridge, MA: MIT Press.

Jurafsky, D., and J. Martin (2008) *Speech and Language Processing: An Introduction to Natural Language Processing, Computational Linguistics, and Speech Recognition*. Prentice Hall.

More detail on gestures can be found int he following text:

Wigdor, D., and Wixon, D. (2011). *Brave NUI World: Designing Natural User Interfaces for Touch and Gesture*. Burlington, MA: Morgan Kaufmann.

The following two papers provide more information on using tools as part of a 3D interface:

Ishii, H., and B. Ullmer (1997). Tangible Bits: Towards Seamless Interfaces between People, Bits, and Atoms. *Proceedings of the ACM Conference on Human Factors in Computing Systems,* ACM Press, 234–241.

Hinckley, K., R. Pausch, J. Goble, and N. Kassell (1994). Passive Real-World Interfaces Props for Neurosurgical Visualization. *Proceedings of the 1994 ACM Conference on Human Factors in Computing Systems (CHI '94),* ACM Press, 452–458.

PART V

DESIGNING AND DEVELOPING 3D USER INTERFACES

Thus far, we have focused on the low-level components of 3D UIs—input/output devices and interaction techniques. Through the guidelines presented in each chapter, we have shown you how to choose devices and techniques for your application that match its requirements and that will result in high levels of usability.

But how do you put all of these components together? What do complete 3D UIs look like? How do you verify that your system is easy to use, efficient, and satisfying? Addressing these questions is the focus of Part V.

As we discussed in Chapter 4, "General Principles of Human-Computer Interaction," we recommend adhering to usability engineering principles (Gabbard et al. 1999) when constructing 3D UIs. This process begins with requirements gathering—an analysis of the existing situation, the problems users are having, the tasks users need to perform, and the characteristics of the users themselves. Next, you develop the design of the system and its UI, and build one or more prototypes that represent the system. Finally, you evaluate the prototype to find usability problems and to assess the quality of your design, a topic we will discuss in the next chapter. In addition, usability engineering uses an iterative process, with multiple design-prototype-evaluate cycles.

In this part of the book, we address parts of this process that are unique to 3D UIs. (For a good overall introduction to usability engineering, we recommend books by Hartson and Pyla (2012) or Rosson and Carroll (2001). Chapter 10, "Strategies in Designing and Developing 3D User Interfaces," deals with the design phase. It presents general design approaches and specific UX strategies that have been proven to work well in 3D UIs—these approaches and strategies can serve as the foundation for a 3D UI design. In Chapter 11, "Evaluation of 3D User Interfaces," we look at how to evaluate 3D UIs, surveying the distinctive characteristics of 3D UI evaluation and various approaches to assessing user experience.

We do not explicitly cover the requirements analysis phase, because 3D UI requirements analysis is very similar to generic requirements analysis processes—you can find more in Chapters 4 and 5, as well as general resources such as in Salvendy (2012). We also do not discuss the details of 3D UI prototyping or implementation. Section 6.6 covers some of this topic with its discussion of input device prototyping.

The current state of development tools for 3D UIs is extremely dynamic and advancing rapidly, especially due to increasing industry interest—there are many 3D modeling tools, programming languages, integrated development environments, toolkits, and libraries for 3D applications. We have chosen to keep our discussion on a high level and focus on 3D UI design, because any specific development information we might present could quickly become obsolete.

CHAPTER 10

STRATEGIES IN DESIGNING AND DEVELOPING 3D USER INTERFACES

This chapter discusses some general strategies and principles for designing 3D UIs. The design strategies we discuss in this chapter are high level and can be used in a wide variety of 3D tasks and applications. Some of these strategies are designed to match 3D UIs to the basic properties of human psychology and physiology; others are based on common sense, rules of thumb, or cultural metaphors.

10.1 Introduction

The previous chapters have focused on foundational knowledge about HCI and human factors and on the basic building blocks common to many 3D UIs: input devices, displays, and interaction techniques for performing basic interaction tasks, such as manipulation and navigation. Although these techniques are essential in designing a variety of 3D interfaces, simply combining them does not necessarily guarantee an intuitive, easy-to-use, and enjoyable user experience.

At a micro-level, the devil is in the details, meaning that the effectiveness and usability of a 3D UI depends on the minute implementation details of interaction techniques, such as the careful choice of parameters and the match between the properties of interaction techniques and input/output devices.

At a macro-level, there are many high-level, general design strategies driven not by the requirements of an interaction task but derived from more general principles, such as the strengths and limitations of human psychology and physiology, common sense, rules of thumb, cultural metaphors, and so on. For example, the basic principles for designing two-handed interaction techniques were developed independently of any interaction task. Rather, they were motivated by the simple observation that people naturally use two hands in real-world activities, so using two hands in a 3D UI might improve usability or performance. Similarly, many of the principles that we discuss in this section are general enough to be applicable to a wide range of interaction tasks.

The strategies and principles discussed in this chapter can be roughly divided into two large groups: **designing for humans** (i.e., strategies to match the design of interaction techniques and applications to human strengths, limitations, and individual differences) and **inventing 3D user interfaces** (i.e., designing techniques based on common sense approaches, creative exploration of 3D UI design, rules of thumb, etc.). Both of these approaches can affect each other.

10.1.1 Designing for Humans

Most interface design principles from general UI literature (Shneiderman 1998) can be applied to the design of 3D UIs. Many of these principles have been studied extensively in the frame of human factors research (Salvendy 2012). Reduction of short-term memory load, consistency of interface syntax and semantics, feedback, error prevention, and aesthetic appeal are as important in 3D interaction as in any other human–machine interface. Expanding to the third dimension, however, brings new challenges, such as designing for user comfort, that require different design strategies that are usually not explored in the traditional UI literature. We have discussed many of these issues in Chapter 3, "Human Factors Fundamentals." In addition, different strategies can be applied to UI design for different user groups, such as children, disabled individuals, or novices.

10.1.2 Inventing 3D User Interfaces

While we've introduced many well-designed 3D interaction techniques in the previous chapters, it is not realistic to propose that they can cover all possible applications. Therefore, it's often necessary to invent new 3D interaction techniques and design for new user experiences. While human factors–based principles can offer valuable insight into how 3D UIs should be designed, they are not always prescriptive (i.e., they do not tell designers how to invent new and enjoyable interaction techniques). Thus, in this chapter we survey some of the more formal methods inspired by human factors research, but also illustrate some of the informal, rule-of-thumb approaches that have often been used in creating new 3D UIs; they can trigger a designer's imagination and provide a starting point for creating new and compelling 3D interaction experiences.

10.1.3 Chapter Roadmap

The chapter begins with a discussion of strategies and principles to match the design of 3D UIs with human characteristics, including issues of feedback, constraints, two-handed interaction, user groups, and user comfort (section 10.2). Section 10.3 is focused on strategies for inventing 3D UIs, such as those that are based on replicating the real world, adapting techniques from 2D interaction, and using magic and aesthetics in 3D UI design. A section of guidelines (section 10.4) summarizes some important ideas discussed in this chapter, as well as some practical tips and techniques for designing interactive 3D applications. Finally, section 10.5 continues our running case studies.

10.2 Designing for Humans

All UIs should be designed in accordance with the most basic characteristics of human physiology and psychology. These **human factors** principles of interface design can be found throughout the literature and have been introduced in Chapter 3. Here we highlight some key principles that arise from a consideration of humans in 3D UI design. Finally, section 10.5 continues our running case studies.

10.2.1 Unconventional User Interfaces

While designing for humans, we tend to optimize interfaces for the limitations of users to avoid drops in performance in difficult or complex usage scenarios. This perspective has been proven effective in many applications, as it reflects how users perceive and process the various sources of information, and control applications. Designers should always include a close analysis of human factors in the various stages of design and evaluation.

However, looking at human factors issues only as potential bottlenecks may also be limiting. For some time, researchers have been looking at the *potential* of the human body, rather than its limitations, as an approach to design novel interaction techniques. This design approach has often led to so-called unconventional user interfaces. Many of the techniques developed in this way did not match traditional UI directions but rather provided alternative ways of input and output to computers.

Interestingly, many of these techniques have actually found their way into mainstream interfaces, including 3D UIs. Two examples are advanced speech systems and vibrotactile cues. Such techniques are often found first in gaming systems, as their unconventional nature offers a compelling way to interact with virtual worlds (Beckhaus and Kruijff 2004; Kruijff 2007). However, they can be found in many other kinds of systems too. For example, it is hard to imagine mobile phones without speech recognition anymore.

The design approach is based on a simple principle: look at the true potential of any of the human sensory and control systems and try to match them with a new technique or a new kind of device. For a closer look at how the approach fits into a complete design and evaluation process, please refer to Kruijff (2013).

10.2.2 Feedback in 3D User Interfaces

Providing effective feedback is crucial in the design of any interface, whether it is a 3D VR or AR system, a desktop 2D GUI, or a simple knob on a stereo system. Feedback refers to any information conveyed to the user that helps the user understand the state of the system, the results of an operation, or the status of a task. This information may come from the system, from the environment, or from the user's own body.

It has long been understood that our ability to self-regulate body movements, such as manipulating objects or walking through the environment, is mediated by feedback-control mechanisms (Wiener 1948). In human–machine interaction, the user controls his movements by integrating various kinds of feedback provided by external sources (e.g., the UI) and self-produced by the human body (e.g., kinesthetic feedback). When interacting with a 3D UI, the user's physical input, such as hand movements, is captured by devices and translated into visual, auditory, and haptic feedback displayed to the user via display devices. At the same time, feedback is generated by the user's own body; this includes kinesthetic and proprioceptive feedback, which allow the user to feel the position and motion of his limbs and body (see section 3.3.3 for more details).

Therefore, one goal of a 3D UI designer is to create an interactive system that provides sufficient levels of feedback to the user and ensures compliance (agreement) between different levels and types of feedback.

Multiple Dimensions in Feedback

Several different dimensions of feedback can be sensed by the user and provided by the interface. We consider two basic classifications of feedback: sense based and system based.

The **sensory dimensions** of feedback include visual, auditory, tactile, and chemical (olfactory and taste) feedback from sources external to the user's body, along with proprioceptive and kinesthetic feedback generated by the user's body in response to limb and body movements. The 3D UI designer has direct control of the external feedback provided to the user. Given the appropriate devices, the 3D UI can provide feedback to most sensory feedback channels, except for self-produced kinesthetic and proprioceptive cues. Providing compliant feedback to multiple sensory channels, such as combining haptic and visual feedback, improves user performance and satisfaction in 3D UIs. Proprioceptive or kinesthetic feedback can provide additional cues to the user, for example, while performing repetitive motions that may eventually lead to so-called muscle memory (Salvendy 2012). Olfactory cues may help improve recall of experiences in 3D applications (Howell et al. 2015)

From a **systems** point of view, feedback can be split into three categories: reactive, instrumental, and operational feedback (Smith and Smith 1987). **Reactive feedback** combines all the self-generated visual, auditory, haptic, and proprioceptive information that results from operating the UI. **Instrumental feedback** is generated by the interface controls and tools operated by the human user, such as the vibration of a pen when writing. Finally, **operational feedback** is feedback that the user receives from the system as the results of his or her actions. For example, when a user manipulates a 3D virtual object with a 6-DOF device, the user gets reactive feedback from moving the device with her arm (in the form of kinesthetic feedback), instrumental feedback from observing the movement of the 6-DOF device and feeling its shape, and operational feedback from observing the motion of the virtual object.

The boundaries of the categories in this classification are a bit fuzzy, but they are still important in analyzing the different techniques for providing feedback to the user and particularly in discussing the main principle in designing feedback—**compliance.**

Feedback Compliance in 3D UIs

The key principle in designing effective feedback for interactive systems is the principle of compliance between different dimensions of the feedback provided to the user. It suggests that for efficient interaction, the 3D UI should *maintain spatial and temporal correspondence between multiple feedback dimensions* that the user receives. For the sensory dimensions, for example, if the visual feedback conflicts with the kinesthetic or proprioceptive feedback generated by the body, then user performance rapidly degrades (Smith and Smith 1987). This would happen, for example, if virtual objects moved in the opposite direction from the hand movement, a condition often called **feedback displacement**.

Because 3D UIs may tend to involve and engage users more than other UIs, a lack of compliance between the sensory dimensions may result not only in decreased performance, but also in much more dramatic effects such as headaches, blurred vision, dizziness, disorientation, or even severe nausea (**cybersickness**). The most basic explanation for cybersickness is a conflict between the feedback from the visual sense and other intrinsic feedback systems, such as the vestibular and proprioceptive systems (LaViola 2000a).

A number of specific types of compliance have been discussed in the human factors and 3D UI literature, and we discuss them in this section.

Spatial Compliance

The types of spatial feedback compliance include directional compliance, also called stimulus-response (S-R) compatibility (Fitts and Jones 1953); nulling compliance; and others. **Directional compliance** suggests that a virtual object should move in the same direction as the manipulated input device. For example, when the user rotates a virtual object using a 6-DOF input device, both the device and the virtual object should rotate in the same direction; that is, they should rotate around the same axis of rotation (Poupyrev et al. 2000). Directional compliance preserves the correspondence between the motions of virtual objects and the observed or felt motion of the physical input device. This allows the user to effectively anticipate the motion of the virtual objects in response to input and therefore plan and execute the desired trajectory of motion. Ensuring directional feedback compliance is important, although it has been shown that humans are extremely adaptable and can compensate for disparities between stimulus and response (Smith and Kosslyn 2013). However, a significant breakdown in directional feedback compliance might result in a decrease in user performance and even in cybersickness such as in the case of navigation without directional compliance (Harris et al. 1999).

Another category of spatial compliances is **nulling compliance.** Nulling compliance means that when the user returns the device to the initial position or orientation, the virtual objects also return to the corresponding initial position or orientation. The importance of preserving nulling compliance depends on the application. It has been shown, for example, that if the device is attached to the user's body, the nulling compliance might be important, as it allows the user to use muscle memory to remember the initial, neutral position of the device and object (Buxton 1986)

On the system level it is also desirable that instrumental and operational feedback are spatially compliant: for example, a virtual hand should be aligned as closely as possible with the user's real hand.

Temporal Compliance and Latency

The most typical example of lack of temporal compliance is latency—the temporal delay between user input and sensory feedback generated by the system in response to it. The investigation of latency was particularly relevant in the early days of VEs, when it was a critical problem because of slower computers and computer graphics rendering hardware. A large number of user studies have investigated the negative effects of latency on performance, in which a range of different measurement methods have been used (Ellis et al. 1999; Allison et al. 2001; Friston et al. 2014). From the sensorimotor point of view, the reason that latency affects user performance is the lack of compliance between internal feedback (e.g., proprioceptive and kinesthetic feedback) and external sensory feedback received by the user (e.g., visual feedback from the system). For example, studies of flight simulators have shown that viewpoint control lags as short as 50 ms have a significant impact on user performance, while latencies that are much longer can lead to oscillations and loss of control (Wickens 1986).

Not only absolute latency but also its variability may affect user performance. Indeed, in most complex computer graphics applications, latency is not constant. Experimental studies have found that at a 20 frames per second (fps) update rate, latency fluctuations as large as 40% do not significantly affect user performance on a manipulation task. At 17 fps, their effect becomes noticeable, and fluctuations become a significant problem at 10 fps (Watson et al. 1997).

With the rapid improvements in computer graphics hardware and software, the problem of latency is lessening. For example, an experimental AR system has an end-to-end latency of 80 microseconds (Lincoln et al. 2016). On the other hand, as rendering performance increases, the requirements for visual realism and environment complexity also increase, so latency should still be considered. Even if users can complete tasks in the presence of latency, relatively low levels of latency can still affect the overall user experience.

The simplest technique for dealing with latency is to increase the update rate by reducing the environment's complexity, using more sophisticated culling algorithms, or rendering the scene progressively (simple rendering during interaction and high-quality rendering during breaks in interaction (Airey et al. 1990). However, culling might not be trivial to perform, especially in AR applications in which users are looking through physical objects. For a discussion of methods, refer to Kalkofen et al. (2011).

Also, note that simply increasing the update rate does not eliminate all the sources of latency. For example, tracking devices have an inherent latency that is not tied to the update rate. Predictive filtering of the user input stream (e.g., tracking data) has also been investigated and has resulted in some success in reducing latency (Liang et al. 1991; Azuma and Bishop 1994). For a more detailed discussion of methods and effects in VR systems, please refer to Allen and Welch (2005), Welch et al. (2007), and Teather et al. (2009). For specific issues in AR tracking, a good starting point is Wagner et al. (2010).

While latency affects user experience in VR systems, in AR systems it can cause even more problems. In particular, offsets (misregistrations) between augmentations and real-world objects due to latency will result in difficulties processing the spatial information. A simple example can be seen in Figure 10.1: with increasing tracking problems, overlaid information cannot be correctly registered.

Figure 10.1 A mockup of an AR application illustrating potential interpretation problems due to tracking accuracy and/or latency (as well as perceptual issues): Where exactly is apartment 6? (Image courtesy of Ernst Kruijff)

Feedback Substitution

In designing and developing 3D UIs, it is often difficult to allow for all possible types of feedback. In particular, haptic feedback often requires devices that are expensive and difficult to operate. In the absence of haptic feedback, feedback substitution principles have often been used. Instead of haptic feedback, additional audio or visual cues can be provided. For example, in a selection task, the action of touching the virtual object can be indicated with a visual highlight (e.g., drawing a frame around the object or changing its color; Figure 10.2). An enhancement of this technique, predictive highlighting (Butterworth et al. 1992), shows the user the 3D object that is likely to be selected if the user continues the operation. This was found to be particularly useful in model editing mode, where the most probable vertex would highlight when the 3D cursor approached it. See section 3.3.5 for additional discussion.

There are many examples of sensory feedback substitution in VR, some of which are surprisingly effective. For example, Kruijff et al. (2016) found that self-motion perception could be increased in the absence of normal vestibular and haptic feedback by playing walking sounds, showing visual head bobbing, and providing vibrotactile cues to the user's feet (using the setup shown in Figure 10.3).

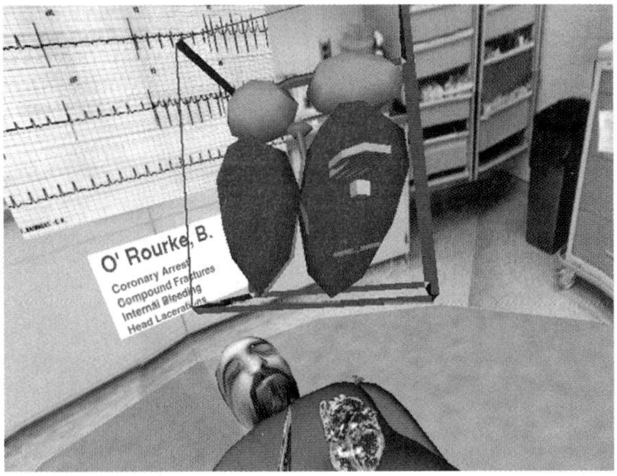

Figure 10.2 Feedback substitution: a visual cue substitutes for haptic feedback when a user touches a virtual object. (Reprinted with permission of HIT Lab, University of Washington)

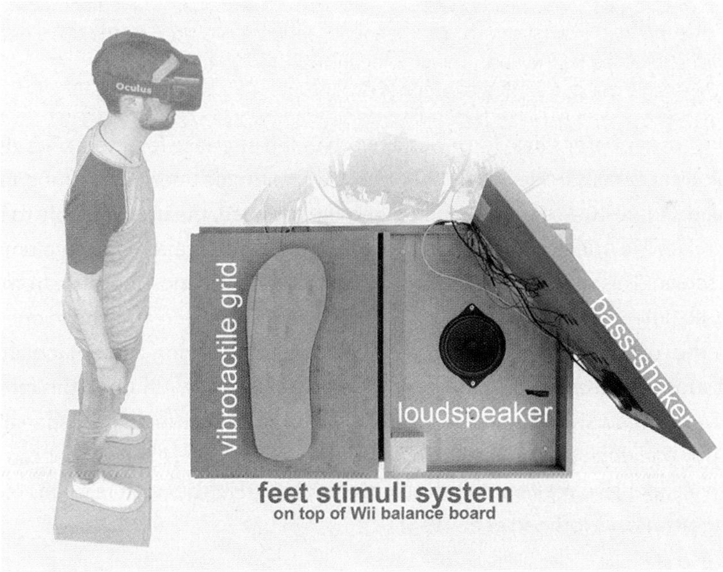

Figure 10.3 A platform that can provide walking sounds and vibrotactile sensations to the feet during lean-based navigation. (Image courtesy of Ernst Kruijff and Alexander Marquardt)

Passive Haptic Feedback

Another method of providing simple haptic feedback is to match the shape and appearance of a virtual object with the shape and appearance of a physical object so that the user can both see and "feel" the virtual object. This approach is called **passive haptic feedback**, or **props**.

Passive feedback is a type of instrumental feedback: it provides users with a tactile sense of the virtual tools they are using. Although this approach is significantly less flexible than general-purpose force-feedback devices, it has been quite successful for real-world 3D UIs.

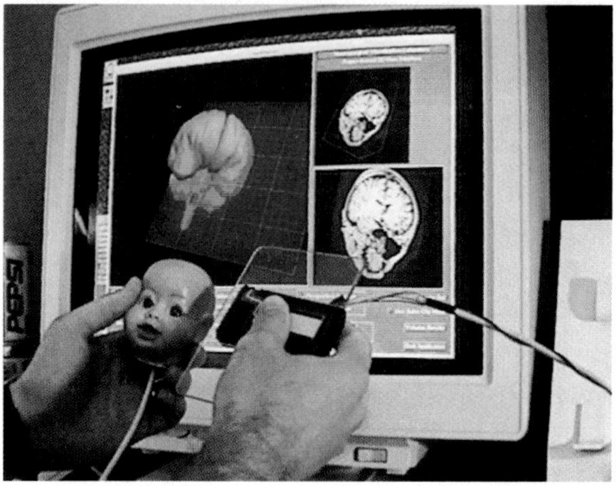

Figure 10.4 Two-handed interface with passive haptic feedback provided by the doll's head and cutting plane tool held by the user. (Hinckley et al. 1994, © 1994 IEEE)

One of the first uses of props in a 3D UI was a two-handed interface for interactive visualization of 3D neurological data (Hinckley et al. 1994). A 6-DOF magnetic tracker was embedded into in a doll's head (Figure 10.4), and by manipulating the toy head, the user was able to quickly and reliably relate the orientation of the input device to the orientation of the volumetric brain data on the screen. This resulted in efficient and enjoyable interaction, because from the user perspective, the interaction was analogous to holding a miniature "real" head in one hand. The tactile properties of the prop allowed the user to know its orientation without looking at the device, so the focus of attention could be kept entirely on the task. Although this interface was nonimmersive, in immersive VR, passive props can be even more effective. By spatially registering tracked physical objects with virtual objects of the same shape, the designer can provide the user with inexpensive yet very realistic haptic feedback. Hoffman refers to this technique as **tactile augmentation** (Hoffman et al. 1998).

Using passive physical props is an extremely useful design technique for 3D UIs. Props provide inexpensive physical and tactile feedback, significantly increasing the sense of presence and ease of interaction (Hoffman et al. 1998). They establish a common perceptual frame of reference between the device and the virtual objects, which in addition to ease of use may make it easier to learn the 3D UI (Hinckley et al. 1994). The introduction of tactile augmentation allows designers to explicitly control the realism of VEs, which can be useful in such applications as the treatment of phobias (Carlin et al. 1997). Passive haptics can also be used to enhance the illusion of redirected walking (Matsumoto et al. 2016), and a single passive haptic prop can be reused multiple times to produce the perception of a much more extensive haptic world (Azmandian et al. 2016).

There are also some disadvantages of using passive haptic feedback. First is the issue of scalability: using multiple movable physical props requires multiple trackers, which might be expensive and difficult to implement. Second, few experimental studies have shown any quantitative improvement in user performance when using props (Hinckley et al. 1997; Ware and Rose 1999). However, the studies did show that users preferred physical props. Props have been pushed forward in particular by the advent of many different kinds of tangible user interfaces (Ishii 2008).

10.2.3 Constraints

In 3D UIs, constraints are usually very narrowly understood as relations between 3D virtual objects in a scene. The theory of constraints, however, is more general and does not necessarily consider the type of objects involved in constraint specification. Constraints are generally defined as a relation between variables that must be satisfied (Marriott and Stuckey 1998). Examples of such relations could be that a line should stay horizontal, that values in spreadsheet cells are always related through a formula, or that pressure in a closed volume should stay below a specified critical level. The objective of constraint theory is the development of algorithms that can find the values of variables satisfying the specified constraints.

For interactive computer graphics, constraints can be defined as relations that define some sort of **geometrical coherence** of the virtual scene during the user's interaction with it. Although the implementation of constraints in interactive 3D computer graphics can use the theory and algorithms developed in constraint theory, from the user-interaction point of view, the way constraints are *applied* is more important than the details of their implementation. The main reason that constraints are used in 3D UIs is that they can significantly simplify interaction while improving accuracy and user efficiency. Several types of constraints can be used in 3D UIs.

Physically realistic constraints are an often-used category. One of the best examples of such constraints is collision detection and avoidance. When collision detection is enabled, the user's freedom of movement is constrained by the boundaries of the virtual objects—the user's virtual viewpoint or virtual hand is not allowed to pass through them. Another typical constraint is gravity—objects fall to the virtual ground when the user releases them. Physical constraints should be used with caution: in some applications, such as training or games, satisfying physical constraints is important because it is a critical part of the experience. However, in other applications, introducing such constraints may make interaction more difficult and frustrating. For example, in modeling applications, it might be convenient to leave objects "hanging in the air" when the user releases them (Smith 1987). Not allowing the user to pass through virtual walls could also lead to feedback incompliance. The flexibility of 3D UIs allows us to selectively choose which physical properties of the physical environment are implemented in the virtual world, and the choice should be based on the requirements of the application.

Constraints are also used to *reduce the number of DOF of the user input* to make interaction simpler. For example, a virtual object can be constrained to move only on the surface of a virtual plane, which makes positioning it easier because the user has to control only 2-DOF instead of 3 DOF. Such constrained manipulation has often been used in desktop 3D UIs to allow effective manipulation of 3D models using a mouse (Bier 1990). Another example is constraining travel to the ground or terrain of the virtual scene. This allows a user to effectively manipulate the viewpoint using only 2D input devices (Igarashi et al. 1998), and it may help users with 3D input devices to maintain spatial orientation.

Dynamic alignment tools, such as snap grids, guiding lines, and guiding surfaces that are well-known in 3D modeling applications, are a more complex way to reduce the required DOF. In this approach, the position and orientation of objects are automatically modified to align them with a particular guiding object, which can be as simple as a grid in space or as complex as a 3D surface (Bier 1986, 1990). With this type of constraint, objects snap to alignment with these guides. For example, objects can snap to an equally spaced 3D grid in space in order to make the alignment of several objects easier, or an object can automatically rotate so that it lies exactly on the guiding surface when the user brings it near to that surface.

Intelligent constraints take into account the **semantics** of objects and attempt to constrain their interaction in order to enforce meaningful relations. For example, a virtual lamp can be constrained to stand only on horizontal surfaces such as tables, while a picture frame only hangs on vertical walls (Bukowski and Séquin 1995).

The disadvantage of all constraints is that they reduce user control over the interaction, which might not be appropriate for all applications. In many applications, therefore, it is important to allow the user to easily turn constraints on and off. However, when the user requirements are clearly understood and interaction flow carefully designed, constraints can be a very effective design tool for 3D UIs.

10.2.4 Two-Handed Control

Using both hands for 3D interaction allows users to transfer their everyday manipulation experiences and skills to interaction with 3D computer-generated environments. Furthermore, two-handed interaction can significantly increase user performance on certain tasks in both real and virtual interaction. For example, it has been shown that a writing task using both hands resulted in 20% more efficient performance than when only one hand was used (Guiard 1987).

Therefore, two-handed or **bimanual** input has been an active topic of investigation in UIs since the early 1980s (Buxton and Myers 1986). The benefits of two-handed input have been demonstrated in various tasks and applications, including both 2D interfaces (Bier et al. 1993) and 3D interfaces (Sachs et al. 1991; Hinckley et al. 1994; Mapes and Moshell 1995; Zeleznik et al. 1997). In this section, we briefly describe some of the important principles that have been proposed for designing bimanual 3D UIs.

Guiard's Framework of Bimanual Manipulation

The theoretical foundation behind most research on bimanual 3D interaction was proposed by Guiard, who studied the underlying mechanisms controlling the distribution of work between the dominant and nondominant hands of humans (Guiard 1987). We introduced Guiard's framework briefly in section 3.5.1.

He observed that some tasks are inherently **unimanual**, such as throwing darts. Other tasks are **bimanual symmetric,** where each hand performs identical actions either **synchronously,** such as pulling a rope or weightlifting, or **asynchronously,** such as milking a cow or typing on the keyboard. A third class of bimanual actions is **bimanual asymmetric** tasks (sometimes called **cooperative** manipulation), in which the actions of both hands are different but closely coordinated to accomplish the same task (Figure 10.5). A familiar example of such an asymmetric bimanual task is writing: the nondominant hand controls the orientation of the page for more convenient and efficient writing by the dominant hand.

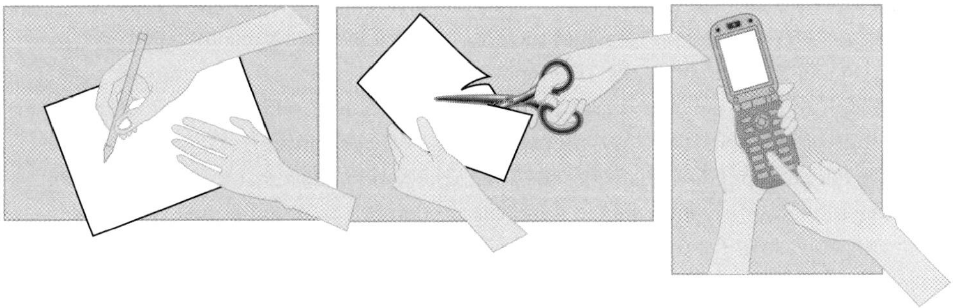

Figure 10.5 Examples of the asymmetric separation of work between hands in bimanual manipulation: the nondominant hand defines a spatial framework for the actions of the preferred hand. (Illustrations by Keiko Nakao)

Guiard proposed three principles that characterize the roles of the hands in tasks involving an asymmetric division of labor (Guiard 1987):

- The nondominant hand dynamically adjusts the spatial frame of reference for the actions of the dominant hand.
- The dominant hand produces fine-grained precision movements, while the nondominant hand performs gross manipulation.
- The manipulation is initiated by the nondominant hand.

We should note, however, that the separation of labor between hands is a fluid, dynamic process, and in complex tasks, hands can rapidly switch between symmetric and asymmetric manipulation modes.

Guiard's principles provide an important theoretical framework for investigating and designing two-handed 3D UIs. In the rest of this section, we discuss some examples of such interfaces, classifying them according to the asymmetric and symmetric division of labor.

Asymmetric Bimanual 3D Interaction Techniques

The bimanual 3D interface for neurological visualization that we discussed above was one of the earliest attempts to develop bimanual interaction techniques based on Guiard's principles. In Hinckley's interface, the nondominant hand controlled the orientation of the 3D volumetric neurological data (using a doll's head prop), while the dominant hand controlled a virtual cutting plane that "sliced" the data and presented slices on the screen for analysis (see Figure 10.4). According to the principles of asymmetric separation of labor, the nondominant hand controlled the gross position and orientation of a 3D virtual workspace, and the dominant hand performed fine operations in that workspace.

The basic method presented above has been explored in a number of 3D interaction systems and for a variety of tasks. A two-handed interface for an immersive workbench display (Cutler et al. 1997), for example, provides tools for two-handed object manipulation and rotation using 6-DOF input devices. The nondominant hand controls the position of a virtual object and the orientation of its rotation axis, while the dominant hand controls rotation around the axis. Zeleznik et al. (1997) propose a similar 3D position and rotation technique using two mice as input devices (Figure 10.6). With the nondominant hand, the user positions a point on a 2D ground plane, creating a vertical axis (left cursor in Figure 10.6), while the dominant hand allows the user to rotate an object around that axis (right cursor in Figure 10.6). Scaling and zooming were implemented in a similar way.

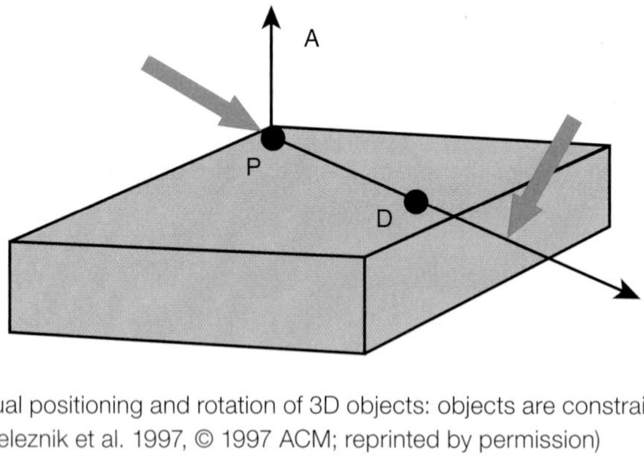

Figure 10.6 Bimanual positioning and rotation of 3D objects: objects are constrained to move only on the plane. (Zeleznik et al. 1997, © 1997 ACM; reprinted by permission)

Virtual menus (see section 9.5) have often been implemented using bimanual manipulation in which the virtual menu is held in the nondominant hand while the dominant hand is used to select an item in the menu (Mapes and Moshell 1995; Cutler et al. 1997). Virtual writing techniques (Poupyrev et al. 1998) use the nondominant hand to hold a tracked tablet input device, while the user writes on the tablet with the dominant hand. Similar two-handed prop-based interfaces are quite common (Coquillart and Wesche 1999; Schmalstieg et al. 1999). The Voodoo Dolls interaction technique that we discussed in Chapter 7, "Selection and Manipulation," (section 7.7.2) is yet another example of using asymmetric bimanual control for object manipulation (Pierce et al. 1999).

A somewhat different two-handed interface has been implemented for desktop 3D viewpoint control (Balakrishnan and Kurtenbach 1999). The nondominant hand controls the 3D position of the virtual viewpoint, while the dominant hand performs application-specific tasks, such as selection, docking, and 3D painting.

A number of user studies have shown that carefully designed asymmetric bimanual interfaces have a significant performance advantage and are strongly preferred by users (Hinckley, Pausch et al. 1997). A study by Balakrishnan and Kurtenbach (1999), for example, found that in a selection task, user performance was 20% faster than a one-handed interface when the user controlled the viewpoint using the nondominant hand and used the dominant hand to perform another task. Ulinski et al. (2007) found that asymmetric bimanual selection techniques were less fatiguing and induced less mental workload that symmetric bimanual techniques.

Symmetric Bimanual 3D Interaction Techniques

Symmetric two-handed manipulation meanwhile has found high acceptance in many gesture-based interfaces. A typical task that has been implemented using symmetric bimanual manipulation is **scaling,** where the user can scale objects by picking up two sides of the object and moving the hands apart or together simultaneously (Zeleznik et al. 1997). A bimanual rotation technique implemented on a workbench display (Cutler et al. 1997) allowed the user to rotate the virtual scene with a steering-wheel gesture. Both of these techniques are examples of synchronous bimanual interaction.

Asynchronous symmetric two-handed manipulation can also be implemented for interaction with 3D environments. For example, the Polyshop system implemented a rope-pulling gesture for 3D travel (see Chapter 8, "Travel," section 8.7.2): the user pulled himself through the environment by pulling on an invisible rope with both hands (Mapes and Moshell 1995).

10.2.5 Designing for Different User Groups

Another important part of 3D UI design is to understand the characteristics of the target user population and design with these user characteristics in mind.

Age

Both information presentation and interaction methods should consider the age of the user. Children often require a different interface design than adults because they are physically smaller, they have a shorter attention span, and the mental model they form about the interaction differs from that of adults. Older users may need text presented in a larger font size, or they may not be able to make movements quickly. More research is needed to determine the effects of age on user experience with 3D UIs, even though some studies involving elderly users have been performed (Bobeth et al. 2012). Design tools such as personas could help to support this process (Woeckl et al. 2012).

Prior Experience with 3D UIs

Targeting a user population that is already proficient with 3D input and output devices allows us to design more complex 3D UIs. Also, observations indicate that experience with console games or desktop 3D computer games can be positively correlated with performance in 3D UIs. On the other hand, 3D UIs for novice users need to be simplified and easily learnable. For more discussion on learning and skills, please refer to section 3.2.3.

Physical Characteristics

Simple things like a user's height can affect the usability of a 3D UI. For example, a basic implementation of the Go-Go technique (see Chapter 7, section 7.4.1) has a fixed threshold at which the nonlinear arm extension begins. Users with shorter arms, therefore, will not be able to reach nearly as far into the environment as other users. In this case, an adaptive threshold based on arm length would be appropriate.

The user's handedness (i.e., his dominant hand) is another example: some input devices are designed only for right-handers. Asymmetric bimanual interfaces must be adaptable for both left- and right-handed users.

Perceptual, Cognitive, and Motor Abilities

The color perception and stereo vision abilities of different users can vary, and this of course affects the choice of a display system. A specific cognitive characteristic affecting 3D UI design is the user's spatial ability (ability to think, plan, and act in a 3D space). If the user population is known to have lower-than-average spatial abilities, a simplified interface for 3D travel and manipulation may be needed (e.g., the use of additional constraints). People with cognitive or motor disabilities may require a simplified interface as well as the use of special-purpose devices.

10.3 Inventing 3D User Interfaces

This section surveys some of the informal approaches that have often been used in creating novel 3D UIs and interaction techniques. These approaches lie in a continuum between strict imitations of reality (naturalism or isomorphism) and magic (nonisomorphism, or things that can't be found in the real world). The approaches presented here should be taken as illustrative examples to help designers and developers ask the right questions that will lead to the development of compelling 3D UIs. Of course, the process of creating something new is difficult to formalize and explain; that is perhaps the most magical, or artistic, part of designing 3D UIs.

10.3.1 Borrowing from the Real World

The most basic, tried-and-true approach is to attempt to simulate, or adapt from, the physical world. In some cases, the goal is to replicate the real world as closely as possible; in other cases, only selected elements of the real world are brought into the VE and creatively adapted to the needs of 3D interaction. In this section, we discuss some of the basic approaches and techniques that have been reported in the literature.

Simulating Reality

Simulating reality is key in all simulation applications, such as flight simulators, medical training, treatment of phobias, some entertainment applications, and human factors evaluations of human-controlled mechanisms such as vehicles (Loftin and Kenney 1995; Carlin et al. 1997; Burdea et al. 1998; Cruz-Neira and Lutz 1999; Ullrich and Kuhlen 2012).

The advantage of using this approach is that the user already knows how to use the interface from everyday experience, so the time spent learning how to use the system can be kept to a minimum. Furthermore, the interface often can be implemented based either on the designer's intuition and common sense or on the clearly specified technical design requirements of the application.

Advanced and special-purpose 3D interaction techniques might not be necessary in such applications. Interaction with virtual space in this type of interface might be frustrating and difficult, but if the real-world interaction is also frustrating and difficult, then this is actually a feature!

Designers may, however, need to compromise on how realistic the simulation needs to be. Because of the limitations of current technology, the simulations that we can create may be far from real-life experiences or prohibitively expensive (e.g., professional flight simulators). In addition, there is some evidence that semirealistic interaction may in some cases provide a worse user experience than interaction not based on the real world at all (Nabiyouni and Bowman 2015). The realism of simulation that the developer should aim for thus depends heavily on the requirements of the application and the capabilities of the technology.

For example, in a VE for entertainment, the goal might be to provide visitors with a first-person immersive experience in an environment that cannot be normally experienced in the real world. Exact visual realism might be less important than responsiveness and ease of learning for this application, and thus interaction can be limited to a very simple flying technique that allows the user to fully experience the environment. As another example, in a medical training simulator designed to teach medical students palpation skills in diagnosing prostate cancer, a realistic visual simulation is not required at all, so only a primitive 3D visual model is needed. A realistic and precise simulation of haptic sensation, however, is a key issue, because learning the feel of human tissue is the main goal of the system (Burdea et al. 1998). On the other hand, in a system developed for treatment of spider phobia, a simple toy spider was used to provide the patients with a passive haptic sensation of the virtual spider that they observed in the VE (Carlin et al. 1997). It was found that this haptic feedback combined with the graphical representation of the spider was realistic enough to trigger a strong reaction from the patient.

These examples demonstrate that the importance of realism is dependent on the application; 3D UIs should deliver only as much realism as is needed for the application. The effect of realism, or level of detail, on user performance, learning, engagement, and training transfer is an important topic of research but is outside the scope of this book. For further reading on this subject, see Luebke et al. (2002), McMahan et al. (2012), Bowman et al. (2012), and Kruijff et al. (2016).

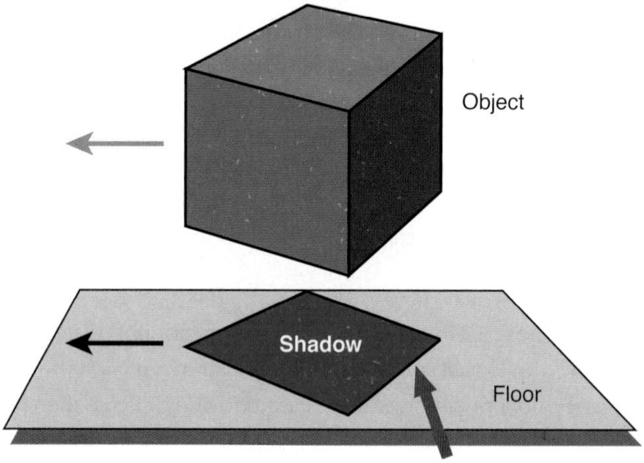

Figure 10.7 Shadows can be used for constrained 3D manipulation. (Herndon et al. 1992, © 1992 ACM; reprinted by permission)

Adapting from the Real World

Instead of attempting to replicate the real world, 3D UIs can also adapt artifacts, ideas, and philosophies from the real world.

The use of **real-world metaphors**—adapting everyday or special-purpose tools as metaphors for 3D interaction—has been a very effective technique for the design of 3D widgets and interaction techniques. For example, a virtual vehicle metaphor has been one of the most often used metaphors for 3D navigation. A virtual flashlight has been used to set viewpoint or lighting directions, and shadows have been used not only to add realism to the rendering but also to provide simple interaction techniques—users can manipulate objects in a 3D environment by dragging their shadows (Figure 10.7; Herndon et al. 1992).

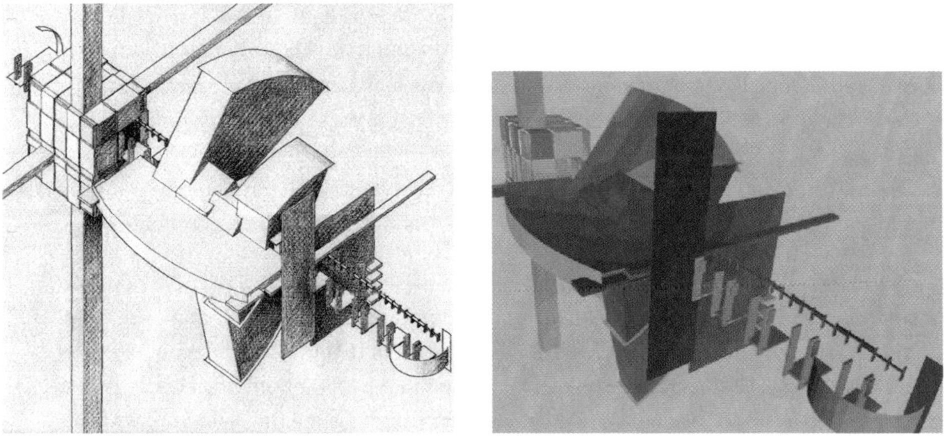

Figure 10.8 Virtual architecture design from architectural sketch (left) to VE (right). (Campbell 1996; reprinted by permission of the author)

As these examples show, the metaphors are only a starting point, and interaction techniques based on them should be carefully designed to match the requirements of the applications and limitations of the technology used. Not just individual tools, objects, and their features but also entire domains of human activity can inspire and guide the design of 3D UIs. Architecture and movies have been an important source of inspiration—movies such as *Minority Report* and *Iron-man* or books by William Gibson (*Neuromancer*) or Neal Stephenson (*Snow Crash*) are just a few of the many examples. The objective is not simply to replicate but instead to creatively adapt the basic principles and ideas in designing 3D UIs and virtual spaces. For example, games have been heavily influenced by the movie culture, exploring transition and storytelling techniques fundamental to film. It has also been observed that both architecture and virtual worlds are based on ordering and organizing shapes and forms in space (Alexander et al. 1977); the design principles from architecture therefore can be transferred to the design of 3D UIs.

Campbell (1996), for example, attempted to design VEs using basic architectural principles (Figure 10.8), suggesting that this would allow users to rely on their familiarity with real-world architectural spaces to quickly understand and navigate through 3D virtual worlds. At the same time, designers of VEs are not limited by the fundamental physical restrictions that are encountered in traditional architecture, giving them new creative freedom in designing 3D interactive spaces. See the discussion of architectural wayfinding cues in Chapter 8, "Travel," section 8.9.2, for more on this topic.

Another common technique for adapting elements from the real world to the design of a 3D UI is to borrow natural physical actions that we use in real life. For example, in the Osmose interactive VE, the user navigated by using breathing and balance control, a technique inspired by the scuba diving technique of buoyancy control (Davies and Harrison 1996).

The user was able to float upward by breathing in, to fall by breathing out, and to change direction by altering the body's center of balance. The intention was to create an illusion of floating rather than flying or driving in the environment. In a more recent example, the Virtual Mitten technique (Achibet et al. 2014) used a mitten metaphor to help users understand the grasping action and haptic feedback provided by a simple elastic feedback device. Since the device only provided one-DOF of feedback, a mitten (which allows grasping only between the thumb and the four other fingers together) was the perfect analogy for this action.

Numerous real-world artifacts and concepts can be used in designing 3D UIs, providing an unlimited source of ideas for the creativity of designers and developers. Because users are already familiar with real-world artifacts, it is easy for them to understand the purpose and method of using 3D interaction techniques based on them. Metaphors, however, are never complete, and an important goal is to creatively adapt and change the real-world artifacts and interactions. It is also difficult to find real-world analogies and metaphors for abstract operations. In such cases, a symbolic representation might be more appropriate.

10.3.2 Adapting from 2D User Interfaces

Adapting interaction techniques from traditional 2D UIs has been another common 3D UI design technique. Two-dimensional interaction techniques have many attractive properties. First, 2D UIs and interaction have been thoroughly studied, and interaction paradigms in 2D interfaces are well established, which makes it relatively easy for 3D interface designers to find an appropriate interaction technique. Second, almost all users of 3D UIs are already fluent with 2D interaction, so learning can be kept to a minimum. Third, interaction in two dimensions is significantly easier than interaction in three dimensions—the user has to manipulate only 2-DOF rather than 6-DOF. Consequently, 2D interaction may allow users to perform some tasks, such as selection and manipulation, with a higher degree of precision. Finally, some common tasks do not scale well into three dimensions. For example, writing and sketching is significantly easier to perform in 2D than in 3D. These considerations have prompted researchers to design 3D UIs that attempt to take advantage of both 2D and 3D interaction techniques, trying to combine these two input styles in a seamless and intuitive manner.

Literal Approach: Overlaying a 2D GUI on a 3D World

With little or no modification, 2D UI elements can be embedded directly into a 3D environment. Certainly, for desktop-based 3D and handheld or head-worn AR applications, this is a natural technique—the 3D scene is rendered in a window, and traditional 2D GUI elements (menus, sliders, etc.) can be attached to this window outside of the 3D environment. A similar approach has been used quite often in immersive VR, particularly for system control tasks and when interacting with inherently 2D information (see Chapter 9, "System Control").

The shortcoming with this approach is that the GUI interaction elements are introduced as a separate layer on top of the 3D world, so it introduces an additional mode of interaction:

the user has to switch into the menu mode and then switch back to 3D UI mode, which also includes the switching between different disparity planes (Kruijff et al. 2010, 2003). The approach also does not scale well to other 2D tasks.

2D GUI as an Element of the 3D Environment

An alternative way to place a 2D GUI into a 3D environment is to render the interface as a first-class object in the 3D world. For example, menus and other interface elements can be rendered on some planar surface within the VR, either as 3D buttons and menus arranged on a plane or as a dynamic 2D texture attached to a polygon (Angus and Sowizral 1996). The user can interact with these 2D UI elements in the same way we interact with them in desktop or tablet environments—by touching or pointing at them on a 2D virtual surface using virtual hand or ray-casting interaction techniques (e.g., Mine 1995b). See Chapter 9, "System Control," section 9.5 for several examples of such 2D menus in 3D environments.

The difficulty with this approach is that there is no haptic feedback, so interacting with the 2D interface might be difficult and frustrating. To overcome this problem, a physical prop—such as a clipboard—can be tracked and registered with the 2D interface so that it appears on top of the clipboard. The user, holding the physical clipboard in one hand, can touch and interact with 2D interface elements using a finger or a pen held in the other hand, which is also tracked. This design approach is sometimes called the pen-and-tablet technique.

One of the first systems that used this approach was implemented by Angus and Sowizral (1996); it provided the immersed user (who was inspecting a virtual model of an aircraft) with a hyperlinked document that included 2D plans, drawings, and other information (Figure 10.9). A similar technique was developed for the semi-immersive workbench environment by Coquillart and Wesche (1999), where instead of using an everyday clipboard, 2D data was spatially registered with a tracked transparent plastic pad. When the user looked through the pad, he perceived the illusion that the 2D information appeared on the pad (more on transparent props below).

The pen-and-tablet technique can be extended by using a touch-sensitive tablet instead of a passive prop. With this active prop, the user can perform significantly more advanced interaction than simply pressing 2D buttons. The Virtual Notepad, for example, allows users not only to view 2D information while immersed in a VE but also to annotate it with 2D drawings (Poupyrev et al. 1998). Another example is the hybrid system developed by Bornik et al. (2006), which uses a special-purpose input device that can be used to interact on a (synced) tablet or directly with the 3D medical content on a stereo screen. Such hybrid systems may offer the best of both worlds, with the precision of a 2D interface and the intuitiveness of a 3D UI (see Figure 10.10)

Figure 10.9 Embedding an interactive 2D interface into a 3D VE.
(Angus and Sowizral 1996, © 1996 IEEE)

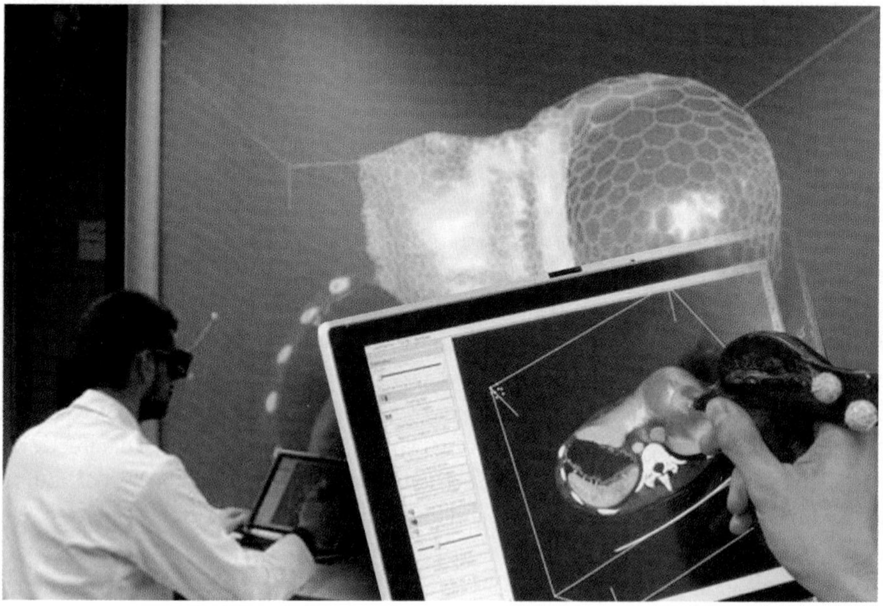

Figure 10.10 The Eye of Ra hybrid interface. (Image courtesy of Ernst Kruijff)

You have probably noticed that we have already discussed the pen-and-tablet idea several times in the context of different tasks. That's because it's a rather generic approach in designing 3D UIs that also incorporates many of the strategies we have discussed before. To summarize, the pen and tablet makes use of

- two-handed, asymmetric interaction
- physical props (passive haptic feedback)
- 2D interaction, reducing the DOF of input
- a surface constraint to aid input
- body-referenced interaction

2D Interaction with 3D Objects

It has been often noted that 3D interaction is difficult: the coordinated control of 6-DOF requires significantly more effort than manipulation of only 2-DOF. Reducing the number of degrees of control is especially crucial when high-precision interaction is needed, such as when creating 3D models or performing virtual surgery. Using constraints (section 10.2.2) is one technique to reduce the number of controlled DOF and simplify interaction. A particular instance of this technique that has been successful is based on constraining input with physical 2D surfaces and gesture-based interaction.

Schmalstieg et al. (1999), for example, developed an effective 2D gestural interface for 3D interaction by using tracked transparent passive props with a workbench display (see Chapter 9, Figure 9.20). The user looks at the 3D environment through the transparent prop (e.g., a simple transparent Plexiglas plate) and interacts with objects by drawing 2D gestures on the prop. The transparent plate acts as a physical constraint for the user input, making drawing relatively easy.

The system determines the objects that the user interacts with by casting a ray from the user's viewpoint through the pen and transparent pad. For example, Schmalstieg et al. (1999) demonstrated how a group of 3D objects can be selected by drawing a lasso around them on the prop.

Transparent props allow the development of very generic techniques that can be used to interact with any 3D objects in the scene. Furthermore, when the position of objects can be constrained to lie on a virtual ground plane, the user can draw 2D gestures directly on the surface of the display, as long as the pen-tracking technology is provided. For example, in Ergodesk, the user interacts in 2D by drawing directly on the display surface (Figure 10.11), sketching 3D models using a three-button stylus (Forsberg et al. 1997). The system is based on the SKETCH modeling system (Zeleznik et al. 1996) that interprets lines as operations and parameters for 3D modeling commands. Creating a cube, for example, requires the user to draw three gesture lines, one for each of the principal axes, meeting at a single point.

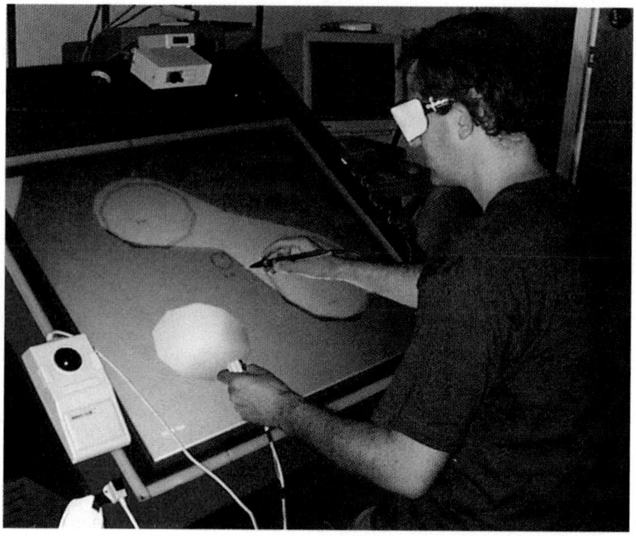

Figure 10.11 Sketching 3D objects directly on the display surface in Ergodesk. (Forsberg et al. 1997, © 1997 IEEE)

The sketching interface is simple to learn and allows the user to easily create 3D objects by sketching them on a 2D physical surface. This is significantly easier then manipulating or sculpting 3D objects directly using all 6-DOF of input. Furthermore, the user can use another hand for performing traditional 3D input tasks, such as navigating or manipulating 3D objects.

10.3.3 Magic and Aesthetics

It has long been argued that the real power of 3D UIs lies not only in simulating or adapting real-world features, but also in creating a "better" reality by utilizing magical interaction techniques (e.g., Smith 1987; Stoakley et al. 1995; Shneiderman 2003). One advantage of magical interaction techniques is that they allow users to overcome many human limitations that are so prominent in the real world: limitations of our cognitive, perceptual, physical, and motor capabilities. The second advantage of this approach is that it reduces the effect of technological limitations by compensating for them with enhanced capabilities of the UI. In fact, most of the interaction techniques discussed in Part IV of this book are magic techniques to some degree. For example, Go-Go (Chapter 7, section 7.4.1) and flying techniques (Chapter 8, section 8.5) enhance our motor capabilities by allowing us to reach further and travel in ways we can't in the real world; the world-in-miniature technique (Chapter 7, section 7.7.2) extends our perceptual capabilities by allowing us to see the entire 3D environment at once; and many system control techniques enhance our cognitive capabilities by visually presenting available choices rather than forcing us to remember them.

There are many approaches that can help to develop new magical techniques. Considering human limitations and looking for solutions that help to overcome them is one possible approach. Cultural clichés and metaphors, such as a flying carpet, can also suggest interesting possibilities for designing magical 3D UIs. For example, the Voodoo Dolls technique (Chapter 7, section 7.7.2) is based on a magical metaphor that suggests that the user can affect remote objects by interacting with their miniature, toy like representations. Because such metaphors are rooted in the popular culture, users may be able to grasp interaction concepts almost immediately.

The relationships between techniques and cultural metaphors, however, can also be a source of difficulties. For example, in order to understand the metaphor of flying carpet techniques—a very popular metaphor in VEs (Butterworth et al. 1992; Pausch et al. 1996)—the user needs to know what a magic carpet is and what it can do. Although some metaphors are quite universal, others might be significantly more obscure. For example, the Virtual Tricorder metaphor (Wloka and Greenfield 1995) is based on imaginary devices from the *Star Trek* television series, which may not be well known by users outside of countries where this show was popular. It is not easy to find effective and compelling metaphors for magical interaction techniques; however, the right metaphor can lead to a very enjoyable and effective 3D UI.

The discussion of realism and magic in designing 3D UIs also directly relates to the **aesthetics** of the 3D environment. The traditional focus of interactive 3D computer graphics, strongly influenced by the film and simulation industries, was to strive for photorealistic rendering—attempting to *explicitly* reproduce physical reality. Although this approach is important in specific applications, such as simulation and training, photorealism may be neither necessary nor effective in many other 3D applications. In fact, modern computer graphics are still not powerful enough to reproduce reality so that it is indistinguishable from the real world, even though realism (especially in games) can already be incredibly high. Furthermore, humans are amazingly skilled at distinguishing real from fake, particularly when it comes to humans; this is why faces rendered with computer graphics often look artificial and therefore unpleasant (the "uncanny valley" effect).

In many applications, however, photorealism may not be entirely necessary: sketchy, cartoonlike rendering can be effective and compelling in communicating the state of the interaction, while at the same time being enjoyable and effective. One example of such an application is a 3D learning environment for children (Johnson et al. 1998).

Nonphotorealistic (cartoonlike) rendering can be particularly effective in drawing humans, because it can suggest similarities using a few strong visual cues while omitting many less relevant visual features. We can observe this effect in political cartoons: even when drawings are grossly distorted, they usually have striking similarities with the subjects of the cartoons, making them immediately recognizable. Simple, cartoonlike rendering of virtual humans or the avatars of other users is also effective from a system point of view, because simpler 3D models result in faster rendering. Thus, more computational power can be dedicated to other aspects of human simulation, such as realistic motion. This allows designers to create effective and enjoyable interfaces for such applications as online 3D communities, chat environments, and games. Research on the effectiveness of virtual humans has also shown that nonphotorealistic virtual characters are more acceptable and more effective in a variety of real-world settings (Bickmore et al. 2009).

Another advantage of non-photorealistic aesthetics in 3D UIs is the ability to create a mood or atmosphere in the 3D environment, as well as to suggest properties of the environment rather than render them explicitly. For example, a rough pencil-style rendering of an architectural model can inform the client that the project is still unfinished (Klein et al. 2000). The possibility to create mood and atmosphere is key in entertainment applications as well as in media art installations. One of the systems that pioneered this broader sense of aesthetics for 3D UIs was Osmose, a VE designed by Char Davies (Davies and Harrison 1996). The aesthetics of Osmose were neither abstract nor photorealistic, but somewhere in between. Implemented using multilayer transparent imagery and heavy use of particle animation, Osmose (see Figure 10.12) provided the user with the impression of being surrounded by the VE, creating a strong sense of being there (i.e., a sense of presence).

Figure 10.12 Vertical tree. Digital frame captured in real time through head-worn display during live performance of immersive virtual environment OSMOSE. (© 1995 Char Davies)

The aesthetic aspect of 3D UI design is an interesting and very important part of compelling, immersive, and easy-to-use interfaces. As the rendering power of computer graphics increases, and therefore the range of tools available to artists and designers broadens, the importance of aesthetics in 3D interaction will continue to grow in the future.

10.4 Design Guidelines

We summarize the discussion above with a number of general guidelines related to design approaches for 3D UIs.

In the design of 2D UIs, a great deal of effort is spent in designing a system that is understandable, intuitive, and well organized, but very rarely do designers have to consider the physical actions users will be performing (although issues such as repetitive stress injuries have made these actions more prominent). In 3D UIs, however, users are often interacting while standing, while wearing or holding heavy or bulky devices, and while moving the whole body. Thus, issues of user comfort and safety are extremely relevant. We offer several practical guidelines for designing comfortable 3D UIs, with a particular emphasis on public installations as an example of 3D UIs for real-world use.

> **Tip**
>
> Move wires and cables out of the way or use wireless solutions when possible; reduce weight of the equipment.

HWDs, trackers, and other input/output devices are typically tethered to the host computer or to an interface box (although wireless devices are becoming more common). One of the most common complaints of VE users is that wires and cables get in the way during system use. If the wires are near the floor, users can trip over them or get them wrapped around their legs when they turn. Hanging wires can get in the way during arm movements. Such situations are annoying, can interrupt the user's interaction, and can reduce the sense of presence. Especially for public systems, it is important to find a cable-management solution, such as hanging cables from the ceiling, to minimize these problems. Care should be taken to leave enough length in the cables to allow users free physical movement.

Hanging wires from the ceiling can also reduce the weight of the equipment worn by the user. Weight is an important problem, especially in immersive VR systems; some 3D input and display devices are heavy. The weight of some HWDs is especially troublesome—even short periods of use can result in user fatigue. In mobile AR systems, the user must also carry the computing and power, so total weight may be even more important. Every effort should be made to reduce the overall weight the user must bear, and supporting comfortable poses for operation also helps considerably (Veas and Kruijff, 2010).

> **Tip**
>
> Provide physical and virtual barriers to keep the user and the equipment safe.

With HWD-based VR systems, the user cannot see the physical world and thus is prone to walk into walls, chairs, tables, or other physical objects. In surround-screen systems, the screens seem to disappear when the virtual world is projected on them, so users tend to walk into the screens, which may damage them. The most common approach to addressing these issues is to establish a safe zone around the user by making a physical barrier, such as a railing, that the user can hold on to. The safe zone should be large enough to allow sufficient physical movement but small enough to keep the user away from any potentially dangerous areas.

Virtual barriers can also be effective. These typically take the form of visuals that appear when a user is approaching the boundary of the safe area. Some systems that include a front-facing camera, allowing the system to fade in a view of the real world when the user is moving close to a dangerous area.

> **Tip**
>
> Limit interaction in free space; provide a device resting place.

The interface design should limit free-space interaction in which the user's hand is not physically supported. For example, the image-plane interaction technique (Chapter 7, section 7.5.1) requires the user to hold her hand in free space to select an object, which over a long period of time is very tiresome. Thus, interaction sequences should be designed so that free-space interaction occurs in short chunks of time with resting periods in between. The user should be allowed to rest her hands or arms without breaking the flow of interaction. Also, consider providing a resting place for a device if it is not attached to the user—this could be a stand, a hook, a tool belt, or some other method for putting a device away when it is not needed.

> **Tip**
>
> Design public systems to be sanitary.

When a large number of users wear, hold, or touch the same devices, hygiene and health issues are important (Stanney et al. 1998). The designer might consider a routine schedule for cleaning the devices. Another approach is to use removable parts that can be disposed of after a single use, such as thin glove liners for glove-based input devices or HWD liners—light plastic disposable caps that users put on before using the HWD. Also, some HWD providers sell face cushion replacements.

> **Tip**
>
> Design for relatively short sessions and encourage breaks.

Cybersickness and fatigue can be a significant problem when using immersive VE systems. Even though graphics, optics, and tracking have greatly improved, many users may still feel some symptoms of sickness or fatigue after 30 minutes to 1 hour of use. In public VR installations, the time that the user spends in the system can be explicitly limited (Davies and Harrison 1996). In other applications, the interface designer can mitigate these problems by allowing the work to be done in short blocks of time.

> **Tip**
>
> Design for comfortable poses.

As we mentioned in our first tip, supporting a comfortable pose can considerably improve user comfort over time. In particular with gestural interfaces and handheld AR interfaces, holding poses or performing actions at a specific height can be very uncomfortable. Consider poses that place the hands at a relatively low, possibly angled position and close to the body (see Figure 10.13; Veas and Kruijff 2008, 2010). Some commercial gesture systems suggest that users rest during gameplay and limit overall duration to avoid any discomfort or repetitive motion injuries.

Figure 10.13 A user holding a handheld AR device at an angled arm pose for user comfort. (Veas and Kruijff 2008, 2010, image courtesy of Ernst Kruijff)

With respect to feedback and constraints, we can provide the following tips.

> **Tip**
>
> Ensure temporal and spatial compliance between feedback dimensions.

It is crucial to ensure the spatial and temporal correspondence between reactive, instrumental, and operational feedback dimensions. In particular, interfaces must be designed to ensure directional compliance between a user's input and the feedback she receives from the system. Reduce latency and use multisensory feedback when appropriate, such as auditory and haptic feedback in combination with visuals.

> **Tip**
>
> Use constraints.

Using constraints can greatly increase the speed and accuracy of interaction in many tasks that rely on continuous motor control, such as object manipulation and navigation. However, also consider including functionality that allows the user to switch constraints off when more freedom of input is needed.

> **Tip**
>
> Consider using props and passive feedback, particularly in highly specialized tasks.

Using props and passive haptic feedback is an easy and inexpensive way to design a more enjoyable and effective interaction. The drawback of props is that they are highly specialized—the physical shape of props cannot change—therefore, they are particularly effective in very specialized applications.

> **Tip**
>
> Use Guiard's principles in designing two-handed interfaces.

Guiard's framework has proven to be a very useful tool for designing effective two-handed interfaces. Use these principles to determine the functions that should be assigned to each hand.

> **Tip**
>
> Consider real-world tools and practices as a source of inspiration for 3D UI design.

Adapting everyday or special-purpose tools as metaphors has been a very effective method for designing 3D interaction techniques. Because users are often already familiar with real-world artifacts, it is easy for them to understand the purpose and method of using 3D interaction techniques based on them.

> **Tip**
>
> Consider designing 3D techniques using principles from 2D interaction.

Two-dimensional interaction techniques have many attractive properties: they have been thoroughly studied and are well established, most users are already fluent with 2D interaction, and interaction in two dimensions is often significantly easier than interaction in a 3D environment.

> **Tip**
>
> Use and invent magical techniques.

The real power of 3D UIs is in creating a "better" reality through the use of magical interaction techniques. Magical interaction allows us to overcome the limitations of our cognitive, perceptual, physical, and motor capabilities. It is not easy to find effective and compelling metaphors for magical interaction techniques, but if one is found, it can lead to a very enjoyable and effective 3D UI.

> **Tip**
>
> Consider alternatives to photorealistic aesthetics.

In many applications, photorealism may not be entirely necessary; sketchy, cartoonlike rendering can be effective and compelling in communicating the state of the interaction while at the same time being enjoyable. Nonphotorealistic cartoon rendering suggests similarities using a few strong visual cues, which results in simple and more effective rendering. Another advantage of nonphotorealistic aesthetics in 3D interfaces is the ability to create a mood or atmosphere as well as to suggest properties of the environment rather than render them explicitly.

10.5 Case Studies

In this section we discuss the design approaches used in our two case studies to help you apply the concepts discussed in the chapter. The case studies are introduced in section 2.4.

10.5.1 VR Gaming Case Study

Many of the 3D UI design approaches discussed in this chapter are reflected in the design of our VR action-adventure game. We make use of two-handed interaction and distinguish between the roles played by the dominant and nondominant hands. The flashlight serves as a constraint to limit the selectable items in the world. Passive haptic feedback is provided by the handheld controllers.

The primary design issue we faced, however, has to do with the naturalism (or *interaction fidelity*) of the 3D UI in the game. And since this is one of the most prominent design tensions faced by many application developers, it's useful to review how that tension was resolved in this particular game design.

Since VR games take place in purely imaginary environments and since there is no expectation on the part of the user that the game world should work exactly like the real world, we as designers had complete freedom to choose the level of naturalism for the various game interactions. Furthermore, the level of naturalism could also vary from one interaction to another (e.g., we chose natural body movements for the primary navigation technique but a fantastical frog tongue shooter for the primary selection technique).

We tried not to abuse this freedom, however. The game does take place in a semirealistic environment, one that players will find somewhat familiar. So if all the rules of real-world interaction and physics were changed, the game would be quite confusing. Like many games, then, we start with a real-world base (you're in a hotel; you see familiar sights; gravity works in the regular way; you can look around and walk around just as you do in real life; you have a flashlight in your hand) and then enhance it (your other hand has a tool that you've never seen before, but if you accept the premise of a frog tongue shooter, it kind of works the way you might imagine; you're carrying items in a bag, but you can also get inside the bag and see all the objects it's holding).

This is an approach we call *hypernaturalism*, which has the nice property that it allows users to make use of their existing knowledge and understanding of the world but is not limited in the same ways that the real world is. Contrast this to the purely natural approach, which attempts to replicate real-world interaction precisely and usually falls short, leading to an inferior user experience. Although it's not always possible to use the hypernatural approach (e.g., a surgical training application should try to replicate real-world interaction as perfectly as possible), it can be a powerful and freeing design strategy for many 3D UI applications.

Key Concepts

- Consider carefully the level of interaction fidelity for your 3D UI. Naturalism is not always the most desirable or most effective approach.
- Especially in games, fun and playful hypernatural interactions can significantly enhance the user experience.

10.5.2 Mobile AR Case Study

The design strategy behind the development of the HYDROSYS system was highly driven by human factors, as we looked closely at perceptual, cognitive, and physical ergonomics issues. As we noted in this chapter, designing the system from a human-factors perspective targets a number of goals there are not always evident in the predominant usability and/or purely performance-driven design approaches taken by many researchers and developers. Human-factors issues are highly related to the different aspects of the AR system: perceptual issues affect the general view management and system control aspects, cognitive issues are prominent in the design of navigation techniques, and physical ergonomics provide design constraints to create the overall system setup. If we had neglected a close analysis of these issues, we would likely have ended up with a system that produced a much inferior user experience!

While human factors problems may not be noticeable by end users of systems that are only occasionally used, our system was used for *longer durations* and exhibited a higher level of *complexity*. Complexity was caused by, among other things, the difficulty of processing the large amount of spatial data and the number of functions accessible to match the users' needs. Longer durations imply a need for guaranteed comfortable use.

To address the various dimensions of human factors, we adopted an iterative design approach. Not solving the human factors issues would diminish the chance of acceptance of the system, as normal mobile devices were already used at the site to access static data in numerical format. We had to show the end users the added advantages of graphical analysis and AR.

We used two specific approaches from this chapter: two-handed interaction and designing for different user groups.

Performing interaction while holding the setup with both hands was possible but difficult, thus limiting performance. We had to reflect on what was more important: user comfort or interaction performance. Our solution was to provide the user with a comfortable option to hold the setup one-handed using a single grip supported by the shoulder strap, while the other hand could be used for interaction. Designers should perform careful evaluation in such situations, especially of user comfort, comparing different physical interaction modes. In the end, data from the user decides the issue, not the designer's intuition. The user may be able to cope with some limitations.

The second issue was user group variance: different users with very different capabilities would interact with the system, posing different requirements. Users varied from environmental scientists to insurance firm analysts and the general public. While most environmental scientists were physically well-trained users with good spatial knowledge of the observed environment, other users were more challenged in these categories. This placed a higher requirement on ergonomic and cognitive issues in comparison to a system used solely by environmental scientists, the users that mainly used the system during the development phases. In many research projects, user variety and involvement during design is limited—often direct colleagues or students are used for feedback. This can lead to systems that do not work for the full range of actual users. In our case, at frequent intervals we interviewed end-users with different backgrounds or invited them to take part in user studies.

Key Concepts

- Human-factors-driven design: designing with perceptual, cognitive, and physical ergonomics in mind has great potential when designing AR systems. While in simple systems these issues may not be evident, when complexity increases, addressing these issues can be a make-or-break item for user performance and acceptance.
- User groups: always consider the full range of potential end-users and involve them frequently in all cycles of iterative system design.

10.6 Conclusion

One of the joys and trials of working on 3D UIs is that the design space is so large and wide open. This provides an opportunity for great innovation but also difficulty in deciding how to begin and determining which ideas are worth pursuing. In this chapter, we've seen some prominent design approaches and strategies that can help designers manage this complexity. But no design is ever perfect the first time; 3D UI developers also need to evaluate their designs and iterate based on the results. Evaluation is the topic of the next chapter.

Recommended Reading

For an excellent review of the basics in feedback-control mechanisms and a discussion of early psychological and human factors experiments in this area, consider the following books:

Smith, T., and K. Smith (1987). "Feedback-Control Mechanisms of Human Behavior." In G. Salvendy (ed.), *Handbook of Human Factors*. G. Salvendy, 251–293. New York: John Wiley & Sons.

Norman, Donald (1988). *Design of Everyday Things*. New York: Basic Books.

For an in-depth discussion of some of the aspects of realism and level of detail and their effect on user performance, see the following book:

Luebke, D., M. Reddy, J. Cohen, A. Varshney, B. Watson, and R. Huebner (2002). *Level of Detail for 3D Graphics*. Boston, MA: Morgan Kaufmann.

Two classic texts on architectural design and philosophy can inspire you to develop new interaction techniques and approaches for planning and developing VEs:

Alexander, C., S. Ishikawa, and M. Silverstein (1977). *A Pattern Language: Towns, Buildings, Construction*. New York: Oxford University Press.

Lynch, K. (1960). *The Image of the City*, Cambridge, MA: MIT Press.

CHAPTER 11

EVALUATION OF 3D USER INTERFACES

Most of this book has covered the various aspects of 3D UI design. However, one of the central truths of HCI is that even the most careful and well-informed designs can still go wrong in any number of ways. Thus, evaluation of user experience becomes critical. In this chapter, we discuss some of the evaluation methods that can be used for 3D UIs, metrics that help to describe the 3D user experience, distinctive characteristics of 3D UI evaluation, and guidelines for choosing 3D UI evaluation methods. Evaluation should be performed not only when a design is complete, but also throughout the design process.

11.1 Introduction

For many years, the fields of 3D UIs, VR, and AR were so novel and the possibilities so limitless that many researchers simply focused on developing new devices, interaction techniques, and UI metaphors—exploring the design space—without taking the time to assess how good the new designs were. As the fields have matured, however, researchers are taking a closer look at the payoff of 3D UI designs in terms of *user experience* (including usability, usefulness, and emotional impact). We must critically analyze, assess, and compare devices, interaction techniques, UIs, and applications if 3D UIs are to be used in the real world.

11.1.1 Purposes of Evaluation

Simply stated, evaluation is the analysis, assessment, and testing of an artifact. In UI evaluation, the artifact is the entire UI or part of it, such as a particular input device or interaction technique. The main purpose of UI evaluation is the identification of usability problems or issues, leading to changes in the UI design. In other words, design and evaluation should be performed in an *iterative* fashion, such that design is followed by evaluation, leading to a redesign, which can then be evaluated, and so on. The iteration ends when the UI is "good enough," based on the metrics that have been set (or more frequently in real-world situations, when the budget runs out or the deadline arrives).

Although problem identification and redesign are the main goals of evaluation, it may also have secondary purposes. One of these is a more general understanding of the usability of a particular technique, device, or metaphor. This general understanding can lead to **design guidelines** (such as those presented throughout this book), so that each new design can start from an informed position rather than starting from scratch. For example, we can be reasonably sure that users will not have usability problems with the selection of items from a pull-down menu in a desktop application, if the interface designers follow well-known design guidelines, because the design of those menus has already gone through many evaluations and iterations.

Another, more ambitious, goal of UI evaluation is the development of **performance models**. These models aim to predict the performance of a user on a particular task within an interface. As discussed in Chapter 3, "Human Factors Fundamentals," Fitts's law (Fitts 1954) predicts how quickly a user will be able to position a pointer over a target area based on the distance to the target, the size of the target, and the muscle groups used in moving the pointer. Such performance models must be based on a large number of experimental trials on a wide range of generic tasks, and they are always subject to criticism (e.g., the model doesn't take an important factor into account, or the model doesn't apply to a particular type of task). Nevertheless, if a useful model can be developed, it can provide important guidance for designers.

It's also important to note that UI evaluation is only one piece of the broader evaluation of user experience (UX). A well-designed UI can still provide a poor user experience if it doesn't provide the necessary functionality to help users achieve their goals in the context of use (usefulness) or if it fails to satisfy and delight the user (emotional impact). Although we focus on UI evaluation in this chapter, production 3D applications should be evaluated with a broader UX focus in mind.

11.1.2 Terminology

We must define some important terms before continuing with our discussion of 3D UI evaluation. The most important term (which we've already used a couple of times) is **usability**. We define usability to encompass everything about an artifact and a person that affects the person's use of the artifact. Evaluation, then, measures some aspects of the usability of an interface (it is not likely that we can quantify the usability of an interface with a single score). Usability metrics fall into several categories, such as system performance, user task performance, and subjective response (see section 11.3).

There are at least two roles that people play in a usability evaluation. A person who designs, implements, administers, or analyzes an evaluation is called an **evaluator**. A person who takes part in an evaluation by using the interface, performing tasks, or answering questions is called a **user**. In formal experimentation, a user is often called a **participant**.

Finally, we distinguish below between **evaluation methods** and **evaluation approaches**. Evaluation methods are particular steps that can be used in an evaluation. An evaluation approach, on the other hand, is a combination of methods, used in a particular sequence, to form a complete usability evaluation.

11.1.3 Chapter Roadmap

We've already covered the basics of UI evaluation in Chapter 4, "General Principles of Human-Computer Interaction," section 4.4.5. Evaluation methods and metrics were also discussed throughout Chapter 3, "Human Factors Fundamentals". We begin this chapter by providing some background information on evaluation methods for 3D UIs (section 11.2). We then focus on 3D UI evaluation metrics (section 11.3) and distinctive characteristics of 3D UI evaluation (section 11.4). In section 11.5, we classify 3D UI evaluation methods and follow that in section 11.6 with a description and comparison of three comprehensive approaches to 3D UI evaluation—sequential evaluation, testbed evaluation, and component evaluation. We then present a set of guidelines for those performing evaluations of 3D UIs (section 11.7). We conclude with a discussion of evaluating the 3D UIs of our two case studies (section 11.8).

11.2 Evaluation Methods for 3D UIs

In this section, we describe some of the common methods used in 3D UI evaluation. None of these methods are new or unique to 3D UIs. They have all been used and tested in many other usability evaluation contexts. We present them here as an introduction to these topics for the reader who has never studied UX evaluations. For more detailed information, you can consult any one of a large number of introductory books on UX evaluations (see the recommended reading list at the end of the chapter).

From the literature, we have compiled a list of usability evaluation methods that have been applied to 3D UIs (although numerous references could be cited for some of the techniques we present, we have included citations that are most recognized and accessible). Most of these methods were developed for 2D or GUI usability evaluation and have been subsequently extended to support 3D UI evaluation.

Cognitive Walkthrough

The **cognitive walkthrough** (Polson et al. 1992) is an approach to evaluating an UI based on stepping through common tasks that a user would perform and evaluating the interface's ability to support each step. This approach is intended especially to gain an understanding of the usability of a system for first-time or infrequent users, that is, for users in an exploratory learning mode. Steed and Tromp (1998) used a cognitive walkthrough approach to evaluate a collaborative VE.

Heuristic Evaluation

Heuristic or **guidelines-based expert evaluation** (Nielsen and Molich 1992) is a method in which several usability experts separately evaluate a UI design (probably a prototype) by applying a set of heuristics or design guidelines that are either general enough to apply to any UI or are tailored for 3D UIs in particular. No representative users are involved. Results from the several experts are then combined and ranked to prioritize iterative design or redesign of each usability issue discovered. The current lack of well-formed guidelines and heuristics for 3D UI design and evaluation makes this approach more challenging for 3D UIs. Examples of this approach applied to 3D UIs can be found in Gabbard et al. (1999); Stanney and Reeves (2000); and Steed and Tromp (1998).

Formative Evaluation

Formative evaluation (both formal and informal; Hix and Hartson 1993) is an observational, empirical evaluation method, applied during evolving stages of design, that assesses user interaction by iteratively placing representative users in task-based scenarios in order to identify usability problems, as well as to assess the design's ability to support user exploration, learning, and task performance. Formative evaluations can range from being rather informal, providing mostly qualitative results such as critical incidents, user comments, and general reactions, to being very formal and extensive, producing both qualitative and quantitative results (such as task timing or errors).

Collected data are analyzed to identify UI components that both support and detract from user task performance and user satisfaction. Alternating between formative evaluation and design or redesign efforts ultimately leads to an iteratively refined UI design. Most usability evaluations of 3D UI applications fall into the formative evaluation category. The work of Hix et al. (1999) provides a good example.

Summative Evaluation

Summative or **comparative evaluation** (both formal and informal; Hix and Hartson 1993; Scriven 1967) is a method for either (a) comparing the usability of a UI to target usability values or (b) comparing two or more configurations of UI designs, UI components, and/or UI techniques. As with formative evaluation, representative users perform task scenarios as evaluators collect both qualitative and quantitative data. As with formative evaluations, summative evaluations can be formally or informally applied.

Summative evaluation is generally performed after UI designs (or components) are complete. Summative evaluation enables evaluators to measure and subsequently compare the productivity and cost benefits associated with different UI designs. Comparing 3D UIs requires a consistent set of user task scenarios (borrowed and/or refined from the formative evaluation effort), resulting in primarily quantitative results that compare (on a task-by-task basis) a design's support for specific user task performance.

Summative evaluations that are run as formal experiments need to follow a systematic process for experimental design. **Research questions** are typically of the form, "What are the effects of X and Y on Z?" For example, a formal 3D UI experiment might ask, "What are the effects of interaction technique and display field of view on accuracy in a manipulation task?" In such a research question, X and Y (interaction technique and display FOV in the example) are called **independent variables**, while Z (accuracy) is called a **dependent variable**. The independent variables are manipulated explicitly among multiple **levels**. In our example, the interaction technique variable might have two levels—Simple Virtual Hand and Go-Go (section 7.4.1)—while the display FOV variable might have three levels—60, 80, and 100 degrees. In a **factorial design** (the most common design), each combination of the independent variables' levels becomes a **condition**. In our example, there would be six conditions (two interaction techniques times three display FOVs).

Experimenters must decide how many of the conditions each participant will experience. If there's a likelihood that participants will have significant learning from one condition to the next, the best approach is a *between-subjects* design, meaning that each participant is exposed to only one of the conditions. If it's important that participants be able to compare the conditions, and if learning is not expected, a *within-subjects* design might be appropriate, in which participants experience all the conditions. Hybrids are also possible, where some independent variables are between subjects and others are within subjects.

The goal of this sort of experimental design is to test the effects of the independent variables on the dependent variables. This includes **main effects**, where a single independent variable has a direct effect on a dependent variable, and **interactions**, where two or more independent variables have a combined effect on a dependent variable. To be able to find these effects, it is critical that other factors besides the independent variables are held constant; that is, that the only thing that changes from one condition to the next are the independent variables. It is also important to avoid confounds within an independent variable. For example, if one compared an HWD to a surround-screen display and found effects, it would be impossible to know whether those effects were due to differences in FOV, FOR, spatial resolution, weight of headgear, or any number of other differences between the two displays. The best experimental designs have independent variables whose levels only differ in one way. Readers wanting more detail on experimental design are encouraged to consult one of the many books on the subject, such as Cairns and Cox (2008).

Many of the formal experiments discussed in Part IV of this book are summative evaluations of 3D interaction techniques. For example, see Bowman, Johnson, and Hodges (1999) and Poupyrev, Weghorst, and colleagues (1997).

Questionnaires

A **questionnaire** (Hix and Hartson 1993) is a written set of questions used to obtain information from users before or after they have participated in a usability evaluation session. Questionnaires are good for collecting demographic information (e.g., age, gender, computer experience) and subjective data (e.g., opinions, comments, preferences, ratings) and are often more convenient and more consistent than spoken interviews.

In the context of 3D UIs, questionnaires are used quite frequently, especially to elicit information about subjective phenomena such as presence (Witmer and Singer 1998) or simulator sickness/cybersickness (Kennedy et al. 1993).

Interviews and Demos

An **interview** (Hix and Hartson 1993) is a technique for gathering information about users by talking directly to them. An interview can gather more information than a questionnaire and may go to a deeper level of detail. Interviews are good for getting subjective reactions, opinions, and insights into how people reason about issues. Structured interviews have a predefined flow of questions. Open-ended interviews permit the respondent (interviewee) to provide additional information, and they permit the interviewer to explore paths of questioning that may occur to him spontaneously during the interview. Demonstrations (typically of a prototype) may be used in conjunction with user interviews to aid a user in talking about the interface.

In 3D UI evaluation, the use of interviews has not been studied explicitly, but informal interviews are often used at the end of formative or summative usability evaluations (Bowman and Hodges 1997).

11.3 Evaluation Metrics for 3D UIs

Now we turn to metrics. That is, how do we measure the characteristics of a 3D UI when evaluating it? We focus on metrics of usability: a 3D UI is usable when the user can reach her goals; when the important tasks can be done better, easier, or faster than with another system; and when users are not frustrated or uncomfortable. Note that all of these have to do with the user.

We discuss three types of metrics for 3D UIs: system performance metrics, task performance metrics, and subjective response metrics.

11.3.1 System Performance Metrics

System performance refers to typical computer or graphics system performance, using metrics such as frame rate, latency, network delay, and optical distortion. From the interface point of view, system performance metrics are really not important in and of themselves. Rather, they are important only insofar as they affect the user's experience or tasks. For example, the frame rate of immersive visual displays needs to be high enough to avoid inducing cybersickness. Also, in a collaborative setting, task performance will likely be negatively affected if there is too much network delay.

11.3.2 Task Performance Metrics

User task performance refers to the quality of performance of specific tasks in the 3D application, such as the time to navigate to a specific location, the accuracy of object placement, or the number of errors a user makes in selecting an object from a set. Task performance metrics may also be domain-specific. For example, evaluators may want to measure student learning in an educational application or spatial awareness in a military training VE.

Typically, speed and accuracy are the most important task performance metrics. The problem with measuring both speed and accuracy is that there is an implicit relationship between them: *I can go faster but be less accurate, or I can increase my accuracy by decreasing my speed*. It is assumed that for every task, there is some curve representing this speed/accuracy tradeoff, and users must decide where on the curve they want to be (even if they don't do this consciously). In an evaluation, therefore, if you simply tell your participants to do a task as quickly and precisely as possible, they will probably end up all over the curve, giving you data with a high level of variability. Therefore, it is very important that you instruct users in a very specific way if you want them to be at one end of the curve or the other. Another way to manage the tradeoff is to tell users to do the task as quickly as possible one time, as accurately as possible the second time, and to balance speed and accuracy the third time. This gives you information about the tradeoff curve for the particular task you're looking at.

11.3.3 Subjective Response Metrics

A subjective response refers to the personal perception and experience of the interface by the user (e.g., perceived ease of use, ease of learning, satisfaction, etc.). These responses are often measured via questionnaires or interviews and may be either qualitative (descriptive) or quantitative (numeric). Subjective response metrics are often related to emotional impact but generally contribute to usability as well. A usable application is one whose interface does not pose any significant barriers to task completion. UIs should be intuitive, provide good affordances (see Chapter 4, "General Principles of Human-Computer Interaction"), provide good feedback, be unobtrusive, and so on. An application cannot be effective unless users are willing to use it. It is possible for a 3D UI to provide functionality for the user to do a task, but a lack of attention to subjective user experience can keep it from being used.

For 3D UIs in particular, **presence** and **user comfort** (see Chapter 3, "Human Factors Fundamentals", sections 3.3.6 and 3.5) can be important metrics that are not usually considered in traditional UI evaluation. Presence is a crucial but not very well understood metric for VE systems. It is the "feeling of being there"—existing in the virtual world rather than in the physical world. How can we measure presence? One method simply asks users to rate their feeling of being there on a 1 to 100 scale. Questionnaires can also be used and can contain a wide variety of questions, all designed to get at different aspects of presence. Psychophysical measures are used in controlled experiments where stimuli are manipulated and then correlated to users' ratings of presence (for example, how does the rating change when the environment is presented in monaural versus stereo modes?). There are also some more objective measures. Some are physiological (how the body responds to the VE, for example via heart rate?). Others might look at users' reactions to events in the VE (e.g., does the user duck when he's about to hit a virtual beam?). Tests of memory for the environment and the objects within it might give an indirect measurement of the level of presence. Finally, if we know a task for which presence is required, we can measure users' performance on that task and infer the level of presence. There is still a great deal of debate about the definition of presence, the best ways to measure presence, and the importance of presence as a metric (e.g., Slater et al. 2009; Usoh et al. 2000; Witmer and Singer 1998).

The other novel subjective response metric for 3D systems is user comfort. This includes several different things. The most notable and well-studied is **cybersickness** (also called **simulator sickness** because it was first noted in flight simulators or **VR sickness** to specifically call out the problem of sickness in the VR medium). It is symptomatically similar to motion sickness and may result from mismatches in sensory information (e.g., your eyes tell your brain that you are moving, but your vestibular system tells your brain that you are not moving). 3D applications may also result in physical aftereffects of exposure. For example, if a 3D UI misregisters the virtual hand and the real hand (they're not at the same physical location), the user may have trouble doing precise manipulation in the real world after exposure to the virtual world, because the sensorimotor systems have adapted to the misregistration. Even more seriously, activities like driving or walking may be impaired after extremely long exposures. Finally, there are simple strains on arms/hands/eyes from the use of 3D devices. User comfort is also usually measured subjectively, using rating scales or questionnaires. The most famous questionnaire is the simulator sickness questionnaire (SSQ) developed by Kennedy et al. (1993). Researchers have used some objective measures in the study of aftereffects—for example, by measuring the accuracy of a manipulation task in the real world after exposure to a virtual world (Wann and Mon-Williams 2002).

11.4 Characteristics of 3D UI Evaluations

The approaches we discuss below for evaluation of 3D UIs have been developed and used in response to perceived differences between the evaluation of 3D UIs and the evaluation of traditional UIs such as GUIs. Many of the fundamental concepts and goals are similar, but use of these approaches in the context of 3D UIs is distinct. Here, we present some of the issues that differentiate 3D UI evaluation, organized into several categories. The categories contain overlapping considerations but provide a rough partitioning of these important issues. Note that many of these issues are not necessarily found in the literature but instead come from personal experience and extensive discussions with colleagues.

11.4.1 Physical Environment Issues

One of the most obvious differences between 3D UIs and traditional UIs is the **physical environment** in which that interface is used. In many 3D UIs, nontraditional input and output devices are used, which can preclude the use of some types of evaluation. Users may be standing rather than sitting, and they may be moving about a large space, using whole-body movements. These properties give rise to several issues for usability evaluation. Following are some examples:

- In interfaces using non-see-through HWDs, the user cannot see the surrounding physical world. Therefore, the evaluator must ensure that the user will not bump into walls or other physical objects, trip over cables, or move outside the range of the tracking device (Viirre 1994). A related problem in surround-screen VEs, such as the CAVE (Cruz-Neira et al. 1993), is that the physical walls can be difficult to see because of projected graphics. Problems of this sort could contaminate the results of an evaluation (e.g., if the user trips while in the midst of a timed task) and more importantly could cause injury to the user. To mitigate risk, the evaluator can ensure that cables are bundled and will not get in the way of the user (e.g., cables may descend from above or a human cable wrangler may be necessary). Some modern systems also help mitigate this issue through the use of wireless technologies. Also, the user may be placed in a physical enclosure that limits movement to areas where there are no physical objects to interfere.
- Many 3D displays do not allow multiple simultaneous viewers (e.g., user and evaluator), so hardware or software must be set up so that an evaluator can see the same image as the user. With an HWD, the user's view is typically rendered to a normal monitor. In a surround-screen or workbench VE, a monoscopic view of the scene could be rendered to a monitor, or, if performance will not be adversely affected, both the user and the evaluator can be tracked (this can cause other problems, however; see section 11.4.2 on evaluator considerations). If images are viewed on a monitor, then it may be difficult to see and understand both the actions of the user and the view of the virtual environment at the same time. Another approach would be to use a green-screen setup to allow the evaluator to see the user in the context of the VE.

- A common and very effective technique for generating important qualitative data during usability evaluation sessions is the "think-aloud" protocol (as described in Hix and Hartson 1993). With this technique, participants talk about their actions, goals, and thoughts regarding the interface while they are performing specific tasks. In some 3D UIs, however, speech recognition is used as an interaction technique, making the think-aloud protocol much more difficult and perhaps even impossible. Post-session interviews may help to recover some of the information that would have been obtained from the think-aloud protocol.
- Another common technique involves recording video of both the user and the interface (as described in Hix and Hartson 1993). Because 3D UI users are often mobile, a single, fixed camera may require a very wide shot, which may not allow precise identification of actions. This could be addressed by using a tracking camera (with, unfortunately, additional expense and complexity) or a camera operator (additional personnel). Moreover, views of the user and the graphical environment must be synchronized so that cause and effect can clearly be seen in the video. Finally, recording the video of a stereoscopic graphics image can be problematic.
- An ever-increasing number of 3D applications are collaborative and shared among two or more users (Glencross et al. 2007; Tang et al. 2010; Beck et al. 2013; Chen et al. 2015). These collaborative 3D UIs become even more difficult to evaluate than single-user 3D UIs due to physical separation of users (i.e., users can be in more than one physical location), the additional information that must be recorded for each user, the unpredictability of network behavior as a factor influencing usability, the possibility that each user will have different devices, and the additional complexity of the system, which may cause more crashes or other problems.

11.4.2 Evaluator Issues

A second set of issues relates to the role of the evaluator in a 3D UI evaluation. Because of the complexities and distinctive characteristics of 3D UIs, a study may require multiple evaluators, different evaluator roles and behaviors, or both. Following are some examples:

- Many VEs attempt to produce a sense of **presence** in the user—that is, a feeling of actually being in the virtual world rather than the physical one. Evaluators or cable wranglers can cause breaks in presence if the user can sense them. In VEs using projected graphics, the user will see an evaluator if the evaluator moves into the user's field of view. This is especially likely in a CAVE environment (Cruz-Neira et al. 1993) where it is difficult to see the front of a user (and thus the user's facial expressions and detailed use of handheld devices) without affecting that user's sense of presence. This may break presence, because the evaluator is not part of the virtual world. In any type of VE, touching or talking to the user can cause such breaks. If the evaluation is assessing presence or if presence is hypothesized to affect performance, then the evaluator must take care to remain unsensed during the evaluation.
- When presence is deemed very important for a particular VE, an evaluator may not wish to intervene at all during an evaluation session. This means that the experimental application/interface must be robust enough that the session does not have to be interrupted to fix

a problem. Also, instructions given to the user must be very detailed, explicit, and precise, and the evaluator should make sure the user has a complete understanding of the procedure and tasks before beginning the session.

- 3D UI hardware and software are often more complex and less robust than traditional UI hardware and software. Again, multiple evaluators may be needed to do tasks such as helping the user with display and input hardware, running the software that produces graphics and other output, recording data such as timings and errors, and recording critical incidents and other qualitative observations of a user's actions.
- Traditional UIs typically require only discrete streams of input (e.g., from the mouse and keyboard), but many 3D UIs include multimodal input, combining discrete events, gestures, voice, and/or whole-body motion. It is very difficult for an evaluator to observe these multiple input streams simultaneously and record an accurate log of the user's actions. These challenges make automated data collection (see section 11.4.4) very important.

11.4.3 User Issues

There are also a large number of issues related to the user population used as participants in 3D UI usability evaluations. In traditional evaluations, participants are gleaned from the target user population of an application or from a similar representative group of people. Efforts are often made, for example, to preserve gender balance, to have a good distribution of ages, and to test both experts and novices if these differences are representative of the target user population. The nature of 3D UI evaluation, however, does not always allow for such straightforward selection of users. Following are some examples:

- 3D interaction techniques are still often a "solution looking for a problem." Because of this, the target user population for a 3D application or interaction technique to be evaluated may not be known or well understood. For example, a study comparing two virtual travel techniques is not aimed at a particular set of users. Thus, it may be difficult to generalize performance results. The best course of action is to evaluate the most diverse user population possible in terms of age, gender, technical ability, physical characteristics, and so on, and to include these factors in any models of performance.
- It may be difficult to differentiate between novice and expert users because there are very few potential participants who could be considered experts in 3D UIs (although this may be changing). In a research setting, most users who could be considered experts might be lab coworkers, whose participation in an evaluation could confound the results. Also, because most users are typically novices, evaluators can make no assumptions about a novice user's ability to understand or use a given interaction technique or device.
- Because 3D UIs will be novel to many potential participants, the results of an evaluation may exhibit high variability and differences among individuals. This means that the number of participants needed to obtain a good picture of performance may be larger than for

traditional usability evaluations. If statistically significant results are required (depending on the type of usability evaluation being performed), the number of participants may be even greater.

- Researchers are still studying a large design space for 3D interaction techniques and devices. Because of this, evaluations often compare two or more techniques, devices, or combinations of the two. To perform such evaluations using a within-subjects design, users must be able to adapt to a wide variety of situations. If a between-subjects design is used, a larger number of subjects will again be needed.
- 3D UI evaluations must consider the effects of cybersickness and fatigue on participants. Although some of the causes of cybersickness are known, there are still no predictive models for it (Kennedy et al. 2000), and little is known regarding acceptable exposure time to 3D UIs. For evaluations, then, a worst-case assumption must be made. A lengthy experiment must contain planned rest breaks and contingency plans in case of ill or fatigued participants. Shortening the experiment is often not an option, especially if statistically significant results are needed.
- Because it is not known exactly what 3D UI situations cause sickness or fatigue, most 3D UI evaluations should include some measurement (e.g., subjective, questionnaire-based, or physiological) of these factors. A result indicating that an interaction technique was 50% faster than any other evaluated technique would be severely misleading if that interaction technique also made 30% of participants sick. Thus, user comfort measurements should be included in low-level 3D UI evaluations.
- Presence is another example of a measure often required in VE evaluations that has no analog in traditional UI evaluation. VE evaluations must often take into account subjective reports of perceived presence, perceived fidelity of the virtual world, and so on. Questionnaires (Usoh et al. 2000; Witmer and Singer 1998) have been developed that purportedly obtain reliable and consistent measurements of such factors. Chapter 3, "Human Factors Fundamentals", Section 3.4.3 also discusses some techniques that can be used to measure presence.

11.4.4 Evaluation Type Issues

Traditional UI evaluation can take many forms. These include informal user studies, formal experiments, task-based usability studies, heuristic evaluations, and the use of predictive models of performance (see Chapter 4, "General Principles of Human-Computer Interaction," and section 11.2 above for further discussion of these types of evaluations). There are several issues related to the use of various types of usability evaluation in 3D UIs. Following are some examples:

- Because of the complexity and novelty of 3D UIs, automated data collection of system performance and task performance metrics by the 3D UI software or ancillary software is nearly a necessity. For example, several issues above have noted the need for more than one evaluator or video recording. Automated data collection can reduce the need for multiple evaluators during a single session. Additionally, automated data collection is more accurate than evaluator-based observations. Task time can be measured in milliseconds (instead of seconds), and predefined errors are always identified and counted. The major limiting factor of automated data collection is the additional programming required to properly identify and record performance metrics. Often this requires close integration with the key events of an interaction technique or interface.

- Evaluations based solely on heuristics (i.e., design guidelines), performed by usability experts, are very difficult in 3D UIs because of a lack of published verified guidelines for 3D UI design. There are some notable exceptions (McMahan et al. 2014; Bowman et al. 2008; Teather and Stuerzlinger 2008; Conkar et al. 1999; Gabbard 1997; Kaur 1999; Kaur et al. 1999; Mills and Noyes 1999; Stanney and Reeves 2000), but for the most part, it is difficult to predict the usability of a 3D interface without studying real users attempting representative tasks in the 3D UI. It is not likely that a large number of heuristics will appear, at least not until 3D input and output devices become more standardized. Even assuming standardized devices, however, the design space for 3D interaction techniques and interfaces is very large, making it difficult to produce effective and general heuristics to use as the basis for evaluation.
- Heuristic evaluations and other forms of usability inspections are analytic in nature and are typically carried out by experts through the examination of prototypes. If very early prototypes are being used (e.g., storyboards or video prototypes), it is very difficult for experts to perform this sort of analysis with confidence, because 3D UIs must be experienced first-hand before their user experience can be understood. Thus, the findings of early heuristic evaluations should not be taken as gospel.
- As we've noted several times in this book, the devil is in the details of 3D UI design. Thus, designers should not place too much weight on the results of any formative 3D UI evaluation based on a rough prototype without all the interaction details fully specified.
- Another major type of evaluation that does not employ users is the application of performance models (e.g., GOMS, Fitts's law). Aside from a few examples (Kopper et al. 2010; Zhai and Woltjer 2003), very few models of this type have been developed for or adapted to 3D UIs. However, the lower cost of both heuristic evaluation and performance model application makes them attractive for evaluation.
- When performing statistical experiments to quantify and compare the usability of various 3D interaction techniques, input devices, interface elements, and so on, it is often difficult to know which factors have a potential impact on the results. Besides the primary independent variables (i.e., interaction technique), a large number of other potential factors could be included, such as environment, task, system, or user characteristics. One approach is to try to vary as many of these potentially important factors as possible during a single experiment. This "testbed evaluation" approach (Bowman et al. 1999; Snow and Williges 1998) has been used with some success (see section 11.4.2). The other extreme would be to simply hold as many of these other factors as possible constant and run the evaluation only in a particular set of circumstances. Thus, statistical 3D UI experimental evaluations may be either overly complex or overly simplistic—finding the proper balance is difficult.

11.4.5 General Issues

General issues related to 3D UI evaluation include the following:

- 3D UI usability evaluations generally focus at a lower level than traditional UI evaluations. In the context of GUIs, a standard look and feel and a standard set of interface elements and interaction techniques exist, so evaluation usually looks at subtle interface nuances, overall interface metaphors, information architecture, functionality, or other higher-level issues. In 3D UIs, however, there are no interface standards. Therefore, 3D UI evaluations most often evaluate lower-level components, such as interaction techniques or input devices.
- It is tempting to overgeneralize the results of evaluations of 3D interaction performed in a generic (non-application) context. However, because of the fast-changing and complex nature of 3D UIs, one cannot assume anything (display type, input devices, graphics processing power, tracker accuracy, etc.) about the characteristics of a real 3D application. Everything has the potential to change. Therefore, it is important to report on information about the apparatus with which the evaluation was performed and to evaluate with a range of setups (e.g., using different devices) if possible.
- In general, 3D UI evaluations require users as participants. It is the responsibility of 3D UI evaluators to ensure that the proper steps are taken to protect these human subjects. This process involves having well-defined procedures and obtaining approval to conduct the evaluation from an Institutional Review Board (IRB) or a similar ethics committee.

11.5 Classification of Evaluation Methods

A classification space for 3D UI usability evaluation methods can provide a structured means for comparing evaluation methods. One such space classifies methods according to three key characteristics: **involvement of representative users**, **context of evaluation**, and **types of results produced** (Figure 11.1).

The first characteristic discriminates between those methods that *require* the participation of representative users (to provide design-or use-based experiences and options) and those methods that do not (methods not requiring users still require a usability expert). The second characteristic describes the type of context in which the evaluation takes place. In particular, this characteristic identifies those methods that are applied in a generic context and those that are applied in an application-specific context. The context of evaluation inherently imposes restrictions on the applicability and generality of results. Thus, conclusions or results of evaluations conducted in a generic context can typically be applied more broadly (i.e., to more types of interfaces) than results of an application-specific evaluation method, which may be best suited for applications that are similar in nature. The third characteristic identifies whether or not a given usability evaluation method produces (primarily) qualitative or quantitative results.

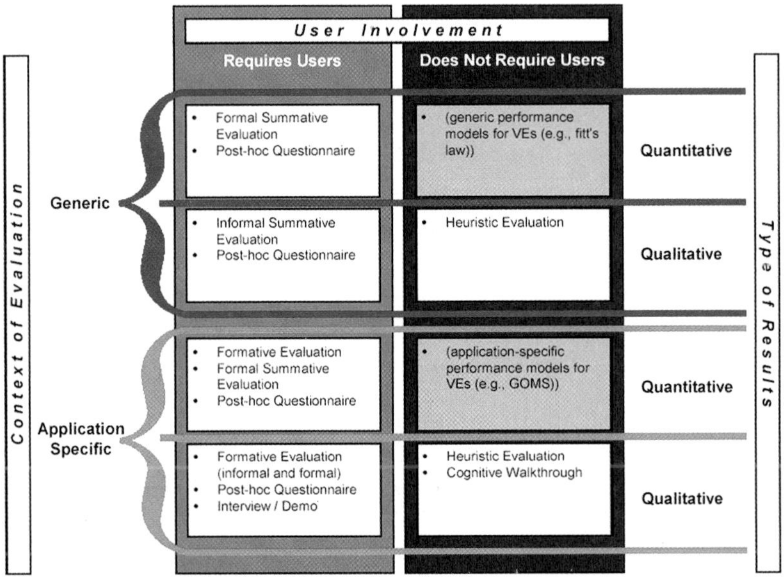

Figure 11.1 A classification of usability evaluation methods for 3D UIs. (Image reprinted by permission of MIT Press and Presence: Teleoperators and Virtual Environments)

Note that these characteristics are not designed to be mutually exclusive and are instead designed to convey one (of many) usability evaluation method characteristics. For example, a particular usability evaluation method may produce both quantitative and qualitative results. Indeed, many identified methods are flexible enough to provide insight at many levels. These three characteristics were chosen (over other potential characteristics) because they are often the most significant (to evaluators) due to their overall effect on the usability process. That is, a researcher interested in undertaking usability evaluation will likely need to know what the evaluation will cost, what the impact of the evaluation will be, and how the results can be applied. Each of the three characteristics addresses these concerns: degree of user involvement directly affects the cost to proctor and analyze the evaluation; results of the process indicate what type of information will be produced (for the given cost); and context of evaluation inherently dictates to what extent results may be applied.

This classification is useful on several levels. It structures the space of evaluation methods and provides a practical vocabulary for discussion of methods in the research community. It also allows researchers to compare two or more methods and understand how they are similar or different on a fundamental level. Finally, it reveals "holes" in the space (Card et al. 1990)—combinations of the three characteristics that have rarely or never been tried in the 3D UI community.

Figure 11.1 shows that there are two such holes in this space (the shaded boxes). More specifically, there is a lack of current 3D UI usability evaluation methods that do not require users and that can be applied in a generic context to produce quantitative results (upper right of the figure). Note that some possible existing 2D and GUI evaluation methods are listed in parentheses, but few, if any, of these methods have been applied to 3D UIs. Similarly, there appears to be no method that provides quantitative results in an application-specific setting that does not require users (third box down on the right of the figure). These areas may be interesting avenues for further research.

11.6 Three Multimethod Approaches

A shortcoming of the classification of evaluation methods discussed in Chapter 4, section 4.4.5, is that it does not convey *when* in the UX lifecycle a method is best applied or *how* several methods may be applied. In most cases, answers to these questions cannot be determined without a comprehensive understanding of each of the methods, as well as the specific goals and circumstances of the 3D UI research or development effort. In this section, we present three well-developed 3D UI evaluation approaches and compare them in terms of practical usage and results.

11.6.1 Sequential Evaluation Approach

Gabbard et al. (1999) present a sequential approach to usability evaluation for specific 3D applications. The sequential evaluation approach is a UX engineering approach and addresses both design and evaluation of 3D UIs. However, for the scope of this chapter, we focus on different types of evaluation and address analysis, design, and prototyping only when they have a direct effect on evaluation.

Although some of its components are well suited for evaluation of generic interaction techniques, the complete sequential evaluation approach employs application-specific guidelines, domain-specific representative users, and application-specific user tasks to produce a usable and useful interface for a particular application. In many cases, results or lessons learned may be applied to other, similar applications (for example, 3D applications with similar display or input devices, or with similar types of tasks). In other cases (albeit less often), it is possible to abstract the results for general use. You should consider an approach like sequential evaluation if you are designing a production 3D application (i.e., a targeted application that will be used in the real world by real users).

Sequential evaluation evolved from iteratively adapting and enhancing existing 2D and GUI usability evaluation methods. In particular, it modifies and extends specific methods to account for complex interaction techniques, nonstandard and dynamic UI components, and multimodal tasks inherent in 3D UIs. Moreover, the adapted/extended methods both streamline the UX engineering process and provide sufficient coverage of the usability space. Although the name implies that the various methods are applied in sequence, there is considerable opportunity to iterate both within a particular method as well as among methods.

It is important to note that all the pieces of this approach have been used for years in GUI usability evaluations. The unique contribution of the work in Gabbard et al. (1999) is the breadth and depth offered by progressive use of these techniques, adapted when necessary for 3D UI evaluation, in an application-specific context. Further, the way in which each step in the progression informs the next step is an important finding: the ordering of the methods guides developers toward a usable application.

Figure 11.2 presents the sequential evaluation approach. It allows developers to improve a 3D UI through a combination of expert-based and user-based techniques. This approach is based on sequentially performing user task analysis (see Figure 11.2, state 1), heuristic (or guideline-based expert) evaluation (Figure 11.2, state 2), formative evaluation (Figure 11.2, state 3), and summative evaluation (Figure 11.2, state 4), with iteration as appropriate within and among each type of evaluation. This approach leverages the results of each individual method by systematically defining and refining the 3D UI in a cost-effective progression.

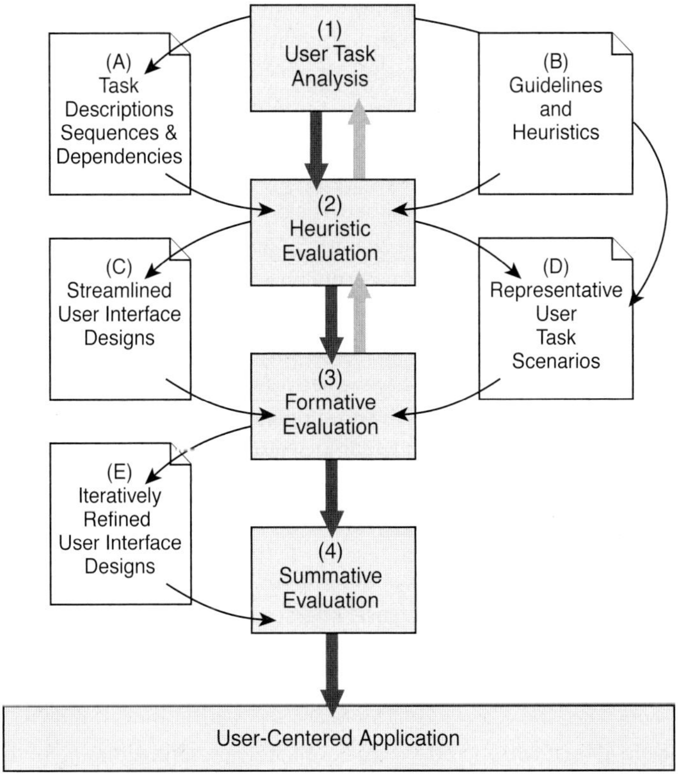

Figure 11.2 Sequential evaluation approach. (Image reprinted by permission of MIT Press and *Presence: Teleoperators and Virtual Environments*)

Depending upon the nature of the application, this sequential evaluation approach may be applied in a strictly serial approach (as Figure 11.2's solid black arrows illustrate) or iteratively applied (either as a whole or per-individual method, as Figure 11.2's gray arrows illustrate) many times. For example, when used to evaluate a complex command-and-control battlefield visualization application (Hix et al. 1999), user task analysis was followed by significant iterative use of heuristic and formative evaluation and lastly followed by a single broad summative evaluation.

From experience, this sequential evaluation approach provides cost-effective assessment and refinement of usability for a specific 3D application. Obviously, the exact cost and benefit of a particular evaluation effort depends largely on the application's complexity and maturity. In some cases, cost can be managed by performing quick lightweight formative evaluations (which involve users and thus are typically the most time-consuming to plan and perform). Moreover, by using a "hallway methodology," user-based methods can be performed quickly and cost-effectively by simply finding volunteers from within one's own organization. This approach should be used only as a last resort or in cases where the representative user class includes just about anyone. When it is used, care should be taken to ensure that "hallway" users provide a close representative match to the application's ultimate end users.

The individual methods involved in sequential evaluation are described earlier in Chapter 4 (user task analysis in section 4.4.2 and heuristic, formative, and summative evaluation in section 4.4.5), as well as in section 11.2 above.

Example of Approach

The sequential evaluation approach has been applied to several 3D UIs, including the Naval Research Lab's Dragon application: a VE for battlefield visualization (Gabbard et al. 1999). Dragon is presented on a workbench (see Chapter 5, "3D User Interface Output Hardware," section 5.2.2) that provides a 3D display for observing and managing battle-space information shared among commanders and other battle planners. The researchers performed several formative evaluations over a nine-month period, using one to three users and two to three evaluators per session. Each evaluation session revealed a set of usability problems and generated a corresponding set of recommendations. The developers would address the recommendations and produce an improved UI for the next iteration of evaluation. The researchers performed four major cycles of iteration during the evaluation of Dragon, each cycle using the progression of usability methods described in this section.

During the expert guidelines-based evaluations, various user interaction design experts worked alone or collectively to assess the evolving user interaction design for Dragon. The expert evaluations uncovered several major design problems that are described in detail in Hix et al. (1999). Based on user task analysis and early expert guideline-based evaluations, the researchers created a set of user task scenarios specifically for battlefield visualization. During each formative session, there were at least two and often three evaluators present. Although both the expert guideline-based evaluation sessions and the formative evaluation sessions were personnel intensive (with two or three evaluators involved), it was found that the quality and amount of data collected by multiple evaluators greatly outweighed the cost of those evaluators.

Finally, the summative evaluation statistically examined the effect of four factors: locomotion metaphor (egocentric versus exocentric), gesture control (controls rate versus position), visual presentation device (workbench, desktop, CAVE), and stereopsis (present versus not present). The results of these efforts are described in Hix and Gabbard (2002). This experience with sequential evaluation demonstrated its utility and effectiveness.

11.6.2 Testbed Evaluation Approach

Bowman and Hodges (1999) take the approach of empirically evaluating interaction techniques outside the context of applications (i.e., within a generic context rather than within a specific application) and add the support of a framework for design and evaluation, which we summarize here. This testbed evaluation approach is primarily aimed at researchers who are attempting to gain an in-depth understanding of interaction techniques and input devices, along with the tradeoffs inherent in their designs as they are used in different scenarios.

Principled, systematic design and evaluation frameworks give formalism and structure to research on interaction; they do not rely solely on experience and intuition. Formal frameworks provide us not only with a greater understanding of the advantages and disadvantages of current techniques but also with better opportunities to create robust and well-performing new techniques based on knowledge gained through evaluation. Therefore, this approach follows several important evaluation concepts, elucidated in the following sections. Figure 11.3 presents an overview of this approach.

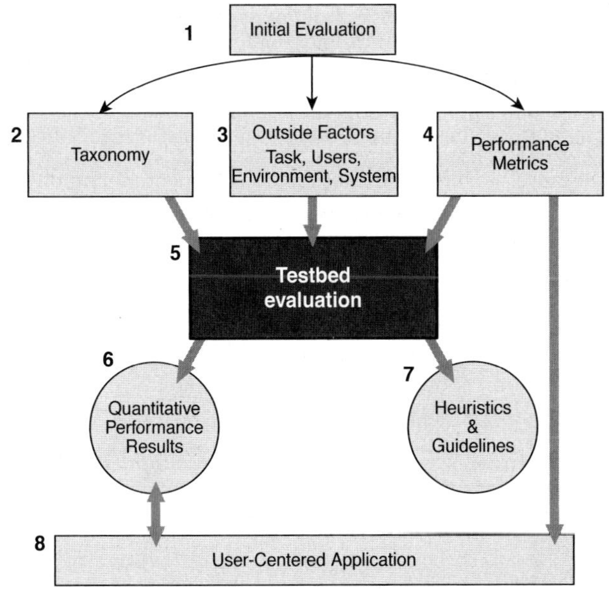

Figure 11.3 Testbed evaluation approach. (Image reprinted by permission of MIT Press and *Presence: Teleoperators and Virtual Environments*)

Initial Evaluation

The first step toward formalizing the design, evaluation, and application of interaction techniques is to gain an intuitive understanding of the generic interaction tasks in which one is interested and current techniques available for the tasks (see Figure 11.3, state 1). This is accomplished through experience using interaction techniques and through observation and evaluation of groups of users. These initial evaluation experiences are heavily drawn upon for the processes of building a taxonomy, listing outside influences on usability, and listing performance measures. It is helpful, therefore, to gain as much experience of this type as possible so that good decisions can be made in the next phases of formalization.

Taxonomy

The next step is to establish a taxonomy (Figure 11.3, state 2) of interaction techniques for the interaction task being evaluated. In particular, the testbed approach uses task-decomposition taxonomies, like the ones presented in Chapter 7, "Selection and Manipulation," (section 7.3.1) and Chapter 8, "Travel," (section 8.3.1). For example, the task of changing an object's color might be made up of three subtasks: selecting an object, choosing a color, and applying the color. The subtask for choosing a color might have two possible technique components: changing the values of R, G, and B sliders or touching a point within a 3D color space. The subtasks and their related technique components make up a taxonomy for the object coloring task.

Ideally, the taxonomies established by this approach need to be correct, complete, and general. Any interaction technique that can be conceived for the task should fit within the taxonomy. Thus, subtasks will necessarily be abstract. The taxonomy will also list several possible technique components for each of the subtasks, but not necessarily every conceivable component.

Building taxonomies is a good way to understand the low-level makeup of interaction techniques and to formalize differences between them, but once they are in place, they can also be used in the design process. One can think of a taxonomy not only as a characterization, but also as a design space. Because a taxonomy breaks the task down into separable subtasks, a wide range of designs can be considered quickly by simply trying different combinations of technique components for each of the subtasks. There is no guarantee that a given combination will make sense as a complete interaction technique, but the systematic nature of the taxonomy makes it easy to generate designs and to reject inappropriate combinations.

Outside Factors

Interaction techniques cannot be evaluated in a vacuum. The usability of a technique may depend on a variety of factors (Figure 11.3, state 3), of which the interaction technique is but one. In order for the evaluation framework to be complete, such factors must be included explicitly and used as secondary independent variables in evaluations. Bowman and Hodges (1999) identified four categories of outside factors.

First, *task characteristics* are those attributes of the task that may affect usability, including distance to be traveled or size of the object being manipulated. Second, the approach considers *environment characteristics*, such as the number of obstacles and the level of activity or motion in the 3D scene. *User characteristics*, including cognitive measures such as spatial ability and physical attributes such as arm length, may also have effects on usability. Finally, *system characteristics*, such as the lighting model used or the mean frame rate, may be significant.

Performance Metrics

This approach is designed to obtain information about human performance in common 3D interaction tasks—but what is performance? Speed and accuracy are easy to measure, are quantitative, and are clearly important in the evaluation of interaction techniques, but there are also many other performance metrics (Figure 11.3, state 4) to be considered. Thus, this approach also considers subjective usability metrics, such as perceived ease of use, ease of learning, and user comfort. The choice of interaction technique could conceivably affect all of these, and they should not be discounted. Also, more than any other current computing paradigm, 3D UIs involve the user's senses and body in the task. Thus, a focus on user-centric performance measures is essential. If an interaction technique does not make good use of human skills or if it causes fatigue or discomfort, it will not provide overall usability, despite its performance in other areas.

Testbed Evaluation

Bowman and Hodges (1999) use testbed evaluation (Figure 11.3, state 5) as the final stage in the evaluation of interaction techniques for 3D interaction tasks. This approach allows generic, generalizable, and reusable evaluation through the creation of testbeds—environments and tasks that involve all important aspects of a task, that evaluate each component of a technique, that consider outside influences (factors other than the interaction technique) on performance, and that have multiple performance measures. A testbed experiment uses a formal factorial experimental design and normally requires a large number of participants. If many interaction techniques or outside factors are included in the evaluation, the number of trials per subject can become overly large, so interaction techniques are usually a between-subjects variable (each subject uses only a single interaction technique), while other factors are within-subjects variables.

Application and Generalization of Results

Testbed evaluation produces a set of results or models (Figure 11.3, state 6) that characterize the usability of an interaction technique for the specified task. Usability is given in terms of multiple performance metrics with respect to various levels of outside factors. These results become part of a performance database for the interaction task, with more information being added to the database each time a new technique is run through the testbed. These results can also be generalized into heuristics or guidelines (Figure 11.3, state 7) that can easily be evaluated and applied by 3D UI developers. Many of the guidelines presented in earlier chapters are generalizations of the results of such experiments.

The last step is to apply the performance results to 3D applications (Figure 11.3, state 8) with the goal of making them more useful and usable. In order to choose interaction techniques for applications appropriately, one must understand the interaction requirements of the application. There is no single best technique, because the technique that is best for one application may not be optimal for another application with different requirements. Therefore, applications need to specify their interaction requirements before the most appropriate interaction techniques can be chosen. This specification is done in terms of the performance metrics that have already been defined as part of the formal framework. Once the requirements are in place, the performance results from testbed evaluation can be used to recommend interaction techniques that meet those requirements.

Examples of Approach

Although testbed evaluation could be applied to almost any type of interactive system, it is especially appropriate for 3D UIs because of its focus on low-level interaction techniques. We'll summarize two testbed experiments that were performed to compare techniques for the tasks of travel (Bowman et al. 1999) and selection/manipulation (Bowman and Hodges 1999).

The travel testbed experiment compared seven different travel techniques for the tasks of naïve search and primed search. In the primed search trials, the initial visibility of the target and the required accuracy of movement were also varied. The dependent variables were time for task completion and subjective user comfort ratings. Forty-four participants participated in the experiment. The researchers gathered both demographic and spatial ability information for each subject.

The selection/manipulation testbed compared the usability and performance of nine different interaction techniques. For selection tasks, the independent variables were distance from the user to the object, size of the object, and density of distracter objects. For manipulation tasks, the required accuracy of placement, the required degrees of freedom, and the distance through which the object was moved were varied. The dependent variables in this experiment were the time for task completion, the number of selection errors, and subjective user comfort ratings. Forty-eight participants participated, and the researchers again obtained demographic data and spatial ability scores.

In both instances, the testbed approach produced unexpected and interesting results that would not have been revealed by a simpler experiment. For example, in the selection/manipulation testbed, it was found that selection techniques using an extended virtual hand (see Chapter 7, "Selection and Manipulation," section 7.4.1) performed well with larger, nearer objects and more poorly with smaller, farther objects, while selection techniques based on ray-casting (section 7.5.1) performed well regardless of object size or distance. The testbed environments and tasks have also proved to be reusable. The travel testbed was used to evaluate a new travel technique and compare it to existing techniques, while the manipulation testbed was reused to evaluate the usability of common techniques in the context of different VE display devices.

11.6.3 Component Evaluation Approach

Another framework-based evaluation approach is to focus on the stages of action and the components that affect those stages. McMahan et al. (2015) provide a system-centric adaptation of Norman's Seven Stages of Action (Norman 2013) called the **User-System Loop** as the basis of this approach (see Chapter 4, section 4.2.2). Every interaction begins with user actions that input devices sense or are manipulated by, which are then interpreted by transfer functions as meaningful system effects. Those effects alter the data and models underlying the simulation's objects, physics, and artificial intelligence. Rendering software captures aspects of the simulation's updated state and sends commands to output devices to create sensory stimuli for the user to perceive.

At each stage of the User-System Loop, there are components that affect the overall interaction and usability of the system. For example, at the output devices stage, the visual display's field of view will affect how much of the 3D UI that the user can simultaneously see. Whether the display is stereoscopic or not will also affect the user's depth cues. At the transfer function stage, if the inputs sensed by the input devices are directly mapped to the effect's output properties in a one-to-one manner, the interaction will afford direct manipulation (Shneiderman 1998). On the other hand, if the inputs are scaled and manipulated in a dramatic or nonlinear fashion when being mapped, the interaction will be a "magic" technique, like the ones described in Chapter 10, section 10.3.3. As discussed in the previous chapters, such changes to the interaction can dramatically affect the user experience.

Evaluating Components

Like testbed evaluation, component evaluation explicitly investigates specific components while keeping other factors the same. First, this helps to avoid confounding variables, or factors not being investigated, from affecting the results of the evaluations. For example, when comparing a surround-screen-based 3D UI to an HWD-based 3D UI, there are multiple confounding variables that may contribute to any significant differences between the UIs, such as field of view, the total size of the visual field surrounding the user, latency, brightness, and the weight of the stereo glasses compared to the weight of the HWD. By explicitly controlling components not being investigated so they are the same, component evaluations avoid potential confounds.

Second, component evaluation yields important knowledge about how to best use components together if the evaluation is used to investigate multiple components. As an example, McMahan et al. (2012) found that conditions with mixed input and output components, such as using a mouse with a visual field completely surrounding the user, yielded significantly lower user performance in a first-person shooter game than conditions with matched pairs of input and output components, such as using a 6-DOF wand with a visual field completely surrounding the user. This interesting result would not have been revealed by a simpler or less-controlled experiment.

Finally, component evaluation will also provide information on the individual effects of a component, if it has no interaction effects with the other investigated components. For example, Ragan et al. (2015) investigated both field of view and visual complexity—the amount of detail, clutter, and objects in a scene (Oliva et al. 2004)—and did not find a significant interaction effect between the components for affecting how users learned a prescribed strategy for a visual scanning task. However, the researchers did find that visual complexity had an individual effect on how users learned the strategy, with users that trained with more complexity better demonstrating the strategy than those that had trained with less complexity.

Applying Component Results

With its focus on controlled experiments to understand the effects of individual components and combinations of components, the component evaluation approach is primarily designed for researchers. It results in general knowledge that can be applied to the design of many 3D UIs.

While the sequential evaluation approach focuses on improving a particular application through iteration and the testbed evaluation approach focuses on characterizing the usability of specific interaction techniques, the results of the component evaluation approach could be used to improve a particular application or to generalize the effects of a specific component for most 3D UIs and 3D interaction techniques. During the design and iterative development of a 3D UI, design choices will present themselves, and the best choice may not be obvious. For example, a large field of view may provide a more realistic view of the VE but may also increase cybersickness. A component evaluation that specifically investigates the effects of field of view could be used to determine if a smaller field of view would still provide a realistic view of the VE while inducing less cybersickness for the given 3D UI application. Alternatively, a series of component evaluations could be used with several 3D UI applications to generalize the effects of field of view and its tradeoffs between realistic views and cybersickness.

Defining Components

A major consideration to using the component evaluation approach is how to define the components that affect each stage of action. For example, the GOMS model (Card et al. 1983), described in Chapter 4, could be extended to define components as the operators required at each stage of action. Component evaluations using this strategy would yield information and knowledge about how elementary actions affect interactions within a system.

A powerful method is to define the components in terms of **fidelity**, or realism (Bowman and McMahan 2007; McMahan et al. 2010, 2012, 2015; McMahan 2011; Bowman et al. 2012; Laha et al. 2013, 2014; Ragan et al. 2015; Nabiyouni et al. 2015). McMahan et al. (2015) have identified three categories of fidelity components based on the User-System Loop—interaction fidelity, scenario fidelity, and display fidelity, which we discuss further in the following sections.

Interaction Fidelity Components

McMahan et al. (2012) define **interaction fidelity** as the objective degree of exactness with which real-world actions are reproduced in an interactive system. For example, the real walking technique (see Chapter 8, section 8.4.1) provides one of the highest levels of interaction fidelity, while the walking-in-place technique (see Chapter 8, section 8.4.2) provides a lower level. Interaction fidelity directly plays a role during the stages of user actions, input devices, and transfer functions.

McMahan (2011) presents a framework of interaction fidelity components referred to as the **Framework for Interaction Fidelity Analysis** (**FIFA**). In the most recent version of FIFA (McMahan et al. 2015), the components of interaction fidelity are divided into the three subcategories of biomechanical symmetry, input veracity, and control symmetry.

Biomechanical symmetry is the objective degree of exactness with which real-world body movements for a task are reproduced during interaction (McMahan 2011). It consists of three components based on aspects of biomechanics: anthropometric symmetry, kinematic symmetry, and kinetic symmetry. The **anthropometric symmetry** component is the objective degree of exactness with which body segments involved in a real-world task are required by an interaction technique. For instance, walking in place has a high degree of anthropometric symmetry because it involves the same body segments (i.e., thighs, legs, and feet) as walking in the real world. The **kinematic symmetry** component is the objective degree of exactness with which a body motion for a real-world task is produced during an interaction. For example, walking in place has a lower degree of kinematic symmetry than real walking, as it does not incorporate the swing phase of the gait cycle and real walking does. Finally, **kinetic symmetry** is the objective degree of exactness with which the forces involved in a real-world action are reproduced during interaction. The Virtusphere, for instance, requires large internal muscle forces to start and stop the device from rolling due to its weight and inertia (Nabiyouni et al. 2015).

McMahan et al. (2015) define **input veracity** as the objective degree of exactness with which the input devices capture and measure the user's actions. It also consists of three components: accuracy, precision, and latency. The **accuracy** of an input device is how close its readings are to the "true" values it senses (Taylor 1997). Accuracy is especially important for interacting with a system that coincides with the real world, such as augmented reality. For AR, aligning virtual images and objects with the user's view of the real world (i.e., registration) is one of the greatest challenges (Kipper et al. 2012). The **precision** of an input device, also called its "repeatability", is the degree to which reported measurements in the same conditions yield the same results (Taylor 1997). A lack of precision is often associated with jitter (Ragan et al. 2009). The last component of input veracity is **latency**, which is the temporal delay between user input and sensory feedback generated by the system in response to it (Friston and Steed 2014). Several research studies have found latency to have a negative effect on user performance (Allison et al. 2001; Ellis et al. 1999).

Finally, McMahan (2011) defines **control symmetry** as the objective degree of exactness with which control in a real-world task is provided by an interaction. In the most recent version of FIFA (McMahan et al. 2015), the control symmetry subcategory has a single component—**transfer function symmetry**, which is the objective degree of exactness with which a real-world transfer function is reproduced through interaction. As most real-world actions do not involve an actual transfer function, McMahan et al. (2015) use the component to compare the transfer functions of interaction techniques to the physical properties affected during the real-world action counterpart.

In summary, McMahan et al. (2015) categorize the components of interaction fidelity as aspects of biomechanical symmetry, input veracity, and control symmetry. These categories directly correspond to the user actions, input devices, and transfer functions of the User-System Loop.

Scenario Fidelity Components

Ragan et al. (2015) define the second category of fidelity components as **scenario fidelity**, which is the objective degree of exactness with which behaviors, rules, and object properties are reproduced in a simulation compared to the real world. For example, VEs designed using basic architectural principles, such as those by Campbell (1996), provide a greater degree of scenario fidelity than VEs designed with impossible architectures, such as the ones created by Suma et al. (2012). Scenario fidelity impacts the data and models underlying the simulation.

Scenario fidelity has not been as extensively researched as interaction fidelity or display fidelity. Currently, its components have only been defined at the high-level categories of behaviors, rules, and object properties (Ragan et al. 2015). **Behaviors** refer to the artificial intelligence properties that control virtual agents and objects within the simulation. **Rules** refer to physics and other models that determine what happen to objects within the simulation. Finally, **object properties** refer to the dimensional (e.g., height, width, shape), light-related (e.g., texture, color), and physics-related qualities (e.g., weight, mass) of objects.

As the components of scenario fidelity have only been loosely defined with three broad categories, there is much research to be done to further identify individual components.

Display Fidelity Components

Finally, the third category of fidelity components is **display fidelity**, which McMahan et al. (2012) define as the objective degree of exactness with which real-world sensory stimuli are reproduced by a system (note that display fidelity has also been referred to as **immersion**; see McMahan et al. 2012 for more discussion). A surround-screen display with a 360-degree FOR and stereoscopic glasses, for example, provides a greater level of display fidelity than a monoscopic desktop monitor. Display fidelity directly depends on the qualities of the rendering software, output devices, and sensory stimuli produced.

Bowman and McMahan (2007) identify many of the components of visual display fidelity, including **stereoscopy** (the display of different images to each eye to provide an additional depth cue), **field of view** (FOV; the size of the visual field that can be viewed instantaneously by the user), **field of regard** (FOR; the total size of the visual field surrounding the user), **display resolution** (the total pixels displayed on the screen or surface), **display size** (the physical dimensions of the display screen or surface), **refresh rate** (how often the display draws provided rendered data), and **frame rate** (how often rendered data is provided to the display).

In addition to visual components, display fidelity also comprises auditory, haptic, olfactory, and gustatory aspects. However, Bowman and McMahan (2007) were focused on visual aspects and did not address the components of these sensory modalities.

Examples of the Component Evaluation Approach

While the component evaluation approach could be used to evaluate nearly any type of interactive system, the fidelity-components strategy specifically targets 3D UIs. It has been used in many studies to investigate the effects and interactions of numerous components of fidelity. These studies can be categorized into three types of evaluations—those investigating components of interaction fidelity, components of display fidelity, and both. Few studies have explicitly investigated the effects or interactions of scenario fidelity.

Investigations of interaction fidelity have mostly compared levels of interaction fidelity holistically rather than varying individual components, due to the integral relationships among the components (for example, it is difficult to alter the kinetics of an interaction without affecting its kinematics). McMahan et al. (2010) compared two techniques based on a steering wheel metaphor to two game controller techniques that used a joystick to steer a virtual vehicle. They found that the steering wheel techniques were significantly worse for the steering task than the joystick techniques, despite having higher levels of biomechanical symmetry and control symmetry. Similarly, Nabiyouni et al. (2015) found that the Virtusphere technique was significantly worse for travel tasks than a joystick technique, despite also having higher levels of biomechanical symmetry and control symmetry. However, they found that real walking, which provides extremely high levels of biomechanical symmetry and control symmetry, was significantly better than the Virtusphere.

Unlike interaction fidelity, specific components of display fidelity have been controlled and investigated. Arthur (2000) evaluated FOV in an HWD at three levels (48°, 112°, 176°) for a visual search task and determined that increasing FOV improved searching within a VE. Similarly, Ni et al. (2006) investigated display resolution at two levels (1280x720 and 2560x1440) and display size at two levels of physical viewing angle (42.8° and 90°) for searching and comparing information within a VE. They found that higher levels of display resolution and display size improved user performance metrics. In the AR domain, Kishishita et al. (2014) showed similar results in that target discovery rates consistently drop with in-view labelling and increase with in-situ labelling as display angle approaches 100 degrees of field of view. Past this point, the performances of the two view management methods begin to converge, suggesting equivalent discovery rates at approximately 130 degrees of field of view.

Finally, some studies have investigated both interaction fidelity and display fidelity. McMahan et al. (2012) controlled both at low and high levels for a first-person shooter game. They varied interaction fidelity between a low level (mouse-and-keyboard technique used for aiming and traveling, respectively), and a high level (6-DOF tracker technique for aiming and the moderate-fidelity human joystick technique (see Chapter 8, section 8.4.2) for travel). They also varied display fidelity between a low level with no stereoscopy and only a 90° field of regard and a high level with stereoscopy and a 360° field of regard. Their results indicated that the mixed conditions (i.e., low-fidelity interactions with a high-fidelity display and high-fidelity interactions with a low-fidelity display) were significantly worse for user performance than the matched conditions (i.e., low-fidelity interactions with a low-fidelity display and high-fidelity interaction with a high-fidelity display).

In most of the case studies above, and others, the component evaluation approach produced unexpected results that provided unique insights. First, results have shown that many components with moderate levels of fidelity can yield poorer performance than those with lower levels (McMahan et al. 2010, 2012; McMahan 2011; Nabiyouni et al. 2015). This could sometimes be due to users not being as familiar with moderate-fidelity interactions as real-world high-fidelity actions or desktop-based low-fidelity interactions, but could also be an inherent limitation of moderate levels of fidelity, which seem natural but are not, similar to the "uncanny valley" effect. Second, several studies have demonstrated that increasing display fidelity normally yields better performance (Arthur 2000; Ni et al. 2006; McMahan 2011; Laha et al. 2014), unless interaction fidelity is also changing (McMahan et al. 2012). These interesting insights would not have been possible without conducting component evaluations.

11.6.4 Comparison of Approaches

The three major evaluation approaches we have presented for 3D UIs—sequential evaluation, testbed evaluation, and component evaluation—take quite different approaches to the same problem: how to understand and improve usability and the user experience for 3D UIs. Sequential evaluation is done in the context of a particular application and can have both quantitative and qualitative results. Testbed evaluation is done in a generic evaluation context and usually seeks quantitative results. Component evaluation can be adapted for a particular application to make a specific design choice, or it can be applied to multiple application contexts to generalize the effects of one or more components. Like testbed evaluation, component evaluation prioritizes quantitative results. All three approaches employ users in evaluation.

In this section, we take a more detailed look at the similarities of and differences between these three approaches. We organize this comparison by answering several key questions about each of them. Many of these questions can be asked of other evaluation methods and perhaps should be asked before designing a 3D UI evaluation. Indeed, answers to these questions may help identify appropriate evaluation methods, given specific research, design, or development goals. Another possibility is to understand the general properties, strengths, and weaknesses of each approach so that the three approaches can be linked in complementary ways.

What Are the Goals of the Approach?

As mentioned above, all three approaches ultimately aim to understand and improve usability and the user experience in 3D UIs. However, there are more specific goals that exhibit differences between the three approaches.

Sequential evaluation's immediate goal is to iterate toward a better UI for a particular 3D application. It looks closely at particular user tasks of an application to determine which scenarios and interaction techniques should be incorporated. In general, this approach tends to be quite specific in order to produce the best possible interface design for a particular application under development.

Testbed evaluation has the specific goal of finding generic performance characteristics of interaction techniques. This means that one wants to understand interaction technique performance in a high-level, abstract way, not in the context of a particular application. This goal is important because, if achieved, it can lead to wide applicability of the results. In order to do generic evaluation, the testbed approach is limited to general techniques for common universal tasks (such as navigation, selection, or manipulation). To say this in another way, testbed evaluation is not designed to evaluate special-purpose techniques for specific tasks. Rather, it abstracts away from these specifics, using generic properties of the task, user, environment, and system.

Component evaluation has the goal of determining the main effects of specific system components and any interaction effects among them for either a specific application context or generally, across multiple application contexts. When conducted for a specific application context, component evaluation can be used to decide upon the best design choices. Alternatively, a series of component evaluations can be conducted across multiple application contexts to develop expectations about how the components will generally affect usability and the user experience in most 3D UIs. These expectations can then be used to create design guidelines such as, "Do not employ moderate-fidelity interaction techniques when familiarity and walk-up usability are important" (McMahan et al. 2012).

When Should the Approach Be Used?

Sequential evaluation should be used early and continually throughout the design cycle of a 3D application. User task analysis is necessary before the first interface prototypes are built. Heuristic and formative evaluations of a prototype produce recommendations that can be applied to subsequent design iterations. Formative evaluations of different design possibilities can be done when the choice of design (e.g., for interaction techniques) is not clear.

By its non-application-specific nature, the testbed approach actually falls completely outside the design cycle of a particular application. Ideally, testbed evaluation should be completed before an application is even a glimmer in the eye of a developer. Because it produces general performance/usability results for interaction techniques, these results can be used as a starting point for the design of new 3D UIs.

Like the testbed approach, component evaluation can be used before the system concept for an application is even written. A series of component evaluations over multiple application contexts will yield knowledge of the general effects of one or more components, which can be expressed as design guidelines. Alternatively, single component evaluations can be used during the development of a 3D application to decide upon unclear design choices.

The distinct time periods in which testbed evaluation and sequential evaluation are employed suggest that combining the two approaches is possible and even desirable. Testbed evaluation can first produce a set of general results and guidelines that can serve as an advanced and well-informed starting point for a 3D application's UI design. Sequential evaluation can then refine that initial design in a more application-specific fashion. Similarly, component evaluation can be used to derive design guidelines concerning specific components that sequential evaluation can rely upon during the initial design of a 3D application. Alternatively, component evaluation can be used during sequential evaluation to make specific design decisions.

In What Situations Is the Approach Useful?

As we have said, the sequential evaluation approach should be used throughout the design cycle of a 3D UI, but it is especially useful in the early stages of interface design. Because sequential evaluation produces results even on very low-fidelity prototypes or design specifications, a 3D application's UI can be refined much earlier, resulting in greater cost savings. Also, the earlier this approach is used in development, the more time remains for producing design iterations, which ultimately results in a better product. This approach also makes the most sense when a user task analysis has been performed. This analysis will suggest task scenarios that make evaluation more meaningful and effective.

Testbed evaluation allows the researcher to understand detailed performance characteristics of common interaction techniques, especially user performance. It provides a wide range of performance data that may be applicable to a variety of situations. In a development effort that requires a suite of applications with common interaction techniques and interface elements, testbed evaluation could provide a quantitative basis for choosing them, because developers could choose interaction techniques that performed well across the range of tasks, environments, and users in the applications; their choices are supported by empirical evidence.

Component evaluation is useful for determining the general effects of one or more system components and establishing design guidelines for how those components should be controlled or fixed in a design. Single component evaluations are also useful for making design choices that directly involve one or more system components, such as what FOV to provide or whether or not stereoscopic graphics should be used.

What Are the Costs of Using the Approach?

In general, the sequential evaluation approach may be less costly than the testbed evaluation approach because it can focus on a particular 3D application rather than pay the cost of abstraction. However, some important costs are still associated with this approach.

Multiple evaluators may be needed. Development of useful task scenarios may take a large amount of effort. Conducting the evaluations themselves may be costly in terms of time, depending on the complexity of task scenarios. Most importantly, because this is part of an iterative design effort, time spent by developers to incorporate suggested design changes after each round of evaluation must be considered.

The testbed evaluation approach can be seen as very costly and is definitely not appropriate for every situation. In certain scenarios, however, its benefits can make the extra effort worthwhile. Some of the most important costs associated with testbed evaluation include difficult experimental design (many independent and dependent variables, where some of the combinations of variables are not testable), experiments requiring large numbers of trials to ensure significant results, and large amounts of time spent running experiments because of the number of participants and trials. Once an experiment has been conducted, the results may not be as detailed as some developers would like. Because testbed evaluation looks at generic situations, information on specific interface details such as labeling, the shape of icons, and so on will not usually be available.

The cost of the component evaluation approach varies, based on when and how it is being used. If a series of component evaluations are being conducted to generalize the effects of one or more components, the cost of the evaluations is similar to that of a testbed evaluation. Difficult experimental designs with many independent and dependent variables usually require large amounts of trials, participants, and time to conduct such a series of component evaluations. On the other hand, single component evaluations used during the design of a 3D application can be less costly than the sequential evaluation approach.

What Are the Benefits of Using the Approach?

For a particular application, the sequential evaluation approach can be very beneficial. Although it does not produce reusable results or general principles in the same broad sense as testbed and component evaluations can, it is likely to produce a more refined and usable 3D UI than if the results of testbed or component evaluations were applied alone. Another of the major benefits of this method relates to its involvement of users in the development process. Because members of the representative user group take part in many of the evaluations, the 3D UI is more likely to be tailored to their needs and should result in higher user acceptance and productivity, reduced user errors, and increased user satisfaction. There may be some transferability of results, because other applications may have similar tasks or requirements, or they may be able to use refined interaction techniques produced by the process.

Because testbed evaluation is so costly, its benefits must be significant before it becomes a useful evaluation method. One such benefit is generality of the results. Because testbed experiments are conducted in a generalized context, the results may be applied many times in many different types of applications. Of course, there is a cost associated with each use of the results because the developer must decide which results are relevant to a specific 3D UI. Second, testbeds for a particular task may be used multiple times. When a new interaction technique is proposed, that technique can be run through the testbed and compared with techniques already evaluated. The same set of participants is not necessary, because testbed evaluation usually uses a between-subjects design. Finally, the generality of the experiments lends itself to development of general guidelines and heuristics. It is more difficult to generalize from experience with a single application.

Like its costs, the benefits of the component evaluation approach vary based on when and how the approach is used. If the approach is used in a series across multiple 3D UI contexts, one benefit is the generality of the results, similar to the testbed approach. Unlike the testbed approach, however, the cost associated with each use of the results is often less, as most results should be relevant to most 3D UIs since they are based on system components that should be present in most 3D UI systems. Another benefit to using the component approach across multiple 3D UI contexts is that general guidelines for controlling that component within 3D UIs should become apparent. Finally, a single component evaluation provides the benefit of revealing the best design choice for a particular 3D application, when that design choice depends upon one or more system components.

How Are the Approach's Evaluation Results Applied?

Application of the results of the sequential evaluation approach is straightforward. Heuristic and formative evaluations produce specific suggestions for changes to the application's UI or interaction techniques. The result of summative evaluation is an interface or set of interaction techniques that performs the best or is the most usable in a comparative study. In any case, results of the evaluation are tied directly to changes in the interface of the 3D application.

The results of testbed evaluation are applicable to any 3D UI that uses the tasks studied with a testbed. For example, testbed results are available for some of the most common tasks in 3D UIs: travel and selection/manipulation (Bowman et al. 2001). The results can be applied in two ways. The first informal technique is to use the guidelines produced by testbed evaluation in choosing interaction techniques for an application (as in Bowman et al. 1999). A more formal technique uses the requirements of the application (specified in terms of the testbed's performance metrics) to choose the interaction technique closest to those requirements. Both of these approaches should produce a set of interaction techniques for the application that makes it more usable than the same application designed using intuition alone. However, because the results are so general, the 3D UI will almost certainly require further refinement.

The results of a series of component evaluations across multiple 3D UI contexts are applicable to any 3D UI system that includes the system components evaluated. As many 3D UI systems include the same system components, the results of the component evaluation may be more generally applicable than the results of the testbed approach. Finally, the results of a single component evaluation can be straightforwardly applied to a design choice based on how to control one or more system components.

11.7 Guidelines for 3D UI Evaluation

In this section, we present some guidelines for those wishing to perform usability evaluations of 3D UIs. The first subsection presents general guidelines, and the second subsection focuses specifically on formal experimentation.

11.7.1 General Guidelines

The general guidelines include less formal modes of evaluation.

> **Tip**
>
> Begin with informal evaluation.

Informal evaluation is very important, both in the process of developing an application and in doing basic interaction research. In the context of an application, informal evaluation can quickly narrow the design space and point out major flaws in the design. In basic research, informal evaluation helps you understand the task and the techniques on an intuitive level before moving on to more formal classifications and experiments.

> **Tip**
>
> Acknowledge and plan for the differences between traditional UI and 3D UI evaluation.

Section 11.4 detailed a large number of distinctive characteristics of 3D UI evaluation. These differences must be considered when you design a study. For example, you should plan to have multiple evaluators, incorporate rest breaks into your procedure, and assess whether breaks in presence could affect your results.

> **Tip**
>
> Choose an evaluation approach that meets your requirements.

Just as we discussed with respect to interaction techniques, there is no optimal usability evaluation method or approach. A range of methods should be considered, and important questions such as those in section 11.6.4 should be asked. For example, if you have designed a new interaction technique and want to refine the usability of the design before any implementation, a heuristic evaluation or cognitive walkthrough fits the bill. On the other hand, if you must choose between two input devices for a task in which a small difference in efficiency may be significant, a formal experiment may be required.

> **Tip**
>
> Use a wide range of metrics.

Remember that speed and accuracy alone do not equal usability. Also remember to look at learning, comfort, presence, and other metrics in order to get a complete picture of the usability and user experience of the interface.

11.7.2 Guidelines for Formal Experimentation

This section presents a number of guidelines for formal experiments to investigate the usability issues of 3D interfaces.

> **Tip**
>
> Design experiments with general applicability.

If you're going to do formal experiments, you will be investing a large amount of time and effort. So you want the results to be as general as possible. Thus, you have to think hard about how to design tasks that are generic, performance measures to which real applications can relate, and a method for applications to easily apply the results.

> **Tip**
>
> Use pilot studies to determine which variables should be tested in the main experiment.

In doing formal experiments, especially testbed evaluations, you often have too many variables to actually test without an infinite supply of time and participants. Small pilot studies can show trends that may allow you to remove certain variables because they do not appear to affect the task you're doing.

> **Tip**
>
> Use automated data collection for system performance and task performance metrics.

As discussed in section 11.4.1, the complexity of 3D UIs can make data collection difficult for evaluators, for they are not able to simultaneously observe the subject's actions and the results of those actions within the 3D UI. A simple yet effective solution to this issue is to program automated data collection methods within the 3D UI software or ancillary software. Such automated data collection methods are more accurate than evaluator-based observations, with time measured in milliseconds and every predefined error being identified. The major limitation of automated data collection is the time and effort required to program the additional data collection methods.

> **Tip**
>
> Look for interactions between variables—rarely will a single technique be the best in all situations.

In most formal experiments on the usability of 3D UIs, the most interesting results have been interactions. That is, it's rarely the case that technique A is always better than technique B. Rather, for instance, technique A works well when the environment has characteristic X, and technique B works well when the environment has characteristic Y. Statistical analysis should reveal these interactions between variables.

11.8 Case Studies

In this section, we discuss the evaluation aspects of our two case studies. Again, if you have not read sequentially through the book, you can find the introduction to the case studies in section 2.4, and the design decisions for the case studies at the ends of Chapters 5–10.

11.8.1 VR Gaming Case Study

As we noted in the introduction to the VR gaming case study, this design is purely a thought experiment. Although we have significant experience in designing 3D UIs, we are not so arrogant as to suggest that the 3D UI design we've presented is the best one or even an especially good one. On the contrary, in our experience, when we imagine 3D interaction in our minds, the interaction concepts can seem really exciting and powerful, but then we find that they don't turn out be nearly as cool or effective when they are actually implemented. That's because it's very hard to imagine all the subtleties of how an interaction will look and feel—we tend to skip over details in our imagination, and the devil is in the details for 3D UI design.

So while this case study should be helpful in seeing how to think about the design of various parts of a complete 3D UI for a VR game, and while several of the interaction concepts we've described would probably work quite well, several rounds of prototyping and formative evaluation would be critical to actually realize an effective 3D UI if this were a real project.

Prototyping is especially important for 3D UIs. While early prototypes of more traditional UIs (desktop, mobile device, etc.) are often low-fidelity paper prototypes or wireframes, it's difficult to apply these approaches to 3D UI prototyping, which often require a more complete implementation. Unfortunately, this means that the early stages of a 3D UI design often can't progress as quickly as traditional UIs, since the notion of rapid throw-away prototypes is less applicable to 3D UIs. Still, 3D UI development tools are becoming more and more powerful, as many game engines gain support for VR, AR, tracking, and the like. And it's still possible to prototype interaction concepts without having high-fidelity representations of the other parts of the game.

In this case study, then, we would suggest starting with working prototypes of the individual interaction concepts (for selection/manipulation, travel, and system control), with some informal formative usability studies and several rounds of iteration to refine and hone them as quickly as possible. In these studies, we would be looking both for large usability problems (requiring significant technique redesign) and for places where the technique's mappings need tweaking.

The next step would be to put all the interaction techniques together into a prototype of the complete UI, using just a couple of rooms that are representative of the entire game. We need to evaluate all the interaction techniques together, because even when techniques are effective on their own, they don't always work well together. In these formative studies, we would look for critical incidents, where interactions break down or don't flow well together. We would also administer standard usability questionnaires.

Once we are happy with the complete 3D UI, we would move on to broader play-testing of several levels of the actual game, looking not just at usability, but at the broader user experience. These evaluations should use members of the target audience for the game, and should make use of standard UX questionnaires and interviews to determine the impact of the game on things like fun, frustration, and emotion.

Key Concepts

The key concepts that we have discussed in relation to our VR gaming case study are

- A 3D interaction concept that seems good in the imagination or on paper does not always translate to an effective implementation. Working prototypes are critical to understand the potential of 3D UI designs.
- Be sure to evaluate the complete UI, not just the individual interaction techniques.
- Start with usability evaluation, but for real 3D UI applications, go beyond usability to understand the broader user experience.

11.8.2 Mobile AR Case Study

Continuing the thread of the Mobile AR Case Study section in the previous chapter, here we will take a closer look at evaluation approaches that affected the analysis of the various perceptual, cognitive, and physical ergonomics issues of the HYDROSYS system.

With regards to perceptual issues, AR systems have been shown to suffer from a range of different problems (Kruijff et al. 2010). In the early stages of development of our system, we performed a user study to address legibility and visibility issues with a rather curious outcome. A simple paper-based experiment used different backgrounds depicting the usage environments, with different structural and color properties. Overlaid on these environments, labels with different color schemes were shown. The results of the informal study with around ten users showed that, not surprisingly, high-contrast combinations were preferred most. Especially those colors that depicted high contrast between the foreground and the background and between the label and text color were preferred. The study also brought out one specific result: the color found to be most visible and legible was pink, as it clearly stood out against the natural background and text was still easily readable. However, we found the color not suitable, as it would not provide a visually pleasing design, at least not in our eyes. In other cultures, however, this color scheme might actually be fully acceptable!

The results might have been different with a different display. For example, using a wide field of view head-worn display, you can visualize information in the periphery. But the outer regions of our visual field react quite differently to colors than our central vision (Kishishita et al 2014), as the ability to perceive colors diminishes towards the borders of our visual field. Additional studies could have been performed to examine this question or the question of label layout with different displays.

Another issue not to be ignored when performing outdoor evaluations is the environmental condition. The biggest challenge of performing perception-driven outdoor experiments in AR is lighting conditions. It is almost impossible to control lighting and related issues (such as screen reflections), even though some methods can be used to minimize effects. For example, you can select similar timeslots on a daily basis when the weather is somewhat similar, controlling better the direction of sunlight. On the other hand, deliberately performing evaluations under different lighting conditions may better reveal the potential and problems of the techniques being evaluated. At a minimum, one should log the outdoor conditions (brightness, possibly the angle of sunlight), to better understand the evaluation outcomes.

Cognitive issues also played an important role in HYDROSYS. We evaluated different techniques to improve spatial assessment of augmented information through multi-camera navigation systems. As we described in Chapter 8, we performed two studies to analyze the effect of different techniques on spatial knowledge acquisition and search performance. The first experiment (Veas et al. 2010) was a summative evaluation in which we compared three different techniques (mosaic, tunnel, and transition). The focus was on assessing which technique was best for knowledge acquisition and spatial awareness, while addressing cognitive load and user preference. The techniques were used in different local and remote camera combinations. We blindfolded users to block acquisition of spatial knowledge between physical locations, and we used rarely visited locations to avoid effects of prior knowledge. Based on the acquired knowledge, we asked the users to draw the spatial configuration of the site.

To measure the spatial abilities of users, participants filled out a SBSOD questionnaire before the experiment. They also rated techniques on subjectively perceived cognitive load using

NASA TLX and RSME scales—see Chapter 3, "Human Factors Fundamentals" for more information on these scales. The experiment illustrated some of the positive and negative aspects of the chosen methods. These scales for addressing spatial abilities and cognitive load are useful and can be reasonably well performed by participants. However, such self-reported measures provide only an initial indication. Objective measures (such as measuring stress with biosensors) would be a good option for coming to more reliable and valid conclusions.

NASA TLX and RSME did not reveal any significantly different results among the techniques. Furthermore, we found the maps highly challenging for interpretation. This was partly because we did not initially provide a legend to inform the participants how to encode the drawing but also because of the difficulty in comparing results. For example, we found noticeable scale and rotation errors. Yet creating a suitable metric to quantify these errors was difficult, as simple offsets would not do them justice. For these reasons, we removed map drawing and RSME scales from the second experiment, where we instead made use of performance time as the main measure.

The experiments revealed the usefulness of addressing user abilities and cognitive load, as technique preference in this case was associated with user capacities. We can also conclude that addressing cognitive issues is not easy, as different users have highly different abilities and interpreting results is not always straightforward. In general, the second experiment provided more valid and reliable results, as we mixed objective and subjective measures. We recommend this approach when analyzing cognition-related issues. Combining subjective and objective methods helps us obtain a more complete understanding.

Finally, addressing ergonomic issues is often disregarded in the design of 3DUIs, even though it can have a major effect on the ease of use and performance of a system. In various informal and formal studies of the Vesp'r and HYDROSYS setups—see Chapter 5, "3D User Interface Output Hardware"—we analyzed two interrelated issues related to ergonomics: grip and pose. The various handheld setups we developed supported multiple grips and poses to enable the user to hold the device comfortably and interact with controllers or the screen. As we discussed in Chapter 3, user comfort is highly affected by both the pose and the duration for which certain poses are held.

As an example of how we included this knowledge in evaluation, in one of our studies users had to compare different grips while performing tasks in different poses (see Figure 11.4). We compared single versus two-handed grips with lower and higher angle postures over a relatively long usage duration. The duration was approximately half an hour; anything shorter would simply not reveal all the key ergonomic issues. Users had to pick up objects from a table and place them on a wall location, forcing them to hold the setup quite high. After the experiment, we asked the users to respond to different questions on, among other things, weight, grip shape, grip material and posture, and user comfort. The experiment revealed the importance of performing longer-duration tests that solely focus on ergonomics, as user comfort and preference varied quite widely. For more details, refer to Veas and Kruijff (2008).

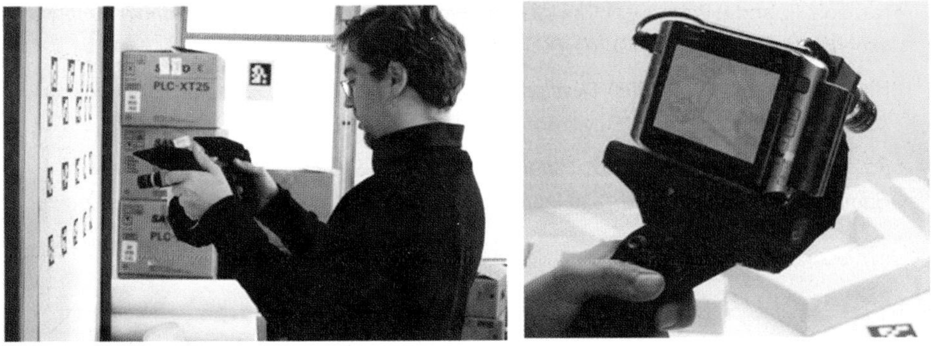

Figure 11.4 Different grips and pose to validate user comfort. (images courtesy of Ernst Kruijff and Eduardo Veas).

Key Concepts

- Perception: verify visual appearance of system control elements and general view management. Be sure to evaluate AR systems in the environment in which the system is deployed. Deal appropriately with outdoor conditions during evaluation as it may bias results.
- Cognition: assess subjective mental load of more complex systems, as it may greatly affect performance. Extend and correlate with objective measures (such as performance or biosensors) where possible to gain more valid and reliable insights.
- Ergonomics: study ergonomics of systems that are used for lengthy time periods. Evaluate long-term usage duration with tasks designed for different poses and grips to assess user comfort and fatigue.

11.9 Conclusion

In this chapter, we have presented an overview of some of the issues surrounding evaluation of 3D UIs. The most important takeaway message is that evaluation is almost always necessary. Despite all the design knowledge, guidelines, and techniques we presented in earlier chapters, initial 3D UI designs require assessment of usability and user experience so that the design can be iterated and improved. In addition, formal experimentation by researchers deepens our understanding of 3D interaction and provides new knowledge, new guidelines, and evidence that can be used to build models and theories.

Recommended Reading

Many entry-level HCI textbooks, such as the following, provide an excellent introduction to usability evaluation and UX engineering:

Hartson, R., and P. Pyla (2012). *The UX Book: Process and Guidelines for Ensuring a Quality User Experience*. Waltham, MA: Morgan Kaufmann Publishers.

Hix, D., and H. Hartson (1993). *Developing User Interfaces: Ensuring Usability Through Product & Process*. New York: John Wiley & Sons.

Rosson, M., and J. Carroll (2001). *Usability Engineering: Scenario-Based Development of Human Computer Interaction*. San Francisco, CA: Morgan Kaufmann Publishers.

Acknowledgment

Some of the content in this chapter comes from a 2002 article by Doug Bowman, Joseph Gabbard, and Deborah Hix that appeared in the journal *Presence*: "A Survey of Usability Evaluation in Virtual Environments: Classification and Comparison of Methods." (*Presence: Teleoperators and Virtual Environments* 11(4): 404–424).

We thank the coauthors and the MIT Press for their generous permission to reuse the material here.

PART VI

THE FUTURE OF 3D INTERFACES

Though 3D UIs have matured over the years, there are still many issues to study. Issues vary from underlying human factors problems to the seamless integration of different universal task techniques into a complex and fluid interface. In this final part of the book, we identify major open questions.

CHAPTER 12

THE FUTURE OF 3D USER INTERFACES

In this final chapter, we present a list of open questions that need to be addressed by researchers, students, or developers. Although we could have listed many more important questions, we've limited this list to those that we consider to be "grand challenge" questions for 3D UIs, in hopes that this will serve as a research agenda for the field.

Although the first edition of this book was published more than ten years ago, several of the questions we posed then are still open and important today. This speaks to the difficulty of some of the major challenges to be solved in this domain. At the same time, the field has changed significantly in the last decade, especially with respect to high-quality consumer-level technologies and real-world applications. With all this change, new challenges have emerged, and so we've significantly updated the list of open questions as well.

Of course, any such list of grand challenges will to some degree be subjective, speculative, and biased by the authors' presuppositions. Despite this, we hope that this list will help you think about the next steps for 3D UIs and inspire you to tackle some of these important issues yourself.

12.1 User Experience with 3D Displays

Although much of this book has been about 3D UIs from the perspective of input devices and interaction techniques, it's undeniable that output hardware (Chapter 5) plays a huge role in the overall user experience for VR, AR, and other 3D UIs. We begin our list of open research questions with display challenges.

How Will Future Visual Displays with Perfect Depth Cues Affect the 3D UI User Experience?

Today's 3D displays have a number of visual artifacts that make them less than realistic. One is the so-called accommodation-vergence mismatch (see Chapter 5, section 5.2.1). Because graphics are displayed on a screen that appears at a fixed depth, the user must accommodate at the depth of that screen to see the graphics in focus. But when stereo graphics are used, the left and right eye images are drawn so that the user's eyes will rotate to see the object at its virtual depth. When the virtual object depth and the screen depth are different, the user's eyes send conflicting signals to the brain about the distance to the object.

Another issue with projected displays (not HWDs) is the occlusion problem. This occurs when a physical object (like the user's hand) passes behind a virtual object. Because the virtual object is actually being displayed on a screen *behind* the physical object, the virtual object is occluded, even though according to the "real" positions of the objects, the physical object should be occluded. The occlusion problem also occurs in AR displays when the system doesn't have sufficient depth information about real-world objects.

Both of these problems could be solved by "true 3D" displays—devices that display the graphics for a virtual object at the *actual depth* of that object, so that light appears to come from the proper points in 3D space and all the depth cues agree. Prototypes of such displays (volumetric, holographic, multifocal, and light-field displays) have been developed (see Chapter 5, section 5.2.2), but they are not yet ready for real-world use, and technical challenges remain.

From a 3D UI point of view, we know very little about user experience with such displays or how to design 3D UIs appropriately for such displays. The assumption is that more perfect depth cues will help users improve their spatial understanding, increase the sense of presence, reduce discomfort, and improve perception of distance and size. But these displays may produce other unforeseen effects, because the visual experience still won't be indistinguishable from the real world in every way (e.g., FOV, spatial resolution, color reproduction, dynamic range, etc.). How will these limitations affect the 3D UI user experience?

How Can We Create Effective Full-Body Haptic Feedback Systems that Don't Encumber the User?

Haptic devices and systems have been developed and researched for decades, but progress is slow. The devices we described in Chapter 5 (section 5.4) are still a long way from producing realistic, general-purpose haptic sensations. Some devices produce very realistic force feedback, but only at a few points and only in a small workspace. Others provide tactile sensations but can't keep users from moving their hand through the virtual object. So one challenge is to develop a haptic system that integrates all the different elements of haptic sensation: resistance, elasticity, texture, and temperature, at any number of points on the user's hand and also on the entire body. To be general-purpose, such a system would have to provide haptic terrain for users to walk on, and so would be integrated with a locomotion system.

There are systems that have attempted to integrate more than one haptic sensation, like the one shown in Figure 5.30, which provides ground-referenced force feedback that keeps the whole hand from going through a virtual object as it moves in space, and grasp feedback that displays forces to the fingers as they grip a virtual object. But these require significant infrastructure and are not at all easy to put on, use, or take off. So a second challenge is the design of usable haptic systems that provide a pleasant user experience. A great deal of interdisciplinary research is needed here.

Can We Build Systems that Immerse All of the User's Senses?

Most VR and AR systems have been designed to provide a virtual stimulus to a single sensory modality (visual), with realistic audio as an add-on if it's considered at all. We have surround-screen displays that flood the user's visual sense with realistic 3D stereo graphics and high-quality HWDs that completely surround the user with realistic virtual worlds. Of course, other sensory modalities haven't been completely ignored. There are spatial audio systems that produce believable sounds from any 3D location, and even haptic devices that display surfaces or textures with passable realism. Less work has been done on smell, taste, or vestibular displays, although we've seen an increasing number of prototypes over the years.

The real challenge, however, is to integrate all of these single-sense display types into a seamless multi-sensory display system. Similar to the Holodeck on *Star Trek*, in such a system, objects and environments would look, sound, feel, smell, and taste completely realistic. One specific challenge is integrating haptics with immersive visuals. The most realistic haptic systems are ground-referenced, while the best immersive visual systems allow free movement by the user. Most haptic devices, because they must sit on a desk or because they require so many wires, mechanical arms, and other hardware, are too complex to integrate with a surround-screen display or HWD. Assuming that we can solve these technical integration issues, the actual interplay of various multisensory cues at a perceptual level is still a subject of research. Assuming that we won't have a perfect multisensory display anytime soon, how will users react to moderate levels of multisensory fidelity?

12.2 3D UI Design

Despite our extensive knowledge of interaction techniques, design strategies, empirical studies, and design guidelines for 3D UIs, there is still much research to be done in the area of 3D UI design.

What Are the Best Mappings Between Devices, Tasks, Interaction Techniques, and Applications?

The point of developing better 3D technology is to enable better 3D applications, but currently we still do not know everything about the usefulness of specific technologies for specific applications. Ideally, we would like to have a set of guidelines (or even an automated process) that, given a description of an application (domain, tasks, users, requirements, constraints), would suggest an appropriate set of devices (input and output) and interaction techniques. In order for this to become a reality, a huge amount of empirical research needs to be performed. We need to compare the usability of various 3D display devices and input devices for particular tasks and domains; we need to evaluate the compatibility of input devices and interaction techniques; and we need to understand the ways in which input and display devices affect each other. It's also unlikely that doing this at the level of whole devices and techniques will fully answer the question, because new devices are always being developed, and two devices of the same general type may have important differences. Thus, this research should really be done on fundamental components or characteristics of display devices, input devices, and interaction techniques. It should examine the effects of these components on both fundamental and compound tasks. The component evaluation approach introduced in Chapter 11, section 11.6.3, is well suited for this purpose.

How Can AR Interaction Techniques Allow Seamless Interaction in Both the Real and Virtual Worlds?

In completely virtual worlds, UI designers can opt for fully natural techniques, or magic techniques, or something in between. In AR, however, UI designers don't have as much freedom, because users will be interacting with real objects as well as virtual ones. In some cases, it may be appropriate and effective to use different methods of interaction in the real and virtual parts of the application, but it is likely that a seamless interface for both parts will be the best choice in most applications. The challenge, then, is to use the same interaction techniques to interact with both physical and virtual objects.

A common way to achieve this is to use a tangible interface, where virtual objects have an associated physical object. To manipulate the virtual object, therefore, the user simply picks up the associated real object. As we've seen, however, magic interaction techniques can be very powerful, so AR researchers should also consider whether it is possible to interact with real objects using magic interaction techniques. As a simple example, note that it certainly makes sense to select both virtual and real objects using a magic technique like ray-casting, as long as the system has knowledge about the objects in the real world.

A fully seamless real-virtual UI may not always be possible. So we also need to consider how users switch between acting in the real world and the virtual world. How much does it disturb the user's flow of action to switch between an AR display and viewing the real world, or between virtual- and real-world interaction techniques?

How Do We Create a Seamless and Consistent 3D UI From a Set of Individual 3D Interaction Techniques?

Part IV of this book presented a large number of individual interaction techniques for the universal 3D interaction tasks and guidelines to help developers choose interaction techniques for their applications. But choosing usable interaction techniques for an application is only half the battle. Just as in the case of individual displays, *integrating* the diverse techniques into a single, seamless 3D UI is another challenge that needs to be addressed.

Take a simple example: suppose you choose the pointing technique for navigation and the ray-casting technique for selection and manipulation and that you are using an input device with only a single button. When the user points in a particular direction and presses the button, what does she mean? She could intend to travel in that direction, or she could intend to select an object in that direction. The integrated 3D UI must disambiguate this action in some way. For example, we could decide that if the user clicks the button quickly, we'll treat it as a selection action, but if the user holds the button down, we'll treat it as a travel action.

One solution to this integration problem is to use integrated or cross-task techniques, which use the same metaphor or action for multiple tasks, but more work is still needed to determine the best ways to integrate techniques in general. A deeper understanding of what techniques work well together as a set is also needed.

How Can We Provide Natural Locomotion Techniques that Allow Travel In Any Virtual Environment?

Physically walking through a virtual world is a compelling experience. Walking provides a fully natural travel technique that users don't have to think about, it enhances the sense of presence, and it improves the sense of scale. But in most VEs, it's not possible to use real walking as the only travel technique, because the tracked area is smaller than the VE. Thus, as we saw in Chapter 8, section 8.4, it has been a long-time goal in the 3D UI community to provide techniques similar to natural walking that enable unrestricted locomotion in a VE of any size and shape.

This has given rise to many locomotion devices that keep users in one place as they walk, but so far none of these devices provide a fully natural walking experience and do not allow for the whole range of human walking movements. The other approach is to use natural walking as the input, but to modify the output in subtle ways to give the user the illusion of walking through an unrestricted space, as in redirected walking techniques. So far, though, redirected walking still requires a large physical tracking space, and there's no general-purpose method that will guarantee that users (a) will never reach the boundary of the physical space and (b) will never notice the redirection.

Both of these approaches still have promise, but there is still a long way to go. A general-purpose, fully natural locomotion device or redirected walking technique is in some sense the "holy grail" of VR travel research.

What Are the Best Approaches for Designing 3D UIs Based On Bare-Hand Input?

Gesture-based interaction has been part of 3D UIs since the beginning. VPL's data glove in the late 1980s was thought to be the most natural way to interact with VR systems. And it certainly makes sense that the most direct way to interact with virtual objects and tools is with our hands—the finely tuned devices that provide strength, precision, and expressiveness in our real-world actions. Hollywood gave us impressive visions of gestural interfaces in movies like *Minority Report* and *Iron Man 2*. But the reality of gesture-based 3D interaction never really lived up to the promise, and most real-world 3D UIs provide interaction through handheld 3D mice, game controllers, or touch screens.

Recently there's been a resurgence of interest in gesture-based interaction because of technological developments that allow much more precise tracking of users' bare hands through optical sensing. Perhaps, it is thought, the reason 3D gestures never took off is that users had to wear cumbersome gloves to use them. Today's markerless tracking systems are significantly different from yesterday's gesture-sensing technologies. There are still technological challenges, however, including the accurate prediction of hand poses in the presence of occlusion, and the precise detection of touch events, such as a pinch between thumb and forefinger.

At the same time, the barriers to gesture-based 3D interaction are not simply technological. Despite its seeming naturalness, it is nontrivial to design gesture-based interactions for many tasks. We don't use gestures for all real-world interactions, so it's not a question of simply replicating the real world. There are tasks in 3D UIs that don't have real-world analogues, including many system control tasks. And there are significant ergonomic barriers—humans cannot hold up their arms/hands in space for long without experiencing fatigue. Although there have been some interesting research prototypes, it remains to be seen whether gestural, bare-hand 3D UIs will become commonplace or whether they will remain a novelty.

How Can We Design "Smart 3D UIs" that Combine Explicit Interaction with Implicit Interaction Based on Machine Learning?

One way to address the problems of gesture recognition and gesture-based interactions that feel natural is through more intelligent interfaces—ones that can infer *user intent* rather than just applying predefined mappings to predefined actions. Machine learning (ML) technology seems to be maturing at the same time as 3D UI technology, so it's natural to think about combining them to enable more powerful 3D interaction.

For example, if the user says "put that there" accompanied by some directional gestures, a traditional interface would require precise specification of the object ("that") and the target location ("there") via accurate pointing gestures at the right time. An intelligent 3D UI, on the other hand, could make predictions about the identity of the object and the target location based on many factors, such as which objects are most likely to be moved, which locations are reasonable places to move the selected object, which objects the user has glanced at over the last few seconds, and how this particular user tends to point. Existing techniques for scene understanding and deep learning can be leveraged to enable such insights.

ML techniques can be used in many other ways for predictions and suggestions that could aid the user and make 3D interactions feel magical, as if the system knows what the user is thinking before the user himself does. And ML perhaps has even more potential to enhance 3D UIs than it does other types of interfaces, because of the complexity of 3D interaction.

But this is a very different style of interaction than today's 3D UIs. Such smart 3D UIs would be based on a combination of explicit input (the users directly indicating what they want to do) and implicit input (the system watching the user to build a model of the user's intent based on learning and probability). Inherently, this means that the user is not fully in control, and the system's actions may not be fully comprehensible. Thus, although we are excited about smart 3D interaction based on ML, it is also a grand challenge for 3D UI designers to ensure that smart 3D UIs provide a great user experience.

How Can We Design Interfaces that Smoothly Transition Between AR and VR?

Today, AR and VR are mostly thought of as two separate experiences enabled by different technological platforms. But of course, AR and VR share many elements (3D graphics, tracking, 3D input). And conceptually, AR and VR can be seen as points on a continuum that specifies the level of mixing between the real world and the virtual world (Milgram and Kishino 1994). So it's highly likely that technologies for AR and VR will eventually merge into one mixed reality (MR) platform, for example an HWD capable of transitioning between fully immersive VR and see-through AR.

This sort of combined platform could be very powerful, especially if it's in a form factor that can be worn all the time, like glasses, as this would allow VR and AR experiences to take place anytime, anywhere, without the need to go to a special room and put on special equipment.

But what does this mean for 3D UIs? If the display transition is seamless, we would also want the interface transition to be seamless. Users who are familiar with the interface for one mode should be able to reuse that knowledge in the other mode. And a dual-mode display is not as useful if users have to pick up different input devices to use in each mode.

At the same time, as we have argued earlier, VR interactions have the potential to be much more expressive and magical than AR interactions, because VR does not have any of the limitations of the real world. 3D UI designers have a balancing act to manage here: interfaces for AR and VR that are consistent and seamless, while still taking advantage of the unique opportunities afforded by each of them.

How Can We Design Expressive General-Purpose Hands-Free 3D UIs?

People are used to working with their hands, and as we saw in Chapter 3, "Human Factors Fundamentals," and Chapter 4, "General Principles of Human-Computer Interaction," there is a long history of research on manual interaction with both real and virtual objects. In some situations, however, a hands-free interface is called for. For instance, how will disabled persons without the use of arms or hands use an interactive VE? How will a vehicle operator interact with an AR system that displays travel information overlaid on the real world? Assistive technology has long been a source of inspiration for hands-free interfaces, where sensory substitution has played a major role. 3D UI designers need to consider novel ways to make use of speech, head movements, eye tracking, and even facial expression to provide input for 3D interfaces.

But of course, in the most extreme situations no body-based input whatsoever (or only a very limited amount) is possible. This is the domain of brain–computer interfaces (BCIs; see Chapter 6, section 6.4.2). Current BCIs are very limited, providing only a very coarse-grained signal that can be used to produce simple triggers or choices between a limited number of alternatives. A great deal of research is needed to be able to use BCIs (perhaps in combination with other inputs such as eye tracking) for general-purpose 3D interactions such as travel and object manipulation. It is likely that machine learning will play a major role in this effort, as computers learn to decipher user intent from complex, noisy brain signals.

Should There be a Standard 3D UI?

Computers would be unusable by the general population if the UI were not standardized to some degree. Desktop computers for many years have used the WIMP (Windows, Icons, Menus, Point and Click) interaction style, and because all applications make use of these same standard interface elements, users can start using applications right away, without lengthy training or reading a manual. The same is true of touch-based interaction on smartphones and tablets—there are de facto standards at play that help users know what to expect and how to interact.

Currently, there is nothing even close to a standard for 3D UIs. The interface is designed and implemented separately for each new application. Some techniques and metaphors have become fairly common, but even when the same technique is used in two different applications, the implementation may be entirely different.

In order to define a standard, we would need much more empirical evidence on the usability of various techniques and metaphors and on the combination of these techniques and metaphors with various devices. In order for a standard to be practical, we would need a set of standard, generic implementations that could be reused in any application.

But perhaps the bigger issue is whether we *want* a standard. One might argue that 3D UIs are much more complex than 2D UIs, that the input and output devices for 3D UIs are too diverse to match up to a single standard, and that 3D UI applications need specialized, domain-specific interface designs for optimum usability.

However, with the advent of consumer-oriented VR and AR systems, there are forces that may be driving us closer to a 3D UI standard. First, the number of "real people" (not just researchers and developers) who are using these systems has grown exponentially, and these users are using many different applications. Second, the systems are trying to provide between-application experiences—basically home worlds where users can launch apps and adjust settings—and these also require their own 3D UI. Making all these experiences comprehensible and usable for consumers will push designers to define at least some ad hoc standards for basic things like selection and menus. Initially, these are likely to be lowest common denominator solutions that will work in any situation and with any technology. It will be challenging to continue to innovate in the huge design space of 3D UIs while still providing a consistent, understandable UI.

12.3 3D UI Development and Evaluation

Beyond hardware technologies and design issues, we also see some grand challenges related to the development process for 3D UIs.

How Do We Enable Rapid Prototyping of 3D UIs?

The UX development lifecycle contains four basic activities: analysis, design, implementation, and evaluation (see Chapter 4, "General Principles of Human–Computer Interaction," section 4.4). Of these, implementation has received by far the least attention by 3D UI researchers. In particular, prototyping methods for the software side of 3D UIs are severely lacking (there are a number of prototyping approaches for 3D input devices; see Chapter 6, section 6.6). 3D interaction designers working on new software-based interaction techniques have limited options for representing the envisioned user experience in a prototype. They can use very low-fidelity paper prototypes (e.g., storyboards) or high-fidelity complete implementations (e.g., an application programmed in a game engine), but moderate-fidelity prototyping tools for 3D UIs are lacking. To make the iterative design and evaluation process work, rapid moderate-fidelity prototyping techniques, which give a good approximation of the interactive user experience without costing much in terms of money or time, are needed.

There are many potential directions here. We might need a platform-independent description language that allows developers to specify 3D UIs without specifying the details of their implementation. Not only would this be a useful abstraction, it would also provide a way for researchers to share the details of their UI designs even though they are using different platforms or engines. It would also be useful to have a plug-and-play 3D UI toolkit that has generic implementations of many common interaction techniques and allows developers to simply choose techniques (and devices) a la carte, resulting in a complete working 3D UI. Generic environments designed for prototyping techniques for particular tasks (e.g., manipulation, navigation) would keep designers from having to custom build a test environment for each prototype. Finally, programming-by-example approaches might be useful to develop working prototypes of gesture-based interfaces without implementing complex gesture recognizers; research in this direction has been promising.

How Can We Effectively Evaluate AR Applications?

Evaluation of VR interfaces can be difficult, as we saw in Chapter 11. But in some ways, the evaluation of AR applications is even more problematic. A typical AR setup might use an optical see-through HWD, so that the user sees graphics overlaid on a direct view of the real world. In this configuration, there is no way for the evaluator to see exactly what the user is seeing, because the evaluator's eyes cannot be at the same location as the user's eyes! If the HWD has a front-facing camera and an eye tracker, the system might be able to approximate the user's view, but the quality of the real-world visuals would be greatly reduced and the perspective will not be exactly the same. This limitation makes it extremely difficult to understand what the user is doing, what problems she is having, or what she is pointing at or talking about.

An alternative would be to give evaluators separate viewpoints into the same augmented scene, using additional HWDs or tracked cameras. This would provide a natural view of the user's actions but still not reproduce what the user is experiencing directly. A combination of the two approaches might be used, but this will require multiple evaluators and/or post-session review to make sense of the data.

Outdoor mobile AR results in additional evaluation challenges. For example, it's not possible to control the environment (weather, lighting, presence of other people in the scene). One approach to address this issue is to run studies in an AR simulation (i.e., simulating AR with VR). AR evaluation methods are an area ripe for further research.

How Can We Perform Longitudinal Evaluation Sessions?

While short-term evaluations have been performed frequently in many different areas, the long-term effects of using particular interfaces are often difficult to grasp. To truly capture these effects, we need longitudinal evaluations, in which the same study participants are observed at regular intervals or continuously over a period of days or weeks. For example, it would be very interesting to look at how task performance in AR improves in a work setting as the user learns the system or at how users' responses to real-world notifications changes over the course of a long VR session.

But longitudinal studies, which are tricky at best with traditional user interfaces, are especially problematic with 3D UIs. The effects of long-term use of VR and AR are still unknown, and evaluators run the risk of adverse effects in participants both during and after the study. Furthermore, many current 3D UIs, especially more experimental ones, do not have sufficient robustness to ensure that they will continue to work flawlessly over the course of a long study. Still, sooner or later we will need to perform such evaluations, especially since 3D UI are rapidly becoming a part of daily life.

12.4 3D UIs in the Real World

It's been sufficient for many years for 3D UI researchers to study single tasks, simple applications, and short-term use, because there were few 3D UIs used for significant activities in the real world. Now, that's all changing due to consumer technologies and high-profile gaming applications. Marathon VR gaming sessions are taking place, people are pulling out their smartphones at all times of the day and in all locations to check their favorite AR game, and even some office workers are hoping to get rid of their desktop monitors altogether and do all of their work in a 3D UI. This brave new world points to some serious research challenges.

What Strategies for Combatting Cybersickness are Most Effective?

Decades of research have gone into measuring and understanding simulator sickness and cybersickness and building up theories that explain why they happen. But ultimately, only a tiny fraction of the population was exposed on a regular basis to stimuli that could make them sick. Now all that has changed. Companies with VR products recognize that this is a serious problem—if someone gets seriously sick when using their system, they may not want to use it again or recommend it to their friends. So not only are companies providing the normal warning messages, they are providing comfort ratings and comfort modes that try to keep the experience from getting anywhere close to making the user sick.

So research on cybersickness now has much more urgency. But it also may need to shift in focus from understanding why people get sick to finding the best methods to prevent people from getting sick. We can't simply tell users not to use the systems or to limit their use. Users want to play intense games in VR, for example. There are some promising methods for preventing cybersickness, including manipulating the environment, changing the travel technique, using anti-sickness medication, providing minimal vestibular cues to minimize cue conflict, or even stimulating the vestibular system directly. The researchers who come up with the most effective methods will have a huge impact on comfort in AR and VR.

What Are the Effects of Long-Duration VR Sessions?

As we discussed above, with today's high-quality and low-cost content, displays, and tracking, many people want to spend significant time in VR. But there has been very little research into long-term use or its effects. This is one reason that we need longitudinal study methods for 3D UIs (see the previous section). Research is certainly needed into user comfort over long sessions, as we explained in the last question, but there are many other possible effects.

How do long exposures to VR affect real-world perception and action, and how long do these aftereffects last? What about task performance—does it improve over the course of a long session due to learning, or does it start to break down after a certain time period? Does the level of presence increase the longer the user is immersed in VR? What are the effects on presence of notifications coming from the outside world? Are there psychological effects of being immersed in realistic virtual worlds that portray violence or scary situations? And how does long-term repeated VR exposure affect social interactions and relationships in the real world? These important questions and many others are now available to be studied for the first time.

What Are the Implications of Always-On AR?

The research opportunities with long-term use of AR are similar, but also subtly different. Instead of "going into AR" for a lengthy but finite session, it appears that people may use AR displays in the future like they use smartphones today. That is, if AR displays are sufficiently comfortable, usable, and useful, users may wear their displays all day long. Certainly research on mobile and wearable interaction is relevant here, but AR adds some new dimensions and is potentially more pervasive than either mobile or wearable devices.

Here, we need to study issues like divided attention—do AR displays distract users from potentially dangerous or otherwise important things in the real world? On the one hand, AR displays should be better than smartphones in this regard, because the real world is always in view, but on the other hand, the augmentations add clutter to the real world and may still be perceived as a separate layer of information, forcing users to choose to attend either to the augmentations or to the real world. Always-on AR also has important social implications, as users pay attention to and interact with their AR device while simultaneously engaging socially with other people. Finally, how do we design microinteractions with AR that enhance people's real-world activities without distracting too much from them?

Can We Quantify the Real Benefits of 3D UIs?

VR, AR, and other 3D UI technologies are still used in relatively few industrial settings (although there have been some notable successes in fields like oil and gas exploration, automotive design, and training/simulation). Industries often perceive these technologies as flashy and good for demonstrations but without sufficient benefit to be used for day-to-day work. Therefore, the challenge for the 3D UI community is to quantify the benefits of these technologies—to demonstrate concrete results that will translate into dollars and cents. For different domains, these benefits might take on different forms. For manufacturers, the benefit might be increased productivity of the workers; for educators, the benefit might be increased student understanding; for scientists, the benefit might be greater insight into a dataset.

These benefits are difficult to prove, but even worse, it is difficult to even design a valid experiment to attempt to measure them. Suppose you run an experiment comparing task completion time on a typical HWD-based VR system and a typical desktop computer system and that you find significantly faster times with the HWD. What would your conclusion be? What caused the difference? Was it physical immersion, head tracking, presence, the use of a 3D input device, the use of a 3D interaction technique, or some combination of these things?

A first step toward quantifying the benefits of 3D UI technologies, then, is to use a methodology that separates all these variables so that we know from where the benefit comes. Again, we point readers to the component evaluation approach in Chapter 11, section 11.6.3. In the example above, a component evaluation might show us that the 3D input device was actually the crucial difference. Then perhaps we could achieve the same benefit by using the 3D input device with a standard desktop display monitor, avoiding the cost, complexity, and potential discomfort of the HWD-based system.

12.5 Applications of 3D UIs

In this final section, we examine research challenges particular to end-user applications of 3D UIs.

How Can We Design 3D UIs for Doing Daily Work?

It should be clear from the discussion so far in this chapter that we believe 3D UIs and related technologies are at an inflection point, where they are on the cusp of exploding into real-world use in a variety of domains. This is already true for gaming and some niche applications in particular industries, but the potential benefits of 3D UIs to the general public in many other settings have yet to be realized.

Researchers over the years have built prototypes of VR and AR applications for work and tasks in areas as diverse architectural design, construction visualization, virtual tourism, medical training, physical rehabilitation, classroom education, on-site data analysis, and intelligence analysis, just to name a few. But many of these applications were designed only as proofs-of-concept, because the time was not right to make them viable for actual work, whether in the office, in the classroom, or in the field. The challenge for 3D UI designers now is to do the difficult and detailed work of designing real-world user experiences, not just toy demonstrations.

Can We Use 3D UIs Themselves as Development and Modeling Tools for 3D UIs?

One interesting potential use of 3D UIs is as a tool to enable the development of more 3D UIs! For instance, what better place to model a scene for a VR application than in VR itself? Or what if teachers could set up an AR exhibit in their classrooms, using an AR system to define where virtual objects should be placed and even how they should behave?

Like many of the applications described in the previous question, there have been a large number of research prototypes, especially VR design tools meant for modeling VR scenes. There has been less research into developing interactive AR and VR applications from within AR or VR, but the concept has been explored to some extent. What hasn't yet been proven is whether these approaches can be used in production to build real 3D applications, and whether it's actually better, in terms of efficiency, understanding, or user satisfaction, to build 3D UIs with 3D UIs.

How Should We Design Social and Collaborative 3D UIs?

Many 3D UI technologies involve a single user by nature. But it doesn't take much imagination to see that these technologies can also be used to connect multiple people or even help them work together. Social and collaborative 3D UIs are definitely coming, and research is needed to make these experiences great.

Some applications are purely social; for example, VR can be used to bring people from all over the world together in the same virtual space. But this raises many questions about how people should be represented (i.e., avatar design), how we give the appropriate social cues beyond speech and coarse-grained gestures, and what the appropriate social protocols are when everyone is virtual (e.g., how do we maintain "personal space" when two virtual characters can inhabit the same virtual space, or how do we have a private conversation when another user can teleport right next to us instantaneously?).

For many 3D UI application areas, collaborative, multiuser work is the norm. Consider automobile manufacturers: when a new car model is being designed, the work is not all done by a single person. A large team of specialists must work together over a long period of time to create the final design. But a collaborative 3D UI for such a team is not trivial—it's not simply the sum of several single-user UIs. Collaboration brings with it a multitude of interface challenges, including the social challenges described above, but also issues such as awareness (Who is here? Where are they? What are they doing?) and floor control (Who is working on that object? How do I get the object?). Increasingly, we are seeing research on social and collaborative VR and AR, but there is still much to be done.

What Is the Killer App for 3D UIs?

Almost all widely successful technologies became successful because of some application of that technology that made everyone feel that they couldn't do without it. For personal computers, the original killer app was the spreadsheet (pioneered in the VisiCalc project), which made complex and tedious business and accounting tasks simple, automatic, and visual—no programming required. The Internet existed for many years before most people were aware of it, but then the World Wide Web and the web browser gave everyone access to massive amounts of information, making the Internet a daily part of life around the world.

So, what about 3D UIs? Will we someday find immersive VR in every home (through the wide adoption of VR-based game consoles)? Will all business professionals need a mobile AR system to keep up? If so, what application is really going to drive this adoption? Or will 3D UIs remain restricted to specialized tasks in a few domains? Of course, this latter outcome would not mean that 3D UIs were a failure—there are many technologies that are used only in specialized contexts (consider submarines, night-vision goggles, and MRI machines) that are considered successful.

The obvious answer to this question is that gaming is the killer app for 3D UIs, and certainly that is the current trend. But gaming technologies have a tendency to come and go, as the console manufacturers look for the latest innovation to help sell the next-generation machines. If AR becomes the preferred portal to all the information in the cloud, then information access may be the killer app for 3D UIs. But the future is uncertain. For 3D UI designers, we say along with Alan Kay, "the best way to predict the future is to invent it."

BIBLIOGRAPHY

Accot, J., and S. Zhai (1997). "Beyond Fitts' Law: Models for Trajectory-Based HCI Tasks." *Proceedings of the 1997 ACM Conference on Human Factors in Computing Systems (CHI '97)*, 295–302.

Accot, J., and S. Zhai (1999). "Performance Evaluation of Input Devices in Trajectory-Based Tasks: An Application of the Steering Law." In *Proceedings of the SIGCHI conference on Human Factors in Computing Systems*, 466–472.

Achibet, M., M. Marchal, F. Argelaguet, and A. Lécuyer (2014). "The Virtual Mitten: A Novel Interaction Paradigm for Visuo-Haptic Manipulation of Objects Using Grip Forces." In *Proceedings of the IEEE Symposium on 3D User Interfaces*, 29–30 March 2014, 59–66.

Adler, H. E. (ed.) (1971). "Introduction: Orientation In Animals and Man." *Annals of the New York Academy of Science*, 188, 3–4. doi: 10.1111/j.1749-6632.1971.tb13084.x.

Agrawala, M., A. C. Beers, I. McDowell, B. Fröhlich, M. Bolas, and P. Hanrahan (1997). "The Two-User Responsive Workbench: Support for Collaboration through Individual Views of a Shared Space." *Proceedings of SIGGRAPH '97*, 327–332.

Airey, J., J. Rohlf, and F. Brooks (1990). *Toward Image Realism with Interactive Update Rates in Complex Virtual Building Environments*. University of North Carolina at Chapel Hill, TR90-001.

Akenine-Möller, T., E. Haines, and N. Hoffman (2008). *Real-Time Rendering*, Third Edition. Natick, MA: AK Peters.

Alahi, A., R. Ortiz, and P. Vandergheynst (2012). "FREAK: Fast Retina Keypoint." In *Proceedings of the IEEE Conference on Computer Vision and Pattern Recognition (CVPR)*, 510–517.

Alakrishnan, Ravin B, and K. Hinckley (1999). "The Role of Kinesthetic Reference Frames in Two-Handed Input Performance." *Proceedings of the 12th Annual ACM Symposium on User Interface Software and Technology*. November 07–10, 1999, Asheville, NC, 171–178.

Alexander, C., S. Ishikawa, and M. Silverstein (1977). *A Pattern Language: Towns, Buildings, Construction.* Oxford University Press.

Allen, B. D., G. Bishop, and G. Welch (2001). "Tracking: Beyond 15 Minutes of Thought." *SIGGRAPH Course #11.*

Allen, B. D., and G. Welch (2005 November). "A General Method for Comparing the Expected Performance of Tracking and Motion Capture Systems. In *Proceedings of the ACM Symposium on Virtual Reality Software and Technology*, ACM, 201–210.

Allison, R., L. Harris, M. Jenkin, U. Jasiobedzka, and J. Zacher (2001). "Tolerance of Temporal Delay in Virtual Environments." *Proceedings of IEEE Virtual Reality 2001*, 247–256.

Altmann, J. (2001). "Acoustic Weapons—A Prospective Assessment." *Science & Global Security* 9, 165–234.

Anabuki, M., H. Kakuta, H. Yamamoto, and H. Tamura (2000). "Welbo: An Embodied Conversational Agent Living in Mixed Reality Spaces." *Proceedings of the 2000 ACM Conference on Human Factors in Computing Systems (CHI 2000), Extended Abstracts*, 10–11.

Anderson, C. (2014). *Makers: The New Industrial Revolution*. New York: Crown Business.

Anderson, J. (1983). *The Architecture of Cognition*. Cambridge, MA: Harvard University Press.

Andre, T. S., R. H. Hartson, S. M. Belz, and F. A. McCreary (2001). "The User Action Framework: A reliable foundation for usability engineering support tools." *International Journal of Human-Computer Studies* 54(1): 107–136.

Andujar, C. and F. Argelaguet (2007). "Virtual Pads: Decoupling Motor Space and VisualSpace for Flexible Manipulation of 2d Windows within VEs." *Proceedings of the 2007 IEEE Symposium on 3D User Interfaces (3DUI' 07)*, 99–106.

Angel, E., and D. Shreiner (2011). *Interactive Computer Graphics: A Top-Down Approach with Shader-Based OpenGL*, sixth Edition. New York: Addison-Wesley.

Angus, I., and H. Sowizral (1996). "VRMosaic: Web Access from Within a Virtual Environment. *IEEE Computer Graphics and Applications* 16(3): 6–10.

Argelaguet, F., and C. Andujar (2013). "A Survey of 3D Object Selection Techniques for Virtual Environments." *Computers & Graphics* 37: 121–136.

Arthur, K. (2000). "Effects of Field of View on Performance with Head-Mounted Displays." Doctoral Dissertation, University of North Carolina at Chapel Hill.

Atkinson, R. C., and R. M. Shiffrin (1971). "The Control of Short-Term Memory." *Scientific American* 224 (2): 82–90.

Ayers, M., and R. Zeleznik (1996). "The Lego Interface Toolkit." *Proceedings of the 1996 ACM Symposium on User Interface Software and Technology* (UIST '96), 97–98.

Azmandian, M., Hancock, M., Benko, H., Ofek, E., and Wilson, A. D. (2016, May). "Haptic Retargeting: Dynamic Repurposing of Passive Haptics for Enhanced Virtual Reality Experiences." In *Proceedings of the 2016 CHI Conference on Human Factors in Computing Systems,* 1968–1979.

Azuma, R. (1997). "A Survey of Augmented Reality." *Presence: Teleoperators and Virtual Environments* 6(4): 355–385.

Azuma, R., and G. Bishop (1994). "Improving Static and Dynamic Registration in an Optical See-Through HMD." *Proceedings of SIGGRAPH '94,* 197–204.

Azuma, R., Y. Baillot, R. Behringer, S. Feiner, S. Julier, and B. MacIntyre. "Recent Advances in Augmented Reality." *Computer Graphics and Applications, IEEE* 21(6): 34–47.

Bacim, F. (2015). "Increasing Selection Accuracy and Speed through Progressive Refinement." Doctoral dissertation, Virginia Polytechnic Institute and State University.

Bacim, F., D. Bowman, and M. Pinho (2009). "Wayfinding Techniques for Multiscale Virtual Environments." *Proceedings of the 2009 IEEE Symposium on 3D User Interfaces*, 67–74.

Bacim, F., M. Nabiyouni, and D. A. Bowman (2014). "Slice-n-Swipe: A Free-Hand Gesture User Interface for 3D Point Cloud Annotation." In *3D User Interfaces (3DUI)*, (2014 IEEE Symposium on), 185–186.

Baddeley, A. (1986). *Working Memory*. Oxford: Oxford University Press.

Baddeley, A. D. and G. Hitch (1974). "Working Memory." In G. H. Bower (ed.), *The Psychology of Learning and Motivation: Advances in Research and Theory*, Vol. 8, 47–89. New York: Academic Press.

Bajura, M., H. Fuchs, and R. Ohbuchi (1992). "Merging Virtual Objects with the Real World: Seeing Ultrasound Imagery within the Patient." *Proceedings of SIGGRAPH '92,* 203–210.

Bakker, N., P. Werkhoven, and P. Passenier (1998). "Aiding Orientation Performance in Virtual Environments with Proprioceptive Feedback." *Proceedings of the 1998 IEEE Virtual Reality Annual International Symposium (VRAIS '98),* 28–35.

Balakrishnan, R., and K. Hinckley (1999). "The Role of Kinesthetic Reference Frames in Two-Hand Input Performance." In *Proceedings of the 12th Annual ACM Symposium on User Interface Software and Technology* (UIST'99), Asheville, NC, 171–178.

Balakrishnan, R., and G. Kurtenbach (1999). "Exploring Bimanual Camera Control and Object Manipulation in 3D Graphics Interfaces." *Proceedings of the 1999 ACM Conference on Human Factors in Computing Systems (CHI '99),* 56–63.

Balakrishnan, R., G. Fitzmaurice, and G. Kurtenbach (2001). "User Interfaces for Volumetric Displays." *IEEE Computer* 34(3): 37–45.

Balakrishnan, R., G. Fitzmaurice, G. Kurtenbach, and K. Singh (1999). "Exploring Interactive Curve and Surface Manipulation Using a Bend and Twist Sensitive Input Strip." *Proceedings of the 1999 ACM Symposium on Interactive 3D Graphics (I3D '99),* 111–118.

Balakrishnan, R., T. Baudel, G. Fitzmaurice, and G. Kurtenbach (1997). "The Rockin' Mouse: Integral 3D Manipulation on a Plane." *Proceedings of the 1997 ACM Conference on Human Factors in Computing Systems (CHI '97)*, 311–318.

Barker, L. (2009). "Measuring and Modeling the Effects of Fatigue on Performance: Specific Application to the Nursing Profession." PhD thesis, Department of Industrial and Systems Engineering, Virginia Tech.

Barrilleaux, J. (2000). *3D User Interfaces with Java 3D.* Greenwich, CT: Manning Publications.

Basdogan, C., and M. A. Srinivasan (2002). "Haptic Rendering in Virtual Environments." K. Stanney (ed.), *Handbook of Virtual Environments: Design, Implementation, and Applications*, 117–134. Mahwah, NJ: Lawrence Erlbaum Associates.

Basu, A., C. Saupe, E. Refour, A. Raij, and K. Johnsen (2012). "Immersive 3DUI on One Dollar a Day." *2012 IEEE Symposium on 3D User Interfaces (3DUI)*, 97–100.

Bau, O., I. Poupyrev, M. Le Goc, L. Galliot, and M. Glisson (2012). "REVEL: Tactile Feedback Technology for Augmented Reality." *ACM SIGGRAPH 2012 Emerging Technologies (SIGGRAPH '12)*. Article 17, 1 pp.

Bau, O., I. Poupyrev, A. Israr, and C. Harrison (2010). "TeslaTouch: Electrovibration for Touch Surfaces." *Proceedings of the 23nd Annual ACM Symposium on User Interface Software and Technology (UIST '10)*, 283–292.

Bau, O., and W. E. Mackay. "OctoPocus: A Dynamic Guide for Learning Gesture-Based Command Sets." In *Proceedings of the 21st Annual ACM Symposium on User Interface Software and Technology*, 37–46.

Baudel, T., and M. Beaudouin-Lafon (1993). "CHARADE: Remote Control of Objects using Free-Hand Gestures." *Communications of the ACM* 36(7): 28–35.

Bay, H., A. Ess, T. Tuytelaars, and L. van Gool (2008). "Speeded-up Robust Features (SURF)." *Computer Vision and Image Understanding* 10(3):346–359.

Beck, S., A. Kunert, A. Kulik, and B. Froehlich (2013). "Immersive Group-to-Group Telepresence." *Visualization and Computer Graphics, IEEE Transactions* 19(4): 616–625.

Beckhaus, S., K. Blom, and M. Haringer (2007). "ChairIO–the Chair-Based Interface." *Concepts and Technologies for Pervasive Games: A Reader for Pervasive Gaming Research*, 1: 231–264.

Beckhaus, S., and E. Kruijff (2004). "Unconventional Human Computer Interfaces." ACM SIGGRAPH Course Notes #18.

Begault, D. R. (1992). "Perceptual Effects of Synthetic Reverberation on Three-Dimensional Audio Systems." *Journal of the Audio Engineering Society* 40(11): 895–904.

Begault, D. R. (1994). *3D Sound for Virtual Reality and Multimedia*. San Diego, CA: Academic Press.

Bell, B., T. Höllerer, and S. Feiner (2002). "An Annotated Situation-Awareness Aid for Augmented Reality." *Proceedings of the 2002 ACM Symposium on User Interface Software and Technology (UIST '02)*, 213–216.

Benko, H., and S. Feiner (2007). "Balloon Selection: A Multi-Finger Technique for Accurate Low-Fatigue 3D Selection." *Proceedings of the 2007 IEEE Symposium on 3D User Interfaces*, 79–86.

Benko, H., Ishak, E.W., and S. Feiner (2005). "Cross-Dimensional Gestural Interaction Techniques for Hybrid Immersive Environments." *Proceedings of IEEE Virtual Reality*, 209–116.

Bertelson, P. (1961). "Sequential Redundancy and Speed in a Serial Two-Choice Responding Task." *Quarterly Journal of Experimental Psychology* 13: 90–102.

Beyer, H., and K. Holtzblatt (1988). *Contextual Design: Defining Customer-Centered Systems*. Vol. 1. San Francisco, CA: Morgan Kaufmann.

Bhowmik, A. (2014). *Interactive Displays: Natural Human-Interface Technologies*. Hoboken, NJ: Wiley.

Bickmore, T. W., L. M. Pfeifer, and B. W. Jack (2009, April). "Taking the Time to Care: Empowering Low Health Literacy Hospital Patients with Virtual Nurse Agents." In *Proceedings of the SIGCHI Conference on Human Factors in Computing Systems*, 1265–1274.

Bier, E. (1986). "Skitters and Jacks: Interactive 3D Positioning Tools." *Proceedings of the 1986 Workshop on Interactive 3D Graphics*, 183–196.

Bier, E. (1990). "Snap-Dragging in Three Dimensions." *Proceedings of the 1990 ACM Symposium on Interactive 3D Graphics* (I3D '90), 193–204.

Bier, E., M. Stone, K. Pier, B. Buxton, and T. DeRose (1993). "Toolglass and Magic Lenses: The See-Through Interface." *Proceedings of SIGGRAPH '93* 73–80.

Bierbaum, C.R., L.A. Fulford, and D.B. Hamilton (1991). *Task Analysis/Workload (TAWL) User's Guide,* Fourth Edition, https://books.google.com/books/about/Task_Analysis_Workload_TAWL_User_s_Guide.html?id=IQRBQAAACAAJ.

Bigdelou, A., Schwarz, L., and Navab, N. (2012). "An Adaptive Solution for Intra-Operative Gesture Based Human-Machine Interaction." *Proceedings of the ACM International Conference on Intelligent User Interfaces*, 75–84.

Biggs, S. J., and M. A. Srinivasan (2002). "Haptic Interfaces:" In K. Stanney (ed.), *Handbook of Virtual Environments: Design, Implementation, and Applications*, 93–115. Mahwah, NJ: Lawrence Erlbaum Associates.

Billinghurst, M. (1998). "Put That Where? Voice and Gesture at the Graphic Interface." *Computer Graphics* 32(4): 60–63.

Billinghurst, M. (2014). "The Glass Class: Designing Wearable Interfaces." ACM SIGGRAPH 2014 Course.

Billinghurst, M., A. Clark, and G. Lee (2015). "A Survey of Augmented Reality." *Foundations and Trends in Human Computer Interaction* 8(2–3): 73–272.

Billinghurst, M., H. Kato, and I. Poupyrev (2001). "The MagicBook—Moving Seamlessly between Reality and Virtuality." *IEEE Computer Graphics and Applications* 21(3): 6–8.

Billinghurst, M., I. Poupyrev, H. Kato, and R. May (2000). "Mixing Realities in Shared Space: An Augmented Reality Interface for Collaborative Computing." *Proceedings of IEEE International Conference on Multimedia and Expo (ICME 2000)*, 1641–1644.

Billinghurst, M., and S. Weghorst (1995). "The Use of Sketch Maps to Measure Cognitive Maps of Virtual Environments." In *Proceedings of Virtual Reality Annual International Symposium* (VRAIS '95), 40–47.

Bimber, O. (2006). "Augmenting Holograms." *IEEE Computer Graphics and Applications*, 26(5): 12–17.

Bimber, O., and R. Raskar (2005). *Spatial Augmented Reality: Merging Real and Virtual Worlds*. Natick, MA: A. K. Peters Ltd.

Bimber, O., B. Fröhlich, D. Schmalstieg, and L. Encarnação (2001). "The Virtual Showcase." *IEEE Computer Graphics and Applications* 21(6): 48–55.

Biocca, F. (1992). "Virtual Reality Technology: A Tutorial." *Journal of Communication* 42(4): 23–72.

Bishop, G., and D. Weimer (1986). "Fast Phong Shading." *Proceedings of SIGGRAPH '86,* 103–105.

Blake, R., K. Sobel, and W. James (2004). "Neural Synergy Between Kinetic Vision and Touch." *Psychological Science* 15(6): 397–402.

Blascovich, J., J. Loomis, A. C. Beall, K. R. Swinth, C.L. Hoyt, and J. N. Bailenson (2002). "Immersive Virtual Environment Technology as a Methodological Tool for Social Psychology." *Psychological Inquiry 13*(2): 103–124.

Blasko, G., F. Coriand, and S. Feiner (2005). "Exploring Interaction with a Simulated Wrist-Worn Projection Display." *Proceedings of the Ninth IEEE International Symposium on Wearable Computers (ISWC'05)*, 2–9.

Blauert, J. (1997). *Spatial Hearing: The Psychoacoustics of Human Sound Localization*. Cambridge, MA: MIT Press.

Bliss, J., P. Tidwell, and M. Guest (1997). "The Effectiveness of Virtual Reality for Administering Spatial Navigation Training to Firefighters." *Presence: Teleoperators and Virtual Environments* 6 (1): 73–86.

Blom, K., G. Lindhal, and C. Cruz-Neira (2002). "Multiple Active Viewers in Projection-Based Immersive Environments." *Proceedings of the Seventh Annual Immersive Projection Technology Workshop*.

Blundell, B. G. (2012). "Volumetric 3D Displays." J. Chen, W. Cranton, and M. Fihn (eds.), *Handbook of Visual Display Technology*, 1917–1931. New York: Springer.

Blundell, B. G., and A. J. Schwarz (2000). *Volumetric Three-Dimensional Display Systems*. New York: John Wiley and Sons.

Bobeth, J., S. Schmehl, E. Kruijff, S. Deutsch, and M. Tscheligi (2010). "Evaluating Performance and Acceptance of Older Adults Using Freehand Gestures for TV Menu Control." *Proceedings of the 10th European conference on Interactive TV and Video*, 35–44.

Bobeth, J., S. Schmehl, E. Kruijff, S. Deutsch, and M. Tscheligi (2012). "Evaluating Performance and Acceptance of Older Adults Using Freehand Gestures for TV Menu Control." In *Proceedings of the 10th ACM European Interactive Conference*, Berlin, Germany.

Bødker, S. (1991). *Through the Interface: A Human Activity Approach to User Interface Design*. Hillsdale, NJ: Lawrence Erlbaum Associates.

Bolas, M. T. (1994). "Human Factors in the Design of an Immersive Display." *IEEE Computer Graphics and Applications* 14(1): 55–59.

Bolt, R. (1980). "'Put-That-There': Voice and Gesture at the Graphics Interface." *Proceedings of SIGGRAPH '80*, 262–270.

Bolter, J., L. Hodges, T. Meyer, and A. Nichols (1995). "Integrating Perceptual and Symbolic Information in VR." *IEEE Computer Graphics and Applications* 15(4): 8–11.

Bordegoni, M., and M. Hemmje (1993). "A Dynamic Gesture Language and Graphical Feedback for Interaction in a 3D User Interface." *Computer Graphics Forum* 12(3): 1–11.

Bornik, A., R. Beichel, E. Kruijff, B. Reitinger, and D. Schmalstieg (2006). "A Hybrid User Interface for Manipulation of Volumetric Medical Data." *Proceedings of the Symposium on 3D user interfaces, IEEE conference on Virtual Reality* 29–36.

Borst, C., and A. Indugula (2005). "Realistic Virtual Grasping." *Proceedings of the 2005 IEEE Virtual Reality Conference (VR '05)* 91–98.

Bott, J., J. Crowley, and J. LaViola, (2009). "Exploring 3D Gestural Interfaces for Music Creation in Video Games." *Proceedings of the ACM International Conference on Foundations of Digital Games*, 18–25.

Bowman, D. (2002). "Principles for the Design of Performance-Oriented Interaction Techniques." In K. Stanney (ed.), *Handbook of Virtual Environments: Design, Implementation, and Applications*. Mahwah, NJ: Lawrence Erlbaum Associates, 277–300.

Bowman, D. A., Coquillart, S., Froehlich, B., Hirose, M., Kitamura, Y., Kiyokawa, K., and Stuerzlinger, W. (2008). "3D User Interfaces: New Directions and Perspectives." *IEEE Computer Graphics and Applications* 28(6): 20–36.

Bowman, D. A., McMahan, R. P., and Ragan, E. D. (2012). "Questioning Naturalism in 3D User Interfaces." *Communications of the ACM 55*(9): 78–88.

Bowman, D., and R. McMahan (2007). "Virtual Reality: How Much Immersion is Enough?." *IEEE Computer* 40(7): 36–43.

Bowman, D., A. Datey, Y. S. Ryu, U. Farooq, and O. Vasnaik (2002). "Empirical Comparison of Human Behavior and Performance with Different Display Devices for Virtual Environments." *Proceedings of the Human Factors and Ergonomics Society Annual Meeting 2002* 2134–2138.

Bowman, D., and C. Wingrave (2001). "Design and Evaluation of Menu Systems for Immersive Virtual Environments." *Proceedings of IEEE Virtual Reality 2001* 149–156.

Bowman, D., and L. Hodges (1997). "An Evaluation of Techniques for Grabbing and Manipulating Remote Objects in Immersive Virtual Environments." *Proceedings of the 1997 ACM Symposium on Interactive 3D Graphics (I3D '97)*, 35–38.

Bowman, D., and L. Hodges (1999). "Formalizing the Design, Evaluation, and Application of Interaction Techniques for Immersive Virtual Environments." *The Journal of Visual Languages and Computing* 10(1): 37–53.

Bowman, D., C. Rhoton, and M. Pinho (2002). "Text Input Techniques for Immersive Virtual Environments: An Empirical Comparison.:" *Proceedings of the Human Factors and Ergonomics Society Annual Meeting, 2002,* 2154–2158.

Bowman, D., C. Wingrave, J. Campbell, and V. Ly (2001). "Using Pinch™ Gloves for Both Natural and Abstract Interaction Techniques in Virtual Environments." *Proceedings of HCI International,* New Orleans, LA.

Bowman, D., C. Wingrave, J. Campbell, V. Ly, and C. Rhoton (2002). "Novel Uses of Pinch™ Gloves for Virtual Environment Interaction Techniques." *Virtual Reality* 6(3): 122–129.

Bowman, D., D. Johnson, and L. Hodges (1999). "Testbed Evaluation of VE Interaction Techniques." *Proceedings of the 1999 ACM Symposium on Virtual Reality Software and Technology (VRST '99),* 26–33.

Bowman, D., D. Johnson, and L. Hodges (2001). "Testbed Evaluation of VE Interaction Techniques." *Presence: Teleoperators and Virtual Environments* 10(1): 75–95.

Bowman, D., D. Koller, and L. Hodges (1997). "Travel in Immersive Virtual Environments: An Evaluation of Viewpoint Motion Control Techniques." *Proceedings of the 1997 IEEE Virtual Reality Annual International Symposium (VRAIS '97),* 45–52.

Bowman, D., D. Koller, and L. Hodges (1998). "A Methodology for the Evaluation of Travel Techniques for Immersive Virtual Environments." *Virtual Reality: Research, Development, and Applications* 3: 120–131.

Bowman, D., E. Davis, A. Badre, and L. Hodges (1999). "Maintaining Spatial Orientation during Travel in an Immersive Virtual Environment." *Presence: Teleoperators and Virtual Environments* 8(6): 618–631.

Bowman, D., J. Wineman, L. Hodges, and D. Allison (1998). "Designing Animal Habitats within an Immersive VE." *IEEE Computer Graphics and Applications* 18(5): 9–13.

Bresciani, J.-P., M. Ernst, K. Drewing, G. Bouyer, V. Maury, and A. Kheddar (2004). "Feeling What You Hear: Auditory Signals can Modulate Tactile Tap Perception." *Experimental Brain Research* 162: 172–180.

Bresenham, J. (1965). "Algorithm for Computer Control of a Digital Plotter." *IBM Systems Journal* 4(1): 25–30.

Brewster, S. (1998). "Using Nonspeech Sounds to Provide Navigation Cues." *ACM Transactions on Computer-Human Interaction* 5(3): 224–259.

Brogan, D., R. Metoyer, and J. Hodgins (1998). "Dynamically Simulated Characters in Virtual Environments." *IEEE Computer Graphics and Applications* 15(5): 58–69.

Brewster, S.A., J. Lumsden, M. Bell, M., Hall, and S. Tasker (2003). "Multimodal 'Eyes-Free' interaction Techniques for Wearable Devices." *Proceedings of the ACM Conference on Human Factors in Computing Systems*, 473–480.

Brooks, F. (1986). "A Dynamic Graphics System for Simulating Virtual Buildings." *Proceedings of the 1986 Workshop on Interactive 3D Graphics,* ACM Press, 9–21.

Brooks, F. (1999). "What's Real about Virtual Reality?" *IEEE Computer Graphics and Applications* 19(6): 16–27.

Brooks, F., M. Ouh-Young, J. Batter, and P. Kilpatrick (1990). "Project GROPE: Haptic Displays for Scientific Visualization." *Proceedings of SIGGRAPH '90,* 177–185.

Brown, L., H. Hua, and C. Gao (2003). "A Widget Framework for Augmented Interaction in SCAPE." *Proceedings of the 16th Annual ACM Symposium on User Interface Software and Technology (UIST '03),* 1–10.

Bruce, V., and P. Green (1990). *Visual Perception: Physiology, Psychology, and Ecology,* Hillsdale, NJ: Lawrence Erlbaum Associates.

Bruder, G., P. Lubas, and F. Steinicke (2015). "Cognitive Resource Demands of Redirected Walking." *IEEE Transactions on Visualization and Computer Graphics* 21(4): 539–544.

Bryson, S. (1996). "Virtual Reality in Scientific Visualization." *Communications of the ACM* 39(5): 62–71.

Bukowski, R., and C. Séquin (1995). "Object Associations: A Simple and Practical Approach to Virtual 3D Manipulation." *Proceedings of the 1995 Symposium on Interactive 3D Graphics (I3D '95),* 102–109.

Bullinger, H., P. Kern, and M. Braun (1997). "Controls." G. Salvendy (ed.), *Handbook of Human Factors and Ergonomics*, 697–728. New York: John Wiley and Sons.

Burdea, G. (1996). *Force and Touch Feedback for Virtual Reality*. Wiley Interscience.

Burdea, G., and P. Coiffet (2003). *Virtual Reality Technology,* Second Edition. New York: John Wiley and Sons.

Burdea, G., G. Patounakis, and V. Popescu (1998). "Virtual Reality Training for the Diagnosis of Prostate Cancer." *Proceedings of the 1998 IEEE Virtual Reality Annual International Symposium (VRAIS '98),* 190–197.

Burdea, G., J. Zhufang, E. Roskos, D. Silver, and N. Langrana (1992). "A Portable Dextrous Master with Force Feedback." *Presence: Teleoperators and Virtual Environments* 1(1): 18–27.

Burr, D., and D. Alais (2006). "Combining Visual and Auditory Information." *Progress in Brain Research* 155: 243–258.

Butterworth, J., A. Davidson, S. Hench, and M. Olano (1992). "3DM: A Three-Dimensional Modeler Using a Head-Mounted Display." *Proceedings of the 1992 ACM Symposium on Interactive 3D Graphics (I3D '92),* 135–138.

Buxton, W. (1983). "Lexical and Pragmatic Considerations of Input Structures." *Computer Graphics* 17(1): 31–37.

Buxton, W. (1986). "There's More to Interaction Than Meets the Eye: Some Issues in Manual Input." In D. Norman, and S. Draper (eds.), *User Centered System Design: New Perspectives on Human-Computer Interaction,* 319–337. Hillsdale, NJ: Lawrence Erlbaum Associates.

Buxton, W. (1992). "Telepresence: Integrating Shared Task and Person Spaces." *Proceedings of the 1992 Graphics Interface Conference*, 123–129.

Buxton, W., and B. Myers (1986). "A Study in Two-Handed Input." *Proceedings of the 1986 ACM Conference on Human Factors in Computing Systems* (CHI '86), 321–326.

Cairns, P., and Cox, A. L. (eds.) (2008). *Research Methods for Human-Computer Interaction*, Vol. 12. New York: Cambridge University Press.

Campbell, D. (1996). *Design in Virtual Environments Using Architectural Metaphor: A HIT Lab Gallery.* Master's Thesis, HIT Lab, University of Washington.

Cao, W., H. Gaertner, S. Conrad, E. Kruijff, D Langenberg, and R. Schultz (2004). "Digital Product Development in a Distributed Virtual Environment." *Proceedings of the IEEE and ACM International Conference on Virtual Reality and its Application in Industry*, 322–326.

Cao, W., H. Gaertner, H., Guddat, A. Straube, S. Conrad, E. Kruijff, and D. Langenberg (2006) "Design Review in a Distributed Collaborative Virtual Environment." *International Journal of Image and Graphics* (IJIG) 6(1): 45–64.

Card, S., J. Mackinlay, and G. Robertson (1990). "The Design Space of Input Devices." *Proceedings of the 1990 ACM Conference on Human Factors in Computing Systems (CHI '90),* 117–124.

Card, S., J. Mackinlay, and G. Robertson (1991). "A Morphological Analysis of the Design Space of Input Devices." *ACM Transactions on Information Systems* 9(2):99–122.

Card, S., T. Moran, and A. Newell (1980). "The Keystroke-Level Model for User Performance Time with Interactive Systems." *Communications of the ACM* 23(7): 398–410.

Card, S., T. Moran, and A. Newell (1983). *The Psychology of Human-Computer Interaction.* Hillsdale, NJ: Lawrence Erlbaum Associates.

Card, S., T. Moran, and A. Newell (1986). "The Model Human Processor." In K. Boff, L. Kaufman, and J. Thomas (eds.), *Handbook of Perception and Human Performance,* Vol. 2, 1–35 Oxford, England: John Wiley & Sons.

Carlile, S. (1996). *Virtual Auditory Space: Generation and Application.* Berlin, Heidelberg: Springer.

Carlin, A., H. Hoffman, and S. Weghorst (1997). "Virtual Reality and Tactile Augmentation in the Treatment of Spider Phobia: A Case Report." *Behavior Research and Therapy* 35(2): 153–159.

Carroll, J.M. (2012). "Human Computer Interaction (HCI)." In Soegaard, Mads and Dam, Rikke Friis (eds.), *Encyclopedia of Human-Computer Interaction.* Aarhus, Denmark: The Interaction Design Foundation. (http://www.interaction-design.org/encyclopedia/human_computer_interaction_hci.html)

Carstensen, P. H., and K. Schmidt (1999). "Computer Supported Cooperative Work: New Challenges to Systems Design." In K. Itoh (ed.), *Handbook of Human Factors.*

Cashion, J., C. Wingrave, and J. LaViola (2012). "Dense and Dynamic 3D Selection for Game-Based Virtual environments." *IEEE Transactions on Visualization and Computer Graphics* 18(4): 634–642.

Cashion, J., C. Wingrave, and J. LaViola (2013). "Optimal 3D Selection Technique Assignment using Real-Time Contextual Analysis." *Proceedings of the 2013 IEEE Symposium on 3D User Interfaces (3DUI '13),* 107–110.

Celentano, A., and F. Pittarello (2004). "Observing and Adapting User Behavior in Navigational 3D Interfaces." *Proceedings of the International Working Conference on Advanced User Interfaces,* 275–282.

Chaffin, D. B., and G. B. Andersson (1991). *Occupational Biomechanics.* New York: Wiley.

Chance, S., F. Gaunet, A. Beall, and J. Loomis (1998). "Locomotion Mode Affects the Updating of Objects Encountered during Travel: The Contribution of Vestibular and Proprioceptive Inputs to Path Integration." *Presence: Teleoperators and Virtual Environments* 7(2): 168–178.

Chee, Y. S., and C.M. Hooi (2002). "C-VISions: Socialized Learning Through Collaborative, Virtual, Interactive Simulations." *Proceedings of the Conference on Computer Support for Collaborative Learning: Foundations for a CSCL Community,* 687–696.

Cheema, S., M. Hoffman, and J. LaViola (2013). "3D gesture classification with linear acceleration and angular velocity sensing devices for video games." *Entertainment Computing* 4(1): 11–24.

Chen, J., and D. A. Bowman (2009). "Domain-Specific Design of 3D Interaction Techniques: An Approach for Designing Useful Virtual Environment Applications." *Presence: Teleoperators and Virtual Environments* 18(5): 370–386.

Chen, K., K. Lyons, S. White, and S. Patel (2013). "uTrack: 3D Input using Two Magnetic Sensors." *Proceedings of the 26th Annual ACM Symposium on User Interface Software and Technology (UIST '13),* 237–244.

Chen, L., H. Wei and J. Ferryman (2013). "A Survey of Human Motion Analysis using Depth Imagery." *Pattern Recognition Letters* 34(15):1995–2006.

Chen, M., S. Mountford, and A. Sellen (1988). "A Study in Interactive 3-D Rotation using 2-D Control Devices." *Computer Graphics* 22(4): 121–129.

Chen, W., N. Ladeveze, C. Clavel, D. Mestre, and P. Bourdot (2015). "User Cohabitation in Multi-Stereoscopic Immersive Virtual Environment for Individual Navigation Tasks." In *2015 IEEE Virtual Reality (VR),* IEEE, 47–54.

Chinthammit, W., E. Seibel, and T. A. Furness (2002). "Unique Shared-Aperture Display with Head or Target Tracking." *Proceedings of IEEE Virtual Reality 2002,* 235–242.

Chiras, D. (2013). *Human Body Systems: Structure, Function, and Environment.* Burlington, MA: Jones & Bartlett Learning.

Cho, I., and Z. Wartell (2015). "Evaluation of a Bimanual Simultaneous 7DOF Interaction Technique in Virtual Environments." *Proceedings of the 2015 IEEE Symposium on 3D User Interfaces (3DUI '15),* 133–136.

Choi, J., and R. Gutierrez-Osuna. (2010). "Estimating Mental Stress using a Wearable Cardio-Respiratory Sensor." *Proceedings of the IEEE Sensors Conference*, Waikoloa, HI, 150–154.

Cholewiak, R., and A. Collins (1991). "Sensory and Physiological Bases of Touch." In M. Heller and W. Schiff (eds.), *The Psychology of Touch*, 23–60. Lawrence Erlbaum.

Chuah, J., and B. Lok (2012). "Experiences in Using a Smartphone as a Virtual Reality Interaction Device." *Workshop on Off-The-Shelf Virtual Reality, IEEE Conference on Virtual Reality* (VR 2012), Orlando, FL.

Chun, W. H., and T. Höllerer (2013). "Real-Time Hand Interaction for Augmented Reality on Mobile Phones." In *Proceedings of the 2013 International Conference on Intelligent User Interfaces*, ACM 307–314.

Clark, F. J., and K. W. Horch (1986). "Kinesthesia." In K. Boff, L. Kaufman, and J. Thomas (eds.), *Handbook of Perception and Human Performance*, Vol. 1: 13-1–13-62. New York: John Wiley & Sons.

Cohen, M., and E. Wenzel (1995). "The Design of Multidimensional Sound Interfaces." In W. Barfield and T. Furness (eds.), *Virtual Environments and Advanced Interface Design*, 291–346. Oxford University Press.

Cohen, M. D., and P. Bacdayan (1994). "Organizational Routines Are Stored as Procedural Memory: Evidence from a Laboratory Study." *Organization Science* 5(4): 554–568.

Colley, S. (2001). *Vector Calculus*, Second Edition. Upper Saddle River, NJ: Prentice-Hall.

Conkar, T., J. Noyes, and C. Kimble (1999). "CLIMATE: A Framework for Developing Holistic Requirements Analysis in Virtual Environments." *Interacting with Computers* 11(4): 387–403.

Conner, B. D., Snibbe, S. S., Herndon, K. P., Robbins, D. C., Zeleznik, R. C., and Van Dam, A. (1992, June). "Three-Dimensional Widgets." *Proceedings of the 1992 Symposium on Interactive 3D Graphics* (ACM): 183–188.

Constantine, L., and L. A. D. Lockwood (1999). *Software for Use: A practical Guide to the Models and Methods of Usage-Centered Design*. New York: Addison-Wesley.

Cooper, A. 2004. *The Inmates Are Running the Asylum: Why High Tech Products Drive Us Crazy and how to Restore the Sanity,* Second Edition. Indianapolis, IN: Sams Publishing.

Cooper, W. (ed.) (1983). *Cognitive Aspects of Skilled Typewriting.* New York: Springer Verlag.

Coquillart, S., and G. Wesche (1999). "The Virtual Palette and the Virtual Remote Control Panel: A Device and Interaction Paradigm for the Responsive Workbench.' *Proceedings of IEEE Virtual Reality '99,* 213–217.

Cree, G. S., and K. McRae (2003). "Analyzing the Factors Underlying the Structure and Computation of the Meaning of Chipmunk, Cherry, Chisel, Cheese and Cello (and Many Other Such Concrete Nouns." *Journal of Experimental Psychology: General* 132(2): 163–201.

Creem-Regehr, S, Willemsen, P., Gooch, A., and W. Thompson (2005). "The Influence of Restricted Viewing Conditions on Egocentric Distance Perception: Implications for Real and Virtual Environments." *Perception* 34, 2, 191–204.

Cress, J., L. Hettinger, J. Cunningham, G. Riccio, G. McMillan, and M. Haas (1997). "An Introduction of a Direct Vestibular Display into a Virtual Environment." *Virtual Reality Annual International Symposium,* IEEE Press, 80–86.

Crichton, M. (1994). *Disclosure.* New York: Knopf.

Crowford, B. (1964). "Joystick vs. Multiple Levers for Remote Manipulator Control." *Human Factors* 6(1): 39–48.

Cruz-Neira, C., and R. Lutz (1999). "Using Immersive Virtual Environments for Certification." *IEEE Software* 16(4): 26 30.

Cruz-Neira, C., D. Sandin, and T. Defanti (1993). "Surround Screen Projection-Based Virtual Reality." *Proceedings of SIGGRAPH '93*, 135–142.

Cuffaro, D. *The Industrial Design Reference & Specification Book: Everything Industrial Designers Need to Know Every Day*. Rockford Publishers, 2013.

Cutler, L., B. Fröhlich, and P. Hanrahan (1997). "Two-Handed Direct Manipulation on the Responsive Workbench." *Proceedings of the 1997 ACM Symposium on Interactive 3D Graphics (I3D '97),* 107–114.

Dachselt, R., and A. Hübner (2007) "Three-Dimensional Menus: A Survey and Taxonomy." *Computers & Graphics* 31(1): 53–65

Daiber, F., E. Falk, and A. Krüger (2012). "Balloon Selection Revisited: Multi-Touch Selection Techniques for Stereoscopic Data. *Proceedings of the International Working Conference on Advanced Visual Interfaces* (ACM): 441–444.

Daneman M, and P. Carpenter. (1980). "Individual Differences in Working Memory and Reading." *Journal of Verbal Learning and Verbal Behavior*. 19:450–466.

Dang, N., M. Tavanti, I. Rankin, and M. Cooper (2009). "A Comparison of Different Input Devices for a 3D Environment." *International Journal of Industrial Ergonomics* 39(3): 554–563.

Darken, R., and B. Peterson (2002). "Spatial Orientation, Wayfinding, and Representation." In K. Stanney (ed.), *Handbook of Virtual Environments: Design, Implementation, and Applications,* 493–518. Mahwah, NJ: Lawrence Erlbaum Associates.

Darken, R., and H. Cevik (1999). "Map Usage in Virtual Environments: Orientation Issues." *Proceedings of IEEE Virtual Reality '99,* 133–140.

Darken, R., and J. Sibert (1996). "Wayfinding Strategies and Behaviors in Large Virtual Worlds." *Proceedings of the 1996 ACM Conference on Human Factors in Computing Systems (CHI'96),* 142–149.

Darken, R., and S. Goerger (1999). "The Transfer of Strategies from Virtual to Real Environments: An Explanation for Performance Differences." *Proceedings of Virtual Worlds and Simulation '99,* 159–164.

Darken, R., and W. Banker (1998). "Navigating in Natural Environments: A Virtual Environment Training Transfer Study." *Proceedings of the 1998 IEEE Virtual Reality Annual International Symposium (VRAIS '98),* 12–19.

Darken, R., W. Cockayne, and D. Carmein (1997). "The Omni-Directional Treadmill: A Locomotion Device for Virtual Worlds." *Proceedings of the 1997 ACM Symposium on User Interface Software and Technology (UIST '97),* 213–221.

Darrah, J., Watkins, B., Chen L., and C. Bonin (2003). *Effects of Conductive Education Intervention for Children with a Diagnosis of Cerebral Palsy:* An AACPDM Evidence Report. American Academy for Cerebral Palsy and Developmental Medicine (AACPDM).

Davies, C., and J. Harrison (1996). "Osmose: Towards Broadening the Aesthetics of Virtual Reality." *Computer Graphics* 30(4): 25–28.

Davis, E. (1996). "Visual Requirements in HMDs: What Can We See and What Do We Need to See?" In J. Melzer and K. Moffitt (eds.), *Head-Mounted Displays: Designing for the User,* 207–249. McGraw-Hill.

Davis, E., and L. Hodges (1995). "Human Stereopsis, Fusion, and Virtual Environments." In W. Barfield and T. Furness (eds.), *Virtual Environments and Advanced Interface Design,* 145–174. Oxford: Oxford University Press.

Davis, E., K. Scott, J. Pair, L. Hodges, and J. Oliviero (1999). "Can Audio Enhance Visual Perception and Performance in a Virtual Environment?" *Proceedings of the Human Factors and Ergonomics 43rd Annual Meeting,* 1197–1201.

Debarba, H., L. Nedel, and A. Maciel (2012). "LOP-Cursor: Fast and Precise Interaction with Tiled Displays using One Hand and Levels of Precision." *Proceedings of the 2012 IEEE Symposium on 3D User Interfaces (3DUI '12),* 125–132.

Defanti, T., and D. Sandin (1977). "Final Report to the National Endowment of the Arts." University of Illinois at Chicago.

Deisinger, J., R. Breining, A. Robler, D. Ruckert, and J. Hofle (2000). "Immersive Ergonomic Analyses of Console Elements in a Tractor Cabin." *Proceedings of the Immersive Projection Technology Workshop*, Ames, Iowa.

Demiralp, C., C. Jackson, D. Karelitz, S. Zhang, and D. Laidlaw (2006). "CAVE and Fishtank Virtual-Reality Displays: A Qualitative and Quantitative Comparison." *IEEE Transactions on Visualization and Computer Graphics* 12(3): 232–330.

Diaper, D., and P. Johnson (1989). "Task Analysis for Knowledge Descriptions: Theory and Application in Training." *Cognitive Ergonomics and Human Computer Interaction* (1989): 191–224.

Dickinson, J. (1976). *Proprioceptive Control of Human Movement*. London, England: Lepus Books, http://eric.ed.gov/?id=ED130997.

DiMaggio, P. (1997). Culture and Cognition. *Annual Review of Sociology*, 23, 263–287.

Dinh, H. Q., Walker, N., Hodges, L. F., Song, C., and Kobayashi, A. (1999). "Evaluating the Importance of Multi-Sensory Input on Memory and the Sense of Presence in Virtual Environments." *Virtual Reality, 1999. IEEE Proceedings*, 222–228.

Dipietro, L., A. Sabatini, and P. Dario (2008). "A Survey of Glove-Based Systems and Their Applications." *IEEE Transactions on Systems, Man, and Cybernetics, Part C: Applications and Reviews* 38(4): 461–482.

Dissanayake, M., P. Newman, S. Clark, H. Durrant-Whyte, and M. Csorba (2001). "A Solution to the Simultaneous Localization and Map Building (SLAM) Problem." *IEEE Transactions on Robotics and Automation* 17(3): 229–241.

Dobashi, Y., T. Yamamoto, and T. Nishita (2003). "Real-Time Rendering of Aerodynamic Sound Using Sound Textures Based on Computational Fluid Dynamics." *ACM Transactions on Graphics* 23(3): 732–740.

Dodgson, N. (2005). "Autostereoscopic 3D Displays." *IEEE Computer* 38(8): 31–36.

Dornhege, G., J. Millán, T. Hinterberger, D. McFarland, and K. Müller (2007). *Toward Brain Computer Interfacing*. Cambridge, MA: MIT Press.

Doug Schuler. 1994. "Social computing." *Communications of the ACM* 37(1): 28–29.

Dourish, P., 2001. *Where the Action Is*. Cambridge, MA: MIT Press.

Downs, R., and D. Stea (1977). *Maps in Minds, Reflections on Cognitive Mapping*. Harper and Row.

Downing, E., L. Hesselink, J. Ralston, and R. Macfarlane (1996). "A Three-Color, Solid-State, Three Dimensional Display." *Science* 273(5279): 1185.

Draper, M. (1995). "Exploring the Influence of a Virtual Body on Spatial Awareness." Master of Science in Engineering, Department of Engineering, University of Washington.

Drasci, D., and P. Milgram (1996). "Perceptual Issues in Augmented Reality." *SPIE Volume 2653, Stereoscopic Displays and Virtual Reality Systems III*, 123–124.

Drew, D., J. Newcomb, W. McGrath, F. Maksimovic, Mellis, and B. Hartmann (2016). "The Toastboard: Ubiquitous Instrumentation and Automated Checking of Breadboarded Circuits." *Proceedings of the 29th User Interface Software and Technology Symposium (UIST 2016)*, 677–686.

Driver, J., and C. Spence (1998). Cross-modal links in spatial attention. *Philosophical Transactions of the Royal Society B: Biological Sciences*. Aug 29; 353(1373): 1319–1331.

Duchowski, A. T. (2009). *Eye Tracking Methodology: Theory and Practice*. Second Edition. London: Springer.

Duchowski, A. T., E. Medlin, A. Gramopadhye, B. Melloy, and S. Nair (2001). "Binocular Eye Tracking in VR for Visual Inspection Training." *Proceedings of the 2001 ACM Symposium on Virtual Reality Software and Technology (VRST 2001)*, 1–9.

Durlach, N. (1991). "Auditory Localization in Teleoperator and Virtual Environment Systems: Ideas, Issues, and Problems." *Perception* 20: 543–554.

Durlach, N., and A. Mavor (1995). *Virtual Reality: Scientific and Technical Challenges.* Washington, D.C.: National Academy Press.

Durso, F. T., Truitt, T. R., Hackworth, C. A., Crutchfield, J. M., Ohrt, D. D., Nikolic, D., Moertl, P. M., and Manning, C. A. (1995). "Expertise and Chess: A Pilot Study Comparing Situation Awareness Methodologies." In D. J. Garland, and M. R. Endsley (eds.), *Experimental Analysis and Measurement of Situation Awareness,* 295–303. Daytona Beach, FL: Embry-Riddle Aeronautical Press.

Dvorak, A., N. Merrick, W. Dealey, and G. Ford (1936). *Typewriting Behavior.* American Book Company.

Ebert, D., E. Bedwell, S. Maher, L. Smoliar, and E. Downing (1999). "Realizing 3D Visualizations Using Crossed-Beam Volumetric Displays." *Communications of the ACM* 42(8): 101–107.

Ellis, S., and B. Menges. (1988). "Localization of Virtual Objects in the Near Visual Field." *Human Factors* 40(3): 415–431.

Ellis, S., B. Adelstein, S. Baumeler, G. Jense, and R. Jacoby (1999). "Sensor Spatial Distortion, Visual Latency, and Update Rate Effects on 3D Tracking in Virtual Environments." *Proceedings of IEEE Virtual Reality '99,* 218–221.

Ellson, D. (1947). *The Independence of Tracking in Two or Three Dimensions with B-29 Pedestal Sight.* Aero Medical Laboratory, Wright Air Development Center, TSEAA-694-2G.

Elvins, T., D. Nadeau, and D. Kirsh (1997). "Worldlets: 3D Thumbnails for Wayfinding in Virtual Environments." *Proceedings of the 1997 ACM Symposium on User Interface Software and Technology (UIST '97),* 21–30.

Enderle, G., K. Kanasay, and G. Pfaff (1984). *GKS: The Graphics Standard, Computer Graphics Programming.* New York: Springer-Verlag.

Endsley, M. (1988). "Situation Awareness Global Assessment Technique (SAGAT)." *Proceedings of the National Aerospace and Electronics Conference (NAECON),* 789–795.

Endsley, M. (2000). "Theoretical underpinnings of situation awareness: A critical review." In M. R. Endsley, and D. J. Garland (eds), *Situation Awareness Analysis and Measurement*. Hillsdale, NJ: Lawrence Erlbaum Associates.

Endsley, M. (2012). "Situation Awareness." In S. Galvendy (ed.), *Handbook of Human Factors and Ergonomics.* Fourth Edition.

Engeström, Y. (1987). *Learning by Expan*ding. Helsinki: Orienta-konsultit.

England, D (2011). Springer Human Computer Interaction Series.

Englebart, D. C., and W. K. English (1968). "A Research Center for Augmenting Human Intellect." *Proceedings of the 1968 Fall Joint Computer Conference,* 395–410.

Ernst, M., and M. Banks. (2002). "Humans Integrate Visual and Haptic information in a Statistically Optimal Fashion." *Nature* 415(6870): 429–433.

Ernst, M., and Bülthoff, H. (2004). "Merging the Senses in a Robust Percept." *Trends in Cognitive Sciences* 8(4): 162–169.

Eubanks, J., V. Somareddy, R. McMahan, and A. Lopez (2016). "Full-Body Portable Virtual Reality for Personal Protective Equipment Training." In S. Lackey, and R. Shumaker (eds.), Virtual, Augmented and Mixed Reality. VAMR 2016. Lecture Notes in Computer Science, Vol. 9740. Springer, Cham.

Fairchild, K., L. Hai, J. Loo, N. Hern, and L. Serra (1993). "The Heaven and Earth Virtual Reality: Designing Applications for Novice Users." *Proceedings of the IEEE Symposium on Research Frontiers in Virtual Reality,* 47–53.

Feasel, J., M. Whitton, and J. Wendt (2008). "LLCM-WIP: Low-Latency, Continuous-Motion Walking-in-Place." *Proceedings of the 2008 IEEE Symposium on 3D User Interfaces*, 97–104.

Feiner, S. K., and C. Beshers (1990). "Worlds Within Worlds: Metaphors for Exploring n-Dimensional Virtual Worlds." In *Proceedings of the ACM Symposium on User Interface Software and Technology.* ACM, 76–83.

Feiner, S., B. MacIntyre, and D. Seligmann (1993). "Knowledge-Based Augmented Reality." *Communications of the ACM* 36(7): 53–62.

Fels, S., (1994). "Glove-Talk II: Mapping Hand Gestures to Speech Using Neural Networks: An Approach to Building Adaptive Interfaces." PhD Dissertation, University of Toronto.

Fels, S., and G. Hinton (1998). "Glove-Talk II: A Neural Network Interface Which Maps Gestures to Parallel Formant Speech Synthesizer Controls." *IEEE Transactions on Neural Networks* 9(1): 205–212.

Figueroa, P., M. Green, and H. Hoover (2001). "3DML: A Language for 3D Interaction Techniques Specification." *Proceedings of Eurographics,* Manchester, UK.

Fitts, P. (1954). "The Information Capacity of the Human Motor System in Controlling the Amplitude of Movement." *Journal of Experimental Psychology* 47: 381–391.

Fitts, P., and M. Jones (1953). "Compatibility: Spatial Characteristics of Stimulus and Response Codes." *Journal of Experimental Psychology* 46: 199–210.

Fitts, P., and M. Posner. (1967). *Human Performance*. Belmont, CA: Brooks/Cole.

Fitts, P., and C. Seeger. (1953). "S-R Compatibility: Correspondence among Paired Elements within Stimulus and Response Codes." *Journal of Experimental Psychology* 48, 483–492.

Fitzmaurice, G. (1993). "Situated Information Spaces and Spatially Aware Palmtop Computers." *Communications of the ACM* 36(7): 38–49.

Fitzmaurice, G., H. Ishii, and W. Buxton (1995). "Bricks: Laying the Foundations for Graspable User Interfaces." *Proceedings of the 1995 ACM Conference on Human Factors in Computing Systems (CHI '95),* 442–449.

Foley, J. (1987). "Interfaces for Advanced Computing." *Scientific American* 257(4): 126–135.

Foley, J., A. van Dam, S. Feiner, and J. Hughes (1996). *Computer Graphics: Principles and Practice.* Reading, MA: Addison-Wesley.

Foley, J., and V. Wallace (1974). "The Art of Natural Graphics Man-Machine Conversation." *Proceedings of the IEEE* 62(4): 462–471.

Foley, J., V. Wallace, and P. Chan (1984). "The Human Factors of Computer Graphics Interaction Techniques." *IEEE Computer Graphics and Applications* 4(11): 13–48.

Follmer, S., D. Leithinger, A. Olwal, A. Hogge, and H. Ishii (2013). "inFORM: Dynamic Physical Affordances and Constraints through Shape and Object Actuation." *Proceedings of the 26th Annual ACM Symposium on User Interface Software and Technology (UIST '13)*, 417–426.

Forman, E., and C. Lawson (2003). "Building Physical Interfaces: Making Computer Graphics Interactive." *SIGGRAPH Course #30.*

Forsberg, A., Prabhat, G. Haley, A. Bragdon, J. Levy, C. Fassett, D. Shean, J. Head III, S. Milkovich, and M. Duchaineau (2006). "Adviser: Immersive Field Work for Planetary Geoscientists." *IEEE Computer Graphics and Applications* 26(4): 46–54.

Forsberg, A., J. LaViola, and R. Zeleznik (1998). "ErgoDesk: A Framework for Two and Three Dimensional Interaction at the ActiveDesk." *Proceedings of the Second International Immersive Projection Technology Workshop,* Ames, Iowa.

Forsberg, A., J. LaViola, L. Markosian, and R. Zeleznik (1997). "Seamless Interaction in Virtual Reality." *IEEE Computer Graphics and Applications* 17(6): 6–9.

Forsberg, A., K. Herndon, and R. Zeleznik (1996). Aperture Based Selection for Immersive Virtual Environments. *Proceedings of the 1996 ACM Symposium on User Interface Software and Technology (UIST '96),* ACM Press, 95–96.

Forsberg, A., M. Kirby, D. Laidlaw, G. Karniadakis, A. van Dam, and J. Elion (2000). "Immersive Virtual Reality for Visualizing Flow through an Artery." *Proceedings of IEEE Visualization 2000,* 457–460.

Forsyth, D., and J. Ponce (2011). *Computer Vision: A Modern Approach*, Second Edition. Pearson.

Foskey, M., M. Otaduy, and M. Lin (2002). "ArtNova: Touch-Enabled 3D Model Design." *Proceedings of IEEE Virtual Reality 2002,* IEEE Press, 119–126.

Foxlin, E. (2002). "Motion Tracking Requirements and Technologies." In K. Stanney (ed.), *Handbook of Virtual Environments: Design, Implementation, and Applications,* 163–210. Mahwah, NJ: Lawrence Erlbaum Associates.

Foxlin, E., and L. Naimark (2003). "VIS-Tracker: A Wearable Vision-Inertial Self Tracker." *Proceedings of IEEE Virtual Reality 2003,* 199–206.

Freeman, A. Davison, and A. Fitzgibbon (2011). "KinectFusion: Real-time 3D Reconstruction and Interaction using a Moving Depth Camera." *Proceedings of the 24th Annual ACM Symposium on User Interface Software and Technology (UIST '11)*, 559–568.

Frees, S., and G. Kessler (2005)." Precise and Rapid Interaction through Scaled Manipulation in Immersive Virtual Environments." *Proceedings of the 2005 IEEE Virtual Reality Conference (VR '05),* 99–106.

Friston, S., and A. Steed (2014). "Measuring Latency in Virtual Environments. *IEEE Transactions on Visualization and Computer Graphics* 20(4): 616–625.

Fröhlich, B., and J. Plate (2000). "The Cubic Mouse: A New Device for Three-Dimensional Input." *Proceedings of the 2000 ACM Conference on Human Factors in Computing Systems (CHI 2000),* 526–531.

Fuentes-Pacheco, J., J. Ruiz-Ascencio, and J. Rendón-Mancha (2015). "Visual Simultaneous Localization and Mapping: A Survey." *Artificial Intelligence Review* 43(1): 55–81.

Funkhouser, T., N. Tsingos, I. Carlbom, G. Elko, M. Sondhi, J. E. West, G. Pingali, P. Min and A Ngan (2004). "A Beam Tracing Method for Interactive Architectural Acoustics." *The Journal of the Acoustical Society of America* 115(2): 739–756.

Gabbard, J. (1997). "Taxonomy of Usability Characteristics in Virtual Environments., Master's Thesis, Department of Computer Science, Virginia Polytechnic Institute and State University.

Gabbard, J., Swan II, J. Hix, D., Kim, S., and Fitch, G. (2007). "Active Text Drawing Styles for Outdoor Augmented Reality: A User-Based Study and Design Implications." *Proceedings of IEEE Virtual Reality Conference*, 35–42.

Gabbard, J., D. Hix, and J. Swan (1999). "User-Centered Design and Evaluation of Virtual Environments." *IEEE Computer Graphics and Applications* 19(6): 51–59.

Gale, N., R. Golledge, J. Pellegrino, and S. Doherty (1990). "The Acquisition and Integration of Route Knowledge in an Unfamiliar Neighbourhood." *Journal of Environmental Psychology* 10: 3–25.

Galitz, W. O. (2007). *The Essential Guide to User Interface Design: An Introduction to GUI Design Principles and Techniques.* Indianapolis, IN: John Wiley & Sons.

Gallistel, C. (1990). *The Organization of Learning*. Cambridge, MA: The MIT Press.

Galyean, T. (1995). "Guided Navigation of Virtual Environments." *Proceedings of the 1995 ACM Symposium on Interactive 3D Graphics (I3D '95),* 103–104.

Garas, J. (2000). *Adaptive 3D Sound Systems.* Kluwer Academic Publishers, http://link.springer.com/book/10.1007%2F978-1-4419-8776-1.

Garcia-Palacios, A., Hoffman, H. G., Kwong See, S., Tsai, A, and C. Botella-Arbona (2001). "Redefining Therapeutic Success with VR Exposure Therapy." *CyberPsychology and Behavior.* 4: 341–8.

Gardner, W. (1998). *3D Audio Using Loudspeakers.* Kluwer Academic Publishers.

Garner, W. (1974). *The Processing of Information and Structure.* Lawrence Erlbaum Associates.

Gaver, William W. (1991). "Technology affordances." In *Proceedings of the SIGCHI conference on Human factors in computing systems,* 79–84.

Gebhardt, S., Pick, S., Leithold, F., Hentschel, B., and Kuhlen, T(2010). "Extended Pie Menus for Immersive Virtual Environments." *IEEE Transactions on Visualization and Computer Graphics* 19(4): 644–651.

Gelfand, S. (1998). *Hearing: An Introduction to Psychological and Psychophysical Acoustics.* Marcel Dekker.

Gibson, J., (1962). "Observations on Active Touch." *Psychological Review* 69(6): 477–491.

Gibson, J. J. (1977). "The Theory of Affordances." In R. Shaw, and J. Bransford (eds.), *Perceiving, Acting and Knowing*, 67–83. Hillsdale, NJ: LEA.

Gibson, W. (1984). *Neuromancer.* New York: Ace Books.

Giesler, A., D. Valkov and K. Hinrichs (2014). "Void Shadows: Multi-Touch Interaction with Stereoscopic Objects on the Tabletop." *Proceedings of the 2nd ACM Symposium on Spatial User Interaction*, 104–112.

Glencross, M., C. Jay, J. Feasel, L. Kohli, M. Whitton, and R. Hubbold (2007). "Effective Cooperative Haptic Interaction Over the Internet." In 2007 *IEEE Virtual Reality Conference*, IEEE, 115–122.

Gleue, T., and P. Dahne (2001). "Design and Implementation of a Mobile Device for Outdoor Augmented Reality in the Archeoguide Project." *Conference on Virtual Reality, Archeology, and Cultural Heritage* *(ACM): 161–168.

Glocker, B., S. Izadi, J. Shotton, and A. Criminisi (2013). "Real-Time RGB-D Camera Relocalization." *2013 IEEE International Symposium on Mixed and Augmented Reality*, 173–179.

Goldstein, E. (2014). *Sensation and Perception,* Ninth Edition. Belmont, CA: Wadsworth.

Golledge, R. (1999). *Wayfinding Behavior: Cognitive Mapping and Other Spatial Processes.* Baltimore: John Hopkins University Press.

Golub, G., and C. Van Loan (1996). *Matrix Computations.* Baltimore: Johns Hopkins University Press.

Gopher, D., and E. Donchin. (1986). "Workload—An Examination of the Concept." In K. R. Boff, L. Kaufman, and J. P. Thomas (eds.), *Handbook of Perception and Human Performance, Vol II, Cognitive Processes and Performance,* 41–49. New York: Wiley & Sons, https://ntrs.nasa.gov/search.jsp?R=19870046254.

Graham, W., C. Thomas, S. Sriram, and A. B. Stephen (2014). "Perception of Ultrasonic Haptic Feedback on the Hand: Localisation and Apparent Motion." *In Proceedings of the SIGCHI Conference on Human Factors in Computing Systems* (CHI '14). ACM, New York, NY, USA, 1133–1142.

Grammenos, G., M. Filou, P. Papadakos, and C. Stephanidis (2002). "Virtual Prints: Leaving Trails in Virtual Environments." *Proceedings of the Eighth Eurographics Workshop on Virtual Environments (VE 2002),* 131–138.

Grassia, F. S. (1998). "Practical Parameterization of Rotations Using the Exponential Map." *Journal of Graphics Tools* 3(3): 29–48.

Grasso, M., D. Ebert, and T. Finin (1998). :The Integrality of Speech in Multimodal Interfaces." *ACM Transactions on Computer-Human Interaction* 5(4): 303–325.

Greenburg, S., and C. Fitchett (2001). "Phidgets: Easy Development of Physical Interfaces through Physical Widgets." *Proceedings of the 2001 ACM Symposium on User Interface Software and Technology (UIST 2001),* 209–218.

Greenburg, S., and M. Boyle (2002). "Customizable Physical Interfaces for Interacting with Conventional Applications." *Proceedings of the 2002 ACM Symposium on User Interface Software and Technology (UIST 2002),* 31–40.

Greunke, L., and A. Sadagic (2016). "Taking Immersive VR Leap in Training of Landing Signal Officers."

Grosjean, J., J-M. Burkhardt, S. Coquillart, and P. Richard (2002). "Evaluation of the Command and Control Cube." *Proceedings of the Fourth International Conference on Multimodal Interfaces (ICMI 2002),* 14–16.

Grossman, T., and R. Balakrishnan (2008). "Collaborative Interaction with Volumetric Displays." *Proceedings of the SIGCHI Conference on Human Factors in Computing Systems (CHI '08)*, 383–392.

Grossman, T., and R. Balakrishnan (2006). "The Design and Evaluation of Selection Techniques for 3D Volumetric Displays." *Proceedings of the 19th Annual ACM Symposium on User Interface Software and Technology (UIST '06)*, 3–12.

Grossman, T., and R. Balakrishnan (2005). "The Bubble Cursor: Enhancing Target Acquisition by Dynamic Resizing of the Cursor's Activation Area." *Proceedings of the SIGCHI Conference on Human Factors in Computing Systems*, 281–290.

Grossman, T., D. Wigdor, and R. Balakrishnan (2004). "Multi-Finger Gestural Interaction with 3D Volumetric Displays. *Proceedings of the 17th Annual ACM Symposium on User Interface Software and Technology (UIST '04)*. 61–70.

Grossman, T., R. Balakrishnan, and K. Singh (2003). "An Interface for Creating and Manipulating Curves Using a High Degree-of-Freedom Curve Input Device." *Proceedings of 2003 ACM Conference on Human Factors in Computing Systems (CHI 2003)*, 185–192.

Guiard, Y. (1987). "Symmetric Division of Labor in Human Skilled Bimanual Action: The Kinematic Chain as a Model." *The Journal of Motor Behaviour* 19(4): 486–517.

Guna, J., G. Jakus, M. Pogačnik, S. Tomažič, and J. Sodnik (2014). "An Analysis of the Precision and Reliability of the Leap Motion Sensor and its Suitability for Static and Dynamic Tracking." *Sensors 14*(2): 3702–3720.

Gupta, S., D. Morris, S. Patel, and D. Tan (2012). "Soundwave: Using the Doppler Effect to Sense Gestures." *Proceedings of the ACM SIGCHI Conference on Human Factors in Computing Systems (CHI 2012)*, 1911–1914.

Hachet, M., Bossavit, B., Cohé, A., and De La Rivière, J. (2011) "Toucheo: Multitouch and Stereo Combined in a Seamless Workspace." *Proceedings of the 2011 ACM Symposium on User Interface Software and Technology*, 587–592

Hachet, M., F. Decle, S. Knodel, and P. Guitton (2008). "Navidget for Easy 3D Camera Positioning from 2D Inputs." *Proceedings of the 2008 IEEE Symposium on 3D User Interfaces (3DUI '08)*, 83–89.

Hachet, M., P. Guitton, and P. Reuter (2003). "The CAT for Efficient 2D and 3D Interaction as an Alternative to Mouse Adaptations." *Proceedings of the 2003 ACM Symposium on Virtual Reality Software and Technology (VRST 2003)*, 205–212.

Hackos, J., and J. Redish (1998). *User and Task Analysis for Interface Design*. New York: John Wiley & Sons.

Hagedorn, J. G., S. G. Satterfield, J. T. Kelso, W. Austin, J. E. Terrill, and A. P. Peskin (2007). "Correction of Location and Orientation Errors in Electromagnetic Motion Tracking." *Presence: Teleoperators and Virtual Environments* 16(4):352–366.

Hainich, R., and O. Bimber (2011). *Displays: Fundamentals and Applications*. Boca Raton, FL: AK Peters.

Hale, K., and Stanney, K. (eds.) (2014). *Handbook of Virtual Environments: Design, Implementation, and Applications*, Second Edition. Boca Raton, FL: CRC Press.

Hall, J. (2015). *Guyton and Hall Textbook of Medical Physiology*, 13th Edition. Philadelphia: Elsevier.

Hamilton, Sir W. (1853). *Lectures on Quaternions*. Hodges and Smith.

Han, J. (2005). "Low-Cost Multi-Touch Sensing through Frustrated Total Internal Reflection." *Proceedings of the 18th Annual ACM Symposium on User Interface Software and Technology (UIST '05)*, 115–118.

Hancock, M., F. Vernier, D. Wigdor, S. Carpendale, and C. Shen (2006). "Rotation and Translation Mechanisms for Tabletop Interaction." *First IEEE International Workshop on Horizontal Interactive Human-Computer Systems (TABLETOP '06)*, 8.

Hanson, A. (1992). "The Rolling Ball." In D. Kirk (ed.), *Graphics Gem III* 51–60. Academic Press.

Harmon, R., W. Patterson, W. Ribarsky, and J. Bolter (1996). "The Virtual Annotation System." *Proceedings of the 1996 IEEE Virtual Reality Annual International Symposium (VRAIS '96)*, 239–245.

Harris, L., M. Jenkin, and D. Zikovitz (1999). "Vestibular Cues and Virtual Environments: Choosing the Magnitude of the Vestibular Cue." *Proceedings of IEEE Virtual Reality '99*, 229–236.

Hart, S. (2006). "NASA- Task Load Index [NASA-TLX]; 20 Years Later." *Proceedings of the HFES Annual Meeting*, 50: 904–908.

Hart, S., and L. Staveland. (1988). "Development of NASA-TLX (Task Load Index): Results of Empirical and Theoretical Research." In P. A. Hancock, and N. Meshkati (eds.), *Human Mental Workload*. 139–183. Amsterdam: North Holland Press

Hartson, H., and P. Gray (1992). "Temporal Aspect of Tasks in the User Action Notation." *Human Computer Interaction* 7(1): 1–45.

Hartson, R., and Hix, D. (1989). "Human-Computer Interface Development: Concepts and Systems for Its Management." *ACM Computing Surveys* 21(1): 5–92.

Hartson, R., and P. Pyla. (2012). *The UX Book: Process and Guidelines for Ensuring a Quality User Experience*. Waltham, MA: Morgan Kaufmann Publishers.

Hartson, R. (2003) "Cognitive, Physical, Sensory, and Functional Affordances in Interaction Design." *Behaviour & Information Technology* 22(5): 315–338.

Hatch, M. (2013). *The Maker Movement Manifesto: Rules for Innovation in the New World of Crafters, Hackers, and Tinkerers*. McGraw-Hill Education.

Hatzfeld, C., and T. A. Kern (2014). *Engineering Haptic Devices: A Beginner's Guide,* Second Edition. London: Springer-Verlag.

Hayes, A. T., C. L. Straub, L. A. Dieker, C. E. Hughes, and M. C. Hynes (2013). "Ludic learning: Exploration of TLE TeachLivE™ and Effective Teacher Training." *International Journal of Gaming and Computer-Mediated Simulations (IJGCMS)* 5(2): 20–33.

He, C., H. Şen, S. Kim, P. Sadda, and P. Kazanzides (2014). "Fusion of Inertial Sensing to Compensate for Partial Occlusions in Optical Tracking Systems." *Augmented Environments for Computer-Assisted Interventions, Lecture Notes in Computer Science* 8678: 60–69.

Hegarty, M., Richardson, A., Montello, D., Lovelace, K., and I. Subbiah (2002). "Development of a Self-Report Measure of Environmental Spatial Ability." *Intelligence* 30: 425–448.

Helms, J. W., J. Arthur, D. Hix, and H. Hartson (2006). "A Field Study of the Wheel—A Usability Engineering Process Model." *Journal of Systems and Software* 79(6): 841–858.

Hemmings, B., and T. Holder (2009). *Applied Sport Psychology: A Case-Based Approach*. New York: Wiley and Sons.

Hendrix, C., and W. Barfield (1995). "Presence in Virtual Environments as a Function of Visual and Auditory Cues." *Proceedings of the Virtual Reality Annual International Symposium'95* (IEEE) 74–82.

Henry, D., and T. Furness (1993). "Spatial Perception in Virtual Environments: Evaluating an Architectural Application." *Proceedings of the 1993 IEEE Virtual Reality Annual International Symposium (VRAIS '93),* 33–40.

Hermann, T., A. Hunt, and J. Neuhoff (2011). *The Sonification Handbook*. Berlin: Logos Verlag.

Herndon, K., A. van Dam, and M. Gleicher (1994). "The Challenges of 3D Interaction." *SIGCHI Bulletin* 26(4): 36–43.

Herndon, K., R. Zeleznik, D. Robbins, D. Conner, S. Snibbe, and A. van Dam (1992). "Interactive Shadows." *Proceedings of the 1992 ACM Symposium on User Interface Software and Technology (UIST '92),* 1–6.

Hesselink, J. Ralston, and R. Macfarlane (1996). "A Three-Color, Solid-State, Three-Dimensional Display." *Science* 273(5279): 1185–1189.

Hick, W. (1952). "On the Rate of Gain in Information." *Quarterly Journal of Experimental Psychology* 40: 199–222.

Hinckley, K., J. Tullio, R. Pausch, D. Proffitt, and N. Kassell (1997). "Usability Analysis of 3D Rotation Techniques." *Proceedings of the 1997 ACM Symposium on User Interface Software and Technology (UIST '97),* 1–10.

Hinckley, K., R. Pausch, D. Proffitt, J. Patten, and N. Kassell (1997). Cooperative Bimanual Action. *Proceedings of the 1997 ACM Conference on Human Factors in Computing Systems (CHI '97),* 27–34.

Hinckley, K., R. Pausch, J. Goble, and N. Kassell (1994). "Passive Real-World Interfaces Props for Neurosurgical Visualization." *Proceedings of the 1994 ACM Conference on Human Factors in Computing Systems (CHI '94),* 452–458.

Hinrichs, U., and S. Carpendale (2011). "Gestures in the Wild: Studying Multi-Touch Gesture Sequences on Interactive Tabletop Exhibits." *Proceedings of the SIGCHI Conference on Human Factors in Computing Systems*, 3023–3032.

Hix, D., and H. Hartson (1993). *Developing User Interfaces: Ensuring Usability through Product and Process.* John Wiley and Sons.

Hix, D., and J. Gabbard (2002). "Usability Engineering of Virtual Environments." In K. Stanney (ed), *Handbook of Virtual Environments: Design, Implementation, and Applications.* 681–699 Mahwah, NJ: Lawrence Erlbaum Associates.

Hix, D., J. Swan, J. Gabbard, M. McGee, J. Durbin, and T. King (1999). "User-Centered Design and Evaluation of a Real-Time Battlefield Visualization Virtual Environment." *Proceedings of IEEE Virtual Reality '99,* 96–103.

Hodges, L., B. Rothbaum, R. Alarcon, D. Ready, F. Shahar, K. Graap, J. Pair, P. Herbert, B. Wills, and D. Baltzell (1999). "Virtual Vietnam: A Virtual Environment for the Treatment of Chronic Post-Traumatic Stress Disorder." *CyberPsychology and Behavior* 2(1): 7–14.

Hodges, L., B. Rothbaum, R. Kooper, D. Opdyke, T. Meyer, M. North, J. de Graff, and J. Williford (1995). "Virtual Environments for Treating the Fear of Heights." *IEEE Computer* 28(7): 27–34.

Hodgson, E., and Bachmann, E. (2013). "Comparing Four Approaches to Generalized Redirected Walking: Simulation and Live User Data." *IEEE Transactions on Visualization and Computer Graphics* 19(4): 634–643.

Hodgson, E., Bachmann, E., and Thrash, T (2014). "Performance of Redirected Walking Algorithms in a Constrained Virtual World." *IEEE Transactions on Visualization and Computer Graphics* 20(4): 579–587.

Hoffman, H. G., D. R. Patterson, M. Soltani, A. Teeley, W. Miller, and S. R. Sharar (2008). "Virtual Reality Pain Control during Physical Therapy Range of Motion Exercises for a Patient with Multiple Blunt Force Trauma Injuries." *Cyberpsychological Behaviour* 12(1): 47–49 (Nov 19).

Hoffman, M., P. Varcholik, and J. LaViola (2010). "Breaking the Status Quo: Improving 3D Gesture Recognition with Spatially Convenient Input Devices." *Proceedings of IEEE Virtual Reality 2010,* 59–66.

Hoffman, H., A. Hollander, K. Schroder, S. Rousseau, and T. Furness (1998). "Physically Touching and Tasting Virtual Objects Enhances the Realism of Virtual Experiences." *Virtual Reality: Research, Development and Application* 3: 226–234.

Hogue, A., M. Robinson, M. R. Jenkin, and R. S. Allison (2003). "A Vision-Based Head Tracking System for Fully Immersive Displays." *Proceedings of Immersive Projection Technology and Virtual Environments 2003,* 179–188.

Hollerbach, J. (2002). "Locomotion Interfaces." In K. Stanney (ed.), *Handbook of Virtual Environments: Design, Implementation, and Applications.* 239–254. Mahwah, NJ: Lawrence Erlbaum Associates.

Höllerer, T., S. Feiner, T. Terauchi, G. Rashid, and D. Hallaway (1999). "Exploring MARS: Developing Indoor and Outdoor User Interfaces to a Mobile Augmented Reality System." *Computers and Graphics* 23(6): 779–785.

Holliman, N., N. Dodgson, G. Favalora, and L. Pockett (2011). "Three-Dimensional Displays: A Review and Applications Analysis." *IEEE Transactions on Broadcasting* 57(2):362–371.

Holmqvist, K., Nyström, N., Andersson, R., Dewhurst, R., Jarodzka, H., and J. van de Weijer (eds.) (2011). *Eye Tracking: A Comprehensive Guide to Methods and Measures.* Oxford: Oxford University Press.

Hongyong, T., and Y. Youling (2012). "Finger Tracking and Gesture Recognition with Kinect." *Proceedings of the 12th International Conference on Computer and Information Technology (CIT '12),* 214–218.

Honkamaa, P., S. Siltanen, J. Jäppinen, C. Woodward and O. Korkalo (2007). "Interactive Outdoor Mobile Augmentation Using Markerless Tracking and GPS." *Proceedings of the Virtual Reality International Conference (VRIC),* 285–288.

Hosseini S. A., Khalilzadeh M. A., and M. Branch. (2010). "Emotional Stress Recognition System Using EEG and Psychophysiological Signals: Using New Labelling Process of EEG Signals in Emotional Stress State." *Proceedings of International Conference on Biomedical Engineering and Computer Science,* Wuhan, China. 23–25 April 2010.

Houde, S. (1992). "Iterative Design of an Interface for Easy 3-D Direct Manipulation." *Proceedings of the 1992 ACM Conference on Human Factors in Computing Systems (CHI '92),* 135–142.

Howard, I. (1991). "Spatial Vision within Egocentric and Exocentric Frames of Reference." In A. Grunwald (ed.), *Pictorial Communication in Virtual and Real Environments*, 338–357. London: Taylor and Francis Ltd.

Howell, M. J., N. S. Herrera, A. G. Moore, and R. P. McMahan (2015). "A Reproducible Olfactory Display for Exploring Olfaction in Immersive Media Experiences. *Multimedia Tools and Applications*, 75(20): 12311–12330.

Hua, C., Ellis, S., and J. Swan II. (2014). "Calibration and Depth Matching Accuracy with a Table-Mounted Augmented Reality Haploscope." In Poster Compendium, *Proceedings of ACM SIGGRAPH Symposium on Applied Perception* (SAP 2014), 127.

Hua, H., C. Gao, F. Biocca, and J. Rolland (2001). An Ultra-Light and Compact Design and Implementation of Head-Mounted Projective Displays." *Proceedings of IEEE Virtual Reality 2001,* 175–182.

Hua, H., C. Gao, L. Brown, D. Ahuja, and J. Rolland (2002). "A Testbed for Precise Registration, Natural Occlusion, and Interaction in an Augmented Environment Using a Head-Mounted Projective Display." *Proceedings of IEEE Virtual Reality 2002,* 81–89.

Huang, J. Y. (2003). "An Omnidirectional Stroll-Based Virtual Reality Interface and Its Application on Overhead Crane Training." *IEEE Transactions on Multimedia 5*(1): 39–51.

Hughes, C., Stapleton, C., Hughes, D., and E. Smith. (2005). "Mixed Reality in Education, Entertainment, and Training." *Computer Graphics and Applications* 25(6): 24 – 30.

Hughes, J. M. (2016). *Arduino: A Technical Reference: A Handbook for Technicians, Engineers, and Makers*. O'Reilly Media.

Hughes, J., A. van Dam, M. McGuire, D. Sklar, J. Foley, S. Feiner, and K. Akeley (2013). *Computer Graphics: Principles and Practice.* Third Edition. Upper Saddle River, NJ: Addison-Wesley Professional.

Hultquits, J. (1990). "A Virtual Trackball." *Graphics Gems I,* 462–463. San Diego: Academic Press.

Huopaniemi, J. (1999). "Virtual Acoustics and 3D Sound in Multimedia Signal Processing." PhD Dissertation, Department of Electrical and Communications Engineering, Helsinki University of Technology.

Hyman, R. (1953). "Stimulus Information as a Determinant of Reaction Time." *Journal of Experimental Psychology* 45: 188–196.

Igarashi, T., R. Kadobayahi, K. Mase, and H. Tanaka (1998). "Path Drawing for 3D Walkthrough." *Proceedings of the 1998 ACM Symposium on User Interface Software and Technology (UIST '98),* 173–174.

Igarashi, T., S. Matsuoka, and H. Tanaka (1999). "Teddy: A Sketching Interface for 3D Freeform Design." *Proceedings of SIGGRAPH '99,* 409–416.

Ingram, R., J. Bowers, and S. Benford (1996). "Building Virtual Cities: Applying Urban Planning Principles to the Design of Virtual Environments." *Proceedings of the 1996 ACM Symposium on Virtual Reality Software and Technology (VRST '96),* 83–92.

Insko, B. E. (2001). "Passive Haptics Significantly Enhances Virtual Environments." PhD Dissertation, Dept. of Computer Science, University of North Carolina at Chapel Hill.

Interrante, V., Anderson, L., and B. Ries. (2006). "Distance Perception in Immersive Virtual Environments, Revisited." *Proceedings of the IEEE Virtual Reality Conference*, 3–10.

Interrante, V., B. Ries, and L. Anderson (2007). "Seven League Boots: A New Metaphor for Augmented Locomotion through Moderately Large Scale Immersive Virtual Environments." *Proceedings of the 2007 IEEE Symposium on 3D User Interfaces (3DUI '07),* 167–170.

Ishii, H. (2008). "Tangible Bits: Beyond Pixels." *Proceedings of the 2nd International Conference on Tangible and Embedded Interaction,* xv–xxv. Bonn, Germany, February 18–20, 2008.

Ishii, H., and B. Ullmer (1997). "Tangible Bits: Towards Seamless Interfaces between People, Bits, and Atoms." *Proceedings of the ACM Conference on Human Factors in Computing Systems,* 234–241.

Ishii, M., and M. Sato (1994). "A 3D Spatial Interface Device Using Tensed Strings." *Presence: Teleoperators and Virtual Environments* 3(1): 81–86.

Israr, A., and I. Poupyrev (2011). "Tactile Brush: Drawing on Skin with a Tactile Grid Display." *Proceedings of the SIGCHI Conference on Human Factors in Computing Systems (CHI 2011),* 2019–2028.

Itoh, Y., and G. Klinker (2014). "Interaction-Free Calibration for optical See-Through Headmounted Displays Based on 3D Eye Localization," *Proceedings of the 2014 IEEE Symposium on 3D User Interfaces (3DUI),* Minneapolis, MN, 75–82.

Itoh, Y., H. Ishii, C. Ratti, B. Piper, Y. Wang, A. Biderman, and E. Ben-Joseph, E. (2004). "Bringing Clay and Sand into Digital Design: Continuous Tangible User Interfaces." *BT Technology Journal* 22, 4 (2004), 287–299.

Ives, B., and M. H. Olson (1985). "User Involvement and MIS Success: A Review of Research." *Management Science* 30(5): 586–603.

Iwamoto, T., M. Tatezono, and H. Shinoda (2008). "Non-Contact Method for Producing Tactile Sensation Using Airborne Ultrasound." In M. Ferre (eds.) Haptics: Perception, Devices and Scenarios. EuroHaptics 2008. Lecture Notes in Computer Science, Vol. 5024. Springer: Berlin, Heidelberg

Iwata, H. (1999). "Walking about Virtual Environments on an Infinite Floor." *Proceedings of IEEE Virtual Reality '99,* 286–293.

Iwata, H. (2001). "GaitMaster: A Versatile Locomotion Interface for Uneven Virtual Terrain." *Proceedings of IEEE Virtual Reality 2001,* 131–137.

Iwata, H., and T. Fujii (1996). "Virtual Perambulator: A Novel Interface Device for Locomotion in Virtual Environment." *Proceedings of the 1996 IEEE Virtual Reality Annual International Symposium (VRAIS '96),* 60–65.

Iwata, H., H. Yano, H. Fukushima, and H. Noma (2005). "Circulafloor: A Locomotion Interface Using Circulation of Movable Tiles." In *Proceedings of IEEE Virtual Reality.* IEEE Computer Society, 223–230.

Izadi, S., D. Kim, O. Hilliges, D. Molyneaux, R. Newcombe, P. Kohli, J. Shotton, S. Hodges, H. Iwata, H. Yano, H. Fukushima, and H. Noma (2005). "Circulafloor." *IEEE Computer Graphics and Applications* 25(1): 64–67.

Izadi, S. D. Kim, O. Hilliges, D. Molyneaux, R. Newcombe, P. Kohli, J. Shotton, S. Hodges, D. Freeman, A. Davison, and A. Fitzgibbon (2011). Kinect Fusion: Real-Time 3D Reconstruction and Interaction Using a Moving Depth Camera. In *Proceedings of the 24th Annual ACM Symposium* on User *Interface Software and Technology* (UIST '11). ACM, New York, NY, USA, 559–568.

Jack, D.; Boian, R., Merians, A., Tremaine, M., Burdea, G., Adamovich, S., Recce, M., and H. Poizner. (2001). "Virtual Reality-Enhanced Stroke Rehabilitation." *Transactions on Neural Systems and Rehabilitation Engineering* 9(3): 308–318.

Jacko, J., J. Yi, F. Saintfort, F., and M. McClellan (2012). Human Factors and Ergonomics Methods." In G. Salvendy (ed.), *Handbook of Human Factors and Ergonomics.*) Hoboken, NJ: John Wiley & Sons.

Jackson, B., D. Schroeder, and D. Keefe (2012). "Nailing Down Multi-Touch: Anchored Above the Surface Interaction for 3D Modeling and Navigation." *Proceedings of Graphics Interface 2012,* 181–184.

Jacob, R. (1995). "Eye Tracking in Advanced Interface Design." *Virtual Environments and Advanced Interface Design.* W. Barfield and T. Furness (eds.), 258–288. Oxford: Oxford University Press.

Jacob, R. (1996). "Input Devices and Techniques." In A. B. Tucker (ed.), *The Computer Science and Engineering Handbook,* 1494–1511. Boca Raton, FL: CRC Press.

Jacob, R., and L. Sibert (1992). "The Perceptual Structure of Multidimensional Input Devices." *Proceedings of the 1992 ACM Conference on Human Factors and Computing Systems (CHI '92),* 211–218.

Jacobs, J., and B. Froehlich (2011). "A Soft Hand Model for Physically-Based Manipulation of Virtual Objects." *Proceedings of the 2011 IEEE Virtual Reality Conference (VR '11),* 11–18.

Jacobson, D. (1996). "Talking Tactile Maps and Environmental Audio Beacons: An Orientation and Mobility Development Tool for Visually Impaired People." *Proceedings of the ICA Commission on Maps and Graphics for Blind and Visually Impaired People,* 21–25 October, 1996, Ljubjiana, Slovenia.

Jacoby, R., M. Ferneau, and J. Humphries (1994). "Gestural Interaction in a Virtual Environment." *Proc. SPIE 2177, Stereoscopic Display and Virtual Reality Systems: The Engineering Reality of Virtual Reality,* 355–364, April 15, 1994; doi:10.1117/12.173892.

Johansen, Robert. (1989). "Groupwise and Collaborative Systems—A Big Picture View." *Global Telecommunications Conference and Exhibition'Communications Technology for the 1990s and Beyond'(GLOBECOM),* 1217–1220.

Johnsen, K., and B. Lok (2008). "An Evaluation of Immersive Displays for Virtual Human Experiences." *IEEE Virtual Reality Conference 2008,* 133–136.

Johnson, A., M. Roussos, J. Leigh, C. Vasilakis, C. Barnes, and T. Moher (1998). "The NICE Project: Learning Together in a Virtual World." *Proceedings of the 1998 IEEE Virtual Reality Annual International Symposium (VRAIS '98),* 176–183.

Johnson, Jeff. (2014). *Designing with the Mind in Mind (Second Edition): Simple Guide to Understanding User Interface Design Guidelines*. Waltham, MA: Elsevier.

Johnson-Laird, P. (1993). *The Computer and the Mind: An Introduction to Cognitive Science (Second Edition)*. Fontana Press.

Jones, H. (2001). *Computer Graphics through Key Mathematics*. London: Springer-Verlag.

Jones, J., Swan J, II, Singh G, Kolstad E, and S. Ellis. (2008). "The Effects of Virtual Reality, Augmented Reality, and Motion Parallax on Egocentric Depth Perception." *Proceedings of the 2008 Symposium on Applied Perception in Graphics and Visualization*, 9–14.

Jones, L. (2008). "Warm or Cool, Large or Small? The Challenge of Thermal Displays." *IEEE Transactions on Haptics* 1(1): 53–70.

Jongyoon C., and R. Gutierrez-Osuna. (2011). "Removal of Respiratory Influences from Heart Rate Variability in Stress Monitoring." *IEEE Sensor Journal* (11): 2649–2656.

Jorgensen, C., K. Wheeler, and S. Stepniewski (2000). "Bioelectric Control of a 757 Class High Fidelity Aircraft Simulation." *Proceedings of the World Automation Conference,* 1–8.

Julier, S., M. Lanzagorta, Y. Baillot, L. Rosenblum, S. Feiner, T. Hollerer, and S. Sestito (2000). "Information Filtering for Mobile Augmented Reality." In *Augmented Reality*, ISAR 2000), *Proceedings of IEEE and ACM International Symposium*, 3–11.

Jurafsky, D., and J. Martin (2008). *Speech and Language Processing: An Introduction to Natural Language Processing, Computational Linguistics, and Speech Recognition*. Prentice-Hall

Kaczmarek, K., J. Webster, P. Pach-y-Rita, and W. Tompkins (1991). "Electrotactile and Vibrotactile Displays for Sensory Substitution Systems." *IEEE Transactions on Biomedical Engineering* 38(1): 1–16.

Kaiser, E., Olwal, A., McGee, D., Benko, H., Corradini, A., Li, X., Cohen, P. and S. Feiner (2003). "Mutual Disambiguation of 3D Multimodal Interaction in Augmented and Virtual Reality." *Proceedings of the 5th ACM international Conference on Multimodal Interfaces* (ICMI '03), 12–19.

Kajastila, R., and Lokki, T. (2009) "A Gesture-Based and Eyes-Free Control Method for Mobile Devices." *Proceedings of the ACM Conference on Human Factors in Computing Systems,* 3559–3564.

Kalkofen, D., C. Sandor, S. White, and D. Schmalstieg (2011). "Visualization Techniques for Augmented Reality." *Handbook of Augmented Reality*, 65–98.

Kalawsky, R. S. (1993). *The Science of Virtual Reality and Virtual Environments*. Wokingham, England: Addison-Wesley.

Kandell, E., Kupfermann, I., and S. Iversen (2000). "Learning and Memory." In E. Kandell, J. Schwartz and T. Jessell (eds.), *Principles of Neuroscience*, Fourth Edition. 1127–1246. New York: McGraw-Hill.

Kane, M., and R. Engle. (2000). "Working-Memory Capacity, Proactive Interference, and Divided Attention: Limits on Long-Term Memory Retrieval." *Journal of Experimental Psychology: Learning, Memory, and Cognition* 26: 336–358.

Kang, H., C. Lee, and K. Jung (2004). "Recognition-Based Gesture Spotting in Video Games." *Pattern Recognition Letters* 25 (15): 1701–1714.

Kapralos B., M. Jenkin, and E. Milios (2003). "Auditory Perception and Virtual Environments." Dept. of Computer Science, York University, CS-2003-07.

Kaptelinin, V., and Nardi, B. A. (2006). *Acting with Technology: Activity Theory and Interaction Design*. Cambridge, MA: MIT Press.

Kaptelinin, V., and B. Nardi (2012). "Activity Theory in HCI: Fundamentals and Reflections." *Synthesis Lectures Human-Centered Informatics* 5(1): 1–105.

Kasik, D., J. Troy, S. Amorosi, M. Murray, and S. Swamy (2002). "Evaluating Graphics Displays for Complex 3D Models." *IEEE Computer Graphics and Applications* 22(3): 56–64.

Kato, H., and M. Billinghurst (1999). "Marker Tracking and HMD Calibration for a Video-Based Augmented Reality Conferencing System." *Proceedings of the 2nd International Workshop on Augmented Reality,* 85–94.

Kato, H., M. Billinghurst, I. Poupyrev, K. Imamoto, and K. Tachibana (2000). "Virtual Object Manipulation on a Table-Top AR Environment." *Proceedings of the IEEE and ACM International Symposium on Augmented Reality.*

Kaufman, N., I. Poupyrev, E. Miller, M. Billinghurst, P. Oppenheimer, and S. Weghorst (1997). "New Interface Metaphors for Complex Information Space Visualization: An ECG Monitor Object Prototype." *Medicine Meets Virtual Reality 5,* 131–140. IOS Press

Kaur, K. (1999). "Designing Virtual Environments for Usability." PhD Dissertation, Department of Computer Science, University College.

Kaur, K., N. Maiden, and A. Sutcliffe (1999). "Interacting with Virtual Environments: An Evaluation of a Model of Interaction." *Interacting with Computers* 11(4): 403–426.

Kaye, J. (1999). "Symbolic Olfactory Display." Brain and Cognitive Science Department. Boston, Massachusetts Institute of Technology.

Keefe, D., D. Acevedo, T. Moscovich, D. Laidlaw, and J. LaViola (2001). "CavePainting: A Fully Immersive 3D Artistic Medium and Interactive Experience." *Proceedings of the 2001 Symposium on Interactive 3D Graphics (I3D 2001),* 85–93.

Kendall, G. (1995). "A 3D Sound Primer: Directional Hearing and Stereo Reproduction." *Computer Music Journal* 19(4): 23–46.

Kendon, A. (1988). "How Gestures Can Become Like Words." In F. Potyatos (ed.), *Crosscultural Perspectives in Nonverbal Communication, 131–141.* Hogrefe.

Kennedy, R., K. Stanney, and W. Dunlap (2000). "Duration and Exposure to Virtual Environments: Sickness Curves during and across Sessions." *Presence: Teleoperators and Virtual Environments* 9(5): 463–472.

Kennedy, R., Lane, N., Berbaum, K., and M. Lilienthal. (1993). "Simulator Sickness Questionnaire: An Enhanced Method for Quantifying Simulator Sickness." *The International Journal of Aviation Psychology* 3(3): 203–220.

Kennedy, R., N. Lane, K. Berbaum, and M. Lilienthal (1993). "A Simulator Sickness Questionnaire (SSQ): A New Method for Quantifying Simulator Sickness." *International Journal of Aviation Psychology* 3(3): 203–220.

Kessler, G., D. Bowman, and L. Hodges (2000). "The Simple Virtual Environment Library: An Extensible Framework for Building VE Applications." *Presence: Teleoperators and Virtual Environments* 9(2): 187–208.

Kessler, G., L. Hodges, and N. Walker (1995). "Evaluation of the CyberGlove as a Whole-Hand Input Device." *ACM Transactions on Computer-Human Interaction* 2(4): 263–283.

Khosrowabadi R., Quek C., Ang K. K., Tung S. W., and M. Heijnen (2011). "Brain-Computer Interface for Classifying EEG Correlates of Chronic Mental Stress." *Proceedings of International Joint Conference on Neural Networks (IJCNN)*; San Jose, CA, USA. 757–762. 31 July–5 August 2011.

Khotake, N., J. Rekimoto, and Y. Anzai (1999). "InfoStick: An Interaction Device for Inter-Appliance Computing. "*Proceedings of Handheld and Ubiquitous Computing: First International Symposium*, 246–258. Berlin: Springer-Verlag.

Kieseyer, U. (2001). *Georges Seurat: 1859–1891: The Master of Pointillism*. Los Angeles: TASCHEN America LLC.

Kim, M. J., and Maher, M. L. (2008). "The impact of tangible user interfaces on spatial cognition during collaborative design." *Design Studies* 29(3): 222–253.

Kim, J., D. Gračanin, K. Matković, and F. Quek (2008). "Finger Walking in Place (FWIP): A Traveling Technique in Virtual Environments." In A. Butz et al. (eds), *Smart Graphics, Lecture Notes in Computer Science #5166*, 58_69. Berlin: Springer.

Kim, Jinwoo, and Jae Yun Moon (1998). "Designing towards Emotional Usability in Customer Interfaces—Trustworthiness of Cyber-Banking System Interfaces." *Interacting with computers* 10(1): 1–29.

Kim, S., A. Israr, and I. Poupyrev (2013). "Tactile Rendering of 3D Features on Touch Surfaces." *Proceedings of the 26th Annual ACM Symposium on User Interface Software and Technology (UIST '13)*, 531–538.

Kindratenko, V. (2000). "A Survey of Electromagnetic Position Tracker Calibration." *Virtual Reality: Research, Development, and Applications* 5(3): 169–182.

Kipper, G., and J. Rampolla (2012). *Augmented Reality: An Emerging Technologies Guide to AR*. Elsevier.

Kishishita, N., Kiyokawa, K., Kruijff, E., Orlosky, J., Mashita, T., and H. Takemura (2014). "Analysing the Effects of a Wide Field of View Augmented Reality Display on Search Performance in Divided Attention Tasks." *Proceedings of the IEEE International Symposium on Mixed and Augmented Reality* (ISMAR'14), Munchen, Germany, 2014.

Kiyokawa, K., and H. Takemura (2005). "A Tunnel Window and Its Variations: Seamless Teleportation Techniques in a Virtual Environment." *Proceedings of HCI International,* Las Vegas, NV.

Kiyokawa, K., H. Takemura, and N. Yokoya (2000). "Seamless Design for 3D Object Creation." *IEEE MultiMedia* 7(1): 22–33.

Klatzky, R., J. Loomis, A. Beall, S. Chance, and R. Golledge (1998). "Spatial Updating of Self-Position and Orientation during Real, Imagined and Virtual Locomotion." *Psychological Science* 9: 293–298.

Klein, A., W. Li, M. Kazhdan, W. Correa, A. Finkelstein, and T. Funkhouser (2000). "Non-Photorealistic Virtual Environments." *Proceedings of SIGGRAPH 2000,* 527–534.

Klein, G., and D. Murray (2008). "Improving the Agility of Keyframe-Based SLAM." In D. Forsyth, P. Torr, and A. Zisserman (eds.), Computer Vision—ECCV 2008. ECCV 2008. Lecture Notes in Computer Science, Vol. 5303. Springer: Berlin, Heidelberg.

Klein, G., and D. Murray (2007). Parallel Tracking and Mapping for Small AR Workspaces. *6th IEEE and ACM International Symposium on Mixed and Augmented Reality*, 225–234.

Kleiner, M., D. I. Dalenback, and P. Svensson (1993). "Auralization: An Overview." *Journal of the Audio Engineering Society* 41(11): 861–875.

Knapp, J., and J. Loomis (2004). "Limited Field of View of Head-Mounted Displays Is not the Cause of Distance Underestimation in Virtual Environments." *Presence: Teleoperators and Virtual Environments* 13(5): 572–577.

Knight, J. (1987). "Manual Control and Tracking." In G. Salvendy (ed.), *Handbook of Human Factors,* 182–218. John Wiley and Sons.

Knoedel, S., and M. Hachet (2011). "Multi-Touch RST in 2D and 3D Spaces: Studying the Impact of Directness on User Performance." *Proceedings of the 2011 IEEE Symposium on 3D User Interfaces (3DUI '11)*, 75–78.

Kohli, L., E. Burns, D. Miller, and H. Fuchs (2005). "Combining Passive Haptics with Redirected Walking." *Proceedings of the 2005 International Conference on Augmented Tele-existence (ICAT '05)*, 253–254.

Koller, D., M. Mine, and S. Hudson (1996). "Head-Tracked Orbital Viewing: An Interaction Technique for Immersive Virtual Environments." *Proceedings of the 1996 ACM Symposium on User Interface Software and Technology (UIST '96)*, 81–82.

Kontrarinis, D., and R. Howe (1995). "Tactile Display of Vibrotactile Information in Teleoperation and Virtual Environments." *Presence Teleoperators and Virtual Environments* 4(4): 387–402.

Kopper, R., D. Bowman, M. Silva, and R. McMahan (2010). "A Human Motor Behavior Model for Distal Pointing Tasks." *International Journal of Human-Computer Studies* 68(10): 603–615.

Kopper, R., F. Bacim, and D. Bowman (2011). "Rapid and Accurate 3D Selection by Progressive Refinement." *Proceedings of the 2011 IEEE Symposium on 3D User Interfaces (3DUI '11)*, 67–74.

Kopper, R., T. Ni, D. Bowman, and M. Pinho (2006). "Design and Evaluation of Navigation Techniques for Multiscale Virtual Environments." *Proceedings of the 2016 IEEE Virtual Reality Conference (VR '06)*, 175–182.

Körner, O., and R. Männer (2003). "Implementation of a Haptic Interface for a Virtual Reality Simulator for Flexible Endoscopy." *11th International Symposium on Haptic Interfaces for Virtual Environments and Teleoperator Systems*, 278–284.

Kosslyn, S. (1993). *Image and Brain.* Cambridge, MA: MIT Press.

Kramer A., and R. Parasuraman (2007). "Neuroergonomics—Application of Neuroscience to Human Factors." In J. Caccioppo, L., Tassinary, and G. Berntson (eds), *Handbook of Psychophysiology*, Second Edition, 704–722. New York: Cambridge University Press.

Kramer, J. (1991). "Communication System for Deaf, Deaf-Blind and Non-Vocal Individuals Using Instrumented Gloves." Patent No. 5,047,952.

Kramer, J. (1993). "Force Feedback and Texture Simulating Interface Device." Patent No. 5,047,952.

Kreitzberg, C. (2008). "The LUCID framework." Cognetics Corporation (2008).

Krueger, M., T. Gionfriddo, and K. Hinrichsen (1985). "VIDEOPLACE: An Artificial Reality." *Proceedings of the 1985 ACM Conference on Human Factors in Computing Systems (CHI '85)*, 35–40.

Krüger, W., and B. Fröhlich (1994). "The Responsive Workbench." *IEEE Computer Graphics and Applications* 14(3): 12–15.

Krüger, W., C. Bohn, B. Fröhlich, H. Schuth, W. Strauss, and G. Wesche (1995). "The Responsive Workbench: A Virtual Work Environment." *IEEE Computer* 28(7): 42–48.

Kruijff, E. (2007). "Unconventional 3D User Interfaces for Virtual Environments." PhD Thesis, Graz University of Technology.

Kruijff, E. (2013). "Human-Potential Driven Design of 3D User Interfaces." *Proceedings of the IEEE International Conference on Artificial Reality and Telexistence* (ICAT 2013), 129-136. Tokyo, Japan.

Kruijff, E., A. Marquardt, C. Trepkowksi, J. Schild, and A. Hinkenjann (2016). Designed Emotions: Challenges and Potential Methodologies for Improving Multisensory Cues to Enhance User Engagement in Immersive Systems. Springer the Visual Computer, doi:10.1007/s00371-016-1294-0.

Kruijff, E., D. Schmalstieg, and S, Beckhaus (2006). "Using Neuromuscular Electrical Stimulation for Pseudo-Haptic Feedback." In *Proceedings of the ACM Symposium on Virtual Reality Software and Technology* (VRST'06), Limassol, Cyprus, 312–315.

Kruijff, E. Wesche, G., Riege, K., Goebbels, G., Kunstman, M., and D., Schmalstieg (2006) "Tactylus, a Pen-Input Device Exploring Audiotactile Sensory Binding." *In Proceedings of the ACM Symposium on Virtual Reality Software and Technology* (VRST'06), 316–319, Limassol, Cyprus.

Kruijff, E., and A. Pander. (2005). "Experiences of Using Shockwaves for Haptic Sensations." *Proceedings of the 3D User Interface Workshop, IEEE Conference on Virtual Reality* (VR 2005), Bonn, Germany.

Kruijff, E., B. Riecke, C. Trekowski, and A. Kitson (2015). "Upper Body Leaning Can Affect Forward Self-Motion Perception in Virtual Environments." *Proceedings of the 3rd ACM Symposium on Spatial User Interaction (SUI '15)*, 103–112.

Kruijff, E., Marquardt, A., Trepkowski, C., Lindeman, R. W., Hinkenjann, A., Maiero, J., and Riecke, B. E. (2016). "On Your Feet!: Enhancing Vection in Leaning-Based Interfaces through Multisensory Stimuli." *Proceedings of the 2016 Symposium on Spatial User Interaction*, 149–158.

Kruijff, E., S. Conrad, and A. Mueller (2003). "Flow of Action in Mixed Interaction Modalities." *Proceedings of HCI International Conference*.

Kruijff, E., E. Swan II, and S. Feiner (2010). "Perceptual issues in Augmented Reality Revisited." *Proceedings of the IEEE and ACM International Symposium on Mixed and Augmented Reality*, 3–12.

Kuipers, J. (2002). *Quaternions and Rotation Sequences: A Primer with Applications to Orbits, Aerospace and Virtual Reality*. Princeton, NJ: Princeton University Press.

Kulik, A., A. Kunert, S. Beck, R. Reichel, R. Blach, A. Zink, and B. Froehlich (2011). "C1x6: A Stereoscopic Six-User Display for Co-Located Collaboration in Shared Virtual Environments." *ACM Transactions on Graphics* 30(6), Article 188, 12 pages.

Kulkanri, A., and H. Colburn (1993). "Evaluation of a Linear Interpolation Scheme for Approximating HRTFs." *Journal of the Acoustical Society of America* 93(4): 2350.

Kulshreshth, A., and LaViola, J. (2014). "Exploring the Usefulness of Finger-Based 3D Gesture Menu Selection." *Proceedings of the ACM Conference on Human Factors in Computing Systems*, ACM, 1093–1102.

Kurtenbach, G., and W. Buxton (1991). "Issues in Combining Marking and Direct Manipulation Techniques." *Proceedings of the 1991 ACM Symposium on User Interface Software and Technology (UIST '91)*, 137–144.

Kuutti, K., (1997). "Activity Theory as a Potential Framework for Human-Computer Interaction Research." *Context and Consciousness: Activity Theory and Human-Computer Interaction* (1996): 17–44.

Laha, B., D. A. Bowman, and J. D. Schiffbauer (2013). "Validation of the MR Simulation Approach for Evaluating the Effects of Immersion on Visual Analysis of Volume Data." *IEEE Transactions on Visualization and Computer Graphics* 19(4): 529–538.

Laha, B., D. A. Bowman, and J. J. Socha (2014). "Effects of VR System Fidelity on Analyzing Isosurface Visualization of Volume Datasets." *IEEE Transactions on Visualization and Computer Graphics* 20(4): 513–522.

Lai, C., R. McMahan, and J. Hall (2015). "March-and-Reach: A Realistic Ladder Climbing Technique." *Proceedings of the 2015 IEEE Symposium on 3D User Interfaces (3DUI '15)*, 15–18.

Lampton, D., B. Knerr, S. Goldberg, J. Bliss, M. Moshell, and B. Blau (1994). "The Virtual Environment Performance Assessment Battery (VEPAB): Development and Evaluation." *Presence: Teleoperators and Virtual Environments* 3(2): 145–157.

Lanman, D., and D. Luebke (2013). "Near-Eye Light Field Displays." *ACM Transactions on Graphics* 32(6): Article 220, 10pp.

Larrue, F., H. Sauzéon, L. Aguilova, F. Lotte, M. Hachet, and B. N. Kaoua (2012). "Brain Computer Interface vs Walking Interface in VR: The Impact of Motor Activity on Spatial Transfer." *Proceedings of the 18th ACM Symposium on Virtual Reality Software and Technology (VRST '12)*, 113–120.

Lascara, C., G. Wheless, D. Cox, R. Patterson, S. Levy, A. E. Johnson, and J. Leigh (1999) "TeleImmersive Virtual Environments for Collaborative Knowledge Discovery." *Proceedings of Advanced Simulation Technologies Conference*, San Diego, CA.

Latoschik, M. (2001). "A Gesture Processing Framework for Multimodal Interaction in Virtual Reality." *Proceedings of the 1st International Conference on Computer Graphics, Virtual Reality and Visualization in Africa,* 95–100.

LaViola, J. (2000). "A Discussion of Cybersickness in Virtual Environments." *ACM SIGCHI Bulletin* 32: 47–56.

LaViola, J. (1999a). "Whole-Hand and Speech Input in Virtual Environments." Master's Thesis, Department of Computer Science, Brown University.

LaViola, J. (1999b). "Flex and Pinch: A Case Study of Whole-Hand Input Design for Virtual Environment Interaction." *Proceedings of the IASTED International Conference on Computer Graphics and Imaging '99,* 221–225.

LaViola, J. (2000a). "A Discussion of Cybersickness in Virtual Environments." *SIGCHI Bulletin* 32(1): 47–56.

LaViola, J. (2000b). "MSVT: A Virtual Reality-Based Multimodal Scientific Visualization Tool." *Proceedings of the Third IASTED International Conference on Computer Graphics and Imaging,* 1–7.

LaViola, J. (2013). "3D Gestural Interaction: The State of the Field." *ISRN Artificial Intelligence*, Vol. 2013, Article ID 514641, 18 pages, 2013.

LaViola, J., Buchanan, S., and Pittman, C. (2014). "Multimodal Input for Perceptual User Interfaces." In A. Bhowmik (ed), *Interactive Displays*, 285–312. Wiley.

LaViola, J., D. Acevedo, D. Keefe, and R. Zeleznik (2001). "Hands-Free Multi-Scale Navigation in Virtual Environments." *Proceedings of the 2001 Symposium on Interactive 3D Graphics (I3D 2001),* 9–15.

LaViola, J., D. Keefe, D. Acevedo, and R. Zeleznik (2004). "Case Studies in Building Custom Input Devices for Virtual Environment Interfaces." *Proceedings of the VR 2004 Workshop on Beyond Wand and Glove Interaction,* 67–71.

Lederman, S., and R. Klatzky (1987). "Hand Movements: A Window into Haptic Object Recognition." *Cognitive Psychology* 19(3): 342–368.

Lederman, S., G. Thorne, and B. Jones. (1986). "Perception of Texture by Vision and Touch: Multidimensionality and Intersensory Integration." *Journal of Experimental Psychology: Human Perception & Performance* 12(2): 169–180.

Lee, C., Y. Hu, and T. Selker (2005). "iSphere: A Proximity-Based 3D Input Interface." In B. Martens and A. Brown (eds.), *Computer Aided Architectural Design Futures 2005,* 281–290. Netherlands: Springer.

Lee, G., Yang, U., Kim, Y., Jo, D., Kim, K., Kim, J., and J. Choi (2009). "Freeze-Set-Go Interaction Method for Handheld Mobile Augmented Reality Environments." *Proceedings of the 16th ACM Symposium on Virtual Reality Software and Technology (VRST '09),* 143–146.

Lee, S., Sohn, M., Kim, D., Kim, B., and Kim, H. (2013). "Smart TV Interaction System using Face and Hand Gesture Recognition." *Proceedings of the IEEE International Conference on Consumer Electronics*, 173–174.

Lee, H., and Woo, W. (2010). "Tangible Spin Cube for 3D Ring Menu in Real Space." *Proceedings of the 28th International Conference on Human Factors in Computing Systems,* CHI 2010, Extended Abstracts Volume, 4147–4152.

Lehrer, K. (1990). *Theory of Knowledge*. London: Routledge.

Lehto, M., Nah, F., and J. Yi. (2012). "Decision-Making Models, Decision Support and Problem Solving." In S. Galvendy (ed.), *Handbook of Human Factors and Ergonomics,* Fourth Edition.

Lenay, C., O. Gapenne, S. Hanneton, C. Genouëlle and C. Marque (2003). "Sensory Substitution: Limits and Perspectives. " In Y. Hatwell, A. Streri and E. Gentaz (eds.), *Touching for Knowing*. 275–292.

Leont'ev, A. (1978). *Activity, Consciousness, and Personality.* Englewood Cliffs, NJ: Prentice-Hall.

Leykin, A. and M. Tuceryan (2004). "Automatic Determination of Text Readability Over Textured Backgrounds for Augmented Reality Systems." *In Proceedings of the Third IEEE/ACM International Symposium on Mixed and Augmented Reality.*

Li, D., Z. Fu, L. Xie, and Y. Zhang (2012). "Comprehensive Comparison of the Least Mean Square Algorithm and the Fast Deconvolution Algorithm for Crosstalk Cancellation." *2012 International Conference on Audio, Language and Image Processing (ICALIP)*, 224–229.

Li, T., and Hsu, S. (2004). "An Intelligent 3D User Interface Adapting to User Control Behavior." *Proceedings of the ACM International Conference on Intelligent User interfaces*, 184–190.

Liang, J., and M. Green (1994). "JDCAD: A Highly Interactive 3D Modeling System." *Computers and Graphics* 18(4): 499–506.

Liang, J., C. Shaw, and M. Green (1991). "On Temporal-Spatial Realism in the Virtual Reality Environment. *Proceedings of the 1991 ACM Symposium on User Interface Software and Technology (UIST '91)*, ACM Press, 19–25.

Lieberknecht, S., A. Huber, S. Ilic, and S. Benhimane (2011). "RGB-D Camera-Based Parallel Tracking and Meshing." *10th IEEE International Symposium on Mixed and Augmented Reality*, 147–155.

Lien, J., N. Gillian, M. Karagozler, P. Amihood, C. Schwesig, E. Olson, H. Raja, and I. Poupyrev (2016). "Soli: Ubiquitous Gesture Sensing with Millimeter Wave Radar." *ACM Transactions on Graphics (TOG)* - Proceedings *of ACM SIGGRAPH 2016* 35(4): Article No. 142.

Lin, M. C., and M. Otaduy (2008). *Haptic Rendering: Foundations, Algorithms and Applications*. Boca Rotan, FL: AK Peters, Ltd.

Lincoln, P., Blate, A., Singh, M., Whitted, T., State, A., Lastra, A., and Fuchs, H. (2016). "From Motion to Photons in 80 Microseconds: Towards Minimal Latency for Virtual and Augmented Reality." *IEEE Transactions on Visualization and Computer Graphics* 22(4): 1367–1376.

Lindeman, R., J. Sibert, and J. Hahn (1999). "Hand-Held Windows: Towards Effective 2D Interaction in Immersive Virtual Environments." *Proceedings of IEEE Virtual Reality '99*, 205–212.

Livingston, M., et al. (2003). "Resolving Multiple Occluded Layers in Augmented Reality." *Proceedings of the 2nd IEEE/ACM International Symposium On Mixed and Augmented Reality*, 56.

Livingston, M., J. Gabbard, J. Swan II, C. Sibley, and J. Barrow. (2012). "Basic Perception in Head-Worn Augmented Reality Displays." In Tony Huang, Leila Alem, and Mark A. Livingston (eds.), *Human Factors in Augmented Reality Environments*, 35–65. New York: Springer.

Loftin, R. B., and P. Kenney (1995). "Training the Hubble Space Telescope Flight Team." *IEEE Computer Graphics and Applications* 15(5): 31–37.

Loomis J., and J. Knapp (2003). Visual Perception of Egocentric Distance in Real and Virtual Environments." In L. J. Hettinger and M.W Haas (eds.), *Virtual and Adaptive Environments*, 21–4. Mahwah, NJ: Lawrence Erlbaum Associates6.

Loomis, J. (2003). "Sensory Replacement and Sensory Substitution: Overview and Prospects for the Future." In M. C. Roco, and W. S. Bainbridge (eds.), *Converging Technologies for Improving Human Performance: Nanotechnology, Biotechnology, Information Technology and Cognitive Science*. Boston: Kluwer Academic Publishers.

Loomis, J., and S. Lederman (1986). "Tactual Perception." In K. Boff, L. Kaufman, and J. Thomas (eds.), *Handbook of Perception and Human Performance*, Vol. 1, 12-1–12-57. New York: John Wiley & Sons.

Lowe, D. (2004). "Distinctive Image Features from Scale-Invariant Keypoints." *International Journal of Computer Vision* 60(4):91–110.

Lucas, J. (2005). "Design and Evaluation of 3D Multiple Object Selection Techniques." M.S. Thesis, Virginia. Polytechnic Institute and State University, Blacksburg, VA, USA.

Lucas, John F., Ji-Sun Kim, and Doug A. Bowman. "Resizing beyond Widgets: Object Resizing Techniques for Immersive Virtual Environments." In *CHI'05 Extended Abstracts on Human Factors in Computing Systems*, 1601–1604.

Lucente, M. (1997). "Interactive Three-Dimensional Holographic Displays: Seeing the Future in Depth." *Computer Graphics* 31(2): 63–67.

Lucente, M., G. Zwart, and A. George (1998). "Visualization Space: A Testbed for Deviceless Multimodal User Interface." *Proceedings of Intelligent Environments '98, The AAAI Spring Symposium Series,* 87–92.

Luebke, D., M. Reddy, J. Cohen, A. Varshney, B. Watson, and R. Huebner (2002). *Level of Detail for 3D Graphics.* New York: Morgan Kaufmann.

Lueder, E. (2012). *3D Displays.* New York: Wiley.

Lund, A. M. (2001) "Measuring Usability with the USE Questionnaire." *STC Usability SIG Newsletter* 8:2

Lynch, K. (1960). *The Image of the City.* Cambridge, MA: MIT Press.

Lyons, K., C. Skeels, T. Starner, C. Snoeck, B. Wong, and D. Ashbrook (2004). Augmenting Conversations Using Dual-Purpose Speech. *Proceedings of the 17th Annual ACM Symposium on User Interface Software and Technology* (UIST '04), 237–246.

MacKenzie, C., and T. Iberall (1994). *The Grasping Hand.* Amsterdam: North-Holland.

MacKenzie, I. (2013). *Human-Computer Interaction: An Empirical Research Perspective.* Waltham, MA: Morgan Kaufmann.

MacKenzie, I. S. (1992). "Fitts' Law as a Research and Design Tool in Human Computer Interaction." *Human Computer Interaction* 7: 91–139.

MacKenzie, I. S. (1995). "Input Devices and Interaction Techniques for Advanced Computing." In W. Barfield and T. Furness (eds.), *Virtual Environments and Advanced Interface Design*, 437–472. Oxford: Oxford University Press.

MacKenzie, I. S., and K. Tanaka-Ishii (2007). *Text Entry Systems: Mobility, Accessibility, Universality.* San Francisco: Morgan Kaufmann.

MacKenzie, I. S., and R. Soukoreff (2002). "Text Entry for Mobile Computing: Models and Methods, Theory and Practice." *Human Computer Interaction* 17: 147–198.

Mackinlay, J., S. Card, and G. Robertson (1990a). "Rapid Controlled Movement through a Virtual 3D Workspace." *Proceedings of SIGGRAPH '90,* 171–176.

Mackinlay, J., S. Card, and G. Robertson (1990b). "A Semantic Analysis of the Design Space of Input Devices." *Human–Computer Interaction* 5(2–3): 145–190.

Macleod, M., R. Bowden, N. Bevan, and I. Curson (1997). "The MUSiC Performance Measurement Method." *Behaviour & Information Technology* 16(4–5): 279–293.

Madgwick, S., A. Harrison, and R. Vaidyanathan (2011). "Estimation of IMU and MARG Orientation Using a Gradient Descent Algorithm." *Proceedings of the 2011 IEEE International Conference on Rehabilitation Robotics*, 1–7.

Maes, P. (1997). "The ALIVE System: Wireless, Full-Body Interaction with Autonomous Agents." *ACM Multimedia Systems* 5(2): 105–112.

Majumder, A., and B. Sajadi (2013). "Advances in Large Area Displays: The Changing Face of Visualization." *IEEE Computer* 46(5):26–33.

Mankoff, J., and G. Abowd (1998). "Cirrin: A Word-Level Unistroke Keyboard for Pen Input." *Proceedings of the 1998 ACM Symposium on User Interface Software and Technology (UIST '98),* 213–214.

Manocha, D., P. Calamia, M. Lin, L. Savioja, and N. Tsingos (2009). "Interactive Sound Rendering." *ACM SIGGRAPH 2009 Courses* (SIGGRAPH '09). ACM, New York, NY, USA, Article 15, 338 pages.

Mapes, D., and J. Moshell (1995). "A Two-Handed Interface for Object Manipulation in Virtual Environments." *Presence: Teleoperators and Virtual Environments* 4(4): 403–416.

Marchal, M., J. Pettré, and A. Lécuyer (2011). "Joyman: A Human-Scale Joystick for Navigating in Virtual Worlds." *Proceedings of the 2011 IEEE Symposium on 3D User Interfaces (3DUI '11),* 19–26.

Marr, D. (1982). *Vision.* New York: W. H. Freeman.

Marras, W. (1997). "Biomechanics of the Human Body." In G. Salvendy (ed.), *Handbook of Human Factors and Ergonomics* 233–267. New York: John Wiley & Sons.

Marras, W. (2012). "Basic biomechanics and workstation design. In G. Salvendy (ed.), *Handbook of Human Factors and Ergonomics*. 347–382. Hoboken, NJ, John Wiley & Sons.

Marriott, K., and P. Stuckey (1998). *Programming with Constraints: An Introduction*. Cambridge MA: MIT Press

Martin J. (1998). "Tycoon: Theoretical Framework and Software Tools for Multimodal Interfaces." In John Lee (ed.), *Intelligence and Multimodality in Multimedia Interfaces*. AAAI Press.

Massie, T. H. (1993). *Design of a Three Degree of Freedom Force Reflecting Haptic Interface*. Cambridge, MA: MIT Press.

Massimino M., and T. Sheridan (1993). "Sensory Substitution for Force Feedback in Teleoperation." *Presence Teleoperators and Virtual Environments* 2(4): 344–352.

Matsumoto, K., Y. Ban, T. Narumi, T. Tanikawa, and M. Hirose (2016). "Curvature Manipulation Techniques in Redirection using Haptic Cues." *Proceedings of the IEEE Symposium on 3D User Interfaces*.

May, J., and D. Badcock (2002). Vision and Virtual Environments. In K. Stanney (ed.), *Handbook of Virtual Environments: Design, Implementation, and Applications*, 29–64. Mahwah, NJ: Lawrence Erlbaum Associates.

Mayhew, D. (1999). "The Usability Engineering Lifecycle." *CHI'99 Extended Abstracts on Human Factors in Computing Systems*, 147–148.

McCormick, B., T. DeFanti, and M. Brown (1987). "Visualization in Scientific Computing." *Computer Graphics* 21(6): 15–21.

McCormick, E. (1970). *Human Factors Engineering*, McGraw-Hill.

McGrenere, J., and W. Ho (2000). "Affordances: Clarifying and Evolving a Concept." In *Graphics Interface*, 2000: 179–186.

McGurk, H., and J. Macdonald (1976). "Hearing Lips and Seeing Voices." *Nature* 264: 746–748.

McMahan, R. (2011). "Exploring the Effects of Higher-Fidelity Display and Interaction for Virtual Reality Games." PhD Dissertation, Department. of Computer Science, Virginia Tech.

McMahan, R. P., A. J. D. Alon, S. Lazem, R. J. Beaton, D. Machaj, M. Schaefer, M. G. Silva, A. Leal, R. Hagan, and D. A. Bowman (2010). "Evaluating Natural Interaction Techniques in Video Games." In *Proceedings of the IEEE Symposium on 3D User Interfaces*, IEEE, 11–14.

McMahan, R., D. Bowman, D. Zielinski, and R. Brady (2012). "Evaluating Display Fidelity and Interaction Fidelity in a Virtual Reality Game." *IEEE Transactions on Visualization and Computer Graphics (Proceedings of IEEE Virtual Reality)* 18(4): 626–633.

McMahan, R., R. Kopper, and D. Bowman (2014). "Principles for Designing Effective 3D Interaction Techniques." *Handbook of Virtual Environments: Design, Implementation and Applications*, 285–311. Boca Raton, FL: CRC Press.

McMahan, R., E. Ragan, D. Bowman, F. Tang, and C. Lai, (2015). "FIFA: The Framework for Interaction Fidelity Analysis" Technical Report UTDCS-06-15, Dept. of Computer Science, The University of Texas at Dallas.

McMahan, R. P., and D. A. Bowman (2007). "An Empirical Comparison of Task Sequences for Immersive Virtual Environments." *IEEE Symposium on 3D User Interfaces, 2007. 3DUI'07...*

McMillan, G., R. Eggelston, and T. Anderson (1997). "Nonconventional Controls." In G. Salvendy (ed.), *Handbook of Human Factors and Ergonomics*, 729–771. New York: John Wiley & Sons.

McQuaide, S., E. Seibel, R. Burstein, and T. Furness (2002). "Three-Dimensional Virtual Retinal Display System Using Deformable Membrane Mirror." *SID Symposium Digest of Technical Papers* 33(1): 1324–1327.

McTear, M. (2002). "Spoken Dialogue Technology: Enabling the Conversational User Interface." *ACM Computing Surveys* 34(1): 90–169.

Medlock, M.C., Wixon, D., McGee, M., and Welsh, D. (2005). "The Rapid Iterative Test and Evaluation Method: Better Products in Less Time." In G. Bias, and D. Mayhew (eds.), *Cost Justifying Usability*, 489–517. San Francisco: Morgan Kaufmann

Melzer, J. (2014). Head-Mounted Displays. In C. R. Spitzer, U. Ferrell, and T. Ferrell (eds.), *Digital Avionics Handbook,* Third Edition, 257–280. Boca Raton, FL: CRC Press,.

Medina, E., R. Fruland, and S. Weghorst (2008). "VIrtusphere: Walking in a Human Size VR Hamster Ball." *Human Factors and Ergonomics Society Annual Meeting Proceedings* 52(27): 2102–2106.

Melzer, J., and K. Moffitt (2011). *Head-Mounted Displays: Designing for the User.* CreateSpace Independent Publishing Platform.

Menashe, I., O. Man, D. Lancet and Y. Gilad (2003). "Different Noses for Different People." *Nature Genetics* 34(2): 143–144.

Meshram, A., R. Mehra, Y. Hongsheng, E. Dunn, J. Franm, and D. Manocha (2014). "P-HRTF: Efficient Personalized HRTF Computation for High-Fidelity Spatial Sound." *2014 IEEE International Symposium on Mixed and Augmented Reality (ISMAR),* 53–61.

Meyer, K., and H. Applewhite (1992). "A Survey of Position Trackers." *Presence: Teleoperators and Virtual Environments* 1(2): 173–200.

Michael, D.C., and P. Bacdayan (1994). "Organizational Routines Are Stored as Procedural Memory: Evidence from a Laboratory Study." *Organization Science* 5(4): 554–568.

Milgram, P., and F. Kishino (1994). "A Taxonomy of Mixed Reality Visual Displays." *IECE Transactions on Information and Systems* E77-D(12): 1321–1329.

Milgram, P., H. Takemura, A. Utsumi, and F. Kishino (1994). "Augmented Reality: A Class of Displays on the Reality-Virtuality Continuum." *Telemanipulator and Telepresence Technologies,* 282–292. SPIE.

Millán, J. (2003). "Adaptive Brain Interfaces." *Communications of the ACM* 46(3): 74–80.

Mills, S., and J. Noyes (1999). "Virtual Reality: An Overview of User-Related Design Issues." *Interacting with Computers* 11(4): 375–386.

Mine, M. (1995a). "Virtual Environment Interaction Techniques." Department of Computer Science, University of North Carolina at Chapel Hill, TR95-018.

Mine, M. (1995b). "ISAAC: A Virtual Environment Tool for the Interactive Construction of Virtual Worlds." Department of Computer Science, University of North Carolina at Chapel Hill, TR-95-020.

Mine, M. (1997). "ISAAC: A Meta-CAD System for Virtual Environments." *Computer-Aided Design* 29(8): 547–553.

Mine, M. (2003) "Towards Virtual Reality for the Masses: 10 Years of Research at Disney's VR Studio." *Proceedings of Eurographics Workshop on Virtual Environments,* 11–17.

Mine, M., F. Brooks, and C. Séquin (1997). "Moving Objects in Space: Exploiting Proprioception in Virtual Environment Interaction." *Proceedings of SIGGRAPH '97,* 19–26.

Moeser, S. (1988). "Cognitive Mapping in a Complex Building." *Environment and Behavior* 20(1): 21–49.

Mohammad Shahnewaz Ferdous, S., I. M. Arafat, and J. Quarles (2016). "Visual Feedback to Improve the Accessibility of Head Mounted Displays for Persons with Balance Impairments." *Proceedings of the 2016 IEEE Symposium on 3D User Interfaces (3DUI),* 121–128.

Monk, S. (2016). *Raspberry Pi Cookbook: Software and Hardware Problems and Solutions,* 2nd Edition. Sebastopol, CA: O'Reilly Media.

Mon-Williams, M., Wann, J. P., and S. Rushton. (1993). "Binocular Vision in a Virtual World: Visual Deficits Following the Wearing of a Head-Mounted Display. *Ophthalmic and Physiological Optics.* 13(4): 387–391.

Moore, A. G., M. J. Howell, A. W. Stiles, N. S. Herrera, and R. P. McMahan (2015). "Wedge: A Musical Interface for Building and Playing Composition-Appropriate Immersive Environments." *2015 IEEE Symposium on 3D User Interfaces* (3DUI), 205–206.

Mouchtaris, A., P. Reveliotis, and C. Kyrakakis (2000). "Inverse Filter Design for Immersive Audio Rendering over Loudspeakers." *IEEE Transactions on Multimedia* 2(2): 77–87.

Mulder, A. (1996). *Hand Gestures for HCI.* School of Kinesiology, Simon Fraser University, Technical Report 96–1.

Muller, Michael J. (1991). "PICTIVE—An Exploration in Participatory Design." Proceedings of the SIGCHI Conference on Human factors in Computing Systems, ACM, 225–231.

Mueller, A., S. Conrad, and E. Kruijff (2003). "Multifaceted Interaction with a Virtual Engineering Environment Using a Scenegraph-Oriented Approach." In *Proceedings of the International Conference in Central Europe on Computer Graphics, Visualization and Computer Vision (WSCG 2003)*, Plzen, Czech Republic.

Mundel, M. (1978). *Motion and Time Study.* Englewood Cliffs, NJ: Prentice-Hall.

Nabiyouni, M., and Bowman, D. A. (2015). "An Evaluation of the Effects of Hyper-Natural Components of Interaction Fidelity on Locomotion Performance in Virtual Reality." *Proceedings of the 25th International Conference on Artificial Reality and Telexistence and 20th Eurographics Symposium on Virtual Environments*, 167–174.

Nabiyouni, M., Saktheeswaran, A., Bowman, D. A., and Karanth, A. (2015, March). "Comparing the Performance of Natural, Semi-Natural, and Non-Natural Locomotion Techniques in Virtual Reality. *IEEE Symposium on 3D User Interfaces (3DUI), 2015*, 3–10.

Naer, M., O. Staadt, and M. Gross (2002). "Spatialized Audio Rendering for Immersive Virtual Environments." *Proceedings of the 2002 ACM Symposium on Virtual Reality Software and Technology (VRST 2002)*, 65–72.

Nahon, D., Subileau, G., and Capel, B. (2015). "'Never Blind VR' Enhancing the Virtual Reality Headset Experience with Augmented Virtuality." *2015 IEEE Virtual Reality (VR)*, 347–348)

Nakamoto, T. (2013). *Human Olfactory Displays and Interfaces: Odor Sensing and Presentation.* Hershey, PA: IGI Global.

Nakamura, S., and Shimojo, S. (1998). "Orientation of Selective Effects of Body Tilt on Visually Induced Perception of Self-Motion." *Perceptual and Motor Skills*, 87(2): 667–672.

Nanayakkara, S., R. Shilkrot, K. Peen Yeo, and P. Maes (2013). "EyeRing: A Finger-Worn Input Device for Seamless Interactions with our Surroundings." *Proceedings of the 4th Augmented Human International Conference (AH '13)*, 13–20.

Nardi, B. A. (1996). "Studying Context: A Comparison of Activity Theory, Situated Action Models, and Distributed Cognition." *Context and Consciousness: Activity Theory and Human-Computer Interaction* (1996): 69–102.

Narumi, T., S. Nishizaka, T. Kajinami, T. Tanikawa, and M. Hirose (2011). "Meta Cookie+: An Illusion-Based Gustatory Display." In R. Shumaker (ed.), *Virtual and Mixed Reality—New Trends, Lecture Notes in Computer Science #6773*, 260–269. Berlin: Springer.

Neale, D. (1998). "Head Mounted Displays: Product Reviews and Related Design Considerations." Blacksburg, Department of Industrial Systems and Engineering, Virginia Tech, HCIL-98-02.

Neuberger, G. (2003). "Measures of Fatigue: The Fatigue Questionnaire, Fatigue Severity Scale, Multidimensional Assessment of Fatigue Scale, and Short Form-36 Vitality (Energy/Fatigue) Subscale of the Short Form Health Survey." *Arthritis Care and Research* 49(S5): S175–S183.

Newell, A., P. Rosenbloom, and J. Laird (1989). "Symbolic Architectures for Cognition." In M. Posner (ed.), *Foundations in Cognitive Science*, 93–131. Cambridge, MA: MIT Press.

Nguyen, H. (2007). *GPU Gems 3.* Upper Saddle River, NJ: Addison-Wesley Professional.

Ni, T., D. A. Bowman, and J. Chen (2006). "Increased Display Size and Resolution Improve Task Performance in Information-Rich Virtual Environments." In *Proceedings of Graphics Interface* 2006, Canadian Information Processing Society, 139–146.

Ni, T., Bowman, D., North, C., and McMahan, R. (2010)." Design and Evaluation of Freehand Menu Selection Interfaces using Tilt and Pinch Gestures." *International Journal of Human-Computer Studies* 69: 551–562.

Ni, T., R. McMahan, and D. Bowman (2008). "Tech-note: rapMenu: Remote Menu Selection Using Freehand Gestural Input." *Proceedings of the 2008 IEEE Symposium on 3D User Interfaces (3DUI)*, 55–58.

Nielsen, J. (1994). "Heuristic Evaluation." In J. Nielsen, and R. L. Mack (eds.), *Usability Inspection Methods*. New York: John Wiley & Sons.

Nielsen, J., and R. Molich (1992). "Heuristic Evaluation of User Interfaces." *Proceedings of the 1992 ACM Conference on Human Factors in Computing Systems (CHI '92)*, 249–256.

Nielsen, J. (1999) "User Interface Directions for the Web." *Communications of the ACM* 42(1): 65–72.

Nilsson, N., S. Serafin, M. Laursen, K. Pedersen, E. Sikström, and R. Nordahl (2013). "Tapping-in-Place: Increasing the Naturalness of Immersive Walking-in-Place Locomotion through Novel Gestural Input." *Proceedings of the IEEE Symposium on 3D User Interfaces (3DUI), IEEE*, 31–38.

Nilsson, N. C., S. Serafin, and R. Nordahl. "A Comparison of Different Methods for Reducing the Unintended Positional Drift Accompanying Walking-in-Place Locomotion." *2014 IEEE Symposium on 3D User Interfaces* (3DUI), 103–110.

Noma, H., and T. Miyasato (1998). Design for Locomotion Interface in a Large Scale Virtual Environment—ATLAS: ATR Locomotion Interface for Active Self Motion. *ASME-DSC* 64: 111–118.

Norman, D. (1988). *The Psychology of Everyday Things*. New York: Basic Books.

Norman, D. (1990). *The Design of Everyday Things*. New York: Doubleday.

Norman, D. (2004). *Emotional Design: Why We Love (or Hate) Everyday Things*. New York: Basic Books.

Norman, D. (2013). *The Design of Everyday Things: Revised and Expanded Edition*. New York:Basic Books.

Norman, D., and D. Bobrow. (1975). "On Data-Limited and Resource Limited Processes." *Cognitive Psychology*, 7:44–64.

Normand, V., C. Babski, S. Benford, A. Bullock, S. Carion, Y. Chrysanthou, N. Farcet, J. Harvey, N. Kuijpers, N. Magnenat-Thalmann, S. Raupp-Musse, T. Rodden, M. Slater, and G. Smith (1999). "The Coven Project: Exploring Applicative, Technical and Usage Dimensions of Collaborative Virtual Environments." *Presence: Teleoperators and Virtual Environments* 8(2): 218–236.

Norton, J., Wingrave, C., and LaViola, J. (2010). "Exploring Strategies and Guidelines for Developing Full Body Video Game Interfaces." *Proceedings of the Fifth International Conference on the Foundations of Digital Games,* June 2010, 155–162.

Noyes, J. (1983). "Chord Keyboards." *Applied Ergonomics* 14: 55–59.

Nurminen, A., Kruijff, E., and E. Veas, (2011). "HYDROSYS—A Mixed Reality Platform for On-Site Visualization of Environmental Data." *Proceedings of the 10th International Symposium on Web and Wireless Geographical Information Systems*, Springer Lecture Notes in Computer Science, 159–175. Kyoto, Japan, 2011

Ohnishi, T., N. Katzakis, K. Kiyokawa, and H. Takemura (2012). "Virtual Interaction Surface: Decoupling of Interaction and View Dimensions for Flexible Indirect 3D Interaction." *Proceedings of the 2012 IEEE Symposium on 3D User Interfaces (3DUI '12),* 113–116.

Ohshima, T., K. Sato, H. Yamamoto, and H. Tamura (1998). "AR2Hockey: A Case Study of Collaborative Augmented Reality." *Proceedings of the 1998 IEEE Virtual Reality Annual International Symposium (VRAIS '98),* 268–275.

Olano, M., and A. Lastra (1998). "A Shading Language on Graphics Hardware: The PixelFlow Rendering System." *Proceedings of SIGGRAPH '98,* 159–168.

Oliva, A., M. L. Mack, M. Shrestha, and A. Peeper (2004). "Identifying the Perceptual Dimensions of Visual Complexity of Scenes." In *Proceedings of the 26th Annual Meeting of the Cognitive Science Society*, 101–106.

Olwal, A., and S. Feiner (2003). "The Flexible Pointer: An Interaction Technique for Augmented and Virtual Reality." *User Interface Software and Technology (UIST) 2003 Conference Supplement,* 81–82.

Omura, K., S. Shiwa, and F. Kishino (1996). "3D Display with Accommodative Compensation (3DDAC) Employing Real-Time Gaze Detection." *Society for Information Display Digest*, 889–892.

Ortega, M. (2013). "Hook: Heuristics for Selecting 3D Moving Objects in Dense Target Environments." *Proceedings of the 2013 IEEE Symposium on 3D User Interfaces (3DUI),* 119–122.

Osawa, N., X. Ren, and M. Suzuki. (2003). "Investigating Text Entry Strategies for an Immersive Virtual Environment." *Information* 6(5): 577–582.

Oviatt, S. (1999). "Mutual Disambiguation of Recognition Errors in a Multimodal Architecture." *Proceedings of the 1999 ACM Conference on Human Factors in Computing Systems (CHI '99),* 576–583.

Oviatt, S., and P. Cohen (2000). "Multimodal Interfaces That Process What Comes Naturally." *Communications of the ACM* 43(3): 45–51.

Paas, F., and J. van Merriënboer. (1993). "The Efficiency of Instructional Conditions: An Approach to Combine Mental Effort and Performance Measures." *Human Factors: The Journal of the Human Factors and Ergonomics Society* 35 (4): 737–743.

Pachella, R. (1974). "The Interpretation of Reaction Time in Information-Processing Research." In B. Kantowitz (ed), *Human Information Processing: Tutorials in Performance and Cognition*, 41–82.

Pai, D. (2003). "Multisensory Interaction: Real and Virtual." In P. Dario and R. Chatila (eds.), Robotics Research. The Eleventh International Symposium. Springer Tracts in Advanced Robotics, Vol. 15. Springer, Berlin, Heidelberg.

Pakkanen, T., and R. Raisamo. (2004). "Appropriateness of Foot Interaction for Non-Accurate Spatial Tasks." *Proceedings of CHI '04 Extended Abstracts on Human Factors in Computing Systems (CHI EA '04),* 1123–1126.

Pang, A. and C. M. Wittenbrink (1997). "Collaborative 3D Visualization with CSpray." *IEEE Computer Graphics and Applications* 17: 32–41.

Patterson, K., P. Nestor, and T. Rogers (2007). "Where Do You Know What You Know? The Representation of Semantic Knowledge in the Human Brain." *Nature Reviews Neuroscience* 8(12): 976–987.

Pausch, R., D. Proffitt, and G. Williams (1997). "Quantifying Immersion in Virtual Reality." *Proceedings of SIGGRAPH '97,* 13–18.

Pausch, R., J. Snoddy, R. Taylor, S. Watson, and E. Haseltine (1996). "Disney's Aladdin: First Steps toward Storytelling in Virtual Reality." *Proceedings of SIGGRAPH '96,* 193–203.

Pausch, R., T. Burnette, D. Brockway, and M. Weiblen (1995). "Navigation and Locomotion in Virtual Worlds via Flight into Hand-Held Miniatures." *Proceedings of SIGGRAPH '95,* 399–400.

Pausch, R., T. Crea, and M. Conway (1993). "A Literature Survey for Virtual Environments: Military Flight Simulator Visual Systems and Simulator Sickness." *Presence: Teleoperators and Virtual Environments* 1(3): 344–363.

Pavlov, I. P. (1927). *Conditioned Reflexes: An Investigation of the Physiological Activity of the Cerebral Cortex*. London: Oxford University Press.

Payne, J., Keir, P., Elgoyhen, J., Mclundie, M., Naef, M., Horner, M., and Anderson, P. (2006). "Gameplay Issues in the Design of Spatial 3d Gestures for Video Games." *Proceedings of ACM Conference on Human Factors in Computing Systems*, 1217–1222.

Peck, T. C., Fuchs, H., and Whitton, M. C. (2009). "Evaluation of Reorientation Techniques and Distractors for Walking in Large Virtual Environments." *IEEE Transactions on Visualization and Computer Graphics* 15(3): 383–394.

Pedro L., I. Alexandra, and B. Patrick (2015). "Impacto: Simulating Physical Impact by Combining Tactile Stimulation with Electrical Muscle Stimulation." In *Proceedings of the 28th Annual ACM Symposium on User Interface Software & Technology* (UIST '15). ACM, New York, NY, USA, 11–19.

Penfield, W., and T. Rasmussen. (1950). *The Cerebral Cortex of Man. A Clinical Study of Localization of Function*. New York: Macmillan.

Periverzov, F., and H. Ilieş (2015). "IDS: The Intent Driven Selection Method for Natural User Interfaces." *Proceedings of the 2015 IEEE Symposium on 3D User Interfaces (3DUI '15),* 121–128.

Perlin, K. (1998). "Quikwriting: Continuous Stylus-Based Text Entry." *Proceedings of the 1998 ACM Symposium on User Interface Software and Technology* (UIST '98), 215–216.

Perlin, K., S. Paxia, and J. Kollin (2000). "An Autostereoscopic Display." *Proceedings of SIGGRAPH 2000*, 319–326.

Péruch, P., M. May, and F. Wartenburg (1997). "Homing in Virtual Environments: Effects of Field of View and Path Layout." *Perception* 26: 301–312.

Pesyna Jr, K. M., Heath Jr, R. W., and Humphreys, T. E. (2014). "Centimeter Positioning with a Smartphone-Quality GNSS Antenna." *Proceedings of the 27th International Technical Meeting of the Satellite Division of the Institute of Navigation (ION GNSS 2014)*, Tampa, FL, 1568-1577.

Peterson, L., and M. Peterson. (1959). "Short-Term Retention of Individual Verbal Items." *Journal of Experimental Psychology*, 58(3): 193–198.

Pfeil, K., Koh, S., and LaViola, J. (2013). "Exploring 3D Gesture Metaphors for Interaction with Unmanned Aerial Vehicles." *Proceedings of ACM International conference on Intelligent User Interfaces*, 257–266.

Pfurtscheller, G., R. Leeb, C. Keinrath, D. Friedman, C. Neuper, C. Guger, and M. Slater (2006). "Walking from Thought." *Brain Research* 1071(1), 145–152.

Pheasant, Stephen, and Christine M. Haslegrave (2005). *Bodyspace: Anthropometry, Ergonomics and the Design of Work, Third Edition.* Boca Raton, FL: CRC Press.

Philbin, D. A., W. Ribarsky, N. Walker, and C. Ellis Hubbard. (1998) "Training in Virtual Environments: Analysis of Task Appropriateness." *Proceedings of the IEEE Virtual Reality Annual International Symposium*.

Phillips, L., Interrante, V., Kaeding, M., Ries, B., and L. Anderson. (2012). "Correlations between Physiological Response, Gait, Personality, and Presence in Immersive Virtual Environments." *Presence: Teleoperators and Virtual Environments* 21(3) (Spring 2012): 119–141.

Pick, S., A. Puika, T. Kuhlen. "SWIFTER: Design and Evaluation of a Speechbased Text Input Metaphor for Immersive Virtual Environments." *Proceedings of the 2016 IEEE Symposium on 3D User Interfaces (3DUI)*, 109–112.

Piekarski, W., and Thomas, B. (2001) "Tinmith-evo5—An Architecture for Supporting Mobile Augmented Reality Environments." *Proceedings of the IEEE and ACM Symposium on Augmented Reality*, 177–178.

Piekarski, W., and B. H. Thomas (2003). "Augmented Reality User Interfaces and Techniques for Outdoor Modelling." In *I3D 2003, ACM SIGGRAPH Symposium on Interactive 3D Graphics*, 28–30 April 2003, Monterey, CA, USA.

Pieraccini, R. (2012). *The Voice in the Machine: Building Computers That Understand Speech*. Cambridge, MA: MIT Press.

Pierce, J., A. Forsberg, M. Conway, S. Hong, R. Zeleznik, and M. Mine (1997). "Image Plane Interaction Techniques in 3D Immersive Environments." *Proceedings of the 1997 ACM Symposium on Interactive 3D Graphics (I3D '97)*, 39–44.

Pierce, J., B. Stearns, and R. Pausch (1999). "Voodoo Dolls: Seamless Interaction at the Multiple Scales in Virtual Environments." *Proceedings of the 1999 ACM Symposium on Interactive 3D Graphics (I3D '99)*, 141–145.

Pique, M. (1995). "Rotation Tools." In A. Glassner (ed.), *Graphics Gems 1*, 465–469. San Diego: Morgan Kaufman Publishers.

Polson, P., C. Lewis, J. Rieman, and C. Wharton (1992). Cognitive Walkthroughs: A Method for Theory-Based Evaluation of User Interfaces. *International Journal of Man-Machine Studies* 36: 741–773.

Posner, M., and S. Boies. (1971). "Components of Attention." *Psychological Review* 78(5): 391–408.

Posner, M., and Y. Cohen. (1984). "Components of Visual Orienting." *Attention and Performance* X 32: 531–556.

Poupyrev, I., and T. Ichikawa (1999). "Manipulating Objects in Virtual Worlds: Categorization and Empirical Evaluation of Interaction Techniques." *Journal of Visual Languages and Computing* 10(1): 19–35.

Poupyrev, I., D. Tan, M. Billinghurst, H. Kato, H. Regenbrecht, and N. Tetsutani (2002). "Developing a Generic Augmented-Reality Interface." *IEEE Computer* 35(3): 44–49.

Poupyrev, I., D. Tan, M. Billinghurst, H. Kato, H. Regenbrecht, and N. Tetsutani (2001). "Tiles: A Mixed Reality Authoring Interface." *Proceedings of INTERACT 2001,* 334–341.

Poupyrev, I., M. Billinghurst, S. Weghorst, and T. Ichikawa (1996). "The Go-Go Interaction Technique: Non-Linear Mapping for Direct Manipulation in VR." *Proceedings of the 1996 ACM Symposium on User Interface Software and Technology (UIST '96),* 79–80.

Poupyrev, I., N. Tomokazu, and S. Weghorst (1998). "Virtual Notepad: Handwriting in Immersive VR." *Proceedings of the 1998 IEEE Virtual Reality Annual International Symposium (VRAIS '98),* 126–132.

Poupyrev, I., R. Berry, J. Kurumisawa, K. Nakao, M. Billinghurst, C. Airola, H. Kato, T. Yonezawa, and L. Baldwin (2000). "Augmented Groove: Collaborative Jamming in Augmented Reality." *SIGGRAPH 2000 Conference Abstracts and Applications,* 77.

Poupyrev, I., S. Weghorst, and S. Fels (2000). "Non-Isomorphic 3D Rotational Interaction Techniques." *Proceedings of the 2000 ACM Conference on Human Factors in Computing Systems (CHI 2000),* 540–547.

Poupyrev, I., S. Weghorst, M. Billinghurst, and T. Ichikawa (1997). "A Framework and Testbed for Studying Manipulation Techniques for Immersive VR." *Proceedings of the 1997 ACM Symposium on Virtual Reality Software and Technology (VRST '97),* 21–28.

Poupyrev, I., S. Weghorst, M. Billinghurst, and T. Ichikawa (1998). "Egocentric Object Manipulation in Virtual Environments: Empirical Evaluation of Interaction Techniques." *Computer Graphics Forum, EUROGRAPHICS '98* 17(3): 41–52.

Poupyrev, I., S. Weghorst, T. Otsuka, and T. Ichikawa (1999). "Amplifying Rotations in 3D Interfaces." *Proceedings of the 1999 ACM Conference on Human Factors in Computing Systems (CHI '99),* 256–257.

Prachyabrued, M., and C. Borst (2012). "Virtual Grasp Release Method and Evaluation." *International Journal of Human-Computer Studies 70*(11): 828–848.

Preece, J., Y. Rogers, and H. Sharp (2002). *Interaction Design: Beyond Human-Computer Interaction.* New York: John Wiley and Sons.

Prince, S., A. Cheok, F. Farbiz, T. Williamson, N. Johnson, M. Billinghurst, and H. Kato (2002). "3-D Live: Real Time Interaction for Mixed Reality." *Proceedings of the ACM Conference on Computer Supported Cooperative Work,* 364–371.

Proctor, R., and K. Vu. (2010). "Cumulative Knowledge and Progress in Human Factors." *Annual Review of Psychology* 61: 623–651

Proctor, R., and K. Vu. (2012). "Selection and control of action." In G. Salvendy (ed.), *Handbook of Human Factors and Ergonomics*, Fourth Edition, 95–116. Hoboken, NJ, John Wiley & Sons.

Pulkki, V., (2001). "Spatial Sound Generation and Perception by Amplitude Panning Techniques." PhD Dissertation, Department of Electrical Engineering and Communications Engineering, Helsinki University of Technology.

Pulkki, V., and M. Karjalainen (2014). *Communication Acoustics: An Introduction to Speech, Audio and Psychoacoustics.* New York: John Wiley & Sons.

Qi, W., R. Taylor, C. Healey, and J. Martens (2006). "A Comparison of Immersive HMD, Fish Tank VR and Fish Tank with Haptics Displays for Volume Visualization." *Proceedings of the 3rd Symposium on Applied Perception in Graphics and Visualization (APGV '06)*: 51–58.

Qian, C., X. Sun, Y. Wei, X. Tang, and J. Sun (2014). "Realtime and Robust Hand Tracking from Depth." *Proceedings of the IEEE Conference on Computer Vision and Pattern Recognition (CVPR)* 1106–1113.

Ragan, E., C. Wilkes, D. A. Bowman, and T. Hollerer (2009). "Simulation of Augmented Reality Systems in Purely Virtual Environments." In *2009 IEEE Virtual Reality Conference*, IEEE, 2009. 287–288.

Ragan, E., D. Bowman, R. Kopper, C. Stinson, S. Scerbo, and R. McMahan (2015). "Effects of Field of View and Visual Complexity on Virtual Reality Training Effectiveness for a Visual Scanning Task." *IEEE Transactions on Visualization and Computer Graphics* (forthcoming).

Ragan, E., R. Kopper, P. Schuchardt, and D. Bowman (2013). "Studying the Effects of Stereo, Head Tracking, and Field of Regard on a Small-Scale Spatial Judgment Task." *IEEE Transactions on Visualization and Computer Graphics* 19(5): 886–896.

Raskar, R., G. Welch, and H. Fuchs (1998). "Spatial Augmented Reality." *Proceedings of the First IEEE Workshop on Augmented Reality*, 63–72.

Razzaque, S., D. Swapp, M. Slater, M. Whitton, and A. Steed (2002). "Redirected Walking in Place." *Proceedings of the 2002 Eurographics Workshop on Virtual Environments,* Eurographics Association, 123–130.

Regenbrecht, H., T. Schubert, and F. Friedman (1998). "Measuring the Sense of Presence and Its Relations to Fear of Heights in Virtual Environments." *International Journal of Human-Computer Interaction* 10(3): 233–250.

Reid, G., and T. Nygren. (1988). "The Subjective Workload Assessment Technique: A Scaling Procedure for Measuring Mental Workload." In P. A. Hancock and N. Meshkati (eds.), *Human Mental Workload,* 185–218. Amsterdam: Elsevier.

Rekimoto, J. (1998). "Matrix: A Realtime Object Identification and Registration Method for Augmented Reality." *Proceedings of Asia Pacific Computer Human Interaction (APCHI '98), 63–69.*

Rekimoto, J. (2002). Smartskin: An Infrastructure for Freehand Manipulation on Interactive Surfaces. In *Proceedings of the SIGCHI Conference on Human factors in Computing Systems*. ACM Press, 113–120.

Rekimoto, J., and K. Nagao (1995). "The World through the Computer: Computer Augmented Interaction with Real World Environments." *Proceedings of the 1995 ACM Symposium on User Interface Software and Technology (UIST '95),* 29–36.

Rekimoto, J., and M. Saitoh (1999). "Augmented Surfaces: A Spatially Continuous Work Space for Hybrid Computing Environments." *Proceedings of the 1999 ACM Conference on Human Factors in Computing Systems (CHI '99),* 378–385.

Ren, G., and O'Neill, E. (2013) "Freehand Gestural Text Entry for Interactive TV." Proceedings of the 11th European Conference on Interactive TV and Video, 121–130.

Renner, R. S., Velichkovsky, B. M., and Helmert, J. R. (2013). "The Perception of Egocentric Distances in Virtual Environments—A Review." *ACM Computing Surveys (CSUR)*, *46*(2): 23.

Rice, A. D., and J. W. Lartigue (2014). "Touch-Level Model (TLM): Evolving KLM-GOMS for Touchscreen and Mobile Devices." *Proceedings of the 2014 ACM Southeast Regional Conference,* 53.

Riecke, B., Feuereissen, D., Rieser, J., and T. McNamara. (2012). "Self-Motion Illusions (Vection) in VR – Are They Good for Anything?" *IEEE Virtual Reality 2012,* 35–38.

Riecke, B. E., H. A. Van Veen, and H. H. Bülthoff (2002). "Visual Homing Is Possible without Landmarks: A Path Integration Study in Virtual Reality." *Presence: Teleoperators and Virtual Environments* 11(5), 443–473.

Riecke, B., Feuereissen, D., and J. Rieser. (2009). "Auditory Self-Motion Simulation Is Facilitated by Haptic and Vibrational Cues Suggesting the Possibility of Actual Motion." *ACM Transactions on Applied Perception* 6(3): 1–22.

Riege, K., T. Holtkamper, G. Wesche, and B. Frohlich (2006). "The Bent Pick Ray: An Extended Pointing Technique for Multi-User Interaction." *Proceedings of the 2006 IEEE Symposium on 3D User Interfaces (3DUI '06)*, 62–65.

Riener, A. (2012). "Gestural Interaction in Vehicular Applications." *Computer* 45(4): 42–47.

Rivers, A., and D. James (2007). "FastLSM: Fast Lattice Shape Matching for Robust Real-Time Deformation." *ACM Transactions on Graphics (TOG)* 26(3): 82.

Robertson, G., M. Czerwinski, and M. van Dantzich (1997). "Immersion in Desktop Virtual Reality." *Proceedings of the 1997 ACM Symposium on User Interface Software and Technology (UIST '97),* 11–19.

Rosenfeld, R., D. Olsen, and A. Rudnicky (2001). "Universal Speech Interfaces." *Interactions* 8(6): 33–44.

Rosson, M., and J. Carroll (2002). *Usability Engineering: Scenario-Based Development of Human Computer Interaction*. San Francisco: Morgan Kaufmann Publishers.

Roussou, M., Oliver, M., and Slater, M. (2008). "Exploring activity theory as a tool for evaluating interactivity and learning in virtual environments." *Cognition, Technology & Work* 10(2): 141–153.

Rubinshtein, S. L. (1946). *Foundations of General Psychology*. Moscow: Academic Pedagogical Science.

Ruddle, R., S. Payne, and D. Jones (1998). "Navigating Large-Scale 'Desktop' Virtual Buildings: Effects of Orientation Aids and Familiarity." *Presence: Teleoperators and Virtual Environments* 7(2): 179–192.

Ruddle, R., S. Payne, and D. Jones (1999). "The Effects of Maps on Navigation and Search Strategies in Very-Large-Scale Virtual Environments." *Journal of Experimental Psychology* 5(1): 54–75.

Sachs, E., A. Roberts, and D. Stoops (1991). "3-Draw: A Tool for Designing 3D Shapes." *IEEE Computer Graphics and Applications* 11(6): 18–26.

Salvendy, G. (1997). *The Handbook of Human Factors and Ergonomics*. New York: John Wiley and Sons.

Salvendy, G. (2012). *Handbook of Human Factors and Ergonomics*. New York: John Wiley and Sons.

Saponas, T., D. Tan, D. Morris, J. Turner, and J. Landay (2010). "Making Muscle-Computer Interfaces More Practical." *Proceedings of the SIGCHI Conference on Human Factors in Computing Systems (CHI 2010)*, 851–854.

Sanders, A. (1998). *Elements of Human Performance*. Mahwah, NJ: Lawrence Erlbaum Associates.

Saponas, T., D. Tan, D. Morris, and R. Balakrishnan (2008). "Demonstrating the Feasibility of Using Forearm Electromyography for Muscle-Computer Interfaces." *Proceedings of the SIGCHI Conference on Human Factors in Computing Systems (CHI '08)*, 515–524.

Savage, V., S. Follmer, J. Li, and B. Hartmann (2015). "Makers' Marks: Physical Markup for Designing and Fabricating Functional Objects." *Proceedings of the 28th Annual ACM Symposium on User Interface Software & Technology (UIST '15)*, 103–108.

Savage, V., S. Follmer, N., Sawant, C. Scharver, J. LiLeigh, A. Johnson, G. Reinhart, E. Creel, S. Batchu, S. Bailey, and B. Hartmann, R. Grossman (2015). "The Tele-Immersive Data Explorer: A Distributed Architecture Makers' Marks: Physical Markup for Designing and Fabricating Functional Objects." *Proceedings of the 28th Annual ACM Symposium on User Interface Software & Technology*, 103–108, 2015.

Sawant, N., C. Scharver, J. Leigh, A. Johnson, G. Reinhart, E. Creel, S. Batchu, S. Bailey, and R. Grossman (2000). "The tele-immersive data explorer: A distributed architecture for collaborative interactive visualization of large data-sets." In *4th International Immersive Projection Technology Workshop, Ames, Iowa*.

Schall G., Mendez E., Kruijff E., Veas E., Junghanns S., Reitinger B., and D. Schmalstieg (2009) "Handheld Augmented Reality for Underground Infrastructure Visualization." *Personal and Ubiquitous Computing* 13: 281–291.

Schell, J., and J. Shochet (2001). "Designing Interactive Theme Park Rides." *IEEE Computer Graphics and Applications* 21(4): 11–13.

Schkolne, S., M. Pruett, and P. Schröder (2001). "Surface Drawing: Creating Organic 3D Shapes with the Hand and Tangible Tools." *Proceedings of the 2001 ACM Conference on Human Factors in Computing Systems (CHI 2001)*, 261–268.

Schmalstieg, D., and T. Höllerer (2016). *Augmented Reality: Principles and Practice*. Addison-Wesley Professional.

Schmalstieg, D., and Wagner, D. (2007). "Experiences with Handheld Augmented Reality." *Sixth IEEE and ACM International Symposium on Mixed and Augmented Reality, 2007. ISMAR 2007*, 3–18.

Schmalstieg, D., A. Fuhrmann, Z. Szalavári, and M. Gervautz (1998). "Studierstube: An Environment for Collaboration in Augmented Reality." *Proceedings of the Collaborative Virtual Environment '96 Workshop.*

Schmalstieg, D., M. Encarnação, and Z. Szalavári (1999). "Using Transparent Props for Interaction with the Virtual Table." *Proceedings of the 1999 ACM Symposium on Interactive 3D Graphics (I3D '99)*, 147–154.

Schmandt, C. (1983). "Spatial Input/Display Correspondence in a Stereoscopic Computer Graphic Work Station." *Proceedings of SIGGRAPH '83,* 253–262.

Schultheis, U., J. Jerald, F. Toledo, A. Yoganandan, and P. Mlyniec (2012). "Comparison of a Two-handed Interface to a Wand Interface and a Mouse Interface for Fundamental 3D Tasks." *IEEE Symposium on 3D User Interfaces* (3DUI 2012), 117–124.

Schulze, J., A. Forsberg, A. Kleppe, R. Zeleznik and D. Laidlaw (2005). "Characterizing the Effect of Level of Immersion on a 3D Marking Task." *Proceedings of HCI International*, Vol. 5.

Schwaiger, M., T. Thuimmel, and H. Ulbrich (2007). "Cyberwalk: An Advanced Prototype of a Belt Array Platform." *Proceedings of the 2007 IEEE International Workshop on Haptic, Audio and Visual Environments and Games (HAVE '07)*, 50–55.

Schwarz, L., A. Bigdelou, and N. Navab (2011). "Learning Gestures for Customizable Human Computer Interaction in the Operating Room." *Proceedings of the Medical Image Computing and Computer-Assisted Intervention*, 129–136.

Schwerdtner, A., and H. Heidrich (1998). "Dresden 3D Display (D4D)." *Stereoscopic Display and Virtual Reality Systems V,* 3295: 203–210.

Scriven, M. (1967). "The Methodology of Evaluation." In R. Stake (ed), *Perspectives of Curriculum Evaluation,* 39–83. American Educational Research Association.

Sedwick, H. (1988). "Space Perception." In K. Boff, L. Kaufman, and J. Thomas (eds.), *Handbook of Perception and Human Performance,* Vol. 1, 1–21. New York: John Wiley and Sons.

Seibel, R. (1963). "Discrimination Reaction Time for a 1,023-Alternative Task." *Journal of Experimental Psychology* 66: 215–226.

Sekuler, R., and R. Blake (1994). *Perception.* New York: McGraw-Hill.

Sekuler, R., Sekuler, A., and R. Lau. (1997). "Sound Alters Visual Motion Perception." *Nature.* 385(6614): 308.

Senders, J., and N. Moray. (1991). *Human Error: Cause, Prediction, and Reduction*. Boca Raton, FL: Lawrence Erlbaum Associates.

Senders, J., J. Christensen, and R. Sabeh (1955). "Comparison of Single Operator Performance with Team Performance in a Tracking Task." Aero Medical Laboratory, Wright Air Development Center.

Serruya, M., N. Hatsopoulos, L. Paninski, M. Fellows, and J. Donoghue (2002). "Instant Neural Control of a Movement Signal." *Nature* 416: 141–142.

Sharit, J. (2012). "Human Error and Human Reliability Analysis." In Galvendy, S. (ed), *Handbook of Human Factors and Ergonomics,* Fourth Edition, 734–800. Hoboken, NJ: Wiley.

Shaw, C., and M. Green (1994). "Two-Handed Polygonal Surface Design." *Proceedings of the 1994 ACM Symposium on User Interface Software and Technology* (UIST '94), 205–212.

Shepard, R., and J. Metzler (1971). "Mental Rotation of Three-Dimensional Objects." *Science* 171: 701–703.

Shepherd G. (2012). *Neurogastronomy: How the Brain Creates Flavor and Why It Matters*. New York: Columbia University Press.

Sheridan, T. (2008). "Risk, Human Error, and System Resilience: Fundamental Ideas." *Human Factors.* 50(3): 418–426.

Sherman, B., and A. Craig (2003). *Understanding Virtual Reality.* San Francisco, CA: Morgan Kauffman Publishers.

Sherrington C.S. 1907. "On the Proprioceptive System, Especially in Its Reflex Aspect." *Brain* 29 (4): 467–85.

Shih, Yi-Hsuen, and Min Liu (2007). "The Importance of Emotional Usability." *Journal of Educational Technology Systems* 36(2):: 203–218.

Shimojo S., and L. Shams, (2001). "Sensory Modalities Are Not Separate Modalities: Plasticity and Interactions." *Current Opinion in Neurobiology* 11(4): 505–509.

Shneiderman, B. (1996). "The Eyes Have It: A Task by Data Type Taxonomy for Information Visualizations." *Proceedings of IEEE Symposium on Visual Languages, 1996,* 336–343.

Shneiderman, B. (1998). *Designing the User Interface: Strategies for Effective Human–Computer Interaction,* Third Edition Boston: Addison-Wesley.

Shneiderman, B. (2000). "The Limits of Speech Recognition. *Communications of the ACM* 43(9): 63–65.

Shneiderman, B. (2003). "Why Not Make Interfaces Better Than 3D Reality?" *IEEE Computer Graphics and Applications* 23(6): 12–15.

Shneiderman, Ben and Catherine Plaisant (2009). *Designing the User Interface,* Fifth Edition. Boston: Addison-Wesley.

Shoemake, K. (1985). "Animating Rotations with Quaternion Curves." *Proceedings of SIGGRAPH '85,* 245–254.

Shoemake, K. (1992). "ARCBALL: A User Interface for Specifying Three-Dimensional Orientation Using a Mouse." *Proceedings of Graphics Interface (GI '92),* 151–156.

Shotton, J., T. Sharp, A. Kipman, A. Fitzgibbon, M. Finocchio, A. Blake, M. Cook, and R. Moore. (2011). "Real-Time Human Pose Recognition in Parts from Single Depth Images." *Communications of the ACM,*56(1):116–124.

Sidorakis, N., G. Koulieris, and K. Mania (2015). "Binocular Eye-Tracking for the Control of a 3D Immersive Multimedia User Interface." *Proceedings of the IEEE 1st Workshop on Everyday Virtual Reality (WEVR),* 15–18.

Siegel, A. (1981). "The Externalization of Cognitive Maps by Children and Adults: In Search of Ways to Ask Better Questions." In L. S. Liben, A. H. Patterson, and N. Newcombe (eds.), *Spatial Representation and Behavior across the Life Span: Theory and Application,* 167–194. New York: Academic Press.

Siegel, A., and Sapru, H. (2010). *Essential Neuroscience*. Baltimore, MD: Lippincott Williams & Wilkins.

Siegl, C., J. Süßmuth, F. Bauer, and M. Stamminger (2014). "Evaluating the Usability of Recent Consumer-Grade 3D Input Devices." *2014 International Conference on Computer Graphics Theory and Applications (GRAPP),* 1–7.

Simeone, A. (2016). "Indirect Touch Manipulation for Interaction with Stereoscopic Displays." *Proceedings of the 2016 IEEE Symposium on 3D User Interfaces (3DUI '16),* 13–22.

Simon, A. and M. Doulis (2004). "NOYO: 6DOF Elastic Rate Control for Virtual Environments.: In *Proceedings of the ACM Symposium* on Virtual *Reality Software* and *Technology* (VRST '04). ACM, New York, NY, USA, 178 181.

Simon, A., and B. Fröhlich (2003). "The YoYo: A Handheld Device Combining Elastic and Isotonic Input." *Proceedings of INTERACT 2003,* 303–310.

Simons, D., and Rensink, R. (2005). "Change Blindness: Past, Present, and Future." *Trends in Cognitive Sciences* 9: 16–20.

Singer, M., Witmer, B., and J. Bailey. (1994). "Development of 'Presence' Measures for Virtual Environments." Poster presented at the Human Factors Society 38th Annual Meeting, Nashville, TN.

Singh, G., Swan II, J. Jones, and S. Ellis. (2012). "Depth Judgments by Reaching and Matching in Near-Field Augmented Reality." *Poster Compendium, Proceedings of IEEE Virtual Reality,* 165–166.

Siochi, A., and D. Hix (1991). "A Study of Computer-Supported User Interface Evaluation Using Maximal Repeating Pattern Analysis." *Proceedings of the 1991 ACM Conference on Human Factors in Computing Systems (CHI '91)*, 301–305.

Slater, M., B. Lotto, M. M. Arnold, and M. V. Sanchez-Vives (2009). "How We Experience Immersive Virtual Environments: The Concept of Presence and Its Measurement. *Anuario de psicología/The UB Journal of Psychology* 40(2): 193–210.

Slater, M., and Usoh, M. (1993). "Representations Systems, Perceptual Position, and Presence in Immersive Virtual Environments." *Presence: Teleoperators and Virtual Environments*, 2(3): 221–233.

Slater, M., B. Spanlang, and D. Corominas (2010). "Simulating Virtual Environments within Virtual Environments as the Basis for a Psychophysics of Presence." *ACM Transactions on Graphics*, 29(4): Article 92, 9 pp.

Slater, M., M. Usoh, and A. Steed (1994). "Depth of Presence in Virtual Environments." *Presence: Teleoperators and Virtual Environments* 3(2): 130–144.

Slater, M., M. Usoh, and A. Steed (1995). "Taking Steps: The Influence of a Walking Technique on Presence in Virtual Reality." *ACM Transactions on Computer-Human Interaction* 2(3): 201–219.

Smith, E., and S. Kosslyn. (2013). *Cognitive Psychology*. Pearson Education.

Smith, R. (1987). "Experiences with Alternative Reality Kit: An Example of Tension between Literalism and Magic." *IEEE Computer Graphics and Applications* 7(8): 42–50.

Smith, T., and K. Smith (1987). Feedback-Control Mechanisms of Human Behavior. In G. Salvendy (ed.), *Handbook of Human Factors*, 251–293. New York: John Wiley & Sons.

Sodhi, R., I. Poupyrev, M. Glisson, and A. Israr (2013). "AIREAL: Interactive Tactile Experiences in Free Air." *ACM Transactions on Graphics (TOG) – SIGGRAPH 2013 Conference Proceedings*, Article 134: 10 pages.

Snow, M., and R. Williges (1998). "Empirical Models Based on Free-Modulus Magnitude Estimation of Perceived Presence in Virtual Environments." *Human Factors* 40(3): 386–402.

Song, D., and M. Norman (1993). "Nonlinear Interactive Motion Control Techniques for Virtual Space Navigation." *Proceedings of the 1993 IEEE Virtual Reality Annual International Symposium (VRAIS '93)*, 111–117.

Sousa Santos, B., P. Dias, A. Pimentel, J. Baggerman, C. Ferreira, S. Silva, and J. Madeira (2009). "Head-Mounted Display versus Desktop for 3D Navigation in Virtual Reality: A User Study." *Multimedia Tools and Applications* 41(1): 161–181.

Sridhar, S., F. Mueller, A. Oulasvirta, and C. Theobalt (2015). "Fast and Robust Hand Tracking Using Detection-Guided Optimization." *Proceedings of the IEEE Conference on Computer Vision and Pattern Recognition (CVPR)*, 3213–3221.

Srinivasan, M., and J. Chen (1993). "Human Performance in Controlling Normal Forces of Contact with Rigid Objects." *Proceedings of* Advances *in Robotics, Mechatronics, and Haptic Interfaces,* 119–125.

Staal, M. (2004). "Stress, Cognition, and Human Performance: A Literature Review and Conceptual Framework." NASA Technical Memorandum—2004–212824.

Stanney, K., and L. Reeves (2000). "COVE Evaluation Report." Orlando, Florida, Naval Air Warfare Center, Training Systems Division.

Stanney, K., M. Mollaghasemi, and L. Reeves (2000). "Development of MAUVE, The Multi-Criteria Assessment of Usability for Virtual Environments System." Orlando, Florida, Naval Air Warfare Center, Training Systems Division.

Stanney, K., R. Mourant, and R. Kennedy (1998). "Human Factors Issues in Virtual Environments: A Review of the Literature." *Presence: Teleoperators and Virtual Environments* 7(4): 327–351.

Starner, T., Leibe, B., Singletary, B., and Pair, J. (2000). "Mind-Warping: Towards Creating a Compelling Collaborative Augmented Reality Game." *Proceedings of the ACM International Conference on Intelligent User Interfaces*, 256–259.

Starner, T., J. Weaver, and A. Pentland (1998). "Real-Time American Sign Language Recognition Using Desk and Wearable Computer Based Video." *IEEE Transactions on Pattern Analysis and Machine Intelligence* 20(12): 1371–1375.

Stassen, H., and G. Smets (1995). "Telemanipulation and Telepresence." *Proceedings of the 6th IFAC/IFIP/IFORS/IEA Symposium on Analysis, Design, and Evaluation of Man-Machine Systems*, 13–23.

State, A., K. P. Keller, and H. Fuchs (2005). "Simulation-Based Design and Rapid Prototyping of a Parallax-Free, Orthoscopic Video See-Through Head-Mounted Display." In *Proceedings of the 4th IEEE/ACM International Symposium on Mixed and Augmented Reality* (ISMAR '05). IEEE Computer Society, Washington, DC, USA, 28–31.

State, A., M. Livingston, G. Hirota, W. Garrett, M. Whitton, H. Fuchs, and E. Pisano (1996). "Technologies for Augmented Reality Systems: Realizing Ultrasound-Guided Needle Biopsies." *Proceedings of SIGGRAPH '96*, 439–446.

Stavness, S., B. Lam, and S. Fels (2010). "pCubee: A Perspective-Corrected Handheld Cubic Display." *Proceedings of the SIGCHI Conference on Human Factors in Computing Systems* (CHI '10), 1381–1390.

Steck, S., and H. Mallot (2000). "The Role of Global and Local Landmarks in Virtual Environment Navigation." *Presence: Teleoperators and Virtual Environments* 9(1): 69–83.

Steed, A., and S. Julier (2013). "Design and Implementation of an Immersive Virtual Reality System Based on a Smartphone Platform." *IEEE Symposium on 3D User Interfaces (3DUI 2013)*, 43–46.

Steed, A., and J. Tromp (1998). "Experiences with the Evaluation of CVE Applications." *Proceedings of Collaborative Virtual Environments 1998*, Manchester, UK.

Stefani, O., and J. Rauschenbach (2003). "3D Input Devices and Interaction Concepts for Optical Tracking in Immersive Environments." *Proceedings of Immersive Projection Technology and Virtual Environments 2003*, 317–318.

Steinicke, F., Bruder, G., Jerald, J., Frenz, H., and Lappe, M. (2010). "Estimation of Detection Thresholds for Redirected Walking Techniques." *IEEE Transactions on Visualization and Computer Graphics* 16(1): 17–27.

Steinicke, F., D. Keefe, A. Krüger, J. Rivière, and H. Benko (2013). "Foreword" to the Special Section on Touching the 3rd Dimension. *Computers & Graphics*, 37(3): A1–A2.

Steinicke, F., K. Hinrichs, J. Schöning, and A. Krüger (2008). "Multi-Touching 3D Data: Towards Direct Interaction in Stereoscopic Display Environments Coupled with Mobile Devices." *Proceedings of the AVI Workshop on Designing Multi-Touch Interaction Techniques for Coupled Public and Private Displays*, 46–49.

Steinicke, F., Visell, Y., Campos, J., and Lécuyer, A. (2013). *Human Walking in Virtual Environments*. New York: Springer.

Stellmach, S., and R. Dachselt (2012). "Looking at 3D User Interfaces." *Proceedings of the CHI 2012 Workshop on The 3rd Dimension of CHI (3DCHI)*, 95–98.

Stephenson, N. (1992). *Snow Crash*. Bantam Books.

Stevens, A., and P. Coupe (1978). "Distortions in Judged Spatial Relations." *Cognitive Psychology* 10: 422–437.

Stiles, R., L. McCarthy, A. Munro, Q. Pizzini, L. Johnson, and J. Rickel (1996). "Virtual Environments for Shipboard Training." *Intelligent Ships Symposium*.

Stoakley, R., M. Conway, and R. Pausch (1995). "Virtual Reality on a WIM: Interactive Worlds in Miniature." *Proceedings of the 1995 ACM Conference on Human Factors in Computing Systems (CHI '95)*, 265–272.

Stoev, S., and D. Schmalstieg (2002). Application and taxonomy of through-the-lens techniques. *Proceedings of the 2002 ACM Symposium on Virtual Reality Software and Technology (VRST '02)*, 57–64.

Stone, D., C. Jarrett, M. Woodroffe, and S. Minocha (2005). *User Interface Design and Evaluation*. San Francisco, CA: Morgan Kaufmann.

Storms, R., and M. Zyda. (2000). "Interactions in Perceived Quality of Auditory-Visual Displays." *Presence: Teleoperators and Virtual Environments* 9(6): 557–580.

Strothoff, S., D. Valkov, and K. Hinrichs (2011). "Triangle Cursor: Interactions with Objects Above the Tabletop." *Proceedings of the ACM International Conference on Interactive Tabletops and Surfaces*, 111–119.

Steuer, J. (1992). "Defining Virtual Reality: Dimensions Determining Telepresence." *Journal of Communication* 42(4): 73–93.

Stuart, R. (1996). *The Design of Virtual Environments*. McGraw-Hill.

Sturman, D. J., and Zeltzer, D. (1994). "A Survey of Glove-Based Input." *IEEE Computer Graphics and Applications* 14(1): 30–39.

Sukan, M., S. Feiner, B. Tversky, and S. Energin (2012). "Quick Viewpoint Switching for Manipulating Virtual Objects in Hand-Held Augmented Reality using Stored Snapshots." *Proceedings of the 2012 IEEE International Symposium on Mixed and Augmented Reality (ISMAR '12)*, 217–226.

Sullivan, A. (2003). A Solid-State Multi-planar Volumetric Display. *Society for Information Display Digest*, 354–356.

Suma, E. A., Lipps, Z., Finkelstein, S., Krum, D. M., and Bolas, M. (2012). "Impossible Spaces: Maximizing Natural Walking in Virtual Environments with Self-Overlapping Architecture." *IEEE Transactions on Visualization and Computer Graphics* 18(4), 555–564.

Sundstedt, V. (2010). "Gazing at Games: Using Eye Tracking to Control Virtual Characters." In *ACM SIGGRAPH 2010 Courses (SIGGRAPH '10)*. ACM, New York, NY, USA, Article 5, 160 pages.

Sutherland, I. (1968). "A Head-Mounted Three-Dimensional Display." *Proceedings of the Fall Joint Computer Conference*, 757–764.

Sutherland, I. (1965). "The Ultimate Display." *Proceedings of the IFIP Congress*, 505–508.

Swain, A., and H. Guttman. (1983). *Handbook of Human Reliability Analysis with Emphasis on Nuclear Power Plant Applications*. NUREG/CR-1278 (Washington D.C.).

Swan, J., Gabbard, J., Hix, D., Schulman, R., and K. Kim (2003). "A Comparative Study of User Performance in a Map-Based Virtual Environment." *Proceedings of IEEE Virtual Reality 2003*, 259–266.

Swapp, D., J. Williams, and A. Steed (2010). "The Implementation of a Novel Walking Interface within an Immersive Display." *Proceedings of the 2010 IEEE Symposium on 3D User Interfaces (3DUI '10)*, 71–74.

Sweller, J. (1994). "Cognitive Load Theory, Learning Difficulty, and Instructional Design." *Learning and Instruction* 4(4): 295–312.

Szalavári, Z., D. Schmalstieg, A. Fuhrmann, and M. Gervautz (1997). "Studierstube: An Environment for Collaboration in Augmented Reality." *Virtual Reality: Systems, Development and Applications* 3(1): 37–49.

Takahasi, M., Fujii, M., Naemura, M., and Satoh, S. (2013). "Human Gesture Recognition System for TV Viewing Using Time-of-Flight Camera." *Multimedia Tools and Applications* 62 (3): 761–783.

Takala, T., and M. Matveinen (2014). "Full Body Interaction in Virtual Reality with Affordable Hardware." *Proceedings of the 2014 IEEE Virtual Reality (VR) Conference*, IEEE, 157.

Talvas, A., M. Marchal, and A. Lécuyer (2013). "The God-Finger Method for Improving 3D Interaction with Virtual Objects through Simulation of Contact Area." *Proceedings of the 2013 IEEE Symposium on 3D User Interfaces (3DUI '13)*, 111–114.

Tan, D., K. Stefanucci, D. Proffitt, and R. Pausch (2002). "Kinesthetic Cues Aid Spatial Memory." *Proceedings of the 2002 ACM Conference on Human Factors in Computing Systems, Extended Abstracts (CHI 2002)*, ACM Press, 806–807.

Tang, Z., G. Rong, X. Guo, and B. Prabhakaran (2010). "Streaming 3D Shape Deformations in Collaborative Virtual Environment." *IEEE Virtual Reality* 2010: 183–186.

Tannen, R. (2009). "Ergonomics for Interaction Designers: Part 3." *Designing for Humans*. January 25, 2009. URL: http://www.designingforhumans.com/idsa/2009/01/ergonomics-for-interaction-designers-part-3.html

Tate, D., Sibert, L., and T. King. (1997). "Using Virtual Environments to Train Firefighters." *Computer Graphics and Applications* 17(6): 23–29.

Tatzgern, M., D. Kalkofen, and D. Schmalstieg (2013). "Dynamic Compact Visualizations for Augmented Reality." *Proceedings of the 2013 IEEE Virtual Reality (VR) Conference*, 3–6.

Taylor, J. (1997). *Introduction to Error Analysis, the Study of Uncertainties in Physical Measurements*, Vol. 1.

Teather, R., and W. Stuerzlinger (2008). "Assessing the Effects of Orientation and Device on (Constrained) 3D Movement Techniques." *IEEE Symposium on 3D User Interfaces (3DUI 2008)*, 43–50.

Teather, R. J., A. Pavlovych, W. Stuerzlinger, and I. S. MacKenzie (2009). "Effects of Tracking Technology, Latency, and Spatial Jitter on Object Movement." In *Proceedings of the IEEE Symposium on 3D User Interfaces*, IEEE, 43–50.

Templeman, J., P. Denbrook, and L. Sibert (1999). "Virtual Locomotion: Walking in Place through Virtual Environments." *Presence: Teleoperators and Virtual Environments* 8(6): 598–617.

Ten Hoope, G., Akerboom, S., and E. Raymakers. (1982). "Vibrotactile Choice Reaction Time, Tactile Receptor Systems and Ideamotor Compatibility." *Acta Psychologica* 50: 143–157.

Teplan, M. (2002). "Fundamentals of EEG measurement." In *Measurement Science Review*, Section 2, Vol. 2, 1–11.

Thibaut, J., G. Bailly, E. Lecolinet, G. Casiez, and M. Teyssier. 2016. "Desktop Orbital Camera Motions Using Rotational Head Movements." In Proceedings of the 2016 Symposium on Spatial User Interaction (SUI '16). ACM, New York, NY, USA, 139–148.

Thomas, B., S. Tyerman, and K. Grimmer (1998). "Evaluation of Text Input Mechanisms for Wearable Computers." *Virtual Reality: Research, Development, and Applications* 3: 187–199.

Thomas G. Zimmerman, Jaron Lanier, Chuck Blanchard, Steve Bryson, and Young Harvill (1986). "A Hand Gesture Interface Device." In *Proceedings of the SIGCHI/GI Conference on Human Factors in Computing Systems and Graphics Interface* (CHI '87), John M. Carroll and Peter P. Tanner (eds.), 189–192. ACM, New York, NY, USA.

Thomas, J. C., and W. A. Kellogg (1989). "Minimizing Ecological Gaps in Interface Design." (IEEE) *Software* 6(1): 78–86.

Thorndyke, P., and B. Hayes-Roth (1982). "Differences in Spatial Knowledge Obtained from Maps and Navigation." *Cognitive Psychology* 14: 560–589.

Tidwell, M., R. Johnston, D. Melville, and T. Furness (1995). "The Virtual Retinal Display: A Retinal Scanning Imaging System." *Proceedings of Virtual Reality World '95*, 325–333.

Tlauka, M., and P. Wilson (1996). "Orientation Free Representations of Navigation through a Computer-Simulated Environment." *Journal of Environmental Psychology* 28(5): 305–313.

Torkington J, Smith S., Rees, B., and A. Darzi. 2001. "Skill Transfer from Virtual Reality to a Real Laparoscopic Task." *Surgical Endoscopy* . 15(10): 1076–1079.

Treisman, A., and G. Gelade. (1980). "A Feature-Integration Theory of Attention." *Cognitive Psychology*. 12(1):97–136.

Tsang, M., G. Fitzmaurice, G. Kurtenbach, A. Khan, and B. Buxton (2002). "BOOM Chameleon: Simultaneous Capture of 3D Viewpoint, Voice, and Gesture Annotations on a Spatially Aware Display." *Proceedings of the 2002 ACM Symposium on User Interface Software and Technology (UIST 2002)*, 111–120.

Tufte, E. (1990). *Envisioning Information*. Cheshire, CN: Graphics Press.

Turk, M., and Robertson,G. (2000). "Perceptual User Interfaces – An Introduction. *Communications of the ACM* 43(3): 32–34.

Turk, M., and V. Fragoso (2015). "Computer Vision for Mobile Augmented Reality." In G. Hua and X.-S. Hua (eds.), *Mobile Cloud Visual Media Computing*, 3–42.

Ulinski, A., Z. Wartell, P. Goolkasian, E. Suma, and L. Hodges (2009). "Selection Performance Based on Classes of Bimanual Actions." *Proceedings of the 2009 IEEE Symposium on 3D User Interfaces (3DUI '09)*, 51–58.

Ulinski, A., Zanbaka, C., Wartell, Z., Goolkasian, P., and Hodges, L. F. (2007). "Two Handed Selection Techniques for Volumetric Data." *2007 IEEE Symposium on 3D User Interfaces*, 107–114.

Ullmer, B., and H. Ishii (1997). "The metaDesk: Models and Prototypes for Tangible User Interfaces." *Proceedings of the 1997 ACM Symposium on User Interface Software and Technology (UIST '97)*, 223–232.

Ullmer, B., and H. Ishii (2001). "Emerging Frameworks for Tangible User Interfaces." In J. Carroll (ed.), *Human-Computer Interaction in the New Millennium*, 579–601. Addison-Wesley.

Ullrich, S., and Torsten Kuhlen (2012). "Haptic Palpation for Medical Simulation in Virtual Environments." *IEEE Transactions on Visualization and Computer Graphics* 18(4): 617–625.

Underkoffler, J., and H. Ishii (1998). "Illuminating Light: An Optical Design Tool with a Luminous-Tangible Interface." *Proceedings of the 1998 ACM Conference on Human Factors in Computing Systems (CHI '98)*, 542–549.

Usoh, M., E. Catena, S. Arman, and M. Slater (2000). "Using Presence Questionnaires in Reality." *Presence: Teleoperators and Virtual Environments* 9(5): 497–503.

Usoh, M., K. Arthur, M. Whitton, R. Bastos, A. Steed, M. Slater, and F. Brooks Jr. (1999). "Walking > Walking-in-Place > Flying in Virtual Environments." *Proceedings of SIGGRAPH '99*, 359–364.

van Dam, A. (1997). "Post-WIMP User Interfaces: The Human Connection." *Communication of the ACM* 40(2): 63–67.

van Dam, A., A. Forsberg, D. Laidlaw, J. LaViola, and R. Simpson (2000). "Immersive VR for Scientific Visualization: A Progress Report." *IEEE Computer Graphics and Applications* 20(6): 26–52.

Vanacken, L., T. Grossman, and K. Coninx (2007). Exploring the effects of environment density and target visibility on object selection in 3D virtual environments. *Proceedings of the 2007 IEEE Symposium on 3D User Interfaces (3DUI '07)*, IEEE, 117–124.

Vasylevska, K., Kaufmann, H., Bolas, M., and Suma, E. A. (2013). "Flexible Spaces: Dynamic Layout Generation for Infinite Walking in Virtual Environments." In *2013 IEEE Symposium on 3D User Interfaces (3DUI)*, 39–42.

Veas, E., and E. Kruijff. (2008). "Vesp'R—Design and Evaluation of a Handheld AR Device." *Proceedings of the IEEE and ACM International Symposium on Mixed and Augmented Reality*, 43–52.

Veas, E., Grasset, R., Ferencik, I, Gruenewald, T., and D. Schmalstieg (2013). Mobile Augmented Reality for Environmental Monitoring. *Personal and Ubiquitous Computing 17 (7), 1515–1531.*

Veas, E., Grasset, R., Kruijff, E., and D. Schmalstieg (2012). "Extended Overview Techniques for Outdoor Augmented Reality." *IEEE Transactions on Visualization and Computer Graphics* 18(4): 565–572.

Veas, E., Kruijff, E. (2010) "Handheld Devices for Mobile Augmented Reality. *Proceedings of the 9th ACM International Conference on Mobile and Ubiquitous Multimedia*. DOI 10.1145/1899475.1899478

Veas, E., Mulloni, A., Kruijff, E., Regenbrecht, H., and D. Schmalstieg. (2010). "Techniques for View Transition in Multi-Camera Outdoor Environments." *Proceedings of Graphics Interface 2010 (GI2010)*, Ottawa, Canada, 193–200.

Vidulich, M., and G. McMillan. (2000). "The Global Implicit Measure: Evaluation of Metrics for Cockpit Adaptation." In P. McCabe, M., Hanson, and S. Robertson (eds.), *Contemporary Economics 2000*, 75–80. London: Taylor and Francis.

Vidulich, M., and P. Tsang. (2012). "Mental Workload and Situation Awareness." In S. Galvendy (ed), *Handbook of Human Factors and Ergonomics*, Fourth Edition. New York: John Wiley & Sons, 243–273.

Viirre, E. (1994). "A Survey of Medical Issues and Virtual Reality Technology." Virtual Reality World, 16–20.

Villarejo, M., Zapirain, B., and A. Zorrilla (2012). "A Stress Sensor Based on Galvanic Skin Response (GSR) Controlled by ZigBee." *Sensors* (Basel) 12(5): 6075–6101.

Vinson, N. (1999). "Design Guidelines for Landmarks to Support Navigation in Virtual Environments." *Proceedings of the 1999 ACM Conference on Human Factors in Computing Systems (CHI '99)*, 278–285.

Vitevitch. M. (2003). "Change Deafness: The Inability to Detect Changes Between Two Voices." *Journal of Experimental Psychology: Human Perception and Performance* 29(2): 333–342.

von Kapri, A., T. Rick, and S. Feiner (2011). "Comparing Steering-Based Travel Techniques for Search Tasks in a CAVE." *Proceedings of the 2011 IEEE Virtual Reality Conference*, 91–94.

Vorländer, M. (2007). *Auralization: Fundamentals of Acoustics, Modelling, Simulation, Algorithms and Acoustic Virtual Reality*. Berlin: Springer.

Vorländer, M., and B. Shinn-Cunningham (2015). "Virtual Auditory Displays." In K. Hale and K. Stanney (eds.), *Handbook of Virtual Environments: Design, Implementation, and Applications*, Second Edition, 87–114. Boca Raton, FL: CRC Press

Vorlander, M., and B. Shinn-Cunningham (2015). Virtual Auditory Displays. In K. Hale, and K. Stanney (eds.), *Handbook of Virtual Environments: Design, Implementation, and Applications*, Second Edition, 87–114. CRC Press.

Vygotsky, Lev Semenovich (1980). *Mind in Society: The Development of Higher Psychological Processes*. Cambridge, MA: Harvard University Press.

Wagner, D., G. Reitmayr, A. Mulloni, T. Drummond, D. Schmalstieg (2010). "Real-Time Detection and Tracking for Augmented Reality on Mobile Phones. *IEEE Transactions on Visualization and Computer Graphics* 16(3): 355–368

Waller, D., E. Hunt, and D. Knapp (1998). "The Transfer of Spatial Knowledge in Virtual Environment Training." *Presence: Teleoperators and Virtual Environments* 7(2): 129–143.

Wang, F.-Y., K. M. C., D. Zeng, and W. Mao (2007). "Social Computing: From Social Informatics to Social Intelligence." *Intelligent Systems* (IEEE) 22(2): 79–83.

Wang, R. Y., and J. Popović (2009). "Real-Time Hand-Tracking with a Color Glove." *ACM Transactions on Graphics (TOG)* 28(3): Article No. 63.

Wang, R., S. Paris, and J. Popović (2011). "6D Hands: Markerless Hand-Tracking for Computer Aided Design." *Proceedings of the 24th Annual ACM Symposium on User Interface Software and Technology*, 549–558.

Wang, X., and B. Winslow. (2015). "Eye Tracking in Virtual Environments." In K. Hale and K. Stanney (eds.), *Handbook of Virtual Environments: Design, Implementation, and Applications*, Second Edition, 197–210. Boca Raton, FL: CRC Press.

Wann, J., and M. Mon-Williams (2002). "Measurement of Visual Aftereffects Following Virtual Environment Exposure." In K. Stanney (ed.), *Handbook of Virtual Environments: Design, Implementation, and Applications*, 731–750. Mahwah, NJ: Lawrence Erlbaum Associates.

Ward, D., A. Blackwell, and D. MacKay (2002). "Dasher: A Gesture-Driven Data Entry Interface for Mobile Computing." *Human–Computer Interaction* 17(2–3): 199–228.

Ward, David, Jim Hahn, and Kirsten Feist. "Autocomplete as a Research Tool: A Study on Providing Search Suggestions." *Information Technology and Libraries* (Online) 31, no. 4 (2012): 6.

Ware, C. (2000). *Information Visualization: Perception for Design*. San Francisco, CA: Morgan Kaufman.

Ware, C., and D. Jessome (1988). "Using the Bat: A Six-Dimensional Mouse for Object Placement." *Proceedings of Graphics Interface '88*, 119–124.

Ware, C., and J. Rose (1999). "Rotating Virtual Objects with Real Handles." *ACM Transactions on Computer-Human Interaction* 6(2): 162–180.

Ware, C., and S. Osborne (1990). "Exploration and Virtual Camera Control in Virtual Three Dimensional Environments." *Proceedings of the 1990 ACM Symposium on Interactive 3D Graphics (I3D '90)*, 175–183.

Ware, C., K. Arthur, and K. Booth (1993). "Fishtank Virtual Reality." *Proceedings of INTERCHI '93*, 37–42.

Watsen, K., R. Darken, and M. Capps (1999). "A Handheld Computer as an Interaction Device to a Virtual Environment." *Proceedings of the Third Immersive Projection Technology Workshop*, Stuttgart, Germany.

Watson, B., V. Spaulding, N. Walker, and W. Ribarsky (1997). "Evaluation of the Effects of Frame Time Variation on VR Task Performance." *Proceedings of 1997 IEEE Virtual Reality Annual International Symposium (VRAIS '97)*, 38–44.

Watt, A., and M. Watt (1992). *Advanced Animation Rendering Techniques: Theory and Practice*. New York: ACM Press.

Weidlich, D., L. Cser, T. Polzin, D. Cristiano, and H. Zickner (2007). "Virtual Reality Approaches for Immersive Design." *CIRP Annals—Manufacturing Technology* 56(1): 139–142.

Weisenberger, J., and G. Poling. (2004). "Multisensory Roughness Perception of Virtual Surfaces: Effects of Correlated Cues." *Proceedings of the 12th International Symposium on Haptic Interfaces for Virtual Environments and Teleoperators Systems*, 161–168 *(HAPTICS'04)*.

Weiser, M. (1991). "The Computer for the 21st Century." *Scientific American* 265(3): 66–75.

Welch, G. (2004). "Tracking Bibliography." http://www.cs.unc.edu/~tracker/ref/biblio/index.html.

Welch, G., and E. Foxlin (2002). "Motion Tracking: No Silver Bullet, but a Respectable Arsenal." *IEEE Computer Graphics and Applications, Special Issue on "Tracking"* 22(6): 24–38.

Welch, G., G. Bishop, L. Vicci, S. Brumback, K. Keller, and D. Colucci (1999). "The HiBall Tracker: High-Performance Wide-Area Tracking for Virtual and Augmented Environments." *Proceedings of the 1999 ACM Symposium on Virtual Reality Software and Technology (VRST '99)*, 1–10.

Welch, G., L. Vicci, S. Brumback, K. Keller, and D. Colucci (2001). "High-Performance Wide-Area Optical Tracking: The HiBall Tracking System." *Presence: Teleoperators and Virtual Environments* 10(1): 1–21.

Welch, R., and D. Warren (1986). "Intersensory Interactions." In K. Boff, L. Kaufman, and J. Thomas (eds.), *Handbook of Perception and Human Performance* 2:25-1–25-36. New York: John Wiley and Sons.

Wellner, P. (1993). "Interaction with Paper on the Digital Desk." *Communications of the ACM* 36(7): 87–96.

Wellner, P., W. Mackay, and R. Gold (1993). "Back to the Real World." *Communications of the ACM* 36(7): 24–27.

Wells, M., B. Peterson, and J. Aten (1996). "The Virtual Motion Controller: A Sufficient-Motion Walking Simulator." *Proceedings of the 1996 IEEE Virtual Reality Annual International Symposium (VRAIS '96)*, 1–8.

Wenzel, E. M., M. Arruda, D. J. Kistler, and F. L. Wightman (1993). "Localization Using Nonindividualized Head-Related Transfer Functions." *The Journal of the Acoustical Society of America* 94(1): 111–123.

Wetzstein, G., D. Lanman, M. Hirsch, W. Heidrich, and R. Raskar (2012). "Compressive Light Field Displays." *IEEE Computer Graphics and Applications* 32(5): 6–11

Whittle, M. W. (1996). "Clinical Gait Analysis: A Review." *Human Movement Science* 15(3): 369–387.

Wickens, C. (1986). The Effects of Control Dynamics on Performance. In K. Boff, L. Kaufman, and J. Thomas (eds.), *Handbook of Perception and Human Performance*, 2:39–60. New York: John Wiley & Sons.

Wickens, C. (2008). "Multiple Resources and Mental Workload." *Human Factors*. 50(3): 449–455.

Wickens, C., and C. Carswell (1997). "Information Processing." In G. Salvendy (ed.), *Handbook of Human Factors and Ergonomics,* 130–149. New York: John Wiley & Sons.

Wickens, C., S. Todd, and K. Seidler (1989). "Three-Dimensional Displays: Perception, Implementation, Applications." Ohio, CSERIAC SOAR-89-01 Wright Patterson AFB.

Wickens, D. (2001). "Workload and Situation Awareness." In P. Hancock, and P. Desmond (eds), *Stress, Workload and Fatigue,* 443–450. Boca Raton, FL: Erlbaum.

Weidlich, D., L. Cser, T. Polzin, D. Cristiano, and H. Zickner (2007). "Virtual Reality Approaches for Immersive Design." *CIRP Annals—Manufacturing Technology* 56(1): 139–142.

Wiener, N. (1948*). Cybernetics, or Control and Communication in the Animal and the Machine*. New York. John Wiley & Sons.

Wigdor, D., and Wixon, D. (2011). *Brave NUI World: Designing Natural User Interfaces for Touch and Gesture*. Burlington, MA: Morgan Kaufmann.

Wilkes, C., and D. Bowman (2008). "Advantages of Velocity-Based Scaling for Distant 3D Manipulation." *Proceedings of the 2008 ACM Symposium on Virtual Reality Software and Technology*, 23–29.

Williams, G., H. Faste, I. McDowall, and M. Bolas (1999). "Physical Presence in Virtual Spaces." *Proceedings of SPIE, Stereoscopic Displays and Virtual Reality Systems VI* 3639: 374–384.

Williamson, B., C. Wingrave, and J. LaViola (2010). "Realnav: Exploring Natural User Interfaces for Locomotion in Video Games." *Proceedings of IEEE Symposium on 3D User Interfaces 2010*, 3–10.

Williamson, B., C. Wingrave, J. LaViola, T. Roberts, and P. Garrity (2011). "Natural Full Body Interaction for Navigation in Dismounted Soldier Training. "*Proceedings of the Interservice/Industry Training, Simulation, and Education Conference*, 2103–2110.

Williamson, B., C., Wingrave, and J. LaViola (2013) "Full body locomotion with video game motion controllers". In F. Steinicke, Y. Visell, J. Campos, and A. Lecuyer (eds.), *Human Walking in Virtual Environments*, Springer, pp. 351–376.

Wilson, A., H. Benko, S. Izadi, and O. Hilliges (2012). "Steerable Augmented Reality with the Beamatron." *Proceedings of the 25th Annual ACM Symposium on User Interface Software and Technology (UIST '12)*, 413–422.

Winfield, L., J. Glassmire, J. Colgate, and M. Peshkin (2007). "T-PaD: Tactile Pattern Display Through Variable Friction Reduction." *Proceedings of the Second Joint Eurohaptics Conference and Symposium on Haptic Interfaces for Virtual Environment and Teleoperator Systems*, 421–426.

Wingrave, C., B. Williamson, P. Varcholik, J. Rose, A. Miller, E. Charbonneau, J. Bott, and J. LaViola (2010). "Wii Remote and Beyond: Using Spatially Convenient Devices for 3DUIs." *IEEE Computer Graphics and Applications* 30(2):71–85.

Wingrave, C. A., Haciahmetoglu, Y., and Bowman, D. A. (2006). "Overcoming World in Miniature Limitations by a Scaled and Scrolling WIM." *3D User Interfaces (3DUI'06),* 11–16.

Winston, P. (1992. *Artificial Intelligence,* Third Edition. Reading, MA: Addison-Wesley.

Wiseman, J. (1995). *The SAS Survival Handbook*. Collins Publications.

Wither, J., R. Allen, V. Samanta, J. Hemanus, Y.-T. Tsai, R. Azuma, W. Carter, R. Hinman, and T. Korah (2010). "The Westwood Experience: Connecting Story to Locations via Mixed Reality." *Proceedings of ISMAR 2010*, 39–46.

Witmer, B., and M. Singer (1998). "Measuring Presence in Virtual Environments: A Presence Questionnaire." *Presence: Teleoperators and Virtual Environments* 7(3): 225–240.

Wloka, M. M., and E. Greenfield (1995). "The Virtual Tricorder: a Uniform Interface for Virtual Reality." In *Proceedings of the 8th annual ACM Symposium on User Interface Software and Technology*, ACM, 39–40.

Woeckl, B., U. Yildizoglu, I. Buber, B. Aparicio Diaz, E. Kruijff, and M. Tscheligi (2012). "Basic Senior Personas: A Representative Design Tool Covering the Spectrum of European Older Adults." In *Proceedings of the 14th Internationals ACM SIGACCESS Conference on Computers and Accessibility*, Boulder, USA.

Wobbrock, J., M. Morris, and A. Wilson (2009). "User-Defined Gestures for Surface Computing." *Proceedings of the SIGCHI Conference on Human Factors in Computing Systems*, 1083–1092.

Wolf, K., and J. Willaredt (2015). "PickRing: Seamless Interaction Through Pick-Up Detection." *Proceedings of the 6th Augmented Human International Conference (AH '15)*, 13–20.

Wolfe, J. (1998). "What Do 1,000,000 Trials Tell Us about Visual Search?" *Psychological Science* 9(1), 33–39.

Wolpaw, J., and E. Wolpaw (2012). *Brain-Computer Interfaces: Principle and Practice*. Oxford: Oxford University Press.

Wormell, D., and E. Foxlin (2003). "Advancements in 3D Interactive Devices for Virtual Environments." *Proceedings of Immersive Projection Technology and Virtual Environments 2003*, 47–56.

Wright, C., Marino, V., Belovsky, S., and C. Chubb. (2007). "Visually Guided, Aimed Movements Can Be Unaffected by Stimulus-Response Uncertainty." *Experimental Brain Research*, 179: 475–499.

Wuest, H., F. Vial, and D. Strieker (2005). "Adaptive Line Tracking with Multiple Hypotheses for Augmented Reality." *Proceedings of the Fourth IEEE and ACM International Symposium on Mixed and Augmented Reality*, 62–69.

Wyss, H., R. Blach, and M. Bues (2006). "iSith-Intersection-Based Spatial Interaction for Two Hands." *Proceedings of the 2006 IEEE Symposium on 3D User Interfaces (3DUI '06)*, 59–61.

Xie, B. (2013). *Head-Related Transfer Function and Virtual Auditory Display*. Plantation, FL: J. Ross Publishing.

Yamada, H. (1980). "A Historical Study of Typewriters and Typing Methods: From the Position of Planning Japanese Parallels." *Journal of Information Processing* 2(4): 175–202.

Yamakoshi T., Yamakoshi K., Tanaka S., Nogawa M., Park S. B., Shibata M., Sawada Y., Rolfe P., and Y. Hirose. (2008). "Feasibility Study on Driver's Stress Detection from Differential Skin Temperature Measurement." *Proceedings of 30th Annual Conference of the IEEE in Engineering in Medicine and Biology Society*, 1076–1079.

Yaras, F., H. Kang, and L. Onural (2010). "State of the Art in Holographic Displays: A Survey." *Journal of Display Technology* 6(10): 443–454.

Yost, W. A. (1994). *Fundamentals of Hearing: An Introduction*, Third Edition. San Diego, CA: Academic Press.

You, S., and U. Neumann (2001). "Fusion of Vision and Gyro Tracking for Robust Augmented Reality Registration." *Proceedings of IEEE Virtual Reality 2001*, 71–78.

You, S., U. Neumann, and R. Azuma (1999). "Hybrid Inertial and Vision Tracking for Augmented Reality Registration." *Proceedings of IEEE Virtual Reality 1999*, 260–267.

Zarchan, P., and H. Musoff (2015). *Fundamentals of Kalman Filtering: A Practical Approach*, Fourth Edition. Reston, VA: American Institute of Aeronautics and Astronautics.

Zeleznik, R., A. Forsberg, and P. Strauss (1997). "Two Pointer Input for 3D Interaction." *Proceedings of the 1997 ACM Symposium in Interactive 3D Graphics (I3D '97)*, 115–120.

Zeleznik, R., and A. Forsberg (1999). "UniCam: 2D Gestural Camera Controls for 3D Environments." *Proceedings of the 1999 ACM Symposium on Interactive 3D Graphics (I3D '99)*, 169–173.

Zeleznik, R., J. LaViola, D. Acevedo, and D. Keefe (2002). "Pop-Through Buttons for Virtual Environment Navigation and Interaction." *Proceedings of IEEE Virtual Reality 2002*, 127–134.

Zeleznik, R., K. Herndon, and J. Hughes (1996). "SKETCH: An Interface for Sketching 3D Scenes." *Proceedings of SIGGRAPH '96*, 163–170.

Zhai, S. (1995). "Human Performance in Six Degree of Freedom Input Control." PhD Dissertation, Department of Computer Science, University of Toronto.

Zhai, S. (1998). 'User Performance in Relation to 3D Input Device Design." *Computer Graphics* 32(4): 50–54.

Zhai, S., and P. O. Kristensson (2012). "The Word-Gesture Keyboard: Reimagining Keyboard Interaction." *Communications of the ACM* 55(9): 91–101.

Zhai, S., and J. Senders (1997a). "Investigating Coordination in Multidegree of Freedom Control I: Time-on-Target Analysis of 6 DOF Tracking." *Human Factors and Ergonomics Society 41st Annual Meeting,* 1249–1253.

Zhai, S., and J. Senders (1997b). "Investigating Coordination in Multidegree of Freedom Control II: Correlation Analysis in 6 DOF Tracking." *Human Factors and Ergonomics Society 41st Annual Meeting,* 1254–1258.

Zhai, S., and P. Milgram (1993). "Human Performance Evaluation of Manipulation Schemes in Virtual Environments." *Proceedings of the 1993 IEEE Virtual Reality Annual International Symposium (VRAIS '93),* 155–161.

Zhai, S., and P. Milgram (1998). "Quantifying Coordination in Multiple DOF Movement and Its Application to Evaluating 6 DOF Input Devices." *Proceedings of the 1998 ACM Conference on Human Factors in Computing Systems (CHI '98),* 320–327.

Zhai, S., and R. Woltjer (2003). "Human Movement Performance in Relation to Path Constraint: The Law of Steering in Locomotion." *Proceedings of IEEE Virtual Reality 2003,* 149–158.

Zhai, S., E. Kandogan, B. Smith, and T. Selker (1999). "In Search of the 'Magic Carpet': Design and Experimentation of a Bimanual 3D Navigation Interface." *Journal of Visual Languages and Computing* 10: 3–17.

Zhai, S., M. Hunter, and B. Smith (2000). "The Metropolis Keyboard: An Exploration of Quantitative Techniques for Virtual Keyboard Design." *Proceedings of the 2000 ACM Symposium on User Interface Software and Technology (UIST 2000),* 119–128.

Zhai, S., P. Milgram, and A. Rastogi (1997). "Anisotropic Human Performance in Six Degree-of-Freedom Tracking: An Evaluation of Three-Dimensional Display and Control Interfaces." *IEEE Transactions on Systems, Man and Cybernetics* 27(4): 518–528.

Zhai, S., P. Milgram, and W. Buxton (1996). "The Influence of Muscle Groups on Performance of Multiple Degree-of-Freedom Input." *Proceedings of the 1996 ACM Conference on Human Factors in Computing Systems (CHI '96),* 308–315.

Zhai, S., W. Buxton, and P. Milgram (1994). "The 'Silk Cursor': Investigating Transparency for 3D Target Acquisition." *Proceedings of the 1994 ACM Conference on Human Factors in Computing Systems (CHI '94),* 459–464.

Zhou, H., and Hu Huosheng (2008). "Human Motion Tracking for Rehabilitation—A Survey." *Biomedical Signal Processing and Control* 3(1): 1–18.

Zilles, C., and J. Salisbury (1995). "A Constraint-Based God-Object Method for Haptic Display." *Proceedings of the 1995 IEEE/RSJ International Conference on Intelligent Robots and Systems,* 146–151.

Zimmerman, T. G., J. Lanier, C. Blanchard, S. Bryson, and Y. Harvill (1987 May). "A Hand Gesture Interface Device." *ACM SIGCHI Bulletin* 18(4): 189–192.

Zwaga, H., T. Boersema, and H. Hoonhout (1999). *Visual Information for Everyday Use: Design and Research Perspectives.* London: Taylor & Francis.

INDEX

Numbers

A

B

C

D

E

F

G

H

I

J-K

L

M

N

O

P

Q-R

S

U

V

W-X-Y-Z